The Witch-Hunt Narrative

The Witch-Hunt Narrative

Politics, Psychology, and the Sexual Abuse of Children

ROSS E. CHEIT

Illustrations by L. Arthi Krishnaswami

OXFORD
UNIVERSITY PRESS

OXFORD
UNIVERSITY PRESS

Oxford University Press is a department of the University of Oxford.
It furthers the University's objective of excellence in research, scholarship,
and education by publishing worldwide.

Oxford New York

Auckland Cape Town Dar es Salaam Hong Kong Karachi
Kuala Lumpur Madrid Melbourne Mexico City Nairobi
New Delhi Shanghai Taipei Toronto

With offices in

Argentina Austria Brazil Chile Czech Republic France Greece
Guatemala Hungary Italy Japan Poland Portugal Singapore
South Korea Switzerland Thailand Turkey Ukraine Vietnam

Oxford is a registered trade mark of Oxford University Press
in the UK and certain other countries.

Published in the United States of America by
Oxford University Press
198 Madison Avenue, New York, NY 10016

CIP data is on file at the LOC

9780199931224

3 5 7 9 8 6 4 2

Printed in the United States of America on acid-free paper

To Kathleen

CONTENTS

Preface   ix
List of Illustrations   xix

PART I   THE RISE OF THE WITCH-HUNT NARRATIVE

1. Introduction: The Infamous Child Sexual Abuse Cases
   of the 1980s   3

2. The McMartin Preschool Case (1983–1990)   17

3. Scrutinizing the Evidence of a National Witch-Hunt   87

4. History Ignored: Silence, Denial, and Minimization   151

Conclusion I   196

PART II   THE TRIUMPH OF THE WITCH-HUNT NARRATIVE

5. The Turning Point: *State v. Michaels*   203

6. Going to Extremes: *State v. Fuster*   283

Conclusion II   355

PART III   RECENT DEVELOPMENTS

7. The Legacy of the Witch-Hunt Narrative   365

Acknowledgments   409
Bibliographic Notes   413
Notes   417
Index   487

PREFACE

Just as this book was being completed, the scandal that has come to be associated with Penn State took a definitive turn. Gerald "Jerry" Sandusky, the football team's defensive coordinator for many years, was convicted of forty-five counts of sexual crimes against children. Soon thereafter, the Freeh Report concluded that "four of the most powerful people" at the university, including Coach Joe Paterno, had covered up the situation and "exhibited a striking lack of empathy for Sandusky's victims."[1] The NCAA quickly imposed severe sanctions, which included a penalty that would provide millions of dollars for child abuse prevention programs. It is, no doubt, the most important child sexual abuse story in recent years. One particular aspect of the story shocked the sensibilities of many: Mike McQueary testified that when he was a graduate assistant at Penn State he saw Jerry Sandusky in the shower with a boy who Sandusky appeared to be subjecting to a sexual assault. McQueary reported the incident to Coach Paterno. Although there are differing accounts about precisely what McQueary said, there is no disagreement about the fact that nobody higher up in the university contacted law enforcement. The criminal trial established that Sandusky sexually abused several more boys after top officials at the university had more than sufficient reason to report him.

What surprised me most about the Penn State story—after spending fifteen years researching and writing this book—was that so many people were flabbergasted that a cover-up like this could occur. Everyone knows, of course, about the massive cover-up of similar events in the Roman Catholic Church. Indeed, a few commentators were quick to draw parallels between the cases by casting football as religion and coach Paterno as the pope. But while we have overcome our collective denial about the possibility that a priest could abuse a child, we have also managed to compartmentalize the lessons from the Catholic Church cases, an issue to which I will return at the end of the book.

Meanwhile, how could child sexual abuse be covered up for as long as it was at Penn State? There are two important answers. First, as Susan Sgroi said decades ago, we abhor child sexual abuse in the abstract but we tolerate it in reality.[2] The abhorrence gets all the publicity. This is how we talk about child sexual abuse—with the language of disgust and disapproval. But that is not how we, as a society, tend to act in specific cases. Instead, we often minimize and deny so as to allow us to avoid seeing things we would rather not see. *Turning a blind eye* to the sexual abuse of children has a long history in this country. So does protecting "upstanding citizens" against such claims. Communities have been known to rally around people convicted of this crime, making arguments to mitigate the punishment because of their "good deeds." There was a particularly egregious version of this response in my home state, Rhode Island, in 1997, when a superior court judge overturned *his own verdict* convicting Father Louis Dunn of rape after receiving an outpouring of letters orchestrated from churchgoers who attested to the ex-priest's character. Though the judge's actions were unprecedented—and eventually overturned by the state Supreme Court[3]—rallying around a convicted child rapist is not at all unusual.

The second reason the events at Penn State did not surprise me stems directly from the argument of this book. We have, over the last twenty years, discounted the word of children who might testify about sexual abuse. We have become more worried about overreacting to child sexual abuse than we are about underreacting to it. The Penn State case is filled with concern on the part of administrators about whether Sandusky was being treated "humanely," with little or no apparent regard for his possible victims. We are far too quick to dismiss the word of a child these days in the name of worrying about "child suggestibility." This development—unlike our contradictory views about sex offenses in general versus sex offenders in particular—is recent. Ironically, an overly dismissive view of children is a function of the very cases that opened the doors to allowing younger children to testify in the first place. Those cases occurred in the 1980s; many of them became infamous, and many were later overturned on appeal. All of those cases have since been cast as wrongful accusations or wrongful convictions, thanks in large part to claims about child suggestibility. Notably, the successful case against Sandusky was built on the testimony of people who were children at the time of the incidents. All were male and at least eighteen at the time they testified. The case might well have come out differently had the facts been the same but the witnesses all adolescents or younger at the time of their testimony.

This book challenges the argument that our society overreacted to the sexual abuse of children and, in the process, engaged in series of "witch-hunts" in the 1980s. Based on the first comprehensive examination of trial court records from those cases, this book argues that the witch-hunt narrative does not do justice to the facts of these cases. The very cases that have been used to justify the claim that children are "highly suggestible" demonstrate how easy it is to make the claim regardless of the evidence. This book does not, however, claim that every controversial conviction from the 1980s was rightly decided, or that every reversal on appeal was misplaced. Rather, it questions the much more extreme claim that there were hundreds or thousands of injustices during this time that were akin to the Salem witch trials. In my view, there *were* some injustices during this period that merit serious concern. Several are detailed in this book. But to claim that those cases define a whole period is to adopt a view not borne out by the evidence.

The research for this book began with the investigation of a single case. At the time, I thought I was writing a book review of *Satan's Silence: Ritual Abuse and the Making of an American Witchhunt,* by Debbie Nathan and Michael Snedeker. The book argues that scores of injustices, akin to the Salem witch trials, were perpetrated around the country in the 1980s through prosecutions for child sexual abuse. The book was dedicated to "the men and women still incarcerated, including those whose names we know," followed by a two-column list of proper names, along with place names in parentheses. Surprisingly, many of those identified on the dedication page were not mentioned in the book; several others were referenced in the book but in no more than a sentence or two. It struck me as strange that the very cases allegedly constituting the strongest and most concrete evidence of a nationwide series of witch-hunts would receive so little attention in a book on the very subject. On closer examination, it appeared that only a few of the cases on the dedication page had been the subject of original research.[4] Although the witch-hunt narrative often refers to "hundreds" of these cases, the same handful of cases are at the core of most publications. Three of them, beginning with McMartin and including Kelly Michaels and Frank Fuster, are the subject of detailed chapters ahead. Before getting to the merits of those cases, however, one might wonder why an allegedly national wave of witch-hunts is routinely illustrated by stories about the same handful of cases.

I decided to look into Robert Halsey's case from nearby Massachusetts. Halsey's name was on the dedication page of *Satan's Silence* but never actually appeared in the book. After reviewing the trial transcript, with the assistance of an excellent research assistant who went to the Berkshires more than once, I found it difficult to imagine why anyone would think that Halsey was anything but guilty, as he was found by jury and by all appellate judicial panels since then. The transcript was filled with cross-corroborating evidence of guilt. The idea of a book review had turned into an article. I called it "The Legend of Robert Halsey."[5]

I then expanded my research horizons to other cases on Nathan and Snedeker's dedication page. I continued to find significant evidence contradicting the conventional wisdom about these cases. This was not my only finding—the wrongful conviction of Bernard Baran is elaborated in Chapter Three—but it was the predominant one. The more this happened, the more important it was that my research should encompass an expansive number of cases in order to be sure I was doing justice to the witch-hunt narrative. The idea was inspired by Darwin's fabled practice of posting for himself notes with any evidence contrary to his own theories or expectations; in this way, "the arguments most easily forgotten" would have to be confronted and explained.[6] I was inclined to doubt the witch-hunt narrative in part from personal experience. I had experienced the preference of many organizations to protect their reputation rather than confront evidence of sexual abuse when I sued the San Francisco Boys Chorus in 1994 for failing to act decades earlier on multiple forms of evidence indicating there was rampant sexual abuse of boys, including me, at their summer camp. I was open about the matter during the pendency of the case, fighting successfully to keep from having the entire matter sealed and insisting on a public apology to settle the suit.[7] But the personal experience that has been far more important, I think, in shaping some of the content of this book is my weekly involvement with the Sex Offender Treatment Program at the Rhode Island Department of Corrections in Cranston. I have been volunteering there since 1998. I teach ethics-related courses designed to help develop cognitive and social skills among men (and two women once, for ten weeks) who tend to see the world in extremely black-and-white terms. I also sit in on core treatment groups from time to time. Through this experience, I have encountered hundreds of sex offenders over the years. I sought the experience largely to help myself understand why anyone commits these crimes. I stayed because the understanding I have gained in answering the question tells me that treatment programs are meaningful and important to public safety.

Meanwhile, the research project expanded to include the list of thirty-six cases that had been made famous in a 1988 series in a Tennessee newspaper. This is when I committed myself to writing at least one book. My focus was on primary documents, not on what people might have to say years after the fact about these cases; I was interested in records of what happened then, at the time of the cases. First and foremost, this meant trial transcripts. Almost all of the cases involved trials. Finding the transcripts was often challenging, particularly for cases that had ended in acquittal or mistrial. Other challenges included protective orders and statutory protections making it difficult, if not impossible, to obtain some transcripts. Almost nothing from the era was computerized, and there were limits to how much assistance even the most cooperative court clerk could provide. Some inquiries had to be made in person; some things had to be viewed in person. Those problems were all solvable, but quite challenging nevertheless. Also, long trials fill lots of boxes. Rarely was there an inventory of any sort, and inevitably there were things missing. These could be significant problems where a trial lasted for many months.

Several years of research demonstrated there were three significant research challenges to this project that I had not fully appreciated: (1) the sheer scale and complexity of the cases, (2) the difficulties locating and copying or inspecting transcripts and related documents, and (3) the limits of written transcripts, particularly of interviews with young children. The scale and complexity problem is apparent in the three major case studies in this book. It also inspired an article about these research challenges.[8] I came to call this work Extreme Research, and I did it for almost fifteen years. During that time, I worked with more than eighty research assistants at Brown University, and I spent a small fortune on photocopying and the transcribing services of court stenographers. It was a massive effort that is still in progress for a few cases. Nevertheless, I am struck by the limitations of what I was able to cover in detail after employing a vast array of resources and research assistants over so many years. I simply did not have the space to cover all the cases I have researched; nor have I finished exhaustively researching every case in the project. Several that merit detailed treatments will be covered in future publications, particularly the Jordan, Minnesota cases and the Snowden case from Dade County, Florida. Some of the cases where I reached a dead-end could undoubtedly still be researched further. Indeed, it was clear that I could probably follow leads for another fifteen years. But there were also basic realities, from research funding to expected mortality, to be considered.

What I set out to do in this research was to assess the actual record in cases and make some independent assessments about the nature and quality of the evidence. Most of the cases analyzed in this book have been held out as modern-day witch-hunts, as cases in which there was no credible evidence of abuse. This view, as described in Chapter One, has been disseminated and accepted so widely that I refer to it as *the witch-hunt narrative*. This narrative appears in newspapers, magazines, and a range of academic publications from psychology and law to history and cultural studies. Some of those publications are now more than twenty years old, but many are much more recent, as the prominent cases in this book continue be discussed by journalists and academics. This book adds to the vast array of publications that already express an opinion about these cases. The book challenges the witch-hunt narrative in a variety of ways. Those familiar with the narrative know where to find an enormous supply of countervailing views to challenge almost all of the views expressed in this book. Readers not familiar with the witch-hunt narrative are encouraged to examine the sources cited in Chapter One.

All readers are cautioned about the limits of even the most comprehensive archival research. These limitations cut against the degree of certainty that should be attributed to some of my conclusions. First, there are inherent obstacles to assessing cases on the basis of a cold transcript and other similarly limited documentary evidence. For the same reason videotapes of interviews with children (or adults) convey far more information than transcripts of the same interviews, viewing the presentation of evidence in a courtroom provides a stronger basis for drawing conclusions about certain evidence than does reviewing the trial transcripts alone. Fortunately, videotapes of interviews were at the heart of some cases, and I had the advantage of viewing such videotapes in two of the three chapter-length cases studies in this book; I heard audiotapes in the other. Still, I did not observe any of the extensive court testimony and therefore have the disadvantage of not observing body language or the intonation of witnesses. A second limitation of transcripts, especially when studied years later, is that they rarely include the exhibits. Transcripts are saved as archival documents in many jurisdictions, but the exhibits are ultimately property of the parties and generally returned to the parties or destroyed once the case (including any possible appeals) is complete. This limitation has particular relevance for medical testimony, where the exhibits (usually photographic slides in child sexual abuse cases) must be available in order to assess the evidence discussed in the transcript. I located slides and medical reports in some instances and consulted more than one expert about those matters, but in many cases the exhibits were not available, which limits the ability to make independent assessments about the evidence. As a reminder, these limitations are pointed out in several places in the text. Finally, there are limitations imposed by the realities of book publishing, dictating that a book covering dozens of cases cannot go into comprehensive detail for every case. Doing so would result in an unfeasibly long book, reading more like a series of books with dozens of case-based narratives than a single book with an overall argument. Accordingly, I have analyzed three cases in chapter-length (or long-form) detail and dozens more in short form, usually a few pages.

The nature of the analysis varies significantly, from chapter-length case studies to short-form treatments, even though many of the cases treated in short form involved extensive research efforts. The primary analytical question in the short-form cases was a threshold question: Was there credible evidence of abuse sufficient to have justified the state in bringing the case to trial? In answering this question, I examined the record as comprehensively as I could. I wanted to know what evidence was put forth and what arguments were made by the defense. But the analysis was not a full-blown weighing of the evidence; nor was the evidence held against the criminal court standard of proof—beyond a reasonable doubt. Instead, I looked to see whether there was evidence that appeared credible to me, and if so, I described its nature. My having concluded that there was credible evidence in a case does *not* mean the defendant was necessarily guilty. But it does mean that in my opinion, as documented by evidence I reviewed, there was sufficient reason for authorities to have investigated and brought charges. This means, by definition, that the case was not a witch-hunt. To the contrary, it is the state's duty to take action when there is credible evidence of child sexual abuse, as with any crime. Evidence that supports my opinions about these cases is described and documented in the text. In no instance are my opinions based on evidence not presented to the reader. But some of the evidence that supports my opinions goes beyond the trial transcripts to include police reports and other administrative records. Such evidence has not been subjected to the rigors of cross-examination, which might well diminish its credibility. Indeed, reasonable people will undoubtedly disagree about whether such evidence should be considered, and if so, how much weight it should be afforded.

The chapter-length cases involve a more detailed engagement of the evidence. This provides a basis for conclusions beyond the low-threshold question explored in the short-form case chapters. As for the long-form case chapters, I sought to ask a higher threshold question: whether there was *substantial evidence* supporting the state's case. A case with substantial evidence involves much more than the showing necessary to justify investigation or even arrest and indictment. It is more than enough evidence to support carrying the charges forward and withstanding a motion to dismiss the case for lack of sufficient evidence. In the course of making these assessments, I employ the terms *credible evidence, corroborating evidence,* and *solid medical evidence*; all of these assessments are my opinion and my opinion alone. The basis for these opinions is explained in the text, and the foundations of these opinions are documented in full. But this evidence could strike others differently. Indeed, some of the jurors in one of these cases, the McMartin trial, and in the retrial reached conclusions that differed from my view elaborated in this book.

My opinion that there was substantial evidence is *not* the same as drawing a conclusion about guilt. I make no pretense of being a prosecutor, judge, or jury. A child sexual abuse case with *substantial evidence* could leave some reasonable people with sufficient doubt that they would not vote to convict under a standard requiring evidence of guilt "beyond a reasonable doubt." This might even be true in cases where there was medical evidence. Although medical evidence can be diagnostic evidence of sexual abuse, it generally speaks to the injury and not to the perpetrator. This issue was particularly relevant in the McMartin case. For all of these reasons, I have tempered my evaluation to stop short of conclusions about the ultimate outcome in two of the three chapter-length cases. (The third case, Frank Fuster, is more definitive for several reasons as described further in that chapter, including a positive STD test involving the throat of his son, who was under his custody and control.)

There is an important difference between scholarly arguments about cases and legal judgments about the same cases. The former do not carry any legal weight, and the latter merit respect for their authority. Reconsidering evidence as done in this book is purely an academic exercise. And no matter how complicated a case may be, the ultimate legal outcome is generally quite clear. Contrast the clear outcome with the mixed messages contained in the procedural history of the first two chapter-length cases. In both cases, some or all jurors voted for guilt beyond a reasonable doubt, but this was not the ultimate legal disposition. In the first case (McMartin), two consecutive juries were divided on some charges, but all of the charges were eventually dismissed; in the second case (Michaels), the jury voted unanimously to convict on almost all of the charges, but a court of appeals reversed the verdict and all charges were later dismissed. In both of those cases, the legal disposition is clear: in the eyes of the law, the defendants are not guilty. In legal terms, those judgments are final and I respect them. That said, it is also true that having charges dropped after a hung jury or having charges dismissed after an appeals court overturns a conviction is not the same thing as being factually innocent. There are rare cases in the criminal justice system where an appellate court or a trial judge directs a finding that a defendant is *innocent*. Much more commonly, however, reversals on appeal are not based on decisions about the facts, and they often allow the possibility of retrial. And acquittals are open to interpretation. In addition to the possibility of a defendant being innocent, there are many pragmatic reasons for a prosecutor choosing not to retry a case that already ended in conviction once. There is a similar range of possible explanations for a not-guilty verdict, which can mean anything from the jury having a very small but reasonable doubt about guilt to the jury concluding the defendant was factually innocent. The defendant is entitled to the presumption of innocence under the law; academics are entitled to consider the range of possible explanations that could lead to legal determinations of not guilty.

The burden of proof in criminal cases is designed to promote the kind of results expressed in Blackstone's formulation that it is *better that ten guilty persons escape than that one innocent suffer*.[9] This is why the state must prove its case beyond a reasonable doubt. The high burden of proof is related to the fact that one's liberty is at stake. But the same facts that might not dispel *all* reasonable doubts might nevertheless be more than legally sufficient for, say, a school board to dismiss a coach.[10] Similarly, a victim (or the family) might well be able to win a civil verdict against a defendant who was found not guilty in criminal court for the same actions. This is precisely what happened in the O. J. Simpson case. There was a "preponderance of evidence"—a common standard of proof in civil cases—to support the conclusion that Simpson was responsible for civil damages, but the jury in the criminal case decided the case had not been proven beyond a reasonable doubt. Of course, many people disagreed with the jury's not-guilty verdict. And even though we can and should be able to debate about the evidence in the case, we should also respect the fact that, in the eyes of the law, Simpson was found not guilty.

The cases in this book are foundational cases in the public discourse about child sexual abuse and about children as witnesses. They have also become an integral part of academic discourse about the suggestibility of children. Much of the discourse is premised on the assumption that these cases did not involve any credible evidence of sexual abuse. I hope this book contributes to a lively debate about the facts of those cases; but whether it does or not, there is plenty of published work to provide any interested reader with a strong dose of opinions other than those advanced in this book. Putting the conventional wisdom to the test of the actual record is, nevertheless, a matter of considerable importance. The extent to which the findings in this book contradict the witch-hunt narrative matters far beyond the historical record. It also matters for how children are viewed as witnesses.

Chapter Seven considers the legacy of the witch-hunt narrative in light of recent developments. The chapter begins with an examination of recent events that have dominated the framing of child sexual abuse in the media: the cases against the Catholic Church and the recent Penn State case. The chapter also examines the worrisome politics of sex offender punishment that have emerged in the last twenty years. The chapter concludes by considering the legacy of the witch-hunt narrative: how it has undermined the credibility of children as witnesses and is taking aim at the institutions and professionals who respond to child sexual abuse complaints.

I close with the hope that anyone who approaches my work with skepticism—and a certain amount of skepticism is always healthy—will hold the witch-hunt narrative to the same standards of evidence and proof that are applied to the arguments in this book. I could not ask for anything more, and I hope that critics of my work will do nothing less.

LIST OF ILLUSTRATIONS

Figures

2.1 McMartin Case Timeline, Initial Complaint to Case
Conclusion. 18

2.2 McMartin Sequence—September Responders as Recorded by
MBPD. 29

2.3 McMartin Interview Sequence—September Responders,
Complainants and Trial. 39

2.4 CII Interview Sequence—All Interviews of Children at CII
Through May 15, 1984. 52

2.5 CII Interview Sequence—Children at Preliminary Hearing. 53

2.6 CII Interview Sequence—Children at Preliminary Hearing,
Trial and Retrial. 54

3.1 Plot of Charlier and Downing's Thirty-six Cases. 90

5.1 Kelly Michaels Case Timeline, Initial Complaint to Conviction. 205

5.2 Kelly Michaels Interview Sequence, Children Interviewed in the
Initial Investigative Phase. 211

5.3 Kelly Michaels Interview Sequence, All Investigative Interviews. 218

5.4 Kelly Michaels, All Children, All Charges by Legal Status (Carried
Forward versus Dropped before Trial). 227

5.5 Kelly Michaels, All Children at Trial, by Status of Charges
(Presented to Jury versus Dropped). 235

5.6 Kelly Michaels, Trial Dispositions by Charge, by Child. 241

5.7 Kelly Michaels Interview Sequence, All Children by Number of
Interviews. 246

5.8 Kelly Michaels Investigative Interview Sequence, Children
Interviewed More than Twice. 248

5.9 Treacy-Child A Excerpt, Reproduced from Ceci and Bruck (1995)
with Source Annotations. 256

5.10   Treacy-Child B Excerpt, Reproduced from Ceci and Bruck (1995)
         with Source Annotations.   259

6.1   Comprehensive Case Timelines, Initial Complaint to Jury
         Verdict.   284

6.2   Overall Attendance Patterns at Country Walk Babysitting
         Service.   287

6.3   Country Walk, Braga Interview Sequence, Children Interviewed Two
         or More Times in August.   303

6.4   Country Walk, Full Braga Interview Sequence.   304

6.5   Country Walk, Braga Interview Sequence, August Detail.   305

6.6   Country Walk, Full Counts, Frank and Ileana, Individual and Group
         Charges.   310

6.7   Country Walk, Full Counts, Individual and Group, Frank only, by
         First Braga Interview, and by Disposition.   326

Tables

1.1   Selected Day Care Sexual Abuse Cases from the McMartin Era.   5

3.1   Charlier and Downing's Thirty-six Cases, by Date and Case
         Features.   91

3.2   Details on Eleven Cases Highlighted by Charlier and Downing.   95

3.3   Details on Names Listed on the Dedication Page of Nathan and
         Snedeker (1995) in Chronological Order.   116

5.1   Kelly Michaels Interview and Charge Information, by Investigative
         Phase.   267

II-1   Application of Ceci and Bruck's "Six Elements" to Three Major
         Cases.   358

II-2   Comparison of Key Features of the McMartin, Kelly Michaels, and
         Country Walk Case.   361

The Witch-Hunt Narrative

PART I

THE RISE OF THE WITCH-HUNT NARRATIVE

1

Introduction

The Infamous Child Sexual Abuse Cases of the 1980s

Child sexual abuse emerged into public discourse in the United States in the early 1980s. A public opinion poll in 1983 indicated that almost all parents were aware of the problem and had seen a story about it in the media. This is a remarkable change from two decades earlier, when the *physical* abuse of children was just being recognized by physicians and sexual abuse was still largely invisible. The only kind of sex crime that was readily acknowledged before then was "stranger danger," which is actually quite rare but seems much more common because of all the attention it receives. Incest, the most prevalent form of child sexual abuse, was the subject of a groundbreaking television movie, *Something About Amelia,* that drew sixty million viewers in the first week of January 1984. Jeffrey Masson's expose about Freud's suppression of the seduction theory was the February 1984 cover story in *The Atlantic.* Masson argued that archival documents proved that Freud had renounced his views about the prevalence of incest in order to curry the professional approval of those who could not accept his initial position. As that story captivated many intellectuals, Wayne Satz, a television reporter in Los Angeles, started a series of graphic stories about an ongoing child sexual abuse investigation concerning the McMartin Preschool in Manhattan Beach, California. An avalanche of media coverage followed and seven people connected to the school—six women and one man—were eventually arrested in what would soon be described as the largest child molestation case in history. The case would come to define an era of prosecutions involving child sexual abuse. It would give rise to competing narratives and competing advocacy organizations. And it would raise important questions about how children disclose sexual abuse, how they should be interviewed, and the role of children as witnesses in court.

The McMartin Case and Others

The allegations in the McMartin case began with claims against Ray Buckey, a twenty-two-year-old college dropout who worked at the preschool founded by his grandmother, Virginia McMartin. Several months later, other teachers at the school were also named as alleged perpetrators, and the claims about the abuse became stranger and more difficult to believe. There were allegations of children being "swapped" between preschools near McMartin. There were allegations of their being transported to other places, including a farm, where children allegedly saw a horse beaten to death in order to keep them quiet. A Sheriff's Task Force was created specifically to investigate "ritual abuse" claims. The term *ritual abuse* carries many different definitions. The most extreme definitions often include a component related to satanism, along with the idea that organized, even intergenerational, groups of people are involved. That view took hold among some parents, therapists, and investigators in the McMartin case. It is encapsulated in the claim that there were tunnels underneath the preschool where children were sexually abused.

After an extended preliminary hearing, the district attorney dropped charges against five of the seven defendants. The case went forward against Ray Buckey and his mother, Peggy Buckey. The decision pleased almost no one. Two polar views of the case had taken hold by then. Those allied with the organization Believe the Children thought that *more* defendants should have been pursued and that none should have been dismissed. Those allied with the defense thought that all of the charges should been dropped, including those against Peggy and Ray Buckey. Those deeply divided perspectives reflected larger differences about how children are viewed. Those allied with Believe the Children took the view that children "do not lie" about sexual abuse. Those allied with the defendants seemed to think that nothing any child said could be believed.

The McMartin case became the defining case of the era. It began in 1983 and ended in 1990. A detailed timeline of the case is presented Chapter Two, which is devoted to the McMartin case. In some respects, there was no other like it in intensity, duration, or scope. On the other hand, the McMartin case was one of a larger group across the country that seemed related. A list of fifteen appears in Table 1.1. A list of thirty-six cases emerged from an investigative series in a Tennessee newspaper in 1988; the first nine found in Table 1.1 are also in that list of thirty-six, which is examined in detail in Chapter Three.

These cases were difficult for law enforcement to investigate and difficult for prosecutors to prosecute because the children were young and the cases were new to the system. When they were filed, the cases were generally seen as evidence that society was taking the protection of children against sexual abuse seriously. But many became the longest trial in the history of their respective

Table 1.1 **Selected Day Care Sexual Abuse Cases from the McMartin Era**

Day Care Center	Year	Location
McMartin	1983	Manhattan Beach, CA
Country Walk	1984	Miami, FL
Small World	1984	Niles, MI
Fells Acres	1984	Malden, MA
Georgian Hills	1984	Memphis, TN
Rogers Park	1984	Chicago, IL
Manhattan Ranch	1984	Manhattan Beach, CA
Craig's Country	1985	Clarksville, MD
Felix's Day Care	1985	Carson City, NV
East Valley YMCA	1985	El Paso, TX
Glendale Montessori	1987	Stuart, FL
Old Cutler	1989	Miami, FL
Little Rascals	1989	Edenton, NC
Faith Chapel	1989	San Diego, CA
Fran's Day Care	1991	Austin, TX

Source: De Young, "Another Look at Moral Panics," 1998

county or state. As they dragged on, the cases became more confounding. In the McMartin instance, it became impossible to believe that all of the allegations were true, but it also seemed unlikely that all of them were baseless. Many jurors voted to convict Buckey on some counts in each of two separate trials. Although he was acquitted of most charges in the first case, Buckey was retried on charges involving three girls. All of those charges ended in a hung jury, with eight voting for conviction on one charge, and fewer than that on all others; a mistrial was declared. All pending charges were dismissed soon thereafter. A trial originally hailed as "the largest child molestation case ever" fizzled entirely.

The Rise of the Witch-Hunt Narrative

The idea that any of the day-care sexual abuse cases that first arose in the 1980s might actually be wrongful prosecutions was never given serious consideration during the earliest phase of the McMartin case. Though news stories during the first few months of the McMartin case included such requisite words as "alleged," it was clear from the initial coverage that the charges were basically accepted as true by those reporting them. When Satz reported the earliest McMartin stories on KABC television, the news anchors weighed in with editorial statements of sympathy and horror after various stories, indicating an endorsement of allegations that had not even become legal charges yet.[1] Writing about the case in April 1984, *People* magazine called the McMartin preschool "a sexual house of horrors."[2] There were isolated voices to the contrary, but they were few and far between.[3] The mainstream media, as media critic David Shaw put it years later, "didn't light a match within three miles of the D.A.'s feet during the first year or two of the case."[4]

The idea that the McMartin case might be a "witch hunt" was first promoted by the "Friends of McMartin" in the summer of 1985. The group, affiliated with the defense in the McMartin case, placed ads in a local newspaper that compared the case to the Salem Witch Trials. The witch-hunt narrative—a view that cases across the country were akin to the Salem witch trials nearly three hundred years earlier—was forged and disseminated over the next few years by a handful of writers. The *San Francisco Examiner* published a series of stories by A. S. Ross under the banner "A Presumption of Guilt" in September 1986, giving voice to the argument that authorities had created "a climate reminiscent of the 17th century Salem witch trials" in these cases.[5] The series included a map with capsule summaries of thirteen "sensational cases across the country." Six of those cases involved day-care settings: the Georgian Hills case in Memphis, Tennessee; the Country Walk case in Dade County, Florida; the Kelly Michaels case in Maplewood, New Jersey; the Fells Acres Day Care case in Malden, Massachusetts; the Small World Preschool case in Niles Township, Michigan; and the West Point Child Development Center from West Point, New York.[6] Several of these, along with the McMartin case, became the core content of the witch-hunt narrative. This narrative argues that coercive and suggestive interviews, conducted by biased interviewers, combined with hysterical parents, overzealous prosecutors, and an unduly credulous media to generate false accusations in cases that had no actual basis in fact.

The next writer to cast these cases as "witch hunts" was Debbie Nathan, who wrote an article called "The Making of a Modern Witch Hunt" in the *Village Voice* in September 1987. Nathan wrote four more articles in the *Village Voice* in 1988, contributing significantly to the nascent witch-hunt narrative.[7] Another early contributor to this narrative was Mary Fischer, a freelance writer who wrote three critical articles about the McMartin case in 1988. The one for *Los Angeles Magazine,* entitled "Media Flip-Flop: Why, Four Years Later the Press Is Taking a Strikingly Different Approach to the McMartin-Preschool Scandal," made the strongest indictment in print of the McMartin case. *60 Minutes* had cast doubt on the McMartin case two years earlier, but "Flip-Flop" was a much more sustained argument.[8]

There were other early voices in the witch-hunt narrative. Mary Pride employed the phrase "child abuse hysteria" in her 1986 book *The Child Abuse Industry*, an attack on child protective service agencies. Pride criticized a national study of family violence by Gelles, Strauss, and Steinmetz as the work of "point men for a whole corps of 'child advocates' who have found a way to impose their elitist, white, upper-class, post-Christian parenting philosophies on the rest of us under the guise of 'fighting child abuse.'"[9] Paul and Shirley Eberle wrote two books that added to the witch-hunt canon, *The Politics of Child Abuse* (1986) and *Abuse of Innocence* (1993). The first was quite similar to *The Child Abuse Industry*; the second blasted the prosecution in the McMartin case on the basis of the Eberles' observations of the trial. None of these early works became influential in the witch-hunt narrative. Pride's writings are best known in the small but avid home-schooling world, where her arguments against intruding on families through child protective services are taken as fundamental beliefs.[10] The Eberles never became a major voice in the witch-hunt narrative either, possibly because of their own dubious history in publication, which included child pornography.[11] Then again, their book about the McMartin case was brought back into print in 2003 by Prometheus Press and is the only book-length treatment of the case in general.[12] Nathan's early witch-hunt writings were undoubtedly convincing to the audience of the *Village Voice,* and Fischer's work had significant influence in Los Angeles, but there was no national voice for the witch-hunt narrative in those years. It remained largely a marginalized view while these highly contested cases moved forward through the legal system.

The turning point in the evolution of the witch-hunt narrative came with the verdict in the McMartin Preschool case. The defendants were acquitted on most charges, and the jury was hung on the rest. A variety of viewpoints about the case were expressed the next day in the *Los Angeles Times.* There was an op-ed maintaining that the system worked, there was one supporting the children, there was an editorial cartoon asking ominously what kind of shadow the case would cast, and, on the front page, there was the beginning of a four-part series by media critic Shaw asking *Where Was Media Skepticism?*[13] This was the last day that such a range of opinions would be expressed on the topic.

Shaw's series proved to be the pivotal piece, scolding the media and his own newspaper for the fiasco that was the McMartin case. He blasted reporters for bias in favor of the prosecution and for giving short shrift to the defense. He chastised Satz, the television reporter who broke the McMartin story, for sensationalism. He criticized Kee MacFarlane, who interviewed many of the children in the case and was later blamed for "implanting" false memories. And he condemned the "pack journalism" that followed. Indeed, Shaw cast the media as a major culprit in the McMartin case, arguing that the five McMartin defendants against whom charges were later dropped might never have been indicted were it not for Satz's intensive and inflammatory coverage before anyone was even charged in the case. The point was well taken, and Shaw's series won a Pulitzer Prize.

Virtually every account written since then has painted the McMartin case as a "witch hunt." The view was memorialized in the award-winning HBO movie *Indictment*. The same perspective was presented in a chapter about the case in Nathan's 1995 book with defense lawyer Michael Snedeker, *Satan's Silence: Ritual Abuse and the Making of an American Witch-Hunt*.[14] This has become the conventional wisdom about a case that was once seen as the biggest child sexual abuse case on record. Steven Mintz's Harvard University Press book *Huck's Raft: A History of American Childhood* enshrines the witch-hunt narrative as the conventional wisdom about the McMartin case.[15]

The 1990s were filled with works that contributed to the witch-hunt narrative. A few reflected original research, most were derivative. There were at least a half-dozen major works in the first half of the 1990s that made significant contributions to this narrative. Together, these works solidified the witch-hunt narrative by providing so many examples, in such a persuasive fashion, that it seemed difficult to imagine how anyone could ever have taken the charges in these cases seriously. By the mid-1990s it was apparent to most casual media observers that the day-care sex abuse cases of the 1980s were something akin to the McCarthyism of the 1950s. They were, as Nathan had put it in 1987, "a modern American witch hunt."

One of the most important contributions to this body of work was an article by Dorothy Rabinowitz in *Harper's* magazine in May 1990 about the Kelly Michaels case, a day-care case from Maplewood, New Jersey. Rabinowitz was the first writer to craft a convincing story of innocence about someone who had been convicted of child sexual abuse.[16] (The conviction was eventually overturned on appeal.) She also championed the cause of Grant Snowden, a police officer who was convicted of abusing children in a home day-care case in South Miami, and the Amiraults from Malden, Massachusetts, through a series of opinion columns on the editorial page of the *Wall Street Journal*. (Snowden was eventually released from prison after a federal appellate court overturned his conviction and the state attorney declined to retry the case, which was by then fourteen years old.[17] The Amiraults lost all of their efforts to overturn their convictions.) In part on the basis of her commentary about these cases, Rabinowitz won a Pulitzer Prize for Commentary in 2001.

Another important contribution to the witch-hunt narrative was made by the PBS program *Frontline*. Producer Ofra Bikel was the first and most prominent critic of the Little Rascals day-care case in Edenton, North Carolina, which also came to be known by the lead defendant's name, Robert Kelly. The first *Frontline* program about the case was in 1991, before Kelly's conviction. (It was later overturned on appeal.) Bikel followed up with two more programs, giving the Edenton case an extraordinary seven hours of national television coverage. It was enough to leave almost any viewer convinced that the defendants were innocent. Bikel produced several additional hours of programming on related topics in the 1990s, adding to the witch-hunt narrative. Peter Boyer, writing in the *New Yorker* and producing programs for *Frontline*, added two more contributions to this narrative with programs that focused on contested child sexual abuse cases linked to Janet Reno when she was state attorney for Dade County, Florida.[18] Those programs live on through program-specific websites created by *Frontline*.

A third major contribution to the witch-hunt narrative came from Lawrence Wright, who wrote a two-part article in the *New Yorker* in 1994 on the conviction of Paul Ingram from Olympia, Washington. The article chronicled how the prosecution of an incest case devolved into an elaborate investigation of a fictional satanic cult. Wright made a convincing case that Ingram was innocent of "everything but suggestibility."[19] The article was later published in expanded form as a book and then made into a movie. Another book, *Making Monsters*, by Richard Ofshe and Ethan Watters, also gave the case significant treatment from the same perspective. But the *New Yorker* version seemed to captivate people the most. It became an iconic article that impressed many people with the dangers of false convictions for sexual abuse.

In 1995, there were several significant contributions to the witch-hunt narrative that solidified it as the dominant discourse on the day-care sexual abuse cases of the 1980s. The major works were (1) Nathan and Snedeker's *Satan's Silence: Ritual Abuse and the Making of an American Witch Hunt*, (2) Ceci and Bruck's book *Jeopardy in the Courtroom: A Scientific Analysis of Children's Testimony,* and (3) Abby Mann's made-for-TV movie *Indictment*, about the McMartin case.

Debbie Nathan, one of the earliest and most frequent contributors to the witch-hunt narrative, teamed up with defense lawyer Michael Snedeker to write a book that is generally considered to be the most authoritative investigation of the day-care sexual abuse cases of the 1980s. There are full chapters about two significant cases (including McMartin), a detailed chapter about cases across the country, and an impressive amount of original source material covering a wide range of topics related to these cases. The book also contains an ominous and powerful dedication page, to fifty-one named individuals who were in prison when the book was first published, all allegedly falsely convicted on charges that included some kind of ritual abuse element. *Satan's Silence* has become a major source for most others writing about these cases.

The other major book published in 1995 covered some of the same cases but from the perspective of academic psychology. Stephen Ceci and Maggie Bruck's

Jeopardy in the Courtroom wove together recent laboratory experiments on child suggestibility with case studies from criminal court. The cases that were relied on most extensively were all day-care sex-abuse cases in the 1980s. The four cases discussed the most were Edenton (the one introduced by Bikel on *Frontline*), Finje (a case in Dade County, Florida, that ended in an acquittal and was also highlighted by *Frontline*), and two that were in the A. S. Ross story in the *San Francisco Examiner* in 1986: the Country Walk babysitting case from Dade County, Florida, also known as the Fuster case, and the Kelly Michaels day-care case from Maplewood, New Jersey. *Jeopardy in the Courtroom* has become highly influential in the field of psychology, representing the mainstream view of "child suggestibility" and children's testimony that was shaped by these cases.

Ceci and Bruck brought to the criticism of these cases the imprimatur of science that had been lacking in the late 1980s. Various mental health professionals had been available for hire as experts by the defense, but these "experts" did not have scientific research to back up their opinions. They criticized interview questions as leading, and they argued that children were highly suggestible; but their expert opinion seemed more a matter of opinion than expertise since there was not a scientific body of literature on the suggestibility of children. (The concept of child suggestibility is essentially that suggestive or coercive questions can cause a child to say and believe things that are not true.) Ceci and Bruck started filling this void in 1993 with an important review article that made suggestibility claims based on recent research.[20] The research was also the basis for a well-known "friend of the court" brief Ceci and Bruck organized in 1993 in the Kelly Michaels case. Their brief sided with Michaels and argued that a combination of suggestive interviewing and interviewer bias made the children's statements unreliable.

Another major contribution to the witch-hunt narrative was *Indictment*, the made-for-TV movie about the McMartin case. Written by Abby Mann and produced by Oliver Stone, the movie adopted the witch-hunt narrative framework and, in the process, made a strong and explicit claim to authenticity.[21] The film barely raised controversy. The only group inclined to raise objections was the organization Believe the Children, which developed serious credibility problems for having endorsed the view that there were tunnels underneath the school in which children were abused in satanic rituals. Their objection to the movie hardly registered.[22] It is one measure of how mainstream the witch-hunt narrative had become. If the underlying dispute was ever a "war," the side that supported the prosecution in these cases had diminished into an isolated group of parents with little credibility or voice. The war was over. The movie won three Emmys, including Outstanding Made for Television Movie. The *Village Voice* gave the movie high praise for two consecutive weeks. "Believe the Movie," Gary Indiana's review proclaimed in a play on Believe the Children. The following week, Ellen Willis wrote that the power of the movie, "enhanced by its meticulous fidelity to the facts, leaves no doubt that the case against the proprietors of the McMartin Preschool was a product of mass hysteria."[23]

There were many other contributions to the witch-hunt narrative in the 1990s. Sauer and Okerblom wrote a series in the *San Diego Union-Tribune* in 1993 that updated a 1988 series in the Memphis *Commercial Appeal* by Tom Charlier and Shirley Downing. Discussing the same group of cases already mentioned, the authors reported there had been "more than 100" of these cases.[24] There were also a host of columnists who found their own "witch hunt" case to tout. Martin Gardner, who had a column in the *Skeptical Inquirer* and in *Scientific American*, wrote about a case near his home in Hendersonville, North Carolina.[25] Thomas Sowell found one through a dissent in which Judge John T. Noonan adopted the witch-hunt narrative.[26] Trevor Armbrister of *Reader's Digest* did original research into the Bobby Finje case in Dade County.[27] There have been important contributions to the witch-hunt canon since 1995, but they are fewer and farther between. There were some acclaimed critiques of the prosecutions in Wenatchee, Washington, particularly a series by the *Seattle Post-Intelligencer*.[28] More recently, Andrew Jarecki's documentary *Capturing the Friedmans* promoted the view that the Friedman case, from 1988 in Great Neck, New York, was a witch-hunt. And in 2009, Sean Penn produced a documentary called *Witch Hunt* about some of the defendants from the Kern County, California, cases in the mid-1980s.

There were also several online sources promoting the idea of a national wave of "witch hunts" involving child sexual abuse claims. These had a significant effect in spreading the witch-hunt narrative. The most important website in the evolution of the witch-hunt narrative does not exist anymore. It was called the Witch Hunt Information Center and was created in 1993. It carried a prestigious mit.edu address because the webmaster, Jonathan Harris, was teaching in the physics department at the time. Under the main title of the site was the following subtitle or statement of purpose: "Information about the modern version of the witch hunts: ritual (and pseudo ritual) sexual abuse trials and those who have been wrongfully imprisoned by them."[29]

There were various links immediately below the statement, six of them about specific criminal cases. Three were well known from the mainstream media: Kelly Michaels, Frank Fuster, and Robert Kelly. The other three were Harris's contribution. Two were cases from Massachusetts: the Amiraults and Bernard Baran. As Harris later explained it, his interest began with the *Frontline* program about Edenton, which prompted him to look into the Amirault case in nearby Malden, Massachusetts. The third case Harris contributed to the witch-hunt narrative involved defendants Patrick Figured and Sonja Hill from Smithfield, North Carolina. Harris labeled their case "outrageous" multiple times. His website provided a very brief description of the facts and links to two legal documents: the appellate decision and the defense brief. He also posted a list of "dubious convictions" that was prepared by Debbie Nathan.[30]

It is difficult to appreciate the power of an early website like the Witch Hunt Information Center. Given an MIT web address, it had authoritative status; dozens of other sites linked to it. It was an early, enterprising use of the web for advocacy purposes, and it had obvious influence. Harris's work has been credited with interesting Rabinowitz in the Amirault case. The site became an authoritative source for some. For example, it contained a brief description of the Robert Halsey case in western Massachusetts. Frederick Crews, writing in the *New York Review of Books*, later claimed that the justice system had "failed" Halsey, a school bus driver whose case had not been written about anywhere as a victim of the child sex abuse "witch-hunts" except the Witch Hunt Information Center.[31] Similarly, after the site provided a description of a case in North Carolina that had not been written about anywhere else, the defendants, Figured and Hill, appeared on Nathan's list of "dubious convictions."

Harris also set up an electronic discussion list called Witchhunt. The idea of such a list was still quite novel in 1993. The internet was just gaining widespread use and engagement by academics. Moreover, the topic was in the news. In its early days, the membership of this list had a remarkable combination of activists and academics. Among the academics were psychology professor Daniel Schacter at Harvard and English professor Frederick Crews at Berkeley, best known for his writings against Freud. Activists included Peter Freyd, a moving force behind the False Memory Syndrome Foundation, and Carol Hopkins, founder of the San Diego–based Justice Committee. The purpose of the electronic list was stated in the form of a question: Is there a child sex abuse witchhunt?[32] The tag line was contained in the subject heading of every posting to the list. In its earliest days, Harris posted a few genuinely skeptical questions about the witch-hunt narrative itself. For example, he asked whether anyone knew of any criticisms of Ofra Bikel's recent television program on Edenton. No responses were forthcoming, although criticisms had been broadcast by the local PBS station.[33] An undergraduate researching the "witch hunt" cases asked for evidence that there had been more than one hundred cases, noting that the major lists of such cases added up to about fifty. There was no reply that provided documentation to support the claim.[34] The members of the list were generally strong proponents of the witch-hunt narrative. They knew the answer to the question "Is there a child sex abuse witch hunt?" These "witch hunters," as those on this list soon came to describe themselves, were increasingly activists who used the internet to exchange information and ideas. Jonathan Harris may have done more than anyone else to disseminate the witch-hunt narrative in the mid-1990s and beyond.[35]

Another unlikely website that played an important role in promoting the witch-hunt narrative was created as a hobby by some professionals in Canada who call themselves the Ontario Consultants for Religious Tolerance. Their site, which is mainly about religion, is large and receives a significant amount of internet traffic. It is not obvious why a site on "religious tolerance" would have anything to do with contested claims of child sexual abuse. One might hypothesize that the connection involved allegations of satanic ritual abuse made against members of the Wicca religion and even the Church of Satan. But rather than confine the coverage on the Religious Tolerance site to such cases, a section of the site is devoted to "43 M.V.M.O. court cases with allegations of sexual abuse and physical abuse of multiple children." (M.V.M.O. means multi-victim and multi-offender.) Eighteen of the forty-three cases are from the United States. The best known in the witch-hunt narrative are all there: Kern County, California; the McMartin Preschool; Kelly Michaels; Country Walk; Edenton, North Carolina; and Amirault. The site explains that because "It seemed obvious to us that grave injustices had been done," the author, Bruce Robinson, eschewed the position that motivates the rest of the site: reporting both or all sides of each issue to "let our readers make up their mind."[36] Harvard psychology professor Daniel Schacter relied on this site in his academic book about memory. So did history professor Philip Jenkins in his Yale University Press book *Moral Panic: Changing Conceptions of the Child Molester in Modern America.*[37]

The witch-hunt narrative is now the conventional wisdom about these cases. That view is so widely endorsed and firmly entrenched that there would seem to be nothing left to say about these cases. But a close examination of the witch-hunt canon leads to some unsettling questions: Why is there so little in the way of academic scholarship about these cases? Almost all of the major witch-hunt writings have been in magazines, often without any footnotes to verify or assess the claims made. Why hasn't anyone writing about these cases said anything about how difficult they are to research? There are so many roadblocks and limitations to researching these cases that it would seem incumbent on any serious writer to address the limitations of data sources. Many of these cases seem to have been researched in a manner of days or weeks. Nevertheless, the cases are described in a definitive way that belies their length and complexity, along with the inherent difficulty in researching original trial court documents.

An Overview of the Book

This book is based on the first systematic examination of court records in these cases. The book argues that even though many cases have been held up as classic examples of modern American "witch hunts," none of them truly fits that description. McMartin certainly comes close. But a careful examination of the evidence presented at trial demonstrates why, in my view, a reasonable juror could vote for conviction, as many did in this case. Other cases that have been painted as witch-hunts turn out to involve significant, even overwhelming, evidence of guilt. There are a few cases to the contrary, but even those are more complicated than the witch-hunt narrative allows. In short, there was not, by any reasonable measure, an epidemic of "witch hunts" in the 1980s. There were big mistakes made in how some cases were handled, particularly in the earliest years. But even in those years there were cases such as those of Frank Fuster and Kelly Michaels that, I believe, were based on substantial evidence but later unfairly maligned as having no evidentiary support.

The argument of the book begins with the McMartin case, the subject of Chapter Two. This is the foundational case in the witch-hunt narrative. Whether or not the narrative applies to other cases, it appears to offer the definitive account of the McMartin case, which ended without a single conviction after once being described as the largest child abuse case in history. The only competing account is a narrative about ritual abuse that was created near the beginning of the case, an account so thoroughly discredited that the witch-hunt narrative became all the more credible. Chapter Two argues that there is a third way to see the case—as it evolved, in stages. By this account, the case began with credible evidence of sexual abuse. Significant evidence was developed in the earliest stages of the case, before it was even referred to the agency that ultimately did hundreds of interviews later blamed for ruining the case. The McMartin case became six parts of overreaction to one part reality, sweeping up six women in criminal charges that never should have been brought. But the strongest evidence—the evidence that started the case—has been lost to history. Recognizing this evidence challenges the witch-hunt narrative in several ways. The McMartin case nevertheless stands largely as a monument to injustice to five, possibly six, of the seven defendants. The uncertainty about whether it is five or six reflects the kind of complexity that is not captured by the witch-hunt narrative. Chapter Two portrays that complexity.

The basic claim of the witch-hunt narrative is that there were at least a hundred, maybe several hundred, cases "just like McMartin." The narrative is a claim about a social phenomenon that swept the country during the McMartin era. The claim has been widely accepted as fact. The best evidence consists of studies of a handful of cases, along with lists of additional case names without any elaboration about the facts. Those sources, even taken at face value, do not add up to one hundred cases. More surprisingly, a substantial number of the cases held up as "witch hunts" actually included credible evidence of abuse, or even something stronger than that. But that is only apparent after doing extensive original research on a substantial number of cases. Chapter Three scrutinizes the claim that there were hundreds of these cases across the country.

The witch-hunt narrative began an account of child sexual abuse over the span of eight or nine years, starting in the early 1980s. It is offered as the sole account of sexual abuse in day-care centers then. There is scant recognition that there were true cases of sexual abuse in day-care centers during the time period—and before, for that matter. The witch-hunt narrative is also a story of overreaction; it often employs such terms as "hysteria" and "panic" to describe the social reactions surrounding these cases. Since child sexual abuse came to be identified with this narrative, there was a sense that our social reactions to the problem were largely panic-ridden. But this account overlooks the social forces that existed before child sexual abuse "emerged" into public discourse. Those phenomena, including silence and denial, continued during the McMartin era. This is part of the unacknowledged history of child sexual abuse, which is the subject of Chapter Four.

Chapters Five and Six take up two other foundational cases in the witch-hunt narrative. They provide an arc from the McMartin case. Seen in this light, the Kelly Michaels case in New Jersey is the turning point. It marked a major shift in the press, in academia, and in the courts. It was the most prominent reversal of a conviction from the 1980s. The shift was precipitated in part by dramatic change in the position of among academic psychologists about the issue of child suggestibility. It was also precipitated by the rise of the witch-hunt narrative in the popular media that began immediately after the demise of the McMartin case. Chapter Five is a systematic analysis of the case. It argues that there was substantial credible evidence of abuse that has been almost entirely ignored, and that there are significant exaggerations and other errors in the widely accepted view of this case.

Chapter Six takes up the Fuster case from Dade County, Florida, also known as Country Walk, after the name of the babysitting service that fostered the complaints in this case. The Fuster case plays a prominent role in Ceci and Bruck's *Jeopardy in the Courtroom*, second only to the Michaels case. The acclaimed television program *Frontline* applied the witch-hunt lens to the Fuster case in two separate episodes. The case is considered by many to be one of the last convictions still standing from the misguided era of the 1980s. Chapter Six takes the opposite view, arguing that there was extremely strong evidence to support this conviction. Indeed, it takes a special kind of bias to minimize or ignore all of the evidence.

Chapter Seven considers how the rise of the witch-hunt narrative has affected how we view child sexual abuse and children as witnesses. It begins with a consideration of two important developments since the end of the McMartin era, the successful civil and criminal cases against Catholic Church priests over child

sexual abuse and the increase in punitive policies aimed at convicted sex offenders. The chapter concludes with an examination of how child-suggestibility
claims have evolved since the Michaels case. Although it has become impolitic
to ask whether children are being unduly discredited in court, there are several
reasons to think they are. The arguments about child suggestibility have evolved
into a much more expansive effort to label children as tainted even in cases with
strong corroborative evidence. There has also been an effort to discredit disclosures simply because they were "delayed." That worrisome development appears
to be part of a larger movement to dismiss the expertise and knowledge of child-
abuse professionals.

2

The McMartin Preschool Case
(1983–1990)

The McMartin Preschool trial is often described as the longest and most expensive criminal trial in American history. There are no official record books for trial costs or trial length, but the McMartin case was a massive criminal trial by any standard. From initial arrest to final disposition of all charges, the case took more than seven years. There was an eighteen-month-long preliminary hearing, and the trial itself lasted more than two years. The case received enormous media attention and became the subject of several books and a made-for-TV movie.[1] It is featured on the Famous Trials website of law professor Douglas Linder and the Crime Library website originally created by CourtTV. In its early stages, the Mc-Martin Preschool case was described as "the largest child molestation case" on record—with multiple perpetrators and hundreds of likely victims. After the case ended without any convictions, it became widely viewed as a witch-hunt.

The case began in August 1983 when a mother named Judy Johnson contacted her son's pediatrician because she thought that the boy, Matthew,[2] had been anally penetrated by "Mr. Ray" at the McMartin Preschool. The name "Mr. Ray" came from her son; Mrs. Johnson did not know Raymond Buckey. Her son had been attending the preschool since June. The investigation that followed eventually included videotaped interviews with hundreds of children who had attended the preschool in the previous decade. Those interviews were conducted almost entirely by a nonprofit agency called Children's Institute International (CII). See Figure 2.1 for an overall case timeline.

On February 2, 1984, a local television station broadcast a detailed story about allegations that were emerging from the supposedly confidential interviews at CII. Although the investigation had been going on for months, there had been no stories in the media. The story immediately became national news even though nobody had yet been indicted and the Grand Jury had not been convened. The interviewers at CII had apparently come to believe that most of the children they had interviewed between November 1983 and January 1984

Figure 2.1 McMartin Case Timeline, Initial Complaint to Case Conclusion.

Overview timeline for McMartin, with breakout timelines for Case Origins and CII Investigation phases of the case.

Case Origins Aug to Oct 1983

CII Investigation
02 Nov 1983 to 30 Jun 1984

Preliminary Hearing
07 Aug 1984 to 09 Jan 1986

First Trial
13 Jul 1987 to 18 Jan 1990

Second Trial
10 May to 28 Jul 1990

| Aug 1983 | 1984 | 1985 | 1986 | 1987 | 1988 | 1989 | 1990 |

Case Origins 12 Aug to Oct 1983

| 1983 | Aug | 1984 | Jan | Feb | Mar | Sept |

Judy Johnson reports suspected abuse
12 Aug

Detective Dye talks to families
24/25 Aug

Search warrant executed
03 Sept

Buckey arrested & released
7 Sept

Manhattan Beach Police Department letter to parents
8 Sept

Tanya Mergili examined at UCLA Medical Center
20 Sept

Last child interviewed by MBPD in September
28 Sept

CII Investigation 02 Nov 1983 to 30 Jun 1984

| 1983 | Dec | 1984 | Jan | Feb | Mar | Apr | May |

First interview at CII
01 Dec

Wayne Satz story aired
02 Feb

Grand Jury
06-22 Mar

National TV coverage begins
05 Mar

115-count indictment
23 Mar

Final CII interview before charges were finalized
10 May

had been sexually abused by various teachers at the preschool in Manhattan Beach, California. The "exclusive" story on KABC-TV reported that sixty children had already been identified as victims. The CII interviews became the primary basis for the criminal charges in the case. They later became the primary focus of the defense.

The case was taken to the grand jury in March 1984. The grand jury indicted seven defendants for sex crimes against children. The primary defendant was Raymond Buckey, the only male who worked at the preschool. Three other members of his family, who also worked at the preschool, were also indicted: his sister, Peggy Ann Buckey; his mother, Peggy Buckey; and his grandmother, Virginia McMartin. Three other teachers at the preschool were also indicted: Betty Raidor, Babette Spitler, and Mary Ann Jackson. Charges would eventually be dropped against five of the seven defendants, with only Ray and Peggy Buckey going to trial. But in 1985, when the case had seven defendants, it was widely held that there were many more defendants yet to be identified. The county sheriff's McMartin Task Force was formed to investigate the case further. At one point, there were more than fifty additional suspects in the case and allegations that children had been taken to a host of locations beyond the preschool. But no further charges were ever brought.

At its height, there were forty-one actual complainants in the McMartin case. Fourteen of those children later participated in the preliminary hearing.[3] The rest of the complainants dropped out of the case for various reasons: some parents decided to pull their children from the increasingly long and highly publicized ordeal, and the DA made the decision to drop other complainants The preliminary hearing lasted eighteen months—far longer than almost all criminal trials in the country. At the conclusion of the hearing, Municipal Court Judge Aviva Bobb ruled there was sufficient evidence to hold all seven of the defendants over for trial. The evidentiary standard required to reach that judgment was low, and the preliminary hearing exposed serious problems with the prosecution's case.

Ira Reiner, the Los Angeles district attorney who inherited the McMartin case when he defeated Robert Philibosian in June 1984, criticized the way in which the case had been investigated and charged. Shortly after Judge Bobb's decision to hold all seven defendants over for trial, Reiner dropped all charges against five of them, famously describing the evidence against them as "incredibly weak." Only Ray Buckey and his mother, Peggy Buckey, would actually go to trial. The case would involve eleven children.

The trial was preceded by a significant sideshow involving a series of tape-recorded interviews between Glenn Stevens, a disaffected prosecutor who quit his job over the case, and Abby Mann, a screenwriter who was developing movie and book ideas that cast the entire case as a witch-hunt. Stevens was one of the

three assistant DAs who were assigned the McMartin case during its most critical stages in the spring of 1984. He left the DA's office in January 1986 after
coming to the conclusion that most, but not all, of the defendants in the case
were innocent. Stevens entered into an agreement to help Abby and Myra Mann
(his wife) write a movie script about the case. Some of the material that he provided to them, including comments made during the tape-recorded conversations, eventually became the focus of a lengthy pre-trial hearing over a motion to
dismiss the case. That hearing occasioned a rare window into what Stevens actually said about the evidence in office memoranda written in late 1985 and early
1986. Contrary to how events were later portrayed in the movie *Indictment*, Stevens wrote that he found the evidence against Ray Buckey to be quite strong.[4]
But he also concluded that the children's statements about all of the other defendants, including Peggy Buckey, were unconvincing. Charges against five of the
female defendants were dropped long before this hearing, but the case went
ahead against Ray Buckey and Peggy Buckey. The motion to dismiss charges
against them, based on tape-recorded conversations between Stevens and the
Manns, was rejected, and Ray Buckey and his mother were then tried for child
molestation.

The trial lasted almost two years, and it ended inconclusively. The defendants
were found "not guilty" on most charges, while others, almost entirely against
Ray, resulted in a hung jury. (The jury also could not reach a verdict on a conspiracy charge against Peggy, but the judge dismissed that charge.) The unresolved charges against Ray involved three girls. Those charges were retried in an
abbreviated trial that began in April 1990 and lasted less than three months. It
ended with a hung jury on all counts. A mistrial was then declared and all remaining charges against Ray Buckey were dismissed, rendering the case a colos-
sal failure by any measure.

The case was filled with strange twists. The lead defense attorney, Danny
Davis, became a witness in the case. The defense filed a motion to disqualify the
Los Angeles District Attorney's Office. Both sides in the case were sanctioned
over various behaviors. Most dramatically, several key actors in the case died an
untimely death: Judy Johnson, mother of the initial child in the case, apparently
died from alcoholism, and two others with connections to the case took their
own lives.[5] An unsolved 1976 murder case was even linked to the McMartin case
at one point.[6]

Several of the McMartin defendants sought unsuccessfully to sue the prosecutors and CII, the organization that interviewed the children in the case, for
monetary damages. A case against Los Angeles County was dismissed because
of sovereign immunity rules that protect government entities against various
kinds of lawsuits.[7] One teacher also tried, without success, to sue CII for defama-
tion. Relying on theories of sovereign immunity, the superior court dismissed

the action on its face, and that result was upheld on appeal.[8] Virginia McMartin, Peggy Buckey, and Peggy Ann Buckey prevailed in a postverdict libel suit against Robert Currie, a parent who made accusations against all three women on various television programs that were aired immediately after the verdicts were announced.[9] Note that charges had long since been dropped against two of these women, and the jury did not return any convictions against Peggy Buckey. Nevertheless, reflecting the deep contradictions surrounding the case, the plaintiffs were awarded one dollar in damages.[10]

The Evolution of the Witch-Hunt Narrative

In 1984, when the case emerged in the media, the coverage was decidedly pro-prosecution. The following year, when the preliminary hearing began, serious criticisms of the case started to emerge in the press. Years later, when the trial was finally winding down, journalists paid homage to the complexity and the confusion of the case. Writing for the *American Lawyer* magazine, Robert Safian authored "McMartin Madness: Ten Days in the Life of the Longest, Most Gruesomely Difficult Criminal Trial Ever." He concluded:

> There are too many inconsistencies in the prosecution's case not to provoke lingering doubts. Yet there is too much conviction and horror in the children's stories of abuse not to look askance at Ray Buckey.[11]

Similarly, after months of observation, Cynthia Gorney wrote a two-part story for the *Washington Post* entitled "The Terrible Puzzle of McMartin Preschool." Spinning a number of alternative views of the case, each with its own plausibility, she suggested:

> . . . that some children were molested in Manhattan Beach . . . and that the disclosing and spreading of those children's reports took place in an atmosphere of such uncontainable and self-feeding alarm that both children and adults lost the capacity to sort the imagined from the real. . . .[12]

That sense of complexity was reflected on the editorial page of the *Los Angeles Times* the day after the original verdicts. There were op-eds with several takes on the outcome of the case. The most popular view was that the DA's office had blown the case. Another view was, "We all wanted the truth but must settle for justice." That point of view was from a legal commentator who thought "the system" worked well.[13] Finally, psychologist and writer Carol Tavris weighed in with an editorial about child suggestibility and the credibility of children as witnesses. She argued, "Our best hope in sorting out these conflicting claims [about children as witnesses] is to try to set aside our prejudices and assess the research evidence for each side." She wrote favorably about research by psychology professor Gail Goodman supporting the view that "very young children do not volunteer information that they feel is embarrassing or shameful" and that they "do not agree with leading questions that are wrong." She ended the column by framing the challenge for the future as being sure that "legitimate concerns about falsely accusing an innocent adult do not cause us to falsely disbelieve an innocent child."

But the sense of complexity and confusion that permeated the end of the case did not linger, even with the inconclusive end to the first and second trials. The day after the verdicts were announced, the *Los Angeles Times* media critic, David Shaw, published the first part in a blistering critique that, ironically, won the *Times* a Pulitzer Prize for criticizing its own coverage. "Where Was Skepticism in the Media?" cried out the first headline. The next day it was "Reporter's Early Exclusives Triggered a Media Frenzy." By the end of the four-part series, Shaw had praised the writers who first adopted the witch-hunt narrative and skewered those who did not.

Positions hardened soon thereafter. "The only evidence against the Buckeys was the children's statements" and they were discredited, Douglas Besharov explained in the *National Review* a month later in February 1990.[14] A few months after that, Dorothy Rabinowitz published an article in *Harper's* about the Kelly Michaels case. She referred to the McMartin case as a modern-day Salem. In June 1990, Debbie Nathan sketched the larger witch-hunt narrative in the *Village Voice* with "What McMartin Started: The Ritual Abuse Hoax."[15]

Nathan's argument gained wider acceptance and eventually became the conventional wisdom. It became as unpopular in the 1990s to be associated with the children's side of the McMartin case as it was to be associated with the defendants in the mid-1980s. Tavris has, in her own words, been "atoning" for her column written the day after the McMartin verdicts expressing concern that children's testimony not be unduly discredited as a result of the case.[16] Writing in *Redbook* in 1992, she warned of the new "witch hunts" against child sexual abuse. "Beware the Incest Survivor Machine," she intoned the following year in the *New York Times Book Review*, arguing that a nefarious network of therapists profited from the child sexual-abuse "industry."[17] In 1997, she explained in an interview how guilty she felt about her 1990 article endorsing psychology professor Gail Goodman's academic research.[18]

Two prominent academic psychologists, Stephen Ceci from Cornell University and Maggie Bruck from Johns Hopkins University, reached very different conclusions from Goodman's about children as witnesses. Goodman's message was essentially positive: children are better witnesses than many people think. Ceci and Bruck's message was much more cautionary: children are highly suggestible. They published an important article about children's testimony in 1993 and a major book in 1995, called *Jeopardy in the Courtroom: A Scientific Analysis of Children's Testimony*. In both of these works, they adopted the view that the McMartin case was a modern-day witch-hunt and drew specific analogies to the Salem Witch Trials.[19] Nathan and Snedeker's book *Satan's Silence* was also published in 1995. It has a chapter on the McMartin case that fits the book's subtitle: *The Making of a Modern American Witch-Hunt*. The third major treatment of the McMartin case in 1995 undoubtedly reached the largest audience—that is, the HBO movie *Indictment*, written by Abby Mann and produced by Oliver Stone. The movie won an Emmy, and reviewers such as Ellen Willis of the *Village Voice* argued that the movie's power "is enhanced by its meticulous fidelity to the facts."[20] "It's rare these days to find, on TV or the larger screen, a work in which fury is a clarifying force," wrote Rabinowitz, who credited the movie with being "a factual account, taken from the record."[21] The complexity and uncertainty that were so prevalent when the case ended were entirely gone. The movie "leaves no doubt," Rabinowitz noted with approval, that the case had *no factual basis*. In sum, in the years since the McMartin case ended the popular narrative that has risen to prominence is that the case lacked *any* factual basis. Instead, it has become the foundational case in the witch-hunt narrative. This narrative is applied so completely to the McMartin case that it may be difficult to imagine there is anything left to say about it. The McMartin case has, quite simply, come to be seen as baseless. Under this view, all of the child molestation charges were "trumped up"; they were a "hoax."

Although the view is widely promoted and accepted, it is contradicted by court transcripts and various other records in the case. Extensive original research reveals that there was considerable evidence against Ray Buckey, and there was also credible evidence to suggest his mother was aware of the situation and helped cover it up. This chapter elaborates the evidence in detail. Five arguments are advanced and documented. First, the evidence involving Judy Johnson's son (the first child in the case) is more compelling than typically portrayed. Second, the early investigation—before CII started interviewing children— uncovered significant evidence of abuse. Third, there were compelling circumstances involving two families who initially supported the defendants and then switched sides. Fourth, the medical evidence, although mixed in quality, was stronger than often portrayed. Fifth, there was considerable evidence that counters the witch-hunt narrative about Ray Buckey's character and about whether he had the *opportunity* to molest children at the preschool. Taken together, these arguments help explain why seven jurors said in a post-verdict press conference that they thought children in the case *had* been abused.

Case Origins: Judy Johnson and Her Son

The McMartin case began in August 1983, when Judy Johnson first suspected that her son, Matthew, had been sodomized at the McMartin Preschool. The evidence supporting her suspicion is largely medical since Matthew was three years old and not very communicative. He apparently told his mother, on August 11, 1983, something about "Mr. Ray" playing with a thermometer. This was in a conversation that began after Matthew's mother noticed some blood on his anus. The boy was examined in short succession by three doctors, first a family physician, then an emergency room doctor, and ultimately a pediatrician with child-abuse experience.

This evidence is ignored in the witch-hunt narrative, which places the focus entirely on Matthew's mother, Judy. Under this view, she was delusional when she made the original complaint about her son, so there is no reason to consider what the doctors who examined the boy actually observed. This story seems plausible because she died of alcohol-related causes in December 1986, and before her demise she lived in a paranoid, reclusive manner. But whether those ills came about during the case or actually predated the original complaint is an important question that has not received serious consideration in the witch-hunt narrative. What is taken as an article of faith—that Judy Johnson was delusional from day one—is flatly contradicted by all of the available evidence.

The evidence concerning Matthew Johnson consisted of more than statements conveyed by his mother. There was medical evidence from several doctors, though virtually all of the medical evidence in the McMartin case would later be dismissed as baseless in the witch-hunt narrative. But that stark position was not even endorsed by Dr. David Paul, the expert the *defense* brought from London to counter the medical evidence in the case.

The McMartin case began with a mother's concern about something very tangible: her son's bleeding anus. This is why Judy Johnson contacted Dr. Richard Segal, Matthew's pediatrician at Kaiser Permanente on August 12, 1983. She reported that Matthew had complained of "rectal discomfort" several times that summer and that she had observed his anus to have "significant redness and occasionally some bleeding." Mrs. Johnson had discussed the matter with Dr. Segal earlier in the summer. That is particularly notable since she would later be characterized as so intent on finding sexual abuse that she had been looking for signs of it all summer.[22] In fact, she did not raise the idea in her discussions with Dr. Segal earlier in the summer. Instead, they discussed the possibility of pinworms.[23] It was only after observing blood again, and then being told by her son something about "having his temperature taken" at school, that Johnson expressed strong suspicions about sexual abuse. Dr. Segal suggested she bring her son to the emergency room.

Dr. Scott McGeary examined Matthew that evening and observed a "band of redness" that "encircled his anus." He described the area as "red and roughened" and concluded that there "appeared to be some friction like trauma to the rectal area."[24] As he later testified, Dr. McGeary "was concerned that there was possible sodomization or at least passage of some object into the child's rectum."[25] The doctor was not a child abuse specialist, so he arranged to have Matthew seen at UCLA. Debbie Nathan, one of the most prominent proponents of the witch-hunt narrative, has suggested that Judy Johnson was unreasonable for taking her son to a special clinic "instead of abandoning her complaint."[26] But Dr. McGeary did not advise abandoning the complaint; quite the contrary, he expressed concern about sexual abuse and referred Johnson to a specialist.

Matthew Johnson was examined at the Marion Davies Children's Clinic at UCLA on August 17. Nathan and Snedeker dismissed the findings from this exam with the claim that "the young intern who examined [the boy] was completely inexperienced at doing sexual-abuse exams."[27] But the "young intern"— actually a resident pediatrician, Dr. Linda Gordon—did not conduct the examination alone. She was joined by the attending physician, Dr. Jean H. Simpson-Savary, a pediatrician who graduated from one of the top medical schools in the country (Johns Hopkins) and had almost five years of experience in pediatrics. Dr. Simpson-Savary described discolored bruising patterns and concluded that the injury was recent, "within the last week, but not recent in sense of hours."[28] She notified the Manhattan Beach Police Department (MBPD) that "the victim's anus was forcibly entered several days ago."[29] Even the doctor hired by the defense years later to challenge the medical evidence in the case agreed that these were "fairly significant findings" of sexual abuse.[30] The significance of those findings might be diminished with more recent knowledge about "normal" anal and genital exams; it depends on precisely what Dr. Simpson saw.[31] Unfortunately, there are no photographs to provide for an independent examination. Nevertheless, the constellation of evidence described on August 12, 1983, would still support a report for suspected child abuse today.

Those facts have not prevented Judy Johnson from becoming the primary scapegoat for the entire McMartin case. Her name is in the title of Nathan and Snedeker's twenty-five-page chapter about the case—the most detailed and documented critique of the case ever published. They claim Judy Johnson had "obvious" mental problems and that her "delusionary statements" launched the case.[32] Abby Mann, who wrote the screenplay for *Indictment*, framed his view of the case around Johnson's "suspect personality."[33] Ellen Willis asserted that the case was "launched by a schizophrenic alcoholic's complaint."[34] But Judy Johnson was never as important to the case as has been claimed; moreover, the chronology of her mental health issues has been inaccurately represented.

Johnson is an obvious candidate for scapegoat given the cause of her death in December 1986 and the nature of her behavior before that. In the summer of 1986, she thought the whole world was out to get her. The McMartin case had been a national news story for well over two years by that point. Johnson asked the DA's office to place her in protective custody because of threats she claimed were verified on her telephone-answering machine. The DA investigator who looked into the matter noted simply, "I made determination her fears were groundless."[35] So there is little question that Johnson's grip on reality was weak in 1986. However, this does not answer the question of whether her mental instability came *after* the McMartin case emerged and evolved or whether it actually *fashioned* the case. That question became the focus of media stories, particularly after her death.

Reporting on the life and death of Judy Johnson in a long story titled "Driven to Her Death," the *Los Angeles Herald-Examiner* indicated that in the first half of 1983 she "was strong and healthy" and that she "jogged constantly, ate health food and reportedly was so averse to alcohol that she brought sparkling apple juice to neighborhood parties. . . ."[36] There is no evidence in the record of the McMartin case that Johnson was mentally unstable when she took her son to the emergency room on August 12, 1983. Indeed, the notes from when prosecutor Stevens first met Judy Johnson confirm she did not present the obvious mental instability that later consumed her. "I found her pleasant and very lucid," Stevens noted at the time.[37] Stevens eventually criticized most aspects of the state's case but *not* Johnson's mental health in August 1983 or her son's medically confirmed injuries.

After leaving the DA's office in January 1986 over doubts about the guilt of most of the defendants, Stevens told screenwriter Abby Mann that the McMartin case pushed Johnson over the edge; the case did not originate in the mind of a mentally ill woman. The transcripts of their conversations over several months demonstrate that the Manns had formed a view of Johnson that went against what Stevens told them on the subject. In one conversation, Stevens pushed Mann to explain why he kept coming back to Johnson. Mann's answer: because she had "a suspect personality." Stevens did not agree; nor did he waiver, in these conversations, in the view that nothing in Johnson's life tainted the origins of the case in August 1983. Stevens even told Mann that Johnson's performance at the preliminary hearing in July 1984 was "Great. She was terrific."[38] Stevens's observation runs so contrary to the witch-hunt narrative that the Manns pointedly asked him at a later date whether there was "anything unusual in her testimony." "No. She did a very good job," Stevens reaffirmed.[39] But that is not how Johnson was portrayed in the movie, or in the witch-hunt narrative at large, where she is routinely described as mentally ill from the start.

There is no doubt that Johnson started drinking after the McMartin case began. She became reclusive and paranoid. There is also no doubt that a case like McMartin could potentially break a person. Paul Bynum, a former MBPD officer who was working as an investigator for the defense in the McMartin case, committed suicide the day before he was supposed to testify in the McMartin case. There were reports of secondary trauma among hardened reporters who covered the case. "The case poisoned anyone who had any contact with it," Judge Pounders, who presided over the first trial, said at one point.[40] Peggy Buckey became paranoid, apparently as a result of the case, and was eventually afraid to leave her house. But none of those effects should be confused with the actual origins of the case. The claim that the McMartin case was started by the delusions of a crazy woman is simply not in line with the facts. Instead, several doctors agreed that Matthew Johnson had apparently been sodomized—recently.

The Early Investigation (Pre-CII)

Judy Johnson's report and the related medical evidence prompted the Manhattan Beach Police Department to take the matter seriously. Ray Buckey was arrested on September 7, 1983. He was released the same day, however, because Matthew had not made any direct statements to the police and he was clearly too young to testify. The medical evidence alone was insufficient to sustain charges. It is not clear whether the police knew this when they arrested Ray Buckey; this was one of the first sexual abuse cases the department had ever faced involving preschool children. Perhaps they arrested Buckey in the hopes he might make an incriminating statement, or maybe they just did not realize that prosecutors could not carry charges forward on the basis of the medical evidence alone.

Whatever the explanation, the police chief, apparently frustrated by the inability to move forward, sent a letter the next day to all of the parents whose names appeared in enrollment records from the preschool. That letter was to become the subject of intense criticism because it named Ray Buckey, described some of the allegations conveyed by Johnson, and requested that parents question their children.[41] The letter was not the first indication to the community that police were investigating the matter, however; a number of families were contacted in late August. Although those families were apparently told not to discuss the matter with anyone, it was later established that Virginia McMartin learned about the investigation before her grandson was arrested.[42]

Precisely how the investigation played out in the immediate aftermath of the now-infamous letter is critical to assessing the evidence in the McMartin case. Most accounts of the McMartin case collapse the time period between when the letter was sent and the first media coverage five months later.[43] There is no question that the dynamics of the investigation changed dramatically with the advent of intense media coverage in February 1984. What is surprising is how little attention has been paid to developments immediately following the September 1983 letter.

The witch-hunt narrative maintains that the letter resulted in no significant disclosures. "Not one child disclosed anything suspicious," according to one account.[44] Mary Fischer put it more starkly in a magazine article still heralded for "debunking" the McMartin case: "What's not commonly known is that with the exception of one child, all of the former preschoolers denied being molested at the school until after they were interviewed at CII."[45] This claim has grown into the widely repeated assertion that the entire McMartin case was "created" months later at CII, where children were first interviewed beginning on November 1.[46] But the initial responses to the September letter were much more significant than is ever acknowledged in the witch-hunt narrative.

A five-page log maintained by the MBPD recorded the telephone responses they received to the letter with short notations of the date and substance of the response. At least eight families are listed as furnishing "positive" responses, usually with an annotation referring to the relevant section of the California Penal Code for child molestation (i.e., "288 PC victim," or "positive 288."). The most specific notation says: "288 victim, touched penis." The remaining "positive" responses are otherwise unelaborated on the log. Several other responses are listed as "possible." A few of those contain a phrase or two of elaboration. The most detailed entry states: "strange behavior—pulls down pants and fondles self. Kisses father in a way not like three-year-old." A few other notations, not labeled as "possible" or "positive," were nevertheless suspicious enough to warrant further investigation. The entry for the Delco family, for example, states, "older daughter says [Ray Buckey] wore no underwear, saw genitals."[47]

There are police reports and, in some cases, other documents for almost all of the families who were recorded as "positive" or "possible" responders in September (see Figure 2.2). Only four of those children became complainants in the criminal case. A fifth September responder was included on the prosecution's witness list in February, but she did not become a complainant in the case. A few other children, who were first identified in September 1983, were listed as likely complainants, when an investigator for the Los Angeles District Attorney's Office started considering specific charges. Those children did not became part of the formal case, but what they said *in September and October 1983* merits attention because any disclosures made during that time directly contradict the notion of the case being "created" at CII months later. Statements made during this time cannot be attributed to media frenzy either, since it would be months

Figure 2.2 McMartin Sequence—September Responders as Recorded by MBPD.

"Positive" and "possible" responses as designated by MBPD log and information forms.

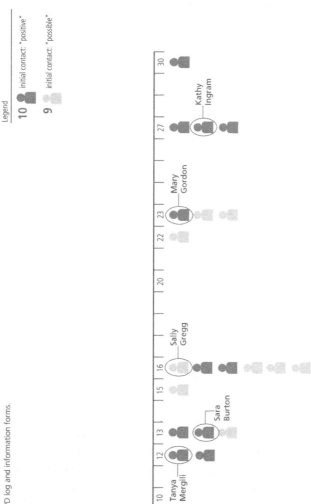

Names for all children referenced in text.
Constructed from MBPD documents.

until there was *any* media coverage. Here is a synopsis of the five children who provided significant responses to the MBPD in September 1983 and later became part of the criminal case.

Tanya Mergili

The first family to provide a "positive" report called the MBPD on Friday, September 9. The MBPD was short-staffed that day because it was a state holiday, California's Admission Day. The Mergilis were told to bring their daughter Tanya in for questioning on Monday, September 12.

The Mergilis were unaware of the investigation that a handful of families learned about in August. Mrs. Mergili learned about the MBPD letter on Friday, September 9, because her daughter was playing with another child from McMartin whose mother received the letter that day. (The Mergilis received their letter the next day.) Mrs. Mergili asked her daughter about the matter, and police notes indicate that Tanya "willingly responded with details of her abuse." The police report indicates that Tanya "mentioned being tied up by Ray Buckey, shut in closets, and playing something called the horsey game."[48] The report also contains the mother's statement that "her daughter related that Raymond Buckey had tickled her in the area of her vagina beneath her clothing."[49]

Tanya Mergili was scheduled to begin a new term at the McMartin Preschool on Monday, September 12. Instead, her parents brought her to the Manhattan Beach Police Department that day. Not surprisingly, the Mergilis decided their daughter would not return to the preschool.[50] Tanya was evaluated at UCLA Medical Center a week later by Dr. Mary Wilson. The interview was videotaped, and the tape received considerable attention in the pre-trial phase of the McMartin case because Tanya was the first child to support the claims made by Matthew Johnson. There are two separate transcriptions of the videotape, one stipulated to by both parties and one prepared specifically by the defense.[51] These documents demonstrate the severe limitations of capturing interactions with a young child in a written transcript. By extension, they also demonstrate the difficulties in interviewing children of this age.

The thirty-page transcript that was agreed to by both sides contains a considerable amount of preliminaries—playing and talking about nothing in particular for the child to become more comfortable with the setting and the interviewer. The first significant passage for the criminal case appears on page 15. That passage, which consumes about half a page, appears to represent several minutes of interaction between Dr. Wilson and the child. But the transcribed statements are all attributed to Dr. Wilson. It is clear from the doctor's words that Tanya was providing relevant demonstrative responses, but those actions are not described in the transcription.[52]

So why don't you show—why don't you show me how—how—how Ray played with you, okay, Tanya, because I really need to talk to you about that.

Is that what he would do?

Huh?

Show me again.

Well, let's pull the dress up so I can really see.

What would he do?[53]

The paragraph breaks contained in this passage suggest there were various pauses. It is not clear, however, what the child was actually demonstrating during this time. Two handwritten annotations, likely made later by Dr. Wilson, add important details that could be verified only by examining the videotape.

So why don't you show—why don't you show me how—how—how Ray played with you, okay, Tanya, because I really need to talk to you about that. [Handwritten note: Tanya demonstrating on dolls—hand under dress and rubbing.]

Is that what he would do?

Huh?

Show me again.

Well, let's pull the dress up so I can really see.

What would he do? [Handwritten note: Tanya's hand rubbing.][54]

A similar interaction occurs a few pages later. The transcription suggests that the child offered further evidence of sexual abuse, although again the specifics remain unclear.

Why don't you show me with the other doll what he would do.

Can you show me with the other doll?

I can help you.

Oh, that's what he would do. Okay.

And would he do anything else?

He'd go like that, huh?[55]

The handwritten notations on this document indicate that the videotape contains important behavioral evidence. In the first sentence above, the notation "hand in pants" was placed above the phrase "what he would do." Moreover, the notation " + rub" was written below the phrase "anything else" in the next to last sentence in the passage above.

There is no doubt how Dr. Wilson at UCLA viewed the substance of the examination. According to the medical report that she wrote: "Tanya described Ray touching penis to rectum, vagina, mouth. Also masturbating himself and touching her."[56] Since the Mergilis were the earliest to respond to the police department, Tanya was clearly one of the most important children in the investigation.

The interviews at CII did not begin, however, until almost six weeks *after* Tanya's interview with Dr. Wilson. By that time, Mrs. Mergili described recent and extremely sexualized behavior by her daughter. One of the behaviors described by one of the parents: "Bending over, spreading her cheeks and saying 'is my hole cute?' Ray-Ray used to like me to do this."[57]

Sara Barton

The second important child from the earliest stages of the case is Sara Barton, who attended the McMartin Preschool from September 1981 until August 11, 1983. She was in Ray Buckey's class in 1982 and she occasionally stayed in the afternoon through 1983, when he was often the only adult at the facility. Sara was recorded as a "positive" response by the MBPD on September 13, 1983. Her parents responded to the MBPD letter by saying their daughter told them she "had seen Ray Buckey's penis and touched same." Mrs. Barton, who would later be criticized as having a "fanatical belief that enveloped their children and demanded their participation,"[58] informed the police that she felt a formal interview was not warranted. Even though she was positive there had been some kind of sexual contact between Ray Buckey and her daughter, she was "concerned about stressing her daughter."

Gloria Barton testified to the grand jury in March 1984 that her daughter had vaginitis in the spring of 1983.[59] She applied over-the-counter medications on Sara repeatedly during that time; they gave relief but then the redness and discomfort would return. Barton testified that the problem continued until Sara started at her new kindergarten in September 1983. During the spring of 1983, Sara also asked her parents to apply medication to her anus. She was apparently unresponsive when asked why she would need medicine on her anus. Her mother testified that Sara replied in the negative when asked if she was constipated. Her parents acceded to applying ointment every time and otherwise let these incidents pass.

In October 1983, Gloria Barton wrote in her diary that she had casually raised questions about Ray Buckey or the McMartin Preschool a few times and that Sara "did not want to talk about him at all."[60] Her mother's conclusion: "We felt we should respect her feelings and dropped the matter." This is apparently how the situation remained until a parent's meeting in mid-November

1983. Leaving the discussion of developments after that date until later, we see clearly that the earliest responses from this child provided relevant evidence for the investigation. The significance of the evidence is unclear, and her parents, though concerned, certainly did not overreact at the time. All of those facts are omitted entirely from Nathan and Snedeker's detailed critique of this child, which relies entirely on later events to discredit the child. Gloria Barton became an outspoken, activist parent who saw a widespread conspiracy behind the McMartin case. Her daughter was listed on some early documents in the case, but she was never one of the named complainants in the case.

Sally Gregg

A third important child who was identified early in the investigation was Sally Gregg, who attended the McMartin Preschool from September 1981 until June 1983. She stayed from 9:00 a.m. to 3:00 p.m. "many days," and Ray Buckey was regularly the only adult in charge of children who stayed after noon. Sally was recorded as a "possible" victim on the MBPD original log on the case. Her parents wrote on the information form they mailed back to the police:

> We are leaving town on 9/14/83 + will not return till 9/22/83. In a preliminary discussion with Sally, she said 'Ray Ray does not wear underpants.' Sally has been overly interested in touching my genital area. This could well be a result of this case. We would like more time to talk to Sally without a heavy cross-examination.[61]

There is no indication in surviving records that the Greggs brought their child into the police station in the weeks after returning to Manhattan Beach. The MBPD eventually wrote a police report about Sally on January 24, 1984. The earliest date detailed in the report is November 28, when Kathy Wilcox, whose child had attended the McMartin Preschool, reported to the police that her daughter said "that Ray would take girls into the bathroom at school and put his finger in their vagina."[62] Karen Wilcox apparently mentioned Sally Gregg, and it appears that the interaction prompted the Greggs to contact CII and schedule an interview.

Sally Gregg was interviewed at CII on January 16, 1984; she was interviewed again at the MBPD on January 24. She became the third of the September responders to become a formal complainant in the criminal trial. She was also one of only nine children who eventually testified at the trial in this case, and one of only three children who participated in the retrial.

Mary Gordon

The fourth response from September 1983 that involved a child who later became a complainant in the criminal case was from the Gordon family, whose five-year-old daughter Mary had attended the McMartin Preschool from 1981 through May 1983. The family's attorney, Robert Hamrick, contacted the MBPD on September 23. He reported that, in response to the MBPD letter, Mrs. Gordon had asked her daughter whether anything bad had happened to her at school. As he reported further, Mary told her mother that Ray Buckey "put his finger down her throat and asked her to pretend that her mouth was a house" and that he put his fingers inside her vagina.[63] Mrs. Gordon later informed MBPD Detective Dye that "upon learning of the finger penetration, she [the mother] didn't pursue further questioning." Mrs. Gregg indicated she "was desirous of avoiding duplication in interviews" and of the emotional impact on the child.[64] The family then went on a trip to England until mid-October.

Mary was interviewed at the MBPD on October 19, a few days after they returned. Her mother advised the reporting officer that Mary was afraid when she came to the station because "she thought she was going to jail." Included in the police report, however, are several incriminating statements Mary apparently made about Ray Buckey: "Mary says the suspect has not fondled her genitals but put his finger inside her pussy." "Mary told [Reporting Officer] further that the suspect called her a bad name, i.e. fucking ass and then spit down her throat."[65] (Mary had been treated with antibiotics in the spring of 1983 for a throat infection.) But the police report also captured the equivocal nature of her statements:

> The victim was very anxious when asked if she had told her mother that Ray had put his fingers here, while pointing to her vaginal area. Mary responded yes, then no, and yes again. Mary then stated that Ray smelled her pussy with his finger and that he put his head down there, referring to her genital area.[66]

Mary was interviewed at CII on November 16; it was one of the earliest of the interviews. In fact, it was *the* earliest CII interview with a child who became a complainant in the case. There are two accounts of the interview, one prepared by the prosecution and one by the defense. In an account by the defense, the tape is summarized as follows: "This child is wild; she runs around the room, screams and yells her answers, hits Kee [MacFarlane, of CII] and is the most vulgar child I've ever seen."[67] Unlike the defense critique of many other interviews, there is no claim that the child was badgered or coerced, just that she was "vulgar." Why the compelling statements made by Mary Gordon would not appropriately raise concerns about possible abuse is never explained.

Sixteen minutes into the interview, while the child is still drawing, she says, without any prompting, "We're going to talk about him, aren't we?" The transcription of the interview indicates that this is what followed:

    I : Yea, why not? Want to draw a picture of Ray Ray or what did you say you want to draw a picture of his dick?
    c: This is what his dick is.
    I : That's what his dick looks like?
    c: No. It's a very long one. Know what it has? See that's him and there is his long dick.
    I : Did anything come out of his long dick?
    c: Yea.
    I : What comes out?
    c: Poo.[68]

This exchange has been read in two entirely different ways. Under one view, the child's most spontaneous and detailed answer ("It's a very long one") demonstrates the girl had seen Ray Buckey's penis. Under a competing view, the "poo" answer casts doubt on the credibility of the statements that came before it. When the interviewer pursued the issue, every question about "poo" resulted in an answer about "his butt." A few minutes later, however, in a conversation about pubic hair on some dolls in the interview room, Mary *denied* that she had seen Ray Buckey naked.

    I : Did Ray Ray have fur on his dick?
    c: No, I haven't ever seen it.
    I : You haven't seen it? I thought you said you saw it?
    c: No, I haven't yet but I can draw it.
    I : How can you draw it if you haven't seen it?
    c: I could just draw it.[69]

Later in the interview, when MacFarlane was using puppets, the transcript becomes harder to follow because the puppets are role-playing. There is also AM radio interference with the audio portion of the videotape at various times. Regardless, this exchange seems to support the idea that Ray Buckey did something inappropriate.

    I : What happened? Did anybody ever touch you?
    c: No response.
    I : You can tell me. [Radio starts up in background]
    c: Ray Ray being mean to me.

I : Show us. Has Ray Ray ever taken his clothes off at school?

C: Yes he has and you know what, they're been bad to me (whispers).[70]

This final response is followed by a series of three statements, all screamed into the microphone: "We had been bad ladies and gentlemen!" "He has been mean to this little girl!" "He touched her in the pussy!" Soon thereafter, the child makes the puzzling statement, "I don't want to play with these shiny guys anymore." While it is unclear why she said "shiny guys," it is quite clear that she wants the questioning ended. "You're almost done," MacFarlane says—but the interview was only about half over. Mary becomes more distracted and uncooperative. "Sorry I have to leave now," she announced as the interviewer tried in vain to figure out what Mary meant by a statement about "a Chinese hair up her butt." One more interaction further captures the ambiguity of this session:

I : Anyone ever put a temperature in there?

C: Tell her to be quiet.

I : Why? You can tell me.

C: (Leaves.)

I : Your mom told you had temperature taken at school. Show me.

C: No way.

I : Someone ever take your temperature like that?

C: No.

I : Didn't you tell your mom that?

C: Someone is on the phone.[71]

The toy telephone was one of many distractions available if and when a child wanted to change the subject. Mary Gordon did this frequently during her interview; she was extremely avoidant at times, and her sporadic moments of screaming are unsettling. In the exchange below, which came near the end of the session, it appears as if she answered "no" automatically and then suddenly remembered an actual game. Her subsequent response about being a cowgirl is delivered in a much different tone from the earlier responses. She was enthusiastic and seems to be recalling the game.

I : I was wondering if anybody ever played games with these?

C: What are they, shoe laces?

I : No, using ropes.

C: No, yea.

I : Really?

C: I'll be this cow-girl and Ray [was an Indian and he] caught me and I was in jail.

I : Tied up?

c : No. I was in jail. Watch me jump this time (runs and jumps in bean bag chair)....[72]

It is not indicated, however, whether the game was in any way sexualized. Indeed, on the basis of the responses in this interview, there is no reason to conclude that it was.

This interview can be seen, alternatively, as incriminating and ambiguous. The most spontaneous and detailed answers were not about sexualized acts, and some of the statements about the alleged sexual acts were confusing in nature, particularly because of the role reversals that occurred with the puppet games. Though some responses could be read as evidence of sexual abuse, it would make sense to characterize this interview as raising the possibility of sexual abuse more than proving it. The statements from Mary that were obtained before November seem much stronger as evidence than the CII interview. Moreover, the CII interview was summarized in a one-page log that appears far more definitive than the actual interview. The defense summary does the opposite, however, making far too strong a claim that the interview contained nothing more than some "vulgar" words. In these varying interpretations, one can see two competing views of the case, neither loyal to its complicated facts.

The circumstances surrounding this family seem particularly compelling because (1) they were not in contact with other families, (2) in their first contact with the police they emphasized the desire to minimize the number of interviews, and (3) their daughter's first statements came early in the investigation. There was also medical evidence, discussed later, to support these claims.

Kathy Ingram

The fifth response in September 1983 involving a child who later became a formal complainant in the criminal case came from the Ingram family. Kathy Ingram started attending the McMartin Preschool in March 1982. She had continuous contact with Ray Buckey throughout that period; he was her teacher for a while and he was in charge of watching her after school the entire time. As her mother indicated in the information form submitted to the MBPD:

> Most of the time my daughter Kathy was left alone there without any other children from hours of approx. 2:30 to 4:00. I was one of the few mothers there that had to work until 4:00—when they closed. Kathy was Ray's student for last part of winter and throughout summer. To our knowledge all was completely innocent.[73]

A week later, however, the MBPD listed Kathy as "possible 288 victim" because she was implicated in statements by three-year-old Valerie Van Holden. The MBPD informed the Ingrams of these statements, and on September 27 they called back to report that their daughter had "seen Ray pull out his penis." An interview was scheduled for the following week. As stated in a document attached to a later search warrant:

> On 10-3-83 your affiant interviewed Kathy Kae Ingram. Kathy told your affiant that Raymond Buckey has touched her pee pee while she was nude and inserted his fingers inside which hurt. Kathy further stated that Ray put his pee pee in hers while facing one another and this act has occurred more than once. Kathy has played doctor and has been tied up by Ray Buckey. [74]

Three other families were recorded in the MBPD log as providing "positive" responses to the September letter. The first one occurred on September 12, the same day the Mergilis came to the MBPD. Roseanne Owen contacted Detective Dye and reported "that her daughter Nina had been tied up in a closet and played a horsey game at the school with Raymond Buckey." Detective Hoag of the MBPD called Owen back the next day, and in that conversation she stated that "additional information obtained from her daughter indicated that Ray tickled her genitals and chest." On September 21, Detective Hoag contacted the Owens to request an interview with Nina; Mrs. Owen "had been reluctant to have Nicolette interviewed." The reluctance to have her child interviewed, combined with the apparent disclosures of abuse that match other descriptions, make these early developments noteworthy even though this child did not become part of the criminal case. Another family, the Goldmans, also provided a positive response on September 13. This family had two girls who had attended McMartin. The Goldmans had taken the younger one out a few months before Ray was arrested; she said the reason involved complaints about Ray, but nothing that raised specific concerns about sexual abuse. She testified at the grand jury, but her daughters did not testify at the preliminary hearing. [75] Nicollete Owens was interviewed at CII and her name appeared on a tentative witness list in February 1984, but she was not ultimately among the forty-one complainants in the case.

The third family to make a positive response in September, but not move forward in the criminal case, was the Van Holdens. Their three-year-old daughter Valerie had been attending the McMartin Preschool since May 1982; their five-year-old son Bobby had attended earlier. Valerie regularly encountered Ray Buckey during afternoon sessions at McMartin. On Friday, September 16, Mrs. Van Holden came to the MBPD and requested that Detective Hoag interview

Figure 2.3 McMartin Interview Sequence—September Responders, Complainants and Trial.

Of the twenty September responders, only one was part of the trial.

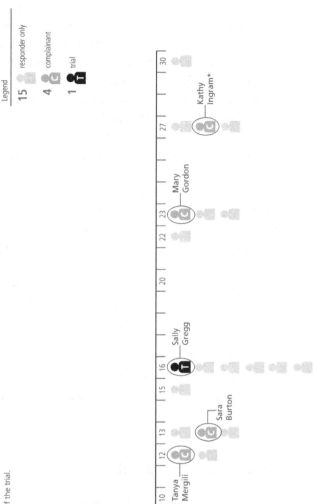

Legend

15 responder only

4 complainant

1 trial

sept 1983

Tanya Mergili

Sara Burton

Sally Gregg

Mary Gordon

Kathy Ingram*

Names for all children who were complainants or went to trial.
Constructed from Los Angeles District Attorney documents.
* Designated as complainant only on the February Witness List.

her children. As the detective later reported, "Bobby and Valerie were both anxious at being separated even briefly from their mother." Conducting an actual interview with each child proved "virtually impossible to do." The detective spent only a few minutes with each child. She reported that Valerie was "totally non-responsive and refused to answer any questions." No information of value was obtained from Bobby. However, the police report indicates that, while at the police station, Valerie told her mother she had touched Ray Buckey's penis.[76] Her mother also reported that Valerie "had tried to kiss [her brother's] penis in the bath tub." These three families were not ultimately involved in the criminal complaint, but all are potentially worth considering in light of the claims that the entire case was created at CII months later.

In sum, at least eight families with children who attended the McMartin Preschool in 1982 or 1983 reported what they viewed as incriminating statements or highly suspicious behavior suggesting sexual abuse at the preschool in response to the MBPD's September letter. These families furnished positive reports or related suspicions at the earliest stages of the McMartin investigation, long before there was any media coverage or "hysteria." Only a few of those children were included in the eventual criminal complaint; four became formal complainants and one was listed as an intended complainant in February (see Figure 2.3). But only one of those children ended up in the actual trial. The police reports from the week immediately following the letter also reveal a phenomenon that has been overlooked in the rush to characterize this time in terms of "hysteria": there were clear signs of parental reluctance to address the issue or to get involved in any way.

The Evaluations at CII

The investigation, which was being handled by the MBPD, soon generated concern and complaints from parents. Detective Hoag questioned children in a fashion that some considered intimidating. These concerns reached the Los Angeles District Attorney's Office, which, through Assistant DA Jean Matusinka, formally requested in mid-October 1983 that CII offer "assistance in conducting and videotaping interviews" in connection with "allegations that several children have been sexually molested."[77] Matusinka made the request "in order to reduce the number of times a child is interviewed" and to ensure that the children were interviewed "in a non-traumatic therapeutic setting." CII had done similar work for at least two years, but never in a case with multiple victims in an institutional setting. Former prosecutor Glenn Stevens, who became disillusioned with the prosecution's case, told screenwriter Abby Mann that Kee MacFarlane had done excellent work in those cases.[78] The witch-hunt narrative never acknowledges this fact. Instead, it sometimes asserts, without any factual basis, that McMartin was CII's first case assessing children for sexual abuse.

What happened at CII formed the basis for the eventual criminal charges. It also became the focus of the defense in the case. It is a core tenet of the witch-hunt narrative that false memories were "implanted" in the children at CII. Actually, the word *implanted* came into use much later; in the early years, the claim was that children had been "brainwashed." Either way, the argument was that children went into CII and suddenly became convinced—or aware, as case supporters might put it—they had been sexually abused at the McMartin Preschool. But there are several reasons to reject the notion that *all* of the allegations in the case were created at CII, a common claim in the witch-hunt narrative. First, there were ten positive and nine probable responders in September who were reported as making statements about Ray Buckey long before CII entered the case. Those are arguably the most important children in the story. Their early disclosures contradict the idea that the entire case was created at CII. Second, there were children who attended McMartin but moved away before the infamous September 1983 letter, and without being interviewed at CII. The universe of those children has been ignored in the witch-hunt narrative, but there is reason to think that children from one or more of those families might have made statements against Ray Buckey.[79] Third, the interview transcripts of children involved in the trial contradict the claim that the entire case was created at CII. It has been claimed, for example, that "Kee MacFarlane was able to extract from these children a tale of satanic horror."[80] Yet a full-text search of the CII interviews with all the children who ended up in the criminal trial reveals that the following words do not appear even once in any of the interviews: *Satan, devil, tunnel, candle, grave, chant, cemetery, robe.* Several of those children eventually made claims that involved such words, but none of those statements originated with the CII interviews. These three arguments are reasons to reject as overly simplistic the view that the case was "created at CII."

What is a more accurate description of what happened at CII? The ability to answer this question is limited by the fact that court records focus on the children who went forward in the legal process. But those children constitute only a small portion of all of the CII interviews, and almost none of them were from the critical early months of the investigation. To understand what happened at CII, the interviews have to be analyzed in chronological order. The content and timing of the earliest interviews is critical to understanding the evidence in the case. How things evolved over time is also important, especially since the interviews went on for months. In the McMartin case, such analysis requires documentation from dozens of CII interviews involving children who were not among the fourteen who participated in the preliminary hearing. Ideally, the analysis would involve the CII videotapes and not just the transcriptions, since videotapes convey tone of voice and nonverbal cues not reflected in transcripts.

Unfortunately, the available records yield an incomplete picture. The analysis offered here is based on records pertaining to many, but not all, of the earliest children in the case. It also includes a thorough review of fifteen videotapes of interviews; the tapes have not been part of any previous examination of the case outside of the actual trial itself. The chapter about the McMartin case in Nathan and Snedeker's book contains descriptions of a few tapes, complete with claims about body language and tone of voice, but those claims were not based on independent analysis of the tapes. Rather, they came directly from the defense and on close examination can be seen to have significant inaccuracies.

A few writers have published specific details about individual children, although not necessarily with a full-fledged attempt to contextualize them. Nathan and Snedeker, for example, give a detailed description of the CII interview with Tanya Mergili that includes the longest excerpt of a CII interview in their book. They make two arguments about the interview: first, that Tanya was coaxed and led into saying "bad" things about Ray Buckey, and second, that it was unclear, at best, whether she understood what it meant to tell the truth. A footnote provides the date of the interview and the child's initials, but no specific page numbers.[81] An independent analysis of this interview, which ultimately included a review of the actual videotape, indicates that Nathan and Snedeker's description of this interview is inaccurate at best. Consider their account of how Kee MacFarlane allegedly suggested and coaxed the girl into saying Ray did something "bad." Here is their unedited account:

> "When Tanya still didn't respond, MacFarlane added that she had seen the little girl's friends from McMartin's, and they told her 'all the bad secrets.' 'We can have a good time with the dolls,' MacFarlane coaxed, 'and, you know, we can talk about some of those bad secrets, if you wanted to. And they could go away. Wouldn't that be a good idea?' Urging puppets on Tanya, she again asked if she knew any bad secrets. 'Uh-uh,' Tanya shook her head. Then maybe she could figure them out, MacFarlane said. She showed off her 'secret machine' and assured Tanya that she would feel better if she told bad things about Ray. 'I hate those secrets,' Tanya finally said, addressing a bird puppet on MacFarlane's hand. 'Ray-Ray did bad things, and I don't even like it.'"[82]

Arguing that the girl's use of the word *bad* was suggested by the interviewer, the authors claim that MacFarlane used the word before it was ever uttered by Tanya. But Nathan does not provide specific citations for any of the statements in quotes; rather, her single footnote cites the entire transcript without any specific page numbers. Nathan's account is offered as a chrono-logical story; however, it ends with the girl "finally" saying that Ray Buckey "did bad things." The actual transcript reveals that this is *not* an accurate chron-ological account of what transpired. In fact, what is represented as the "final" comment—about Buckey doing "bad things"–came *before* MacFarlane ever uttered the word *bad*. MacFarlane used the word for the first time at the bottom of page 36. But *before* that statement, Tanya said that she didn't like Ray be-cause "He did bad things."[83]

Nathan and Snedeker also inaccurately conveyed a later exchange, where MacFarlane is ascertaining whether the child understands the concept of truth telling. Beyond raising questions about the accuracy of Nathan and Snedeker's reporting, this example demonstrates a stunning insensitivity to the kinds of miscommunication that can occur with children. According to the authors:

> [MacFarlane] asked Tanya, 'Do you know the difference between the truth and a lie? What's a lie?' 'Umm, it has big teeth, and it—and it's kind of brownish,' answered the girl. At that, MacFarlane asked whether Tanya had 'told the truth to the secret machine.' The girl was mute. She only nodded, with her mouth wide open.[84]

After checking this description against the actual interview, the transcript leaves no doubt that Tanya understood the difference between the truth and a lie. The reader would never know this, however, because Nathan and Snedeker omitted nearly *three pages of follow-up questions* after the "big teeth and brownish" com-ment. The two pages following further reinforce that Tanya understands she gets punished if she lies. Nathan omits any description of these statements, implying instead that MacFarlane moved directly from the "big teeth and brownish" com-ment to her question about whether Tanya told the truth. Avoiding any acknowl-edgment of the intervening three-page exchange leaves the reader with a serious misimpression.[85]

There is a sensible and seemingly obvious explanation for the child's answer, which otherwise appears to be a non sequitur: what she heard MacFarlane say is "what's a lion?" instead of "what's a lie?" Accordingly, her answer is accurate and makes sense. It is unclear whether Nathan and Snedeker even considered this expla-nation. It is even less clear why they omitted the series of questions that followed, since those questions were obviously designed to clarify whether the child under-stood the concept of truth telling. Immediately after the "big teeth and brownish" comment, MacFarlane asked "If you tell a lie, what would you—what would be a lie?"[86] The girl replied: "If you didn't tell the truth." MacFarlane then asked: "If I told you that Mr. Bird was pink, would it be the truth or a lie?" "A lie," the girl answered, correctly.[87] But these details are not included in Nathan and Snedeker's account.

November 1983

A detailed, chronological analysis of the content and progression of interviews at CII reveals a period of limited disclosures and palpable frustration on the part of the interviewers, followed by an incredible expansion of the case beyond all reason, beginning *before* the case broke on television on February 2.

The CII interviews began on November 1, 1983. Fifteen children were interviewed that month. The interviews lasted between forty-five and ninety minutes each. Many of these interviews were exemplars of patience. MacFarlane spent a significant amount of time playing and making the child feel comfortable; eventually, she would draw a picture of a human body and establish what awareness and vocabulary the child had for sexual parts. She would then ask about games that had been played at the school. *Did you play any games at school? What were they called? How do you play that? Did children have their clothes on?*

There is no comprehensive account of the content of all fifteen interviews in November. By several measures, however, these interviews were surprisingly unproductive. None of the first seven children interviewed at CII became formally involved in the criminal proceedings. Only three children interviewed in November moved forward in the case: Mary Gordon, Kathy Ingram, and Trisha Walters. They were number eight, nine, and eleven in the interview sequence. The first two had been September responders, so they have already been discussed. The third attended McMartin the day before she was interviewed. She was arguably the most important child in the state's case at the eventual trial, the only one interviewed at CII in 1983; the rest were all first interviewed there in 1984—most well after the story became a major media event.

Trisha Walters made several statements that had a combination of relevant specificity and childlike authenticity. She said, for example, that Ray had "stuck fingernails in my back." Her back, as she later clarified, included her "bottom." She said as well that Ray stuck a "pencil" in her bottom. (It is not uncommon for children to describe anal penetration by an object or finger as being either a nail or a stick, since they produce the kind of pain a child would associate with those items.[88]) A MBPD police officer who later viewed the videotape of this CII interview wrote: "In substance, the victim related the following: Ray touched the victim's vagina with his finger, he penetrated the victim's anus with his penis, a finger, and an object."[89] Judging from the transcript of the interview, it would seem more accurate to use the word *or* than *and* at the end of the sentence just reported. That said, the interview contained many important statements included in the police report, such as "Trisha said Ray wore no underwear" and "Trisha was threatened by Ray that he would slug kids if they told." In conversations with screenwriter Mann, Glenn Stevens referred to this interview as the prosecution's "best tape."

One might question these statements, of course, particularly given that Trisha's parents had provided a negative response to inquiries about the matter a couple months earlier. This is why the medical evidence is so important; it could constitute a physical basis for allegations that might otherwise seem difficult to believe. When Trisha was examined by Dr. Astrid Heger at CII on January 7, 1984, the girl asked the doctor to check her eyes because she was concerned about the "gray stuff" that had gotten into them. Dr. Heger considered it one of the strongest spontaneous statements made to her by any of the approximately 150 children she examined. "The only thing I can think of is that somebody ejaculated on Trisha's face," Dr. Heger later testified.[90] The medical evidence from her physical examination caused even the defense expert, who later examined this evidence, to agree that the combination of findings on the girl would be "strongly suggestive of penetrative injury."[91]

The rest of the fifteen children interviewed at CII in November said little or nothing incriminatory, yet it is clear from the existing records that MacFarlane concluded that virtually all of these children had been sexually abused at the McMartin Preschool. Some of the November interviews were with children so young that their responses were minimal and difficult to understand; children so young were not likely to end up as witnesses in a criminal trial. Valerie Van Holden, for example, was interviewed on November 7. She wore roller skates through the entire interview, which was disjointed and confusing but contains fragmentary statements that raise obvious concern, including something about Ray Buckey "sticking his pee-pee."[92] Other children may have been reluctant to talk. The first girl interviewed in November, Ella Baldwin, denied that any of the games at school were sexualized. She made no clear incriminating statements, and many of her responses were soft and unintelligible. The interview ended when Ella said "I wanna go."[93] Shortly before that request, MacFarlane asked, "Didn't you tell your mommy some things?" Whatever she had told her mother, she did not repeat it in this interview.

Signs of frustration on the part of the interviewer are apparent in the November sessions. By the end of the month, there was an obvious sense, reflected in the questions, that MacFarlane had decided the children were holding back. On November 29, when interviewing Sonny Landell, she asked twice whether someone had told the child not to talk. Twice the girl said no, adding once "I just don't want to talk."[94] MacFarlane then employed a kind of peer pressure, telling Sonny that her older sister "told already." (This is not an accurate description of the transcript of the interview with the older sister, who was vague and equivocal.) Sonny used dolls shortly thereafter in a fashion that has been interpreted by some as demonstrating knowledge of sexual abuse. But standing alone, the "knowledge" proved very little; nor did these interviews contain significant disclosures. The next day, interviewing five-year-old Mark Janes, MacFarlane told the boy that "other kids told her" he was there because of some "naked games." When the boy maintained he did not remember any naked games, MacFarlane called him a "scaredy cat."[95] This inappropriate use of name calling and pressure foreshadows the worst of what would happen at CII over the next several months. Children were pressured and otherwise manipulated into "telling" things, often in language that, on reflection, seems to be mostly innuendo and adult interpretation more than anything child-based and specific.

In sum, a few children made incriminating statements in their interviews at CII in November; others reportedly made incriminating statements to their parents but were unwilling to repeat them at CII. But most children seemed to have nothing to say. Rather than conclude at the end of November that the McMartin case was small, the CII staff seems to have concluded the opposite: the case was much larger than anyone imagined, and many or most of the children were not disclosing, probably out of fear. The children must have been threatened into silence, they reasoned. This explanation made sense to the adults, but the concept definitely emerged in the *questions* posed in CII interviews long before it appeared in any answers.

December 1983

The quality of the interviews deteriorated in December. Many contained the kind of pressure tactics used at the end of November. In some instances, they contained unfounded assertions made by the interviewer that "all the other kids" had talked, sometimes allegedly about the specific child being interviewed. There were also repeated references in many of the December interviews to the idea that the children had been threatened not to talk. "Someone told you not to tell, didn't they?" MacFarlane asked Penny Bailey in the first interview of December. She denied it. The five-year-old girl eventually indicated that Ray Buckey's penis touched her. But this occurred immediately after the child indicated he had touched her *with his foot*. The child provided no details, and it is impossible to ascertain whether the statement is an actual memory or simply an assent to a leading question.[96]

Statements by the interviewer about alleged threats came to be paired with assurances that "telling yucky secrets" would "make them go away." The microphone on the table in the interview room became known as the "yucky secrets machine." MacFarlane was particularly relentless with Jenny Brown on December 7, badgering her repeatedly throughout this interview, and calling her "a scaredy cat" for not saying anything. Then she played on the child's sense of guilt: "Jenny won't help me," MacFarlane's puppet intoned. "Nobody's helping me."[97] But the child was not moved to say anything. Instead, she endured sustained pressure, including questions at the end of the session from her mother.

The girl whispered to her doubting mother that she was not touched, placing clear emphasis on the word "not." None of this seemed to affect the interviewer's conclusion that the child had been sexually abused at school.

A few of the interviews in December stood out as being much more open-ended and less coercive, but a small fraction of the sixteen children who were interviewed that month. Several of those children made statements that might have supported a criminal complaint, but most came after the child was pressured in ways that are now recognized as inappropriate. Only two of the children interviewed in December became complainants in the case: Tanya Mergili and Sara Barton. Notably, both of them had been identified almost three months earlier, during the week of September 12. It is unclear why these two early responders in September were interviewed at CII in December instead of November. But their not being interviewed in November demonstrates that the CII interview sequence was correlated only loosely with the sequence of responses in September, if at all.

The remarkable bottom line for the interviews at CII in December was that *they did not generate a single new complainant in the case.*[98] Indeed, most of these interviews were surprising for how little they actually contained in the way of clear incriminatory statements. Although the December interviews did not generate any new complainants for the criminal case, they were apparently vital in expanding the case to include five female teachers at the school and Virginia McMartin, the wheelchair-bound woman who founded the preschool. According to a handwritten list prepared by MacFarlane several months later, the interviews in early December contained the first statements that implicated any teachers beyond Ray Buckey. By her account, the case started to expand on December 5 and increased noticeably the following week:

> 12/5 Bobby Vickers: "Peggy didn't touch but watched Ray do it"
>
> 12/7 Tanya Mergili: "Miss Peggy saw things happen" (Ray molesting Tanya)
>
> 12/12 Sara Barton: Betty took pictures during NMS [Naked Movie Star] game
>
> 12/12 Barry Gregg: Betty touched his heiney, exposed herself, tied him up, took naked pictures, drove him to a house
>
> 12/13 Betsy Lawton: Peggy took nude photos; Peggy was naked
>
> 12/13 Otis Lawton: Babs [Babette Spitler] played NMS game—she was naked[99]

The phrases cited above came directly from the logs of the videotapes. Those logs were created contemporaneously by the person operating the video camera and were originally intended to serve as indices, not as synopses; combined with a number on the VCR counter, the entries would allow someone to find the place in an interview where a subject or phrase was discussed. But they came to be used for much more than that—all to the detriment of the case.

The children who first implicated the female teachers would seem to be pivotal in the case. Two of them, Tanya Mergili and Sara Barton, became complainants, but neither one actually went to trial. The available written records on the remaining children are more limited. Fortunately, the copies of videotaped interviews that I obtained in the course of this research contain four interviews from early December, including Bobby Vickers and Tanya Mergili.

A close examination of the interview with Vickers reveals that the claim that he incriminated Peggy Buckey is significantly overstated. What actually transpired was ambiguous. It was more than fifty minutes into an interview in which Bobby had said almost nothing about the school or any bad activities there when MacFarlane asked about "yucky secrets." The boy responded quite earnestly: "One time, [another boy at the preschool] took off his clothes before he went swimming and everyone saw him."[100] He also indicated that he knew what "bad touch" meant. "We saw a movie about that at McMartin," he said. He proceeded to say something about a boy whose father didn't want him to tell, but the interviewer cut off the story. After asking again whether Miss Peggy was ever naked— the boy answered "no"—this exchange occurred:

KEE: Did Miss Peggy ever touch anybody?
BOBBY: No.
KEE: Did she ever watch?
BOBBY: Yes.
KEE: Did she watch when the kids were being touched?
BOBBY: Yes.
KEE: Do you think that she ever took her clothes off?
BOBBY: No—only when she was going to go swimming.

The interviewer returned to the topic later and asked questions to clarify or verify this earlier response.

KEE: Did Miss Peggy do anything bad?
BOBBY: No.
KEE: Did she know what Mr. Ray did to you?
BOBBY: Yes.
KEE: How come she didn't do anything to help you?
BOBBY: Because she didn't know.
KEE: Did she ever see any of those touchings that happened to Bobby?
BOBBY: Nope.

This exchange certainly contradicts the idea that Bobby incriminated Peggy Buckey in any meaningful way. The most that can be said is that his statements on this topic were contradictory. It appears he was most adamant and persuasive in the second exchange. But however one interprets these contradictions, it is not reasonable to boil this exchange down to *Peggy didn't touch but watched Ray do it*. Yet this is how the video log reads for this section.

There was also a diversion near the end of this interview that bears mentioning. Bobby was asked about going to Ray's house. He said they had gone in a car. "And then they went off the cliff," he added. The remark did not cause the interviewer to pull back, change directions, or even pause. Over the next few minutes, Bobby poured out details about a "spooky, haunted house" with windows that opened by themselves. "There might be ghosts," he said. "Mr. Ray pushed the button and the trap door opened into the alligator pit," he continued. The notion that certain questions might encourage a child to spin a story, so to speak, did not seem to be considered in general. The interviewer clearly did not believe there was an alligator pit, but there is no indication that this interview gave pause to the CII staff to consider why a child might say such a thing and how this might affect the evaluation process. Instead of this interview marking the beginning of a period of increased caution in the CII evaluations, this was apparently when the idea took hold that the case involved multiple defendants and multiple crime scenes (both at and away from the preschool).

The same kind of problem exists with Tanya Mergil's statements about Peggy Buckey's involvement. The most important part of her interview, according to the CII staff, was reduced to *Miss Peggy saw things happen*. Here is the interaction from which the phrase emanated:

Q: Did Ray-Ray ever take you some place?

A: No, no, no, no, no.

Q: Did all those bad things just happen at school?

A: Yes.

Q: Oh. Where were all those other teachers when those bad things were happening?

A: I don't know, but—

Q: Did Miss Peggy ever see any? Did she see anything?

A: Yes.

Q: She did?

A: Uh-huh.

Q: Did she ever play any of those bad games, too?

A: Oh, no.

Q: No. Did she get mad at Ray-Ray?

A: Yes.

Q: Oh. She didn't—she didn't want him to play?

A: Right.

Q: Do you think she ever saw the kids naked?

A: No, no, no, no, no.

Q: She wasn't there?

A: Nope.[101]

Of course, in a literal sense, Peggy Buckey *did* "see things happen" every day. But the follow-up questions that were appropriately aimed at fleshing out the meaning of this vague statement seem to make it clear that Miss Peggy did *not* witness any alleged acts of abuse. According to the response above, she did not play any of the bad games or see any of the kids naked. She was not there. The most one could fairly say is that Tanya said something ambiguous about Peggy that was contradicted by follow-up questions.

None of this is to deny that Tanya made credible statements on videotape at UCLA in September and again in this CII session in November. Notably, none of those statements were about the involvement of Miss Peggy or any other teacher besides Ray Buckey. The notation on the log from this CII interview misrepresented the actual content. Accordingly, the log notes seem to reflect more about the biases of the CII staff than they do about the actual substance of the interviews. The biases account for so much of what eventually happened in the case, however, that this insight is useful in understanding CII's role.

In early to mid-December, the CII staff formed the view that the case involved most or all of the female teachers. They also came to believe that these women were involved in making child pornography. An economic motive might help explain actions that otherwise seemed incomprehensible. Three of the first six children alleged to have incriminated the female teachers also allegedly made statements about taking pictures. See the phrases emphasized by bold print from the log notes (previously presented in this chapter) below:

12/5 Bobby Vickers: "Peggy didn't touch but watched Ray do it"

12/7 Tanya Mergili: "Miss Peggy saw things happen" (Ray molesting Tanya)

12/12 Sara Barton: **Betty took pictures** during NMS [Naked Movie Star] game

12/12 Barry Gregg: Betty touched his heiney, exposed herself, tied him up, took **naked pictures**, drove him to a house.

12/13 Betsy Lawton: **Peggy took nude photos**; Peggy was naked

12/13 Otis Lawton: Babs played NMS game—she was naked[102]

Although the phrases in bold seem to convey the underlying content in abbreviated form, they actually convey just the subject matter of the questions. In all three instances, the topic was introduced by the questioner and the responses were either ambiguous or otherwise less than corroborative. But the log conveys the opposite. Indeed, given how critical these supposed statements were to the evolution of the case—since they were apparently the first children to implicate the female teachers—it is telling that none of these children became part of the criminal case. Though virtually all of the children interviewed in December were considered by the staff at CII to have been victims of sexual abuse, none of them—save Tanya Mergili (who came forward in early September)—became part of the criminal case. By any objective standard, these interviews were unproductive. MacFarlane was clearly frustrated that the children had so little so say.

January 1984

The pace of interviewing increased dramatically over the next four months (see Figures 2.4 to 2.6). The most children were interviewed in April, which also yielded more actual complainants than any other month. Figures 2.5 and 2.6 illustrate how the children in the case were drawn largely from those interviewed at CII in February, March, and April—all months after the case became a major media story. The interviewing at CII continued for several more months but the criminal case was built entirely on the statements of children interviewed at CII before May. Nobody seemed to wonder why the bulk of the children who were eventually involved in the criminal proceedings emerged five and six months into the investigation. The notion that all of these children had been scared into silence was one possibility. Another was that their "disclosures" were the product of influences separate from any actual abuse. But this explanation did not receive any consideration in 1984, when the criminal case took shape.

Several aspects of the interviews changed in January. First, the nature of the children's statements became much more bizarre than anything said in November or December. The first child interviewed in January told Kee MacFarlane that Peggy Buckey was "a naked horsey rider."[103] He said that "Babs, Betty and Peggy scared kids" but "not Ray." His statements got stranger and stranger; at one point, he said Miss Virginia killed animals at school. Later, he talked about going on a freeway to a church, to a hotel, and to a car wash with "mean people." There are so many seemingly fantastic claims in this single interview that it is difficult to imagine sorting out the truth in any of the more plausible sounding statements. This boy was included in the original complaint but was not among the children who went through the preliminary hearing.

Second, rigidity and overconfidence on the part of the interviewers took root in January. In comparison to the earlier interviews, it is clear that that the

Figure 2.4 CII Interview Sequence—All Interviews of children at CII Through May 15.

This figure represents the 226 interviews conducted at CII before the charges were finalized in the case.
Approximately 178 interviews occured from May 15 through December, but none of those children were part of the case.

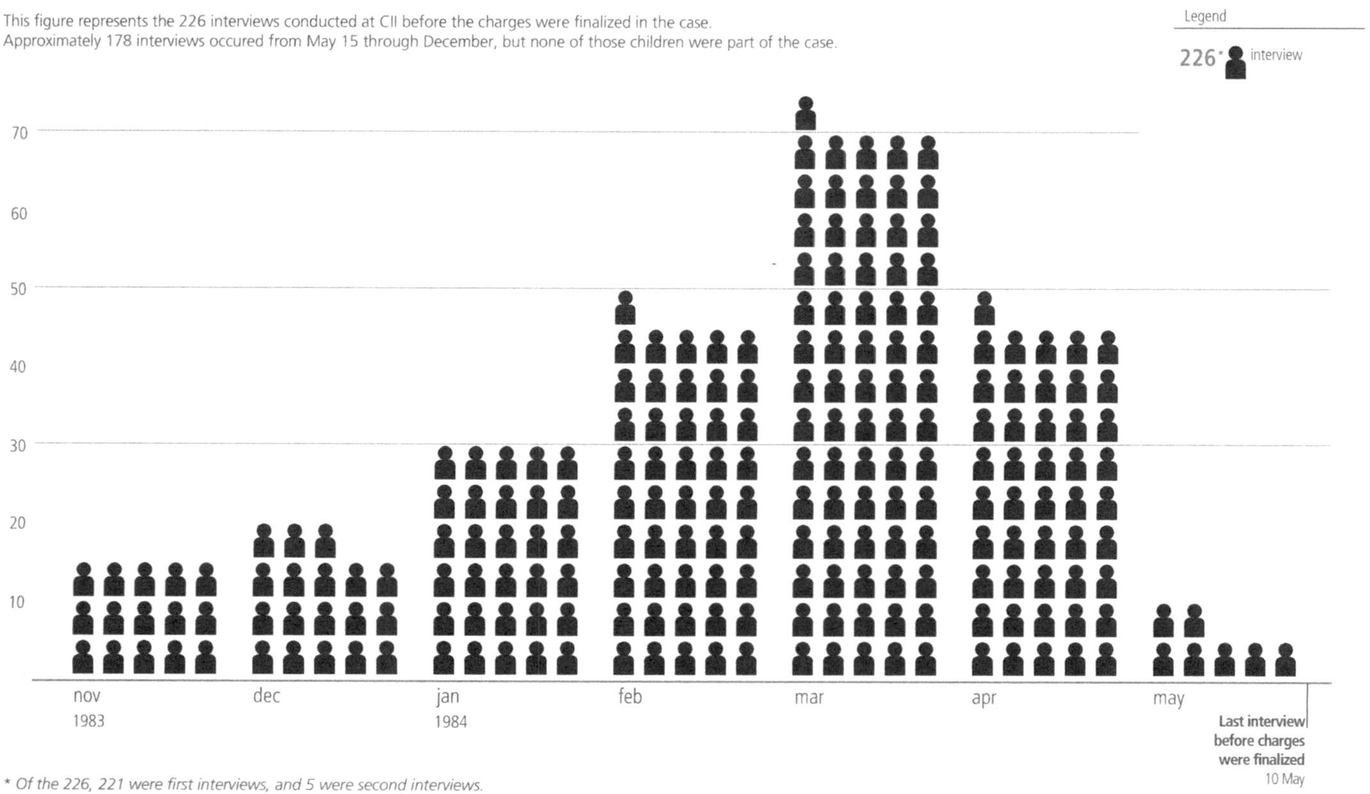

* Of the 226, 221 were first interviews, and 5 were second interviews.
Compiled by author from assorted CII documents.

Figure 2.5 CII Interview Sequence—Children at Preliminary Hearing.

Icons do not represent the order of interviews within the month.

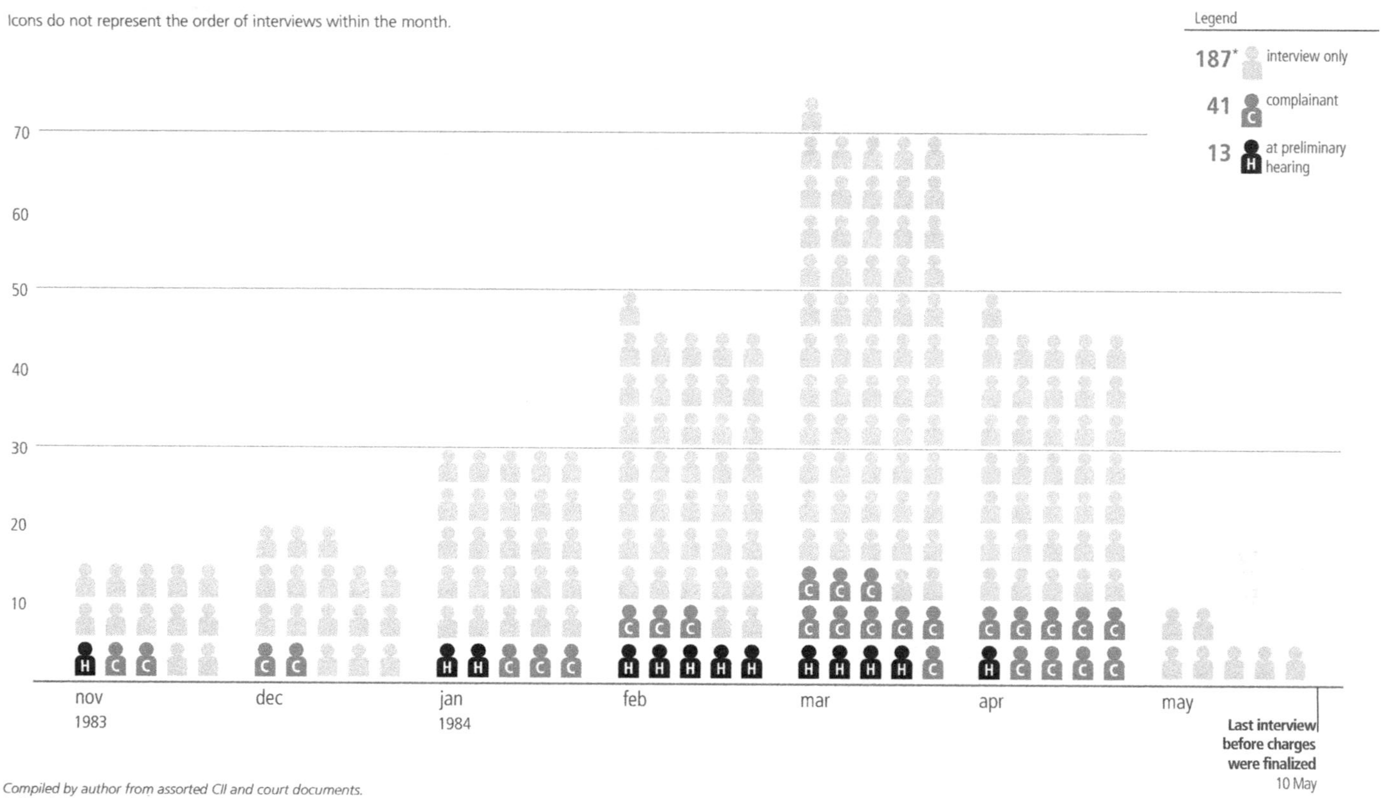
Legend
187* interview only
41 complainant
13 at preliminary hearing
70
60
50
40
30
20
10
nov
1983
dec
jan
1984
feb
mar
apr
may
Last interview before charges were finalized
10 May

Compiled by author from assorted CII and court documents.
** Five children were interviewed twice.*

Figure 2.6 CII Interview Sequence—Children at Preliminary Hearing, Trial and Retrial.

Icons do not represent the order of interviews within the month.

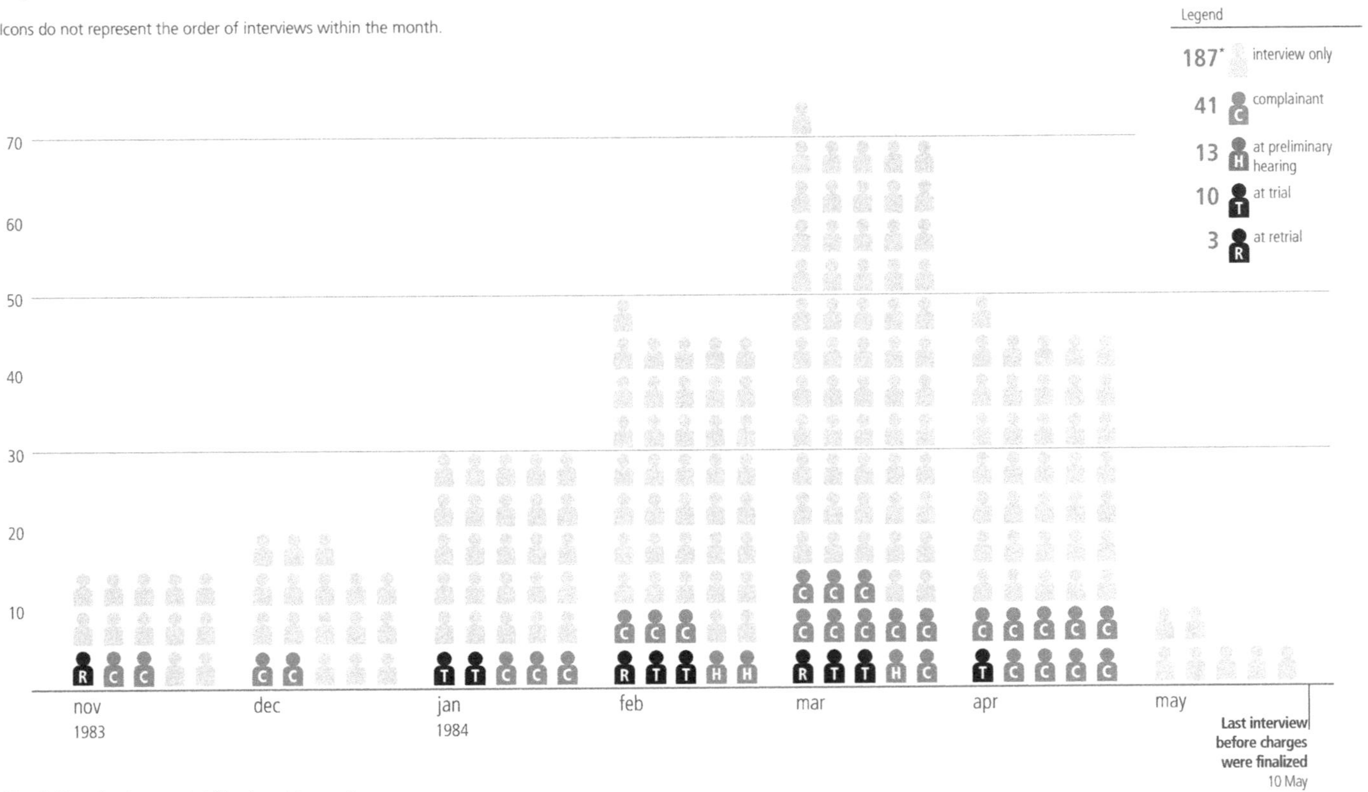

Legend

187*	interview only
41	complainant
13	at preliminary hearing
10	at trial
3	at retrial

Last interview before charges were finalized
10 May

nov 1983 dec jan 1984 feb mar apr may

70
60
50
40
30
20
10

Compiled by author from assorted CII and court documents.
* Five children were interviewed twice.

interviewer's expectations became much stronger. The interviews in this time period do not read as though the interviewer was trying to find out what happened; it is as if the interviewer already knew what happened and wanted the child to affirm it. This does not mean every single interview in January should be disregarded. Breanna Chapman, who attended the McMartin Preschool in January, emerged as one of the most compelling witnesses in the case in connection with events that resulted in the school closing "voluntarily" on January 12.

Her parents, Ellen and Terry, were staunch supporters of the Buckeys in the fall of 1983. Breanna attended McMartin until mid-January 1984, when she made a disclosure to her mother that was quickly corroborated by medical evidence; the school closed down a few days later. The evidence concerning this child has not been acknowledged in the witch-hunt narrative, even though it is contained in the grand jury notebooks and was well known enough that it was referenced in outtakes of the *60 Minutes* episode about the case in December 1986.[104] But, as explained below, the jury never heard this evidence.

It is fair to say that after the September letter from the MBPD, the parents who continued sending their children to the McMartin Preschool were supporters of the McMartins who had concluded that there was no basis to the allegations. Indeed, Ellen Chapman told one of the investigators for the district attorney that in the fall of 1983 she was "totally appalled that people were going to discredit the school."[105] She even recommended the preschool to a friend after learning about the investigation. She was so loyal to the school that she made nothing of a strange remark of Peggy Buckey's about the allegations.[106] She didn't even entertain the possibility of sexual abuse when, on the evening of January 6, 1984, her daughter screamed in pain as she urinated. Her mother bathed her, applied some cream, and "noticed that she was very red and very swollen."[107] When she asked her daughter if anyone had hurt her, Breanna replied that "Ray had spit in her face and hurt her arm."[108] Chapman later testified that she assumed Breanna must have been referring to a playground mishap with a child named Ray. She did not connect the genital discomfort with this comment because Breanna spoke only of a hurt arm. It is important to remember that the story about McMartin had not yet been in any media coverage. Whatever was brewing at CII was unknown to all but a handful of insiders. To McMartin loyalists, the September letter was ancient history.

If, as is often alleged, there were parents of children attending the McMartin preschool who were bent on extracting disclosures of sexual abuse from their children, Chapman was clearly not one of them. Indeed, she took her daughter *back* to McMartin on January 12.[109] Later that day, however, Breanna told her Mr. Ray had hurt her private parts. The meaning of Breanna's words was apparently so clear that they almost instantly turned Chapman from a diehard McMartin supporter to potentially the most convincing witness for the state.[110] She withdrew Breanna from the McMartin Preschool, and Peggy Buckey closed it down two days later. Breanna was examined at the medical office of Dr. Myron Mitzenmacher on January 28. The exam revealed an enlarged vaginal opening and markedly red mucous membranes. Later, a colposcopic exam by Dr. Astrid Heger found a "remarkable scar" that, given its stage of healing, was diagnosed as "between two and four weeks" old.[111]

Chapman recounted those facts to the grand jury in March.[112] But Breanna, who had just turned four, was considered too young to testify. Her older sister Nancy, who was almost seven, was interviewed, and she was slated to testify instead. However, she became one of the untold casualties of the McMartin case: Nancy literally had a nervous breakdown in June 1984, was hospitalized after a period of continuous vomiting and dehydration,[113] and was subsequently removed from the witness list. Ellen Chapman still testified at the preliminary hearing, but all she was allowed to say in her direct testimony, given that her daughter was not a complaining witness, was that Breanna attended McMartin in the fall of 1983, that Peggy Buckey made a strange comment in the fall about "checking Ray for hard-ons," and that her daughter left the school on January 12, 1984. The normally contentious defense attorneys, who drew cross-examination of some children out for more than a week, didn't ask Chapman a single question. This eliminated any danger that she would be given the opportunity to explain why her daughter left McMartin and what Dr. Heger observed when examining the child shortly after her complaints in January 1984. The jury never heard any of that.

Other than Breana Chapman, however, there were enough problems with the interviews in January that they are generally not useful in assessing whether or not a child was sexually abused. The problems with "source attribution" apparently increased in January as more parents sent their kids to CII, and more parents told other parents about their experiences. There are several examples in the interview transcripts where a child makes it clear that his or her seemingly incriminatory statements against Ray Buckey or others are based on something told to the child by a parent (*My mommy told me Ray touched kids*). Although the case still had not yet generated any media attention, it was creating considerable interest and conversation in the community. A parents' meeting at UCLA Medical Center in late October drew parents from about a dozen families; scores more attended the community meeting in Manhattan Beach on January 24. Those developments made it more likely that a child generating specific claims in January might have heard that information from someone else, rather than actually having experienced it. Most likely, *the child's parent* heard it from someone else's parent.

February Onward

An interview with a six-and-a-half-year-old boy during the first week of February involved the same problem. During the interview, conducted by MacFarlane, the boy made a number of specific statements about Ray "touching kids," including a seemingly telling response that "something came out" of Ray's penis. But in the time *after* the interview, while the tape was still running, the boy contradicted everything he had just said. He told Sandy Krebs, another CII interviewer, that he was not scared to answer MacFarlane's questions, that he had never seen Ray's (alleged) gun, that he was not actually at the McMartin Preschool for long, and that Ray did not hurt him or threaten him.[114] These statements were apparently ignored by the CII staff.

The next three months were the most important in the overall process, by two measures: total number of interviews and total number of complainants generated for the criminal case. These months were also when the CII interviews deteriorated in several ways. Most significantly, the interviewers had clearly reached the conclusion that there had been massive abuse at the preschool; they could not possibly be said to have an open mind about the interviews during these months. I have reviewed the videotapes of two interviews in February, one in March, and two in April. All involved children who became complainants in the case. None of the interviews had the feeling of open-ended inquiry that characterized some of those from November. To the contrary, they seemed aimed at getting the child to confirm that something bad happened, to say it on videotape. These interviews are filled with inappropriate questions.

The interview with Miranda Chase on April 3, 1984, is representative of some of the worst practices in the CII interviews. It also contains a particularly striking example of how the interviewers ignored statements that did not fit their own view of the case. Miranda was nine years old at the time; she had attended the McMartin Preschool from August 1977 until June 1979. As the defense later pointed out, Ray Buckey was still in high school during the time covered by some of the complainants in the case, including Miranda.

Miranda was strikingly older than the children in all of the other tapes I was able to review. She is described in Dr. Heger's medical evaluation, which was conducted on April 23, as "a bright cooperative nine year old who was able to volunteer a tremendous amount of information." The CII interview starts with a remarkable statement that is quite unprompted and involves considerable detail. It is all about how a friend of hers got "sick" because of all this stuff about McMartin. "His mind is playing tricks on him and he thinks things happened that never happened," she explains. "Hmmmm. I didn't talk to him," Krebs replies and lets the subject drop.

The interviewer and the girl then drew for more than ten minutes, making small talk about drawing. Eventually, Krebs gave Miranda a human figure she drew and prompted the girl to label various parts of the body: belly button, eyes, nose, mouth, fingers. With specific prompting, she added "boobs" and then "vagina." A few minutes later, Krebs brought out school pictures from various classes and years at McMartin. "Ray's in jail," Miranda said energetically and without any prompting. When shown a picture of some or all of the adults charged in the case, she added, again without any kind of prompt, "I'm glad he's in jail [pointing to Ray], but I'm not so sure about them" and pointed to several other adults. Krebs also let this remark pass, declining to inquire about the "not so sure" part.

Miranda then told her about a child she should interview. The girl once spent the night at Ray's house and later said "Ray's going to be my boyfriend." (There is no additional information in available records about this lead.) Apparently aware that she was supposed to say something about Ray Buckey, the girl then said, again without any specific prompt, that Ray "was dishonest." This time, Krebs followed up and asked for an explanation. The girl launched into a long story about how Miss Virginia would give Ray suckers, but the children were not supposed to eat them. Once Miss Virginia was gone, Ray said, "you guys can go eat some suckers."

Krebs abruptly said something about how helpful puppets have been and directed Miranda's attention to a host of puppets on the couch. They each selected one and Krebs started talking through her puppet to Miranda's puppet. She told the puppet how the older children can help out more because they are smarter, they can talk better, and they have better memories. Then she gave Miranda's puppet "a pretty blue pointer" and said: "We know somebody scared people; told them not to tell." She asked Miranda—again, through her puppet—to point out anyone like that in the photo. Miranda pointed immediately to Ray. "Anyone else?" Krebs asked. "Miss Betty, I think," she responded with equivocation. Krebs replied with enthusiasm: "You know what, Wookie [the puppet Miranda was holding], that's what all the other kids said! You're going to be a big help."

Miranda was then asked a series of very leading questions. "What did they say to Miranda when she was little to make her scared?" She responded with something about "don't go home" that did not quite make sense. "Did they say to Miranda that she might get hurt?" This is when Miranda said something about a bomb threat. "Getting rid of these secrets is kind of neat. And everybody's doing it." This is when Miranda said something about Ray letting children go swimming in the pool naked. Krebs proceeded to ask more leading questions, such as, "Who tickled the kids?" Miranda was given huge praise for her answers. "Congratulations, what a brave bear," she is told after nodding in response to a question as to whether Ray did any "tricky tickling" of Miranda. Krebs later employed some of the worst kind of leading questions, ones with forced-choice answers, such as "Which hurt more, the bottom or the vagina?" Either answer, of course, "confirmed" the implication contained in the question. This interview ended with Krebs giving excessive praise: "You really did a good job! You really did a good job! You're terrific!"[115] Two weeks later, when Miranda was evaluated by Dr. Heger, the cooperative fourth-grader repeated much of what she said to Krebs. The adults were apparently so taken by the articulateness of this nine-year-old that they did not take her negative responses to heart. What seems most convincing from her interview is that Ray Buckey gave children suckers when he was not supposed to; he also apparently let children swim in the pool naked. But almost this entire interview is ambiguous, contradictory, and overly leading. The single-mindedness of the interviewer is apparent throughout. Miranda Chase was included in the forty-one complainants; she was not, however, one of the fourteen who testified at the preliminary hearing. It is not clear why she dropped out of the case between the grand jury proceedings and the preliminary hearing.

In retrospect, the mistakes made during this critical phase of the CII evaluations seem fairly clear; what remains less clear is why such a shaky foundation of interviews resulted in seven defendants being charged and in official claims that far more people were probably involved. In other words, why did so many people come to believe, based on so little evidence, that there *had* been such widespread abuse? The answer is complicated and involves a confluence of factors that are analyzed next. First and foremost was the role of medical diagnosis.

Contested Medical Evidence

Medical evidence played a critical role from the beginning. The case was referred to the Manhattan Beach Police Department after an evaluation of Matthew Johnson, conducted at UCLA's Medical Center, yielded evidence that the boy had likely been sodomized. Several other children, interviewed later in the case, were also examined by pediatric specialists at UCLA. The vast majority of medical evaluations in the case, however, were conducted through CII—the same organization that interviewed hundreds of children in the case. These medical examinations were conducted by Drs. Astrid Heger and Bruce Woodling. Dr. Heger was a young pediatrician with strong credentials; she graduated at the top in her medical school class at the University of Southern California in 1972 and started working at CII in 1983. Dr. Woodling had gained some experience—and later, notoriety—for his testimony in the Kniffen and McCuan cases in Bakersfield, California.[116] Together, they helped pioneer the use of the colposcope, a medical instrument that combines binocular magnification with the power of photography, in evaluating the possibility of sexual abuse.[117]

The medical evaluations conducted through CII played a significant and complicated role in the McMartin case. On the one hand, it is clear with the benefit of hindsight that Drs. Heger and Woodling overdiagnosed abuse in the children who were interviewed at CII. The overdiagnosis became apparent as advances in medical knowledge demonstrated that some medical findings clinicians considered to be related to sexual abuse were also found in nonabused children. The overdiagnosis helps explain why parents became convinced that their children had been sexually abused, even if their statements at CII were ambiguous or strained credulity. Yet, these shortcomings do not mean their evaluations should be rejected out of hand. The changes in medical knowledge that occurred between 1984 and the late 1980s, particularly two well-known studies by Dr. John McCann, discredited *some* "findings" from the early 1980s, but they did not dismiss all relevant medical knowledge from that era.[118]

The significance of evolving medical knowledge in the McMartin case cannot be ascertained without case-by-case analysis of the constellation of findings reported for each child. The first original effort at such analysis—given here— reveals that a considerable amount of the evidence presented in the McMartin case would still be considered strong today. Unfortunately, any close inquiry into this medical evidence is limited in at least two ways. First, although there is fairly extensive information about the fourteen children involved in the preliminary hearing and even more information about the subset that went to trial, there is only scattered information available for the rest of the children who were evaluated by CII. Second, even though medical reports and related documents were entered into the court record for many children who did not end up in the trial, the photographic slides that were entered as exhibits in support of those records are not in the court archives. It is a standard practice that transcripts are retained by the court while exhibits are destroyed or returned to the parties soon after the case is over.[119] With one exception, none of the photographic slides were available to this researcher. Despite those limitations, there is considerable documentation in the court record concerning some of the most significant children in the case, particularly Matthew Johnson and the three girls who were involved in the original trial and the retrial. Information about the earliest children involved in the case was also obtained from various sources.[120]

The Overdiagnosis Problem

Just as the interviewers at CII "found" indications of child sexual abuse in interviews that do not, on close examination, support the conclusion, the physicians at CII "found" medical evidence of sexual abuse in an astonishing number of children. Medical records for most of these children were never part of the criminal proceedings, so it is not possible to assess the details. There are some aggregate claims, however, that indicate there was a significant problem of overdiagnosis in medical evaluations conducted between January and May 1984. Two claims about the widespread prevalence of medical evidence have been cited in various writings about the McMartin case. One is that Dr. Heger found medical evidence in 80 percent of the 150 children she examined; the other is that the "majority" of the 400 children evaluated at CII had medical indications of sexual abuse.[121] The latter statement was made by Kee MacFarlane in congressional testimony in September 1984.[122] Information about most of these evaluations remains elusive because most of the children who received medical examinations through CII were never part of the criminal proceedings. The case had forty-four children at its height and Dr. Heger apparently evaluated thirty of them. Most of those children were diagnosed with having medical signs of sexual abuse. Dr. Heger has since published a peer-reviewed article concluding that approximately 5 percent of sexually abused children actually have medical signs of abuse. So even if all thirty children whom Dr. Heger examined early in the case were actually sexually abused, one would expect, u*nder current understandings concerning this kind of evidence*, that no more than a few would present with medical indications.

Why did the CII "find" such widespread indications of abuse? The primary reason is that the prevailing clinical understanding of sexual abuse was quite limited in 1984. Doctors knew what they often saw in sexually abused children, but there had not yet been studies examining the prevalence of such findings in "normal," or nonabused, children. Clinicians were aware of this problem. Drs. Heger and Woodling had written about the need for such studies.[123] Early examples of this kind of study include McCauley, Gorman, and Guzinski's prospective case-control study conducted at the University of Maryland Hospital in Baltimore between July 1984 and May 1985.[124] The study was conducted to evaluate use of a blue dye as a method of detecting lacerations, but it also provided scientific proof concerning the significance of fourchette lacerations in girls under ten years old. The incidence of lacerations "in the sexually abused group was 55 percent, whereas none of the control children had any lacerations detected."[125] In short, this study confirmed the common-sense conclusion that lacerations in the genitalia are not normal. The study also confirmed that physical signs were present in a minority of confirmed cases. The percentage of cases thought to have meaningful physical findings has gone down as knowledge advances in the field. Astrid Heger was lead author on a study published in 2002 that concluded, on the basis of a sample of 2,384 children, referred for suspected sexual abuse, there were "abnormal medical findings in only 5.5%" of the cases.[126]

There were several beliefs in the medical community in the 1980s that later proved to have much less basis than findings concerning certain lacerations in young girls. One involved the "normal" opening of the hole in the hymen. Pediatrician Hendrika Cantwell published an article in 1983 that argued openings larger than 0.4 mm are abnormal.[127] It was eventually proven that "normal" (nonabused) children could also have a large hymenal opening. Studies of "normals" also dispelled notions about "neovascularization" and "vaginal ridges and notches" as evidence of abuse. Most famous were the McCann studies that dispelled some conventional wisdom about anal findings.[128] What Woodling described as an "anal wink" response occurs more often in nonabused children than Woodling or others ever knew. Advancements in knowledge have also produced results that challenge the witch-hunt narrative. For example, there have been controlled studies of the reliability of genital exams in the context of sexual abuse. Atabaki and Paradise found that physicians with experience evaluating cases of suspected abuse evinced *less diagnostic bias* than did physicians with less experience.[129] It makes common sense that experience improves the knowledge of physicians, but the witch-hunt narrative definitely tells a different story: one in which child-abuse professionals, pejoratively known as the "child abuse industry," are considered most "prone" to "finding" abuse whether or not it exists because it is supposedly in their professional interest to do so. Instead, this study demonstrates that professionals are generally more conservative. At least they are now. It is clear in retrospect that some clinicians were overdiagnosing sexual abuse in the mid-1980s.

The consequences of the problem were enormous in the McMartin case. A medical diagnosis of sexual abuse is an extremely powerful way to convince parents that his or her child has been sexually abused, almost regardless of what the child said on tape at CII. Statements that contained direct denials of abuse, clear equivocations, contradictions, and even fantastic details would not likely raise enough skepticism to overcome such "findings." To the contrary, the medical diagnosis apparently "validated" the content of the interviews. What parent, faced with a medical diagnosis, would decide that his or her child has not been abused because the CII interview contained leading questions, or the child's answers were less than clear and convincing?

In this way, the overdiagnosis of children who did not move forward in the case caused far greater harm than overdiagnosis of the children who did. The evidence concerning children who moved forward was subject to cross-examination and critique by the defense. Because the proceedings lasted so long, it was also subject to Dr. Heger's frank testimony about changes in medical knowledge since the original examinations. The diagnosis of children who did not become part of the case had the effect of convincing a host of parents that their children had been abused. Had the same parents been faced with only the CII interviews, they might have been far more skeptical about how those interviews were being interpreted.

Relevant Medical Evidence

The witch-hunt narrative has used the fact that medical knowledge became more conservative over time—learning that some medical indications associated with sexual abuse were sometimes found in nonabused children—to reject all of the medical evidence in the McMartin case. But this is an overstatement of the studies of "normal" children. Moreover, the argument does not account for the medical findings on Matthew Johnson; the defense's own medical expert agreed that they were significant. The witch-hunt narrative has employed a different argument to dismiss the medical evidence concerning Matthew, arguing essentially that it should have been much more dramatic. Nathan and Snedeker asserted that the kind of sexual abuse Judy Johnson suspected her son had endured "can be expected to leave horrific anal tears and bruising" and that such abuse "often maims or kills."[130] Since Matthew was neither maimed nor killed, the argument goes, he must not have been sodomized. But the single publication on which they relied for this argument merely says that "Children, who are smaller and unwilling, experience more pain and injury."[131] It says nothing about being maimed or killed. Moreover, the article—which is actually about the behavior of child molesters, not the injuries sustained by their victims—cites several studies that directly contradict Nathan's claim.[132] The defense's own expert rejected Nathan's claim, although this has never been recognized in the witch-hunt narrative. [133]

Beyond the evidence concerning Matthew Johnson, some of the most relevant medical evidence in the case involved three girls.[134] A majority of the jurors in the first trial found the evidence pertaining to these girls convincing enough to vote that Ray Buckey was guilty beyond a reasonable doubt. The jury in the second trial also split on those charges. The witch-hunt narrative relies heavily on Dr. David Paul, who came from England to testify for the defense, for the claim that there was no credible medical evidence in the case. But he did not reject all of the evidence concerning these girls. Moreover, it is not clear how much weight his opinion should receive. The nature and extent of disagreements concerning these girls is considered here.

Sally Gregg

Sally Gregg was the only September responder who ended up in the actual trial. This is the family to indicate by mail that "in a preliminary discussion with Sally, she said 'Ray Ray does not wear underpants'" and that "we would like more time to talk to Sally without a heavy cross examination." Sally was not interviewed in the earliest phase of the CII interviews. Instead, she was fortieth in the CII interview sequence, interviewed on January 16, 1984.[135] Her medical examination was conducted by Dr. Heger about six weeks later, on March 2. Dr. Heger testified at the grand jury that Sally's hymenal opening was "one-and-a-half times" the normal size, that she had many areas of "rounding" on the hymen, and that there were "multiple scars" in various locations around the opening of the hymen. Dr. Heger also testified there was a scar located posteriorly, that is, in the anus.[136] Several years later, in her testimony at the first trial, Dr. Heger acknowledged that some of the vaginal findings mentioned at the grand jury were no longer considered indications of abuse. But she also testified that the anal findings on Sally were still consistent with blunt force penetrating trauma. She testified further that causes other than sexual abuse, such as diarrhea, could not have caused these findings.[137]

Three other doctors testified at trial about the photographic slides that formed the basis of Dr. Heger's conclusions: two for the prosecution (Drs. Woodling and Gordon) and one for the defense (Dr. Paul). Dr. Gordon testified that he saw "extraordinary injury to the anal verge." He testified further that given those findings there was a "very high probability that Sally was a victim of anal penetration." He noted the anal area was "grossly abnormal in its pattern" and showed "evidence of significant injury." He also testified that he saw thickened tissue, "broad base large wedges pointed into the anal opening," as well as a "markedly abnormal anal opening showing evidence of injury and trauma to the anal verge."[138] Dr. Woodling, who examined a photograph in a three-dimensional viewer, testified that the picture of the anal area showed a "marked deformity"; he said this suggested "multiple traumas" had occurred in the area. He testified further that an anal scar could clearly be observed, extending toward the anal funnel. Dr. Woodling called it a "significantly scarred anus" and said it was "significantly deformed."[139] Dr. Paul contradicted these three doctors, testifying at the first trial that the slide reflected a "perfectly normal" anus. On cross-examination, however, he also identified as "perfectly normal" a photograph of an anus from a British medical journal article that, unbeknownst to him, was about cases of *corroborated* trauma from sexual abuse.[140]

Dr. Heger's testimony in the second trial clearly took into account the changes in medical knowledge since 1984. She discussed the vaginal findings, particularly the scarring,[141] which would still be considered significant, but her testimony focused on the anal findings, which were even more clearly abnormal. When testifying about the vaginal findings, she noted that some, particularly scarring, were significant and some, like rounding, were no longer considered relevant.[142] She testified that the minor findings in Sally included a hymenal diameter of 0.6–0.7 cm and the rounding of the hymenal edge.[143] She maintained that the vaginal area was nevertheless abnormal, describing it as "deformed" in the sense that it was "disrupted and transected looking vestibular mucosa or hymen . . . it's a scarred hymen."[144] She described it as being a scar half a centimeter to a centimeter posteriorly away from the vagina on the anus.[145] Finally, she testified specifically in relation to the new studies of "normals" that she felt "very confident that the major findings in [Sally] G. would be supported by any of [the] studies" of nonabused children.[146] In other word, studies of nonabused children did *not* find these kinds of medical indications.

Trisha Walters

Among the eleven children who eventually went to trial, Trisha Walters appeared earliest in the CII interview sequence. She was interviewed on November 22, 1983, and her medical exam was conducted by Drs. Heger and Woodling on January 7, 1984. This is the girl who spontaneously asked Dr. Heger to examine her eyes. When Dr. Heger inquired why, the four-year-old said Ray's "gray tinkle" got in her eyes and her hair, and she was afraid she might go blind.[147] The jury was admonished not to take this statement into account because it was hearsay evidence.

Dr. Heger testified at the grand jury that Trisha's hymenal opening was "one-and-a-half times" what she thought was normal. She also noted there was rounding of the hymen and "neovascularization."[148] These findings would be considered nonspecific today; that is, they would *not* be considered indicative of sexual abuse. But Trisha also had several scars and healed lacerations of the hymen. There was one at the 3 o'clock position and another in between 3 o'clock and 4 o'clock. Dr. Heger testified as to an "impressive" scar at 6:30 that extended into the vagina.[149] These findings *would* still be considered significant today. During the second trial, Dr. Heger emphasized them; she testified there was a crescent-shaped scar that came across the hymen at 5 o'clock and extended across the "actual edge of the hymen."[150] There was another scar at 7 o'clock and a scar in the posterior fourchette.[151] Her conclusion was that the medical findings were "consistent with sexual assault."[152]

There were no slides taken of Trisha Walters; the colposcope in Dr. Heger's office did not yet have a camera in early January, 1984.[153] Instead, she drew a diagram based on what she saw through the colposcope. Dr. Paul testified that if the findings that she drew were present, it would also be consistent with sexual abuse. He later claimed that such findings would be consistent as well with "normal wear and tear."[154] It is difficult to ascertain what kind of "wear and tear" Dr. Paul thought a four-year-old girl would have sustained. No other doctor provided any testimony that supported this peculiar claim.

Dr. Paul's testimony in the second trial was inconsistent with that in the first trial, as he testified that there were no signs in the medical reports consistent with penetrative abuse through the hymen or the anus.[155] On cross-examination, however, he allowed that *if* the exam by Drs. Heger and Woodling was accurate, and there was damage to the posterior fourchette, this *would* be a significant finding.[156] Finally, he admitted that the combination of findings on the girl—scarring to the posterior fourchette as well as scar tissue—was "strongly suggestive of penetrative injury." Thus, in the end he conceded that if Dr. Heger's findings were accurate, her conclusions would be correct.

Allison Brown

The third girl involved in both trials was Allison Brown, who was first interviewed at CII on March 13, 1984. Her initial medical examination was less than
a month later, on April 8. Allison attended the McMartin Preschool from 1981
to 1983. She had nightmares during her time at McMartin about someone
coming into her house at night; her father actually nailed her bedroom window
shut during that time to ease her mind. The findings on Allison were, in retrospect, quite mixed. Several findings—"rounded hymen," neovascularization—
were considered significant in 1984 but would not be considered important by
the time of the second trial. Dr. Heger addressed those changes directly in the
second trial. Several of the original findings involved scarring.[157] There was a tear
to the posterior fourchette (the mucous membrane forming the posterior margin
of the vulva). Dr. Heger testified that "to a medical certainty" these were not the
kind of scars that could have been self-inflicted or accidentally incurred.[158]
Dr. Paul did not reject those findings entirely; rather, he testified he could not
tell if there were one or more scars. Multiple scars would presumably be a stronger finding than a single scar. But allowing that there was at least one scar seems
to indicate there was some kind of attendant injury.

Whatever the number of scars, it is important to consider the weight that
should be given to Dr. Paul's testimony. The witch-hunt narrative seems to accept
it all without question, and apparently without looking closely enough to see
that he did not reject all of the state's evidence. There is no question he made
statements that were eminently quotable. He was also firm in his opinions, con-
cise in his statements, and unfailingly British in delivery ("You have to be jolly
careful" about magnifying photographic images, he said at one point[159]). But his
critique of the colposcope, however quotable, was deeply flawed. The colposcope became the basis for controlled studies about "normals." It is also what
allowed the findings in the McMartin case to be examined by other doctors.

It is not surprising that Dr. Paul knew little about the colposcope. He was
trained in the 1950s and the device did not start being used in the United States
until the early 1980s. One of the strangest arguments offered against the medical
evidence in the McMartin case is against the colposcope, a medical instrument
"now accepted as the standard of care in most referral centers in the world."[160]
Debbie Nathan claimed that use of the device was inspired by the dubious practices of a Brazilian doctor named Wilmes Teixeira.[161] But the colposcope was not
introduced to the medical community in the United States by Teixeira's article;
the instrument was already well established for use in cervical pathology and for
"the diagnosis of early carcinoma in situ."[162] The absurdity of criticizing the colposcope is that the device itself is what allowed Dr. Paul to review the evidence
in the McMartin case. It is also what allowed the studies by McCann and others

of "normals." Every advance in medical knowledge in this area is based, in part, on the colposcope. Dr. Heger's use in 1984 was pioneering and prescient.

Dr. Paul also had some decidedly unusual methods—such as inserting his finger into a child as a way of measurement. The witch-hunt narrative was quick to label a Minnesota pediatrician, who testified for the state in the Jordan cases, as a *child abuser* for having engaged in this practice.[163] But the narrative heaps only praise on Dr. Paul, despite this unusual practice, along with his inexplicable objection to taking a medical history from a child, and his absurd claims about assessing the honesty of children by observing their "eye contact."[164] Although Dr. Paul faded from the field after his appearance in the McMartin case, Dr. Heger went on to considerable professional prominence. She coauthored a major textbook on evaluating sexually abused children and was the medical expert who helped identify problems at Children's Hospital in San Diego in 1992.[165] She was also one of the peer reviewers of the famous McCann study.[166] Her original evaluations of children in the McMartin case were definitely overstated, but there was also considerable evidence that remained significant over time on all three of these girls.

Beyond the three girls who participated in both trials, there was medical evidence presented for most of the remaining children who participated in the first trial. Two of the boys were reported to be "within normal limits"; that is, their medical evaluations resulted in no medical evidence of sexual abuse. The medical evidence concerning the five other children involved in the first trial varied considerably. There were definitely issues of overdiagnosis, but there was also medical evidence that seems significant even with the benefit of advancements in medical knowledge since 1984. There was medical evidence worthy of consideration on at least five of the other children in the first trial.[167] Among these children, there are findings that would still be considered significant today contradicting the central claim in the witch-hunt narrative: that there was virtually no meaningful medical evidence of sexual abuse in the case.

Many of the earliest children in the case also had positive medical findings. Unfortunately, much of that evidence was not fully developed. Of course, evidence involving children who became complainants but dropped out before the preliminary hearing was never subject to cross-examination. Nevertheless, it is important to consider such evidence since the witch-hunt narrative denies the existence of any evidence of abuse. In fact, the medical evaluations of some of the earliest children in the case help explain how and why the case moved forward. There were five September responders who became complainants; only one, Sally Gregg, actually testified at the preliminary hearing. She also went on to trial and retrial, and the medical evidence in her case has already been discussed. Documents indicate that three of the other important September responders had medical signs of sexual abuse as well.[168] The fourth, Tanya Mergili, had some suspicious medical findings, but nothing as strong as with the other three.[169] Finally, there was relevant medical evidence concerning Kathy Ingram, whose family responded to the MBPD in late September 1983. The girl's mother indicated she had a chronic thin watery discharge with a distinctive odor. Dr. Heger told the grand jury that she saw "numerous scars surrounding the entire entrance through the girl's hymenal opening," and some of them "crossed the hymen and had been torn."[170] One of the reported findings is more ambiguous; a "scalloped hymen," though considered relevant at the time, was shown to be far more common in nonabused children than ever known. Another finding on Kathy Ingram was also, in retrospect, given too much importance at the time: neovascularization. This was thought to be a sign of new blood vessels, but it can also be congenital. Nevertheless, if the scarring evidence was accurate, it would still be considered highly significant today. Indeed, it would be unthinkable for authorities to ignore evidence of this nature.

In sum, the medical evaluations helped to support the state's case in McMartin—and, ironically, they also helped to undermine it. The latter effect was ultimately more powerful, since the overdiagnosis of many children in early 1984 fueled the idea that the case involved dozens, if not hundreds, of children. It also gave parents a strong reason to believe their children must have been abused, regardless of what else they said about the matter. The damage caused by the overdiagnosis was enormous, and it undoubtedly helped doom the case. But the witch-hunt narrative that has since emerged does an injustice in the other direction: it ignores or dismisses credible medical evidence of sexual abuse that would still be recognized today.

The Confluence of Forces Beyond CII

The mistakes that were made at CII are pivotal to explaining how the McMartin case spun out of control. The interviewers, in an earnest attempt to avoid dismissing children's voices, "heard" far more than they were actually told. Convinced that the children were afraid to talk, they coaxed responses that seemed to confirm their view. Faced with the implausible idea that all of the teachers in the school participated in the abuse, they came up with a conspiracy theory about a national network of child pornographers. These problems were compounded significantly when medical evaluations "confirmed" that most of the children interviewed in the first few months at CII had been abused. Children who made few incriminating statements, if any, were seen in an entirely different light because the evaluators "knew" they showed medical signs of abuse. The chance that parents might view the CII videotapes skeptically was virtually eliminated when they were presented with medical evidence "confirming" the abuse. The toxic combination of these problems explains a lot about why the case went so wrong. But three factors external to CII are also important to understanding the story. First, there were activist parents and therapists who provided substantial reinforcement to an emerging view of the case in 1984. Second, a barrage of national publicity that came long before a grand jury was ever convened changed the dynamics of the case in such a way as to accentuate the extremes. Finally, the Los Angeles District Attorney's Office, which was responsible for actually charging and prosecuting the case, failed in a variety of ways.

Parent-Investigators and Activist-Therapists

One factor that undoubtedly influenced the content and intensity of beliefs that developed around the McMartin case was the role of parent-investigators and activist-therapists. Parents started becoming investigators in middle to late December 1983, when the idea that the McMartin case involved activities beyond the school grounds first began to take shape. Various houses in and around Manhattan Beach were mentioned as possible places where children had been taken. Some parents drove their children around Manhattan Beach and surrounding communities, asking them to point out places they may have been taken. A number of the children apparently provided affirmative answers, further fueling the idea that the case involved parties well beyond the preschool. In late December, various parents start reporting addresses of suspect houses to the MBPD. This soon evolved into the reporting of suspects in general, as parents reported license plates of "suspicious" individuals, an assessment made on the basis of how their child reacted to, say, a stranger in a pizza parlor. The documentation of these events is all in the form of police and DA's investigator notes. From existing records, it is impossible to know what these children were actually asked or how they actually answered.

It is also difficult to ascertain how much of this amateur investigation was requested or encouraged by authorities. Some of it definitely was. A number of parents were given photographs of buildings to show their children; the photos came from the MBPD and were circulated in December 1983 and January 1984.[171] But some of the parents took matters into their own hands. One of the parents who played a leading role in these efforts was Robert Currie, who was portrayed in the movie *Indictment* as yelling at the chief of the Manhattan Beach Police Department:

> I'm going to ask you, this is about the thousandth time, for the grand jury transcripts and the police report. I mean, if you won't pursue this, we'll conduct our own investigation!

Investigator notes from the DA's office indicate that Robert Currie was providing the FBI with photos of possible additional suspects as early as February 3, 1984—the day the case began receiving intensive media coverage. Sociology professor Jeffrey Victor eventually identified Currie as one of the "carriers" of the satanic cult legend that swept through this community.[172] Currie led a group of parents who started to dig at the site of the preschool in 1985 because they were convinced they would find dead animals, killed to scare the children into silence. Some of these parents also believed there were tunnels underneath the school where children had been abused. The district attorney's office had the area cordoned off and conducted their own dig—which did not turn up any evidence of tunnels. They did find some tortoise shells, which were the subject of considerable attention at the eventual trial with competing experts arguing about whether the turtles had died of natural causes.

Another parent who was extraordinarily involved in the early investigation was Madeline Randle, whose daughter attended the preschool with Tanya Mergili. Randle's amateur investigative work was dutifully reported to the DA's investigator. She was one of the parents who drove children around Manhattan Beach and surrounding areas to see if particular houses looked familiar. Two notations from police investigative notes in early January reveal the extent of her activity:

> 1/6/84 Randle: "Daughter Molly picked a yellow house. 829 2nd Str. Hermosa Beach as place where Ray took her." "Girls independently ID same house."
>
> 1/11/84 Randle: "2 more licenses for Jean." "Molly IDs all three houses with absolutely no help from mother."[173]

The final notation might be a reference to some photos of buildings prepared by the MBPD. There is no question that Randle went overboard in her efforts. Through her own "investigation," this parent convinced herself that the case involved numerous buildings beyond the preschool; this "fact" alone helped reinforce the view that the case had to have multiple defendants. On February 16, she provided "a two-page handwritten letter re a dark skinned oriental they saw @ Cocos in M.B."[174] She also supplied a license plate number for the "suspects." This letter was received the same day the investigator received a two-page communication from Judy Johnson about satanic cults. The prosecution would later be charged with withholding vital evidence from the defense by not disclosing Johnson's strange allegations. It is not clear whether Randle's equally dubious theories were ever disclosed to the defense. But the fact that she was writing about a suspicious "dark skinned oriental" at the same time Johnson was imagining satanic cults indicates that something was in the air. Something was happening in the community. Johnson's statements in February were just one of many such claims, none of which ever amounted to anything.

The parent-investigators reinforced the sense that the CII view of the case was correct. These parents "confirmed" places, and they helped account for the fact that the formal investigation spread to Harry's Market, a Nautilus gym, several farms, and various churches and day-care centers. Parents also became a political force, lobbying on issues including a bill to allow children to testify by closed-circuit television. The most ardent of this group financed another effort to find tunnels under the school in 1990. Curiously, the most active parents did *not* actually have children in the case.[175] But they certainly had an effect on how the case was perceived. Some of these parents also formed an organization called Believe the Children, a support group for parents of children in day-care abuse cases; it also had the stated goal of addressing the "sexual and ritual exploitation of children." Believe the Children began in Manhattan Beach and was later run out of Chicago, the location of the Rogers Park case (discussed in Chapter Three). The organization had, at most, several hundred members and a very limited budget. Richard Beck recently cast such groups as right-wing, but nothing in their newsletters supports this claim.[176]

Therapists also exerted influence on parents and investigators by adding a professional stamp of approval to various claims, particularly the focus on satanic ritual abuse. They were not part of the criminal case, however, and their records would be subject to discovery only in civil litigation, which never came to pass; so they were largely hidden from view. But they were deeply involved. A small number of therapists accounted for all of the children at the preliminary hearing. One therapist, Cheryl Kent, was seeing nine of the fourteen children in the preliminary hearing.[177] Wade Green, who was discredited at the preliminary hearing after making increasingly implausible claims, had Michele Dugan as a therapist. According to Glenn Stevens, the prosecutor who quit his job during the case, these therapists used devil puppets in their therapy.[178] Stevens also noted that "most or all the children who made tunnel claims were going to the same therapist." Documents from the DA's office support this observation. Many of these therapists also met as a support group. Even though the need for support makes sense, it is likely to create a dangerous echo chamber of sorts if appropriate precautions are not taken. When various children described similar but implausible things, these therapists viewed it as proof of the widespread existence of their theory—rather than proof that their theory had taken hold of their view of the case. The therapists got so caught up in the satanic abuse theme that some of them persisted well into the 1990s with their conspiratorial theories.[179]

It should be noted, however, that the extremism was not limited to one side. There have been a number of dubious conspiracy-theory claims made by case critics as well. When there was a fire at the McMartin school site on April 8, 1984, the Eberles jumped to the conclusion that a roving band of crazed

McMartin local parents "torched" the school.[180] But, as reported in a local newspaper on May 26, the man arrested for the arson had no connection to the McMartin case.[181] Yet the implication that "McMartin parents" torched the preschool has become part of the urban folklore of the witch-hunt narrative. The arson is described in the same misleading way in the movie *Indictment*, which was promoted and praised on the basis of its alleged fidelity to the facts. Curiously, Abby Mann also had a suspicious fire at his own house. This was in 1993, when *Indictment* had just started filming. Mann rushed to judgment and blamed crazed McMartin parents. He later blamed the U.S. attorney, when the FBI concluded there was no link between the suspicious fire at his house and the parents in the McMartin case.[182]

Massive Media Coverage

"The gaze of the world is a fickle, intoxicating thing," Lisa Belkin wrote in 1999 about the effects of national media attention on a public-housing lawsuit in Yonkers, New York. When television cameras turned their attention to Yonkers, "they magnified and electrified events, changing the body language of the combatants and sharpening the tone of their words."[183] The media attention on Yonkers was nothing compared to what happened fifteen years earlier in the McMartin case. On February 2, 1984 the beginning of the rating sweeps week, the ABC television affiliate in Los Angeles aired the first in a series of "exclusive" stories about sexual abuse at the McMartin Preschool. The stories were long, detailed, and sensationalistic. The reporter, Wayne Satz, claimed that sixty children—basically the total number of children interviewed at CII since November 1, 1983—had been sexually abused at the McMartin Preschool and scared into silence through physical threats and the killing of small animals (rabbits, turtles).

These stories had the requisite number of qualifiers to protect the station against libel actions, but they nevertheless left the distinct impression that the allegations were true. And this is precisely how they were seen. The regular Channel 10 news anchors weighed in with dismay and editorial-like approval of the reporting.[184] The stories were "exclusives." Satz had some kind of "exclusive" access to someone (or more than one person) at CII. Because they were "exclusives," the rest of the media was reduced, at least initially, to the role of reporting on KABC's stories. It is not clear whether Satz was given access to the CII videotapes or whether he relied on sources at CII that described the children's interviews to him. Whatever the specific basis for these stories, they were definitely prepared with the knowledge and assistance of Kee MacFarlane.[185] Night after night, there were new stories at the beginning of the broadcast. In retrospect, what is most remarkable about the airing of these stories is that they were aired before the case was even sent to a grand jury. No one had yet been arrested.

KABC later placed full pages advertisements touting their McMartin coverage under the headline "Sometimes Being the Only One With All the Serious News Makes Us Feel Lousy." "We feel lousy because the story is so awful," the ad continued. But, as the ad explained, the story "has to be told because it can be the catalyst to provoke public outrage demanding better protection of our children." It is no wonder the media was later accused of participating in a moral crusade. KABC basically took credit for launching a crusade.

The early media coverage, which appeared to document widespread sexual abuse at the McMartin Preschool, enraged parents who understandably felt that "nothing was being done" about a seemingly widespread problem. After all, by the time these stories aired, it had been almost four months since Assistant DA Jean Matusinka referred the case to CII, and the investigation had produced no arrests. The Satz stories fueled the idea that there was much more to the case than had been reported. After the first story was broadcast, the DA's chief investigator started receiving phone calls that reflected a new level of fear and paranoia. Investigator Brunetti's notes, dated 8:00 p.m. on February 2, contain a report of "a scary man at Magic Pizza."[186] The parents furnished a license plate number. The next day, Robert Currie was giving photos of possible additional suspects to the FBI. Within two weeks, numerous mothers were calling the DA's investigator to report all kinds of fantastic things. These stories were mutually reinforcing, and a view formed that it was the largest child sex-abuse case in history.

The intense media spotlight magnified the forces that rushed the case to the grand jury and resulted in such broad indictments. There were almost a dozen national news stories about the McMartin case in the month of March. Glenn Stevens later described it as a period of "intense pressure" at the DA's office. This is when some of the worst and most fateful decisions about the case were made—from what charges to present to the grand jury to how to handle the question of bail.

The period of most intense media coverage—the time from which almost all the egregious examples of media stories are taken—was surprisingly short for a case that lasted seven years. The months of February through May 1984 were by far the worst time in this regard, though the period is described as much longer in the witch-hunt narrative. Philip Jenkins has claimed there were "high-profile national stories *throughout 1984.*" Curiously, he cites four media reports in support of the proposition: three from the first week in April 1984 and one from the third week in May.[187] In fact, coverage of the McMartin case dropped off significantly during the final six months of 1984. The national media had nothing to report again until January 1985, when the first child testified in the preliminary hearing. But there was intense coverage from February 2 through the end of May. Emotions were running high, and the media was in a frenzy. When Stevens went to the McMartin preschool to film the layout in early May, his notes indicate "Residents seem angry. Media arrives by helicopter."

That the period of media excess lasted months, not years, does not diminish the damage done in the critical period when the McMartin case was charged and bail decisions were made on the seven defendants, five of whom were initially held without bail. Two of those five were in the McMartin family; the other three (Betty Raidor, Babette Spitler, and Mary Ann Jackson) were unrelated teachers. The injustice to those teachers cannot be overstated.

In short, the media was a major culprit in the McMartin case. It might even seem like the primary culprit at first glance—but the stories could not have been done without cooperation from one or more people at CII. Moreover, the case would not have become a case without the decisions made by the Los Angeles DA. The complicity of CII in these stories is arguably more objectionable than the stories themselves because social workers at CII had a professional obligation to keep details of the investigation confidential.

David Shaw, media critic for the *Los Angeles Times*, won a Pulitzer Prize for criticizing his own newspaper's coverage of the McMartin case. Although his four-part series, which began the day after the original McMartin verdicts, was actually broader than that, Shaw laid considerable blame for the McMartin debacle at the media's credulous early acceptance of virtually everything said against the defendants. The argument has considerable force.

Prosecutorial Failures

The DA's actions in the case came after various other actors—particularly CII staff, a number of therapists, and the media—had wreaked havoc. Those forces created enormous pressure to bring a significant number of charges soon. Of course, this does not absolve the prosecutors of responsibility for their mistakes. Indeed, the Los Angeles District Attorney's Office bears primary responsibility for three of the worst mistakes in the McMartin case: failing to supervise the CII process, charging the case without adequately reviewing the evidence, and approaching the case in political, not professional prosecutorial, terms. Avoiding any of these mistakes might have resulted in a narrowly charged case that did not involve fantastic claims and include inappropriate defendants. Those mistakes were all much worse than what later became the rallying cry for criticisms of the prosecution: their failure to provide the defense with notes concerning Judy Johnson's February 1984 rantings.[188]

Neglecting to Supervise the CII Process

Although the DA's office invited CII to evaluate children in the McMartin case, there was no clear agreement in advance about the scope or purpose of the CII interviews. The interviewers did not see themselves, at least originally, as investigators; they were evaluating children and supplying information to the DA. But the interviews soon became investigative. The CII interviewers even showed the children "photo lineups" of possible suspects and places. Some, or possibly all, of those photos originated with the MBPD; it is not clear from available records what role was played by the DA's office. But either they facilitated a bad idea or they failed to see how the investigation was being compromised.

Overall, the LA District Attorney's Office paid scant attention while the process evolved at CII between November 1983 and early February 1984. They did not review interview tapes and they did not offer feedback, but rather relied almost entirely on reports from CII. Those reports were not informed by forensic considerations. The impressions of interviews, often reduced to shorthand notations in the video log, ended up playing far too large a role in shaping the case. How the children were interviewed became the focus of the defense in the case. This was a direct function of the DA's office allowing the process to move along for months without paying close attention, let alone offering a prosecutor's skepticism to evidence they would have to defend in court.

Charging the Case Without Reviewing the Evidence

The DA's office was caught unprepared when the media spotlight hit them on February 2, 1984, with a story that suggested there was widespread sexual abuse at the McMartin Preschool and the government was dragging its feet in response. The most active parents had already been busy for weeks "investigating" the case and organizing other parents. The early stages of organizing meant convincing other parents to have their children evaluated at CII. The success of the effort is demonstrated through the remarkable fact that CII never solicited anyone to come in for an evaluation but ultimately interviewed more than four hundred children. There were some referrals through the DA's office, but in December 1983 and January 1984 it appears the long waiting list that developed was generated almost entirely by parents being convinced by other parents to participate.

While that process was still in progress, the DA's office rushed the case to the grand jury. The CII investigation, or evaluation, was still very much in progress; in fact, they had interviewed only about half of the children they would ultimately evaluate.[189] Remarkably, the DA's office took the case to the grand jury in early March without having reviewed almost any the CII videotapes, which were supposedly the state's primary evidence. The DA's investigator had obtained statements from Kee MacFarlane about the content of the interviews, but they had not independently reviewed the evidence.[190] As MacFarlane told it, the videotapes documented children who were initially too scared to talk but who, through skilled questioning and the use of puppets, ultimately unburdened themselves of various "yucky secrets." But those videotapes ended up being most useful to the defense. The DA's office did not realize the problems posed by the tapes until well after they had charged the case. This is probably the most egregious error in the case because it did not involve a judgment call, or possibly a good-faith difference of opinion. It was pure shoddiness.

This dereliction of duty was compounded when prosecutors filed an additional two hundred counts against the defendants in May. Twenty-four children were added to the case. Investigative notes from the DA's office indicate they "processed" twenty-seven names at a two-hour meeting in May. This meant no more than an average of about five minutes to discuss an interview, the medical evidence, and the likely nature of parental cooperation for each child. This abbreviated "processing" was, at least for questions concerning the content of the children's allegations, based entirely on the videotape log notes and the recollections of the interviewers. There was no independent review of the actual interviews until after the charges were finalized. The new charges added the potential of prison sentences in the hundreds of years. Stevens later admitted it was "a huge rush" to announce those charges and the potential sentences.[191] Inventory logs indicate he had not yet reviewed *any* of the CII videotapes at the time.

The grand jury, which met for only a few days in March, became what lawyers sometimes call a runaway train. They indicted someone the district attorney did not ask them to indict: Virginia McMartin, the wheelchair-bound grandmother. All told, the grand jury indicted seven people: Ray Buckey; his sister, Peggy Ann; their mother, Peggy; their grandmother, Virginia; and three other teachers from the preschool, Babette Spitler, Mary Ann Jackson, and Betty Raidor. A review of the grand jury transcripts reveals a combination of relevant medical evidence on some children, and cursory but reinforcing testimony from eighteen children and some parents. Much of the testimony focuses on Ray and Peggy Buckey, but apparently the grand jury also brought charges against anyone else a child named. The prosecutors had decided that the would-be allegations against Virginia McMartin were not credible, or perhaps they simply shied away from the specter of charging a grandmother. But the grand jury saw no reason to draw distinctions between possible defendants and took a kind of all-or-nothing approach. Ironically, by accepting "all" of the claims, they helped to ensure that ultimately "none" would result in convictions.

Politics over Professionalism

Political factors were also apparently more important than professional ones when it came to key decisions in the Los Angeles County District Attorney's Office. Rushing the case to the grand jury in early March was undoubtedly a product of the media coverage and the attendant need for Robert Philibosian, the elected district attorney, to show he was "doing something." This was apparently more important than taking the considerable time it would have required to evaluate the case thoroughly before going to the grand jury. The DA also made a critical decision that has largely been lost to history: he brought in prosecutors with experience in handling "high-profile" cases, mostly murder cases. The new prosecutors added the two-hundred-plus charges in May. Beyond rushing the case to the grand jury, the DA, who was up for election in June 1984, blatantly used the case for publicity. He appeared at court hearings and frequently gave press conferences in the hallway. Philibosian's media strategy did not succeed; he lost the election to Ira Reiner.

The Brutal Preliminary Hearing

Although the actual trial did not begin until 1987, there is a good argument that the case was effectively over in January or February 1985. This is when the first two children testified at the preliminary hearing. It is also when it became apparent that the prosecution would not be able to prove its case beyond a reasonable doubt. Some of the children's testimony included incredible claims that *had* to create reasonable doubt (one boy testified that his teacher took him to a cemetery, where human bodies were exhumed and cut with knives to scare the children). It also became clear in the preliminary hearing that the CII interviews, on which the case largely rested, actually raised more questions than they answered.

The hearing lasted seventeen months and was the longest preliminary hearing in California history. There were several explanations for its taking so long. First, the parents of some children helped to delay the case in order to lobby the California legislature for adopting new provisions for children to testify by closed-circuit television. Second and more important, there were seven defendants, which meant every witness was subject to possible cross-examination by seven defense lawyers.

The most important developments in the case occurred during this pre-trial period. First, the number of complainants was winnowed from the original forty-one to fourteen who actually testified at the preliminary hearing. Second, the number of defendants was also brought down significantly. Although the preliminary hearing resulted in a technical victory for the prosecution—that is, all seven defendants were held over for trial—in perhaps the most dramatic single moment in the case, District Attorney Reiner dropped charges against five of the defendants shortly after the preliminary hearing ended. The story behind the dismissal of charges against most of the defendants is explained in the witch-hunt narrative; the winnowing of complainants is not.

The preliminary hearing is best remembered for the fantastic claims made by several children. The second boy on the stand said he had been forced to drink rabbit's blood. He made the statement during his fourteenth day on the stand.[192] Another boy testified he had watched as McMartin teachers dug up corpses and mutilated them to scare the children. As prosecutor Stevens put it, "the kids are falling apart."[193] A contributing reason was that the preliminary hearing was brutal; the children who testified at the hearing were savaged by the process of cross-examination. The second boy was on the stand for seventeen days, sixteen of them in being cross-examined. "Trial by ordeal" is how John Jackson described the process in the Torrance (California) *Daily Breeze*.[194] In another story about how the children were experiencing "a legal battering," *People* magazine focused on a thirty-two-minute span during which defense attorney Danny Davis used the word *kill* twenty-four times while questioning a young girl.[195] The prosecution pleaded without success for the judge to constrain cross-examination. Some parents withdrew their children from the case because they saw what happened to the first few children in the preliminary hearing. Others refused to go forward without being able to have their children testify by closed-circuit television. Their concerns were not exaggerated. Even after defecting from the DA's office, Stevens described what happened to the children as "inhumane" and how Danny Davis acted as "monstrous."[196] This aspect of the case is not included in the witch-hunt narrative.

Remarkably, there was no real strategy to presenting the children's testimony at the preliminary hearing. "The press kept asking why [Walter Gorman] was first in the preliminary hearing," Stevens later told Abby Mann. The boy did not do particularly well as a witness, and the press assumed that the prosecution would open with its strongest witness. It did not. "He was the only kid there that was ready," Stevens later explained.[197] Why the prosecution was not prepared with its witnesses, let alone how they neglected to consider the order of the evidence they presented, remains unclear.

The damage done by those errors is clearer. One can easily see why so many people think that most of the children in the McMartin case made claims about satanic practices and tunnels—things that were inadvertently highlighted in the preliminary hearing. There was no strategic effort to select children whose interviews would be the least susceptible to attack: the earliest and the most spontaneous. Indeed, the earliest interviews were underrepresented at all stages of the case. The thirty-four children interviewed at CII during the first two months accounted for only four of the forty-one criminal complaints in the McMartin case, and only one of these four children made it to trial. On the other hand, more than 70 percent of the forty-one complainants were interviewed after Wayne Satz broke the story on television in early February 1984. The significance of these facts was not appreciated at the time.

The preliminary hearing was a ferocious attack on many adults as well. Parents reported various intimidating tactics by the defense, which was admonished for the investigators they hired.[198] One parent, whose daughter reportedly touched Ray's genitals in the spring of 1983, testified he felt as though *he* were being put on trial.[199] Similarly, the defense put MacFarlane and the rest of the CII staff on trial. They inquired into whether she had been sexually abused as a child and into the details of her relationship with Satz, the reporter who broke the case. There were long sidebars about the appropriateness of these excursions into issues of admittedly remote relevance. Judge Bobb was generally ineffective in containing these detours.

After the judge ruled that none of the remaining complainants could testify by closed-circuit television, the state rested its case. Fourteen children had testified; none of the remaining children was called. Given what was described as "a mass defection of witnesses," it is not clear how many of those children would have participated if allowed to testify by closed-circuit television. The lowest estimate I have found is six; the remainder presumably dropped out of the case for other reasons. Whatever the number, the judge was required to dismiss all of the charges related to these children.

The decision to drop charges against five of the seven defendants stood in sharp contrast to the implications of holding them over for trial. Judge Bobb's decision to hold them over meant she found probable cause to think the defendants were all guilty; Reiner's decision to drop the charges meant he did not think there was sufficient evidence to prove the allegations. Calling the evidence against the five defendants "incredibly flimsy," Reiner dismissed all of the charges against them. This decision was not a reaction to the judge so much as the end result of the internal discontent on the part of Glenn Stevens. In the six months since claiming that "the kids are falling apart," he had second thoughts about the evidence. His expression of those misgivings, offered within the confines of the DA's office, resulted in a dramatic story in a local newspaper. "McMartin Quandary," the *Daily Breeze* announced in an exclusive headline on September 25, 1985. The story reported that one of the McMartin prosecutors was having second thoughts about some (possibly most) of the charges. The DA called for "a candid and complete" evaluation of the evidence.[200] It resulted in a confidential memorandum written in December in which Stevens detailed two conclusions: (1) he did *not* find the evidence against the female defendants to be credible enough to justify charges, and (2) he still thought there *was* sufficient evidence to convict Ray Buckey. Stevens resigned in early 1986 and, as his collaboration with Mann deepened, he slowly changed his mind about Ray Buckey.[201] The beginning of the trial was a year away, but the dismissal of so many charges caused *Newsweek* to report in January 1986 "A Child-Abuse Case Implodes."[202]

The Trial and Retrial

The prosecution went forward to trial with eleven of the fourteen children who were involved in the preliminary hearing. The trial was preceded by a highly publicized motion to dismiss, based largely on the tape recordings of conversations between former prosecutor Stevens and screenwriter Mann and his wife and co-author, Myra. The tapes, which were supposedly made confidentially, were interviews of Stevens by the Manns. Stevens had already signed a secret agreement to sell his story to the Manns and share in the profits of any book or movie.[203] The Manns ultimately turned the tapes over to the defense.[204] They were publicized largely for the obvious and highly unusual story line, involving a prosecutor who switched sides in the middle of a case. The Manns made it clear to Stevens that he would be the hero in their movie, and this is how he was ultimately portrayed. But the hearing revolving around his conversations with the Manns was embarrassing to Stevens in several ways. First, it demonstrated his raw ambition as a prosecutor; he described "what a rush" it had been to charge the original defendants with enough counts to translate into hundreds of years in potential sentences. He also described the McMartin case as "just a career stepping stone."[205] Further, the hearings revealed that Stevens still thought Ray Buckey was guilty when he participated in a toast with the Manns to the acquittal of all defendants.[206] Before leaving the district attorney's office, Stevens wrote a confidential 113-page memo to Gil Garcetti, chief deputy DA, dated January 10, 1986, analyzing the evidence in the case and detailing the problems with how it was investigated. He rejected various claims (among them the idea that children were taken from the preschool to other locations) as "totally unbelievable," but not the entire case. His bottom line was clear: "It is my opinion that Raymond Buckey did in fact molest some of the children at the school."[207] Stevens later allowed that he anticipated receiving "substantial additional sums of money" from the movie, although he had made it clear to the Manns he "can't be made to look like I have any pecuniary interest in the outcome of the case."[208] Although the hearings deflated the value of the much-hyped Mann-Stevens tapes, they did not move the judge. After a three-month hearing, Judge Pounders ruled that the case should, at long last, go to trial.

The trial took two years. The main component was the child witnesses, but an extraordinary amount of time was also spent on medical testimony and on the testimony of social workers and psychologists. There were even several days devoted to battling veterinary testimony, concerning animal bones found in the ground at the preschool. Many of these arguments had been aired at the preliminary hearing. A new claim by the defense, one that would become a mainstay in the witch-hunt narrative, was that many of the charges against Ray Buckey could not have occurred because he was not working at the preschool at the time.

These arguments were popularized by Mary Fischer in a story in *LA Magazine* that included a chart entitled "Where Was Ray?" The chart detailed the attendance periods for eleven children in the trial, arrayed along a timeline conveying that Ray Buckey was "at McMartin Preschool" from 1981 through summer 1983, with the first six months of 1981 designated as "A.M. only."[209] By this reckoning, three of the children at trial attended the preschool *before* Ray was ever there. The claim grew slightly in the movie *Indictment*; actor James Woods, who starred in the movie, claimed, with characteristic indignity, that Ray Buckey was charged with crimes against "four kids who never met him." The *LA Magazine* article has since become a foundational article in the witch-hunt narrative.[210]

This claim was undermined at trial, where prosecutors introduced extensive evidence that placed Ray at the preschool before 1981. The evidence included visual aids for the jury that contradicted the chart in *LA Magazine*, backed up by pay stubs, entries in Virginia's journal, photographs, and testimony by parents corroborating the fact that Ray Buckey was at the preschool before 1981. He just was not there *full-time* before 1981, but he was there doing odd jobs, hanging around, and working as an aide in a class with children who, according to the witch-hunt narrative, had never met him. Several parents who were never part of the criminal proceedings, and who told the MBPD they had no information about sexual abuse at the preschool, verified that Ray was at the preschool in 1980 and earlier.[211] A former college student testified that, as part of a class at El Camino College in the fall semester of 1980, she observed at the McMartin Preschool. This was more than a year before the *LA Magazine* chart places Ray "at" the school, but the ex-student testified she saw him there on many occasions between September and December (1980) "observing and helping out."[212]

There was also extensive evidence concerning his character and behavior. Was there any reason to think he might be the kind of person to sexually abuse children? This is inevitably an important question for the jury in any child molestation case. Had there been any complaints or concerns about Ray Buckey? The question is particularly relevant in cases with multiple complainants. In this case, the answer to both questions was yes, but you would never know it from the witch-hunt narrative. Nathan and Snedeker assert that "when [Ray] took a job at his family's preschool, the move was hailed as evidence that Ray was finally figuring out what to do with himself."[213] It is not clear from this oblique assertion to whom this was hailed as such evidence, or why they needed it.[214] But there was evidence introduced in the trial to contradict that view. There had been concerns raised about Ray Buckey's behavior around children, both by his family and by others. Darlene Gregg testified that Betty Raidor, a teacher at the school, registered "concern" about Ray. One of his friends told the police that Ray was abusing alcohol at the time, and possibly much stronger drugs.[215]

Neighbors remember him throwing violent temper tantrums outside, screaming and crying "I hate my life." There was also an entry in Virginia McMartin's preschool-related dairy about Ray having "troubles" in April 1981.[216] In short, the record is replete with evidence that supports the conclusion, included in one case study written about the McMartin case, that Ray Buckey was "a strange and troubled individual, who, even if not a child molester, had no business being entrusted with the care of young children."[217]

More significantly, there had been prior complaints about Ray Buckey— specifically about inappropriate exposure of his genitals in various situations. Several neighbors told police that he masturbated in his bedroom in plain view of the neighbors, declining to pull down shades or turn off lights.[218] Donna Ennis, a mother otherwise unconnected to the case, testified she scolded Ray in 1981 for not keeping his genitials covered during pre-match exercises with eleven- and twelve-year-old girls on a soccer team he helped coach.[219] Donald Spitler, husband of McMartin teacher Babette Spitler, was the main coach. Ennis testified she told Buckey "he ought not to be on a girls' soccer team if he was not going to wear underwear" and she complained directly to Donald Spitler, who apparently made sure Buckey wore sweat pants at future events.[220] Brett Weisberg, who worked briefly as a teacher's aide at the McMartin pre-school, testified that Ray would sit so as to expose his genitals and frequently had a child on his lap.[221] There was even a notation in Virginia McMartin's diary in the spring of 1983, months before the case broke, about an incident involving a child touching Ray's penis. (McMartin later blamed the girl's father and spoke of the incident as if Ray played no role whatsoever.[222] The girl's father, inciden-tally, had picked her up one day from the preschool and found Ray "in the middle of the playground," with children around, "exposed and not wearing underwear."[223])

Testimony from two loyalist parents who stuck with the McMartins long after the letter from the MBPD revealed a bizarre response from Peggy Buckey to the charges against her son. According to Ellen Chapman, Peggy Buckey told her:

> . . . she would—she had been molested as a child herself, that she would be aware of anything like this going on. That she would always continually watch Ray when the children were sitting on his lap or hanging on his neck, um, that if he ever had a hard-on, that she would have noticed it.[224]

Trisha Walters's mother had a similar story. She once saw Ray with kids on his lap reading *Playboy* magazine. Peggy, apparently not the least surprised, told the mother she "would take care of it." Mrs. Buckey later testified she did not think Ray's behavior was a problem:

Q: What would you say about a teacher of children that age who would be reading *Playboy* magazine while students are in the classroom?

A: I believe it's a very popular magazine, so I really wouldn't have much to say about it.

She was also asked whether she would be upset if children could see the genitals of a teacher. Making a reference to "modern bathing suits," Mrs. Buckey responded: "I don't know how the poor little kids could help but see everything there is to see if they go to the beach."[225]

The proceedings involved excruciatingly detailed testimony on the smallest points. As the trial dragged on, press coverage became more episodic. The overall question, as most people saw it, was simply whether the jury would believe the children. But the jury was being asked a much more specific question that involved the exacting burden of proof in any criminal case: whether the state had proven the defendant guilty of specific charges *beyond a reasonable doubt*. By 1989, when the case had dragged on for years and children had made so many dubious statements it was impossible to know what to believe, the only drama for assorted observers of the trial was whether the jury would reject all the charges, or end in a mistrial because they could not agree. Those seemed like the most likely outcomes.

What actually happened is a combination of the two. The jury rejected fifty-two of the charges, voting unanimously to acquit Ray and Peggy Buckey of a host of child molestation charges. They jury could not reach a unanimous verdict on twelve child molestation charges involving Ray Buckey and one conspiracy charge involving his mother.[226] Judge Pounders dismissed the conspiracy charge, ending all charges against Peggy Buckey. The results involving Ray Buckey were less clear, especially given the number of charges on which the jury could not agree. At a press conference shortly after the verdict was announced, seven jurors made it clear they thought that children *had* been sexually abused.[227] They just were not certain enough about the details to convict on a "beyond a reasonable doubt" standard of proof.[228] "I never voted innocent; I voted not guilty," said juror Sally Cordova. Asked directly whether she was convinced Ray Buckey was *not* guilty, Cordova responded: "I am not."[229] Juror Julie Peters said "the verdicts should not be considered a victory for the defense." Several jurors also made it clear they had doubts about the case largely because of the CII tapes, which "did not help me. They gave me a lot of reasonable doubt," Peters said. This is what makes the case a tragedy. Despite the best intentions of the interviewers, their efforts actually made the case unwinnable and gave the witch-hunt narrative its signature song.

The verdict was received with shock and outrage by some parents of children in the case, and some parents of children who were never in the case. But there is little evidence that this view captured public opinion at large. There were commentaries on whether courts were sufficiently child-centered, or put differently, whether they were too adult-centered to be fair to children. Outspoken parents who thought Ray Buckey—and maybe even Peggy Buckey and others—should have been convicted were quoted extensively on television in the days after the verdict arguing for a retrial. There were also voices in favor of dropping the remaining charges. An editorial in the *Washington Post* praised the jury.[230] The DA decided to retry Ray Buckey, assigning new prosecutors to the case. There was an abbreviated trial held in the spring and early summer of 1990, where the lead prosecutor misstated some basic facts in his opening statement, raising questions about whether the DA's office was dedicated to the retrial. In what seemed a fitting conclusion at the time, the jury ultimately deadlocked on all eight charges, although the extent of the split varied significantly by charge. (The strongest vote for the prosecution was 8-4 on one charge involving the first girl; the strongest vote for the defense was 11-1 against conviction on all three charges involving the third girl.) "I don't know that you can get 12 people together to agree on this case," said juror Lloyd, who voted for conviction on the one charge that he concluded was "spontaneously disclosed."[231] Everyone agreed there should not be a third trial. Within hours, the Los Angeles County District Attorney's Office announced it was dropping all remaining charges against Ray Buckey. Seven years of proceedings, $15 million in public expenditures—most of which funded the defense—resulted in not a single conviction.

Conclusions

The McMartin case was doubly unjust. First, it was unjust to the defendants who were charged without sufficient evidence or adequate investigation. Several defendants were held without bail, some for an extended period of time. Babette Spitler had her children taken away for a while, and Peggy Ann Buckey, Ray's sister, lost her teaching credential. (It was later reinstated.[232]) There was an unfathomable personal and financial toll to these people, who were falsely accused in an environment where they were publicly castigated before they were even charged with anything. For most of the defendants, the case was a monumental injustice.

But the case was also unjust to children. Some were brutalized by the judicial process, particularly in the preliminary hearing. Although that was widely recognized when it occurred in 1985, it was long since forgotten by the end of the McMartin case in January 1990. There were also children who had been sexually abused but who never received justice and instead have been demeaned by the witch-hunt narrative's assertion that the entire case was a "hoax."

The McMartin case began as a morality play about the failure to protect children. It ended as a morality play about the failure to protect civil liberties. The final step in the evolution of how the case has come to be remembered was the complete negation of the evidence of abuse elaborated in this chapter. This development marked the triumph of the witch-hunt narrative. It also marked a change in attitude about the case from one of complexity and confusion—which characterized the case in its later stages—to one of moral clarity. In this regard, the case came full circle.

It is ironic that those who saw the inappropriateness of the original moral framework were not more suspicious of the stark opposite view. Not surprisingly, both caricatures are inadequate representations of the complicated underlying facts. This chapter ends, then, with the puzzle posed by the juxtaposition of the considerable evidence of guilt in the case with the rise of a witch-hunt narrative that denies all of the evidence. Just as one must ask how supporters of the prosecution were able to ignore the seemingly obvious problems with the case, it is important to ask how case critics have been able to minimize or deny all of the evidence of guilt.

The most obvious reason the witch-hunt narrative has become dominant is that it is by far the larger of the two opposing stories. Five or six defendants[233] were charged with heinous crimes they did not commit, and dozens of others were cast under a cloud of suspicion for the flimsiest of reasons while the Sheriff's Ritual Abuse Task Force followed dozens of "leads." If there has to be one simple storyline for the McMartin case, the witch-hunt narrative fits much better than the alternative. The alternative—focusing on the evidence of abuse and the travails of the children—is undoubtedly the smaller story. But it is an important story, nonetheless.

Why haven't both stories been maintained, side by side, for history? The McMartin case was, after all, a dual tragedy. It was tragic for the defendants who should not have been charged, and it was tragic for the children who were mistreated and those who were never appropriately vindicated. But only one of those tragedies has been remembered over time. The most general explanation is that dual tragedies are cognitively and politically difficult to acknowledge. It is difficult to worry about defendants who should not have been charged *and* about children who were never vindicated, particularly since measures to remedy one problem might been seen as exacerbating the other one. The first problem seems to cry out for more skepticism about children's testimony, while the second cries out for taking children more seriously. Political interests have organized around these problems, as well. The members of VOCAL (Victims of Children Abuse Laws) are not concerned about children's testimony being summarily dismissed; they are worried about it being accepted too readily. Conversely, members of Believe the Children never evinced any concern about accusations or charges that had no merit; they were focused entirely on the social forces that would minimize or deny the extent of child sexual abuse. As perplexing and challenging as these dual tragedies are, they are not impossible to comprehend together. Indeed, most writing about the case during its final stages conveyed this sense of complexity.

A more specific explanation about why this did not continue is that there has been a crusade to promote the witch-hunt narrative. The view that the case was complicated and conflicting has been lost to history by design, not by accident. A narrative without ambiguity is far more compelling—in court, in print, and in the movies—than a narrative that acknowledges injustice on both sides. The moving forces in promoting the witch-hunt narrative include journalists, defense lawyers, and defense-oriented expert witnesses. What is remarkable is that these actors seem to mirror, in fervor and tactics, the very things they claim to abhor. Instead of disregarding evidence that might point away from guilt, they disregard evidence that points toward it. Instead of automatically believing any child accusation, they seem to automatically believe the denial of any adult. Instead of assuming all of the medical evidence presented by the prosecution must be true, they take the position that it should all be rejected. In this way, the Mc-Martin case provided the foundation for a witch-hunt narrative that would eventually extend well beyond the case.

3

Scrutinizing the Evidence of a National Witch-Hunt

The witch-hunt narrative is a national claim. It is a claim about social trends, the central one being that there were scores of cases just like the McMartin case. In 1987, Debbie Nathan used the phrase "junior McMartins" to describe what she called "a nationwide rash of similar cases."[1] It has since become widely accepted that there were at least one hundred such cases between 1984 and about 1990.[2] They are sometimes referred to as "the day-care sexual abuse cases of the 1980s" and have also been referred to as the "ritual abuse cases of the 1980s," or even the "Satanic ritual abuse cases of the 1980s," although those definitions include cases well beyond the day-care setting. Social psychologist Mary de Young combined most of those labels (and more) into a single book title: *The Day Care Ritual Abuse Moral Panic*. The book repeats the claim that "a hundred or more day care centers and preschools around the country" were investigated for "ritual abuse" during the 1980s.[3] The prominent academic psychologists Stephen Ceci and Maggie Bruck concur in an article that refers to "the McMartin case and *hundreds* of others like it."[4] Carol Hopkins, who founded something called the Justice Committee, has claimed there were one thousand false convictions during this era.[5] Paul Craig Roberts, a syndicated columnist for the *Washington Times*, made an even stronger claim, asserting that there were two thousand such cases.[6] Although claims about the overall number of cases vary, there seems to be almost universal agreement that these cases stemmed from the McMartin case and that there were more than a hundred of them.

This chapter scrutinizes the best evidence that has been put forth for those claims. There are two particularly important lists of case names in the witch-hunt narrative: (1) a list of thirty-six cases from an investigative series in a Memphis, Tennessee, newspaper in 1988; and (2) a list of fifty-four names (representing twenty cases not contained on the first list) in Debbie Nathan's 1995 book with defense lawyer Michael Snedeker called *Satan's Silence: Ritual Abuse and the Making of an American Witch Hunt*.[7] These lists carry the authoritative weight that comes with details such as a full name and accompanying place name. Even though these lists, in the aggregate, do not come close to supporting the claims about hundreds of these cases, they nevertheless constitute an impressive accumulation of case names. However, an intensive examination of these lists reveals they are not well researched; nor, more importantly, do they provide strong support for the witch-hunt claim. The lists are wrong in many instances and are dubious in others, and although they are occasionally largely correct, it is not often enough to support the claim of a national trend. There were, indeed, some frighteningly mismanaged cases during this time, and some charges were brought without sufficient justification. But a few lightning strikes do not create a national lightning epidemic.

Charlier and Downing's List of Thirty-six Cases

Two reporters for a Tennessee newspaper were the first to make an extended argument that there was a national pattern of witch-hunts following the McMartin case.[8] In "Justice Abused: A 1980's Witch-Hunt," a six-part series published in the *Commercial Appeal* in January 1988, Tom Charlier and Shirley Downing purported to identify thirty-six cases around the country that demonstrate this phenomenon. The article had a national map plotting the cases, a full page with abstracts of them, and other graphs and text that seemed to make a convincing argument that investigations across the country had found little or no evidence of sexual abuse but had resulted in a significant number of false accusations or convictions.

The series has become one of the foundational works in the witch-hunt narrative. It has been referred to as "the most comprehensive" source on the daycare sexual abuse cases of the 1980s.[9] Ellen Willis, Nathan's editor at the *Village Voice*, called it "a fine investigative series."[10] A journal published by defense psychologist Ralph Underwager claimed, incorrectly, that the series won a Pulitzer Prize.[11] Law reviews, academic journal articles, and various books have subsequently relied on this list as authoritative.[12] One book even reproduced the summaries of Charlier and Downing's thirty-six cases as a long appendix[13]; this single source accounts for more than a dozen footnotes in the chapter of Nathan and Snedeker's book which also argues that these cases constitute a national trend. None of the sources just mentioned have expressed any doubt about the quality or accuracy of the reporting. To the contrary, the series has been held up as the "most in-depth treatment of these cases."[14]

These uncritical endorsements notwithstanding, a close examination of the cases covered in this series reveals that this list is deeply flawed. Some problems are apparent simply by examining the article on its face.[15] Charlier and

Downing's claim that the thirty-six cases prove a nationwide trend over four years is contradicted by the actual distribution of these cases over time. Thirty-one of the cases are dated by the authors as beginning in a twenty-six-month period between August 1983 and September 1985; there are only three cases for the twenty-seven remaining months covered by the article (see Figure 3.1). But without a graphic representation of the distribution over time, it is not clear to most readers that almost all of the evidence Charlier and Downing offer to prove an alleged four-year trend is from the first two years.

Charlier and Downing's list also appears to be padded through the inclusion of cases that never involved an arrest, let alone prosecution. What kind of witch-hunt or "justice denied" results in no charges whatsoever? Sixteen of the cases never got to the stage of a trial; charges were dropped in some cases and they were never brought in others. One-third of the cases resulted in a conviction, seemingly undercutting the claim of "justice abused." Table 3.1 lists the cases by place name, as they are identified by Charlier and Downing. Notably, only a handful of the cases involved charges "taking place on a large scale," something the article claimed was a feature of these cases. In explaining the series, the authors said that a "pattern emerged . . . most cases evolved from a single incident involving one child, but investigations often triggered runaway inquiries that fed on publicity and parents' worst fears." But many of the thirty-six cases involved a single alleged perpetrator, some involved two, and it is impossible to ascertain the number in several. Only *four* cases clearly involved a large number of alleged perpetrators: the Manhattan Beach case (McMartin); the Kern County cases; the Jordan, Minnesota, cases; and the Memphis case (Georgian Hills). The vast majority of the thirty-six cases in this series do not fit the pattern. Many also do not fit another theme that is repeated throughout the series: day-care abuse. At least ten—almost a third of their evidence—have nothing to do with day-care centers.

The most significant problems, however, are apparent only after doing research. One problem that becomes clear on researching secondary sources is what I call satanic exaggeration. As it turns out, fewer than one-quarter of the thirty-six cases actually fit the primary theme of the series, which combined the idea of witch-hunts over child sexual abuse with claims of ritualistic or satanic overtones. Some of the cases Charlier and Downing discuss had nothing to do with satanic or ritualistic abuse.[16] Moreover, several that *did* involve such elements were clearly based in reality. The Richmond, Virginia, "case" is described as follows:

> Two children believed to have been sexually abused by family members began telling of rituals they allegedly took part in a year earlier. They said they had been forced to witness the slaying of a child, a friend of

Figure 3.1 Plot of Charlier and Downing's Thirty-six Cases.

Plotted by Charlier and Downing date and whether the case went to trial.
Charlier and Downing provide dates and details for only 34 cases.

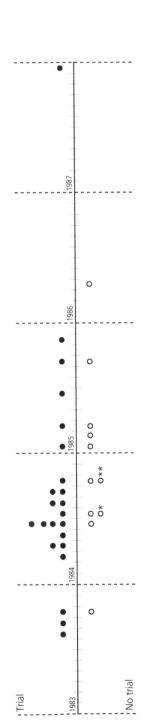

* Designated "summer 1984" by Charlier & Downing.
** Designated "fall 1984" by Charlier & Downing.

Table 3.1 **Charlier and Downing's Thirty-six Cases, by Date and Case Features**

Name	Date	Day care?	Actual trial?	Convictions by judge or jury?
Manhattan Beach, CA	Aug 1983			No
Jordan, MN	Sept 1983	No		No
San Geronimo, CA	Oct 1983		No	No
Bouse, AZ	Oct 1983	No	No	No
Honolulu, HI	Mar 1984			No
Pico Rivera, CA	Apr 1984	No	No	No
Chicago, IL	Apr 1984			
Reno, NV	May 1984			
Spencer Township, OH	June 1984	No	No	No
Memphis, TN	June 1984			
Sacramento, CA	June 1984	No	No	No
Bakersfield, CA	June 1984[a]			
Cincinnati, OH	June 1984	No		No
West Point, NY	July 1984		No	No
Memphis, TN[b]				No
Essex County, NJ	July 1984	No		
LA County, CA	Summer 1984		No	No
Miami, FL	Aug 1984			
Niles, MI	Aug 1984			
Malden, MA	Sept 1984			
Indianapolis, IN	Sept 1984	No		No
LA County, CA	Oct 1984		No	No
Atherton, CA	Oct 1984	No	No	No
Richmond, VA	Fall 1984	No	No	No
Memphis, TN[b]			No	No
Fort Bragg, CA	Jan 1985		No	No
Clarksville, MD	Jan 1985			
New Braintree, MA	Feb 1985		No	No
Wilkes-Barre, PA	Mar 1985		No	No

(continued)

Table 3.1 (**continued**)

Name	Date	Day care?	Actual trial?	Convictions by judge or jury?
White Plains, NY	Mar 1985			
El Paso, TX	June 1985			
Carson City, NV	Sept 1985			
Coos Bay, OR	Sept 1985	No	No	
Maplewood, NJ	Nov 1985[c]			
Sequim, WA	Apr 1986	No	No	
Roseburg, OR	Dec 1987[d]			

[a] Bakersfield actually began in 1982.

[b] Two Memphis cases do not appear on the page with blurbs for each case. If they are the two cases that were connected to Georgian Hills; one was dropped, the other resulted in an acquittal.

[c] Maplewood actually began in May 1985.

[d] Roseburg actually began in July 1987.

theirs whose decomposed body had been discovered in the woods. . . . The police found burn rings—similar to those left by candles—on the floor of the apartment where the acts were said to have occurred. But the police couldn't tell whether the children were telling the truth or fantasizing. No charges have been filed in the girl's slaying.[17]

The authors never explain why this case was included in their "Justice Abused" series. A dead body was found, the children "were believed to have been sexually abused," and nobody was charged. The injustice appears to have been to the victims. Similarly, the Atherton, California, "case" allegedly involved wild allegations made by a girl after a dead cat was found in her locker at school. The authors do not contest the fact that the case involved something that would merit investigation—a dead cat in a locker. Moreover, they do not explain why a case in which the district attorney considered the evidence insufficient to prosecute anyone would merit inclusion in a series about "justice abused."

A third "case" that fails after basic research of secondary sources is Spencer Township, which the authors incorrectly list as June 1984. (The events occurred in June 1985.) This is Charlier and Downing's entire description:

Sheriff James Telb and his deputies dug up a swamp in a wooded area, searching for the graves of 50 to 60 people allegedly slain in satanic rites. Despite days of digging, no bodies were found. There were no arrests.[18]

What the authors neglect to acknowledge is that the search was prompted by a confirmed kidnapping case. The search was conducted near a home that had reportedly been abandoned by LeRoy Freeman, who was wanted in the abduction of his seven-year-old granddaughter, Clara Freeman.[19] The girl had been missing for two years and was last seen when he took her on his first court-ordered visitation. "We never said we had cult killings," Sheriff Telb explained when the swamp was searched. "We have a missing child and an awful lot of informants saying this is a burial ground."[20] The authorities also had apparent evidence of cultlike activity of some sort.[21] While playing up the satanic allegations and ignoring the facts that prompted the dig, Charlier and Downing never mentioned what was uncovered in the swamp: "a headless doll with nails driven through its feet and a pentagram attached to its arm, a nine-foot wooden cross with ligatures attached" along with hatchets and knives, and an anatomy dissection book.[22] In October 1988, the missing girl was located in Huntington Beach, California. Freeman pleaded guilty to child stealing two months later.[23]

The claim that all thirty-six cases are bound together by satanic or ritualistic allegations is summarized in a dramatic table labeled Similar Tales. The text at the top reads "Some details occurred over and over in children's statements about alleged abuse," and the table itself lists several dozen "elements" of such cases, with numerous place names or defendants' names listed after each element.[24] For example, one entry in the table reads "Children taken to mortuary: McMartin, Grenada, Torrance, Rolling Hills Estates, Bakersfield." The table creates a powerful impression. "Perhaps the most striking feature of these allegations," law professor Denis Brion would later write, relying entirely on this table, "was the fact that the details of these bizarre activities were altogether similar despite the wide geographic dispersion of these episodes."[25]

But a close examination of the table reveals several problems. First, the "elements" used to weave these cases together are extremely overinclusive. Some are not remotely satanic or ritualistic. A case could be tagged as having "ritualistic" elements for something as common as "activities in the basement" or "Barbie dolls." It apparently made no difference to Charlier and Downing that the day-care operation in the White Plains case, for example, *was* in the basement of Jeanette Martin's house. Similarly, the authors do not explain what is unusual, let alone ritualistic, about children reporting Barbie dolls at a day-care center. Other elements in this table reflected aspects widely known to be involved in the most ordinary child sexual abuse cases. The Bronx case, for example, is noted for only one so-called element, allegations involving oral sex. That is a common type of sexual abuse, and certainly not a marker of anything ritualistic. Similarly, there is nothing ritualistic, or even all that unusual, about "Activities during naptime or trips to rest room"—but seven cases in the table are linked by this feature. A case could be labeled as having ritualistic features if a child claimed to have been pinched or physically abused in any way.

Some of the seemingly least-plausible features in Charlier and Downing's account are employed in a misleading manner. The Richmond case, for example, is listed for one element: "stabbed, or murdered babies or children." But by Charlier and Downing's own account, this case revolved around the discovery of a girl's dead body. So this was not a wild, uncorroborated tale. Other elements were apparently constructed with satanic exaggeration in mind. "Animal sacrifice," for example, clearly suggests something ritualistic, but cases were tagged with this purported element whether or not there were allegations of "sacrifice." There was evidence in the Craig case, for example, that the children saw and maybe even handled a dead rabbit, but nobody described it in terms of sacrifice.

What is most striking about this table is apparently overlooked by the many writers and scholars who have since cited it without skepticism: even by Charlier and Downing's inflated accounting, many of the thirty-six cases involve only one or two of these elements—and many more apparently didn't involve any. Eleven of the cases included in this table have only one or two of the forty-one listed "elements." In short, a handful of the thirty-six cases account for the vast majority of the entries—and several of those cases are never discussed in the article. [26]

But this has not prevented writers and scholars from exaggerating the claims in this article. In a stunning example of satanic exaggeration, Michael Phillips, referring to Charlier and Downing as the "most comprehensive source" on the matter, claimed that "nearly all of the cases they investigated alleged Satanism and pornography."[27] In fact, by Charlier and Downing's account, eight of the original thirty-six cases involved allegations of child pornography—and at least one of those cases never had any claims remotely related to Satanism. In other words, seven cases have been exaggerated into a claim that is five times larger than what the article actually supports. This is without examining the extent to which Charlier and Downing overlooked evidence of guilt in those cases.

Although the series has become famous for the list of thirty-six cases, the actual coverage of those cases varied from extensive to negligible. Three cases received extensive treatment in the series: the McMartin case (Manhattan beach); the Jordan, Minnesota cases; and the Georgian Hills case (Memphis). Eight others are "profiled" in the series, each receiving a few hundred words of coverage (see Table 3.2). The remaining twenty-five received very little coverage. Many are mentioned only in short abstracts that fill one full page in the

Table 3.2 **Details on the Eleven Cases Highlighted by Charlier and Downing**

Name	Date	No. Defendants	Actual trial?	Significant evidence of abuse?	Unjustified criminal charges?
Manhattan Beach, CA	Aug 1983	7	Yes	Yes	Yes
Jordan, MN	Sept 1983	28	Yes	Yes	Yes
Chicago, IL	Apr 1984	1	Yes	Yes	No
Memphis, TN	June 1984	4	Yes	Yes	Yes
Sacramento, CA	June 1984	2	No	No	Yes
Cincinnati, OH	June 1984	4	Yes	No	Yes
Bakersfield, CA	June 1984	35	Yes	Yes	Yes
Malden, MA	Sept 1984	3	Yes	Undetermined	Undetermined
Fort Bragg, CA	Jan 1985	2	No	Yes	No
Clarksville, MD	Jan 1985	2	Yes	Yes	No
Sequim, WA	Apr 1986	2	No	Yes	No

series. For those cases, it is difficult to ascertain much about the underlying facts or the specific nature of Charlier and Downing's concern. The plan for this book evolved into an effort to research all thirty-six cases. Almost fifteen years of effort produced extensive information on most of these cases, but not all. Some of the research was still in progress when this book went to press, and a few cases proved impossible to crack. One of the eleven cases highlighted in the series—those from Jordan, Minnesota—will be the subject of a separate publication. Extensive research into the Jordan cases reveals substantial evidence of abuse alongside strong evidence that there were unjustified charges.

What is most striking about the highlighted cases is how many involved significant evidence of abuse. There are two clear exceptions; notably, neither one occurred in a day-care setting, although that is the stated theme of the article at times. One was in Cincinnati, involving the Isaac Wise Temple summer camp. It ended in acquittals, so there is no official transcript of the proceedings. But local newspaper coverage of the trial indicates the charges in this case were highly suspect and should never have been brought.[28] The other case that clearly did not involve any plausible evidence of abuse is from Sacramento, where charges were dropped after it became clear to Municipal Court Judge Ronald Robie that the children had been told by their grandmother to make baseless charges.[29] No other case in the series is similar. Beyond these, however, there was credible evidence of abuse in all of the other highlighted cases that I have analyzed. As explained in the previous chapter, the evidence was restricted to one defendant in the McMartin case. Indeed, as indicated in Table 3.2 and elaborated in this chapter, several of these cases involved credible evidence of abuse *and* they involved unjustified charges. The "justice abused" in those cases had two dimensions, but only one of those problems was acknowledged by Charlier and Downing.

At least three of the highlighted cases did not involve any unjustified charges. There was a solid basis for charging the defendants in the cases from Chicago, Clarksville, and Sequim, Washington. Nobody was ever charged with a crime in the Fort Bragg case, where the license revocation proceedings for the Jubilation Day Care Center stemmed from proven claims of sexual abuse by the owner's niece.[30] Beyond the cases already mentioned, there were two others that involved some unjustified charges: Memphis and Bakersfield (Kern County). But as explained below, both of those cases (or groups of cases, in the Kern County instance) also involved credible evidence of abuse.

Six of the ten cases in Table 3.2 are discussed in this chapter: Memphis, Jordan, Chicago, Clarksville, Sequim, and Bakersfield. (The McMartin case, of course, has already been discussed.) All six involved more evidence of abuse than has ever been recognized in the witch-hunt narrative. Three additional cases from the list of thirty-six that also involved substantial evidence of abuse are discussed in this section as well: West Point, New York; Niles, Michigan; and White Plains, New York.

BALLARD

Location	Memphis, TN
Institution	Georgian Hills
Date	1984
Lead Def.	Frances Ballard

The Georgian Hills Early Childhood Center case began on May 31, 1984, just as the charges in McMartin were being finalized. A four-year-old girl told her mother that her vagina hurt; she quickly volunteered that Frances Ballard had put her fingers in it. Ballard was a fifty-five-year-old woman who had never worked outside the home until taking a job at Georgian Hills in 1983. The center was run by the Georgian Hills Baptist Church and had about 120 students. Ballard, who had cared for children in her home for years without incident, was a devout Baptist and, according to multiple sources, a "stern" preschool teacher. She was the last person one might suspect of being a child molester. But there was medical evidence that appeared to support the sexual abuse claim; according to her family physician, the little girl's hymen was torn.

After an initial investigation that involved about a dozen children, Frances Ballard was arrested on June 12, 1984, and charged with four counts of sexual abuse involving four children, among them the original girl. The investigation continued, and there was a bureaucratic struggle between the child protective service agency and law enforcement over the ownership and administration of the investigation. Law enforcement took charge, and in a few months there were far more complainants, and eventually more defendants. In October, Ballard was charged with thirty-eight additional counts of sexual abuse involving nineteen children. The following month, the investigation spread to the Daybridge Learning Center, where children had been sent from Georgian Hills. After suspicions were raised there, fifteen staff members were suspended and then fired in a move that, in retrospect, seems like a clear indication of a case run amok. Six months later, three more defendants were indicted for sexual abuse related to the charges in the Ballard case: Betty Stimson, the Georgian Hills director; her son Jeff; and Rev. Paul Shell, pastor of the Georgian Hills Baptist Church. These charges were brought almost exactly a year after the investigation began. Why did the investigation last so long? If Betty Stimson was involved in events at the same time and place as Frances Ballard, why did it take a year of interviews to find out? Those questions were not being asked in 1985.

The criminal trials did not reveal much about the larger investigation, but there is an important document uncovered in a subsequent civil suit: a letter from local investigators to Special Agent Kenneth Lanning of the FBI, providing a confidential "synopsis of the case and the problems encountered" in early February 1985, several months before the additional adults were charged. That letter indicated children had "required a lot more leading than would be desirable with older victims" and "it appeared that some information may have been coerced or improperly extracted from the children."[31] Given this candid assessment of the problems with the investigation, it seems remarkable that, instead of reassessing the case in full, authorities went ahead and indicted three more adults a few months later.

Betty Stimson's case came to trial first, in March 1987, two years after the charges were brought. The trial was interrupted when a child left the stand in tears; the proceedings were suspended and charges were eventually dropped. Charges were also dropped against Pastor Shell; Jeff Stimson was acquitted. But the case against Ballard went forward. When the trial began on October 27, 1987, the charges were whittled down to eleven victims.

There were, on close examination of the trial transcript, a host of problems with the charges against Ballard. First, it was difficult to believe she actually had the opportunity to commit all of these crimes. Only three of the eleven children were in her regular class; two others had her for something called Mother's Day out. This leaves six of the eleven children whose only other time for possibly encountering Ballard was 7:00 to 7:30 a.m. But a few of those students were never there at seven, leaving it unclear when she would even have had the opportunity.[32] Second, several children said Ballard had driven them to places away from the school. This has been known to happen at day care centers, but because of terrible eyesight Ballard never had a driver's license. She also had a complicated medical history that included multiple surgical scars, skin grafts, and other distinguishing marks that were described in embarrassing detail at trial. But not a single child who claimed to have seen her naked remarked about any markings that would apparently have been both noticeable and unusual.

There were various statements in the case that seem satanic in nature. From Charlier and Downing's description, one would think the children's testimony was filled with these elements. Six of the children at trial said nothing of the sort. But there was also testimony about an "exploded hamster" and a "blood man." The "Satanic tint," as one investigator called it, was there from the day when Mrs. Ballard was arrested. There was extensive testimony at trial about something she said in the police car, rebuking the devil.[33] The testimony was inconclusive, but investigators thought the devil was so significant to the case that it was the first word on a list of catch words distributed to parents and others. By my count, only one child actually invoked the devil in describing anything related to sexual abuse, saying that "the Devil would turn [him] into fire" if he told about what Frances Ballard did to him.[34] Authorities seemed particularly baffled by the satanic aspects. The lead investigator commented, in the confidential letter to the FBI, that "all of this is in direct contradiction to the atmosphere of the Southern Baptist Church that houses the day care."[35] Indeed, Ballard's outcry about the devil makes more sense as the response of a religious woman than it does the implied confession of a child molester. The intensely religious environment certainly made the devil references more likely, not less. This was proven years later in a study that found children in highly religious settings were more likely to invoke the devil.[36]

Although the "fantastic" elements of the case were arguably overplayed, two other elements of the case have received limited attention: the earliest statements, in June 1984, and the medical evidence. Both provide evidence supporting the charges but are omitted from the witch-hunt narrative. The origins of the case are not fully documented in the trial, but I located records documenting ten interviews conducted between June 6 and June 22, 1984. The records are not transcriptions; rather, they were prepared from audiotapes. The case was ultimately overturned on appeal, in part because the tapes were recorded over before they could be supplied to the defense.[37]

What is most noteworthy about the accounts in June is how "garden variety" they were. There were no references to Satanism or the devil. But there were some powerful exchanges, as when Wayne Hargrove was asked if Miss Frances ever kissed him. His answer was recorded as:

Is anybody gonna get mad at me, mommy's gonna get mad at me, I don't like to talk about what, Yep, she does kiss me. Like a man and a woman.[38]

He followed-up with a statement about Ballard kissing "my dingaling."

Many of the children in the case were examined by a family physician, and a significant number were also examined by Dr. David Muram, a child-abuse pediatrician at the University of Tennessee. Dr. Muram's testimony in the case was quite conservative. The family physician of the first girl in the case reported that her hymen was "torn." Dr. Muram, a specialist in child abuse, testified the girl had a "notch in the hymen, which may or may not represent a tear," at 3 o'clock.[39] The most significant medical findings were probably the "depressed scar at 11 o'clock" on Cameron Bennett's anus. More of this scar was on the exterior of the anal canal, basically ruling out the possibility of constipation as a cause.[40] Dr. Muram's testimony was similarly guarded for other children. He described the anal findings on Charlie Higgins as "possible" sexual abuse.[41] For Brooke Northrup, he described labial adhesions, which "can be a normal occurrence or can result from friction-type dry intercourse." He cited a study concluding that the incidence of labial adhesions was five times higher in sexually abused kids. Noting a small scar on the midline of her rectum, Dr. Muram concluded there was "possible sexual abuse."[42] It is not a strong finding, but there were enough children with such findings to raise important questions that the witch-hunt narrative ignores.

In the end, the jury did not see the case as a witch-hunt or as a proven case of mass molestation. Instead, the jury acquitted Ballard on fifteen charges and found her guilty on one count of sexual abuse concerning one boy—a boy who apparently said early in the investigation that "You don't understand. Her husband's old and she had to have someone to love her, nobody loves her. I have to be her helper and I have to love her."[43] It is a puzzling result because there does not appear to be anything about this count making it far worthier of credence than most everything else in the case. Apparently, the jury was reluctant to let Ballard off completely, but they were also extremely ambivalent regarding the children's testimony. The conviction was later overturned on appeal and the prosecution declined to retry Ballard.[44]

Charlier and Downing's series is most remembered and cited for the claims about national trends, but the most original and extensive reporting was specifically about the Georgian Hills case. It has become the definitive explanation; there has been no other major published account. But Charlier and Downing's version does not convey that any of the earliest statements in the case were clear and without fantastic elements, or that several children in the case had medical findings relevant to sexual abuse. Those facts make the case the complicated conundrum it appeared to be at the time, rather than the one-dimensional witch-hunt story it eventually became. Like the McMartin case, however, the extent of the wrongful prosecutions was much larger than the rest of the story. It is impossible to defend the charges brought a year into this investigation, let the alone the firing of fifteen people at Daybridge; there were terrible costs inflicted on innocent adults. The complication is that it also seems likely some children were sexually abused. It appears the reality of the injustice to adults drove Charlier and Downing to overgeneralize from Memphis to the country. Though they saw similarities to the McMartin case in dozens of instances, the Ballard case was actually more like McMartin than any other cases that Charlier and Downing covered. Accordingly, their article gave the rest of the country an overstated claim about national witch-hunts that would have been far more fitting had it focused largely on the case in Memphis.

There are three cases on the list of thirty-six that involved *more* defendants than four as in the Georgian Hills case. One is McMartin Preschool, discussed in the previous chapter, with seven defendants. The other two were far larger than McMartin, although neither was actually based at a day-care center and neither was really a single case. There were a set of related cases in Jordan, Minnesota, that involved twenty-eight defendants and another set in Bakersfield, California (also referred to as Kern County), with thirty-five defendants. Both of these "cases" received significant attention in the *Commercial Appeal* series. As with McMartin and Georgian Hills, they both included prosecutions that should never have been initiated. But they also involved more evidence of sexual abuse than has been recognized in the witch-hunt narrative. The Jordan cases are discussed briefly below and those in Kern County are discussed later in the chapter.

JORDAN

Location	Jordan, MN
Institution	none
Date	1983-84
Lead Def.	Robert & Lois Bentz

The Jordan, Minnesota, cases were the first "mass child molestation" cases to come to trial after McMartin catapulted the issue of child sexual abuse into the national consciousness in the winter of 1984. They were also the first cases to come to a conclusion, albeit an abrupt and puzzling one. "Jordan" was not a single matter, but a series of cases against twenty-four defendants.

Some were against individuals, but most were against couples. The defendants were generally categorized into two "rings." The case originated with the lead defendant, James Rud, who lived in a trailer park described by the Minneapolis *Star-Tribune* as being "on the wrong side of Jordan's tracks" and populated by "a transient population who people don't trust."[45] The case then spread to the better-established part of town. The case against Robert and Lois Bentz, who were not among the first group of defendants, was the first one to come to trial. The three major television networks carried national news stories about the beginning of the trial during the third week of August 1984. It would be two years before the McMartin trial actually began and four more years before it ended ambiguously; in less than two months, however, all of the criminal cases filed in Jordan would be over. The Bentzes were acquitted in late September 1984 and charges against the remaining twenty-one defendants were dropped in mid-October amid reports about wild stories children told about undetected child murders. Rud was the only defendant whose case ended in a guilty verdict. He completed his sentence in 2011 and has since been held through Minnesota's civil commitment procedure.

The state attorney general, Hubert Humphrey III, examined the situation and declined to refile any of the sexual abuse charges. He explained his decision in the February 1985 *Report on Scott County Investigations*, commonly known as the Humphrey Report. The report concluded there was no credible evidence of child murders and the investigative process in the case was flawed in ways that made the refiling of charges inadvisable. The report also noted that "some" children had definitely been abused in Jordan but concluded it was not possible to assess how many.[46]

Some of the former defendants joined Ralph Underwager, the defense psychologist from the Bentz case, to launch an advocacy organization called VOCAL, standing for victims of child abuse laws. A petition was filed with Minnesota Governor Rudy Perpich requesting the removal of County Attorney Kathleen Morris for filing the Jordan cases. Former defendants also initiated a federal lawsuit alleging civil rights violations. Although they did not prevail in federal court, and the inquiry into the county attorney did *not* recommend Morris's removal, VOCAL prevailed where it matters most: in the court of public opinion. The Jordan cases have come to be known as "witch-hunts," which is how they were described by Charlier and Downing in 1988. Philip Jenkins, a professor of history and religion, drew an explicit parallel between the Jordan cases and the Salem witch trials, concluding, "almost all of the testimony that led to 25 indictments on very grave charges was invented."[47]

But the witch-hunt version of the Jordan cases does not do justice to the underlying facts. There are two sources of information beyond the Humphrey Report that were based on careful, systematic examinations of the factual record. Neither source supports the witch-hunt narrative as the best explanation of what happened in Jordan. The Olson Commission was created in response to the petition that accused County Attorney Morris of making arrests without probable cause. The commission found little evidence to substantiate the claim; in fact, by the time the hearings were over, Morris was being accused of the opposite—improperly dropping solid criminal cases.[48] A federal court in the Eighth Circuit also evaluated a broad array of documents underlying the Jordan investigation while adjudicating civil rights claims brought by many of the former defendants. Relying on a detailed examination of the underlying factual record, the court concluded the wrongful prosecution claims were without merit. The appellate decision reads like the report of the Olson Commission; that is, one is left wondering why so many prosecutions were dropped, not why they were brought in the first place.[49] Neither source applies this conclusion across the board; and both found considerable fault with how the investigation was conducted. What the Olson Commission and the Humphrey Report demonstrate, however, is that the witch-hunt narrative has reduced a complicated double tragedy to a simplistic one-line story.

The Jordan cases were flawed in ways that ultimately diminished the credibility of some key children. In addition to the murder allegations, there were other children subjected to repeated interviews that ultimately diminished their credibility. A few therapists played a significant and improper role in the process. But considering the array of evidence—medical, physical, adult, and child (at various stages of the interview process)—the witch-hunt narrative is misplaced.

The overinterviewing aspect of these cases is important because it led to fantastic claims that ultimately spoiled the case. The mother of one child indicated that her daughter had been interviewed "at least thirty and possibly as many as fifty times" by Scott County authorities."[50] But how widespread was this problem? Every witch-hunt account of the Jordan cases glosses over the question, acting as if all of the children were "brainwashed," as was asserted by defense psychologist Underwager. The Humphrey Report did not attempt to answer the question, simply reporting a few startling anecdotes instead. The Olson Commission took a more systematic view, identifying ten children in the case who had been subject to more than twelve interviews. The commission concluded there was still sufficient basis for proceeding against nine defendants, even if all the children subjected to the most repetitive interviews were excluded from testifying. What is clear on close examination is that the intensive interviewing phase of the case came late in the process. It does not make sense to automatically disregard statements children made in the fall of 1983 simply because some of them they started making fantastic claims six to nine months later. The earliest statements are the most important to analyze in cases where children have been subject to repetitive interviews, since they are least affected by this problem. Tellingly, critics of the Jordan case have never tried to take into account the earliest statements that formed the basis for the Jordan cases.[51]

When the Jordan cases were dismissed, the outcome was generally seen by those in Minnesota as unsatisfactory and unsettling. Josephine Marcotty, a reporter for the Star Tribune, predicted the legacy of Jordan would be "one of confusion."[52] This has not turned out to be the case. What was so perplexing at the time has, deceptively, become much starker over the years. Now the witch-hunt narrative prevails as exemplified by Charlier and Downing's account, written four years later, which did not acknowledge that there was credible evidence against any of the defendants beyond James Rud.

ROGERS PARK

Location	Chicago, IL
Institution	Rogers Park JCC
Date	1984
Lead Def.	Deloartic Parks

The Rogers Park Jewish Community Center case began the first week of April 1984 when a mother named Brenda Voigt reported that her four-year-old daughter told the janitor, while leaving her preschool, to leave her alone. The girl told her mother that the man tickled her. Asked where he tickled her, the girl's answer included her vagina. Voigt complained directly to the school and then to the Department of Children and Family Services. Charlier and Downing's description of the case states:

> Children soon began to accuse teachers of abusing them in satanic rituals. No teachers were arrested. [The janitor] was acquitted. The Illinois Department of Children and Families concluded that most of the 246 allegations against other staff members were unfounded. In February 1986, prosecutors dropped remaining charges.[53]

The implication by Charlier and Downing is that the outcome was appropriate. There is no sense in their reporting that children may have been sexually abused. Their account is accurate in describing fantastic statements and expanding allegations, including ritual abuse claims. It was widely reported in the media that children made statements about "animal mutilation and satanic rituals of an almost medieval quality."[54] The details about those statements remain vague as they were all part of the confidential DCFS investigation. But the statements were never used against anyone in a judicial context. The investigation involved eighty-eight children; interviews were conducted in late April 1984 and occurred in an environment of publicity and intense parental interest.

An internal DCFS report in June 1984 indicated there was credible evidence "that nineteen children were abused at the Center." Those findings were controversial within the agency. A state-level review reversed the conclusions months later, and cases that had been deemed "indicated" were reclassified as "unfounded."[55] The school was reopened. On the basis of existing records, it is not possible to piece together precisely what went wrong in the investigation. But this much seems clear: too much of the investigation was delegated to someone who was not qualified to conduct it.[56] Complaints pertaining to a small number of children, including the original girl, moved ahead against Deloartic Parks, the janitor. The case went to trial in criminal court, and several families pursued civil claims. None of the civil cases went to trial, however, and it is impossible to ascertain from court files what the ultimate settlements and dismissals mean. Moreover, the available evidence from the Parks trial is limited, owing to difficulties in getting the full stenographic record converted into an actual transcript.[57]

The witch-hunt narrative ignores the evidence that moved law enforcement to bring criminal charges against Parks. First, there was medical evidence pertaining to the first girl in the case, and to another girl, Jane Cranshaw, who testified at Parks's criminal trial. She experienced medical problems in the spring of 1984 and went to the doctor's office four times in four months. She had a sore throat and upper respiratory tract problems during this time, but the doctor also noted she was not gaining weight. Her mother brought her daughter back on April 6 with the girl's complaint that it hurt when she urinated. Laboratory tests were "grossly positive for leukocytes." "It is very unusual for children to have pus cells in their urine," the doctor explained when he testified.[58] The doctor raised sexual abuse as a possibility. *This was before anything had been said publicly about the possible sexual abuse at Rogers Park day care.* Her labia were "intensely inflamed." Emergency Room Dr. Lorraine Ling, who saw the girl later that day, testified she suspected the girl "was sexually abused, but not to a medical certainty."[59]

The other child with strong medical indications was Sophie Voigt, the little girl whose mother heard her tell Deloartic Parks to leave her alone as she was departing school one day in early April. This girl had been to her family doctor on March 12 for a rash that had not gone away for two weeks. She came back on April 9, when the doctor noted "multiple erythematous lesions on Sophie's right labia majora and the adjacent inner aspect of the right thigh."[60] He prescribed some medicine. The Voigts came back several days later, after Sophie told her mother Parks had tickled her "on the vagina." The doctor did a genital examination and reported:

> With separation of the labia majora, the labia minora were exposed and found to be intensely erythematous with a white exudate upon them. The hymen ring was not intact and the gaping vaginal walls were also noted to be intensely inflamed.[61]

These findings were cited in a DCFS report that described the interviews with this girl in a single sentence: "In two separate interviews, both using anatomically correct dolls, Sophie told Detective Keenan and DCFS Worker Robinson that Mr. Parks lifted up her dress and tickled her vagina."

There is additional evidence bearing on the question of guilt in this case. Parks flunked a lie detector test. According to the police report, the polygrapher concluded that he "was not being truthful" about a general question concerning touching children's genitals and two specific questions about touching the Voight girl.[62] Lie detector results are always mentioned in the witch-hunt narrative when they might support the defendant, but they are conspicuously absent when defendants fail them. The judge who heard the case did not present the acquittal as an exoneration; instead he remarked about how about "these are not easy cases to decide."[63] As Judge Jack G. Stein concluded, "There is a reasonable doubt in my mind, so I have no choice but to discharge."[64] It is important to understand the evolution of an investigation that could spawn the kind of outlandish allegations reported in this case. It is also important to keep in mind the evidence that those problems arose in the context of a real child sexual abuse case. If cases labeled as a witch-hunts are actually botched investigations of real sexual abuse, then the defendants who go free do so under false pretenses. That is arguably what happened in the Rogers Park case, although neither side would characterize it this way. A core group of parents were dedicated to believing every word the children said, and the witch-hunt narrative has cast Parks as the victim regardless of the evidence of abuse. Given such evidence, this would seem to be an example of a case where the acquittal of the defendant reflects the price we pay for ensuring that convictions occur only when there is an extremely high confidence level in the conclusion. Attaining this level of confidence in any case pitting a child's word against that of an adult is bound to be difficult, but such is not the story Charlier and Downing told.

CRAIG'S PRE-SCHOOL

Location	Clarksville, MD
Institution	Craig's Country Pre-School
Date	1985
Lead Def.	Sandra Craig

The Craig's Country Pre-School case is one of eight cases profiled by Charlier and Downing. Their 250-word account paints a dreamy picture of Craig's as "a place where children learned to operate computers and studied French." Out of nowhere, they imply, a little girl began to accuse Sandra Craig of sexual abuse, apparently without any corroborating evidence. But as reported in the *Washington Post* nearly nine months before publication of the Charlier and Downing series:

> Accusers and defenders of Sandra Craig have expressed dismay with what they saw as the failures of police and the County Department of Social Services, which had investigated a report of abuse involving a five-year-old girl at the center more than a year before it was closed, without notifying other parents.[65]

This case had additional features Charlier and Downing did not report. In day-care abuse cases such as Georgian Hills, there are serious questions about whether there was an opportunity for the defendant to commit acts of sexual abuse without being detected. In this case, however, there was extensive testimony about children being sent upstairs to Mrs. Craig's room for discipline.[66] This practice violated the staffing plan for the facility, which stated that Sandra Craig would always be downstairs and no children would be upstairs. There were also a series of former employees who started working at Craig's Pre-School and left after becoming uncomfortable with her harsh demeanor. One former employee described how Craig's treatment of disruptive children left them looking "frightened," and her quite uncomfortable.[67]

None of this proves sexual abuse, of course. But the most powerful evidence for the prosecution was never mentioned by Charlier and Downing: the "graphic testimony of a medical expert," which was also described in the Washington Post. Dr. Charles Shubin, a pediatric specialist, testified:

> that his examination of the 6-year-old girl and the three other children who testified that Craig had abused them produced evidence of internal scarring that suggested that they had been molested in a "remarkably consistent manner."[68]

He observed a "very clear healed injury" in the vagina of the first girl in the case, concluding that "beyond a reasonable degree of medical certainty" some object "would have to be pushed into this child with penetrating force" to cause this kind of injury.[69] The girl testified she had been touched in her "privates" with a "stick."[70] She was the only complainant in the case because the judge had ruled that charges involving other children had to be tried separately. But medical reports for three other children with similar injuries were admitted since they were so consistent.[71] The defense was left to argue that perhaps all four children had likewise been abused elsewhere.

The "satanic or ritualistic" feature that Charlier and Downing highlight is one child's statement that Sandra Craig killed a rabbit. They did not mention that there *was* a rabbit at the day care, it died at the school, and one of the parents of a child who attended the day-care handled it.[72] (This was not part of the charges.) The conviction in this case was reversed on appeal over objections to the use of closed-circuit television. This is the only one of the contested child sexual abuse cases from the 1980s to end up before the U.S. Supreme Court. Their decision in *Maryland v. Craig* is known for the issue about closed-circuit television.[73] What has been lost in all discussions of this case is the evidence that four children who attended Craig's sustained surprisingly similar penetrative injuries.

The prosecution declined to proseute Sandra Craig a second time; five years had elapsed since the original trial. Charges against Craig's son were dismissed in 1987 when the accusing child in the case was deemed incompetent to testify.[74]

CORA'S DAY CARE

Location	Sequim, WA
Institution	Cora's Day Care
Date	1986
Lead Def.	Ralph Priest

The Cora's Day Care case was also profiled in Charlier and Downing's series. It is notable as well for being one of only two of the thirty-six cases that began after 1985. The authors summarize this case as follows:

The case surfaced after an area woman placed her 2-year-old granddaughter in the day care center for the first time. After a two-hour stay, the grandmother noticed redness in the girl's vaginal area. Medical tests found no evidence of abuse, but word spread among parents of possible problems. . . . Suspicions focused on Ralph Priest [Cora's son]. They also assert that this occurred at a "highly-regarded day care center."

In fact, there had been previous complaints of physical abuse by Ralph Priest, whose medical history included severe mental instability and a finding that he was dangerous to others. A state worker who visited the day-care center in 1978 observed Priest in the "back forty" waving a rake or stick at children. Later that year, a pediatrician diagnosed choking injuries in a girl who attended the day care.[75] Interviewed again on April 29, 1986, the doctor was disturbed that Cora Priest still had a day-care license after the 1978 incident. He examined two girls who attended the day care in 1986 and concluded there *had* been sexual abuse.

Charlier and Downing reported that "suspicions focused on Ralph Priest," but they omitted any mention of his criminal history and mental illness. In subsequent civil litigation, Cora Priest confirmed that Ralph first exhibited signs of emotional problems in 1970.[76] He was diagnosed in 1975 as paranoid schizophrenic. After being arrested for criminal activities in 1979, he pleaded insanity and was hospitalized at Western State Hospital until 1984. He then moved back to Cora Priest's house, where he a started a fire and was allegedly hallucinating; he was rehospitalized. Soon after his release, he was charged with simple assault and then voluntarily committed to Olympic Memorial Hospital. After a seventy-two hour observation period, he was found to be a danger to others.[77] Ralph Priest applied for SSI, listing "mental problems," and it was determined that he met the criteria for incapacity; a state DHSD document from July 1985 lists "manic depression, disorientation, bizarre behavior, a danger to himself and others."[78] It was determined that he required protective supervision twenty-four hours a day. Instead, he moved back to his mother's house, where he had contact with the children in the day care, sometimes alone, during the period when these allegations arose. In an article that discredits the allegations of abuse in this case, defense psychologist Underwager summarized all of the information described in this paragraph as follows: [Priest] "had a history of alcohol problems, had recently lost his job, and therefore was living at home during the day."[79]

According to Charlier and Downing, the case stalled when Clallam County Prosecutor David Bruneau "convinced a local court to drop charges of indecent liberties against the Priests."[80] But this is not an accurate representation of what the prosecutor said at the time. His explanation, contained in a contemporaneous article in the Seattle *Post-Intelligencer*, specifically said "the four alleged victims were too traumatized to testify."[81] Several children in the case were diagnosed with posttraumatic stress disorder.

In sum, there is ample evidence to challenge the witch-hunt narrative about this case. If anything, the state was too easy on Cora's Day Care in 1978. As a result, a dangerous, mentally ill man who should never have been alone with children was placed in that position. But there is one nagging problem: bizarre claims related to Satanism emerged later in the case. How prevalent were those claims, and why did they happen? First, not all of the children made them, but at least one mother in particular became an "investigator," much like some of the parents in the McMartin case, taking the child to the cemetery and churches to seek "confirmation" that he had been there. Those developments definitely undermined the criminal case. But the tragedy is not that Ralph Priest was accused; it is that those children were left alone with a man considered dangerous to himself and others.

NILES

Location	Niles, MI
Institution	Small World Preschool
Date	1984
Lead Def.	Richard Barkman

The Small World Preschool in Niles Township, Michigan, was not highlighted by Charlier and Downing, but it is on their list of thirty-six and is often mentioned in the witch-hunt narrative. This case, which occurred between 1984 and 1985, involved two defendants: Richard Barkman, twenty-eight, a teacher at the school, and his wife Rebecca, thirty-two, the director. The case began with a single complaint and soon expanded to enormous proportions. According to an academic study of the case, "The investigation began with four children, spanned eight months, and involved interviews with a total of 106 alleged victims."[82] By one official count, sixty-two children indicated in interviews with various state agencies that they had been sexually abused at the preschool. Richard Barkman was charged with nineteen counts of sexual abuse involving four boys and five girls' Rebecca Barkman was charged with two misdemeanor counts of failing to report suspected child abuse. Nobody else was charged. There was one criminal trial before a jury, involving the charges concerning a four-year-old boy. Richard Barkman was convicted and sentenced to fifty to seventy-five years in prison. The remaining charges were then dropped, including those against Rebecca Barkman.

Barkman's conviction was overturned by the Michigan Court of Appeals in September 1988. The court ruled that the trial judge had improperly limited cross-examination of the child witness.[83] The state was allowed to retry Barkman after he had served five years in prison, subject to the appellate court's decision. Instead, Barkman pleaded no contest to one count of assault with intent to commit first-degree sexual conduct with a four-year-old girl in exchange for time served and five years of probation.[84] Both sides received something, but neither side could be considered victorious. Nevertheless, the case has been classified as a witch-hunt.

There are significant research challenges involved in trying to study this case at large. Criminal charges were brought in connection with nine children, but charges related to eight were dropped after the original case ended in a conviction and long sentence. The trial transcript from the case provides considerable information about the four-year-old boy's complaint, but it contains nothing about the four-year-old girl connected to the post-appeal plea agreement. It also says nothing about the other seven children involved in criminal charges. Beyond the criminal case, there were thirty-nine children involved in civil suits. Almost all of the records from the civil suits are sealed or in private hands and subject to attorney-client privilege.[85]

Existing sources offer three reasons to conclude that the statements leading to criminal charges were credible. First, the case did not expand beyond the Barkmans. Second, it did not involve repetitive interviews before children made disclosures; the MDMH Report indicates that 83 percent of disclosures were on the first interview.[86] Third, there was consistency across statements. Significantly, four organizations were involved in the case and the disclosure rate did not vary by agency, providing a kind of check that did not exist against Children's Institute International in the McMartin case.

Yet, there are obvious reasons to question the credibility of some children in this case. It strains credulity to think that the children were, without anyone detecting these events, driven away from the preschool to photography sessions in barns and made to watch Richard Barkman snap the heads off chickens. But how significant were such claims in the case? By one measure—the amount of negative publicity generated—they were enormous. But Charlier and Downing said nothing about the frequency or context of these statements. They do not consider how many children made implausible statements and what role, if any, they played in any criminal or civil claims.

It appears that Charlier and Downing's account is quite exaggerated. They state that "the children" said they were driven to photography sessions and "made to watch as Barkman snapped the head off a chicken." A summary of statements by eighty-four children interviewed by DSS includes the word *chicken* twice— once involving allegations of actually cutting the wings of chickens.[87] There is no evidence that "the children" in this case made such claims. But there is evidence in the MDMH Report that a sizable number of children made fantastic claims. Twenty-eight made statements that were classified as "ritual/bestiality."[88] It should be reiterated that 106 children were interviewed, so those statements were not a significant part of what all of "the children" said, which is what Charlier and Downing suggest. In overall terms, it appears the majority of children who made incriminating statements in the case did *not* make the kind of statements that Charlier and Downing cite as reason to label the case a witch-hunt. Those could well represent all of the children who were involved in the criminal charges.

Beyond issues concerning the testimony of children, the witch-hunt narrative contains two instances of glossing over contrary evidence and a significant omission. The first inaccuracy is that Barkman "passed a polygraph test." Actually, he told police he was willing to take a test, and it was scheduled for two days later, at which time he declined to take it.[89] Later he arranged through his own lawyer to have one administered. The state had no input into the questions or the process and did not accept the results, which Barkman claimed as proof he was telling the truth when he denied sexually abusing children. The second problem is the inaccurate claim that there was "no medical evidence" in the case. It does not appear that anyone making this claim has actually reviewed the medical files of the children in the criminal and civil cases. From the files I was able to examine, the four-year-old boy at trial had a period of excruciating difficulty with bowel movements; he was found to have a fecal impaction. This is consistent with sexual abuse, but there are other possible causes as well. A five-year-old boy who was also involved in the criminal proceedings had a healed anal fissure at the 6 o'clock position. This is not *diagnostic* of sexual abuse, but it is consistent with it. Interpretations based on this evidence may vary, but the witch-hunt narrative does not allow anyone to consider it, preferring instead to omit it.

Another important set of omissions concerns Barkman's temperament and the history of complaints at Small World. It is clear from evidence developed in the criminal case that Richard Barkman did not have a personality suitable for working with small children. He had a terrible temper and was fired from a coaching job after throwing a tantrum (and a telephone). Moreover, the preschool had been the subject of two separate complaints about him in the previous two years. There was a complaint on June 29, 1982, from an anonymous witness stating she heard Richard Barkman slap one child on the head; two children (anonymous) who reported being spanked at school; a child being put in a garbage can as a punitive measure.[90]

A separate report in February 1983 cited an anonymous witness saying her daughter had been taken off the premises for lunch without her permission, and that Richard Barkman had kissed her on the mouth.[91] These previous complaints against him obviously do not prove the later allegations, and none gave rise to any kind of separate charges, but they are worth mentioning since the lack of prior complaints is regularly used as an argument against the credibility of abuse allegations in day-care settings.

With sufficient access to relevant documents, one could spend years analyzing the complete scope of this case, the evolution of the charges and statements, and the differences between children. This would likely lead to a more nuanced view of the case. But even without such intensive inquiry, an examination of a range of original documents paints a picture that is more complicated than the witch-hunt narrative. This appears to be a case with "fantastic" statements *and* credible evidence of sexual abuse—a combination never recognized in the witch-hunt narrative.

WEST POINT

Location	West Point, NY
Institution	West Point Child Development Ctr.
Date	1984
Lead Def.	none

The West Point Child Development Center case is not among a handful of cases commonly mentioned in the witch-hunt narrative, but it appears on Charlier and Downing's list of thirty-six. Although barely remembered today, it received a considerable amount of publicity in its time. It was the subject of an article in *Newsweek* in July 1985 and an article in *Redbook* in January 1986, and it was one of two major case studies in a chapter of David Hechler's prophetic 1988 book, *The Battle and the Backlash*.[92] Those works were all sympathetic to the view that children had been sexually abused at the West Point Child Development Center. They did not cast the case as a witch-hunt. To the contrary, there was the sense that too little was being done to address definite abuse.

But the case was also mentioned in one of Debbie Nathan's earliest witch-hunt articles, and it later appeared on Charlier and Downing's list. As they explained, "allegations grew to include several children, animal sacrifices, pornography and rituals involving people wearing bloody Dracula-type masks." Nobody was charged in the case. Charlier and Downing's three-sentence description ends, "An investigation concluded there were indications of abuse but insufficient evidence to prosecute."[93] The nature of those "indications" is not explained. Nor is any rationale provided for why a case with "indications of abuse" but no actual charges would be included in a series about "justice abused."

The case began on July 27, 1984, when a three-and-a-half-year-old girl came home from a full day at the West Point Child Development Center and screamed with pain while urinating in the bathroom. Her mother observed that she was bleeding from her vagina and so immediately took her daughter to Keller Army Hospital. The girl told a technician and the doctor that her "teacher did it." She also told the doctor, "She put a pen in my touchy." The doctor observed that the girl had lacerations in her vaginal canal and indicated on the report that these internal injuries had most likely occurred within two to four hours before 5:15 p.m.[94] The only place the girl had been during that time was the day-care center.

About two weeks later, another child made statements to her parents about being touched sexually by a "teacher" at the day care. She and her family had been on vacation in late July and early August and they did not know about the girl who went to the emergency room on July 27. But the second girl did not name the same teacher who had been implicated earlier. Her father, a U.S. Army doctor, was convinced by statements from his daughter that she had been sexually abused. The teachers at the center were questioned by investigators from the army, administered lie detector tests, and quickly cleared as suspects. Two of the teachers were later reconsidered as suspects, but nobody was ever charged or disciplined. The doctor soon came to the conclusion that the army was intent on minimizing or denying child sexual abuse.[95]

Ultimately, the FBI undertook a massive investigation that included 950 interviews and the screening of about fifty children by a child psychologist. There was never a public accounting of any sort, but the core number of victims was apparently around a dozen. A briefing memo to the FBI director, after twenty-eight children had been screened, stated that ten were "probably victims" and an additional eight were either abused or witnessed sexual abuse of other children.[96] There were nine parties to the settlement of the civil suit. Two prominent families in the criminal case did not participate fully in the civil case; they actually withdrew from it. In other words, there were eleven key children in this case, although only one or two were ever publicly identified. Unfortunately, little information is available about these children and their statements. A grand jury in the Southern District of New York heard evidence about this case for ten months before U.S. Attorney Rudolph Giuliani declared that there was insufficient evidence to bring charges. He noted there *was* credible evidence that children had been sexually abused, but he said one couldn't be "absolutely sure" of who did it.[97] (The law does not require "absolute certainty"; it requires certainty beyond a reasonable doubt.)

So why is the West Point case on the witch-hunt list? Because a number of children made ritualistic allegations. How extensive and significant were those statements? There is apparently no way to ascertain the answer. The videotapes of child interviews are under seal, and the FBI's own reports are subject to redaction, which is substantial. The source of Charlier and Downing's description is likely a self-selecting group of parents who started seeing the case as ritualistic. They made claims in the public realm—claims that I think strain credulity. One of the first parents involved in the case became thoroughly convinced that the abuse at West Point was "ritualized" and "satanic," part of a national network of pedophiles who worked out of day-care centers. Other parents followed suit.

In short, the West Point case was a mixture of incredible claims and verified abuse. Some parents, faced with a nonresponsive bureaucracy that seemed to be stonewalling, succumbed to conspiracy theories of the case. Their exasperation was at least partially based on realities that have not been recognized in the witch-hunt narrative. And an important part of the story of this case—a part that distinguishes it from being a witch-hunt—is the failure to hold a perpetrator responsible for, at the very least, inflicting vaginal puncture wounds on a little girl.

WHITE PLAINS

Location	White Plains, NY
Institution	home day care
Date	1985
Lead Def.	James Watt

Another case from the list of thirty-six that contradicts the arguments in Charlier and Downing's series is from White Plains, New York. It involved an unlicensed day-care center in the basement of Jeanette Martin's house, which was raided on May 3, 1985—the day after a three-year-old boy who attended the day-care was admitted to an emergency room for injuries caused by anal penetration.[98] The police found James Watt, a thirty-four-year-old man who rented a room in the house, wrapped in a blanket in a cold, dirty basement with fourteen young children, some naked, who were watching television. Watt told the police it was "choir practice." On the basis of initial interviews with the children, Watt was arrested on May 8 and charged with sexual assault. The case was presented to a grand jury in July. Watt was then indicted on thirteen additional counts involving six children between August 1, 1984 and December 31, 1984.

Three of those children tested positive for venereal diseases. One girl had no hymen, and a skin tag on her anus that was suggestive of anal penetration.[99] The grand jury also indicted Jeanette Martin on three counts of rape, two counts of child sexual abuse, and one count of child endangerment. A twenty-count indictment several months later added additional sexual abuse charges against Watt, involving eight more children from before 1984. Three of those children *also* tested positive for venereal disease. Watt challenged the indictments for lack of specificity as to the dates of the alleged crimes. This would be his primary defense throughout the case: that the dates were not specific enough for him to provide a defense. Such an argument would make sense if Watt had no connection to the location and was, accordingly, hampered in his ability to provide alibi evidence that might place him elsewhere. But there was uncontested evidence that he had lived at the house since 1981, regularly drove a van that picked up and delivered some of the children, and was involved in the daily supervision of children during the entire time period covered by the charges. There were two other defendants in the case; charges against Jeanette Martin's husband, Harold, were eventually dropped, and James Freeman, who also lived in the house, was acquitted of child endangerment. Watt's trial began in April 1986 and lasted for nine months. Though children were the primary witnesses, various adults also testified, including parents, investigators, and two doctors who testified about the venereal diseases and related medical evidence. The jury convicted Watt of nine counts of rape, four counts of sodomy, and one count of child endangerment. Jeanette Martin was acquitted on the rape charges and convicted of child endangerment; the jury did not convict her on the charge that she held several children down while Watt raped them, even though Watt was convicted of rape in those instances.

Charlier and Downing impugned the case because one of the defense lawyers claimed that children made "bizarre" statements. None of the allegedly bizarre statements are mentioned in their article. Nor do any bizarre statements appear in the appellate documents filed by Watt, in the transcript portions that I located, or sixty-one assorted newspaper stories about the case. The same defense lawyer is quoted in several of those stories saying that children should *never* be allowed to testify in court.[100] He is also quoted making a statement that itself might well be labeled bizarre, asserting that "if [Watt] committed the crimes, he was a victim of circumstance."[101] He never explained why "circumstances" would be to blame for sexually abusing children. Watt appealed his conviction and succeeded in having most charges dismissed on the grounds that the time frame specified in the indictment was too broad. The New York Court of Appeals, the state's highest court, upheld the charges involving a five-month time frame, and the case was heralded an important accommodation to child victims.[102] Charlier and Downing justify the inclusion of this case on a "ritual abuse" list because there were "activities in basement," allegations of "sodomy," and something about urination. But there was nothing about urination in the charges, there is nothing bizarre about sodomy allegations in a sexual abuse case, and the daycare *was* located in the basement. James Watt is also listed in the dedication of Nathan and Snedeker's book, but there are no details in the book about the case. The advocacy group that now promotes the witch-hunt narrative, the National

Center for Reason and Justice, also apparently considers Watt a victim. They rely on a freelance journalist, Lona Manning, whose website entry about the case is based on five articles from the *New York Times* and a few quotes from the same defense lawyer who thinks that *all* child-abuse cases are "incredibly weak" and that children should never be able to testify in court.[103] Notably, the two *New York Times* articles about the case that mention six children having venereal diseases are not quoted or otherwise acknowledged on the site.[104] All of the medical evidence, including the anal scar on the girl whose charges were never overturned, must be ignored in order to assert, as Manning does, that a case like that of James Watt "has all of the hallmarks of a ritual abuse panic mass molestation case."[105]

Nathan and Snedeker's Dedication Page

No writer has done more to perpetuate the view that scores of people were falsely imprisoned on charges involving satanic ritual abuse in the 1980s than Debbie Nathan. She published her first article on the theme four months before the Charlier and Downing series was published. Focusing on a single case from El Paso, Texas, where she lived at the time, Nathan argued that there was a "nationwide rash" of these cases. She proceeded to identify six cases by name, notably Kelly Michaels and Country Walk—each the subject of an entire chapter later in this book. In her next paragraph, these cases were all labeled "junior McMartins" and described as "an epidemic." The other cases mentioned by name included Jordan, Minnesota (discussed earlier in this chapter and to be written about in a future publication), where there was substantial evidence of sexual abuse, and West Point (also discussed earlier in this chapter), where there was clear medical evidence of sexual abuse but no actual arrests. This leaves two cases that might conceivably support Nathan's nationwide claim: the Barkman case in Niles, Michigan (discussed earlier in this chapter), and the Amirault case in Malden, Massachusetts (to be discussed in a later publication). In short, Nathan's first article claimed there was a national trend, on the basis, at best, of a handful of cases. But few of those cases actually support the claim, if any.

Nathan's 1995 book with defense lawyer Michael Snedeker contains a longer list of names that has been widely cited as evidence of the nationwide trend of witch-hunts involving child sexual abuse claims. The list was presented on the dedication page of their book, "to the men and women still incarcerated, including those whose names we know." Information about those cases is contained in Table 3.3. Unlike the Charlier and Downing list—where many of the "cases" did not even involve criminal charges—Nathan and Snedeker's list consists entirely of people who were actually in prison at the time of publication, making it a

Table 3.3 **Details on Names Listed on the Dedication Page of Nathan and Snedeker (1995) in Chronological Order**

Place Name	Defendant Name	Number of names	Year	Wrongful Convictions?
Kern County, CA	Multiple names	9	1982–85	Yes and No
Malden, MA	Amirault	1	1984	Undetermined
Lanesborough, MA	Baran	1	1984	Yes
Miami, FL	Fuster	1	1984	No
Bainbridge Island, WA	Runyan	1	1985	No
White Plains, NY	Watt	1	1985	No
Dayton, OH	Wilcox	1	1985	Likely not
Great Neck, NY	Friedman	1	1987	No
Vancouver, WA	Malcom	1	1987	No
Olympia, WA	Ingram	1	1988	Likely not
Edgewood, IA	Schildmeyer	1	1988	No
Smithville, NC	Figured/Hill	2	1989	No
Edenton, NC	Kelly/Wilson	2	1989	Undetermined
Stuart, FL	Toward	1	1989	No
Austin, TX	Kellers	2	1991	No
Lanesborough, MA	Halsey	1	1992	No
Hendersonville, NC	Parker	2	1992	Likely not
Houston, TX	Perkins	1	1992	Undetermined
Lowell, MA	Souzas	2	1992	Undetermined
Lorain, OH	Smith	1	1994	No
Wenatchee, WA	Multiple names	18	1995	Yes and No

much stronger list on its face. One book reviewer cited this list, along with the phrase "whose names we know," as evidence that there must be a national trend much larger than the names listed.[106]

Lists with complete names and specific places look authoritative. They have a certain precision: *Michael Joseph Schildmeyer (Edgewood, Iowa)*. But there is much less here than meets the eye. First, the list is strangely disconnected from the book. Twelve of the cases included on the dedication page are not even listed in the book's index, even though the index includes cases that are mentioned on just a single page.[107] Moreover, two of the cases are included in the index but cannot fairly be counted as being covered in the book.[108] And none of the names from the Wenatchee case, which accounts for one-third of the names on the list, are even cited in the book; instead, the Wenatchee cases are discussed once, in a sentence that is in parentheses.[109] There are also two puzzles in this list, both involving cases with two defendants, only one of whom is included on the list.[110] A skeptic might wonder why so few of the allegedly "phony" ritual-abuse cases listed on the dedication page are actually included in a book that argues there was a nationwide trend of such cases.

The *Satan's Silence* list suffers from two of the same problems as the list compiled by Charlier and Downing. First, it is filled with exaggeration regarding satanic elements. Most of the cases on this list have nothing to do with satanic ritual abuse claims. Second, the list features cases in which there was substantial evidence of guilt. I have done enough research on seventeen of these twenty-one cases to reach at least a tentative conclusion about whether the case involved a wrongful conviction.[111]

That judgment is tentative in four cases. In the Aldridge and Wilcox case from Dayton, Ohio, one judge overturned the criminal convictions but another rejected the defendants' subsequent claim for civil damages, finding there was actually substantial evidence of their guilt.[112] Similarly, Lawrence Wright made a convincing case in the *New Yorker* that the Ingram case from Olympia, Washington, involved a wrongful conviction, but Karen Olio and William Cornell published a subsequent article that raises substantial doubts about Wright's claim.[113] The Parker case from North Carolina was described by Martin Gardner in the *Skeptical Inquirer* as a wrongful conviction, but newspaper accounts and appellate documents suggest it was not.[114] The conclusion is tentative because the transcript is not currently available; the only available copy is in the possession of a defense lawyer who was unwilling to make it available for fear it might damage his client's ongoing efforts to overturn his conviction.[115]

Finally, it would take many years to research the Wenatchee cases thoroughly, but there is evidence to suggest that labeling the entire matter a witch-hunt is highly inappropriate. A local television station broadcast a prison interview with an adult woman who had pleaded guilty and—even after all the criticism of the case—maintained that she and other adults had engaged in sexual contact with numerous children.[116] It is also apparent that there were false convictions in Wenatchee, spurred by a sheriff who would later be discredited in many ways.[117] The false conviction problem has been expounded on in the media and in a book by a defense lawyer. What has been lost in those accounts is any sense that some of the cases were well founded, that some were rightly not overturned, and that some were never even challenged.

Only three of the seventeen cases involved wrongful conviction. The clearest case is Bernard Baran, discussed below. The two others were massive cases that involved wrongful convictions *and* well-founded ones: Kern County, the earliest cases of all, and Wenatchee, from 1995. Even if all four of the "undetermined" cases were wrongful convictions, this would mean only seven of the twenty-one cases bear out the argument of Nathan and Snedeker's book. In short, the dedication page, which has persuaded so many people with its specificity and length, actually provides surprisingly limited support for the primary thesis of the book. The rest of this chapter provides case-by-case details that support this conclusion, analyzing the cases in chronological order.

KERN COUNTY

Location	Kern County, CA
Institution	none
Date	1982-85
Lead Def.	Kniffens & McCuans

A series of cases from Kern County, California, were the earliest and most problematic of the child molestation cases of the 1980s. Eight "organized sex rings," allegedly involving fifty-four identified adults, were listed by law enforcement officials in the Bakersfield newspaper story in January 1985.[118] Two months later, the County Sheriff's Office organized a special task force to investigate claims that there was organized satanic abuse in the county. The task force almost immediately referred eleven new complaints to the District Attorney's Office. Prosecutors rejected those complaints, and within four months the task force was disbanded. A grand jury in Kern County then requested that the California Attorney General's Office investigate the role of various Kern County agencies in this fiasco. The *Report on the Kern County Child Abuse Investigations*, published in September 1986, delivered a strong indictment of how children had been interviewed and child molestation complaints investigated. But the report did not take a position on specific cases.

At least twenty-six people were eventually convicted of child molestation in connection with the cases in Kern County. By 1996, eighteen of those defendants had their convictions overturned. The number includes two couples, the Kniffens and the McCuans, who were first charged in April 1982. Their cases have been the primary focus of the witch-hunt narrative about Kern County. They were the subject of a chapter in Nathan and Snedeker's books, they accounted for most of a similar chapter in Edward Hume's book *Mean Justice,* and they have been featured in two movies.[119] None of those accounts do justice to the facts of the McCuan part of the case. Instead, they ignore or minimize the actual origins of the case and the quality of the medical evidence. Accounting for those facts presents a far more complicated picture than the witch-hunt narrative presents, including the unavoidable conclusion that the McCuans' girls had been sexually abused for years.

John Stoll's conviction in Kern County in June 1984 has also received considerable attention in recent years. He was the subject of a *New York Times Magazine* article in 2004 and was featured in Sean Penn's 2009 movie *Witch Hunt*.[120] Although these accounts provide persuasive evidence that Stoll was falsely convicted, neither one tells the complete story of the evidence against his codefendant, Grant Self, who has also been embraced in the witch-hunt narrative.

The Kniffen and McCuan Cases

The Kniffen and McCuan cases began as an intrafamilial sexual abuse case in the McCuan family. The primary victims were two young girls, identified by Debbie Nathan as Bobbie and Darla, the daughters of Deborah and Alvin McCuan. The children's mother was the daughter of Gene and Linda Barbour, who divorced when Deborah was a child. Linda then married Rod Phelps. Gene remarried twice; his third wife was Mary Ann Barbour. Mary Ann suspected that Bobbie and Darla were being sexually abused by Phelps, their stepgrandfather. Mary Ann Barbour is the focus of the witch-hunt narrative, which argues, just like the claim against Judy Johnson in the McMartin case, that the case began in the imagination of a mentally unstable woman. As Edward Humes put it, "the events that triggered the Bakersfield Witch Hunt occurred in January 1980" and started with "an obsessed woman named Mary Ann Barbour."[121] But the story did *not* begin in January 1980. There are important events and facts that preceded Barbour's would-be imaginings about child sexual abuse. First, there is substantial evidence that Deborah McCuan, the girls' mother, was determined to minimize or ignore their abuse at the hands of her stepfather, Phelps, well before 1980. When Barbour told Deborah McCuan *in 1979* that Bobbie had visible vaginal bruises from what she thought Phelps was doing to the child, Deborah reportedly responded that Bobbie "had a lot of accidents."[122] Deborah later told Mary Ann that what Phelps had done was "no big deal." This was not the only time Deborah McCuan used the phrase to minimize child molestation. Deborah had accused Phelps of sexual abuse when she was younger, but the case was dropped when she recanted. When later confronted by Detective Glen Johnson about the discrepancy between her denial and an earlier sworn statement about Phelps, Deborah "stated that she had testified that Rod had not molested her because 'it was no big thing.'"[123] It is no wonder Mary Ann Barbour was worried about those girls. Their mother had sworn to having been abused by Rod Phelps, she had later minimized the matter, and she was then leaving the girls with him.

Second, it turns out that Deborah McCuan took Bobbie to the doctor some months *before* being confronted by Mary Ann Barbour about this in 1980. Records never mentioned in the witch-hunt narrative indicate that it was for some kind of injury to the girl's "pubic area." Deborah apparently told the doctor that her daughter had sustained injuries "falling on a wire fence." The pediatrician who examined the girl months later concluded that the vaginal injuries she observed at that time could not possibly have been caused by such an accident because there were no skin lacerations.[124] When Dr. Squyres informed McCuan in 1980 that her daughter had medical signs of sexual abuse, Deborah expressed disbelief and asked if maybe the findings could be explained "due to a fall."[125] They could not. In short, the would-be imaginings of Mary Ann Barbour had strong foundations in fact. McCuan, on the other hand, seemed to be imagining every possible alternative explanation to avoid facing the idea that her own daughters were now the ones being sexually abused by her stepfather.

The McCuan girls were interviewed by the Kern County Sheriff's Office in October 1981. The incident report indicates Bobbie McCuan disclosed that Rod Phelps, her stepgrandfather, had molested her two years ago and that her father, Alvin McCuan, had been molesting her about once a week since then.[126] Darla also said that "her dad and her grandfather rub between her legs" and "rub their 'hotdog' there." The girls were put in shelter care and Child Protective Services was notified. There is conflicting evidence about where the girls lived between then and April 1982. The April date is critical because, as Judge Jon E. Stuebbe explained years later, "that is when the case changed from two victims and two suspects to seven more victims and nine named and numerous unnamed suspects."[127] It was during interviews in April 1982 that the girls named the Kniffen boys, Brian and Brandon, as victims, and their parents, Scott and Brenda, as perpetrators. Notably, the judge reviewing the case years later concluded that "the earliest stages of the investigation" were sound. The initial "interviews and notes appear to have sought to find out what, if anything, happened," he concluded, adding that "there does not appear to have been a preconceived conclusion during this period up until April, 1982." Those conclusions alone would seem to implicate Alvin McCuan and Rod Phelps, since the McCuan girls made detailed incriminating statements in October 1981 (and earlier) that have never been impugned.

But the Kniffen boys were in a much different position. They were taken into custody on April 7, 1982, and their parents were eventually prosecuted on the basis of a recorded statement from the boys taken on April 13. The five days of interviewing that occurred in the interim are not well documented, but there were tapes and transcripts of interviews with the Kniffen boys in mid-April. When Judge Stuebbe reviewed those years later in a proceeding challenging the convictions, he concluded "the questions themselves were almost always suggestive of the answer" and "questions that were answered 'wrong' were asked again."[128]

The troublesome convictions here were against the Kniffens, not the McCuans. The Kniffens also made their statements after being taken away from their parents by the state. None of those concerns apply to the statements in October 1981 by the McCuan girls. Indeed, Edward Humes, who is quite critical of this case in his book *Mean Justice*, allows that in the girls' first interviews "the only molesters mentioned were the father and grandfather."[129] Humes uses this fact to question the validity of all of the allegations that emerged as the investigation unfolded over the next few months. But he never comes to terms with another implication of those initial interviews: even if "the only molesters" were Rod Phelps and Alvin McCuan, then Mary Ann Barbour's concerns *were* well taken and the case did not originate in wild imaginings.

The medical testimony in the Kniffen and McCuan case has also been the source of considerable criticism, for one reason: Dr. Bruce Woodling was the primary medical expert for the prosecution. Woodling had a novel clinical "test" that later made him the object of derision in the witch-hunt narrative. He employed something that became known as the "anal wink" test (although Woodling actually called it the "wink response" test).[130] The idea behind the test was that stimulation to produce a reflex response of the sphincter muscle would basically have one of two results: there would be tightening among those who had not had regular anal penetration and an actual gaping, or opening, among those conditioned to this response. Dr. Woodling testified that both Brandon and Brian Kniffen had a "marked" response to this test with significant "gaping." Critics have since argued that the "wink response test" was not scientifically validated. The criticism is well taken. But this does not mean that anal "gaping" is an insignificant finding; when verified, it can be quite significant.[131] The problem with Woodling's "test" is that it was too subjective. But the same objection can be made to several of the quirky procedures employed by Dr. Paul, the medical expert for the defense in this case and in McMartin, including what he called the "lateral traction test" and his insertion of fingers in the anus to "test" for anal tone.[132] But Dr. Paul's testimony should not be rejected entirely because of these faults. (He was correct, for example, in stating that synechia—intrauterine adhesions—are not a relevant finding and that formation of the hymen varies significantly.) By the same token, one should not automatically dismiss every observation made by Dr. Woodling.

The expert who testified for the state at a hearing years after the original convictions agreed that what Dr. Woodling described in one of the Kniffen boys—anal dilation over 20 mm without stool present—was significant because "it appears to be a learned response to the body to avoid injury from repeated sodomy." The judge who overturned the convictions in those proceedings noted it is "clear that even under the most recent medical studies" the dilation that Woodling reported observing would still be considered "a very strong indication" of sodomy.[133]

The medical testimony about the McCuan girls was even stronger. After all, the case began with Mary Ann Barbour's concern about *vaginal bruising*. For all of the attention focused in the witch-hunt narrative on her medical records, there has been surprisingly little attention to precisely what the medical records reflect about the McCuan girls. Humes, who devotes almost twenty pages to the Kniffen and McCuan case, allows in a single sentence that the girls saw "a doctor, who found bruising and swelling and concluded that [Bobbie] had, indeed, been molested."[134]

That is an understatement, to say the least. Dr. Carol Squyres, the pediatrician who had examined the girls in 1980, found them to be extremely abnormal in 1982. She had examined "hundreds of vaginas" in her pediatric practice and testified that "prepubital children do not look like" these young girls. More specifically, she testified that Bobbie's "hymen had been transected," cut at the edges at approximately 4 o'clock and 8 o'clock—findings that would still be considered abnormal today.[135] Dr. Squyres also made statements that would not be considered appropriate now; she testified that sexual activity causes vaginal "rounding," when this is no longer considered a medical indication of abuse.[136]

According to the trial testimony, Dr. Woodling's colposcopic images in 1982 documented vaginal scarring in Bobbie. Dr. Squyres examined these slides[137]; she was in the unique position of having a comparison to her observations two years earlier. The time period is significant because the girls supposedly had no exposure to Phelps during this time—but they had continuous contact with their own parents, who were named as defendants in 1982.

The testimony that compares the 1982 findings to those of 1980 has never been mentioned in the witch-hunt narrative. Dr. Squyres observed "gaping" of the anal area in 1982 that was not present in 1980. She testified that in all her years of practice she had never seen a child who had an anal lining like that in the pictures of Bobbie.[138] In her view, some kind of trauma to the area would have to be the cause. She also testified that she could not see Bobbie's vagina in 1980 without spreading apart the labia. In the pictures in 1982, however, she could see the vaginal mucosa without spreading the labia. This would be a highly unusual finding, but it cannot be confirmed without reviewing the actual slides.

In fact there is strong reason to conclude the McCuan girls were subject to repeated sexual abuse in the period between 1980 and 1982. Even the doctor who testified for the defense concurred with some of these findings. Nathan and Snedeker allow that this concurrence "buttressed intimations of incest in the McCuan family and seriously weakened Alvin and Debbie's protestations of innocence."[139] They do not explain why, given this conclusion, they included both of the McCuans on the dedication page of their book. Further, they do not disclose that Snedeker was representing the Kniffens and McCuans at the time. It would be a violation of Snedeker's ethical obligations to clients, especially during their appeal, to incriminate them; this demonstrates an inherent limitation when a defense attorney coauthors a book that analyzes cases involving his clients.

The focus of the witch-hunt narrative has been on the mental stability of the grandmother, who made a report in January 1980 and then fell apart when she concluded that authorities were doing little in response. It would appear from the medical evidence that her fears were well founded and that the witch-hunt narrative has now enshrined the result that worried her the most: the abuse of the McCuan girls would be minimized or denied. This is not to deny that the case expanded beyond all reason and that there are serious questions concerning the Kniffen boys. Those questions are more perplexing than they are clear. Both of these individuals recanted their statements and they apparently recanted their recantations at some point as well.[140] As the judge put it in 1996, in reversing the convictions of the Kniffens and the McCuans:

> It may be that all of the acts reported actually occurred and that later recantations by Brandon and Brian Kniffen are fabrications as a result of family pressure or personal guilt.[141]

In short, the proceeding that set all four defendants free was a repudiation of how the state interviewed the children in April 1982 and later, but it was not a declaration of the defendants' innocence. Indeed, the McCuan girls never recanted. But this is not reflected in the witch-hunt narrative.

John Stoll and Grant Self

John Stoll was charged in June 1984 with abusing numerous children, including his own son. Four other adults were charged as well: Grant Self, Timothy Palomo, Margorie Grafton, and Glenda Manners. Stoll succeeded in having his conviction overturned in 2004, after serving more years than anyone in the contested Kern County cases. Palomo and Grafton's convictions were reversed by the California Supreme Court in 1989 on the grounds that the trial court improperly excluded a defense psychologist who would have testified that the defendants' personality tests revealed "no signs of 'deviance' or 'abnormality.'"[142] (Ironically, the same people who excoriate pediatricians for diagnosing sexual abuse without the benefit of controlled studies are silent on the lack of "scientific proof" for profile evidence.[143]) As Judge Malcolm M. Lucas noted in dissent, the psychologist was "unable to cite any studies on the validity of the subject tests as applied to individuals charged with either child abuse or incest."[144] Notably, Grant Self's conviction was not overturned in the same case. Instead, he served out his sentence and was then held through the civil commitment statute. He later filed a lawsuit in state court, seeking to set aside his 1984 conviction connected to John Stoll.[145]

Stoll's conviction was set aside because of the recantation of four adults who accused him as children. One of those adults is particularly persuasive because a poem that he wrote as a child supports the idea that he provided false testimony and felt guilty about it at the time. But however persuasive one finds those recantations, there is additional evidence that should also be considered: Stoll's own son has not recanted. The witch-hunt narrative seems to assume that his son's position, which has not wavered over time, should not be taken seriously. But there is no explanation why the charges involving his son should be rejected, other than the fact that children unrelated to Stoll have since recanted. Then again, most, and maybe all, of the charges against him were baseless. This view is supported by the $5.5 million that Kern County officials agreed to pay Stoll in a civil case claiming damages for wrongful conviction.[146]

There is also the matter of Grant Self and Glenda Manners. The witch-hunt narrative never acknowledges the complete story about these two people. Glenda Manners is generally omitted from the discussion entirely. She is not mentioned in Maggie Jones's lengthy story, nor in the chapter about Bakersfield in Nathan and Snedeker's book. Her name does not appear on any of the lists in the witch-hunt canon, even though she was convicted of abusing one of the same children that Grant Self was convicted of abusing. Self, on the other hand, is widely labeled as a witch-hunt victim. Carol Hopkins of the Justice Committee organized a vigil for "innocent victims" including Self.[147]

A few accounts in the witch-hunt narrative allow that Self has a relevant criminal past. According to a detailed internet account that circulated on the witch-hunt list, he had "a few prior troubles with the law and was forbidden by his parole from being around children."[148] Writing in the New York Times, Jones allowed that Self had "a previous conviction of molestation" but said nothing else about it.[149] Those are both serious understatements. Self had more than "a previous conviction" or "prior troubles." He had multiple prior convictions involving sexual contact with multiple children each time. His first arrest for sexually abusing children was in 1976, with three boys (two ten-year-olds and an eight-year-old). Self was charged with oral copulation. He pled to contributing to the delinquency of a minor and was sentenced to one-year suspended and ninety-days in jail. Self was placed on three years of probation, and while on probation he was apprehended for his second sexual offense children—in 1979. Again there were three victims, all boys under the age of fourteen. Self took pictures of some of the acts and instructed one of the boys to take other photographs documenting the sexual activities.[150] The police recovered the photographs, which prove this case beyond any doubt. Self received an eight-year suspended sentence and was sent to a state mental facility.

He was released in 1983 and was supposedly under "supervision" when he moved in with a woman who had a nine-year-old boy. Self was working for John

Stoll at this point, and eventually started renting the pool house in his backyard. By one account, he did so as a ruse because the terms of his community release would not have permitted him to live with a woman who lived with a nine-year-old boy. Jones reported that "Stoll didn't know" that Self had a criminal record or that a mother had recently complained to the sheriff's office that Self had "inappropriately touched her son." The woman with the nine-year-old was Glenda Manners, the boy's maternal grandmother. It was in connection with this child that *she* was charged with two counts of felony lewd and lascivious behavior and one count of child endangerment. The latter charge stemmed from Manners having "twice witnessed without comment as Self sexually molested [the boy]."[151] Manners did not contest those facts on appeal; nor did she ever challenge her conviction. All that she appealed was the court's denial of probation.[152]

The crimes Glenda Manners observed Grant Self commit were *not* at the pool house in John Stoll's backyard, although Self apparently listed the pool house as his official residence at the time. Maybe Self sexually abused the boy at Manners's apartment but did not do the same thing at a pool house that attracted multiple children—although his prior convictions involving multiple children would suggest otherwise. Maybe Stoll unwittingly helped Self perpetrate a ruse concerning his supervised release,[153] although it would seem one would be aware if the person allegedly renting the pool house in the backyard did not actually live there. And maybe what Manners saw are things that Stoll knew nothing about. But the witch-hunt narrative never acknowledges these uncertainties, let alone attempt to address them. Instead the narrative has ignored Manners and embraced Self. Bruce Robinson opines, through his popular "religious tolerance" website, that Self is "not guilty of the crimes" and adds that in all likelihood "no molestations occurred."[154] Nathan and Snedeker dedicated their book, in part, to Self—a man who is unquestionably a serial child molester (two of his convictions rested, separately, on photographic evidence and on an adult eyewitness[155]). The earliest of his convictions for child sexual abuse was a guilty plea that he has never contested. Self was held in civil commitment after his prison term ended. In a civil commitment proceeding in 2000, Self denied having any sexual interest in children; he had no explanation for 115 disciplinary charges in prison, including possession of "full frontal nude photographs of children."[156] Self succeeded in getting one of his 1984 convictions set aside—the one connected to John Stoll. The boys in the case, except Stoll's own son, had recanted their testimony. Self then sued Kern County for civil damages and in March 2013 the county agreed to pay him $725,000.[157] What is perhaps most remarkable about this settlement is that it occurred after Self had been arrested again on child sexual abuse charges—this time in Jackson County, Oregon. Four months after settling his civil case against Kern County, Self pleaded guilty to using a child in a display of sexually explicit conduct (a class A felony in Oregon) and two related felonies. He was sentenced to seventy months in prison and three years of post-prison supervision.[158]

Both Nathan and Snedeker and Humes have argued that the excesses of the prosecutions in Bakersfield launched a wave of witch-hunts across the country. What they actually helped launch was a witch-hunt *narrative* that is so expansive it cannot or will not distinguish between those with legitimate claims of innocence and those who are clearly guilty. The Kniffens and Stoll may well qualify as the former, although this is not entirely clear; but the McCuans and Self certainly do not. There are other Bakersfield defendants, such as Richard Charles Bishop, who also photographed his abusive acts, whose convictions have, appropriately, never been overturned.[159] And there are confusing cases, as with the Pitts case, where convictions were overturned for prosecutorial misconduct and "three of six child victims recanted."[160]

There is no question that the problems identified in the 1986 report on Kern County were serious. They painted a picture of "one of the clumsiest and most destructive child abuse investigations in American history."[161] The harm done to the falsely accused in these cases was enormous. But there is also no question that the evidence of guilt in some of these cases has been ignored or distorted in the subsequent witch-hunt narrative.

BARAN

Location	Pittsfield, MA
Institution	Early Childhood Development Ctr.
Date	1985
Lead Def.	Bernard Baran

The brief description of this case in *Satan's Silence* gives no special reason to think that Baran's conviction was wrongful, but research into the complete trial transcript and other related documents reveals that the outcome was indeed a miscarriage of justice. There is, however, one important way in which the facts differ from the witch-hunt narrative: the case had nothing to do with ritual abuse.

Bernard Baran was working as an assistant at a day-care center in Pittsfield, Massachusetts, when he was accused of child molestation. The case began with a four-year-old boy who contracted a venereal disease. His mother notified authorities that her son had been sexually abused by Baran at the day-care center. An investigation ensued, and charges involving five other children were added. Baran was tried and convicted in a matter of months.

But nothing in this case is as it initially appears. The strongest statement made by the first boy to complain was taken by William Baughan, a Department of Social Services (DSS) investigator who "substantiated" the sexual abuse claim and referred it for prosecution. But the person the child named in that report was not Bernard Baran. It was the boy's mother's boyfriend, who lived with them at the time. He was never charged with any crime, although the matter was re-ferred to prosecutors after DSS substantiated a complaint involving him.[162] She had already vehemently accused Baran, of course. But what, if anything, her son actually said about Baran became more doubtful over time.

During the trial, the boy did not implicate Baran on the stand, and all charges connected to him were dismissed. Nevertheless, Judge William Simons allowed medical testimony to support the prosecutor's preposterous argument that the first boy got his venereal disease from Baran *because* Baran was gay and therefore at higher risk himself. Any gay person who works with children is assumed guilty under this approach. The prosecutor, Daniel Ford, even suggested that Baran—who tested negative for gonorrhea—might have taken penicillin between volun-tarily talking to the police and being arrested a few days later. But Baran is aller-gic to penicillin; this fact is stamped on his medical records.[163]

The prosecution seemed to be fueled by homophobia. The prosecutor told the jury that a gay man working in a day-care center was like "a chocaholic in a candy store." (The prosecutor later claimed that he was addressing whether Baran had the *opportunity* to commit the crimes, but the underlying homopho-bia is apparent.) Moreover, the bigoted man who led the original charge against Baran—the stepfather of the first boy—complained bitterly about having a gay man employed at the day-care center. A few weeks later, he accused Baran of child molestation.

The DSS report that pointed the finger *away* from Baran was dated January 17, 1985—a day before the pre-trial hearing began in Baran's criminal trial. Cu-riously, the report was not stamped as "received" at the district attorney's office until a day *after* the entire trial *ended*, about two weeks later. The report was ap-parently stamped, filed . . . and buried. The defense was never given a copy, and the mother's boyfriend, named by DSS, was never prosecuted. The critical memo was uncovered years later by lawyers representing the insurance compa-nies of the day-care center. Faced with a lawsuit from the family of the first boy, the insurance lawyers did the kind of thorough investigation that was never done in the first instance. Several civil cases eventually settled for nuisance value.

Still, one might wonder, how did charges with such misguided beginnings spread to five other children? One answer is that they did not. The five other children at trial said surprisingly little that actually incriminated Baran. The three older children—two were then four-year-olds and one was five—have all given reasons to doubt that Baran abused them. One boy said so little on the stand that, like the first boy, charges related to him were dismissed. Another boy, added the day of trial, barely said more, but records uncovered in the civil cases docu-ment his repeated retractions. The civil investigation also uncovered evidence that the oldest girl told a therapist that "her mother led her to believe that if she didn't say the right words they wouldn't get a lot of money." The remaining two child witnesses were three-year-old girls. One clearly did not prove she was competent to testify.[164] The other was asked, "If someone asks you a question and you know what the answer is, what should you do?" "Bernie touched me," she responded.[165] Both were allowed to testify. There is much more that could be said about the weaknesses in this evidence. Baran's motion for a new trial contains hundreds of pages of "new" evidence from the civil case, plus 392 pages obtained under defense subpoena. The subpoenaed documents are sealed, but several, quoted liberally in the motion, add substantial weight to the already strong case for a new trial.

The Baran case is a challenge to those sympathetic to either side of the witch-hunt narrative. Those sympathetic to Baran seem to have a difficult time accepting the STD test and the implication, borne out in the DSS memo, that the original child in this case was sexually abused—though not by Baran. But someone got away with sexually abusing a child in this case. Those sympathetic to the prosecution have an even larger challenge. There are substantial reasons to think Baran was wrongfully convicted. Those who have defended the conviction point to the "admission" Baran made in 1989 in order to be transferred from the general prison population to the Massachusetts Treatment Center. Baran, who took the stand to proclaim his innocence at trial, told a newspaper reporter years later he made those statements after repeated assaults in prison.[166] Baran prevailed in reversing his conviction years after this section was written. He was freed from prison in 2006.[167]

RUNYAN

Location	Bainsbridge Island, WA
Institution	home day care
Date	1985
Lead Def.	Debbie Runyan

This case is listed on the dedication page of Nathan and Snedeker's book, but it is not discussed in the book. Debbie Runyan was convicted in January 1986 of molesting five girls, including her two daughters, at a day care she ran out of her home. The allegations surfaced when Runyan went on vacation and a distant relative took care of the children. The woman was startled by how sexualized the children were. One girl tried to grab the woman's breasts, another tried to French kiss her, and a third frequently masturbated. After finding a vibrator in drawer *in the day care*, she conveyed her concern to a parent of one girl. The mother's four-year-old girl had experienced constant redness and vaginal pain that year and two serious bladder infections, one very recently. She had also come home once with choke marks on her neck. Runyan told her mother another child had done it.[168] She attributed the other problems to general hygiene.

Detectives who then interviewed the children were told that Runyan often took the children into the bathroom, locking the door. One child described hearing "buzzing" behind the bathroom door when this happened. Another child described being abused by a "rolling pin, except it was flat on top." Other children said they were abused with "sticks." (The authorities found three vibrators and other sexual paraphernalia in the house.) Runyan's seven-year-old daughter said children were tied up in the garage and described green and white plaid cloth strips used to tie them up. Runyan's roommate turned over strips of that kind, which she said she found in Runyan's bedroom. Runyan's younger daughter used the phrase "monster mommy in the garage."[169] And a pediatrician testified that there were signs of physical abuse in three of the five girls.

It is not clear why this case appears in the dedication of *Satan's Silence*. The case is not discussed in the book; it is not even spelled correctly on the dedication page (where one sees "Runyon"). The most likely reason is that Runyan's name appears in Mark Pendergrast's book *Victims of Memory*. But he provided no analysis either; Runyan is just one of several names listed in a single paragraph that has no accompanying documentation.[170]

The children's statements in the case contained unusual and verified details, from the vibrators to the plaid strips of cloth, and there were medical findings to bolster their testimony. Moreover, as reported at the time, Runyan admitted under cross-examination that "she had lied on numerous occasions to family, friends, and police."[171] Indeed, her protestations of innocence grew stranger over time. She originally claimed that she was "set up" by her ex-husband.[172] She never specified how he accomplished this feat since the charges were corroborated in various ways and included several children beyond their own. After her conviction, Runyan expanded her conspiracy theory to include the argument that the prosecutor and trial judge acted for "political reasons."[173] As she made these fantastic claims, her lawyer withdrew from the case, citing "ethical" considerations. In a nine-page decision upholding Runyan's conviction, a unanimous three-judge panel concluded "the record in this case is overwhelming."[174] As they summarized the trial record: it reflects that "children were tied up, gagged and physically injured by Runyan's abuse."[175]

A post-conviction proceeding five years later resulted in an evidentiary hearing to consider Runyan's claim that her oldest daughter had recanted.[176] Runyan's older daughter was clearly troubled about testifying against her mother. The day she testified, a reporter who covered the entire trial wrote that she was "pale and uncomfortable on the witness stand" and "constantly stared at her mother." Nevertheless, the daughter testified she had seen two girls tied up, and "she identified strips of cloth that allegedly had been placed in the mouth of one child."[177] The court found that her affidavit was consistent with memory problems she expressed to her therapist in 1993, but it was "equally clear that her testimony at trial was truthful."[178] None of the other girls who testified at trial have claimed memory loss or otherwise recanted their testimony, including Runyan's *other* daughter.

FRIEDMAN

Location	Great Neck, NY
Institution	none
Date	1987
Lead Def.	Arnold and Jesse Friedman

Jesse Friedman is also listed on the dedication page of *Satan's Silence*, although his case was not discussed in the book. Friedman was apprehended in connection with an investigation that originated in 1987 as a child pornography investigation against his father, Arnold Friedman, who was a well-respected teacher in Great Neck, New York. The elder Friedman held after-school computer classes in the basement of his house. He had an interest in child pornography and ordered some from a source that turned out to be law enforcement; they subsequently raided his house. One of the items agents seized was a list of students in the after-school computer classes. Those students were subsequently interviewed, and some revealed they had been sexually abused in the basement of Friedman's house. As more victims were identified, Jesse Friedman, then seventeen, was identified as a participant in the abuse. Jesse eventually pleaded guilty to twenty-five counts of sexual abuse and was sentenced to six to eighteen years in prison. He told the judge, "I am sorry for my actions," and asked for "assistance with my problem," a request to be sent to a federal institution with sex-offender treatment. His father, then fifty-eight, pleaded guilty earlier to distributing child pornography through the mail and to multiple counts of child sexual abuse. He was sentenced to ten to thirty years.

The case was not highly contested at the time; after all, the defendants pleaded guilty. And for at least five years after those guilty pleas, nothing was written to suggest the outcome was inappropriate. Arnold Friedman sent some kind of "open letter" protesting his innocence, but even those who have come to support Jesse Friedman have not challenged his father's conviction by guilty plea. Nevertheless, Nathan included Arnold and Jesse Friedman's names on a list posted on the "Witch Hunt Information Center" in 1994. Because the case was not discussed in the book, it is difficult to know why Nathan considered the convictions to be inappropriate. The answer emerged in 2003 with the release of Andrew Jarecki's movie *Capturing the Friedmans*. Nathan appears in the film and argues that the Friedman case was part and parcel of the "sex-abuse hysteria" that was sweeping the country at the time. Her role in the film has never been fully explained. After the film was released, Richard Hankin, an editor and producer of the film, described Nathan as "a friend of the [Friedman] family" and as "an intermediary" in the project, raising questions about how the project evolved.[179] Nathan appears in the film as an expert on witch-hunts. She is not identified in the film as a friend of the family.

Capturing the Friedmans raises many questions about the case, but it purports not to take a side. The film was marketed with the tagline "Who Do You Believe?" Whereas the film gives voice to several officials who stand by the conviction, there is no question that it leaves the impression that the case was a miscarriage of justice. Three main objections are put forth in the film. First, investigators are criticized for pressuring the adolescents whom they interviewed. One family that secretly taped the interrogation of their son is featured prominently in presenting the argument that teenage boys were pressured to say they were abused. Second, there is a claim that the police manufactured or exaggerated claims about child pornography in the house. Finally, the film presents portions of a videotaped interview with one of the complainants from the time, who describes being sexually abused at the Friedmans' house but seems to say his recollections of the abuse emerged only after being hypnotized.

On their face, all three of these claims challenge the credibility of the state's version of events. On closer examination, however, there is much less here than meets the eye. Moreover, some relevant facts are left out of the movie. For instance, it omits any mention of a third defendant, outside the family, who pleaded guilty. When confronted with this startling omission, Jarecki responded that Ross Goldstein "did not want to appear" in the film.[180] Why this would prevent someone who was making a film they describe as a documentary from *mentioning* him has never been explained. The importance of Goldstein was acknowledged in Jesse Friedman's motion for a new trial, filed after the movie was released. In summarizing the facts, Friedman's lawyers allowed that "Jesse knew how detrimental the testimony of this adult witness might be at trial."[181] The film also omits any mention of the two lie detector tests Jesse Friedman failed. Jarecki later defended this choice on the grounds that *he* thought the results were inconclusive.[182] He did not explain how the editorial choice squares with the idea that the audience was supposed to decide whom to believe. The film also omits any of the dramatic videotape of Jesse describing his own sexual abuse by his father, and his participation in sexual abuse of boys in his family home, on the *Geraldo* program.[183] Nathan claimed in a 1994 posting on the Witch-Hunt List that the only reason Jesse Friedman gave the interview was the hope that it "would help him during sentencing."[184] In the same post, she claimed the interview was his lawyer's idea and Jesse "felt betrayed because he still ended up with a harsh sentence." But the interview was conducted *after* Friedman was sentenced, not before.[185] And Jarecki agreed, in a public session after screening the movie in New York City, that Jesse Friedman's lawyer counseled *against* the interview.[186] Jesse recanted his confession while in prison. As reported in *Newsday*, Friedman said he "lied to manipulate the media so that people would feel sorry for [me]."[187] The explanation could be equally true of Friedman's current claims of innocence.

The film also casts doubt on the child pornography claim by showing a picture of an empty table and challenging the description of a police investigator that there was a "foot high stack" of such material in plain view. But a year after the film was released, Jesse Friedman's lawyers made a different claim in their appeal: they described the materials as "approximately twenty magazines containing nude photos of adolescent and teenage males." In other words, the quibble seems to be whether twenty magazines constitute a "foot-high stack." (Nathan claimed in 1994 that it was "two or three old magazines.") Jesse's lawyers also argued that these materials were not "interspersed" with classroom materials but rather "were all found behind the piano in Arnold Friedman's private study." They made no mention of the pornographic games found on disks that *were* interspersed with materials in the classroom.[188]

Finally, the most important claim in the movie, at least from the point of view of challenging Jesse Friedman's conviction, involved hypnosis. The film features portions of a videotaped interview with a man identified as Gregory Doe, who makes statements to the effect that he did not remember being abused until after being hypnotized. Testimony obtained through hypnosis is not considered reliable and would be inadmissible in most states. Friedman's lawyers told the *New York Times* "they have obtained evidence indicating that some of the other youths who accused the Friedmans" had been hypnotized before testifying to the grand jury.[189] But there are serious questions about the accuracy of the presentation of Gregory Doe in the movie, and no actual evidence was ever offered to prove *other* complainants had been hypnotized. To the contrary, Dr. Joyce W. Parks filed a sworn affidavit in 2004 stating unequivocally that Doe was her patient and "at no time during this patient's treatment did I ever use hypnosis."[190] Moreover, Friedman's own lawyer cast doubt on the film, describing it as "reliable evidence of nothing." In a hearing on October 3, 2007, Friedman's lawyer said it was fair to characterize the film as "containing interviews, cut and spliced, and taken out of context."[191] It is not known whether the interview with Doe was subject to such techniques. What is clear is that Friedman's lawyers provided no evidence to support their claim that any other complainant in the case had been subject to hypnosis. Accordingly, the court turned down their request to reopen the case.

Other events have cast further doubt on the thoroughness and balance of Jarecki's research. When the film was nominated for an Academy Award, six of the complainants from the time came forward to say it "omitted or distorted important evidence about their cases."[192] Their statements raised important questions about how many of the victims Jarecki actually interviewed. There were fifteen complainants in the case. The film never addressed this question, but Jarecki told an interviewer after the film was released that he had interviewed "more than three" of them. He later filed an affidavit on Jesse Friedman's behalf saying he interviewed "approximately five" of the complainants.[193] It is difficult to imagine how Jarecki could be so unsure of exactly how many of the original complainants he actually interviewed. Moreover, even if it was five, this would mean he interviewed only one-third of the original victims. In other words, Jarecki found "no evidence" of Friedman's guilt, but he never talked to most of the people who could provide such evidence. Jarecki interviewed far more adults who never complained as children that they were abused at the Friedmans.

Recent developments largely support the argument that Jesse Friedman was *not* the victim of a witch-hunt. In response to a federal appellate court decision that questioned, but did not overturn, the verdict, the Nassau County District Attorney's Office re-opened the case and convened an independent panel of experts to guide an inquiry into the conviction.[194] The nearly three-year investigation ended in June 2013 with the release of a 155-page "Conviction Integrity Review" that concluded "by any impartial analysis, the re-investigation process . . . has only increased confidence in the integrity of Jesse Friedman's guilty plea and adjudication as a sex offender."[195] Among other conclusions, the reviewers found: (1) no evidence that improper police questioning materially tainted the investigation, (2) no credible evidence that hypnosis was used on any complainant, and (3) Friedman's guilty plea was not a product of coercion. The report detailed new information that further supports the outcome of the case, including an incriminating statement by Jesse Friedman's uncle and a psychological evaluation in 1988, never released by the defense, that Jesse Friedman was a "psychopathic deviant" whose personality was "consistent with someone who was capable of committing the crimes with which he was charged."[196] The review also criticized Andrew Jarecki for "misrepresenting Judge Boklan" in *Capturing the Friedmans*.[197] One important development, discussed in the report, could be seen as supporting Jesse Freidman's position: Ross Goldstein, the third defendant in the case who pleaded guilty, has since recanted his admission of guilt. For several reasons, the reviewers did not consider Goldstein's recantation reliable, including his inability to explain the things he originally told Andrew Jarecki—things Jarecki chose to leave out of the movie.[198] The Case Advisory Panel that oversaw the review included Barry Scheck, the defense lawyer who co-founded the Innocence Project. The Advisory Panel issued a unanimous statement that the Review Team's conclusion that Jesse Freidman was guilty was "reasonable and supported by the evidence."[199] The report is not a binding legal decision and Jesse Friedman has vowed to continue to seek to overturn his conviction through the court system.[200]

Marilynn Malcom's name is also on the dedication page of Nathan and Snedeker's book, although the case is not discussed. Michael Snedeker, Nathan's co-author, represented Malcom years later at a clemency hearing, although this too is not disclosed in the book. Malcom was convicted in 1988 of twelve felony counts of

MALCOM

Location	Vancouver, WA
Institution	Rainbow Christian Daycare
Date	1987
Lead Def.	Marilynn Malcom

child sexual abuse, involving seven victims including her daughter Julia, then eight years old, and her son Kevin, then twelve. The other children, all younger, attended the Rainbow Christian Daycare Center in her home in Vancouver, Washington. The case began in late January 1987, when one of the children who attended the day care watched a video about sexual abuse and strangers. This boy told his mother about sexual games involving Malcom's daughter and other boys. She called a friend, whose son also attended the day care, and her son apparently confirmed the gist of the story (although the second boy said he was not involved). These mothers phoned the Clark County Sheriff the next day.

One of the boys apparently repeated the story about sexualized games at Malcom's house; the other one did not. Malcom, as would later be documented, soon "took a number of steps attempting to stifle the investigation."[201] This included telling at least three other parents not to let their children be interviewed by the police. These allegations should be handled within the church, she told them. She told another neighbor she was adamant she was not going to let the police talk to her daughter, Julia.

Detective Sharon Krause interviewed Marilynn Malcom and, separately, Julia Malcom on February 6. The girl apparently told the detective she had been molested by her brother and that she told her mother about it. Her mother denied any knowledge. Four days later, Marilynn Malcom called Detective Krause and said her daughter had fallen off a stool and "hit herself on the heel" and was bleeding from her vagina. Malcom said she did not want to touch her daughter "because of what has been going on."[202] The detective told Malcom to take her daughter to the doctor, who later reported that Julia was "too uncomfortable for him to do the exam" and that Julia wanted Detective Krause to "hold her hand and help her while at the doctor's, not her mother."[203] The girl was examined, under a sedative, two days later by Dr. Brigitte I. Mengelberg, who reported there was significant evidence of anal and vaginal trauma.[204]

While the investigation continued, the younger children who attended the day care implicated Kevin and then Marilynn Malcom. Kevin confessed to sexual activities with young boys at the day care and pleaded guilty in Juvenile Court on April 20, 1987. That afternoon, Detective Krause interviewed Julia again. The eight-page report of this interview indicates that Julia disclosed "there had been a number of sexual contacts between her and her mother which occurred over several years of time."[205] She also made statements indicating her mother had sexual contact with several children at the day care. Kevin then confirmed that his mother was involved in the abuse. Marilynn Malcom was charged with sexual abuse against her son, daughter, and other children later in April.

The parents of some of the children who attended the day care continued to question their children in the coming weeks. The state would later describe what happened as "an investigator's nightmare," including the claim that Marilynn Malcom killed a little girl. One parent was described as "hindering the investigation by her improper questions and lack of cooperation with the prosecutor's office."[206] A few parents also started complaining that Detective Krause did not believe their children. The detective interviewed one of the boys on June 2, at which time he retracted recent allegations and said he lied about many things because of pressure from his parents. Notably, he did not recant the basic claims against Kevin or Marilynn Malcom.

Malcom was charged with sexual abuse of all of the children, but the trial and the main witnesses were her own two children, who never made the most fantastic allegations and who were much older than the other children. Malcom was convicted by a twelve-person jury. She was then evaluated in advance of sentencing. The Sentencing Report and Psychological Evaluation noted "indications of deception" in response to the relevant questions about sexual activity. The examiner, whose credentials, methods, and findings were never challenged in any later proceedings, concluded this was "a clear-cut case of old-fashioned denial."[207] The conclusion was seconded by Dr. Kirk Johnson, who had been hired by Malcom's mother and concluded, after reviewing the same materials, that Malcom was "highly manipulative." Years later, after her release from prison, Malcom claimed in an editorial in the local newspaper that those reports "were not accepted by Judge Morgan."[208] The claim is flatly contradicted by the Findings of Fact and Conclusions of Law signed by Judge J. Dean Morgan on February 5, 1988, in support of a sentence with "aggravated circumstances."[209] Malcom's conviction was upheld on appeal, although she also claimed years later in a petition for clemency that she had been "without recourse in the appellate court."[210]

The clemency petition—prepared by Michael Snedeker—included a report from a medical expert who contradicted the report about Julia's injuries and a statement of recantation by Julia Malcom. The recantation was reportedly written by Marilynn Malcom, not by Julia.[211] And it was written after Julia started rooming with a woman who had become Malcom's friend in prison. When prosecutors asked Julia if they could interview her about her alleged retraction, she said yes—but later her lawyer indicated "he had reconsidered and would not allow an interview."[212] Her attorney also denied access to the two counselors and their records from 1987 to 1995, when Julia was treated for sexual abuse by her mother.[213] Prosecutors sought those records in the hopes of finding detailed information that would contradict the "retraction."

There are several reasons the recantation is suspect. First, the claim that her incriminating statements were made after repeated, coercive police interviews is not supported by the report of the interview of April 20, 1987. This is the first time she was asked about abuse by her mother, and she made a detailed statement. Second, her recantation is contradicted by statements her brother swore she made in family counseling sessions that he also attended.[214] Third, her recantation is contradicted by statements by a close friend who swore Julia confided in her when they were sixteen years old about sexual abuse by her mother when she was a child. The same friend reported that shortly before the recantation Julia told her not talk to anyone who was trying to keep her mother in prison—a request eerily similar to Marilynn Malcom's request to all of the parents not to speak to police when the case was first investigated. This friend also reported that Julia said her mother was going to get out of prison and sue the state, and they were going to "get a lot of money and move to Montana."[215] There are, of course, obvious reasons for a family member to recant truthful disclosures about abuse. Possible motivations include a desire to reunite, feelings of guilt, and coercion by the perpetrator. Another is the hope of monetary gain. All of those possibilities potentially fit this case.

Dr. Steven Gabaeff, the medical expert offered on Malcom's behalf, disagreed with all of the findings from the examination of Julia in 1987. Without an independent assessment of the slides, which are not part of the public record, it is impossible to evaluate this disagreement. But it is worth noting that the doctor did not try to provide any explanation for why Julia was bleeding from her vagina; nor did he try to explain how his view that her findings were normal would be consistent with the symptom. He also did not provide any opinion about Malcom's absurd claim that her daughter's vaginal bleeding was caused by falling off a stool.

Snedeker offered the clemency board an affidavit from Maggie Bruck, a psychology professor at Johns Hopkins University, who concluded that none of the statements from anyone in the case were reliable—except the recent recantation by Julia Malcom. Bruck's lengthy analysis of whether the interviews with the children were coercive was silent on the possibility that coercion might be involved in this would-be recantation. Nor did Bruck comment on the discrepancy between Julia's claim that she "had no sexual knowledge" at age eight and therefore could not possibly have made those statements to Detective Krause, and the assertion *in her recantation* that she was raped by a babysitter at age four and still remembers how painful it was. Notably, neither Julia's older brother nor any of the others involved in the case have ever recanted. Anita Peterson, chair of the Clemency and Pardons Board and also a psychologist, stated she "had some considerable problems" with Bruck's report after she "went back and cross-checked Dr. Bruck's assertions."[216] Peterson concluded that Bruck had "lost her objectivity." The board voted 4-0 to deny the petition.

There is no doubt that some of the parents in this case damaged the state's case by overinterviewing their children. But the charges against Marilynn Malcom pre-dated those events, and her conviction was based on the testimony of her own two children, who never made such claims. The older child has always stood by his testimony, and the would-be recantation of the younger one is dubious on many levels. Malcom's subsequent efforts to overturn her conviction in federal court have all failed.

GLENDALE MONTESSORI

Location	Stuart, FL
Institution	Glendale Montessori School
Date	1987
Lead Def.	James Toward

James Toward's name is also on the dedication page of Nathan and Snedeker's book, although the case as well is not actually discussed. It stems from abuse allegations at the Glendale Montessori School in Stuart, Florida, where James Toward was headmaster. The first official record that there might be sexual abuse at the preschool came through the Child Abuse Registry Hotline on June 25, 1987. The caller reported highly sexualized behavior by a two-and-a-half-year-old girl. She lay on top of her mother and started "pumping" her; when her mother asked what she was doing, the little girl said "screwing." The girl also asked her mother to put her hand in the child's panties and "make her feel good." When asked if someone did this to her, the girl said "Mr. T," the name children used for James Toward.[217] The police interviewed these parents, who apparently removed their child from the school. Nothing else happened at that point, even though the case would later be said to have all the markings of a modern witch-hunt. But the witch-hunt narrative has never acknowledged this initial warning sign or the minimal response to it. Another complaint about possible sexual abuse at Glendale Montessori was received on the Child Abuse Registry Hotline two months later, on August 21. A police investigator contacted the parents of a four-and-a-half-year-old boy who had "feigned illness, screamed, cried and locked himself in the bathroom" to avoid going to school. The parents called the hotline after their son grabbed his father's hand and rubbed it against the boy's genitals. The boy told his mother he learned that from "Mr. T." Neither of these early disclosures could possibly have been caused by repetitive interviews or public hysteria. The reports occurred the same day as the observed behavior, and the matters had not yet become public. The following day, a search warrant was executed at the home of James Toward. The boy had told authorities he was taken to Toward's house, where he and several other boys were photographed naked, wearing masks, bandanas, and cowboy hats. The boy said those items would be found in the closet of a spare bedroom. According to the search affidavit, costume masks, bandanas, and cowboys hats "were located where the child had described." The child was also "able to describe the entrance to the home," even though Toward told the police he had never taken children from the school to his home.[218]

A third complaint pertaining to the Glendale Montessori came on September 11, 1987, when the Stuart Police Department received a call from a woman in Tennessee, who was visiting her mother in Knoxville and had not been in Florida during the events in late August. They reported that on September 3, the grandmother had taken their son to see a pediatrician about an upper respiratory infection. In the examination room, the boy reportedly said "in a very frightened voice, Nana, he won't have to touch my penis will he?" When asked why he didn't want the doctor to touch his penis, the boy reportedly said it was a "secret" that "I can't tell you." His parents arranged for the boy to see a social worker in Knoxville. After that visit, the boy told his mother that he had been to "Mr. T's" house and "we were touching." He said that "Miss Brenda," who worked at the preschool, made him take off his clothes. The parents, who had never given permission for the boy to visit Toward's house, contacted the Stuart Police Department.[219]

The police proceeded to interview children and talk to parents. The investigation went on for months before James Toward and Brenda Williams were charged with the sexual abuse of six boys. As the investigation continued, other teachers were considered suspects; one lost her teaching license in what was perhaps the most dubious aspect of the case. Brenda Williams eventually pleaded guilty in June 1989 and was sentenced to ten years in prison.

There was a pre-trial hearing in Toward's case in August 1989, lasting eight days and including testimony from all of the children connected to the original charges and some of their parents. The state also introduced sworn statements from teenagers, who claimed Toward had offered them "money or gifts for sex." They described Toward's sexual behavior as "sick" and "freakish." Prosecutors stated the intention to introduce this evidence if the defense raised Toward's character as an issue.[220] This is relevant only to the extent that Toward's "proper British demeanor" led some to conclude he could not possibly commit such crimes.

There was also significant circumstantial evidence concerning the claim that Toward had made, and disposed of, child pornography material in the months before his arrest. The six boys testified they were photographed by a "movie camera" and by a camera where the picture "came right out."[221] There was also testimony at trial from a clerk who sold Toward a Polaroid camera two years earlier. The clerk remembered Toward because he made repeated references to sex when he bought the camera.[222] But the camera was never recovered. Nor did the police find the video camera described by the children. They *did* find the original box for the video camera in Toward's attic.[223] Toward claimed he never owned either one. We will never know how he would have tried to explain that fact, or the evidence concerning his safety deposit box. A bank clerk testified she saw "bundles of cash and videotapes" in his safety deposit box on several occasions in 1986. Bank records showed that Toward's wife, Rosario, opened the box six days after his arrest. By the time police executed a search warrant, the box was empty.[224] Faced with this evidence, Toward entered into a plea agreement in exchange for a twenty-seven-year prison sentence, ten years of probation, and an agreement not to prosecute his wife. He also waived the pre-sentence report, which assured that "character evidence" against him would not become part of the official record.

The case became more contested in the years after his conviction, when additional civil suits were filed by families who were never involved in the criminal case. One of those lawsuits, filed three years later, was "aggressively defended" by an insurance company.[225] Insurance companies, which quickly paid as much as $1 million in settlements to some of the original complainants in the criminal case, viewed some of the later civil claims as baseless. Given the legal requirement to handle claims in "good faith" and the danger of paying enormous punitive damages if they are found to be in "bad faith," one can reasonably assume that the evidence for some of the later claimants was weak. By the same token, however, the earlier claims were paid quickly and to the satisfaction of the plaintiffs.

Toward first became part of the witch-hunt narrative when his name appeared on lists prepared by Professor Mary de Young, who never provided any supporting details or original documentation.[226] The False Memory Syndrome Foundation (FMSF) started writing about the case in 2008, after someone they described as a "retracting student" reportedly contacted them. It is not clear why this person, who has never identified himself or herself publicly, would be considered a "retractor" since, by the person's own description, the family never participated in any charges or lawsuits. It is unclear, in other words, that there were any charges to retract. But this person apparently recalled being subject to hypnosis in an effort to uncover memories of abuse at the school. The FMSF also advanced the argument that there were "suggestive interviews," purporting to quote numerous snippets from an interview that is never footnoted.[227] But none of these claims deal directly with the children who had withdrawn from the preschool *before* any charges were made public, or with the fact that specific items described in the original search affidavit were found in a search of Toward's house, a place he said the children had never visited.

Toward made no effort to challenge his guilty plea, so the facts of the case were not subjected to any post-conviction judicial scrutiny. Instead, he offered his own version of the facts, without the danger of cross-examination. Toward later claimed he did not even know he had pleaded guilty to child sexual abuse. But the actual transcript of that proceeding proves otherwise.[228] Toward declined all interview requests from journalists over the years, making an exception for a writer who befriended his wife and who recently wrote sympathetically about his allegedly false conviction.[229]

When Toward's prison sentence ended in 1999, the state petitioned to hold him under involuntary civil commitment. The petition included psychological evaluations by Alan J. Waldman, M.D., and Ada Rameriz-Brouwer, Ph.D., both of whom concluded Toward was a pedophile who was likely to reoffend.[230] There were extended legal proceedings and appeals, first over whether this petition violated the original plea agreement, and then over various aspects of the civil commitment law in Florida known as the Jimmy Ryce Act, which itself changed over time. Toward was released in 2010, at age eighty, with strict conditions, including immediate deportation to England and an order, which cannot possibly be enforced, for sex offender counseling.

SCHILDMEYER

Location	Edgewood, IA
Institution	Sunshine Preschool
Date	1989
Lead Def.	Michael Joseph Schildmeyer

This is another case included on the dedication page of *Satan's Silence* without providing any details or referencing any source material, so it impossible to know why Nathan concluded this was a false conviction. The case had not appeared on any other lists of alleged false convictions when *Satan's Silence* was published. It did appear, however, on a list of "ritual child abuse" convictions prepared by Believe the Children and available online.[231] The only source about this case on that site was a single newspaper article.[232] Presumably, Nathan included the case because Believe the Children listed it as a true conviction for ritual child abuse.

Neither Nathan nor Believe the Children is right about this case. Nathan is wrong in claiming it was a false conviction; Believe the Children is wrong is claiming it was a ritual-abuse conviction. The case began in April 1989, when a four-year-old boy in Edgewood, Iowa told his parents about a man named Mike at the Sunshine Preschool and Day Care Center who made him do things he did not like and made him promise not to tell anyone. The center was an unlicensed home day-care center operated by Kim Schildmeyer, who opened the business in 1988, the same year she married Michael Schildmeyer. On the basis of the statements from the four-year-old boy, Michael Schildmeyer was arrested on April 4, 1989, on a single charge of second-degree sexual assault. He was tried and convicted by a jury in July; the primary witness was the four-year-old boy.

But the state's case also included testimony from Janet Fitzpatrick, an employee at the center who testified that on five to ten occasions she had seen him take the four-year-old into the bathroom and shut the door; sometimes when they re-emerged, she said, it appeared the boy had been crying.[233]

Schildmeyer denied the charges and testified that the boy "could have become confused over incidents in which Schildmeyer helped the victim with a zipper after he urinated."[234] In point of fact, there is no evidence that the boy would have required that kind of assistance; moreover, the boy's testimony specifically included Schildmeyer sucking his penis, which the boy called his "nubbin."[235] According to an Iowa assistant attorney general who reviewed the evidence in the case, the initial statements "were entirely unsolicited and spontaneous and remained substantially consistent through trial."[236] The Iowa Court of Appeals agreed, noting it was impressed with the boy's "consistency, recall, endurance under pressure."[237] There were no allegations of ritualistic abuse in this case.

What began as a straightforward case with one allegation, however, later "exploded from one case into many others," according to Delaware County Attorney Jim Nussle, who requested the assistance of the Iowa Division of Criminal Investigation. According to the *Des Moines Register*, children "reported drugging, animal slayings, and illicit photos" taken at the center.[238] The "explosion" apparently originated in the investigation by the Iowa Department of Human Services, which continued to investigate the case after Schildmeyer was arrested and charged in connection with the four-year-old boy. As later described by the Iowa Department of Justice:

> This investigation took the form of videotaped interviews with approximately forty-five children. Many of the children were interviewed on two or three occasions during this process, with the majority of the DHS interviews taking place during the months of May and June 1989.[239]

The videotapes were never used in any administrative and judicial proceedings, so it is not possible to assess the specific content of the children's statements or the nature of the questions. The Iowa Department of Justice, which reviewed all of this evidence and much more, concluded:

> While several of the children have reported further abusive incidents, it is difficult to determine in our opinion if these reports are the result of actual abuse or if they result from suggestions, references and questions raised with the children or in their presence during the past year and a half since the original disclosure.[240]

This aspect of the investigation demonstrated how difficult it is to interview a significant number of young children. Having conducted the kind of careful evaluation of the evidence that was lacking in the early stages of the McMartin case, the decision was made that additional charges could not be proven. The children's statements, beyond the original four-year-old, were not sufficiently credible and consistent. In other words, this case seems to demonstrate a careful and sound response to what was apparently a problematic DHS investigation. A similar approach in the McMartin case might have resulted in a conviction based on a few of the September responders and no further action.

The Schildmeyer case is complicated. It involved the original charge and an extensive investigation afterward. The original charge had no satanic or ritualistic overtones, and the evidence of guilt was strong enough that it is absurd to classify the case as a witch-hunt. The investigation that followed the charges is much more problematic and difficult to evaluate. It clearly involved fantastic statements, but these statements were not taken at face value. To the contrary, they were apparently seen as lacking in credibility, so it does not make sense to call even this part of the case a witch-hunt.

FIGURED & HILL

Location	Smithville, NC
Institution	Miss Polly's Day Care
Date	1989
Lead Def.	Patrick Figured & Sonja Hill

Patrick Figured and Sonja Hill's names are also contained in the list at the front of *Satan's Silence* of those supposedly wrongfully incarcerated for ritual abuse, but they are never mentioned in the book. There is no indication Nathan did any original reporting on this case. The case was, however, featured earlier by Jonathan Harris, webmaster of the Witch Hunt Information Center, who called the decision upholding their conviction "outrageous."

Sonja Hill's mother ran an unlicensed day care out of her rural home in Smithville, North Carolina. Patrick Figured, who was married to someone else, was intimately involved with Sonja Hill at the time. Figured and Hill were charged in connection with the sexual abuse of three children at the day care in July 1988. Figured agreed to plead guilty to three counts of first-degree sex offense (one for each child) in exchange for a life sentence and an agreement *not* to proceed against Hill. The district attorney, who was leaving office soon, broke this agreement by recharging Hill four months later. As a result, Figured was eventually allowed to withdraw his plea. He was later found guilty by jury. Hill pleaded guilty to lesser charges. One wonders why Jonathan Harris and Debbie Nathan have rallied around Figured or Hill.

The answer appears to stem from the "bizarre" aspects of this case: to wit, all three children testified that Figured abused them with a screwdriver, two of the children described abuse involving dog urine, and one child described abuse with a candle. There was also testimony about a cape and a mask, things that the child, who went into detail, clearly understood as Halloween costumes. (It is clear from his full statements that the child did *not* think Figured was the devil or part of some cult.) Seizing on a brief (and insignificant) passage about "submissive dogs" and urination, Harris dubbed *State v. Figured* the "outrageous appellate decision of the decade."[241]

Harris provided links to the defendant's brief on appeal—apparently the extent of his research into this case—but not to the court's unanimous decision upholding the conviction. He made only selective use of the court's decision, which held that there was such overwhelming evidence of Figured's guilt that any error involved in admitting some psychological testimony was immaterial to the outcome.[242] The court described the extensive evidence of *opportunity* (since Figured purported to offer alibi evidence) and reported there was corroboration of the abuse by medical evidence. Harris described the medical evidence as "no more than medical signs (anal dilation) which are found in about 1/3 of nonabused children."

But this trial took place in 1992. The doctors who examined the children were quite familiar with the McCann study, which compared the genitalia and anuses of abused and non-abused children. Although McCann's study, and others like it, caused professionals to discount the strength of certain findings, the study should not be read, as Harris and others do, to dismiss *any* evidence of anal laxity.[243] What Dr. Sherry L. St. Claire found for one of the two children she examined in this case was recorded in Duke Medical Center notes as "extremely abnormal anal exam." She testified that the boy's "soft tissue area was gone, that his blood vessels were enlarged and that his anal canal was so wide that she could see into his bowels. Dr. St. Claire testified this was one of "the most significant medical exams she has ever seen" in all her years of examining children as part of the Duke Child Protection team.[244] The other boy was seen separately by Dr. Marcia Herman-Giddens, a professor of pediatrics at Duke University. The doctor observed anal muscles that opened so wide as to reveal the anal canal. She testified to seeing "an area of healing trauma inside the anal canal" and ruled out the (slim) possibility of congenital pigmentation when she observed further healing. These injuries were consistent with the use of a screwdriver. They required, according to Dr. Herman-Giddens, "some force object from outside the body." These are not injuries commonly, or even rarely, found in non-abused children.

The defendant had more than ample opportunity to abuse these children, although Harris suggests, without specific support, that there were only "rare occasions" when Figured was in the house. In fact, Pat Figured moved to North Carolina over Memorial Day weekend in 1988. He was unemployed and needed a place to live. He "stayed at the day-care home frequently until he got a job," and thereafter several witnesses testified they saw his distinctive white Corvette there frequently "during the daytime."[245]

This case was not born of an overanxious parent, as is often claimed about day-care abuse cases. Rather, it began with persistent and unexplained symptoms that caused a mother to take her daughter to the pediatrician in July and August 1988, after her daughter complained that her "lulu" (vagina) hurt. The medical evidence was strong, and there is no good reason to think this case was an injustice.

KELLERS

Location	Austin, TX
Institution	Fran's Day Care
Date	1991
Lead Def.	Daniel & Francis Keller

The Kellers were convicted in 1992 of aggravated sexual assault of a young girl who attended their home day-care business, Fran's Day Care, in Travis County, Texas. The Kellers were not charged with fantastic or incredible crimes but were also charged with sexually abusing two boys; those charges were dismissed after the Kellers received forty-eight-year sentences in the first case. There was substantial evidence in the first case that went far beyond the girl's statement, including medical evidence of vaginal injury and a detailed adult confession by a friend of the Kellers who participated in the abuse on at least one occasion. Debbie Nathan does not provide any reason for including the Kellers in the dedication page of her book, but it is apparent that the Keller case became part of the witch-hunt narrative through a single article in *Texas Monthly* entitled "The Innocent and the Damned."[246] Although that article raises questions about claims made by some children months after the case began, it does not impugn the basic evidence on which the Kellers were convicted.

The case began on August 15, 1991, when a mother picked up her three-year-old daughter at the day care and the girl said that she did not like "Danny." Her mother inquired why and the girl reportedly said Danny "had hurt her and pulled down her panties and he poo'd and pee'd on her head."[247] Later that day, the girl cried when she urinated, screaming "it hurts, it hurts." The girl was taken to Brackenridge Hospital, where the emergency physician found medical evidence that was unusually strong for a sexual abuse case. Dr. Michael Mouw testified that he observed "a tear of the posterior fourchette" and "what appeared to be lacerations of the hymen at three and 9:00."[248]

The investigation against Daniel Keller quickly expanded to include other alleged victims and perpetrators. Three other adults were indicted for sexually abusing children at Fran's Day Care: Douglas Perry, a friend of the Kellers, and two other adults. Perry provided a written statement to investigators in July 7, 1992, describing a Friday afternoon in August 1991 when he was present at the Kellers, along with the other adults. Perry described a beer party that resulted in several adults sexually abusing a girl and a boy who were under the Keller's care. According to Perry, "Fran had a pen and was sticking it in and out of the little girl's vagina."[249] This account was entirely consistent with the fresh injuries on the girl who was taken to the emergency room after screaming in pain when she went to the bathroom that evening. Perry identified the girl when shown a videotape.

The investigation grew to include at least forty-two children who had attended Fran's Day Care. Some number of those children eventually made claims that were bizarre, and from my perspective impossible to believe. Some number of parents came to describe the case in terms of ritual abuse. An article in the local newspaper detailed those claims after the Kellers had been convicted.[250] Five parents spoke to the newspaper; they represented a total of four children and claimed that these children had, among other things, witnessed the murder of a baby, taken airplane rides, and dug up graves. Apparently on the basis of those statements and the fact that the Kellers were convicted, the case was considered by some to be proof of satanic ritual abuse in a day-care setting.[251] But the outlandish claims were not part of the original criminal case against the Kellers, and they apparently involved only a small number of the parents and children who were interviewed in the case.

The trial highlighted some of the difficulties with child witnesses. A five-year-old girl who testified "alternately denied and admitted that anything bad happened to her." The most incriminating statement that she made "was not admissible evidence because the child whispered the statement to her sister" and the court reporter was not able to record it.[252] But there was also the testimony of the emergency room doctor and of the Kellers' friend, Perry, who had recanted his written confession by the time of trial; even Gary Cartwright, who criticized many aspects of the case, called the confession "hard to refute." Perry eventually pleaded guilty to indecency with a child by contact, and charges against the other two adults were dropped because the primary evidence against them was the recanted confession.[253] The Kellers were both convicted by jury. They appealed, raising various objections, including the use of Perry's confession. But they did "not question the sufficiency of the evidence to sustain the convictions."[254] They lost their appeal.

Given the number of adult participants described by Perry, one family later brought a civil action seeking monetary damages for their failure to report the abuse. They alleged that Francis Keller had confided with Perry's wife "with regard to Daniel Keller's abusive habits towards children."[255] There was also Perry's statement about the adults present at the beer-and-sex party that Friday afternoon in August 1991. The civil case went all the way to the Texas Supreme Court, which overruled an appellate decision that would have allowed the plaintiffs a chance to prove their case. The Texas Supreme Court agreed that the plaintiff's children "are within the class of persons whom the child abuse reporting statute was meant to protect, and they suffered the kind of injury that the Legislature intended to prevent." The court also agreed that the situation described constituted a violation of the child-abuse reporting law, but disagreed that the law created a private right of action for civil damages. "It would take a stone heart not to sympathize with the . . . family," the *Austin American-Statesmen* editorialized before concluding there were sound public policy reasons for not allowing this kind of lawsuit.[256]

It would appear that those citing the Keller case as a "wrongful conviction" have not actually read the *Texas Monthly* article. Cartwright does *not* proclaim the Kellers innocent on all counts. Rather, he argues that "parents have convinced themselves that the couple are guilty of much worse" than sexual abuse. Cartwright argues that "what started as a simple accusation—'Danny hurt me'— became an avalanche of charges that overwhelm the senses." His story is a cautionary tale about the escalation of sexual abuse charges. But it is not a wrongful conviction story. Cartwright acknowledges:

> There is certainly evidence that the [name omitted] girl was sexually abused—the medical report, Doug Perry's statement, the child's own allegations, which were unusually lurid and detailed for such a case.[257]

He cautions that "it is important when investigating allegations like those against the Kellers to distinguish between sexual abuse and the far more bizarre satanic ritual abuse."[258] The caution is appropriate for those who would list this case as proof of satanic ritual abuse in day-care centers. But it is also appropriate for those, like Nathan, who include this case on a list of false convictions. The actual conviction in this case was solid and did not involve any claims of satanic ritual abuse. The *Austin Chronicle* wrote a story about the case in March 2009, claiming it was "likely" that the Kellers were innocent. The article claimed that Dr. Mouw "wasn't sure" if he would have come to the same conclusion today as he did in 1991.[259] But his reported explanation—that he knows more now about "normal variants" in hymens than he did then—does not make sense. First, Dr. Mouw testified to more than a "laceration of the hymen at three and 9:00," which is not a "normal variant" of the hymen. Second, he also testified to a "tear of the posterior fourchette." This has nothing to do with the hymen and would still be considered an indication of abuse. The reporter states that Dr. Mouw "was contacted" for the story; there is no indication he had the medical report when responding to their questions. Since his original testimony made it clear that he "didn't have any independent recollection" of the exam and "would have to review the record," there is no reason to think a conversation about the case eighteen years after the fact should be given any weight.

HALSEY

Location	Lanesborough, MA
Institution	Lanesborough Elementary School
Date	1992
Lead Def.	Robert Halsey

Robert Halsey is also listed at the front of *Satan's Silence* as someone wrongly incarcerated, but the case was not discussed in the book or in any of Nathan's other writings. This case name also likely came directly from Jonathan Harris's Witch Hunt Information Center. But Harris cited nothing more than an innocuous article in the *Boston Globe* to support his claim that the case was a witch-hunt.[260] A careful analysis of the trial transcript indicates there was overwhelming evidence of Halsey's guilt.

Robert Halsey, sixty, was a part-time bus driver in western Massachusetts in 1990, when he was given a route that covered a remote part of Lanesboro, where he was a lifelong resident. The "bus" was actually a GM Suburban van, and the route covered the homes of a handful of kindergartners who arrived at school shortly after noon every day and left after 3:00 p.m. Sometimes, Alex and Wade Watkins, five-year-old twins, were the only passengers in Halsey's van. He drove this route for the entire 1990–91 school year, and part of the following year. In February 1992, Halsey was transferred to a different route, but the circumstances surrounding his transfer were kept quiet for almost a year.

The case began eleven months later, shortly after Alex and Wade Watkins's father handed out cigars in celebration of a new birth in their family. With cigar smoke permeating the house, the twins suddenly began talking about their former bus driver, also an avid cigar smoker; Halsey smoked cigars on the bus, and sometimes he used lit cigars to intimidate the children. The twins described various forms of physical abuse on the bus, including restraints with rope and duct tape, and abuse with a plastic baseball bat. They also described (in the words of a child) being anally raped by Halsey in a wooded area next to a desolate road he often used as a shortcut. Mr. Watkins contacted the police immediately. This all happened over a weekend, and the boys each received a simple forensic interview on Monday morning.

There were no repeat interviews, the boys disclosed significant details after the most open-ended questions, and they were interviewed almost immediately after disclosure. The session lasted forty-five minutes, during which time Alex told a detailed story of physical and sexual abuse. He described, among other things, being taken off the bus, near the pond on Nobody's Road, and sexually abused and humiliated in the woods. Interviewed separately, Wade told a similar story. He said Halsey "put his finger in my butt" many times.

The police arrested Halsey that night at his home. After waiving the right to an attorney, Halsey gave a bizarre statement filled with non sequiturs, sexual innuendo, and lies.[261] Halsey was charged with multiple counts of rape, assault, and battery. Parents soon learned that Halsey had been transferred in 1992 after a young girl's parents lodged a complaint about inappropriate "tickling." It turns out Halsey had also been removed from the approved driver list in bordering Mt. Greylock School District.

The main witnesses in the case were the twins. Alex Watkins described a varied pattern of what adults would see as humiliation, intimidation, and physical and sexual abuse. He also described being anally penetrated: "He told me that he was sticking his finger in my butt."[262] He described going to Halsey's house as well on occasion and being forced to sit in a box of smelly kitty litter while Halsey played pornographic videotapes. Wade, his brother, described, among other things, Halsey putting candy "down his pants" and masturbating in front of them on the bus. The third child to testify, Lucy Cohen, had moved to Florida with her family *before* Halsey's sudden reassignment in February 1992. Interviewed by police in Florida, where the family had not maintained contact with anyone near Pittsfield, Lucy quickly corroborated several aspects of the twins' story, including how Halsey would take children off the bus one at a time, near a pond.

The children's testimony was corroborated by physical evidence. For example, the twins described being chased by a grocery cart in the area off Nobody's Road in 1990–91. One of the two men who live on that road testified he found a cart in the same location in 1991. He also found pornography in the area, but this testimony was prohibited because the children did not mention pornography in the woods—just at his house. The twins further described an impressive constellation of items later found in Halsey's home: guns, knives, duct tape, and rope. Though those items might seem commonplace, the descriptions in some cases were quite specific. A small black pocketknife and a swordlike dagger with a hand on the handle, for example, were among the items that matched the descriptions provided by the boys. The twins also provided an accurate description of Halsey's house—a place Halsey claims they had never been to. They gave accurate descriptions of the *inside* of the house.

The medical evidence that the twins had been sexually abused was beyond dispute. A pediatric specialist testified that both boys had multiple lacerations inside the anus. In both cases, the lesions were in a pattern considered by the American Academy of Pediatrics to be "diagnostic of penetration by a foreign object into the anus." All the defense could do was suggest that the boys might have been raped by someone else—but these insinuations were not supported by actual evidence. The boys' pediatrician testified to having made additional physical findings that were "supportive," but not diagnostic, of sexual abuse. Once, their mother was so worried about both twins having an itchy and irritated anus that she discussed the matter with the pediatrician. The doctor told her it was either pinworms or sexual abuse. The mother considered the possibility of sexual abuse and eliminated it because she could not imagine it happening either at school or at home, let alone "en route." As a result, the boys took medicine for pinworms.

Halsey was convicted, sentenced to two consecutive life terms, and lost all subsequent appeals. But none of these facts have kept Halsey's name out of the witch-hunt narrative. He has been "sponsored" by the advocacy organization that embodies the narrative.[263] They have apparently relied on an account written by the same freelance writer who wrote about James Watt, without mentioning that six children in the case contracted venereal disease. Her account of Halsey's case is equally flawed, leaving out virtually all of the evidence of guilt.

SMITH & ALLEN

Location	Lorain, OH
Institution	Head Start Program
Date	1993
Lead Def.	Nancy Smith & Joseph Allen

Nancy Smith's name is also on the dedication page of Nathan and Snedeker's book, but her case is not discussed. Her co-defendant, Joseph Allen, is not listed on the dedication page, but the National Center for Reason and Justice, an organization with which both Nathan and Snedeker are affiliated, has championed his case as a false conviction. Smith was a bus driver for the Head Start Program in Lorain, Ohio; the case began when a child told her parents in May 1993 that Smith had taken children to Allen's house, where they were bound, molested, and raped by the two adults. Smith and Allen were convicted by a jury, and their convictions were upheld on appeal in 1996.[264]

Smith has always maintained she did not even know Allen. This was her primary defense at trial, along with an attack on the credibility of the child witnesses. Allen's main argument on appeal was that it was unduly prejudicial to allow a witness to testify about how Allen raped her in 1985. (Allen pleaded guilty to those charges.) The case is complicated and merits more detailed attention than space allows here, but it is worth mentioning because of various strange statements made by some children. Before Allen was identified, several children described him as a "black man with spots," and others said he was a "white man painted black." These statements, which appear inconsistent and unlikely at first glance, were borne out when Allen was identified and apprehended. He is a black man with skin pigmentation problems; his face, legs, shoulders, hands, ankles, knees, buttocks, and penis all appear to be covered with white spots.

Furthermore, before Allen was apprehended, several children said he had dressed up like a woman in a pink dress and that he sometimes wore a strange mask; these are both the kind of details that Charlier and Downing labeled as "fantastic." Several children also described a "book" with pictures of a man shot in the head by a gun. During a voluntary search of Allen's house the police later found a *High Society* magazine with a picture of a man shot in the head, but they did not locate a mask or a dress. However, a second, more thorough search, executed with a search warrant, located a pink dress (size sixteen) and a mask with a snake on it.[265] One of the children was shown the mask by the police and asked if it was the one Allen had worn. The child said yes but that the eyes on top of the snake lit up and were pink. The police had removed the pink eyes, which were battery operated.

Although Smith maintains she did not even know Allen, there has been no other explanation advanced for how the children from her bus would have ended up at Allen's house. More importantly, three separate adults testified they had seen Smith and Allen together in different settings, including on the bus. The child suggestibility arguments that have dominated the witch-hunt narrative about this case cannot account for why children would be able to describe Allen's unusual physical features or the unusual items, later recovered from his house, before the police ever identified him.

Smith and Allen's convictions were set aside in an unusual proceeding in 2009 that was supposed to involve resentencing.[266] The state appealed the outcome, and their convictions were reinstated by the Court of Appeals. This outcome was upheld by the Ohio Supreme Court.[267] Smith, who had been free since the 2009 ruling, was resentenced in June 2013 in a deal that gave her credit for time served and assured she would not be sent back to prison.[268] Two months later, the Ohio Parole Board voted 9-2 against clemency in the form of a pardon.[269] Allen was resentenced to 10 to 25 years (with credit for time served) on October 1, 2013 in a deal that includes giving up any further appeals and resigtering as a sex offender for ten years after he is released from prison.[270]

Conclusion

The claims of a national witch-hunt are much stronger than the evidence that has been offered in support. There are no national data; instead, there are scores of comparisons to McMartin and various lists of people who were allegedly falsely accused or convicted. But the comparisons do not stand up to close analysis. There were clearly some poorly investigated and poorly charged cases, but fewer and far between what the witch-hunt narrative claims. There is no evidence of one hundred cases or, as some have claimed, hundreds or even thousands of such cases.

4

History Ignored

Silence, Denial, and Minimization

The witch-hunt narrative drowned out all accounts of social and legal responses to child sexual abuse in America during the McMartin era. There is no sense in the narrative that there were competing social forces concerning child sexual abuse during the period. There is no sense that, at the same time there were problematic prosecutions, real child sexual abuse was being minimized and denied. Indeed, there is little or no acknowledgment of the social forces that prevailed before child sexual abuse became "recognized" in the mid-1980s. Instead, the witch-hunt narrative is presented as if the social forces prevailing before 1984—ones that remain rather mysterious in nature—magically disappeared as soon as there was widespread publicity concerning child sexual abuse. The social forces that explain why child sexual abuse existed for so long without publicity or social recognition are never addressed, except in a condescending fashion. The idea that social forces denied the sexual abuse of children is treated pejoratively, with the word *denial* often placed in quotes, at least concerning any claim that denial still pervades our culture.[1] The idea of "sex-abuse hysteria" is presented as if child sexual abuse went from not being reported to being over-reported. The witch-hunt narrative also conveys the idea that child sexual abuse went from being rarely punished to being all-too-severely punished. And it suggests that the so-called ritual day-care abuse cases began with the McMartin case. There is no recognition that there were proven cases of sexual abuse in day-care centers before the McMartin case, sometimes even including features that were later generally written off as "fantastic."

This chapter considers the extensive evidence from the McMartin era that contradicts the witch-hunt narrative. It surveys the extent to which child sexual abuse was minimized and denied during the same time period in which cases like McMartin unfolded. This chapter argues that even at the height of social concern about—and occasional overreaction to—child sexual abuse, there were also significant social pressures to minimize and deny such abuse. By this account, the contemporary history of child sexual abuse is far more complicated than the witch-hunt narrative allows. Some parents and professionals were too quick to believe the most incredible statements in some cases, but there were parents unwilling to believe solid evidence of sexual abuse in other cases. At the same time people demanded the harshest sentences in some cases, they rallied around admitted pedophiles and pleaded for leniency in other cases. And at the same time the allegations in some cases were criticized for being completely implausible, other cases were proving that factors labeled "bizarre" and "incredible" exist in reality. This is the unacknowledged history of our social and legal responses to child sexual abuse in America.

The Reality of Day Care Abuse

The witch-hunt narrative explains allegations of sexual abuse in day-care centers in the 1980s in terms of moral panic. According to this view, although social anxieties about day-care centers were building, it was not until the McMartin case that people started alleging sexual abuse at day-care centers—and they did so falsely, on the basis of unfounded fears. Under this explanation, the allegations had little or nothing to do with actual abuse. Sociology professor Mary de Young, a leading proponent of this approach, attributes day-care abuse claims to the fears created when "working parents reluctantly began transforming the almost covenantal duty of caring for their young children into businesslike contractual arrangements with day care providers."[2] Likewise, Debbie Nathan casts day-care workers as "symbols, products of a century's worth of American social and political history that has lately culminated in a new body of thought."[3] Recently, Richard Beck cast these concerns about day-care abuse as a contrivance by the political right.[4] None of these authors offer any recognition of the *actual* dangers posed by these "symbols." Labeling cases with words such as *hoax* and *witch-hunt* conveys the impression that all of these cases were entirely without factual basis. But there were real cases involving sexual abuse in day-care centers before and during the McMartin era.

Pre-McMartin

The McMartin case is often written about as if it were the first in which there were allegations of sexual abuse in a day-care center. Nathan suggests this view by labeling cases after McMartin as "junior McMartins." She also wrote an article entitled "What McMartin Started."[5] The idea that McMartin was the first such case is critical to the theory that fears about sexual abuse in day-care centers were *exclusively* a function of social anxieties and not based on any real danger. Beginning the discussion of day-care abuse with McMartin makes it much easier to discredit almost any other case that came afterward. The rhetorical device is so powerful that Charlier and Downing misstated the chronology of the cases in their series in an apparent effort to make McMartin appear to be first.[6] Recognizing various cases that arose before McMartin complicates matters significantly; it would then be necessary to acknowledge that, whatever our fears, some day-care abuse cases were based in reality. Recognizing that fact would make it difficult to write off similar claims as "fantastic" without a careful analysis of the factual basis for every claim. And it would be clear that children might be abused over a period of time yet not disclose the abuse, even in an institutional setting.

It turns out that the McMartin case was not the first in which widespread sexual or physical abuse was alleged in a day-care center. There were earlier cases with overwhelming evidence, cases that it would be nearly impossible to miss by doing even basic newspaper research. One of the most significant began just a few months before the first complaint in the McMartin case. Stephen Boatwright was arrested in Reno, Nevada, and charged with child molestation at the Papoose Palace Academy in late April 1983. Boatwright, who later pleaded guilty, lured as many as seventy children, over several years, into a basement storage area he called "the fort."[7] Beyond proving that claims of sexual abuse in day-care centers are not automatically "fantastic," this case also demonstrated that such abuse could occur without being detected quickly or easily. Boatwright fooled parents and the abuse went undetected for several years without any children disclosing it.

Other examples abound, but they tend to have been subject to only minimal local media coverage. Beryl Bishard, for example, the operator of Nanny's Day Care in Radcliff, Kentucky, was convicted of child abuse in 1981 that included tying children with medical gauze and forcing objects into their mouths.[8] David H. Perry, operator of two nursery schools in Gloucester County, Maryland, pleaded guilty to sodomy and sexual assault of children under his care between 1979 and 1981.[9] Raymond Kuemin pleaded guilty to criminal sexual conduct against three children at the state-licensed day care run by his wife in Niles, Michigan.[10] George and Betty Warnock, who ran an unlicensed day-care center in Polk County, Iowa, were convicted in 1982 of child abuse that included the use of handcuffs and locking children in small wooden boxes.[11] Those who view day-care abuse entirely through the lens of sociological theory would later label allegations of this nature as "fantastic" and "highly improbable."

The Papoose Palace case in Nevada was not the first verified case of *sexual* abuse in a day-care center. David Perry, the operator of two nursery schools in Gloucester County, New Jersey, pleaded guilty to sexual assault charges in November 1983. Some of the thirty-six counts, which spanned more than two years, involved assaults in the basement of a church.[12] ("Activities in basement" was one of Charlier and Downing's "fantastic" elements.) Thomas Max Hetherington was charged with seventy-four counts of child molestation involving girls aged two to eleven. The abuse took place over a three-year period at his wife's day-care center in Ramona, California; Hetherington pleaded guilty in 1982.[13] A similar case in New Mexico demonstrated how poorly equipped government was to deal with allegations of sexual abuse in day-care centers in the early 1980s. In March 1982, Thomas McKeg was charged with thirty-seven counts of sexual abuse involving children ages three to five. He pleaded guilty or no contest to nine of the charges. The case attracted the attention of the New Mexico legislature and the attorney general's office because the first complaint about McKeg was made in August 1981, yet the center remained open for almost a full year, leading to numerous molestations that could have been prevented.[14] These cases not only demonstrate that children were being sexually abused in day-care centers before the McMartin case but also highlight the inadequate response that often followed disclosures of abuse.

These early cases also show the relative ease with which child abusers operated for years, even after detection. Eleanor Nathan—who was ultimately convicted of murdering an eleven-month-old boy and abusing dozens of other children in her care—operated for a surprisingly long time in California without being apprehended. Although she was under suspicion after the infant's death, it was not until three additional children ended up in the emergency room that the Department of Social Services closed her day-care operation. One of those children lost sight in an eye; another was taken to the emergency room with symptoms diagnosed as strangulation.[15] This was not Eleanor Nathan's first encounter with the law. Her day-care operation, in San Mateo, California, was investigated in the early 1970s when five separate complaints were filed in connection with a series of injuries to children in her care. An infant died in her care at that facility, but no charges were filed and the complaints were not pursued, apparently because Nathan had moved out of town. Another complaint was filed against her shortly after she opened her day-care center in Concord, California, in 1977. Apparently no action was taken on that complaint either. It was not until another child, the eleven-month-old boy, was dead and three more were injured that Eleanor Nathan was apprehended.

The pre-McMartin cases demonstrate a lot about the social and psychological forces that worked against disclosure and "recognition" of day-care abuse. They also stand as evidence against the claim that anyone charged with sexual abuse in a day-care center after the McMartin case began was probably the victim of a "junior McMartin." These varied cases illustrate that abuse in day-care centers was a proven phenomenon before McMartin began, so instead of dismissing such claims out of hand, it is necessary to judge allegations of day-care abuse with careful attention to the facts. Most important, these cases counter the claim that allegations of sexual abuse in day-care centers are, by their nature, so implausible as to be incredible.

During McMartin

Whereas the witch-hunt narrative never denies the existence of child sexual abuse in general, it never really acknowledges sexual abuse in the day-care setting. None of the major writings in the narrative contain explicit acknowledgment of *any* verified case of sexual abuse in a day-care setting during the era of McMartin. Nathan and Snedeker bury their acknowledgment of the Papoose Palace case in Nevada in a footnote that avoids identifying the case by name.[16] Debbie Nathan told an interviewer that the Bernard Baran case in 1985 was "the first daycare conviction we could find," ignoring the Papoose Palace case and others.[17] The internet-based Witch Hunt Information Center used the same label to describe the Baran case.

There was a major national study of abuse allegations in day-care centers that covered 1983–1985. The study, conducted by David Finkelhor and Linda Meyer Williams under the auspices of the Family Research Laboratory at the University of New Hampshire, focused on cases "substantiated" by state child protective service agencies.[18] The researchers, who identified 270 such cases, surveyed day-care licensing offices and child protective service offices in all fifty states, but some states did not respond and others did not have centralized data.[19] By extrapolating from the states with the most complete information, they estimated there were 500 to 550 cases in the three-year period. The study excluded small-scale operations (fewer than six children). These numbers put the Charlier and Downing series into context. Their list of thirty-six cases, analyzed in Chapter Three, involved approximately twenty-four cases in day-care settings; and Charlier and Downing covered a four-year time period, not three years as this study did. The study of 270 cases (from a likely universe of more than five hundred) demonstrates that the cases identified by Charlier and Downing were the statistical exception, not the rule. The witch-hunt narrative focuses on approximately one dozen cases from the middle to late 1980s; this national study suggests there were at least twenty times as many day-care abuse sexual abuse cases in just three of those years. The official data the authors obtained allowed a comparison of substantiated cases versus total allegations in seven states. The substantiation rate for sexual abuse allegations in day-care centers during the time period was 21 percent. In other words, there was one substantiated case for every five reports. This finding contradicts the claim by proponents of the witch-hunt narrative that investigators are prone to "find" abuse wherever they look. These aggregate numbers demonstrate that investigators were more than willing to conclude that allegations were apparently unfounded. Of course, some of the reports that were screened out might have been factually true. It would be impossible to ascertain this without research into files that are confidential and unlikely to still exist. The point is, these data do not bear out a story of overzealous investigators who always "find" sexual abuse, whether or not it exists.

Few of the 270 substantiated cases generated headlines or resulted in any of the indicia of "moral panic" or "hysteria." Half of the substantiated day-care abuse cases in their three-year study resulted in no publicity at all, and often with just a license revocation but no criminal prosecution. These findings challenge the witch-hunt narrative, which describes the social climate exclusively as one of overreaction. The study identified thirty-two substantiated cases of day-care abuse with multiple perpetrators. Those are the kinds of cases Charlier and Downing said they were addressing in their series. But in exactly half of the cases in the national study—which were all "substantiated" by child protective services—the investigation ended without any criminal charges. Those cases also contradict the assertion that overzealous prosecutors were anxious to bring such cases regardless of the evidence. The witch-hunt narrative offers no theory to explain these contrary results, since it never predicts lack of publicity or a decision not to prosecute cases that meet the standard for substantiation.

The Finkelhor and Williams study also demonstrated that there were verified cases in which one or more of the following were involved: (1) female perpetrators, (2) abuse that went undetected over a long period of time, and (3) allegations considered "far-fetched" or implausible by proponents of the witch-hunt narrative that were proven to be true. This study has been criticized most for its conclusions about "ritual" abuse claims. What the authors actually said about the subject has been exaggerated and distorted for the apparent purpose of branding them as gullible and dismissing the entire study as worthless. It is important to remember, then, what the authors actually said immediately after observing that "some ritualistic element was noted by investigators" in thirty-six substantiated cases. They added that "what was happening in those cases is not usually very clear" and then proceeded to offer a typology of three kinds of ritualistic abuse. The first category fit the idea—held by some at the time, but clearly discredited since—that "large-scale organizations or cults" had infiltrated day-care centers. The authors did *not* endorse this idea but instead reported it as a position that "some investigators believe." The other two types of ritual abuse were markedly different: one was called pseudo-ritualistic abuse, and the other, psychopathological ritualism.[20] These two categories provide a much more realistic notion of what has been lumped together under the label of "ritual abuse." Those seeking to dismiss the report summarily ignore these distinctions and their implications.

Finkelhor and Williams's study used pseudonyms for all of the cases except McMartin and Country Walk. The study has been severely criticized for counting the McMartin case as substantiated, since the witch-hunt narrative is built on the idea that there was absolutely no evidence of abuse in the case.[21] Chapter Two demonstrates why the narrative is wrong about this. But Finkelhor and Williams can be faulted for counting the case as having more than three hundred victims. In their defense, the study was based on how cases were classified by public authorities. Nevertheless, it was well known when the book was published in 1988 that (1) the McMartin case was hotly contested, (2) most of the original defendants had been dropped, and (3) the case was an extreme outlier in their data.

A brief survey of cases identified through press accounts and legal records during this era further demonstrates the reality of day-care abuse in the McMartin era. Here are a few examples of identified cases that are never acknowledged in the witch-hunt narrative but are useful in understanding the phenomenon.

Seering Family Day Care (Contra Costa County, California, 1984)

Flora and William Seering's day care license was revoked by the California Department of Social Services "primarily upon allegations that [William] had sexually abused a four-and-one-half-year old girl." The girl testified, and "although there were some inconsistencies in her testimony, the girl said that Bill had hurt her between her legs with a needle, had tied her up, and touched her."[22] Dr. David A. Kerns, medical director of ambulatory services at Children's Hospital in Oakland, testified to a "sharp angular defect of the hymen" that "speaks for some sort of sharp object having done it." The Seering's objections on appeal concerned the use of closed-circuit television and the admission of expert testimony that relied on child abuse accomodation syndrome. The medical evidence was not contested and has not since been discredited. The pressing question is why there was no criminal prosecution. The answer likely speaks to the difficulties in relying on the statements of such a young child even when there is strong medical evidence.

Fairmont Baptist Church (San Diego, 1984)

Bus driver Vasco W. Walter, Jr., "confessed to substantial acts of molestation, including fondling and oral copulation" over the period June 1984 through December 1984.[23] The idea that a bus driver might commit such acts of sexual abuse is precisely the fact pattern that retired English professor Frederick Crews labeled as "far-fetched" in the *New York Review of Books,* after an essay promoting the witch-hunt narrative.[24] This case, like the Halsey case, involved not only the sex crimes but the culpability of those who supervised him. Even "after receiving numerous warning signs" regarding Walter's unfitness to supervise children, church leadership placed him in charge of religious training for children at the church.[25]

Pearl Lee Mitchell licensed day care (St. Petersburg, Florida, 1985)

The seventy-seven-year-old husband of the day-care operator was arrested for sexual abuse of girls aged two to four. Court records indicate that his wife "had caught her husband in several sex acts with young girls over the past years." Richard J. Mitchell entered pleas of no contest.[26] This is the kind of crime that might seem unbelievable both for the age of the perpetrator and the age of the victims. But there is no doubt that it occurred.

Bo Peep Day Nursery (Harford County, Maryland, 1988)

This case involved allegations of physical and sexual abuse at the Bo Peep Day Nursery. The charges originally involved four girls; they expanded to include five or six other children who attended the facility. A complaint in July 1987 resulted in a four-day hearing before the Harford County Health Office, followed by a seven-day hearing before the Department of Health and Mental Hygiene. The hearings included a considerable amount of hearsay evidence. The mother of a five-year-old girl testified her daughter said, "Mom, will you lick my butt" and something about sucking her mother's finger "until the stuff comes out."[27] The mother of another girl testified that her daughter described how an employee would pinch her "twinkie" (her term for vagina) and "put a black stick in her" during naptime.[28] This girl was seen by her pediatrician about a painful urination problem before the allegations became public. The owners of the facility objected to the use of hearsay evidence. They also presented a psychologist who considered some of the children's statements inconsistent or so implausible as to be flawed. For example, a girl who said she had been hurt in the vagina insisted that blood had come from her knee. The hearing officer discounted the psychologist's arguments because they did not take into account the developmental level of each child. The statement about blood "could quite possibly result from having blood drip on her knee"; a child this age "would quite naturally believe she was bleeding from the knee," he opined.[29] Two pediatricians were part of an interdisciplinary team that evaluated nineteen children who attended Bo Peep in the summer of 1987. One was Dr. Charles Shubin, who had examined between two thousand and three thousand children for evidence of sexual abuse. The doctors concluded that eight of the children (seven of them female) exhibited physical findings consistent with sexual abuse; this included "vaginal scars and tears and anal gaping and scarring."[30]

The hearing officer concluded that several children with no other connection to each other gave "remarkably consistent" stories, and that a preponderance of the evidence supported the revocation of the license. Defense lawyers called it a "witch hunt."[31] The administrative licensing decision was overturned in Circuit Court on issues having to do with the use of hearsay evidence; that decision was overturned by the Maryland Court of Appeals.[32] There was a criminal investigation, but no charges were filed. It is not clear whether this is because parents were unwilling to allow their children to testify, or the children were not considered likely to be considered competent. There were civil suits settled out of court. The case is notable for the care taken by the hearing officer to consider the developmental stages of the children and not to simply judge their testimony as if it had been provided by an adult. The case also highlights the significance of hearsay evidence in child sexual abuse cases. Several of the children made explicit statements that would cause any parent deep concern. Although the rights of defendants might well keep those statements out of criminal court, their potential relevance seems clear in this case.

Bethel Baptist Church (Fruitport, Michigan, 1989)

Two juveniles were accused of molesting approximately fifty young children in the church nursery center between 1985 and 1988. This is precisely the kind of abuse the witch-hunt narrative would claim is unlikely to have occurred over such a long period of time without someone detecting it or disclosing it. But that is what happened. The case is verified through the confession of the perpetrators. One of them revealed details during court-ordered therapy at a residential treatment facility; the other later pleaded guilty to criminal charges.[33]

These examples contradict the witch-hunt narrative in various ways. They are most important for illustrating the difficulties in detecting and prosecuting this kind of abuse—even in the years when the witch-hunt narrative claimed sex-abuse hysteria was sweeping the country.

The Reality of "Fantastic" Elements

Writers who promote the witch-hunt narrative often employ the word *fantastic* to describe various allegations. Charlier and Downing's series is best remembered by the "fantastic elements" they utilized to link cases across the country. Nathan and others also use the device of describing cases as "ritual abuse" and then dismissing them on the grounds that there is no evidence such cases occur. But those arguments have been used to dismiss cases with features that *have* been proven to be true.

"Fantastic" Elements in Real Cases

Skepticism about widespread claims of satanic and ritual abuse became the dominant position in the 1990s—and for good reason. The idea that a network of organized pedophiles infiltrated day-care centers in the 1980s deserves to be dismissed. As Kenneth Lanning wrote in the FBI's *Investigator's Guide to Allegations of "Ritual" Child Abuse*, "some professionals, in their zeal to make American society more aware of [the sexual victimization of children], tend to exaggerate the problem."[34] Lanning concluded, after years of reports of widespread satanic ritual abuse, that no evidence "of a well-organized satanic cult" had been found in any of the cases. This report was followed two years later by a study funded by the National Center on Child Abuse and Neglect (NCCAN). Described in the press as "the first empirical study of [the] actual prevalence" of ritual abuse, its findings were hailed as evidence that "organized satanic cults don't exist."[35]

But these two reports were careful to distinguish between conspiratorial claims involving *networks* of perpetrators that had infiltrated day-care centers and claims of individual cases involving satanic or ritualistic *elements*. The NCCAN study made it clear that it found "convincing evidence of lone perpetrators or couples who say they are involved with Satan or use the claim to intimidate victims."[36] The primary author of the report described an intergenerational ritualistic case, including black robes and candles, with medical evidence of chlamydia, a sexually transmitted disease, in five children's throats.[37] So, too, an investigation in Utah uncovered a case in which three adult woman recalled satanic sexual abuse as children involving "robed ceremonies, alters, [sic] candles, animal sacrifices and extreme physical and sexual abuse."[38] The attorney general's office interviewed the suspects and reported that "both the mother and father admitted to serious sexual and physical crimes against the children and named several other individuals who were involved."[39] The statute of limitations prevented prosecution. Those cases did not involve "organized cults" but nevertheless stand for the proposition that children *have been* sexually abused in ritualistic or satanic ways, and therefore claims involving such elements should not automatically be written off as "fantastic" and unrelated to reality.

The FBI *Investigator's Guide* distinguishes between claims that were physically impossible or had never been proven (e.g., cannibalism and the sacrificing of babies) and the ritualistic claims that were "possible and probable" or corroborated (i.e., child pornography, cases involving victim threats and manipulation).[40] This guide also contains an entire section on "Alternative Explanations," which explores six reasons for a child possibly claiming something fantastic or ritualistic that is not literally true. What is most important about the analysis has been lost entirely in the witch-hunt narrative: some explanations are consistent with the child having been sexually abused, and others are not. The explanation it described as "most controversial and least popular" is one that suggests there was no abuse: "overzealous intervenors" who misinterpreted, embellished, or otherwise subtly affected the child's statements. Other explanations, however, such as "normal childhood fears," suggest there *was* actual abuse; children "might describe their victimization in terms of evil that they understand." So even though this guide has become best known for its official skepticism of claims of ritual abuse, it actually recognized many activities described as ritual abuse *and* it cautions that there might be plausible explanations for children making such statements in other cases with sexual abuse. There has been research since publication of the guide bearing out the reality of sexual abuse in cases where children make "fantastic" statements.

Those distinctions have been ignored in the witch-hunt narrative. A. S. Ross, who wrote the first investigative journalistic piece challenging the existence of ritual abuse cases,[41] wrote eight years later in *Redbook* that investigators had "not found any physical evidence to support the existence of such cults or their practices." Writing in the online magazine *Salon*, David Futrelle summarized the NCCAN report in 1997 as having "examined over 12,000 accusations of ritual abuse, finding no physical evidence to back up any" of the claims. In fact, the executive summary of the NCCAN report that he purports to summarize contradicts this extreme claim. More stridently, Howard Fishman argued that all claims of satanic ritual abuse are "a delusion suffered and/or fostered by rabid, drooling fanatics."[42] But there are actually two kinds of fanatics in this debate: the ones who still cling to allegations of cult conspiracies and the sacrificing of babies, and those who deny all claims of ritualistic sexual abuse.

Many of the elements Charlier and Downing called fantastic have been proven to exist in actual cases.[43] To listen to the most virulent of the denials, however, one would think that no adult has ever committed a sex crime with some of the more extreme items on their list, such as devil worship. But there are many proven cases in the public record. For example, Bradley James Key and Michael Paul Dillard were convicted of child endangerment for satanic rituals that injured three young adolescent boys in Pike County, Ohio. The rituals involved candles, incantation, pentagram drawings, and bloodletting. One boy "had hot candle wax dripped in the shape of a cross on his chest, back and genitals."[44] The unacknowledged history of child sexual abuse also includes cultlike cases with multiple perpetrators. In November 1991, a terrified twelve-year-old girl fled to a women's shelter in Johnstown, Pennsylvania, to escape a group of adults she was convinced had supernatural powers. She told stories of being subjected by her "parents and neighbors to ritualistic torture that included bloodletting with a sword, hot needles under their fingernails, sodomy." It is precisely the kind of case that would-be skeptics deny. But the evidence proved to be overwhelming. Rickie Jay Gaddis had physically and sexually abused seven children for at least eighteen months. He used "ceremonial swords" to draw blood to pour on the grave of a daughter killed in a fire three years earlier. A boy had been tattooed in one of these "ceremonies," and the children had been sodomized. The police found everything the girl described, including the swords.

According to Detective Richard Rok, "the thing that still bothers me the most about all of this is that so many people knew about this, yet did nothing."[45] The county child protective service agency had a file on Gaddis "for years" but had taken no action even though a school nurse reported suspicions about the family almost three years earlier. Several of the defendants pleaded guilty. Gaddis was found guilty of more than 150 counts of "horrific sexual, physical, and emotional abuse" ranging from terrorist threats to rape, incest, and involuntary deviant sexual intercourse. Later upholding these convictions, Judge Tamilia noted that one "victim's testimony was corroborated by the testimony of three eyewitnesses."[46] The court rejected the claim that evidence of "terroristic threats" and "instilling fear and menace on the victims" was unfairly prejudicial. To the contrary, the court found it was directly relevant to the charges.

Another case like this emerged in Florida. Eddie Lee Sexton, Sr., also ran his family like a cult, subjecting them to the kinds of rituals that Nathan and others claim is only imaginary. But the horrors were real, including a nine-month-old child who was murdered and buried on Sexton's command at a Florida campground, where the family was fleeing from child-abuse charges in Ohio. Skipper Lee's body was found where Sexton's daughters said it had been buried. The senior Sexton, who told his children he was the devil, inflicted horrendous tortures on his family, including sexual abuse. Two adult sons testified about rituals in which they drank deer's blood and joined hands around a dead cat.[47]

Similarly, a "ritual abuse" case with satanic elements was verified in San Diego, where two defendants were charged in 1986 with threatening and sexually abusing seven boys and girls (ages eleven to fourteen) who lived in the same apartment complex. Robert Wilkins was convicted by a jury of multiple counts of "forcible oral copulation" and "committing a lewd and lascivious act with a child under fourteen by force or duress" and sentenced to forty-six years. His conviction was upheld on appeal.[48] Lori Bartz was charged with the same offenses plus false imprisonment and assault with a deadly weapon. As reported in the *San Diego Union-Tribune*, Bartz "used satanic rituals to frighten and intimidate some of the victims into performing sex acts."[49] She pleaded guilty to nine charges in exchange for the dropping of sixty-two charges and the state's agreement not to seek a sentence longer than fifty years. After being sentenced to forty-eight years, she appealed on the grounds that the sentence was cruel and unusual given her "lack of intelligence and emotional immaturity." The appellate court found although she "'almost' believe[ed] true the fantasy world she created," her sentence was appropriate because the victims were particularly vulnerable, she took advantage of a position of trust, and she engaged in a pattern of violent conduct that indicates a serious danger to society.[50]

In Northern California, there was the case of Daryl Ball, Jr., and Charlotte Mae Thrailkill, with multiple child victims (ages five to eight) and allegations of

threats and other kinds of abuse labeled as "ritualistic." The prosecution described those elements and cited the Finkelhor study specifically to explain that
"these cases are distinguished from the incest model by the extreme terror shown
by the victims."[51] The factual allegations are precisely the kind that Nathan dis-
avows, having criticized Finkelhor for "believing" (as she put it) that ritual abuse
cases actually exist. This case was classified as ritual abuse primarily because the
children were threatened, with several testifying they were tied with rope. The
preliminary hearing, which lasted throughout August 1987, was the longest preliminary hearing in Sonoma County history. Some of the children broke down
and were removed from the case[52]; medical evidence was presented that corroborated the abuse.[53] Both defendants later pleaded guilty to "forcible lewd and
lascivious conduct" involving five children.[54] In 1998, Thrailkill became the first
woman in California to be declared a sexually violent predator after she decided
not to contest the state's petition. She asked to be sent to a state hospital.[55]

There are even verified cases of sexual abuse in the context of organized cult
activities.[56] The existence of these cases does not prove anything about *other*
cases, of course, but it does demonstrate that such things are possible. Since cases
with similar allegations have been uniformly dismissed as fantastic, the existence
of proven cases demonstrates that automatic rejection on such grounds is inappropriate. In sum, there is extremism on both sides of the ritual abuse controversy. On the side that included the organization Believe the Children, seemingly
anything a child said, no matter how implausible, was taken at face value. Prosecutor Kathleen Morris suspected, at least for a time, that there was baby killing in
Jordan, Minnesota, without any reports of missing babies or evidence of their
death. On the other hand, the witch-hunt narrative has adopted the position that
children's statements involving ritualistic elements that have been proven in real
cases are nevertheless so "bizarre" as to discredit the child automatically.

The Child Pornography "Myth"

There has also been minimization and denial of child pornography as an element
in child sexual abuse cases. Charlier and Downing, for example, lump allegations
of child pornography with the most bizarre and far-fetched claims. Philip Jenkins and others have made similar arguments, relying on the dubious work of
Lawrence Stanley, who coined the phrase "child pornography myth" in an article
in *Playboy* magazine.[57] The proof that Stanley offered for this "myth" is the same
handful of day-care cases that have been widely distorted in the witch-hunt narrative: McMartin, Jordan (not actually a day-care case), Amirault, Edenton, and
Country Walk. In all of these cases, there were statements by some children
about having been photographed in the nude—but no photographs were ever
recovered. As a result, the witch-hunt narrative argues that such charges, at least

in connection with day-care or other multiple victim cases, are without any foundation in fact. Debbie Nathan asserts that "there has not been a single case" in which allegations of child pornography were "physically substantiated."[58]

But these arguments overlook a host of cases with precisely the kind of evidence Nathan and Mark Pendergrast deny. Charles Bishop, one of the Kern County defendants, was convicted largely on the basis of the pornographic pictures he took of his victims.[59] Grant Self, whose name appears on the dedication page of Nathan's book, had two prior convictions that included similar photographic evidence.[60] A connection between child pornography and day-care abuse was also established before the McMartin case began through a confirmed case at Isabel's Day Care, not far from Manhattan Beach, California. The case began when a three-year-old girl told her mother in 1981 that "James [the owner of her day-care center] took pictures of my butt today." When the police executed a search warrant, they found thousands of sexually explicit photos and slides of past and present students. Edwin James Meacham, a biochemist with a doctorate from the University of Southern California, did not disavow the pictures; instead, he claimed he was "doing research." Many of the pictures were taken in the bathroom of the day-care center. (Remember that Charlier and Downing included "activities in bathroom" *and* "nude photography" as incredible or fantastic elements of ritual abuse cases.) Meacham was convicted of child pornography in May 1982, and his conviction was upheld in 1984 in an opinion that is readily available through standard legal research.[61] This was not the only case in which there were proven allegations of child pornography in a day-care context. In January 1984, still a month before the McMartin case hit the news, Robert McMormick, a forty-three-year-old teacher at the ABC Scholar Day Care Center, pleaded guilty to "sexually abusing and/or taking the nude photographs" of preschoolers in Prince George's County, Virginia.[62]

Another relevant case consistently overlooked by those purveying the "child pornography myth" involved the Rainbow Day Care Center in Fort Lauderdale, Florida. John W. "Jack" Shaver, owner of the center, was arrested in 1990 after he retrieved pictures of naked children from a photo lab. When police searched his home, they found thousands of pictures and negatives of naked children, along with pornographic magazines depicting children engaging in sexual acts; twenty parents picked out their children in Shaver's enormous collection of nude photos.[63] Shaver's case demonstrates how such predators are able to elude punishment, even when their behavior raised suspicions and resulted in multiple allegations over the years. Shaver escaped no fewer than *four* times in the years before he was apprehended at the Rainbow Day Care Center. Before moving to Florida, he lived in Hawaii, where he volunteered at a day-care center in 1979. He was asked to leave that position because the director was "uncomfortable" with how he handled the children. He then opened the Kailua Beach Preschool.

In 1983, he lost his license for that facility after Honolulu police received complaints that Shaver was "washing off [young girls] by rubbing, tickling and running his hands up [their genitalia]." (Again, the "activity" was in the bathroom—something Charlier and Downing would label "fantastic.") Shaver pleaded guilty to a misdemeanor and paid a $200 fine.

Two years later he bought a day-care center near Fort Lauderdale. The criminal background check revealed nothing because he had never been convicted of a felony. In 1986 and 1987, during the height of the "panic" about day-care sexual abuse, two unrelated parents complained to child protective services that Shaver had touched their children inappropriately. Neither case went forward, though, because the agency concluded the evidence was insufficient. When Shaver was finally apprehended in 1990, his defense attorney argued, audaciously, that Shaver was the victim of a "panic."[64] This argument rings hollow in light of his previous history; but it also defies reality given the outcome of his case. A circuit judge dropped twenty-eight of the twenty-nine charges of possessing child pornography pursuant to a state appellate court decision that defendants can be charged with only one count of child pornography no matter how many photographs they possess. (Shaver had more than two thousand pictures in his possession.) At the same time Southern Florida was supposedly in the grips of "hysteria" over child sexual abuse, Jack Shaver received *probation* in exchange for his guilty plea.[65]

A similar case in Massachusetts bears out the connection between day-care abuse and child pornography—and the difficulty in getting people to take it seriously. Robert Shell of Arlington, Massachusetts, was investigated by the Department of Social Services in 1988 for allegedly abusing his own children. The case was not considered strong enough to prosecute, but it was sufficient for DSS to issue a cease-and-desist order when Shell began operating a family day-care center in Arlington. DSS employees warned parents who were entrusting their children to Shell that he posed a serious danger; some parents did not want to hear the warnings. The director of family day-care licensing reported that, despite the "hysteria" supposedly infecting Massachusetts at the time, "we were told by at least one parent that she could do whatever she wanted to do with her kids and that she didn't believe it."[66] Shell, who worked as a custodian at several day-care centers, was arrested in 1990 after an investigation into a series of larcenies at day-care centers in Lexington and Burlington. The police seized photos of naked children between the ages of nine months and three-and-a-half years in the act of being sexually abused. Shell met several of the victims through his work at various day-care centers. He pleaded guilty to thirty-five charges, including indecent assault of two girls under the age of *four*.[67]

The prevalence of child pornography in Southern California at the time of McMartin is illustrated by the fact on the same day the defendants were being arraigned in the McMartin case, there was also a probation violation hearing in Los Angeles County Superior Court for Allan Licht, who had been prosecuted for child pornography in 1981 after authorities seized forty thousand pictures of boys engaging in sexual contact "with men and one another." Licht's probation violation hearing involved charges that he developed photographs of a similar nature for a Vancouver travel agent.[68] Catherine Stubblefield Wilson was also prominent in Southern California at this time. The mother of five, who prosecutors claimed made $500,000 per year by supplying child pornography across the country, had a customer list of thirty thousand people. Wilson distributed films with titles such as "Little But Lewd" and "Kinder Orgy." (A jury deadlocked eleven to one for conviction after the first trial. Prosecutors moved ahead with a retrial, and Wilson ended up pleading guilty to a single count of child pornography.)

One might wonder, in light of these cases, how Lawrence Stanley supported his oft-cited claim of a "child pornography myth." The answer is partly that Stanley was describing how effective law enforcement officials had been in driving "commercially produced magazines such as Lollitots, Baby Love and Nudist Moppets" out of the market. What replaced that market, Carol McGraw documented in the Los Angeles Times in 1985, was "a thriving cottage industry that creates its own pornography and distributes it through an informal but extensive underground."[69] This is what Stanley minimizes. A close reading of his "award-winning" article in Playboy reveals that Stanley's own estimates contradict the idea of a child pornography "myth."[70] After debunking some overstated claims about the size of the child pornography business, Stanley allowed that "a small, essentially insignificant group by some estimates as few as 5,000 people" are involved in child pornography. Stanley does not explain why thousands of child pornographers constitute an "insignificant" number, but his statement nevertheless provides a basis for concluding that thousands of children are victimized in the production of child pornography. It turns out Stanley's interest in child pornography was neither academic nor detached; it was economic and personal. Stanley is a self-proclaimed "girl-lover," who produced a variety of magazines with pedophile themes, sold pictures of young girls at nudist camps, and produced a newsletter called Uncommon Desires—"the voice of a politically-conscious girl-love underground."[71] Stanley does not consider child pornography to be a social harm in the first place. It is no wonder he minimizes the size of the industry. What is surprising is how many others have relied on him as some kind of expert.

This discussion of ritual elements and child pornography is probably the section of this book that is most likely to be misrepresented by proponents of the witch-hunt narrative. The narrative uses a kind of guilt-by-association to discredit cases (and people) by associating them with credulous acceptance of all sorts of "ritual abuse."[72] So I will close this section by reemphasizing that this is *not* an endorsement of any theories about networks of organized groups that infiltrated day-care centers. Rather, it is a plea for those who want to engage this issue with an open mind to pay attention to the FBI report that is misrepresented almost as often as it is cited. Elements that have been labeled as ritualistic *have* occurred in documented cases, and accordingly, children who make statements about such elements should not be dismissed out of hand.

What Hysteria?

The witch-hunt narrative says in no uncertain terms that hysteria about child sexual abuse swept the country in the 1980s. It was supposedly strong enough to create allegations of sexual abuse out of nothing; Professor Stephen Ceci uses the phrase "air of accusation."[73] There are two serious flaws with this claim. First, there is almost no evidence to support it, in exact times and places when this phenomenon was supposedly at work. Second, this account of the 1980s does not recognize the forces of secrecy, silence, and disbelief that produced an air of denial around child sexual abuse during the same era. The reality is that serious sexual abuse allegations were often ignored, sometimes for years, at the time this hysteria was allegedly occurring. The hysteria claim also overlooks the difficulties in prosecuting cases and the remarkably lenient sentences that were commonplace for those convicted of sexually assaulting children.

Places Allegedly in the Grip of Hysteria

Even in specific communities where "sex abuse hysteria" was supposedly the worst, there is little evidence to support the witch-hunt narrative. The unacknowledged history of the communities in which the most infamous cases occurred actually contradicts the narrative. What happened in the McMartin case spread to only a handful of other preschools in Southern California, and it caused significantly less damage than is often claimed. Beyond McMartin, there is no evidence that the Kelly Michaels case caused any kind of outbreak of false accusations in New Jersey. To the contrary, there is a powerful story that disproves the hysteria hypothesis. Similarly, events in Dade County (Florida) and Boston during the middle to late 1980s provide considerable evidence that contradicts the witch-hunt narrative.

Southern California at the Time of McMartin

The McMartin case is the premier example of social hysteria over child sexual abuse. Many accounts claim that "hysteria broke out" when the Manhattan

Beach Police sent the letter of September 8, 1983. But, as demonstrated in Chapter Two, the letter resulted in less than is ever recognized. The preschool remained open throughout the fall, it was many weeks before there was a meeting among parents, and the story did not reach the newspapers or television until five months later.

There *was*, however, a kind of social contagion in the McMartin case once it was the subject of intense media coverage, resulting in some nearby preschools being implicated as well. At the height of the belief that there was a broader conspiracy afoot—something many people, including investigators, believed in 1984 and 1985—several other day-care centers were named in connection with the McMartin case. Prosecutors claimed at one point that children had been "swapped" between the McMartin Preschool and the Manhattan Ranch Preschool.[74] A few other schools were named at various points by parents connected to the McMartin case. But this was nothing like the claims that quickly became part of the witch-hunt narrative. Richard Wexler asserted that the McMartin investigation "spread to sixty-four other daycare centers; seven of them closed."[75] In point of fact, the investigation spread to *seven* other South Bay schools, and three of those preschools never reopened. There is no evidence of the case spreading beyond that.

Seven South Bay preschools are often lumped together in stories about this era, but what happened at the preschools varied significantly, reflecting a complex social reality that is not captured in the witch-hunt narrative. The first case to arise elsewhere in the South Bay began with a mother's call on March 28, 1984, to the Lomita Sheriff's Station to report suspected sexual abuse at the Peninsula Montessori School No. 2 in Rolling Hills. The timing of the call alone, coming at the peak of the most intensive and pro-prosecution coverage of the McMartin case, raises obvious concerns about the possibility that it was caused by overreaction. But what this mother reported would likely lead any good parent to be concerned. She observed her four-year-old daughter "lying on top of her brother and simulating sexual intercourse" and then "kissing her younger brother's penis saying 'Let's make love.'" Her daughter had been attending the preschool since September 1983; her three-year-old son had started attending in December. This behavior is far beyond the bounds of what is recognized as normal sex play in young children. Claudia Krikorian, the owner of the school, did not cooperate with the investigation at first. There was an administrative finding that she impinged on the investigation in two ways: (1) the suspect was tipped off about the investigation, making the subsequent search essentially futile; and (2) she did not supply authorities with a complete list of students attending the school.[76] (Krikorian was never charged with any crimes.)

The primary children in the case were interviewed in a matter of days, not months. The case did not expand beyond the students in the 1983–84 class. The interviewing was done by two seasoned deputy sheriffs, women with a combined twelve years' experience and more than one thousand child abuse investigations. They interviewed nine children, six of whom were medically examined by Dr. Carol Berkowitz at Harbor-UCLA Hospital. The suspect, a teacher's aide who was immediately fired, had started working at the school in September 1983.

The first child was interviewed by Los Angeles County Deputy Sheriff Susan McGirt two days after the initial report. This child identified the teacher's aide as the person who taught her the behavior that startled her mother.[77] McGirt attempted to interview the second child, but the boy was completely nonverbal. His mother reported he said that the same teacher's aide had shown him pictures of people in the nude.[78] The mother of another child reported that her son, who attended the school from September 1983 through February 1984, came home from the school [one day in January] and told her he had seen a 'naughty' or 'dirty' picture at school. At the time the mother assumed that "a teenager passing by the school had shown him the picture."[79] McGirt reported that this child stated the same teacher's aide "showed him and another child a picture of a 'naked lady.'" McGirt also "received information concerning other children" from psychologist Dr. Helena Barry. It included statements by one child about being taken to a house with two swimming pools, where a "black man with a mean face and long hair" was present.[80] Some aspects of the child's testimony strained credulity on their face. Nevertheless, there was medical evidence in the case. Six children were examined for indications of sexual abuse by Dr. Carol Berkowitz and nurse Mary Logan at Harbor-UCLA Hospital. Those medical examinations concluded that four of the children examined had been sexually abused. The findings on one child were described as "severe," labeled as "supportive of chronic sexual misuse including sodomy."[81] There were "no hymenal remnants visible" on this child, a finding that would still be considered significant today.

After considering all of the evidence, an administrative law judge found that the first child "was molested by [the teacher's aide] on the campus of the R.H. School." The judge found that four other children had been sexually abused, although "it was not established that these children were molested by [the teacher's aide]."[82] These conclusions seemed carefully tailored to the quality of the evidence, and of course they were under a standard of proof for a civil action, not the much higher "beyond a reasonable doubt" standard for criminal court. The charges did not spread to other teachers, and the nature of allegations that were accepted was not fantastic or incredible in any way.

The parents of several children brought a civil lawsuit against Krikorian and the school. Krikorian countersued. The teacher's aide refused to answer any questions, citing his constitutional right against self-incrimination. (He was later deported.) After taking depositions from two of the children, the insurance

company settled the case for $1 million, over Krikorian's objections.[83] The supe-
rior court eventually decided Krikorian could get her license back. She expressed
concern that her name would be forever linked to sexual abuse, even though
there was never any evidence she was aware of abuse. Indeed, her position was
that no abuse ever occurred. Nevertheless, it may well be that the failure of justice in this case was in the decision not to prosecute the aide.

The second case related to McMartin involved Michael Ruby and the Manhattan Ranch Preschool. Again, charges focused on a single teacher. This suspect
was ultimately charged and tried; the eleven-week jury trial ended in a hung jury.
The district attorney decided not to retry the case and then dropped all charges.
Deputy District Attorney Lisa Hart said the decision not to retry was not a
matter of "pulling out" but rather was out of "consideration for the children."[84] It
is impossible to evaluate the merits of the case without gaining access to the
daily trial transcripts, which were sealed by Judge Bob T. Hight. It should be
noted, however, that Manhattan Ranch Preschool did not close permanently—
it was sold and remained open during the investigation and subsequent trial—
and the charges against Ruby did not spread.

The third case with links to McMartin involved the St. Cross Church in Hermosa Beach. The day-care center at the church was first implicated in April 1985
by one of the children in the McMartin preliminary hearing. There is no question that claims made about the church in the McMartin case were beyond far-
fetched. One child in the preliminary hearing in the McMartin case testified
about witnessing satanic rituals at the church including black robes and drinking
blood.[85] Nevertheless, there are significant omissions in the witch-hunt account.
First, it should be noted that the St. Cross day-care center was not closed by the
state. (The following year, it was closed voluntarily by the board of directors.)
Second, Faye Fiore reported in the *Daily Breeze* that two men confessed to sexual
abuse occurring at St. Cross Church in the 1980s but their statements were
beyond the six-year statute of limitations in effect at the time of the acts.[86] Apparently, the hysteria that is claimed to have gripped the area during this time did
not prevent those confessed incidents from happening. As nobody was ever
charged and the center was not closed by the state, this case does not provide
much support for the witch-hunt narrative.

The fourth case with links to McMartin was a twenty-two-pupil preschool in
Manhattan Beach called Learning Game. According to newspaper reports, three
of five children who made statements relating to abuse of some sort also indicated something about the McMartin Preschool as well. A memo by the Los
Angeles County Sheriff's Task Force in December 1985 stated that two preschools were being investigated beyond McMartin and Manhattan Ranch: "One,
the Learning Game Preschool, is clearly linked to McMartin. The other, Children's Path Preschool, is not." The Learning Game was closed in December

1984, and it never reopened. No charges were brought against anyone. On the basis of available information, this seems to be strong evidence of overreaction to the McMartin case; the school was closed owing to uncorroborated claims that were never proven.

The fifth preschool mentioned in connection with McMartin—Children's Path, also in Manhattan Beach—was closed for two weeks and then reopened as Creative Kids. There was no hysteria; the sentiment of the parents was all in favor of reopening. Even if the initial revocation was without substantial basis—and there is nothing in available records to support the claim that there was sexual abuse at this preschool—the disruption was minimal, and no one was charged, let alone prosecuted.

The sixth preschool, Children's Path in Hermosa Beach, provides support for the witch-hunt narrative. It was closed temporarily and was going to reopen, having changed one or more staff members. A small group of parents discouraged the owners from reopening, however, through outrageous forms of protest such as "wanted" posters depicting teachers from the preschool. Such actions demonstrate the fever of emotions that ran through the immediate community. However, news reports indicate there was medical evidence of abuse.[87] It does not appear that the state overreacted, but the case is complicated and there is almost no available original documentation to help verify published reports.

The seventh preschool case in the South Bay linked to McMartin provides the strongest evidence in favor of the witch-hunt narrative. It involved Peninsula Montessori School No. 1 in Torrance. The school was also owned and operated by Claudia Krikorian, owner of the Peninsula Montessori School No. 2 in Rolling Hills, where allegations of sexual abuse had been made against a teacher's aide months earlier. A review of the charges involving the Torrance school bears out the claim that the state officials were being overzealous and unreasonable. Krikorian was written up for missing floor tiles in a classroom, for a cement stairway with a crack, and for a toilet bowl that smelled of urine. But the primary charge in overall significance was that an employee of the school had sexually molested four students. No charges were ever brought against him, and Krikorian appealed the temporary order of suspension to an administrative law judge. There was an eleven-day hearing in October 1985. Two months later, the judge upheld the license revocation in a fourteen-page decision that contains no discussion of the factual basis for the sexual abuse claims, even though they were the focus of almost the entire evidentiary hearing. Instead, Judge Richard Lopez simply stated, "it was established by direct evidence" that each child had been sexually abused.[88] Krikorian appealed the decision to superior court, where, eighteen months later, Judge H. Walter Croskey overturned the ruling. His eighteen-page decision said "each of the four girls who testified presented serious credibility problems," and he provided relevant details about each girl's testimony. "The concerns that all serious persons involved in this field have toward possible manipulation of child witnesses," he reasoned, "would be aroused by the facts in this case." The judge concluded that the children's testimony was "totally unconvincing."[89] Although it would require a complete examination of the transcripts of the October 1985 hearing to evaluate this decision independently, the opinion is persuasive and provides enough details to conclude that Montessori No. 1 was the worst local case to occur in the wake of McMartin. Although no criminal charges were brought, a man's reputation was damaged and Claudia Krikorian had to spend a significant amount of money to defend her business.

This was the last of the preschool cases directly linked to McMartin. Indeed, Bob Williams, who wrote a series of articles critical of the McMartin case for the *Los Angeles Times*, reported that "by the end of 1985, the tide of allegations began to recede."[90] The "cloud seems to have lifted," he later quoted a Torrance preschool operator as saying.[91] Real damage was done in the case of several preschools, but the nature and extent of the damage has been exaggerated in the witch-hunt narrative. The reach of the social hysteria beyond the McMartin case was significant, but also highly localized and included at least two cases in which there was credible evidence of abuse.

Criminal charges were brought in three other cases in Southern California that had been mentioned along with the McMartin case in various news stories. There was no claim that the McMartin case was literally related to these cases, but since they were mentioned together in media stories these are cases most likely to exhibit the kind of hysteria attributed to the McMartin case. Henry Lawson was charged with child molestation at the Little Angels Preschool in Lynwood, some fifteen miles from Manhattan Beach. Campbell Greenup was charged with molesting girls, aged five to seven, at his Greenup School in Northridge; and four adults were arrested in Pico Rivera on the basis of some fantastic claims, including satanic ritual abuse, made by neighborhood children. Lawson eventually pleaded guilty after a judge ruled that his confession to police would be admissible. Greenup, who claimed he was the victim of a "political witch-hunt," was convicted by jury of molesting six girls four to eleven years old.[92] Charges against the adults in Pico Rivera were quickly dropped, and they were eventually awarded $9.9 million in damages. Their case is mentioned frequently in the witch-hunt narrative; it is case number six in Charlier and Downing's series. The other two cases are never mentioned.

Beyond the most localized effects, which have themselves been exaggerated, there is no evidence of a wave of unjustified arrests or convictions for child sexual abuse in Southern California at the time of McMartin. To the contrary, the claim that the McMartin case had a major impact across California, or even across Southern California, is not borne out by data from the California

Department of Social Services (DSS). There were 220 complaints statewide in 1985 and 240 in 1986. There were in that period thirty-eight thousand licensed day-care facilities in California.

New Jersey at the Time of Kelly Michaels

The local response to the Kelly Michaels case (the subject of Chapter Five) was much less intense than the local response to the McMartin case; it did not spread to *any* nearby day-care centers. No cases have been held up as examples of day-care centers wrongfully closed or wrongfully accused in the wake of the Kelly Michaels case. Nevertheless, Dorothy Rabinowitz described the "social climate" at the time of the Michaels case as "more virulent than the Asian flu."[93] She did not offer any evidence from New Jersey at the time of the Michaels case to support this claim. The Charlier and Downing list of thirty-six contained two New Jersey cases: one was Michaels, and the other, which preceded the Michaels case, involved a camp counselor. There was no connection between the two cases, however, other than the fact that Ralph Underwager—a controversial psychologist who became a prominent defense expert through the Jordan, Minnesota, cases—testified for the defense in both of them. There is simply no evidence in New Jersey of what Rabinowitz called a "national pathology" at the time of the Michaels case.[94] No similar allegations emerged from any of the thousands of day-care centers covered by the same large media markets that include Maplewood, New Jersey. No explanations have been offered as to why this alleged "social contagion" never expanded beyond this single facility.

In fact, through a coincidence of names, there was something akin to a natural experiment to test the claim that there was a "climate of hysteria" in New Jersey at the time of the Kelly Michaels case. It stems from the coincidental fact that there was a Wee Care Child Care Center in Clifton, New Jersey—less than fifteen miles from the Wee Care Day Nursery where Kelly Michaels worked in Maplewood. (There was also a Wee Care Nursery School in nearby South Orange, run by the same organization that ran the Wee Care in Maplewood.) The fascinating but unnoticed "natural experiment" sheds light on whether strong concern about possible sexual abuse in a day-care center in New Jersey, when the Kelly Michaels case was unfolding, was likely to generate false allegations through anxious questioning by parents. When news of the Kelly Michaels case was first reported by a local newspaper in nearby Clifton in mid-August 1985, Leslie Kropinack, director of the Clifton school, was "besieged" with calls. "Several dozen parents were 'quite upset' after reading about the charges last week," she said.[95] They thought the charges stemmed from the Wee Care Child Care Center in Clifton. Of course, if there really were mass hysteria around Maplewood in the summer of 1985, then allegations of some sort would have been generated against at least one staff member at the day-care center. But that did not happen. Some, perhaps all, of the anxious parents in Clifton undoubtedly asked their children if anything bad had happened to them at school. Some undoubtedly used leading questions and were unwilling to accept an initial denial. But not a single one of those inquiries resulted in a reported accusation, even though this is the most common explanation in the witch-hunt narrative for how these cases begin.

Dade County at the Time of Country Walk

Strong rhetoric has also been used to assert there was public "hysteria" over child sexual abuse in Dade County, Florida, at the time of the Country Walk case (the subject of Chapter Six). Peter Boyer claimed, in his 1998 *Frontline* program called "The Child Terror," that a "fever in Miami" lasted from 1984 through 1991. The unusually long time period—eight years—was apparently selected to link the Bobby Finje case (which ended in an acquittal in 1991) with two cases from 1984 that Boyer cited as the proof of this "fever." The cases from 1984 were Country Walk and a home day-care involving Grant Snowden. Neither the Country Walk case nor the Snowden case has been accurately portrayed in the witch-hunt narrative.[96] But for the purpose of examining the broader claim about sex abuse hysteria, what is most interesting is the lack of *any* additional cases to prove the existence of a trend that allegedly lasted for eight years. Dade County is one of the largest in the United States; there were thousands of day-care centers in Dade at the time of Country Walk and thousands more home babysitting services. Yet, as far as can be ascertained from all major sources in the witch-hunt narrative, not a single one of those centers or babysitting services joined the three cases that Peter Boyer linked together years later.

There were three other day-care sexual abuse cases that received media attention in Miami in 1984. None of these cases provide support for the witch-hunt narrative. Indeed, all of them suggest the existence of social forces that run counter to those embodied in the witch-hunt narrative. The first of the three cases, in chronological order, involved allegations of sexual abuse at the Lehrman Day School, run by Temple Emmanuel in Miami.[97] The case had several notable features: it stayed out of the newspaper until the Country Walk case broke months later. The allegations did not expand or spread beyond the original claims. And most significantly, the case involved unequivocal medical proof of sexual abuse. The two-and-a-half-year-old boy who made the first allegations tested positive for gonorrhea of the throat. But the case turned out to prove the difficulty of prosecuting child sexual abuse cases, particularly with young victims. Even though the child had incontrovertible medical evidence and identified the suspect, there was insufficient evidence to prove a criminal case.[98] The boy was developmentally too young to testify, so the case was dismissed.

There were two other day-care cases involving allegations of abuse in the local news during the time of Country Walk. The first one, which emerged in August 1984, when Country Walk began generating headlines, involved the Turtle Top Day Nursery. The State Department of Health and Rehabilitative Services (DHRS) closed the school pending an investigation of "allegations that children have been severely spanked by the 70-year old owner."[99] A week later, Circuit Court Judge Richard Hickey allowed the center to reopen, finding that the state had not gathered "substantive evidence" against A. Andrew Berent.[100] The DHRS investigators eventually collected statements from six children who had allegedly been "beaten, humiliated, and molested" by Berent.[101] The state scheduled a hearing to present the evidence in February 1985, and the center closed voluntarily a few weeks before the hearing. Accordingly, the evidence was never presented in a legal setting. No criminal charges were brought, and there is no other available information about the case beyond the media coverage. But it would hardly seem to be evidence of hysteria.

The final case arose in mid-July 1985 and involved the Hazel Crawford Day Care Center. This one is particularly important because it involved some of the same members of Janet Reno's staff who have been accused of "witch-hunting" in the Country Walk case. The case began with the arrest of Stephen Bergman by the North Miami Police Department, which charged he had sexually abused a four-year-old girl earlier that week.[102] In what might be the surest sign of an overreaction, two judges separately denied Bergman bail the next day. (Three days later, he was ordered released on his own recognizance.) A month after that, however, Christopher Rundle, an assistant state attorney for Dade County, announced that the state had *declined* to file charges.[103] He defended the initial arrest, explaining that the standard of evidence to arrest someone is much lower than the standard for filing a criminal case. Clearly, the state concluded that the child's statement was not clear or convincing enough to warrant prosecution. Some parents expressed outrage at the decision, and the family of the four-year-old girl filed a civil lawsuit against the Bergmans. Eventually, a six-person jury "took twenty minutes to clear a former North Miami Beach day care center operator of wrongdoing."[104] This decision was rendered in 1989, two years before the "fever" that allegedly gripped Southern Florida had broken. It would appear that the "hysteria" in this case involved one family; their initial statements were (appropriately) taken seriously by law enforcement, but after careful and expedient review it was decided not to prosecute. This seems to be the appropriate decision, and it was made by the same actors who Peter Boyer and others have claimed were so biased that they constantly "found" sexual abuse where it did not exist. It is difficult to square these three cases with the claim that the county was infected by hysteria during this time.

Boston at the Time of Amirault

The most publicized of day-care sexual abuse allegations in Massachusetts involved the Fells Acres Day School in Malden, Massachusetts, near Boston. The first allegations were made in the fall of 1984. The prosecution against the Amirault family, who owned and operated the center, lasted for years as there were ultimately four separate trials, all ending in conviction. Dorothy Rabinowitz has made the claim that the Amiraults were tried and convicted at a time when hysteria was rampant in Massachusetts.[105] Under this view, the social hysteria must have existed for more than five years, since that is how much time elapsed between the first trial and the final conviction. Without such an expansive view, it is difficult to explain how hysteria could account for the defendants all being convicted at their second trials.

But the evidence for sex abuse hysteria in Massachusetts is almost nonexistent. An article in the *Boston Globe* at the height of publicity about the Amirault case indicated that thirty-five facilities in Massachusetts had been investigated and four had been closed.[106] The Office for Children had jurisdiction over more than ten thousand day-care facilities at the time. The three facilities beyond the Amirault case have never been mentioned in the witch-hunt narrative, and there is no evidence in the public record to suggest they involved false accusations.

The possible exception is Caring for Kids, a day-care facility in Braintree, Massachusetts, that was included on Charlier and Downing's list of thirty-six cases. The allegations began with two children and eventually involved three others, although the parents of two of the children observed videotapes of their children being interviewed and concluded that no abuse had occurred. The community, however, was not "hysterical." Eighteen parents of children who attended the day-care centers testified in *favor* of Deborah Wingard, who operated two facilities under the name Caring for Kids. It is difficult to assess the case from existing DSS records alone, since they do not include a transcript of the ten-day administrative hearing. But Chief Administrative Magistrate Christopher F. Connolly, who presided over the appeal of the license suspension, concluded in July 1985 that "no sexual or physical abuse of children occurred at Caring for Kids, Inc."[107] A spokesman for the state licensing board said this was the system operating as it should; the licenses had been temporarily suspended for good cause and both were later reinstated after further investigations. There was no foregone conclusion of abuse since precisely the opposite was actually concluded. The center did not reopen, because Wingard moved away. Whatever one concludes about the underlying merits, the idea that the greater Boston area was swept up in some kind of mass hysteria does not fit the facts.

The only case beyond McMartin where the complaints at one facility actually spread to another one is the Georgian Hills case in Memphis, home of Charlier and Downing's newspaper. What happened in that case was a terrible injustice; fifteen employees at the Daybridge Daycare Center lost their jobs. But there were no other cases from the time period that had localized effects as severe as these two, and there is no evidence of widespread hysteria even in the same times and places where it was supposedly the worst.

"Air of Denial"

Beyond the evidence about specific places, there are powerful social forces, never acknowledged in the witch-hunt narrative, that also contradict the claims of "hysteria" and overreaction to allegations of child sexual abuse. Those forces were at work throughout the time of the alleged "modern American witch-hunts." Their origin is in the era before child sexual abuse was "recognized" as a social problem. The primary forces are secrecy, silence, and disbelief. These forces foster an "air of denial," the polar opposite of the "air of accusation" that practically defines the witch-hunt narrative.

Recognizing these factors is critical to placing the witch-hunt narrative in context. Vital to this understanding is some historical perspective that is sorely missing from the narrative. The emergence of the McMartin case coincided with the recognition of child sexual abuse as a social problem. A pivotal event in the process of social recognition was the television movie about incest called "Something About Amelia." Broadcast on January 9, 1984—less than a month before the first stories about the McMartin case were aired—the movie addressed what the *New York Times* called "undoubtedly the biggest of social taboos."[108] As nervous as the topic made television reviewers, it garnered an enormous audience, and hotlines were flooded with calls afterward. Later that month, Jeffrey Masson made headlines with scholarly revelations from the Freud archives about how Sigmund Freud lost his nerve and, in the face of intense criticism, turned away from recognizing the importance of child sexual abuse.[109] An excerpt from Masson's book *The Assault on Truth: Freud's Suppression of the Seduction Theory* was the cover story in *The Atlantic* magazine in February. The biggest of social taboos was suddenly in the news.

In understanding the events that came afterward, we should give consideration to the vast history during which child sexual abuse was not "recognized." The era is sometimes described such that it seems as if the only thing lacking was an "understanding" of the problem. This argument has been advanced in defense of the Catholic Church. For example, Philip Jenkins has written that the Church was essentially "guilty of applying standards that had prevailed before the revolution in social sensibilities."[110] (He squares this position with the fact that child sexual abuse has long been a crime by labeling it illegal "in the technical sense.") But there was also a remarkable denial of what was obvious—in broken bones, in venereal disease, and in incest victims. The "discovery" of the physical abuse of children came when pioneers in the field refused to ignore the implications of x-rays documenting broken bones. Masson reconstructed the efforts of two early French physicians to recognize the physical and sexual abuse of children in the late 1800s. Dr. Ambroise Tardieu recognized that the sexual assault of girls was often overlooked; similarly, Dr. Paul Brouardel was often "drawing the attention of his audience at autopsies to the abuse of children by their parents and teachers."[111] It would be more than fifty years before Dr. John Coffee, a radiologist in the United States, wrote an article in 1946 about abnormal bone fractures in infants.[112] It has been reported that the journals' editors "were so alarmed" at the implications of the study that "the eventual article did not contain references to intentional abuse."[113] Sixteen years later, Dr. Henry Kempe and his colleagues coined the phrase *battered-child syndrome* for the clinical condition of children who have suffered serious physical abuse.[114] The power of denial prevailed during those decades. History professor Lynn Sacco has documented how, during the twentieth century, "doctors refused to consider the possibility of incest" when new diagnostic procedures revealed gonorrhea infections in "respectable" families.[115] Rather than revise their views about the prevalence of incest, doctors speculated that perhaps the disease was transmitted by toilet seats. Harvard psychiatrist Judith Herman has written about how the profession still considered incest to be a rare occurrence, with a prevalence of maybe one in a million children, as recently as the 1950s.[116] This perception was off by a staggering amount—a multiple of tens of thousands.[117] Historian Linda Gordon has documented how case workers in Boston, during the Progressive Era, construed father-daughter incest as an encounter between a seductive and sexually precocious girl and a relatively innocent man.[118] Another historian, Estelle Freedman, has recounted how a major study of child sexual abuse and incest in the1950s described the majority of victims as "seductive" and "flirtatious," stigmatizing the victims as the perpetrators.[119] The social forces of silence and denial that explain this history should be kept in mind when considering the abrupt cultural change to the intense media spotlight on sexual abuse in January 1984.

None of those forces are acknowledged in the versions of history that describe the middle to late 1980s as a period of witch-hunts over child sexual abuse. Instead, the entire view of our social response to child sexual abuse is wrapped up in words such as *hysteria*. Indeed, the witch-hunt narrative is built on the notion that child sexual abuse suddenly became overreported. A primary target in this narrative is Dr. Roland Summit, a psychiatrist who published an influential article in 1983 about what he called the "Child Abuse Accommodation Syndrome."[120] Summit advanced a theory about how children come to "accommodate" sexual abuse—that is, how sexual abuse can continue to be perpetrated without children telling anyone. The first component in his framework is secrecy. Summit theorized that "attempts by the child to illuminate the secret will be countered by an adult conspiracy of silence and disbelief."

Lee Coleman, a psychiatrist hired by the defense in the Country Walk case and many others, began attacking this idea in 1986. Speaking at a convention of the political advocacy group Victims of Child Abuse Laws (VOCAL), Coleman allowed that this dynamic might happen within families, but he mocked the idea that it would happen in other contexts as "totally ludicrous." It "makes absolutely no sense," he argued, that this would happen when the allegation involves a teacher, coach, or virtually anyone else who might be accused in an institutional context.[121] Coleman and others have belittled the idea of "denial," arguing instead that, particularly in an institutional context, adults invariably overreact to children's disclosures rather than ignore or deny them. The "air of accusation" is a primary component in the hysteria claim that has been widely accepted in the years since the McMartin case ended. Richard Gardner made this argument in his 1991 book *Sex Abuse Hysteria: Salem Witch Trials Revisited*. Charles Krauthammer relied on the same idea to argue in 1993 that "we have become exquisitely over-sensitized" to child abuse.[122]

There is no question that the McMartin case *was* characterized by an air of accusation in the months when the case became a national news story and was rushed to the grand jury. The concept has little or no application, however, to many other cases advanced by the witch-hunt narrative, where the initial accusations involved one or two related people and did not spread beyond that, regardless of the intensity of community concern and publicity. Moreover, the opposite phenomenon—an air of denial—is apparent in countless institutional abuse cases. This is what explains hundreds of pedophile priests who operated with impunity for decades in a variety of jurisdictions. It also explains how hundreds of pedophile Boy Scout leaders could operate for decades without being apprehended.[123]

The air of denial is fueled by a sense of disbelief that adults, particularly those in positions of trust, could do horrible things to children. This is precisely how Barry Seigel, in his book *A Death in White Bear Lake*, explained a family physician seeing horrendous physical signs of abuse but not comprehending that the cause was intentional.[124] There was a "sense of disbelief" that anything so awful could be happening. The same phenomenon explains how Waneta Hoyt could be accepted as "the unluckiest woman in America" when she actually killed all five of her children over time.[125] Her family was long considered as case evidence that Sudden Infant Death Syndrome must be genetic. The physicians' "disbelief" of the abuse hypothesis in both cases might be written off as a product of the time. The murder described in Seigel's 1990 book was more than twenty-one years old; Hoyt's crimes also went undetected for nearly twenty years. But a comprehensive study of death certificates published by the Gannett News

Service in 1990 concluded that at least half of child-abuse deaths go undetected. This study was based on 49,569 death certificates in 1987, one of the years the witch-hunt narrative places at the height of hysteria about child abuse.[126] Yet, when writing about the exaggerated abduction figures that were widely accepted in the early 1980s, Philip Jenkins concluded that "children are at a low risk for homicide."[127] In his careful analysis of official statistics, there is no mention of the idea that such statistics might significantly underreport this crime. The reasons for the underreporting subvert his entire argument about hysteria.

A sense of disbelief can also arise if the person charged with sexual abuse does not fit social stereotypes of sex offenders. This sense of disbelief is particularly likely to happen in institutional settings because offenders tend to "groom" both victims and parents in order to avoid detection. An academic study of admitted child molesters examined this process in detail; the men studied "described themselves as charming, nice, and likeable."[128] Norman Watson, who molested hundreds of boys over several decades as a Little League coach, described the same process in a 1999 prison interview with *Sports Illustrated*.[129] Watson molested boys without any consequences through all of the years described as "hysterical" by Drs. Coleman and Gardner—and he was in the same part of Southern California described as the epicenter of this phenomenon. Watson was apprehended because a man he had molested twenty-three years earlier, and whose children had reached Little League age, hired a private investigator to look into his "nagging" and unresolved feelings about the matter.

A football coach in Pennsylvania was apprehended in a similar, but less deliberate, way. Richard Hoffman wrote a personal memoir that involved abuse in his childhood. He did not know that the abuser, John E. Feifel, was still coaching (and still abusing boys), but his book resulted in the man's apprehension and conviction.[130] The witch-hunt narrative contains no social or psychological explanations for how such abuse could go on undetected for so many years, particularly years when sex abuse hysteria supposedly gripped the country. The reality is that the witch-hunt narrative is underinclusive and incomplete. However accurate its description is in a few select cases, it misses important dynamics that explain many other cases. The disbelief that a "respectable" person would sexually assault a child was widespread during the 1980s (and later), and it worked in the favor of many child molesters.

This myth has been used in telling many of the alleged witch-hunt cases—as if having a steady job or being a professional rules out being a child molester. In fact, the cover of respectability is often an integral part of grooming parents, avoiding detection, and manipulating victims. In her initial article about "Junior McMartins," Debbie Nathan argued that these cases were impossible to believe in part because the alleged perpetrators were "white and middle class"—"in short, the last people you'd associate with sleazy trench coated pedophiles."[131]

This time-worn cliché of pedophiles fails to recognize how child molesters actually gain access to children. It is not by lurking around in "sleazy trench coats." From detailed interviews with child molesters in treatment, Carla Van Dam documents how they "groom adults" in order to obtain access to children; the grooming involves presenting yourself in a likeable way and "providing timely and appreciated assistance." As an assistant prosecutor in Delaware explained, "Nice guys make good child sex abusers. Kids don't like mean, nasty guys."[132] Neither do the adults who are critical to gaining access to children. Nathan's way of thinking is precisely what pedophiles bank on—that they appear to be so unlikely to have sexual interest in children that any allegations to this effect are quickly dismissed as improbable.

The witch-hunt narrative also suggests that children easily disclose sexual abuse, dismissing the significance of the forces of secrecy, fear, and shame. Consider this explanation by Professor Maggie Bruck in the Edenton, North Carolina, daycare case involving Robert Kelly:

Q: Would it be fair to say that one of the least favorite subjects, ah, to talk about, whether it's with their own parents or, ah, stranger would be anything that occurred to them of a sexual nature?

A: Oh, I don't agree with you, Mr. Hart. I think that children, in fact, love to talk about those kind of things especially among themselves....

Q: Tell me, Doctor, from your experience how great a time would a child have going and telling her friends and neighbors and other people about having someone stick his finger up their butt, how much glee would be involved in that?

A: You know, I don't know, Mr. Hart, but if they get a good laugh from their friends and if it could be something that would make them a really important kid and that their friends could all jump in and say is that what happened to you, I've got an even better one, it would be a really great topic of conversation.[133]

But survey evidence illustrates quite the opposite. Victims of sexual abuse typically do not "love to talk about it"; rather, they avoid reporting and often disclose the information to no one.[134] Aside from the issues of embarrassment and humiliation that Bruck does not recognize, children who report sexual abuse can also face indifference, or worse. Turning a blind eye against such allegations is the response in many institutions where the allegations are seen primarily as a threat to the organization's well-being. It is a common dynamic in families as well. Pursuing allegations against "upstanding" perpetrators can trigger hostility and pressure to drop the charges. In short, although the witch-hunt narrative is built around the idea that an "air of accusation" has led to countless false accusations, this account overlooks powerful countervailing social forces that often create an air of denial and indifference.

Examples of this kind of denial abound, even in the years when the witch-hunt narrative claims there was hysteria in the opposite direction. James Joseph O'Boyle, a respected police officer in East Rockhill Township, Pennsylvania, counted on this phenomenon while abusing scores of boys in the 1980s. "Denial was just the reaction O'Boyle correctly assumed people would have," wrote Stephen Fried in a chilling investigative story in *Philadelphia* magazine.[135] "There were cops who looked the other way, employers who didn't make routine background checks, reporters who knew but didn't or couldn't write the story."[136] A comparable case emerged from Hapeville, Georgia, in 1994, when Walter P. West pleaded guilty to thirty-three counts of child molestation, ending a long pattern of sexual abuse that covered all the years of the McMartin case. "Officials were told of numerous accusations of possible child abuse by a Hapeville police officer but failed to act," reported the *Atlanta Constitution*.[137]

In 1986, Calvin Trillin described a case in *The New Yorker* in which authorities in the Mormon Church and local law enforcement in Redmond, Oregon, turned a blind eye on a "valued member of the community," Ed Dyer. Dyer was scoutmaster of the church's Boy Scout Troop 26. In 1982, the parents of a boy in the troop informed the local bishop that Dyer had made sexual advances toward their son. After establishing that "there were other stories," the church asked Dyer to resign. They did not inform local authorities, however; nor was Dyer excommunicated. "It's just something you don't want to believe has happened," a church member later explained to Trillin.[138] A year after that, the church undertook a more serious investigation, resulting in a thirty-page dossier, including tape recordings, proving "a pattern that went back at least twenty-five years." Dyer was eventually "disfellowshipped" from the church, but he continued to have access to boys through his work with the U.S. Forest Service. In the spring of 1984, when the McMartin case was all over the national news, someone in the church with detailed information about Dyer tried to get the Redmond Police to investigate the matter. But nothing happened. The reason was never specified. Trillin speculated that:

> The police were reluctant to launch a vigorous investigation of good old Ed Dyer or that, like some members of the church, they were simply unable to face the possibility that what was being said about the man who had been entrusted with so many boys for so many years was true.[139]

That such sentiments would prevent action from being taken in a case involving a man with a long, documented history of predatory behavior contradicts everything the witch-hunt narrative claims about social responses to child sexual abuse in 1984. When new allegations reached the state police more than a year later, Dyer was arrested. After pleading guilty to two counts of second-degree sexual abuse, Dyer was sentenced to a total of twenty days, with three years of probation—less than three weeks in jail.

Faced with a child disclosing sexual abuse, many adults would respond, both within families and in institutions, by avoiding "getting involved." Mandatory reporting laws are aimed at addressing this problem. The witch-hunt narrative is built around the idea that sexual abuse is often tragically overreported. But this position overlooks the immense evidence of underreporting. Survey data consistently indicates that mandated reporters underreport their suspicions. A Rand Corporation survey of twelve hundred pediatricians, child psychologists, social workers, school principals, and child-care providers found that about 40 percent "had at least once suspected child abuse but failed to report it."[140]

Though there are penalties for failure to report suspected cases of child abuse, there are few reported cases of prosecution for failure to report. And the few cases that have gone forward have generally been unsuccessful even in the face of substantial evidence—bearing out a social reluctance to punish anyone for this behavior. Jason Berry, in the first major exposé of the Catholic Church, documented widespread failure to report known pedophiles. Patrick Boyle, reporting on more than two hundred confidential files, described a similar phenomenon in the Boy Scouts. Reflecting the social reluctance to criticize those who fail to act, a book review of *Scout's Honor* said it "falls short on the level of outrage" provoked by Berry's book because "the sins seem primarily ones of omission."[141] Many of those sins of omission occurred in the mid-1980s, when cases like Mc-Martin and Jordan, Minnesota, were dominating the news.

Similar events occurred in Florida. In April 1988, an anonymous source informed local police about a complaint made to school authorities by the parent of a second-grade girl at the Nativity School in Hollywood. The school principal had not informed authorities, as required by law, of the complaint against Edward Charles White, known to the students as "Mr. Ed." Detectives eventually discovered that White had been "discharged or terminated" from four other schools in the archdiocese between 1962 and 1976. Church records did not include any explanation. The investigation led to White's arrest on charges of sexually abusing twelve children. Some charges had to be dropped because of a restrictive statute of limitations; White pleaded guilty to others. The Hollywood police said that officials of the Nativity School "should be charged with failing to report suspected child molesting."[142] As a local newspaper editorial pointed out, "no one at Hollywood's Nativity School wanted to think the unthinkable." No one was charged; yet this unwillingness to "think the unthinkable" took place during the time when Peter Boyer later claimed a "fever" of sex-abuse hysteria was gripping South Florida.

A case that became public in the small town of Boulder, Montana, also demonstrated the power of denial during the same era. Douglas Marks, a "widely
admired" elementary school teacher and member of a prominent local family,
was arrested in 1989 on four counts of felony sexual assault against four of his
students between 1985 and 1989. Marks had been sexually abusing children for
decades; court records listed twenty-two accusations dating back to 1956.
County Attorney Rich Llewellyn identified forty-five victims, but there were
probably many more. The fathers of two of the boys involved in the 1989 charges
had themselves been victims. The extent to which officials turned a blind eye to
Marks is stunning. He was first apprehended for sexual abuse in 1959; no charges
were brought, but he was forced to take an "indefinite leave" from Jefferson High
School. He was later hired at the elementary school.

Over the years, "people went to officials and said things, but nobody paid attention."[143] Paul Myrhow, who was molested by Marks in the early 1980s, reported him in 1985 to Daryl Craft, a longtime friend who had become deputy
sheriff. As reported in the press years later, "Craft did not doubt the story—he,
too, had been molested by Marks." But the complaint did not result in an arrest.
Myrhow went back to authorities in 1989. The four charges that were later
brought against Marks were all based on events that had occurred since his
report in 1985. Marks pleaded guilty to four counts of felony sexual assault and
was sentenced to twenty years.[144] School board chairman David Reiter said later
"it was fairly common knowledge of his sexual preferences." Why was nothing
done, even after a report in 1985? "I think there is a tendency for everyone to
submerge these bad thoughts," he said.[145] In other words, even at a time of alleged hysteria about child sexual abuse, it was easier to turn a blind eye than deal
with a known pedophile.

The same disturbing behavior was documented through an eight-month investigation by two reporters at the *Arkansas Democrat-Gazette* who examined
allegations of sexual misconduct against school teachers. They concluded,
"When teachers are accused of sexual misconduct, some school officials and
school boards quietly sidestep legal and ethical issues to protect their schools
from scandal."[146] The study was published in 1996, four years after Dr. Richard
Gardner flatly asserted it is "no longer the case" that those revealing sexual abuse
will be met with a disbelieving community. Gardner claimed the opposite was
true, that police and child protective services were more likely to "accept as valid
even frivolous and absurd accusations."[147] But Hargrove and Roth found that
"sexual allegations by students have been greeted with shrugs, although a teacher's files indicated previous sex-related complaints." There is no reason to think
this phenomenon was peculiar to Arkansas.

The witch-hunt narrative is further contradicted by the intense pressure families have experienced to withdraw sexual abuse charges, particularly against

"beloved" figures like coaches, teachers, scout leaders, and choir masters. When a twelve-year-old girl in Florida disclosed that Ronald Bach, a popular physical education teacher at Miami Springs Middle School, had sexually abused her, the community rallied around *Bach*. The family was ostracized. Later, Bach pleaded guilty.[148] A family in Barrington, Rhode Island, experienced the same thing when their child spoke out against Carlton Bittenbender, a popular Boy Scout leader who has since been proven to be a serial child molester.[149] To these families, the witch-hunt narrative is a cruel misrepresentation of social pressures that, in their experience, are the complete opposite of "overly sensitive" to sexual abuse.

Difficulties Prosecuting Child Abuse

The witch-hunt narrative also contains a significant myth about prosecuting child sexual abuse: that these cases are somehow "easy." Kim Hart of VOCAL was quoted in Charlier and Downing's series as saying that legal reforms to accommodate child witnesses are "just an easy way to get an easy win."[150] Debbie Nathan's first article in her witch-hunt oeuvre was captioned: "Gayle Dove and Mickey Noble had their day in court. But what difference does that make, when you've been labeled a daycare child molester?"[151] In other words, defendants stand virtually no chance of prevailing when charged with sexual abuse in a daycare center. This is a convenient argument to make when one is arguing that someone was falsely convicted. But Nathan provided no data on conviction rates to support her claim. Entirely lost in the witch-hunt narrative is a sense of how hard it actually is to win a child sexual abuse case. In the case Nathan wrote about, Noble's conviction in that trial was overturned on appeal, and she was acquitted in a second trial, seemingly contradicting the notion that these charges bring an automatic conviction. Dove's conviction was overturned on appeal; she was convicted a second time, and the conviction was also overturned on appeal. Charges were later dropped. The case poses an important question about uses and limits of evidence concerning children not named in the charges at hand.[152] Reasonable people can disagree about where courts should draw such a line. Seeing the case for those issues, however, highlights the difficulty in proving sexual abuse cases involving multiple children, something never acknowledged in the witch-hunt narrative.

The complexity and challenge of proceeding with young victims has been overlooked by proponents of the witch-hunt narrative. Many states also had age limits or competency requirements that kept children under the age of seven out of court. It was effectively open season on those children since they had little possibility of legal recourse. States that switched to a case-by-case approach accommodated younger children, but some children will always be too young to testify. In some cases this problem has been misinterpreted as evidence of a witch-hunt. The Presidio Child Development Center case in San Francisco is a primary example. Six children tested positive for a sexually transmitted disease and dozens more were thought to have been sexually abused in 1986, but charges were dropped (because the children's testimony was "too vague.") That fact apparently explains why this case has appeared on several lists of so-called witch-hunts. But as Captain David Fox, a physician and father of children who attended the facility, told the press, "Just because this case didn't reach prosecution, doesn't mean that it didn't happen."[153] Unfortunately, this distinction is often blurred in the witch-hunt narrative, where dropping charges is routinely considered as proof that charges had no basis in fact.

Cheryl McCall highlighted a similar tragedy in the December 1984 issue of *Life* magazine, describing a case prosecutors declined to accept because the witnesses were too young, even though the family court had found:

> that over a period of three years [a father] had sexually abused his daughters in many ways, cruelly forced them to take part in and observe other vile acts and permitted his uncle similarly to abuse the girls in his presence.[154]

These kinds of stories are told in the media only relatively rarely; indeed, they have been overshadowed in an avalanche of articles about hysteria and witch-hunts.

Another case like this, also lost to virtually every historical account of daycare abuse in the 1980s, is the Sugar Plum School House in Lake Worth, Florida. The case began when a mother alleged that her three-year-old daughter told her "Ba Ba Blue" had "poked a hole in her bottom." The mother indicated that the man who co-owned and operated the center responded to that name. The girl was examined by Dr. Donald T. Drummond, who found a tear in her hymen that indicated recent trauma.[155] The man was arrested November 23, and the school held an informational meeting for parents on November 27. At least two other families came forward after the meeting. Their children were interviewed by the police, and both children apparently implicated the same man.[156] An investigation by Child Protective Services resulted in a finding that sexual abuse was "indicated."[157] Using enrollment information provided by the Department of Health and Rehabilitation, the state attorney's office endeavored to contact 120 people. A small number were never reached, but virtually everyone who was reached reported their child had indicated nothing about abuse. It is worth pondering the significance of this result since the argument in several other cases is that anxious parents caused their children to respond in the affirmative. These parents were presumably no less anxious or concerned, and yet this widespread parental interview process produced no additional reports.

These results apparently puzzled the grand jury as much as they puzzled a reporter who later obtained as many documents as possible. The grand jury issued two findings on March 17, 1989: (1) the owner and operator of the school was "completely innocent" of any and all charges, as were other teachers and staff at the school; and (2) the child who triggered the investigation "has been sexually abused."[158] Perhaps the child was abused elsewhere; perhaps the grand jury was wrong about part of its findings. Either way, the age of the child made it impossible to ascertain with any more certainty where and how she sustained what one expert diagnosed as a repeated trauma to the vagina. The failure of justice in this case, however, was to the child whose story has been lost in accounts of the 1980s that reflexively label day-care cases as witch-hunts.

Courts have made various accommodations for children as witnesses since the early 1980s. Many states had "corroboration requirements" that required evidence beyond a child's word in order to file sexual abuse charges. Elizabeth Holtzman, the Brooklyn district attorney, told the *New York Times* in July 1983 that there were "at least 24 cases in the borough last year that could not be prosecuted" because of this requirement.[159] Jeanine Pirro, chief of the Domestic Violence Prosecution Unit in Westchester County, estimated that twenty cases a month could not be prosecuted because of this requirement. These numbers would translate into thousands of cases across the country that could not be pursued even though prosecutors thought the evidence was strong. Yet in the absence of such a requirement, there were jury instructions that routinely warned jurors in child molestation cases that without corroboration the word of a child was not as worthy of belief as the word of an adult. The "cautionary instruction" that was used in California reads:

> Corroboration of the testimony of a child under the age of fourteen years upon and with whom a lewd and lascivious act is alleged to have been committed is not essential to a conviction. However, a charge of committing a lewd and lascivious act is one which is easily made and, once made, is difficult to defend against even if the person accused is innocent. The law requires that you examine with caution the testimony of the child with whom the lewd and lascivious act is alleged to have been committed.[160]

This instruction tilts the proceedings in favor of the defendant. Although the California Supreme Court ruled in 1975 that this instruction was inappropriate, Judge Bob Hight agreed to use this instruction ten years later in Michael Ruby's case, stemming from Manhattan Ranch Preschool.[161] The case went to trial while the McMartin case was still in preliminary hearing stage, and it ended in a hung jury. Reforming such laws, as happened throughout the country during the Mc-Martin era, did not magically eliminate the prejudices that created them in the first place. But to listen to the witch-hunt narrative, one would think any accusation by a child is almost automatically believed in court.

Another accommodation that courts made to the testimony of children was to loosen requirements about specifying the precise dates of any alleged misconduct. Children do not have datebooks; nor do they have the same sense of time that adults do. Many cases in the 1980s were dismissed, or the conviction was reversed, on the grounds that the time frame had not been specified narrowly enough. The Tots 'N' Toddlers Center in Berlin, New Jersey, was closed in March 1985 by a superior court judge after an investigation by the New Jersey Division of Youth and Family Services. A grand jury indicted Robert and Nancy Knighton on charges of sexually abusing seven children between 1981 and 1984. The criminal charges were eventually dismissed, however, because of an appellate decision in a separate case requiring the prosecution to specify the exact days when the alleged abuse occurred. Requirements about specifying the time and date of the allegations were later relaxed in child sexual abuse cases. Some of the convictions against James Watt (discussed in Chapter Three) in White Plains, New York, were overturned on the same grounds, even though a number of those charges included strong medical evidence of abuse. (Watt's conviction was upheld on one charge.) One of the "Bronx Five" cases was also overturned on these grounds. The first sentence in the appellate court decision reads:

> The record in this case unequivocally indicates that defendant, a teacher's aide at the Puerto Rican Association for Community Action Day Care Center (PRACA), engaged in criminal activity involving the rape, sodomy and sexual abuse of innocent, defenseless children between the ages of three and five years.[162]

But the court then indicated it was forced to reverse the convictions because the charges were framed as a "continuing course of conduct" and the "time interval alleged in each count was so excessive as to be unreasonable." The court's own reading of the facts suggests this case was not a witch-hunt but rather a monument to the difficulty in charging a case that involves young children.

There was a final reform, widely supported by parents and many legislators in the 1980s, that was supposed to ease the discomfort of testifying in court. Many states adopted laws permitting children to testify by closed-circuit television. This would allow them to testify without having to stare at the defendant or appear in the actual courtroom. The use of closed-circuit television was seen by many as an infringement on a defendant's right to confront witnesses, even though the reform did not exempt the child from cross-examination; it only exempted the child from having to look directly at the defendant.[163] But prosecutors in many cases were too worried that convictions won through closed-circuit television would be voided. And indeed, this is what happened. The Craig's Preschool case, analyzed in Chapter Three, was remanded to the trial court on grounds that had nothing to do with the strength of the state's evidence; the court required "case-specific findings" to justify the use of closed-circuit television, and the prosecution later decided against trying to reconvict Craig.[164] The U.S. Constitution was read to require the confrontation of witnesses in person, unless there is a specific showing that doing so would be traumatic. The catch-22 is that proving the existence of trauma basically requires a process resembling the kind of trial one is presumably trying to avoid. So even if the state prevails, the end result is still two court proceedings, not one. This explains why one of the major innovations in the 1980s, designed to minimize trauma, is almost never used.

Nevertheless, the witch-hunt narrative still insists that the law unduly favors children. The accused, the argument goes, is "presumed guilty" and has the difficult burden of proving his or her innocence.[165] In reality, there was no change in the extraordinary burden of proof the state carries in criminal cases: it must prove the case *beyond a reasonable doubt.* And even though various reforms allowed some of these cases to be brought—unlike in earlier years, when they were virtually prohibited by law—the difficulties involving children as witnesses remained. Children are not as articulate as adults; they are much easier targets for defense attorneys on cross-examination. There is a general tendency, borne out in jury simulation studies, to consider older witnesses as more credible than younger ones.[166] Children are also more prone to be intimidated by courtrooms and court procedures than adults. Although programs have been developed to familiarize children with courtrooms in advance of testifying, nothing has been done to reduce the stress of cross-examination. Even Charlier and Downing note that "defense lawyers have little trouble confusing and discrediting small children on the stand," although they did not appear to take that into account in their analysis of cases. Some of the most bizarre statements made in the actual proceedings in the McMartin case were from children in the preliminary hearing who were subject to cross-examination by seven lawyers. One child was cross-examined for more than fifteen days. Countries such as New Zealand have designed procedures for limiting cross-examination of children, but the prevailing sense in the United States is that such measures would violate a defendant's right to "confront" witnesses. How this position undercuts the effectiveness of children as witnesses, and leaves some parents unwilling to subject their children to such procedures, is never acknowledged in a narrative that claims child molestation cases are "easy" to win.

Children have also been known to freeze on the stand, resulting in the dismissal of the case. Warren Poole, a police officer in Lynn, Massachusetts, was charged with molesting a young girl. She froze on the witness stand in the summer of 1988 and charges were dismissed. Poole was arrested again in 1989 when a videotape was located that documented his raping the same girl in the fall of 1988.[167] This time, he pleaded guilty. But rarely is there a second chance like that one.

Even though various reforms made it possible to file charges in the day-care sexual-abuse cases of the 1980s, facilitating the filing of charges is not the same as making it easier to win such cases. The high-profile child sexual abuse cases were often the first time young children had been witnesses or complainants in criminal proceedings in their respective states. Several of these cases demonstrate the difficulty of prosecuting such charges even after the reforms of the 1980s. First, some children are just too young to testify. The Maine Supreme Court overturned the conviction of a man who confessed to child molestation, reasoning that without the young child's testimony it was not clear that a crime had been committed.[168] In a 1992 case in Delaware "state prosecutors gave a man his freedom in exchange for a signed statement admitting that he repeatedly had raped his daughter when she was 3."[169] The agreement caused such an outcry that the attorney general released a statement explaining the difficulties in prosecuting such cases.

Second, in order to protect defendants, courts generally have not admitted the same types of evidence that would be most likely to allow disbelieving jurors to see a defendant as a potential child molester. Evidence of prior acts, in other words, though undoubtedly relevant to assessing allegations, is generally considered too prejudicial to defendants to allow into evidence. The *Miami Herald* described a case in which a father of four was being tried for assaulting an eleven-year-old girl who had been riding her bicycle. The jury, which ultimately settled on a lesser offense, was not allowed to be informed of the defendant's conviction five months earlier for assaulting a different eleven-year-old girl on a bicycle.[170]

In an essay about one of the lesser-known cases of sexual misconduct by a priest, Paul Wilkes wrote in *The New Yorker* about Father Ronald Provost, who was charged with "posing" a ten-year-old boy for semi-nude photographs. The jury was not allowed to hear that pornographic pictures of young boys had been discovered in his room at Our Lady of Mt. Carmel in 1979, or that he had been "sent away for treatment" to the House of Affirmation. The jury was also prohibited from hearing about the hundreds of pictures found in his possession when he was arrested; only the pictures involving this single child would be admitted. The defense lawyer had successfully isolated the charges in the case "as though they were a single, aberrant—even accidental—episode."[171] Viewed this way, almost any act of sexual abuse, other than an attack on a stranger, is likely to seem like a single aberrant act. In the name of protecting the defendant, courts prevent introduction of evidence that would put those acts into context. (The judge found Provost guilty and issued a ten-year suspended sentence.)[172]

Finally, rules about hearsay evidence often come into play in child sexual abuse cases. The Charlier and Downing article reported that twenty-seven states had expanded the traditional hearsay exceptions to allow parents to testify about statements made by their children. But the hearsay evidence rule can nevertheless be an impediment to prosecution. Charges were dropped in a locally publicized child molestation case after a Michigan Supreme Court decision was seen as prohibiting the use of a detailed statement by a babysitter as to what a four-year-old girl told her about things her mother said were "secret."[173] Similarly, a judge in Prince William County, Virginia, decided that fourteen-year-old Kristi Kauffmann's diary could not be admitted in a prosecution against her father, Paul. Kristi committed suicide and the *Washington Post* described her diary as "a grim portrait in depression and fear that she said was caused by her adoptive father's sexual assaults."[174] Prosecutors also had a statement from Paul Kauffmann admitting "that he had been fondling his daughter for nearly three years." But a statement by the defendant alone is not sufficient to sustain a conviction under Virginia law, so the case against Kauffmann was dropped. Hearsay statements were allowed in some of the cases discussed in Chapter Three, but a number of those cases were overturned on that basis. This would-be reform has done little to make it easier to win such cases. The witch-hunt narrative misrepresents what prosecutors have always known: these cases are extremely difficult to win.

Leniency for Child Molesters

Those claiming hysteria over child sexual abuse are often careful to add that they abhor "real" sexual abuse. The same can be said of society as a whole. As Suzanne Sgroi observed in 1978, "the sexual abuse of children is a crime that our society abhors in the abstract but tolerates in reality."[175] But beyond the rhetoric, the evidence that actually bears out this abhorrence is thin at best. In fact, there is significance evidence to the contrary—evidence that we actually tolerate child sexual abuse and minimize the offense *in specific cases*. When the defendant is not an abstraction, but an actual adult, the result is often to embrace the guilty. Minimal punishments are meted out in many instances, even though the crime as a whole has the reputation of carrying extremely severe penalties. None of the factors described here would exist, especially during the 1980s, if the witch-hunt narrative accurately characterized social responses to child sexual abuse in America.

The strongest and most direct evidence of tolerating child sexual abuse is the extent to which "respectable" child molesters are embraced and supported even *after* they are proven guilty. The phenomenon played out in detail not far from Jordan, Minnesota, at precisely the same time as that case. Curiously, the

Jordan case is mentioned in virtually every contemporary account of child sexual abuse in America, while the Minneapolis Children's Theatre case almost never is. It resulted in a book whose title summarizes the phenomenon: *Hating the Sin, Loving the Sinner.*[176] When the theatre's director, John Donahue, was apprehended in 1984 for sexually abusing students, the *New York Times* described the theater as "widely respected" and the defendant as the recipient of a Margo Jones Award, "among the most prestigious awards in American Theatre."[177] The article reported the considerable concern about the impact the arrest would have on a major theatre company with "a full-time staff of 100" and an annual budget of $2.7 million. It was eventually revealed that Donahue had been charged with felony sodomy of a student at Carl Sandburg Junior High School in 1961, before he started the Children's Theatre in Minneapolis. (He pleaded guilty to the reduced charge of indecent liberties and received a one-year suspended sentence with ninety days in jail.) It also became clear there were numerous prior warnings and complaints about his behavior at the Children's Theatre. The father of one boy warned Donahue to leave his son alone in 1978, and a complaint was made to the Hennepin County District Attorney's Office. The Minneapolis police declined to take action, apparently because of "Donahue's prominence in the community."[178] Another complaint reached the board of directors, which dropped the matter after Donahue told them there was "no problem."

So many adults were aware of the situation that two teachers were later charged with violations of the Mandatory Reporting Act. Those charges were dropped, however—"with the greatest reluctance," according to the judge— because the statute was considered unconstitutionally vague.[179] When it came time to sentence Donahue, who pleaded guilty, Judge Charles A. Porter Jr. noted "the disturbing fact that collectively this community knew what was going on." Incredibly, the judge argued that Donahue should not "be made a scapegoat for what happened," as if his crimes were committed by someone else. The judge sentenced him to one year in prison; Donahue served eight months. Marvin Costello described the outcome as clear evidence of "society's ambivalence" about these cases.[180]

The same phenomenon occurred with priests, teachers, coaches, and scout leaders. For example, in June 1985, at the height of accusations in the McMartin case, David Slone pleaded guilty to molesting students at Falls-Lakeview School and at the Trinity Baptist Church in Norman, Oklahoma. According to local newspaper, although Slone admitted to at least eight victims, he "continued to get strong support from some parents, children and officials of the church and at the school."[181] In Inverness, Florida, after Mitchell Matthews was convicted of eight counts of sexually abusing boys, "members of his church stood beside their choir director" and wrote letters to the judge urging probation instead of prison time.[182] The willingness of adults to embrace the guilty is directly related to the kind of grooming of parents that helps provide child molesters with access to children. The disbelief that Debbie Nathan expressed about charges against reputable, middle-class citizens who do not wear "sleazy trench coats" helps reinforce this point.

Although there are occasional cases where the defendant is vilified, the fact remains that perpetrators of child sexual abuse are often defended and embraced even after it is clear they are guilty. The witch-hunt narrative provides no explanation for this phenomenon—and this is because its existence is frighteningly similar to the phenomenon that leads to underreacting, not overreacting, to child sexual abuse.

Finally, the actual punishments meted out to child molesters by the criminal justice system often contradict the witch-hunt narrative, which predicts severe punishment as the end product of "sex abuse hysteria." Richard Gardner, who coined this phrase, made an empirical claim in the *Wall Street Journal* that our society has become so hysterical about child sexual abuse that child molesters "on average" serve longer prison sentences than murderers. Gardner claimed that his references were "available on request," but his response to a request from this author produced only an example of one long sentence: Robert Kelly's in the Edenton, North Carolina, day-care abuse case.[183] A comprehensive examination of all sentences for murder and for child molestation over a nine-year period in Rhode Island revealed that Gardner's claim was extremely exaggerated. Child molesters often receive probation, but murderers never do; child molesters often receive minimal sentences, but murders almost never do.[184] It is a testament to the uncritical acceptance of the witch-hunt narrative that Gardner's exaggerated claim was published in the *Wall Street Journal* without documentation or subsequent correction.

It does not require an original study to get a sense of the phenomenon. Newspaper stories are filled with examples of leniency to child molesters during the McMartin era. In the fall of 1983, Albert Breto pleaded guilty in Santa Ana, California, to forty-six counts involving sex crimes against two minors. He received five years of probation after Superior Court Judge Robert Green described Breto as "a gentle person" who "promised he would not engage in sexual activity" with any other minors.[185] That same week, Eugene Gold, who served four terms as Brooklyn district attorney, received probation in exchange for acknowledging "unlawful sexual conduct" with a ten-year-old girl.[186] In June 1984, near the height of the McMartin publicity, Samuel L. Jones, a Burbank, California, airport official, received probation after pleading guilty to felony charges of lewd and lascivious acts with pre-teenage boys. "This man could not suffer more consequences than he already has," his lawyer told the court, employing a logic that would insulate anyone with an important job from actually having to go to prison.[187] Similar evidence can be found in Minnesota, and probably anywhere else in the country. At the time the Jordan case was beginning, a local television station did a documentary about:

> two men—one a city official, another a doctor, both liked and respected in their small Minnesota towns—who went virtually unpunished after it was discovered that they molested adolescent boys.[188]

Systematic studies further contradict the notion that child molesters generally receive extraordinarily long sentences. The American Bar Association's Center on Children and the Law conducted a study in the early 1990s that included an examination of 954 case files from ten DA's offices around the country. The cases occurred in years that Gardner claimed were characterstic of "sex abuse hysteria." Yet, the researchers found that defendants who plead guilty or were found guilty at trial received prison or jail sentences in 59 percent of the cases. In other words, forty-one percent of the guilty avoided incarercation.[189] The distribution of sentences was strongly skewed to the low end. Thirty-six percent of the guilty were sentenced to one year or less, and twenty-two percent were sentenced between one and five years.[190] *Eight* percent received more than twenty years in prison, the kind of strict sentence the witch-hunt narrative claims to be characteristic of sex offenders.[191] The *Boston Globe* found similar results in a comprehensive study done right at the time the Amiraults were first being tried in Middlesex County. Those defending the Amiraults have since portrayed 1986 as a time when hysteria about child molestation gripped Massachusetts. But the *Globe* found that one out of three convicted child molesters did not go to jail at all that year; they received probation instead. Only one in ten was sentenced to more than five years in prison.[192] What kind of sex abuse hysteria is there if thirty to forty percent of convicted child molesters avoid prison and the vast majority of those sentenced receive a light sentence? Wouldn't the hysteria result in a high incarceration rates and lengthy sentences? What generally happens in reality is the opposite.

One consequence of minimal punishments is that they allow, and perhaps even embolden, repeated child sexual abuse. There are myriad cases on record in the 1980s and 1990s where a person who was apprehended for a sex crime against a child turns out to have been apprehended earlier without any significant consequences. This was the case with James Rud, the central character in the Jordan, Minnesota, cases. He had two prior convictions for sex crimes against children in the five years before his arrest in Jordan; both had resulted in probation. So, too, when John Shaver was apprehended in Fort Lauderdale, Florida, in 1988. His day-care center license had been revoked in Hawaii in 1983 after allegations of improperly touching little girls. In 1985, he opened the Rainbow Learning Center in Fort Lauderdale. The police investigated Shaver in Florida as well; three women who worked for him and at least one girl he cared for expressed concerns to police "about how Shaver handled little girls."[193] But there in Florida, in the midst of the so-called sex abuse hysteria, the investigation was closed. Similarly, when Richard Plass, a biology teacher and assistant principal at Stuyvesant High School in Manhattan, pleaded guilty in 1999 to sexually abusing a fifteen-year-old girl, it was reported that complaints about him had been filed by female students at the high school in 1985 and 1992.[194] If sex-abuse hysteria really was sweeping the country in the late 1980s and early 1990s, one wonders why there were no charges in these cases during that time.

Conclusion

None of this is to deny the combination of elements in the McMartin case that caused five teachers to be unjustly charged with crimes. There was overzealousness among many parties in that case. And the dynamics of the case can be found, to a lesser extent, in a handful of others around the country. But there were not hundreds, or even dozens, of cases like that. There were, in contrast, strong forces of minimization and denial at work during the same time period. The grains of truth in the witch-hunt narrative do not prove a major social trend. Rather, they demonstrate that competing social forces can coexist. At the same time Betty Raidor was unjustly being denied bail in the McMartin case, a man in Memphis, Tennessee, named David Slater, who had sexually assaulted a twelve-year-old over an extended period of time through his position in the Big Brother program, was avoiding jail, receiving probation instead and ordered to seek psychiatric treatment.[195] As serious and problematic as they were, the pockets of overreaction to child sexual abuse in the 1980s existed in a sea of minimization and denial of the very phenomenon. These forces are so powerful that they help explain why the witch-hunt narrative itself is so exaggerated.

CONCLUSION I

The McMartin preschool case came to define an era of child sexual abuse cases that began in 1983 and drew to a close in the early 1990s. These cases coincided with the "recognition" of child sexual abuse in America. Two important implications of this fact have been lost in subsequent discussions of these cases. First, the front-line psychologists, social workers, and law enforcement agents who were asked to respond to sexual abuse were pioneers. There were no protocols for interviewing children, few physicians had extensive knowledge about child sexual abuse, and experience with children as witnesses in court was extremely limited. Many of the professionals who found themselves in this difficult position were later criticized for aspects of how they responded. But few critics seem to remember what was being asked of these people: to respond to a problem that was suddenly recognized as serious, with little guidance and few precedents.

Second, there were powerful forces of secrecy and denial that explained why sexual abuse was not "recognized" before the mid-1980s. Those who promoted the witch-hunt narrative arising during this time never confronted what it meant that sexual abuse had been ignored or dismissed for so long. There were multiple reasons for the deafening silence around this issue. The perpetrators of abuse rely on secrecy, and they are skilled at coercing children into silence by various means. Some instill fear in their victims, some instill a sense of guilt or shame, and others rely on the sense of helplessness that comes from convincing children that nobody will believe them. Bystanders also play a role in maintaining silence. Some children speak up, and even when they do not, there are often signs that suggest abusive behavior might be occurring. But bystanders too often turn a blind eye, finding it easier to minimize or deny their suspicions than to confront the enormity of what is occurring. None of these dynamics disappeared simply because this taboo topic became a subject of public discourse in the mid-1980s.

The McMartin case began with a credible medical report and soon involved statements by several additional children supporting the suspicion that children attending the McMartin preschool had been sexually abused. The case spun out of control for a range of reasons, directly related to the fact that sexual abuse had just been "recognized." Pediatricians involved with the case overdiagnosed children largely because there was not a solid base of information about the genitals of non-abused children. Interviewers who were too sure that the children must have been abused read nonresponsive answers as an indication of fear. They were also too literal in interpreting fantastic statements. When similar statements were made in other cases around the country, some people concluded that the similarities had to mean the cases were connected. This led to some of the greatest excesses of the case—the period when many were convinced that day-care centers had been infiltrated by an organized group of people who abused children ritualistically.

But those excesses have been exaggerated in various ways. The infamous claim that there were tunnels under the McMartin preschool, often attributed to hundreds of children, was made by only a handful. The LA County Sheriff's "Ritual Abuse Task Force" took its charge seriously and credulously in 1985. It was disbanded at the end of the year without bringing any charges. Indeed, by 1986 there was a State Attorney General's Report about the significant problems with child sexual abuse investigations in nearby Kern County. Charges against five of the seven defendants in the McMartin case were dropped that year as well. The case dragged along for so many years that Dr. Heger, who evaluated many of the children in early 1984, eventually testified about how medical knowledge had evolved since then. Acknowledging that information about non-abused children had made the medical evaluation of children more conservative, she also verified how some evidence was still considered significant.

The witch-hunt narrative that grew out of the McMartin case tells a different story. Labeling the entire case a "hoax," it dismisses all of the medical evidence out of hand. Relying on the mistakes of interviewers who entered the case in November 1983, it dismisses children who made statements two months before that. The witch-hunt narrative goes much farther, extending the claims about McMartin to cases across the country, arguing there was a national epidemic of cases "just like McMartin." Despite the prominent academics and journalists who have rebroadcast it, the evidence for the claim is remarkably thin. Although the notion of there being hundreds or thousands of such cases is widely accepted, the number of specific cases offered as evidence is nowhere near that number. A few dozen cases, at most, have been offered as proof of this national witch-hunt. However, as detailed in Chapter Three, the evidence pertaining to those specific cases that would support the claims of a witch-hunt ranges from limited to nonexistent.

These cases were some of the most complicated and lengthy criminal proceedings in American history. There are more than a hundred thousand pages of
transcripts in the McMartin case alone. Several of the other most commonly
mentioned cases have transcripts in the range of fifty thousand pages. Beyond
court transcripts, there are a host of peripheral documents, ranging from police
reports and medical reports to information from civil cases that shed light on
how these cases began, how they were investigated, and how they evolved. None
of these cases can be encapsulated fairly with a simple story.

But the witch-hunt narrative, which has been accepted as the best explanation
of these cases, does precisely that—it tells a simple story. It claims these cases
share essential similarities that make them functionally alike. The rhetoric to that
effect is as simple as it is unequivocal: cases across the country were "clones,"
"cookie-cutter copies," and "just like McMartin." The foundation for these claims
has never been subject to careful scrutiny. By her own account, which became
clear only in recent years, Debbie Nathan argued that the Michaels case was a
cookie-cutter copy of the McMartin case *before* she ever researched the Michaels
case.[1] Other magazine writers published strikingly similar claims, providing a set
of definitive statements about lengthy and complicated cases without even reviewing the court transcript. In some instances, it was not even available when
the writer claimed to have conducted research and established that the case was
all a witch-hunt.

It is a testament to the power of the witch-hunt narrative that these accounts
have been accepted so readily. It might also be a function of the fact that doing
this kind of research is difficult. This book represents the first effort to comprehensively research the cases that serve as the foundation of the witch-hunt narrative. It is the culmination of fifteen years of locating, accessing, and analyzing
transcripts and related documents in the cases that form the basis for the narrative. The challenges in this kind of research are enormous. With an army of
research assistants and a substantial budget for photocopying and travel, it still
was not possible to cover a few dozen cases completely. But none of these challenges or limitations is mentioned in the works that are the foundation of the
witch-hunt narrative. Indeed, none of the magazine articles about the case
were based on a comprehensive examination of trial transcripts. Yet these accounts have been accepted, repeated, and enshrined in the academic literature
of fields ranging from sociology and law to psychology and English, where
they are written about in the extreme language of the witch-hunt narrative.

The result is a deeply flawed account of these cases and of the time period.
The witch-hunt narrative offers a simple and satisfying explanation, one that has
deep roots in the American experience. But it does not do justice to the facts of
these cases, including McMartin. The cases examined in Chapter Three are
among those offered as the best evidence of the witch-hunt narrative. These are

the cases that should serve as the empirical foundations for the claims the narrative advances. That is, they should *all* provide strong support for the narrative, especially since the claims of hundreds of cases rest on lists that together cite not more than several dozen. Yet, almost none of the cases on those lists support the narrative's claims. As demonstrated in Chapter Three, even the cases with the worst problems also involved evidence of abuse. And the lesser-known cases, which have received almost no attention in the witch-hunt canon, involved surprisingly little evidence for the claim that they were "hoaxes" or lacked a basis in fact.

The witch-hunt narrative was first written by journalists, and then adopted by academics. It was never based on comprehensive research of multiple cases. From the vantage point provided by fifteen years of in-depth, original research, I would say the narrative certainly appears to have begun with a conclusion and then sought information to support it, using documents and claims provided by defense lawyers as primary sources, and even as coauthors and "fact checkers." It is, in short, the defense view of history. In this way, the witch-hunt narrative is guilty of the same shortcomings it criticizes. While claiming that prosecutors and interviewers consistently minimize or deny evidence that does not support their position, the proponents of the witch-hunt narrative have done the same thing in the direction of the defense. Instead of disregarding evidence that might point away from guilt, they disregard evidence pointing toward it. Instead of automatically believing any statement from a child, they seem to automatically believe the denial of any adult. Instead of assuming all the medical evidence presented by the prosecution must be true, they take the position that it should all be rejected.

The structure of the witch-hunt narrative makes for powerful reading, but it creates a distorted picture of these cases and of the time period in which they existed. The McMartin case is told in an exaggerated form that ignores all the evidence of guilt. But the Papoose Palace case from Reno, Nevada—which proves that sexual abuse can occur in a day-care center on a wide scale, for years, without detection—is forgotten. The Jordan, Minnesota, cases are similarly described in a manner that ignores evidence of guilt. But the Minneapolis Children's Theatre case, which demonstrates how adults turn a blind eye to abuse, is forgotten. The wild claims made by some parents in West Point are recounted in detail, while the fact that a girl had a puncture wound to her vagina that almost certainly occurred at the day-care center is forgotten, along with the fact that nobody was ever apprehended. Claims about child pornography that were made in some cases but never proven are well preserved in the witch-hunt narrative, but the realities of Jack Shaver's case—multiple complaints that were ignored, lenient penalties on more than occasion, and child pornography that involved day care—are lost to history.

The witch-hunt narrative is not just an inaccurate view of the cases it describes; it is an inaccurate view of the time period in which they occurred and the social forces at play. These inaccuracies matter for reasons far beyond the historical record. These cases have had a major influence on the field of psychology and on the perception of children as witnesses. Those issues are best illustrated through the Kelly Michaels case, the subject of the next chapter. The implications of what happened in that case are the subject of the remaining chapters in the book.

PART II

THE TRIUMPH OF THE WITCH-HUNT NARRATIVE

5

The Turning Point

State v. Michaels

The Kelly Michaels case became a turning point in the public discourse about child sexual abuse in America. Unlike many other cases from the 1980s, which ended in hung juries or acquittals, the Michaels case, which emerged in 1985, ended in a resounding guilty verdict in 1988. It appeared to be a textbook conviction in the kind of day-care sexual abuse cases that had made headlines but posed great difficulties for prosecutors. Learning from some of the mistakes in other cases, the prosecutors in the Kelly Michaels case successfully discredited Ralph Underwager, then one of the leading defense psychologists on child suggestibility, and won a sweeping jury verdict.

But everything changed on appeal. In a dramatic decision in 1993, the New Jersey Appellate Division overturned the conviction and endorsed the concept of pre-trial "taint hearings" to ascertain whether children had been so "tainted" by the interview process that they should not be allowed to testify at trial. The New Jersey Supreme Court upheld the decision, and charges against Kelly Michaels were eventually dropped. The view that the case was all a witch-hunt has since become the conventional wisdom.

This chapter argues that the conventional wisdom is wrong. On the basis of a comprehensive examination of the record, it is apparent that the witch-hunt narrative omits key facts and distorts others—all in favor of the theory that the case can be explained entirely by "child suggestibility." The actual evidence in the case has been overshadowed by academic research purporting to demonstrate that children were highly suggestible under conditions much less intensive than what happened in the Kelly Michaels case. But the critical claim that compares the approach in their experiments to what was actually done in the case is not borne out by the record of the case.

The Case and the Conviction

Margaret Kelly Michaels, who was known as Kelly, moved to New Jersey in the summer of 1984 when she was twenty-two years old and a few credits short of graduating from college. In September she took a job as a teacher's assistant at the Wee Care Day Nursery in Maplewood, a prosperous suburb of New York City. The day-care center was operated out of St. George's Episcopal Church, a sprawling three-story building that rented rooms on two floors to the day-care center. Soon after starting at Wee Care, Kelly Michaels became a classroom teacher; she replaced a teacher who left unexpectedly. Michaels had her own classroom and a naptime group with some of the same children, and she took care of children in the late afternoon when the center was nearly deserted. Two events in late April 1985 are critical to the case that soon developed: Kelly Michaels left Wee Care abruptly, and shortly thereafter a four-year-old boy blurted out something disconcerting while having his temperature taken anally at his pediatrician's office. A basic timeline of the case appears in Figure 5.1.

Key Events in Late April 1985

Kelly Michaels left her job hastily at the end of April, about six weeks before the school year was over. The hastiness is reflected in the fact that she gave two weeks' notice and then departed *before* what she said would be her final day. By her description at the time, the departure was for "personal" reasons. That is the word she used in a letter to the school's director on April 15. Two days later, in a letter to parents, Michaels said she "had been experiencing serious personal difficulties which have now made it imperative for me to leave Wee Care as soon as possible."[1] Michaels did not explain what she was "experiencing" at the time that made it so "imperative" to leave Wee Care immediately. She would later claim her decision to leave Wee Care was a simple matter of leaving one job in favor of a better one. But according to Stephanie Lorman of the Community Day Care Center in East Orange, the "better" job that Kelly Michaels accepted was temporary; it would last only through September 1985, and it paid essentially the same as the job at Wee Care.[2]

Michaels never explained convincingly why a temporary job, at essentially the same pay, was so much better than her current job that it would prompt her sudden departure weeks before the end of the school year. Of course, she did not owe anyone an explanation, but the prosecution would later argue that one reason made particular sense: Michaels had been playing sexualized games with the children, she could see that various children were acting out, and she was fleeing the scene. There was strange additional evidence that also fit this theory better than any other explanations that have since been offered: Michaels told a

Figure 5.1 Kelly Michaels Case Timeline, Initial Complaint to Conviction.

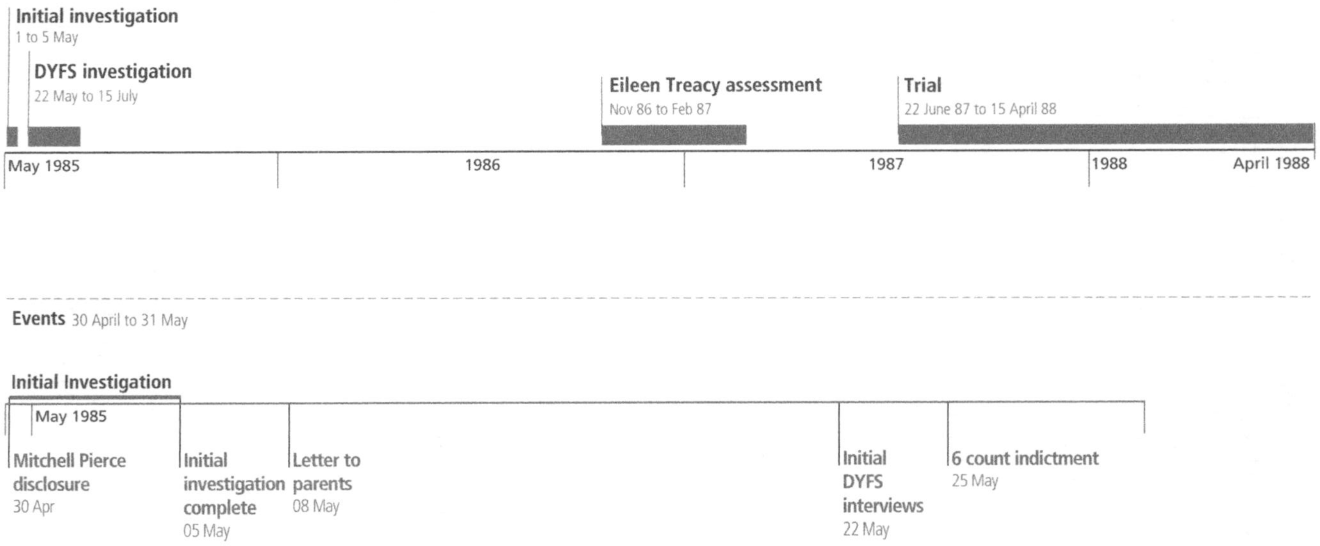

Initial investigation
1 to 5 May

DYFS investigation
22 May to 15 July

Eileen Treacy assessment
Nov 86 to Feb 87

Trial
22 June 87 to 15 April 88

| May 1985 | 1986 | 1987 | 1988 | April 1988 |

Events 30 April to 31 May

Initial Investigation

May 1985

Mitchell Pierce disclosure
30 Apr

Initial investigation complete
05 May

Letter to parents
08 May

Initial DYFS interviews
22 May

6 count indictment
25 May

mother on April 19 that she was leaving early because she was "bleeding from the rectum, a lot."[3] Whatever the reason for her departure, the investigation in the case was triggered days later when a four-year-old boy made a spontaneous statement at his pediatrician's office. On April 30, 1985, Dorinda Pierce took her son Mitchell[4] to the pediatrician because he had a rash. While the medical assistant was taking his temperature rectally, Mitchell said "this is what my teacher does to me at school." Laura Hadley, the medical assistant, testified that the thermometer was in his rectum for "about a half a minute" before the child made this statement.[5] Asked specifically about where her hands were, Hadley indicated she was "holding the thermometer" with one hand and "watching my watch" with the other hand.[6] (This testimony would later be overlooked completely by the witch-hunt narrative.) Hadley then asked the boy, Which teacher? He said, "Kelly." Hadley mouthed to Pierce, who was also in the room, "Who is Kelly?" Dorinda indicated she did not know any "Kelly." As it turns out, Kelly Michaels was Mitchell's "naptime" teacher, but she was not his classroom teacher, so the name did not sound familiar to his mother. Seeking to clarify, the medical assistant asked *what* Kelly did. The boy responded: "Her takes my temperature every day at school." There was little doubt to the nurse or the mother that the child was indicating he was anally penetrated by someone named Kelly.

Mrs. Pierce later testified that after lunch the same day, when she asked her son what happened at naptime, he "leaned against the refrigerator, put one leg up and started rubbing his genitals." He then stated "she used the white jean stuff," adding "you have to be real careful not to get it on your pants."[7] His mother was not sure what "white jean stuff" meant, but the overall meaning of his words was clear. She called her pediatrician back to ask for advice. He told her to call the New Jersey Department of Youth and Family Services (DYFS) and report that her son had possibly been sexually abused at Wee Care. Those events all occurred within three hours of the office visit. What unfolded after the phone call spanned nine years. First there was an investigation, and then there was a lengthy pre-trial period, followed by a nine-month trial. Five years later, there were two high-profile appeals.

The Initial Phase of the Investigation

The first phase of the investigation began when Richard Mastrangelo, an investigator for the Essex County Prosecutor's Office, was notified about the matter by Lou Fonolleras from the DYFS Institutional Abuse Unit. Fonolleras had first spoken to Dorinda Pierce, whose call was on the advice of her pediatrician. Cases in the Sexual Abuse Unit of the Essex County Prosecutor's Office were assigned chronological numbers beginning with the new year. The call about

Mitchell Pierce's statement was given the internal case number 402. Though it was the 402nd case of the year, it was the only one to eventually become a national news story.

Sara Sencer-McArdle, the assistant prosecutor assigned to the case, had handled hundreds of child sexual abuse cases by the time this one arrived.[8] But she had never had an "institutional abuse" case. So this was the first time she faced questions about how to coordinate an investigation with another agency. DYFS had jurisdiction to investigate claims of child maltreatment at nursery schools because they licensed such facilities. The agency could revoke a license, it could assess fines, and it could mandate changes such as removing an employee or changing procedures. This mission, though, differs considerably from that of the criminal justice system. The purpose of a DYFS investigation is to identify and rectify problems, not to assess innocence or guilt for purposes of punishment. The burden of proof before taking an official action is "a preponderance of the evidence," an evidentiary standard much less demanding than the "beyond a reasonable doubt" standard in criminal proceedings.

The Essex County Prosecutor's Office was not inclined to work with DYFS. Their inclination was to complete their own investigation without any outside interference. As Lisa Manshel reported, in one of the two books written about the case, Sencer-McArdle asked Fonolleras to hold off on his investigation.[9] He agreed at first, but the agreement lasted only three weeks. During this time, the prosecutor's office conducted its own investigation and presented the evidence for an indictment based on the testimony of three children.

The criminal case began to take shape on Thursday, May 2, when Mitchell Pierce was interviewed by detective George McGrath and assistant prosecutor Sencer-McArdle. Mitchell indicated that his teacher at school took his temperature rectally. He demonstrated with a doll and stated, as he had with his mother, that Kelly used "gasoline." The prosecutor asked if his temperature was taken in his mouth. "No. You can't put gasoline in your mouth," he replied. "Her takes it in my bum," he explained.[10] The prosecutor would later confirm that temperatures were *not* taken rectally at Wee Care, but instead with a plastic strip on the forehead. If Mitchell's naptime teacher was inserting something into his rectum, it was not an approved action. Mitchell also named two other boys as being "hurt" by Michaels: Eddie Nathanson and Sam Raymond. The investigation had its first two leads. These disclosures became the core of the original charges against Kelly Michaels.

One of these leads produced nothing at the time; the other provided the basis for additional charges. Eddie Nathanson was the second child interviewed, and he did not disclose anything. Sam Raymond was interviewed by Mastrangelo, of the Essex County Prosecutor's Office, on May 3. Sam's mother, Jackie, later testified that she learned there were sexual abuse allegations at Wee Care on April 30 when Arlene Spector, director of the preschool, informed her husband in person.[11] The next day, Jackie Raymond asked her son "if he had any problem with anybody in school." As she later summarized his response: "He told me that one of the teachers at school had touched him on the behind and in his penis and kicked him a couple of times." When asked to describe this exchange in more detail, she added:

> He told me in spurts of the moment, like different intervals. He ran behind the couch, hid, he started crying and then finally he just sat there when I walked behind the couch and he told me that he was hurt by a teacher at school.[12]

The five-year-old boy made similar statements at the prosecutor's office: "Kelly kicked me," he said, and she touched "on my private area." How often did this occur? "Once," he responded. He also said Kelly had once locked him in a closet. These statements would be the basis for one count of second-degree sexual assault (touching his penis) and one count of child endangerment (locking him in the closet).

An additional boy—not one of the two mentioned by Mitchell—also emerged in the first days of the investigation. At this point, there had not been any kind of announcement or press coverage concerning allegations of sexual abuse at Wee Care. The other parents of children at Wee Care who knew about the allegations in the first few days in May 1985, beyond the parents of the boys already interviewed, were those on the board of directors of the nursery school. The board oversaw Wee Care facilities in Maplewood and South Orange, New Jersey, and several board members had children at the Wee Care facility in Maplewood. One was Debbie Cook, whose five-year-old son Cody was also in Michaels's naptime group. On May 2, the Cooks opened a conversation with their son about the teachers at school. Later that evening, Cody's father wrote a three-page single-spaced description of what then happened. The handwritten statement indicates that these parents, like Dorinda Pierce, were not aware that their child even had contact with someone named Kelly at Wee Care.

> I asked who all of the teachers at school were and proceeded to name the ones I knew; Nancy, Arlene, Rosita, Barbara Crystal & Joan. Cody then said I'm forgetting someone and I said who? He said, Kelly. I asked, who's she? He said the Nap Teacher.[13]

As Cody's father described it, his son avoided his gaze and started kicking the table when asked about Kelly. He wrote further:

I told him whatever he told me was O.K. whether anything happened or not, but I needed to know the truth. He hung his head and said "Oh, you mean about Kelly touched my private parts." I asked, "Did Kelly do that?" He said "yes, and she also told me not to tell my parents & that I had to keep it a secret."[14]

This statement was possibly the most jarring to the boy's father, but something stranger was yet to come. When the boy was asked how Kelly touched his private parts, he provided a most unlikely answer: *with a spoon*. His father's handwritten statement continues:

I said, "with a spoon?" He said yes. I then asked what do you mean? He got up from his chair, and walked over to the drawers by the sink, got out a spoon, and said like this.[15]

The boy repeated those details the next day and demonstrated on a doll what happened with the spoon, which was essentially that Michaels had lifted his scrotum with the utensil. This was the first child to mention utensils as part of the sexual acts involving Michaels. Although the claim would eventually be made that investigators induced children to make allegations of this sort, there can be no question that the original allegations about utensils came from a child's statement to his parents before he was formally interviewed in the case. Cody Cook's father gave a statement to Detective Mastrangelo at the prosecutor's office that contained the same essential facts. Asked whether he had anything to add, he said:

Yes, both last night at home, and today with Det. McGrath, Cody said that Kelly had told him to keep it a secret. And when he told me what took place in school last night, he hung his head down and looked pained. Previous to that he had been very nervous and figidy [sic]. In my mind, his body language, at these critical moments, underscore [sic] the truthfulness of his statements.[16]

One more boy was also interviewed in the first week of May. Max Rooney was a good friend of Sam Raymond's, and Max's father was co-president of the board of directors of Wee Care. Max's parents were asked if they would bring their son to the prosecutor's office on Sunday, May 5, when Sam was going to return for a second interview that was to be videotaped.

Unfortunately, there were problems with the videotape equipment. The "recorded" statement of Sam Raymond was determined to be unusable shortly after it was taken. The prosecutor had to conduct the same interview a second time if there was any hope of capturing his statements on tape. (It probably could not be used as evidence, anyway, given the rules against hearsay evidence.) The boy reportedly said much less in the second interview than he did in the first; his affect was apparently much different as well.[17] Things went even worse with Max. The "Patricia Crowley" book about the case, written under that pseudonym by the mother of Martha Landez, includes the following account, which suggests how emotional the topic of sexual abuse was for many parents:

> Next it was Max Rooney's turn. But he appeared terrified, and was reluctant to respond to even the simplest questions about school. So Sara brought Sam Raymond back into the room, hoping that Max would say that nothing bad happened to his friend when he talked about Kelly.
>
> But when Sam Raymond described for Sara how Kelly fondled the boys with spoons, Max Rooney denied it.
>
> Sam Raymond looked puzzled. "Yes, Max, it did so happen," he said.
>
> Max turned his fearful face to his friend and said softly, "Sam, I said no."
>
> At this point, Sara decided to intervene. "Okay, little boys," she said. "Just tell the truth."
>
> Michael Rooney Max's father, standing out in the hall listening, was outraged. He had had enough. It seemed to him like Sara was bullying his child into talking when the child was obviously petrified. He smashed the baseball bat over the staircase banister, and began to scream obscenities at a startled Sara.[18]

Max Rooney did not play any further role in the case, so there is no testimony or other court documentation that would provide critical purchase in assessing this claim. It is impossible to know for sure whether Max "appeared terrified" or was "obviously petrified." It is also not possible to know why his father reacted so violently to the statement "Just tell the truth." Indeed, this incident and the addendum that Cook offered to his statement about Cody's disclosure demonstrate how significant nonverbal qualities can be in describing and interpreting children's statements. These examples also demonstrate the limits of reviewing such issues entirely on the basis of written transcripts and related documents.

The original Wee Care case, then, was based on three of the five boys interviewed in the first few days of May. See Figure 5.2 for a depiction of the interview sequence for the five boys who were first interviewed in early May. All three of them gave clear statements about sexual abuse at the hands of Kelly Michaels in their first contact with authorities. The first one originated in a spontaneous statement at the pediatrician's office, and the other two each came in response to

Figure 5.2 Kelly Michaels Interview Sequence, Children Interviewed in the Initial Investigative Phase.

Each icon represents one interview. The space between 5 and 22 May is not drawn to scale.

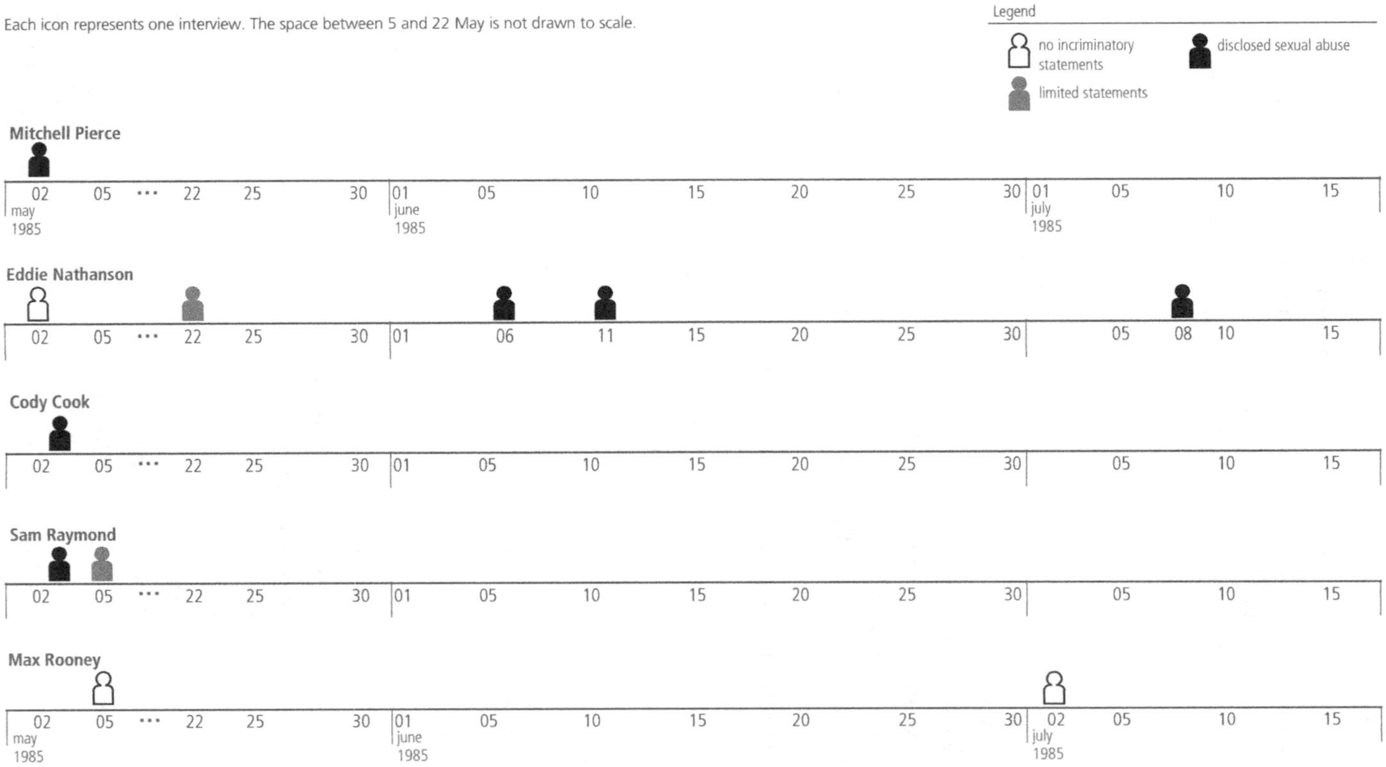

Compiled by author from original documents.

a question from a parent. The statements of these boys would form the basis for a six-count indictment that was handed down by a grand jury on May 24. Unknown at the time, two more grand juries would be convened—one in July, the other in November—and more indictments would follow. Twenty-eight more children would be added to the case through this process. But statements by three boys—obtained long before any publicity about the case, and even before the director of the preschool sent a letter to parents—were the core of the original case against Kelly Michaels.

The Subsequent Investigation

The prosecutor's office did not look beyond the three boys for additional victims, or even seek to reinterview either of the boys who did not make any kind of a disclosure. Investigators interviewed a few more adults in preparing the case for the grand jury, but no more children were interviewed by the Essex County Prosecutor's Office in May. The prosecutors had "stepped back" from further investigation of the case.[19] This was not a formal designation, of course; rather, it was a practical reality in an office overburdened with other cases. Two events caused the matter to reverberate in the community after the five boys were interviewed. The first was a letter about the matter sent on May 8 to all the parents with children at Wee Care in 1984–85. Second, there was a meeting for parents on May 15. The letter to parents indicated that the prosecutor's office was conducting an investigation "regarding serious allegations made by a child against a former employee of the Maplewood Center."[20] It promised communication in the future when more information was available, but the letter otherwise provided no details. It did not name the suspect; nor did it request that parents do anything.

The letter raised concerns among parents, for obvious reasons. On receiving it, many parents phoned each other, comparing notes and seeking information. Although this information was not formally released, there is evidence that many parents were aware that the alleged victims were all boys.[21] This caused some parents of girls at Wee Care to decide it was not necessary to attend the parents' meeting on May 15. Even some parents with boys at Wee Care skipped this meeting, but many of the parents were in attendance.

The board of directors wanted to have a meeting for parents, but they were painfully aware of the tension between investigating a criminal case and providing information to those affected by the investigation. The board president informed the audience on May 15 "that both the Maplewood Police Department and the Essex County Prosecutor's Office had requested that we not have any meeting at all."[22] The main speaker for the meeting was Peg Foster, a social worker whose mission was to address child sexual abuse issues in general without addressing anything about the status of the case. The minutes of this meeting indicate that "as expected, parents raised many questions that Board members could not answer for fear of endangering the investigation."[23]

Foster is reported to have emphasized that parents should not interrogate their children and that "they should be good listeners."[24] She also described various behavioral symptoms that might be of concern, emphasizing that *changes* in behavior are what is relevant. It was not clear to parents whether the allegations were current or not. Kelly Michaels's connection to this letter was not widely known then. The whole thing was played down by Arlene Spector, director of the preschool, who was quoted as saying: "It was very benign stuff. On a scale of one to ten, I'd say it was about a three."[25]

Fonolleras, the DYFS investigator who originally notified the prosecutor's office about the statement by Mitchell Pierce, entered the case on May 22. The prosecutors had asked him to hold back on his investigation. But after three weeks of waiting, he received approval to commence his own investigation from a DYFS supervisor who knew the prosecutors did not have the power to prevent DYFS from doing so. Fonolleras reportedly informed the Essex County Prosecutor's Office, "I'm coming in, whether you like it or not."[26] He drove to the school and started looking around. After examining the premises, he proceeded, with the assistance of Spector, to call Eddie Nathanson's mother for permission to interview the first boy who denied any involvement when interviewed earlier at the prosecutor's office.

According to Fonolleras's description, Eddie "refused to give information" at first. They played, they made drawings, and Eddie eventually "admitted seeing Kelly Michaels massage Sam Raymond and Mitchell Pierce's buttock and backs and that she inserted her index finger into their anus."[27] But he denied any personal victimization. Fonolleras then tried to interview Ralph Gans, a classmate and friend of Eddie's. Ralph was "visibly upset and angry at being questioned" about Michaels, and he ran out of the room when her name was mentioned.[28] On the basis of this one-day visit, Fonolleras submitted a report to his supervisors that described concerns about lack of adequate supervision of children at Wee Care. He made no findings concerning abuse and did not schedule any more interviews. This is important to remember, since Fonolleras is eventually cast as an interviewer with such a strong "confirmation bias" that he found sexual abuse everywhere he looked. That certainly is not what happened on May 22.

Fonolleras returned to Wee Care on June 6, prompted by a telephone call from Eddie Nathanson's mother, indicating that Eddie had made statements at home indicating Kelly Michaels had sucked his penis ("a lot, a lot") and scraped the boys' nipples "with a fork."[29] Critics of the case often mention the fact that Eddie's mother read him a book called *No More Secrets for Me*.[30] They do not tend to mention the reasons that it seemed possible that Eddie might, in fact, be keeping secrets. First, he was one of two children named by the first boy in the case, and the other boy confirmed the abuse when first questioned. Second, Eddie had had an unexplained, chronic rash in his anal area that spring.

Fonolleras described Eddie as "frightened and very shaken" on June 6. With the aid of dolls, however, the boy made numerous statements about sexual abuse. These included several mentions of utensils. Eddie's statements matched what had seemed to be the most unbelievable aspect of Sam Raymond's disclosure to his parents the night of May 2: sexual abuse with a spoon. (There is no evidence that Fonolleras knew the content of Raymond's statement to police.) Eddie also described rubbing a spoon on Michaels's vaginal area. Fonolleras's notes from this interview contain additional statements about abuse with utensils: Eddie indicated that Michaels had put her finger and a "knife handle" in his anus. He also reported that she had said: "Let's play nurse. I'll take your temperature. You feel warm."[31] Additionally, "Eddie told me he was naked in the music room, had been hit with a wooden spoon." Fonolleras asked the boy "to show me where it was."[32] Eddie took him to the church choir room, a third-floor room that was off-limits to the children at Wee Care.

Fonolleras interviewed two other children that day: Ralph Gans, Eddie's friend, and Julia Tilden, the first girl interviewed in the investigation. Ralph had run out of the room when Fonolleras tried to interview him on May 22. On June 6, Ralph stayed in the room and reportedly made numerous statements about sexual abuse by Michaels. These statements were noteworthy for two reasons. First, he also mentioned utensils, particularly knives. Second, he implicated "various girls," according to Fonolleras's notes. One girl, Tilden, was named several times in connection with sexual acts. She was interviewed later that day. Fonolleras's notes from this interview indicate that Julia also stated Kelly Michaels had used a knife and her finger to penetrate girls and boys. She also specified "the music room" and added a detail that became the symbol for those who criticized the case: she said that Michaels had played the piano in the nude, specifically playing the song "Jingle Bells." Perhaps even more striking, for its resonance with prior statements from several other children, is this question and answer from the statement Julia Tilden gave at the prosecutor's office six days later:

Q: Does Kelly play nurse with you?
A: Takes my temperature, with a spoon, on my front bottom.[33]

But Julia did not end up being in the case, and I have been unable to find anything in the record to explain why.

The next day, Fonolleras interviewed four girls at Wee Care. The first was Nora van Haley, who had been mentioned the day before by one or both of the boys. Nora's mother was telephoned on June 6 to request permission for her daughter to be interviewed at school. Her mother declined, insisting on meeting Fonolleras first. This happened the following morning, and Nora was the first interview of the day.

Eileen Treacy, a psychologist who later evaluated children for the prosecution, summarized the disclosures contained in Fonolleras's notes:

> Knife in vagina; fork handle in [Max Rooney's] butt & other boys; hurt her in piano room; nude pileup w/silverware.[34]

Max Rooney was, by then, the only one of the original five boys who had not disclosed abuse. His original interview was the one cut short when his father lost his temper. What is striking about the content of these early statements is the consistency of the strangest elements in other disclosures: the utensils and sexualized games in the "piano room."

Fonolleras interviewed three other girls that day: Cassie Bond-Foley, Lucy Deacon, and Jessie Shaw. Cassie had been mentioned earlier by Eddie Nathanson. Again, there are statements about utensils in his notes: "she described having a knife put into her" and being "hit on the genitals with a wooden spoon." Perhaps most strikingly, "she also saw [Kelly] nude, sitting and playing Jingle Bells." Once again, a bizarre element that is otherwise almost impossible to believe was mentioned by more than one child. There was not really a formal interview with Lucy Deacon, but an attempted interview: Fonolleras described the girl as "too scared" and ended the effort in less than five minutes. The other girl, Jessie Shaw, apparently made some kind of disclosure; this much is clear from her mother's later testimony.[35]

When the day ended on June 7, the case was destined to expand beyond the original indictments. In two days, Fonolleras had interviewed two boys and five girls. Both boys made statements about sexualized games, including abuse with utensils. The boys named several girls who also participated, and those girls were interviewed within one day. Four of the five girls interviewed then made statements, with overlapping details, that would be the basis for criminal charges. The second grand jury was not convened until July, but these children would account for the first charges presented.

It is clear from the later accounts by Martha Landez's mother that at the time the parents still had no sense that the "former employee" might be implicated in anything involving more than a few boys.[36] A local newspaper reinforced this idea when it reported, in a brief story on June 7, the filing of a six-count indictment against Kelly Michaels for sexually abusing three boys.[37] Children were still attending Wee Care in the first week of June, and the board of directors had just gone through a long argument about whether or not to proceed with an annual fundraising event in June. They decided against it, but the fact there were strong advocates of "business as usual" demonstrates that the charges against Michaels had not become an obsession among Wee Care parents.

The investigation expanded the next week. Fonolleras conducted seven interviews in the two days at the end of the first week in June; there were fourteen interviews conducted between Monday and Thursday of the second week of June. Six of those interviews were with children who had not previously been interviewed. The others were second or third rounds, but this was because the Essex County Prosecutor's Office had come back into the case that week after hearing a report from Fonolleras on June 7. The investigators from the prosecutor's office needed to take their own statements; they could not recommend criminal charges to be based on statements they never heard. Several children, then, repeated to a police investigator what they had already told the DYFS investigator. These second interviews were *not* prompted by the lack of disclosure in the first interview, as the witch-hunt narrative would later claim. To the contrary, they were conducted because there *had* been earlier disclosures.

The fact that some children made statements to police investigators after being interviewed by DYFS illustrates why it is impossible to characterize the "average" interview in the case. The interviews did not all have the same purpose; why children were interviewed varied. Sometimes a second interview followed a first one in which there was a disclosure; at least a few times, the second interview was a subsequent attempt to find out whether a child who did not originally disclose anything untoward nevertheless had relevant information.

Recognizing these differences, we can still find some patterns to the interviews. Dr. Karen Burton, who reviewed transcripts of twenty-six interviews with children for the defense, wrote a memo describing the "basic format characterized by most but not all of the interviews." First the child would be asked to draw his or her family and then be asked to draw Kelly; the interviewer would ascertain what words the child used for various body parts, and the children would be asked general question (e.g., Did you see Kelly do anything bad?) and then more specific ones (e.g., Did you ever see Kelly doing something funny with peanut butter?).[38]

By the end of the second week in June, the original case had expanded to include two more boys as victims—Eddie Nathanson, Ralph Gans—and the several girls who they mentioned and who made independent statements corroborating details about abuse with utensils and sexualized games in the choir room. Several children (Cody Cook, Lucy Deacon, and Eddie) made incriminating statements to one or both of their parents before being interviewed by authorities. Others made statements to their parents immediately after being interviewed. It was apparent to investigators that the case was larger than a few boys, although no one knew how much larger.

The Investigation Intensifies and Then Deteriorates

The nature and intensity of the investigation eventually changed, shifting from being focused on the evidence obtained in earlier interviews to being essentially universal. Every child who attended Wee Care would be interviewed, whether or not investigators had reason to think the child had been abused. But this was a DYFS goal, not one adopted by the prosecutor's office—a distinction later to be lost in all that was written about the case.

The interviewing increased the next week (see Figure 5.3). There were fourteen interviews the week of June 10 and twenty-three the week of June 17. The intensity of the matter also increased in the community. A board meeting with parents was held on June 10. Two more parents' meetings followed in June— one on Friday the 14th, the other Monday the 17th—both with Dr. Susan Esquilin, a psychologist. On June 21, the *Star Ledger* reported that additional charges would be filed against Michaels.[39]

As the investigation expanded to include all of the children, it reached many who did not allege any kind of abuse. This happened at the same time Fonolleras was becoming convinced that most, if not all, of the children at Wee Care had been sexually abused by Michaels. The belief led to interviews where some children where prompted and pressured inappropriately. A prime example is Fonolleras's interview with Brian Murphy,[40] an almost-five-year-old who attended Wee Care for the final two months of the 1984–85 school year. "Don't be a baby," Fonolleras scolded the boy, who was apparently running around the room during the interview. "Come here. Seriously, we are going to need your help on this," he said. This interview has been cited frequently by critics of the case because early in the interview, when Fonolleras is asking the boy to name various body parts, Brian says, pointedly, "Stop, you're teaching me stuff." Fonolleras's ham-handed reply: "You got to learn somehow."[41]

Lou Fonolleras clearly grew less open to the idea that any children were *not* her victims. He ultimately "substantiated" sexual abuse in connection with fifty-one children. His explanation for reaching this conclusion about children who did not disclose abuse appears, in retrospect, to yield much better evidence of his bias than of Michaels's guilt. For example, after interviewing one boy on June 19, Fonolleras wrote that he "was obviously quite shaken, and this investigator felt strongly that he wanted to relate his knowledge, but was afraid of upsetting his family."[42] In other words, the child did not make any incriminating statements but the investigator "felt strongly" that the child was withholding things. Fonolleras even opined that the boy's parents "refused to accept his possible victimization and projected those feelings onto him."[43]

Figure 5.3 Kelly Michaels Interview Sequence, All Investigative Interviews.

Each icon represents one interview. Some children appear more than once. The vertical stacks of icons indicate the number of interviews in one day. The space between 5 to 22 May is not drawn to scale.

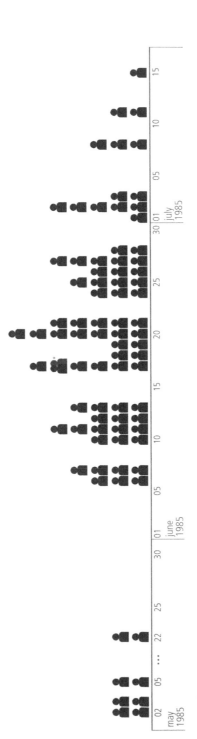

* Two children were interviewed in a single session on *June 17.*
Compiled by author from assorted court documents.

Another troublesome example is the interview with Clare Williams, a girl who Kelly Michaels regularly babysat. She denied any victimization, but Fonolleras wrote in his report:

> There is a slight possibility that Kelly may have respected her relationship with the family . . . but this investigator finds it difficult to believe that she would have had the conscience to exercise discretion.[44]

There were also instances where Fonolleras told a child that Kelly was "bad." A prime example: "Everyone knows you didn't do anything wrong. Kelly did. She took advantage of you kids," Fonolleras told Tracy Hayes. None of these examples is defensible. Indeed, any one of them could be used as an argument to discredit subsequent statements from the child. But in analyzing the actual criminal case, it is vitally important to ask whether these examples involved children whose statements actually formed the basis for charges against Kelly Michaels. The answer is no. *None of the examples cited above involved a child who was actually in the criminal case.* The objectionable content in these interviews might be why they were not included. More likely, it is because these children had no relevant information. This does not excuse the specific tactics with individual children, but neither should it be a reason to abandon the entire case. Rightfully, none of the children mentioned above was taken to the grand jury, and none appeared in any of the indictments—although several would later be included in the witch-hunt narrative about the case. Additionally, these examples all came from the late stage of the investigative interviews: Elliot Sanders was interviewed on June 19, Clare Wolfe on June 20, Tracy Hayes on June 25, and Brian Murphy on June 26.[45] These examples are strong evidence of overzealous interviewing, but this should not be confused with evidence of an all-encompassing problem in a case that originated with three separate disclosures in early May—weeks before Fonolleras interviewed any children.

The "hearsay knowledge" that appears in some of the investigative interviews is also consistent with the idea that the investigation reached a point of worse-than-diminishing returns. "My mommy told me Kelly did bad things," Clare Williams told Fonolleras. Ruby Watson said "My daddy told me Kelly did bad things." Shayla Palimieri indicated that "Tracy Hayes told me that Kelly touched private parts." Those statements, also later cited by case critics, are reason to worry about any subsequent "disclosure" made by these children since it is apparent that the reason they associate Michaels with wrongdoing is that someone told them so. But again, *none* of these children was taken to the grand jury and none of their statements formed the basis for any charges in the case, even though several of these children would later figure prominently in the witch-hunt narrative about the case. Notably, all of the examples of supposed hearsay knowledge that have been identified in the case were from the late stages of the investigative interview sequence.[46] If there was a time, then, when a significant number of parents were anxious to have their children interviewed solely for the fact they attended Wee Care—and not because of statements by other children—it was the third week of June, right after consecutive parents' meetings on June 14 and 17. Between June 18 and June 28 there were thirty-two investigative interviews, which is slightly less than the total number of interviews conducted between May 2 and June 17. Twenty-two of those sessions were with children being seen for the first time. Some of the remaining ten, however, were second interviews with children who did not disclose any sexual abuse the first time. Two of those children, P. J. Isaacs and Brenda Mendes, made statements that caused them to be included in the charges and subsequent trial. The interviews with both those children would become common examples in the witch-hunt narrative and would repeatedly be described, inaccurately, as being typical of the case.

The investigation started wrapping up by the July 4 weekend. Four children who had not been previously interviewed were questioned between July 1 and 3. Six more interviews were conducted after that weekend, all with children who had previously been interviewed. With the exception of one boy, the children interviewed at that point had already made substantive statements concerning Michaels. Several of these interviews were in advance of the grand jury, which began hearing testimony on July 11. Although criticisms would later be made about multiple interviews in the case, those critics would never address how many of the children who were interviewed more than once had disclosed sexual abuse in the first interview. Nor would they confront how many children disclosed abuse early in the investigation. The final investigative interview was July 15. Fifty-one children had been interviewed; from the very first investigative interview with Mitchell Pierce, there had been eighty-three interview sessions in the case.[47]

There would ultimately be three grand juries in the Michaels case: the one that handed down the six-count indictment in May involving the three boys, the one that heard evidence throughout July, and a third that heard evidence in November. The indictments generated through the final two were unsealed in December, adding 229 counts and twenty-eight children to the original case. Twenty children ended up in the eventual trial.

One additional child merits attention, since he was never interviewed by Fonolleras but by some accounts became the most important witness in the case as a result. He was, as Lisa Manshel put it, "a major choke point in the defense's suggestibility theory"; he became "the tactical star witness"[48] but is generally not acknowledged fully in the witch-hunt narrative. David Applegate was mentioned

early in May when Rebecca Flora told her mother she had seen David naked at
school. Rebecca's mother telephoned David's mother, who she did not otherwise know, to alert her to this statement. Notably, Judy Applegate did not take
the comment very seriously. She later testified: "I actually said to her, you know,
kids go the bathroom. I'm not going to get upset over it and she shouldn't
either."[49] Accordingly, she did not attend the parents meeting in mid-May. When
another mother called her on June 13, however, she decided to speak directly to
her son, who had been home sick with chickenpox since early that month and
had not been interviewed by anyone. As explained through her testimony at
trial:

Q: What did you say?
A: I said David, the other kids are telling their mothers about the bad things
   that happened at school.
Q: And what was David's reaction?
A: David's eyes opened up like saucers and he said they are?[50]

This hearsay testimony was permitted, after an objection by the defense, because
it was offered to prove the sequence of events that led to the emergence of David's disclosure, not to prove the underlying claim. After allowing Applegate to
consult her diary from the time, this exchange occurred:

Q: Did you ask him at that time what Kelly did to him?
A: Yeah.
Q: What did he tell you?
A: That she put things in his tushie and this was the very first thing he told
   me that day, and then the next few days were primarily identifying the
   objects, the forks, the spoons and knives, Legos....[51]

This child was never interviewed by Fonolleras or anyone else at DYFS. His parents, both lawyers, worried about overinterviewing. When the family later filed
a civil claim, the insurance company settled quickly, and reportedly for the largest amount of money that any family received. This may help explain why this
boy's circumstances have never been fully described by proponents of the child-
suggestibility defense. The basis for the defense simply does not apply to him.
Nor does it explain why, on June 8 or 9, her son "would not let [his mother] near
him with a thermometer."[52]

Ceci and Bruck's amicus brief, filed years later, dismisses this child without
ever acknowledging, let alone responding to, any of these facts. Instead, his
initial disclosure to his mother is presented, without any supporting evidence, as
an example of "peer pressure." According to Ceci and Bruck:

this child finally disclosed to his mother after she had told him that others had mentioned him as a participant. The above evidence suggests that this strategy may co-opt children into making false reports.[53]

But that misstates the evidence about David's disclosures. According to the evidence at trial, Applegate did *not* tell David that others had mentioned him *as a participant*. And she certainly did not describe the actions David later elaborated. Moreover, it is clear that Applegate's initial inclinations were all against believing allegations of sexual abuse.[54] There is no reason to believe that merely telling her son that other boys had told their mothers "about the bad things that happened" would *create* an allegation of sexual abuse, particularly with these kinds of specific allegations, which turned out to be entirely consistent with statements already made to authorities by other children.[55]

Eileen Treacy Evaluates the Children

Almost a year after the charges were finalized, the prosecutor's office hired Eileen Treacy, a doctoral candidate in psychology, to evaluate the children who were included in the charges. Treacy evaluated these children between November 1986 and February 1987. These interviews were *not* part of the investigation; the charges had been finalized in December 1985. Treacy assessed, first, whether it would be too traumatic for each child to testify; she also assessed whether the child's behavior was consistent with sexual abuse, and she evaluated the extent to which the child was susceptible to suggestion. She interviewed sixteen of the twenty children who went to trial. Her suggestibility analysis would later be ignored completely by critics of the case, who would focus entirely on her analysis of each child's behavior. She interviewed children from one to three times and submitted detailed reports to the state about the developmental capacity of every child.

Treacy followed a model widely used in sexual abuse cases in New York Family Court, referred to as "validation."[56] The label is unfortunate because it conjures up a rubber stamp, not a thorough and logical process. In fact, the validation process involves, among other things, a comprehensive analysis of "confounding" variables—that is, other possible stressors and causes apart from sexual abuse that might explain any observed behavioral changes. Treacy testified at length about the process, which is still widely accepted and employed in New York courts. There are four components.[57] First, the evaluator considers the child's statements to her, along with demeanor or affect. Second, the evaluator looks for signs of four of the five phases of child-abuse accommodation syndrome.[58] Third, the evaluator asks parents for information about *changes* in behavior; children must have demonstrated changes in behavior in at least five areas to be considered significant in this area. (The idea behind the checklist is consistent with something the defense psychologists in the case agreed on: sexual abuse is likely to result in changes in children's behavior.) Finally, the evaluator conducts a "confounding variable" analysis. The logic of this inquiry is also supported by a defense psychologist in the Kelly Michaels case who, in his own survey of nursery school behavior, found it necessary to ask whether the children had experienced other life traumas that might account for various behaviors.[59] If all four inquiries point in the same direction, the validation process results in a finding that the child's behavior is *consistent* with sexual abuse, but not dispositive. Treacy did not "vouch" for children; instead, she concluded that the behavior of fourteen children who ended up in the trial was "consistent with sexual abuse." Those children displayed enough behavioral changes that could not be explained away by other factors. Her conclusion was equivocal on one child and negative on another; that is, she could not rule out other possible causes of the child's behavior.[60] Four of the children who were in the trial were never evaluated by Treacy.

One aspect of this analysis that would be overlooked entirely later by critics of the case is that Treacy specifically considered whether suggestibility might account for each child's statements and behavior. Passages from her report about David Applegate, the child who was never interviewed by DYFS, demonstrate the point:

> In another attempt to test his suggestibility, I asked him about what happened to him in the bathroom (as he had not disclosed anything about the bathroom). David did not accept the suggestion. He clearly denied that anything happened to him in the bathroom.
>
> When I told him that Kelly was saying that the children were making a mistake and all of this did not happen, David said that she was not telling the truth.[61]

Treacy's reports on other children contain similar accounts of asking purposely leading questions containing incorrect information. In the reports located in the course of this research, there were no examples in which a child accepted the suggestion and parroted back the misinformation supplied by Treacy. Yet this is precisely the mechanism that, according to the witch-hunt narrative that later developed around the case, explains every single allegation in the case. The narrative has never explained how children could be so susceptible to suggestion when being interviewed by investigators yet never succumb to suggestion while being interviewed by Treacy.

The Charges and the Trial

Lou Fonolleras ultimately "substantiated" sexual abuse by Kelly Michaels against fifty-one children at Wee Care. He characterized the evidence as "overwhelmingly evident" in his final report. He also noted that "approximately another ten children and their parents have been interviewed and deemed not to have been involved."[62] But the DYFS findings were independent of the criminal investigation. "Substantiating" claims at DYFS did not trigger any additional proceedings.[63] The Essex County Prosecutor's Office would decide how many of those children should be included in a criminal complaint. Given the much higher standard of proof in criminal cases, prosecutors are not supposed to bring charges unless they believe a reasonable jury could find the defendant guilty "beyond a reasonable doubt."[64] It is not clear how many of the fifty-one made credible statements in the first place. My own assessment is that a handful definitely did, and possibly as many as two dozen more, but not many more than that. Certainly not all fifty-one, as Fonolleras concluded; but also not zero, as the defense urged.

The Actual Charges

Translating children's statements into specific criminal charges is particularly difficult in cases involving young children. The Michaels case unfolded during a time when prosecutors around the country were addressing those issues for the first time. Given the developmental capabilities of small children, it was clear that applying the same rules used for adult witnesses would not be appropriate. Children simply are not capable of specifying dates, for example, in the same fashion as adults. A recent appellate decision on the issue in New Jersey mirrored the rules developing in other states: courts would not require the same degree of specificity in naming the dates of alleged offenses when children were involved.[65]

Deciding what charges to bring and how many counts of each charge was far more complicated than specifying a range of dates for the alleged offenses. There were two relevant charges in the New Jersey criminal code concerning child sexual abuse: first- and second-degree sexual assault. The difference was that first-degree charges involved penetration, second-degree charges, sexual touching. The criminal code also contained a third-degree charge called child endangerment. Almost all of the charges ultimately brought in the case were under one of the three statutes.

The widespread allegations about sexual touching with utensils posed an unusual challenge. Was it necessary to specify whether the charge involved a fork or a spoon? There was a danger that charges written too broadly might be thrown out on appeal for being too vague. But narrowly drawn charges also posed dangers. If a child's original statement involved a spoon, but the child testified at trial that the abuse involved a fork, would this be considered such a different act that it should have been charged separately? The prosecutors decided it did. As Lisa Manshel explained:

> The appellate section of the Prosecutor's Office instructed Sara [Sencer-McArdle] to charge the first-degree crimes by the instrument. Instead of charging one count of vaginal penetration and one count of anal penetration for each girl, Sara was to charge up to three separate counts for vaginal penetration (fork, knife, and spoon) and up to three separate counts for anal penetration (fork, knife, and spoon). If she charged the penetrations by orifice alone, the variety of instruments that might be mentioned in testimony could confuse the jury or cause appellate problems down the road.[66]

This legal consideration multiplied the total number of charges. The large number of charges in the case has been cited to suggest that the state alleged that the abuse was, improbably, a daily occurrence. In fact, the legal demands involved in charging the case caused a multiplicity of charges for single events.[67] Ultimately, some children were connected with only a few charges, and others were named in a dozen or more. The most common charges involved sexual abuse with plastic utensils (spoons, knives, forks). A handful of the child endangerment counts contained grotesque charges involving urine or feces, and a few—the ones that received the most publicity, particularly after the conviction—involved the claim that Michaels had played the piano in the nude.

In short, the large number of counts in the case did not translate into as many corresponding sexual abuse events because the state charged alternative counts to minimize potential "appellate problems" concerning lack of specificity. Had the state actually claimed there was daily abuse of twenty children over 150 days, there could have been more than ten thousand counts in the indictment. Instead, at its height, before various children dropped out of the case, there were 235 counts. This was an average of seven or eight counts per child, which actually meant no more than *a few claimed incidents for each child*. The 165 counts that made it to trial clearly did not translate into "daily" or even "frequent" incidents.[68] Basically, the state charged that Michaels abused children occasionally during naptime and in after-school settings. It was, they claimed, "opportunistic" abuse.[69]

Children Dropped from the Case

Eleven of the thirty-one children named in the charges were dropped from the case before trial (see Figure 5.4). Those children accounted for sixty-seven counts. Ten of the eleven children were initially named in the second or third indictment. One child, Cody Cook, was from the first indictment. Cody's father got a promotion and the family moved away.[70] The paucity of available records about these children renders it impossible to ascertain the specific reasons each one was dropped from the case. In a few cases, the reason is documented. Two children were dropped from the case because Treacy, the psychologist who evaluated the child witnesses for the state, deemed them too emotionally distraught.

There were also other reasons children were dropped from the case. One involved the use of hearsay evidence—charges based entirely on statements that a child made to an adult, not to an investigator—for which they were ultimately dropped from the case. The law requires direct testimony from the victim. There are hearsay exceptions that allow spontaneous utterances during medical examinations to be used as evidence, but generally adults are not permitted to testify about allegations made to them by a child. That appears to explain why John Allister was dropped from the case. He denied any victimization in two interviews with Fonolleras, but in an interview on July 6 his mother provided a detailed statement about disclosures she said John had made at home.[71] When Fonolleras tried to interview John again in July, the boy was beyond resistant; he unleashed a series of obscenities and acted wildly until the interview was terminated. Five counts against Michaels were included in the second indictment on the basis of what John's mother told the grand jury. Presumably it was determined that the New Jersey case law would not sustain charges based on that evidence alone, so those counts were eventually dropped.

The parent who wrote a book about the case mentioned two other reasons children were dropped: "because the youngsters were simply too immature" and in some cases "the children themselves refused to testify."[72] The former reason apparently explains why Dana Drew was dropped from the case. She was not able to provide any kind of narrative account to the grand jury; her testimony consisted entirely of single-word answers and shakes or nods of the head.[73] In short, there are a number of reasons for these children being dropped from the case. Some of them might have strengthened the state's case; others undoubtedly would not have.

The State's Case

The case against Kelly Michaels went to trial with 165 criminal counts involving twenty children. The prosecutors were not sure, however, how many of those

Figure 5.4 Kelly Michaels, All Children, All Charges by Legal Status (Carried Forward versus Dropped before Trial).

Children are arranged by phase in order of date of initial interview.

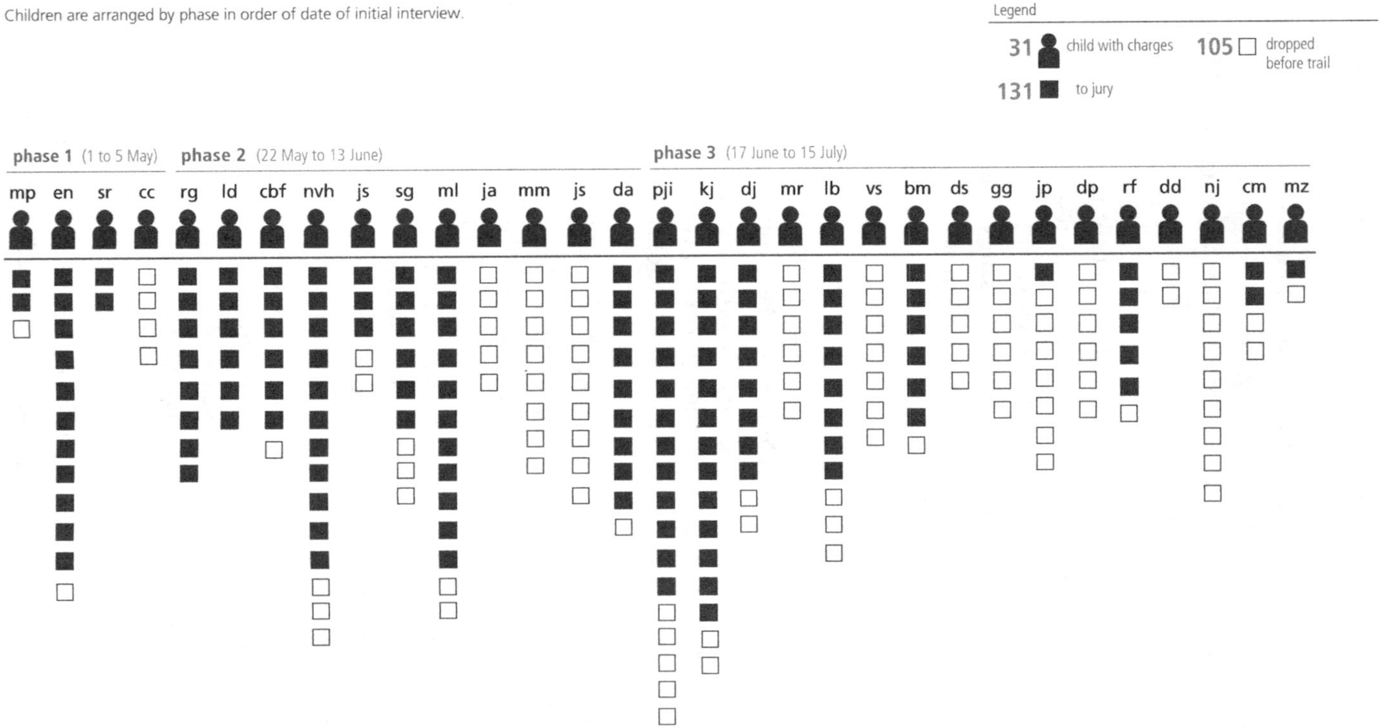

Legend

31 🧍 child with charges   105 ☐ dropped before trail

131 ◼ to jury

phase 1 (1 to 5 May)   phase 2 (22 May to 13 June)

phase 3 (17 June to 15 July)

Compiled by author from original documents.

children would actually testify. Some parents were concerned about how testifying at trial might affect their children, and some of the children had expressed ambivalence. Most had been seeing mental health professionals, who agreed that testifying in open court might be particularly difficult for some children. The case became a battleground over the recent New Jersey statute that provided for the possibility of children testifying by closed-circuit television. The trial judge decided the issue in favor of the prosecution, allowing the children to testify this way at trial. The issue would be raised again on appeal. Meanwhile, nineteen of the twenty children testified in the judge's chambers through closed-circuit television. The other child, Martin Zeitz, did not actually testify. Charges pertaining to him went forward on the basis of other testimony that apparently averted the prohibitions against hearsay evidence.

Because of the number of complainants, the state's case was massive in size. There were ultimately 105 witnesses for the prosecution, 254 exhibits, and twenty weeks of testimony. The core of the case was the testimony of nineteen children, along with their parents. Five therapists, all with a doctorate in psychology, also testified, plus Eileen Treacy, a master's-level psychologist who would finish her doctorate while the case was on appeal. The only potential witnesses of importance who did *not* testify were Peg Foster, the social worker who spoke at the first parent's meeting, and Detective Mastrangelo. Although this leaves the historical record less complete, those individuals were not necessary for introducing the children's statements. Lou Fonolleras testified, of course, as did Detective McGrath.

The gist of the state's case, as told through the children's testimony, was that Michaels played various sexualized games with children. Most of those activities were described as happening either at naptime or in the choir room, presumably in the late afternoon. Many children testified that plastic utensils were employed during these games. The jury not only heard from the children but also heard testimony from parents about statements children made at home. Even the claims that seemed most incredible were generally voiced by more than one child. This did not necessarily mean they were true, of course; the defense would argue that any concordance was evidence of "taint" or "cross-contamination." Beyond this core of narrative evidence, the prosecution presented three kinds of additional evidence: (1) extreme behavioral evidence, (2) medical evidence, and (3) evidence concerning Michaels's "motive."

Extreme Behavioral Evidence

Most of the children at trial exhibited extreme behavior during the 1984–85 school year. Mitchell Pierce's grandfather testified that the boy's behavior changed so dramatically in early winter 1985 he "wondered if Mitchell had sustained some mental damage that we did not know about when we saw this stark change."[74] Similarly, David Applegate's parents witnessed something far beyond a nightmare: night terrors with uncontrollable shaking upon waking. Greg Guild became so aggressive in the winter of 1985 that the boy's bus driver told his mother "she had never seen a child behave like this, and she didn't know what happened to him."[75] His mother took him to a doctor. Debra Schultz's father recounted for the grand jury how his daughter refused to allow her parents to take her temperature with a rectal thermometer in either March or April 1985, even though they had always used this kind.[76] The family later dropped out of the case, so no additional information is available in the record.

Overall, parents of thirteen children at trial reported either "that their children were afraid of nap time at school or complained nearly every day about taking a nap at school."[77] The issue became so apparent that one teacher jokingly called it the "nap rebellion." Children who usually wanted to take their nap rebelled. Nobody identified it as a problem with Michaels herself, but there is no question that the unusual behaviors surrounding the naps she supervised were noted at the time. Even more significant, the naptime rebellion ended after she left Wee Care. A woman who worked there in January 1985 and then again in May 1985 testified that the difference was significant.[78]

Several children also acted frantically or in a highly sexualized manner during the investigative interviews. The most extreme behavior was exhibited by Jacob Peyton, who was almost four and hypersexually out of control. He groped two interviewers and his mother in a sexualized manner. Jacob was interviewed on June 20 by Detective Mastrangelo and social worker Foster. It was one of the longest of the transcribed interviews, with the child distracted and uncooperative. The most noteworthy event took place when the boy was left alone with Anne Felsten, a psychology graduate student. The tape recorder malfunctioned, but she was able to record her recollections of the incident shortly thereafter. "I was still shaking," she later testified. The full single-spaced page of her dictation reads, in part:

> At first he just played a little bit, he was making a drawing but then a he moved over to me and he placed his hand inside my blouse and touched my breasts. At that time I asked him who he touched liked that and he said "You." And I said, "All right, did you touch anyone else like that?" And he said, "You know." And I said, "Can you tell me." And he said, "You know who." So I said, "Can I guess." And he said, "Yes." So we went through some names, "Susan." "Linda," and the answers to those names was "No." When I said, "Kelly," he said, "Yes."[79]

The boy's sexualized behavior extended beyond fondling Felsten. He repeatedly demanded, "Take off your clothes"; she reported, "His aggressiveness about wanting me to take my clothes off became greater and greater."[80] She introduced an anatomically detailed doll (the use of which is the subject of considerable disagreement). As two academic psychologists who later became critical of the case argued:

> Children insert fingers or objects into the doll's openings for the same reason they would insert a finger into the hole of a doughnut; it is there, it is something to manipulate.[81]

Their caution about interpreting such actions is well taken, but exaggerated. In the study they cite, only 18 percent of nonabused children did this.[82] The argument does not appear to explain a child who "practically ripped the clothes off" the doll and proceeded to spread the doll's legs and lick the vaginal area, which is what Jacob Peyton did. Or the child who grabbed Fonolleras's genitals. These incidents are remarkable not only for the highly sexualized behavior and subsequent disclosure. The Felsten incident is also notable because she did precisely what critics of the case later claimed never happened in the case: she asked the child about other adults. The boy singled out Kelly Michaels in that conversation. Two days after the Felsten incident, the same boy tried to insert an emery board dipped in Vaseline into his mother's vagina.[83] Several days later, at a follow-up interview, he grabbed Fonollares's genitals while showing him how Old McDonald was played by the defendant at Wee Care.[84]

This was not the only child to act in an extreme fashion during one of the interviews. Ralph Gans "ran out of the room" every time Michaels's name was mentioned on May 22. Knowing this, of course, places the fact that he was interviewed twice in a different perspective. The first interview ended abruptly; it was nothing like the "exhaustive questioning" critics would later claim all children endured before making any kind of incriminatory statement. Another boy, Justin Lang, "became frantic when Kelly's name was mentioned" in a brief interview on July 1. He returned the next day. According to the DYFS report, "when Kelly's name was mentioned, he began turning over furniture and screaming. The interview was terminated immediately."[85] He was never part of the criminal charges. Similarly, John Allister's interview is filled with extreme language and behavior. "You son of a bitch," this preschooler yelled repeatedly. He later screamed, "You fuck head." "Why are you trying to hit me?" the interviewer later asked.[86] There was no disclosure in this interview, and this child was not part of the eventual trial.

Other dramatic examples of hypersexualized behavior include Rebecca Flora's in therapy. Dr. Jeryl Rempell, a psychologist, testified that at her first session she "was bouncing all over the place" and kept putting her hands on him "as if she was fondling me." This had "a different quality to it" from a hug, he noted. In fact, in his extended experience with hundreds of children, this was the first time a child had done such a thing in therapy.[87] The parents of two other children at trial (Lucy Deacon and Brenda Mendes) testified their children tried to French-kiss family members. Lucy also attempted to lick between her mother's legs. Rebecca Flora's parents testified that she frequently tried to grab them in a sexual manner. Finally, P. J. Isaacs's mother testified that her son once asked her, "Would you like me to put this [baster toy] in your tushie so you can feel healthy too?"[88]

Of course, these behaviors are not conclusive proof of abuse. But neither should they be denied or written off as everyday behavior. Indeed, the peer-reviewed literature on this subject supports the conclusion that the kinds of behavior observed in the Michaels case were truly extreme. A survey of the frequency of sexual behaviors in 251 preschool children concluded that the most extreme found in the Michaels case were "very uncommon." Attempts to touch adults' genitals—something several children did during the interview process, and others did to their parents—were observed in fewer than 1 percent of the children.[89] None of the many child-suggestibility studies later cited by critics of the case ever mention children sexually assaulting the researchers or repeatedly kicking and hitting them, so presumably these behaviors are so rare in nonabused children that researchers virtually never see them. Knowing that this cohort of children was characterized by a significant amount of such extreme behavior does not prove the underlying charges. But it certainly makes them more plausible.

Medical Evidence

Many of the children in the case registered complaints about genital soreness in the months before Michaels left the day-care center. Eddie Nathanson, one of the original five boys interviewed in the case, had two documented pediatric visits for postural dermatitis (an itchy anus) in the winter of 1985.[90] Mitchell Pierce also complained of a "sore rectum" that winter. His mother testified about how her son "used to ask if he needed his temperature taken."[91] David Applegate's mother testified that his "anus was always sore" in the winter of 1985.[92] Sam Raymond also complained about a "sore bottom" for about six weeks in March and April of 1985. The problem was gone in May.[93]

There was also medical evidence involving three other girls who testified against Michaels. Dr. Anna Haroutunian, director of the Child Abuse Program for Children's Hospital of New Jersey, examined two girls in the case. She found the evidence on Rebecca Flora to be most compelling. The doctor testified that the child's hymenal orifice was "well over a centimeter in diameter," or "clearly wider than a child of this age would have." She concluded there were "abnormal genital physical findings, most likely secondary to child sexual abuse" and that there was no apparent physical reason for her enuresis and encotrosis.[94] The defense's own medical expert, Dr. Winston S. Price, did not deny there were significant findings indicating trauma and healing. All he could say for the defense was, "It's very difficult to make a definitive statement about when those particular abnormal findings occurred."[95] Rebecca Flora also had a series of documented visits to the pediatrician precisely during the final two months before Michaels's abrupt departure in late April. As Dr. Price acknowledged, her doctor recorded visits for "red, inflamed vulva" on March 16 and "red vaginal area" on March 30. He ordered urine culture tests on April 3 and again on follow-up.[96] The problem went away in late April.

Dr. Haroutunian testified cautiously that the findings on Cassie Bond-Foley could be "a slight developmental variation" or might "represent an area of healed trauma." Moreover, she testified:

> To me, it would raise a question of abuse even if I didn't know any history. If I saw this child on a routine exam and saw this finding I would have to raise the possibility of sexual abuse happening.[97]

Two other girls at trial had notable medical histories. Martha Landez had documented vaginal and rectal pain in the winter. Her doctor later reported she had no hymen. The other girl, Brenda Mendes, experienced "vaginal bleeding and soreness" between February and April 1985. At least two of the children who were named in the original indictments, but later dropped from the case, also had medical evidence that is worth mentioning. Debra Schultz had such "a sore tushie" in the winter that her father took her to the emergency room.[98] Another boy, Greg Guild, complained to his mother during the winter that his rectum was sore. His mother testified he asked her "to put something on it, put medication on it, which he never requested before, and he also told me his penis hurt." There are no additional details about this boy because he later dropped out of the case. Inquiring whether it was clear these signs caused concern well before the Michaels case became news, a grand juror asked his mother whether she took him to the doctor at the time. The mother replied, "Yes."[99]

Kelly Michaels's Motive

The children's statements, bolstered by adult testimony and medical evidence, would never be able to answer a critical question about Kelly Michaels herself. Perhaps the most pressing question for many observers of the case was, Why? Why would she do it? Of course, the crime of child sexual abuse is never easy to explain. It is undoubtedly harder in the case of female offenders, who make up a statistically small percentage of sex offenders against children. Those who later rallied around her often noted how "all-American" Michaels looked.[100] The prosecution undoubtedly understood they needed to provide some kind of insight into the psychological explanation for the charges. As it turned out, a psychiatric evaluation by the defense helped with some insight.

The first psychological evaluation of Michaels, conducted by a defense-paid psychiatrist, provided considerable reason for concluding that Michaels might have had a mental state conducive to playing sexualized games with children. The evaluation by Dr. Murray Bartky, conducted on December 14, 1985, and January 3, 1986, found "areas of pathology, particularly in the sexual area." Dr. Bartky described Michaels's psychosexual development as "stunted and conflicted" and called her "sexually confused." Perhaps most telling were statements Michaels made about the charges. As quoted in Dr. Bartky's report, she said:

> It was a small school. All of the children knew about their body. They had a normal and natural curiosity. These parents, they were working and don't know what is normal and natural.[101]

It is not clear what Michaels was trying to convey in these statements about "natural curiosity" and what the children "knew about their body." Moreover, what could she possibly have meant about "these parents" not knowing "what is normal and natural"? Dr. Bartky concluded: "She does not seem rational in these statements."

The testimony of Charlene Munn, a woman Michaels befriended in jail, supplied further evidence that Michaels had a belief system that could allow her to sexually abuse a child. Munn testified that Michaels told her "I didn't mean to harm those children."[102] Unlike jailhouse-informant evidence, which can often be dismissed as self-serving, this testimony could not be dismissed on that ground. Munn had already been sentenced when she testified, and she had already pleaded guilty when first interviewed by investigators. Her ten-year minimum sentence bears out her not making any deals in exchange for her testimony.[103] The defense tried arguing that Michaels did not associate with other prisoners. In fact, she did correspond with Munn after she was released on bail. She also bought cigarettes for her in prison.[104]

The jury did not hear additional evidence concerning disturbing sexual behavior in Michaels's family. The state offered evidence about her being groped by her father during an early jail visit. The incident was documented at the time, and the prosecution found out about it only because a correctional officer in a barber shop was overheard talking about it.[105] The evidence was offered in a hearing outside the presence of the jury. The judge deemed it too prejudicial to present to the jury, but he made it clear, in ruling to keep the evidence out, that:

the out of the ordinary came about because of an anonymous tip to the State about matters which I've not allowed us to go into for the protection of your client. . . . But the reason it came about was because of conduct between your client and her father.[106]

But the jury did hear the unusual response Michaels gave Dr. Stanley Brodsky, when asked if she had been sexually abused as a child; she said she had "no recollection."[107] The state also presented considerable evidence that Michaels's behavior at Wee Care was strange, to say the least. One teacher vividly remembered her saying "for all they know, I could be abusing children." Michaels agreed on the stand that she made this statement but said the comment was taken "out of context."[108] Another teacher remembered her unprompted announcement one day that she was not wearing any underwear. A teacher's aide, only fifteen years old at the time, remembered Michaels trying to get her to talk about what she did sexually with her boyfriend. Michaels also wrote a "poem" in her preschool roll book that contained arguably lurid lines.[109] Her evasive answers about this "poem" strain credulity; she claimed she could not remember writing the words, even though she agreed that they were in her handwriting.[110]

When the prosecution rested its case, Judge William Harth dismissed thirty-eight counts. Some of those charges, according to Lisa Manshel, "had been substantiated only by what children said on the audiotapes, and Harth would not allow such hearsay material to be considered as proving the truth of a charge."[111] The judge also dismissed some of the "terrorist threat" charges because the children testified Michaels had threatened their parents, while the actual legal charge alleged she had directed threats at the children. There remained 131 counts, spread across the children and not resulting in any child being eliminated from the case (see Figure 5.5). One child stands out, however, at this stage: Jacob Peyton. Seven of his eight counts were dismissed, leaving a single count of third-degree child endangerment; no other child had so many counts dismissed.[112] His testimony did not back up his interview statements, and his interview statements came from a second interview where the interviewer was exasperated and the boy was acting in a difficult manner. Maybe some of his behavior was actually posttraumatic stress disorder, or maybe he was simply a hyperactive and difficult child. Whatever the explanation, he was unusual among the children in the trial for being considered least credible to the court. In the witch-hunt narrative that later developed, however, he is one of the children most frequently quoted from the case. But there are never accompanying contextual details; to the contrary, Jacob is presented in a way that suggests he is representative of the children in the case.

Figure 5.5 Kelly Michaels, All Children at Trial, by Status of Charges (Presented to Jury versus Dropped).

Children arranged in phases by date of initial interview, with charges at trial.

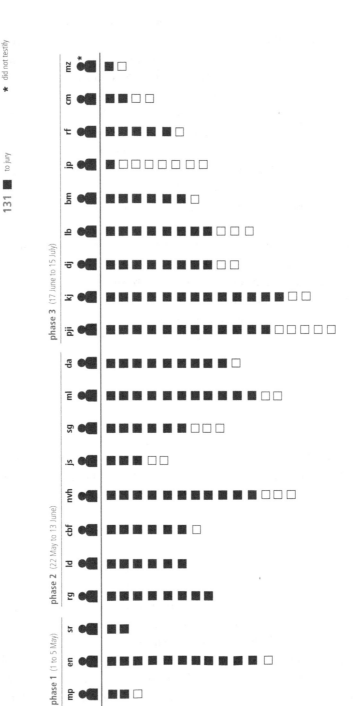

Kelly Michaels's Defense

There was serious disagreement within the defense team about whether to rely on a "diminished capacity" defense, or even to plead insanity. The lawyer who favored the insanity defense left the team in early June 1986, citing "differences in defense strategy."[113] The strategy they chose instead was to call the case a witch-hunt and blame the parents and investigators for the substance of the children's statements. "Throughout this country we have a witch-hunt type mentality," defense lawyer Harvey Meltzer told the jury in his opening statement.[114] He harped on selected instances of clear prodding by investigators and then argued that *all* of the children made their statements in order to please adults. Placing the blame squarely on the adults, Meltzer referred to the children's statements as "learned responses to specific questions." He reminded the jury that "children are very, very suggestible."[115]

The defense offered alternative arguments: first, the sexual abuse did not occur, and second, even if it did occur, Michaels did not perpetrate the acts. The bulk of the defense, however, denied the abuse entirely. One strand of the argument involved "opportunity," another "plausibility." The opportunity argument was that it would have been impossible for these acts to have occurred without detection. The plausibility argument was based on the lack of medical injuries, specifically given the allegations about abuse with utensils. But the crux of the defense was expert testimony impugning the children's statements.

Dr. Ralph Underwager

The defense relied on three experts. The first was Dr. Ralph Underwager, a psychologist who attacked the investigative interviews in the case as highly suggestive, even coercive. It was a defense that was being honed in the McMartin case in California and had already been successfully employed in the lead case (*State v. Bentz*) in the so-called sex ring case in Jordan, Minnesota. Underwager, who lived in Northfield, Minnesota, was the defense expert in the nearby case. He quickly developed a specialty in testifying for the defense in child sexual abuse cases, and he apparently came to see the growth of his business not as a measure of the rise in awareness and prosecution of child sexual abuse but as evidence of a national witch-hunt. He also became controversial for his willingness to use extreme rhetoric. He told a national television audience, for example, that the interviews with children he had reviewed in the Jordan cases "mirrored those of Red Chinese brainwashing."[116] In October 1993, when the Kelly Michaels case was between the Appellate Division and the New Jersey Supreme Court, Underwager became a magnet for intense criticism when an interview given in 1991 was published in the winter 1993 issue of a Dutch magazine called *Paidika: The Journal of Paedophilia*. In it, Underwager was quoted as saying:

Paedophiles spend a lot of time and energy defending their choice. I don't think that a paedophile needs to do that. Paedophiles can boldly and courageously affirm what they choose. They can say that what they want is to find the best way to love. I am also a theologian and as a theologian I believe it is God's will that there be closeness and intimacy, unity of the flesh, between people.[117]

Underwager had not made these views widely known in the mid-1980s when he was one of the experts of choice for child sexual abuse defendants around the country. Nevertheless, there was a wealth of information in the late 1980s that cast doubt on his expertise. The Essex County Prosecutor's Office put an extraordinary amount of effort into preparing to cross-examine him.[118] The cross-examination of Ralph Underwager lasted eight excruciating days. Glenn Goldberg extracted a series of embarrassing admissions from Underwager. No, he had never published any studies on child suggestibility. No, he had not reviewed significant materials about the children or the parents in the case. No, he had never visited the Wee Care facility in the process of concocting a "time and motion" study that purported to prove Michaels could not have abused the children. No, he had not counted the number of times children provided answers about sexual abuse in response to open-ended questions. From these and other responses, one of the prosecutors would later refer to Underwager as a "witch doctor" in his closing argument. The appellate court ruled that this reference was not unfairly prejudicial; rather, it had a basis in Underwager's own testimony.[119]

Dr. Jonas Rappeport

The second expert witness for the defense was Dr. Jonas Rappeport, a forensic psychiatrist from Baltimore. Dr. Rappeport had a national reputation for his work as medical director of the American Academy of Psychiatry and the Law, a group that certified specialists in forensic psychiatry. He was hired to provide a "profile" of child molesters—one that, he would presumably argue, did not fit Kelly Michaels. Claiming that women do not fit the profile, his testimony would apparently provide a defense for any woman charged with a sex crime against children. Judge Harth was not persuaded; there simply was not sufficient foundation for "proposed testimony on the profile of an abuser."[120] The testimony was not allowed.

Dr. Rappeport testified anyway. Without the profile argument, he made many of the same claims that Underwager did. It was Rappeport's view that the children in the case had "been so traumatized since this whole thing started, anything they say now is invalid."[121] His evaluation of Michaels was also included in the three-part appendix to a defense brief on appeal. This document contains an extraordinary example of unfounded speculation about what happened when

Mitchell Pierce was at the pediatrician on April 30, 1985. In the "Discussion" section of his report, Rappeport stated:

> My impression of what could have and probably did happen in this situation is as follows: I believe that when [Mitchell Pierce] was having his temperature taken rectally at his pediatricians, the nurse placed her hand upon his back (the usual practice when taking the rectal temperature of a restless child) he stated "that's what my teacher does to me at naptime at school." The child certainly may have believed that lying on your tummy with someone's hand on your back was "taking your temperature."[122]

For all the common sense that may appear to bolster his "impression," Rappeport's speculation is contradicted completely by testimony that was available for him to review. The statement taken on May 8, 1985, from the medical assistant Laura Hadley, made it clear she did *not* have a hand on the boy's back when he uttered this statement. She later testified that her routine involved one hand on the thermometer while she monitored the watch in her other hand.[123] Rappeport's willingness to reconstruct events in the light most favorable to Michaels, notwithstanding direct evidence to the contrary, calls into question the rest of his expert opinions in the case.

Dr. Elissa Benedek

The third expert witness for the defense, Dr. Elissa Benedek, was a board-certified psychiatrist in adult, child, and forensic psychiatry. She had impressive credentials. She was an officer in the American Psychiatric Association and had consulted in five other day-care abuse cases and testified in a sixth. Benedek was hired to assess the demeanor and affect of the children in the case. At least, that was the basic substance of her testimony. She did not actually evaluate the children in person; rather, she evaluated their testimony in the case. She described David Applegate's testimony in court, which she reviewed on videotape, by saying it "showed very little affect."[124] She also described his testimony as "carefully rehearsed," although, as one of the prosecutors quickly objected, she had no factual basis for the conclusion.

The impact of her conclusions was diminished significantly by her limited review of the case. While she reviewed grand jury testimony and "portions" of other testimony in the case, she reviewed the videotaped testimony of only *two* children in the case (David Applegate and P. J. Isaacs.). Her knowledge of the case was surprisingly limited, but her opinions were surprisingly broad—and inaccurate. At one point, she asserted that "Parents were sent a letter and told their kids had been abused." But the letter of May 8 did not tell parents their children had been abused; it said there had been unspecified allegations involving "a former employee." Judge Harth directly asked the witness whether she had read the letter. She replied she had not; she was apparently referring to some kind of article—that is, a secondary source—about day-care abuse cases. Perhaps she was thinking about the McMartin case; but even that letter did not tell parents their children had been abused.

Kelly Michaels

To court observers, the highlight of the case was when Michaels took the stand in her own defense. She offered repeated and emphatic denials of all the charges. She also denied ever discussing her case with inmates or guards at the Essex County Jail, although she acknowledged writing a letter to Charlene Munn, who earlier testified that Michaels told her "she didn't mean to hurt the kids the way she did."[125] The cross-examination was marked by several strange exchanges. Michaels testified in a deposition in August 1987 that she had seen a doctor after her conversation with Marilyn Schuster about bleeding from her rectum. But she was unable to name the doctor. Six months later, at trial, she still did not know the name. "What have you done to locate the doctor?" asked Glenn Goldberg, who wanted to subpoena any such evidence. "I didn't make any effort to find this doctor for you," she replied.[126] Asked why she had not informed her family doctor of the problem that had apparently caused bleeding, Michaels replied "it wouldn't be something that I would go to visit him for." Otherwise, the cross-examination was limited by the extent to which Michaels did not remember things. She "didn't specifically recall" if she had rubbed children's backs. She also had "no recollection" of what was written in her roll book. "It's my writing definitely," she allowed, "but I had no memory of if I copied it from something else, if it was mine." Asked whether she had children make believe they were dogs and cats, Michaels responded "I don't recall."[127] Her emphatic denials about having ever sexually abused the children may have been undercut by her extensive lapses of memory. The witch-hunt narrative overlooks these issues and argues, instead, that Michaels is credible because she "passed" a lie detector test.[128] In fact, the results of the lie detector test were determined to be "inconclusive."[129]

The Verdict and Sentence

The jury was asked to decide on 131 charges. They deliberated for thirteen days and appear to have gone through the evidence methodically. The defense actually objected to their method; an Associated Press story reported that the defense "objected yesterday to allowing the jury to alternate between deliberations and reviewing videotaped testimony of the children."[130] The story also reported that jurors had already reviewed "tapes of children interviewed by investigators from the prosecutor's office in 1985." Those include important interviews early in the sequence of events.

The verdict was an overwhelming victory for the prosecution. Its details bear examination. The jury clearly treated the children as individuals (see Figure 5.6). They also made their own judgments about the credibility of individual charges. Although it has scarcely been reported, the jury rejected what were arguably some of the most "fantastic"—or, at least, difficult to believe—charges in the case. Had the case been built entirely on such charges, it is safe to say Michaels would not have been convicted. Indeed, eleven of the seventeen not-guilty verdicts involved those kinds of charges.[131] By contrast, only two of the forty-eight counts of first-degree sexual assault resulted in a not-guilty verdict. The jury also paid close attention to the legal distinctions between first- and second-degree sexual assault, convicting Michaels of the less-included second-degree charge in nineteen counts in which she was charged with first-degree. Those variations account for about one-quarter of the charges. The jury found Michaels guilty as charged for the remaining 96 of the 131 counts.

Perhaps the most telling aspect of the jury verdict is how it varied by child. The jury clearly made decisions by child and by charge. As indicated in Figure 5.6, the jury found Michaels guilty as charged on all of the charges connected with seven children. (Two of those seven children had only one count each and were largely peripheral to the case.) There were five children, then, who accounted for multiple charges and for whom the jury convicted on every count as charged. Those children were apparently considered highly credible by the jury. That assessment also applies to several other children in the case. For example, the jury found Michaels guilty as charged on eight of nine counts involving David Applegate, with a guilty verdict on a lesser-included sexual assault charge for the other count. Similarly, the jury found Michaels guilty as charged on ten of eleven counts involving Eddie Nathanson.

Contrast those outcomes to the verdicts related to three girls, who were believable enough for the jury to agree on convictions but mostly for lesser charges than requested by the prosecution. In the case of Martha Landez, eight charges of first-degree sexual assault went to the jury. They found Michaels *not* guilty on one charge and guilty of the lesser-included offense on the other seven. This does not mean the jury found Martha unbelievable. If that were the case, they would have found Michaels not guilty on more than one count. Either Martha did not say enough to support first-degree charges, or perhaps she said enough but this still left too much room for reasonable doubt among jurors. The verdicts involving Johnny Shaw were similarly mixed. The jury found Michaels not guilty of a single count of third-degree child endangerment; they also found her not guilty on the two first-degree charges, but guilty of the lesser-included offense

Figure 5.6 Kelly Michaels, Trial Dispositions by Charge, by Child.

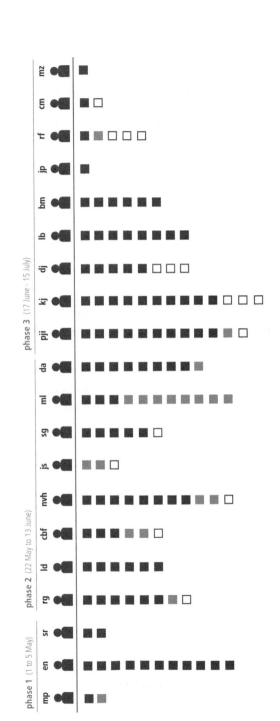

Compiled by author from original documents.

and of a separate count of the second degree. Similarly, with Cassie Bond-Foley, there were three counts involving first- or second-degree sexual assault that went to the jury. The jury did not convict as charged on any of those counts; rather, they found Michaels *not* guilty on one count and guilty of the lesser-included offense on the other two.

Three children stand out as the only ones with multiple charges that resulted in not-guilty verdicts. For the charges involving Rebecca Flora, the jury found Michaels not guilty of three of five charges (two third-degree charges and one second-degree). They also found Michaels not guilty of a first-degree charge but guilty of the lesser included offense of second-degree sexual assault. The only count on which the jury returned a verdict of guilty as charged was a single count of third-degree child endangerment. Similarly, the jury convicted Michaels of four of the seven counts involving Dennis Jones. They found her not guilty on three charges of a grotesque nature: second-degree sexual assault (licking rectum), third-degree child endangerment (choking), and third-degree child endangerment (drinking urine). But the jury convicted Michaels as charged on one count of first-degree sexual assault and three counts of third-degree child endangerment. Similarly, the jury rejected three grotesque charges involving Dennis's sister, Kimmy, but convicted as charged on seven counts of first-degree sexual assault.

All told, Michaels was convicted of 115 charges. She was sentenced to forty-seven years in prison and would be eligible for parole in fourteen years. By all appearances, it was a successful prosecution of a difficult case.

The Witch-Hunt Narrative and the Appeal

Rewriting the Story of the Case

The first writer to apply the witch-hunt narrative to the Kelly Michaels case was Debbie Nathan, who did so immediately after Michaels was convicted. Writing in the *Village Voice*, where she had recently applied the same framework to a day-care abuse case in El Paso, Texas, Nathan came to the defense of Michaels in the summer of 1988.[132] The local reporters who sat through the trial came to think there was substantial evidence of guilt in the case; none editorialized against the prosecution or the verdict. Nathan characterized them as gullible. Her article about the Michaels case, written without access to the complete trial transcripts, was based largely on an interview with Michaels and on materials about the children's interviews that she obtained from the defense. Nathan argued that the Michaels case was "a cookie-cutter copy" of the one she had written about in Texas. Investigators used a "preconceived approach," she argued, that assumed the children had been abused.[133]

She also had biting criticisms of Eileen Treacy, the psychologist who assessed the children and testified for the state about children's developmental capabilities. Nathan claimed that Treacy had "exaggerated information about credentials" and that a judge in another case had criticized her questions as improperly leading.[134] The heart of Nathan's argument was that the investigative interviews were all leading and suggestive, eliciting responses that the questioners essentially provided to the children. She described the content of the interviews as:

> filled with confused children who have little to say despite being told things like Kelly is bad, Kelly hurts kids, Kelly is in jail, and the police need help trying to make sure she stays there.[135]

The article included an excerpt from an investigative interview in which a young girl, Debra Schultz, said "I think I really forgot" the accusations she had apparently made days earlier. "Why do you believe me to know things?" she asked the interviewer at one point. Nathan argued that "other children were told that after they said how Kelly hurt them, they could have toy police badges."[136] She also reported uncovering something about Lou Fonolleras that was apparently not known by his own supervisor: he had been sexually abused as a child and, remarkably, had brought up his personal experience in at least one of the interview sessions. He told Natalie Jenkins "a little secret," all about something that happened to him as a child.[137] There is no question this was inappropriate, even in an era without clear protocols for interviewing children. But Nathan did not mention that neither Schultz nor Jenkins was actually involved in the trial. This was typical of the problems with the witch-hunt narrative that built up around the case.

On its face, Nathan's article made a strong case that Michaels was the victim. Surprisingly, Nathan's article is not the one best remembered, or even most influential, in creating the witch-hunt narrative that eventually became the conventional wisdom about this case. Dorothy Rabinowitz claims this distinction for an article in *Harper's* almost two years later called "From the Mouths of Babes to a Jail Cell."[138] The article marked a watershed moment in the media. It also helped mobilize a group of New York intellectuals and civil libertarians, including the family that owned the *Village Voice*, to promote the Kelly Michaels Defense Committee.[139] This committee resulted in Morton Stavis, a famed civil liberties lawyer, taking over the appeal initiated by the Public Defender's Office.

The Rabinowitz article appeared in the wake of the denouement of the Mc-Martin case in January 1990—an event that dramatically altered how the media viewed child sexual abuse cases. There were many articles in the wake of the McMartin verdicts that promoted the witch-hunt narrative to explain the Mc-Martin case, and Rabinowitz's article did likewise to the Michaels case. Although

Nathan had already raised doubts about the case, Rabinowitz argued forcefully that Michaels was factually innocent. She eventually won a Pulitzer Prize for a body of work at the *Wall Street Journal* that included similar commentaries on behalf of defendants in other high-profile child sexual-abuse cases. This article was the foundational piece in that oeuvre, and it gained immediate attention.[140]

Both of these influential articles mischaracterized how the case began. Rabinowitz wrote that it began with a "bizarre misunderstanding" about what Mitchell Pierce said while the medical assistant at his pediatrician's office took his temperature rectally.[141] Rabinowitz apparently adopted Jonas Rappeport's speculation that Mitchell was referring to having his back rubbed. (The claim was flatly contradicted by the testimony of the two adults who were in the room when Mitchell's temperature was taken.[142]) She then discredited all of the later charges in the case with the stunning claim that "the jury eventually rejected the charge" that began the whole case.[143] Given the importance of the first child in any case with multiple complainants, it would be quite significant if the original charge resulted in a "not guilty" finding. But that did not happen. The jury found Kelly Michaels guilty of second-degree, instead of first-degree, sexual assault on that charge. In other words, they concluded there was felonious sexual touching, but not penetration. Rabinowitz later claimed Michaels had been "acquitted of the original charge"—failing to note that she was guilty of a lesser included felony involving sexual touching. Labeling this verdict as a "rejection" of the original charge is beyond misleading. It was also indicative of how the rest of the case would be misrepresented.

The mass media started lining up on Michaels's side. Mike Taibbi, a New York City television reporter, did a two-part story that endorsed Rabinowitz's view in August 1990. This was the first television program to broadcast audio excerpts from the children's interviews, which were all under seal. In September 1990, the Kelly Michaels case was referred to as part of "the Salem Epidemic" in the *National Review*.[144] In 1991, the nationally televised program *48 Hours* broadcast a story about the case that featured Rabinowitz at the beginning of the program saying "I believe that Kelly Michaels is entirely innocent."[145] The program included excerpts from two investigative interviews. The first one demonstrated what reporter Bernard Goldberg described as "investigators asking children to demonstrate how Kelly molested them." This is the entire snippet:

UNIDENTIFIED MAN #1: Now did Kelly do any bad things to you?
UNIDENTIFIED CHILD #1: No.
CHILD #1: No.
MAN #1: How come you don't want to tell me what all your friends already told me?

CHILD #1: (unintelligible)

MAN #1: You want a badge?

CHILD #1: Yeah.

MAN #1: We will get you a badge if you help us, if you help—if you be a little detective with us.[146]

The only effort Goldberg made to put this tape into context was the statement that "In many of the tapes, the children repeatedly deny they were abused." There was no indication of how often this was not true; nor did Goldberg address whether this child ever made any allegations or played any role in the case. In fact, the child did not make any accusation, and he was never part of the criminal case. But it was powerful television. Nevertheless, these stories painted an extremely misleading picture.

Five major inaccuracies in the witch-hunt narrative about this case are elaborated below:

Inaccurate Claims About the Interviews

The basic claim of the witch-hunt narrative is that the children in the Kelly Michaels case were subjected to repetitive interviews before ever disclosing sexual abuse. Virtually all popular critiques of the case make this claim. "The most startling thing," according to Nathan, "was that *none* [of the children] had spoken of the abuse to parents and teachers—until after investigators had interviewed them repeatedly."[147] Rabinowitz argued that the charges were the product of investigators "who convinced parents and children alike." She claimed the children were "confused, had nothing to say, or flatly denied that anything had happened to them."[148] These descriptions are patently untrue for the three boys whose statements formed the basis of the original indictment.

The witch-hunt narrative makes even stronger claims about the rest of the investigation. For example, Nat Hentoff argued in the *Washington Post*: "These interrogations went on for a two-year period. The questioning was intense."[149] But the witch-hunt narrative is contradicted by a simple mathematic reality. There were eighty-three investigative interviews, combining the DYFS and police interviews.[150] There were fifty-one preschoolers in full-time attendance at Wee Care in 1984–85, and every child, except David Applegate, was interviewed at least once. It would have required 102 interviews just to interview every child twice. Nearly half the children did not have a second interview. Twenty-one children had two interviews during this time period; five other children had more than two investigative interviews (see Figure 5.7). It is impossible to reconcile Figure 5.7 with the

Figure 5.7 Kelly Michaels Interview Sequence, All Children by Number of Interviews.

Each icon represents one interview. The vertical stacks of icons indicate the number of interviews in one day. The space between 5 to 22 May is not drawn to scale.

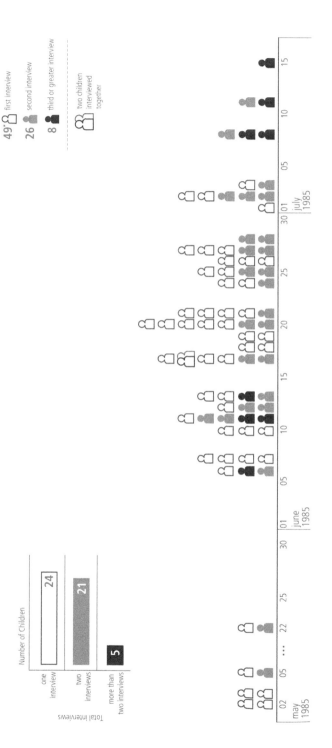

* Fifty children had first interviews; two children were interviewed in a single session on June 17.
Compiled by author from assorted court documents.

claim that "the children" in the case disclosed only after weeks or months of repetitive interviews. If investigators were so intent on "finding" abuse, why were so few of the children who did not disclose abuse brought back for a second interview? If repetitive interviews explain the disclosures in the case, how does one explain the significant number of children who made disclosures on their first interview?

The children who were interviewed twice (or more) were divided almost evenly between those who went to trial and those who did not. If investigators were so intent on "finding" abuse, why weren't *any* of the children who did not disclose abuse in the second interview brought back for a third interview? For the investigative stage of the case, the "repetitive interviewing" claim simply does not fit the facts. Despite the overblown claims that all the children were subjected to repetitive interviews before making any disclosures, the fact is that only *five* were interviewed more than twice in the investigative phase.

Focusing directly on the children who were interviewed the most during the investigation demonstrates that none of these children were subject to as many interviews as has been claimed *before they first disclosed abuse* (see Figure 5.8). Four of the five children who were interviewed more than twice by investigators were part of the criminal trial. One child, John Allister, was dropped before the case went to trial.[151] The circumstances surrounding the other four children are all different. One child, Martha Landez, disclosed sexual abuse *in her first interview* on June 10, before the two heated parents meetings in June. She was the thirteenth child interviewed in the case. Landez had complained of vaginal and rectal pain during the year and repeatedly asked to have her temperature taken during the winter of that year. I was unable to locate any documentation of the content of the second interview, which occurred on June 12 with Peg Foster. The next day, Martha gave a statement to police investigator Evelyn Catalano. Perhaps it would have been better to eliminate one of these interviews, or even to combine all into one. But by no stretch of the imagination did she disclose after weeks or months of repetitive interviews.

The third child, Rebecca Flora, was first interviewed on June 21 by Foster and Rich Mastrangelo and was "nonresponsive." Her mother took Rebecca to Dr. Susan Esquilin on June 30. This is the one child involved in the eventual trial who is described as having first disclosed to Dr. Susan Esquilin, a psychologist. She was interviewed again on July 3 by George McGrath. Early in the interview, McGrath asked, "Was Kelly your teacher?" Rebecca responded, "Yeah, but she did a lot of bad things to me."[152] Moments later the

Figure 5.8 Kelly Michaels Interview Sequence, Children Interviewed More than Twice.

Each line represents one child. Each icon represents one interview.

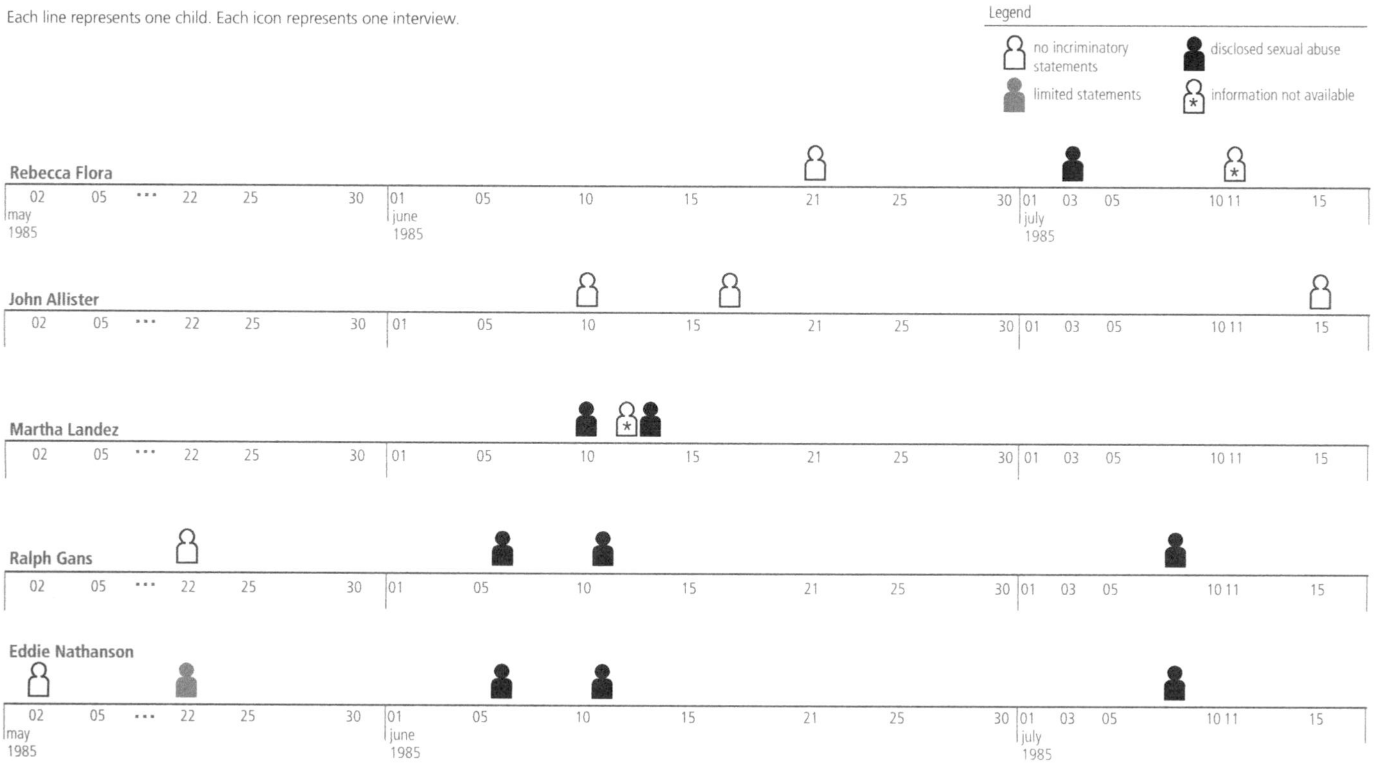

Compiled by author from original documents.

child said Kelly did *not* do any bad things to her. Much later, this exchange occurs:

R: Do you know what?

G: What?

R: Kelly did a lot of bad things to [another child][153]

G: Oh yeah, what did she do?

R: She hit her.

G: How?

R: With a knife.

G: Where did she put the knife?

R: On her tooshie.

On the final page of the interview transcript, Fonolleras indicates that he talked to Rebecca while McGrath was speaking with her mother. According to Fonolleras, the girl "informed me that she had been hurt with the fork in her vaginal area." Court records indicate there was a third interview on July 11, but I was unable to locate any additional documentation of this interview. Rebecca's disclosure, then, came after one interview. But the interview of July 3 was certainly problematic. She was inconsistent and unclear, and it remains questionable at various points whether she was talking about herself or someone else. Rebecca was one of the youngest children in the case, she exhibited some of the most extreme behavior, and she was probably one of the weakest witnesses. Arguably, she should not have been included as a complainant. As it turns out, she was not an effective witness; the jury rejected most of her charges.

The remaining two children who were interviewed more than twice in the investigative phase of the case were Eddie Nathanson and Ralph Gans. Eddie had the most investigative interviews in the case, having been interviewed five times. He was also one of two boys named by Mitchell Pierce on the first day of the case. (The other, Sam Raymond, confirmed the abuse, and his father wrote a lengthy statement that night.) Eddie did not disclose anything untoward on May 2 but was interviewed again on May 22, when Fonolleras entered the case. In that interview, Eddie told Fonolleras that Michaels had inserted her finger into the anal area of the boys whose charges were already before the grand jury. He also said Michaels would say, "Let's play nurse—I'll take your temperature—you feel warm." But he denied personal victimization.[154] Eddie was interviewed a third time on June 6 because his mother called DYFS to say he had disclosed that Michaels had sucked his penis and abused various boys with utensils. His two subsequent interviews involved disclosures.

It should be noted that Fonolleras did not seek to have Eddie Nathanson interviewed after the second interview on May 22. Although some critics of the case have blamed Eddie's mother for his statements, the explanation cannot account for how Eddie was able to show Fonolleras the choir room on June 6. That room, hidden away on the third floor, was supposedly out of bounds for the preschool. Nathan has argued that some children who talked about the room were taken there by Fonolleras—but this did not occur until later in June.[155] Also, the witch-hunt narrative never acknowledges that Eddie had a persistent and documented anal rash in 1984–85.

Ralph Gans was the only child other than Eddie who was interviewed more than three times by investigators. He was also involved in the earliest part of the overall investigation. His chronological number in the case was six, and he was first interviewed on May 22, Fonolleras's first day of interviews. Ralph kept running out of the room when Kelly's name was mentioned, so the interview was terminated. Fonolleras did not schedule a follow-up interview. When he returned to interview Eddie Nathanson, however, he also ended up interviewing Ralph because Eddie specifically mentioned his involvement. Ralph made extensive disclosures on June 6 about abuse with utensils and about the "pile-up" game they played in the music room. His third interview was a police statement five days later, and it was consistent with his earlier disclosure. He was brought back one more time for a joint interview with Eddie; Fonolleras hoped to learn more about the games from the boys together. Neither of Eddie's third and fourth interviews was an effort to obtain a disclosure from a child who had said nothing; he had already made significant statements in his second interview.

In short, the children depicted in Figure 5.8 were interviewed more often in the investigative phase of the case than any other children in the case. These children are differently situated, both in terms of when they entered the case and when, in the sequence of interviews, they disclosed sexual abuse, if they did. Of the four children at trial, the latest disclosure was in the third interview. But this was true for only one child; the rest disclosed earlier in their respective interview sequence, rendering even these children less subject to "repetitive" interviews before disclosing than has been claimed by proponents of the witch-hunt narrative.

Beyond the inaccuracies of the claim about the "repetitive" interviews, the narrative has misrepresented the content of various interviews. The Rabinowitz article included five mini-excerpts from an interview with P. J. Isaacs, one of the nineteen children who testified at the trial. The excerpts portray a child who did not want to answer any questions, who said he wanted to go home, and who made incredible statements such as "I saw her penis" and "No, she peed on me!" P. J. eventually said Kelly Michaels put a fork "in my heinie," but Rabinowitz said this was said "in an obviously playful, make-believe tone." Perhaps most damning, she reported that the interview ended with the boy shouting "It's all lies!"[156] To be sure, these excerpts alone provided ample reason to be concerned. But the transcript of the interview with this boy (who Rabinowitz calls "Luke") contradicts several of her claims about the interview. First, by running questions together and moving the timing of the child's answer, the Rabinowitz version makes it appear the child provided meaningless answers when in fact the answers were actually quite clear.[157] Rabinowitz also misstated the flow of this interview. She quoted three questions near the very beginning of the interview and then stated, "Fonolleras *at this point* handed Luke an anatomically correct doll, then proceeded with this questioning" (emphasis added). In fact, by the designated Q&A numbering, more than sixty questions separated these events.

Rabinowitz also claimed that "the session ends with Luke shouting 'It's all lies.'" But neither the prepared transcript of the interview nor the annotated version of the transcript—which the defense appended to their appellate brief—bears this out. The last six lines of the interview transcript are quoted below. The two statements in brackets were added by hand to the version submitted by the defense, and the numbering appears on the document:

> [208Q] LOU: Did she pinch you anywhere? No? Do you remember anything else that happened [that you're afraid to tell me about?]
>
> [208A] CHILD: No.
>
> [209Q] LOU: Do you want to go?
>
> [209A] CHILD: Yeah, I want to go home.
>
> [210Q] LOU: Let me get you up, come on. So you don't have anything else to talk to me about. [Tell your mother to come in.]
>
> [UNNUMBERED] LOU: End of statement.[158]

The defense undoubtedly would have made a notation if the child screamed "It's all lies" and it was somehow left out of the state's transcript. But there is no evidence in the transcript that the child said any such thing in this interview. Rabinowitz has claimed that "jurors never saw the record of the interrogations. That's the key point."[159] But the trial transcript, which Rabinowitz also claims to have reviewed, proves otherwise. This interview was played to the jury on November 5, 1987, a transcription of the interview was entered as Exhibit J-9, and there were almost fifty pages of questions to Folloneras about the interview. There is not a single mention of "It's all lies." Rabinowitz's erroneous claim was also featured by Nat Hentoff in the *Village Voice*; the "It's all lies" statement was highlighted as a pull-out quote.[160] Although Hentoff also claims to have examined the interview transcripts, the fact remains that this statement does not appear in the interview from which he purports to quote.

The error apparently stems from conflating two events: this investigative interview and the boy's grand jury testimony, which is described in Lisa Manshel's book. According to Manshel, the boy screamed "Lies! Lies! Lies!" while testifying before the grand jury. The prosecutor then asked a neutral question: "OK.

Then what did Kelly do?" to which the boy responded, "No. It's the truth."[161] If this is the incident that Rabinowitz and Hentoff confused with the interview from which they purported to quote directly, then both writers omitted an important follow-up question and answer. One also wonders how closely these critics actually read the transcripts they purported to have researched if their confusion stemmed entirely from a secondary source.

Evidence Allegedly Kept from the Jury

Rabinowitz has also claimed "jurors never saw the record of the interrogations."[162] Evidence from the investigative interviews, she argues, would have proven the child-suggestibility defense, but the evidence was somehow kept from the jury. Mike Taibbi, a WCBS television reporter, made the same claim in August 1990, asserting that "the jury only heard the children's final version, long after the incidents took place."[163] This claim is critical to lending plausibility to the child-suggestibility defense. It is much easier to understand how a jury might fail to detect a massive case of child suggestibility if all they ever heard were the children's final statements at trial. It is also much easier to second-guess a jury verdict if it was based on incomplete information in the first place. If, however, the jury actually *had* all of the relevant evidence, plus the advantage of seeing and hearing the witnesses live, then it is difficult to understand how the jury could be so wrong—or how those who never saw the witnesses could have so much better an understanding of the evidence. Those questions disappear, however, if one can claim critical information was withheld from the jury.

The claim that the jury was kept in the dark about the investigative interviews is false. The Essex County Prosecutor's Office objected to Taibbi's error and pointed out that investigative tapes *were* played for the jury. In February of the following year, WCBS issued a correction on the "News at Five."[164] But the myth lives on. "I saw what the jurors did not see," Rabinowitz asserted on *CNN*, staking a claim to having reviewed investigative interviews that were kept from the jury.[165] But the jury listened to tape recordings of the investigative interviews and were supplied with the same transcriptions that the defense later attached to their appellate brief. The *CNN* interviewer, wondering why the jury would not also see such evidence, was told something vague by Rabinowitz about the hearsay evidence rule.[166] But what Rabinowitz did not explain is that the hearsay rule prevented only *the state* from introducing the tapes from the investigative interviews; it did not prevent the defense from presenting them. Indeed, the tapes were at the core of the defense in the case. Not only were these tapes introduced at trial but, as reported in Lisa Manshel's 1990 book, the prosecution specifically requested "that the judge instruct the jury that the state could not have introduced these tapes."[167] The prosecution did not want the jury to think what Rabinowitz later urged the public to believe: that the state had tried to keep the tapes out. It is worth noting that the defense "strenuously objected" to this instruction.[168] Apparently, they wanted to create the same phony aura which others have since perpetuated, that the state was trying to hide the same interviews they had voluntarily recorded. The defense could not provide a convincing reason for keeping the jury in the dark about this rule, so the tapes came in *with* the state's requested instruction that informed the jury that the state was not allowed to introduce them.

The same evidence many claim was kept from the jury was reviewed again during the process of jury deliberations. That the jury took these issues seriously is best evidenced in their requests for complete playbacks of each child's testimony *and* various investigative interviews during the thirteen days of deliberation. The Associated Press reported on March 31, 1988, that the defense "objected yesterday to allowing the jury to alternate between deliberations and reviewing videotaped testimony of the children."[169] The story also reported that jurors had already reviewed "tapes of children interviewed by investigators from the prosecutor's office in 1985." What the jury did not see were interviews with children who were not involved in the case; those interviews, without ever being identified as such, form the core of the witch-hunt critique of the interviews.

Inaccurate Claims About Eileen Treacy

Eileen Treacy's role in the case has been criticized as much as, if not more than, Lou Fonolleras's role. The criticisms levied at Treacy range from attacks on her credentials and professionalism to the claim that she implanted ideas in various children. Ceci and Bruck have argued Treacy did "some of the most suggestive interviews" in the Michaels case. They describe her role as extensive, claiming that "all but three of the 20 children were interviewed by Eileen Treacy at least twice before the trial."[170] The implication seems to be that as many as seventeen of the children were interviewed by Treacy more than twice. Actually, the number is four, and *none* was interviewed more than three times. And four children at trial—not three, as claimed—were never interviewed by Treacy. Moreover, as indicated in the case timeline (Figure 1.1), Treacy entered the case after the investgation was completed and the charges had been finalized.

None of Treacy's interviews are included in the three-volume appendix to the defense brief to the Appellate Division, which is represented as containing "all known recorded interviews of the children in the Wee Care case."[171] Since almost all of Treacy's interviews *were* taped and transcribed, a skeptic might wonder why *none* of her interviews were included. Those interviews were memorialized more systematically than the DYFS interviews, so the reason cannot be that they were unavailable. Moreover, Treacy was a major object of criticism, so the reason cannot be that her interviews were considered unimportant. The most reasonable explanation may be that those interviews do not bear out the criticisms that have been lodged.

The attacks on Treacy's credentials and professionalism have been withering. In 1988, Nathan wrote that "not until it was too late to attack her credibility did the defense discover that Treacy's curriculum vitae contained exaggerated information about credentials."[172] Jonathan Harris, who created the influential internet Witch-Hunt Information Center, called her a "fringe psychologist" and a "dangerous fruitcake."[173] More recently, Rabinowitz expressed nothing short of outrage that Treacy continues to testify in cases. According to Rabinowitz, Treacy was "so discredited as a witness" that "people wanted nothing to do with her" when the state of New York hired her in State v. Carroll, a 2000 case in which Rabinowitz concluded that the defendant was falsely convicted of sexually abusing his stepdaughter.[174]

These are remarkably unfair criticisms. When Treacy testified in the Carroll case, she had testified hundreds of times in New York and never been reversed on appeal. She had conducted training seminars on developmental psychology and sexual abuse for law-enforcement officials in twelve New York counties for almost twenty years. Further, she had taught psychology at Lehman College and had extensive clinical experience with child sexual abuse. Her dissertation was an evaluation about foster-parenting sexually abused children.[175] Not a single word of the dissertation has ever been criticized by those who have attacked Treacy's credentials and expertise. What was the "exaggerated information about credentials" that Nathan ominously alleged and Rabinowitz later repeated? Her vitae listed a "postgraduate course" at St. Joseph's College in Connecticut that Nathan claims was actually an "intensive weekend seminar."[176]

The claim that Treacy was a "true believer" and always "found" sexual abuse is similarly unfounded.[177] It is contradicted by the record of published court decisions in New York. In one case, decided around the time of the Michaels trial, Treacy's testimony was influential in the court's decision not to substantiate sexual abuse.[178] This case did not deter detractors from continuing to claim she is a "rogue therapist" who finds abuse in "everything a child does" during an evaluation, as Rich Lowry claimed in the National Review in December 1994.[179] Earlier that year, however, the New York Law Journal reported "Ms. Treacy could not validate because she believed that there was a significant probability that the child was coached and prepared for the assessment."[180] Evidence that contradicts the "true believer" claim apparently does not influence those who make this charge. In this way, the would-be "skeptics" have become true believers of their own, apparently impervious to evidence that contradicts their beliefs.

The intense hostility against Treacy reflects the larger politics surrounding law reform and sexual assault. Treacy played a central role in changing legal responses to sexual violence in New York over the last twenty-five years. While heading the New York City Advisory Task Force on Rape in 1983, she provided striking testimony to a joint legislative committee hearing in favor of eliminating the corroboration requirement in child sexual-abuse cases. Her testimony at trial in *People v. Taylor* helped set the New York precedent for allowing rape trauma syndrome evidence in trials. In *Taylor*, she testified it was common for a rape victim to appear quiet and controlled following an attack; she also explained why a rape victim might be initially unwilling to name an attacker whom she knows personally. "Rape is a crime that is permeated by misconceptions," the appellate court noted, allowing trauma syndrome evidence to counter "cultural myths that still affect common understanding of rape and rape victims."[181] One of the purposes for which the state hired her as an expert witness in the Michaels case was to counter similar myths surrounding child sexual abuse.

She was also hired specifically to assess whether suggestibility might account for the children's statements in the case. In fact, she *tested for suggestibility* in ways that have never been acknowledged in the witch-hunt narrative. Ceci and Bruck have argued, for example, that nobody in the case ever asked questions challenging the children's statements. Emphasizing the importance of this technique, they have said, "When an interviewer avoids confirmatory bias by posing and testing alternative hypothesis, the suggestive techniques do not seem to result in serious problems."[182] The claim that Treacy did not test alternative hypotheses is contradicted by the detailed reports she prepared on each child. Those aspects of her interviews have never been acknowledged. Instead, a picture has been painted in the witch-hunt narrative that Treacy implanted ideas and even created charges that appeared in the case.

The most detailed critique involves two interview excerpts that are said to "give a flavor of the interactions" between Treacy and the children she evaluated, and they appear to be quite damning. Both passages require detailed analysis, since a close examination of transcripts prepared for the case reveals that appearances can be quite deceiving.[183] The interaction with "Child A" comprises approximately ten questions and answers. The questions are clearly leading and the answers are generally negative or "I don't know." But a comparison of this excerpt to the written record[184] reveals that this "excerpt" is actually a composite of eight snippets taken from two different dates and various pages, and they are not always presented in chronological order (see Figure 5.9). Ceci and Bruck included ellipses for six of these discontinuities, but no reader would reasonably expect that these snippets are from different dates or are out of chronological order. Further, the necessary ellipses are missing in two places in this twenty-line excerpt, leaving even the most careful reader with the impression of an excerpt more intact than it actually is. These mistakes are particularly striking since Ceci and Bruck state they "lightly edited these transcripts for dysfluencies and redundancies, but [...] never altered the meaning."[185]

Figure 5.9 Treacy-Child A Excerpt, Reproduced from Ceci and Bruck (1995) with Source Annotations.

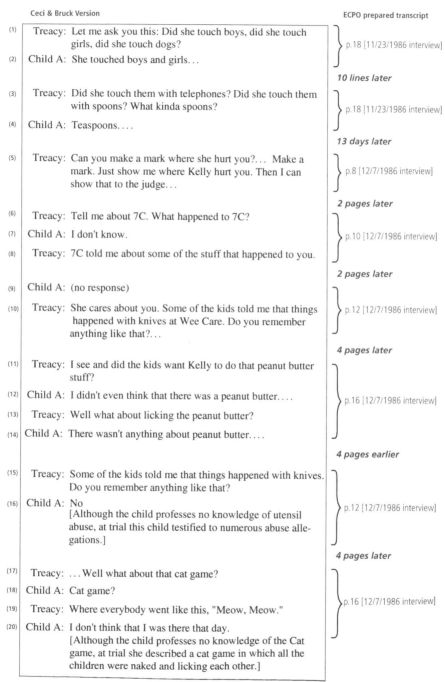

Ceci & Bruck Version   ECPO prepared transcript

(1) | Treacy: Let me ask you this: Did she touch boys, did she touch girls, did she touch dogs?
(2) | Child A: She touched boys and girls...

p.18 [11/23/1986 interview]

10 lines later

(3) | Treacy: Did she touch them with telephones? Did she touch them with spoons? What kinda spoons?
(4) | Child A: Teaspoons....

p.18 [11/23/1986 interview]

13 days later

(5) | Treacy: Can you make a mark where she hurt you?... Make a mark. Just show me where Kelly hurt you. Then I can show that to the judge...

p.8 [12/7/1986 interview]

2 pages later

(6) | Treacy: Tell me about 7C. What happened to 7C?
(7) | Child A: I don't know.
(8) | Treacy: 7C told me about some of the stuff that happened to you.

p.10 [12/7/1986 interview]

2 pages later

(9) | Child A: (no response)
(10) | Treacy: She cares about you. Some of the kids told me that things happened with knives at Wee Care. Do you remember anything like that?...

p.12 [12/7/1986 interview]

4 pages later

(11) | Treacy: I see and did the kids want Kelly to do that peanut butter stuff?
(12) | Child A: I didn't even think that there was a peanut butter....
(13) | Treacy: Well what about licking the peanut butter?
(14) | Child A: There wasn't anything about peanut butter....

p.16 [12/7/1986 interview]

4 pages earlier

(15) | Treacy: Some of the kids told me that things happened with knives. Do you remember anything like that?
(16) | Child A: No
[Although the child professes no knowledge of utensil abuse, at trial this child testified to numerous abuse allegations.]

p.12 [12/7/1986 interview]

4 pages later

(17) | Treacy: ...Well what about that cat game?
(18) | Child A: Cat game?
(19) | Treacy: Where everybody went like this, "Meow, Meow."
(20) | Child A: I don't think that I was there that day.
[Although the child professes no knowledge of the Cat game, at trial she described a cat game in which all the children were naked and licking each other.]

p.16 [12/7/1986 interview]

JEOPARDY IN THE COURTROOM 116

This questionable editing significantly changes how one reads and understands the content of the interview. Consider the first place where material was removed by editorial choice, between lines [2] and [3] in Figure 5.9. Here is the same passage, with the material omitted by Ceci and Bruck highlighted in bold:

TREACY: Let me ask you this. Did she touch boys? Did she touch girls? Did she touch dogs?

CHILD: She touched boys and girls.

TREACY: She touched boys and girls. **And where did this touching take place?**

CHILD: **At Wee Care.**

TREACY: **At Wee Care. Did it happen in like the kitchen? Where did it happen?**

CHILD: **In the piano room.**

The editing removed an open-ended question ("And where did this touching take place?") and a leading question that purposely contained false suggestion ("Did it happen in the kitchen?"). It is noteworthy that the child did *not* say "yes, it happened in the kitchen." Instead, the child said "in the piano room"—an answer that Treacy did not suggest. The added significance of the piano room is that it was named by other children who stayed late in the afternoon on occasion.

As indicated in Figure 5.9, the second "question" in this excerpt is reported as three continuous, run-on questions: "Did she touch them with telephones? Did she touch them with spoons? What kind of spoons?" The child's one word answer ("teaspoons") appears to be the sole response after a sequence of questions that ended with *what kind* of spoon. In other words, the interview appears to have led the child to a choice of spoons. But the transcript reveals otherwise:

TREACY: Did she touch their butts with her body or other stuff?

CHILD: Other stuff.

TREACY: Like what? Like blocks?

CHILD: No.

TREACY: How about things I have over there?

CHILD: No I forgot. I think I forgot, I'm not sure.

TREACY: You're not sure. Are you getting uncomfortable?

CHILD: No.

TREACY: OK, did she touch them with toys?

CHILD: No.

TREACY: Did she touch them with telephones?

CHILD: No.

TREACY: No. Did she touch them with spoons?
CHILD: Yes.
TREACY: What kind of spoons?
CHILD: Teaspoons.[186]

Editing this exchange to compress several separate questions into one uninterrupted bunch changes the appearance of the interaction from unobjectionable to highly objectionable. Academic psychologists Deborah Poole and Michael Lamb, who have written extensively about interviewing children, clearly counsel against the kind of multiple questioning created in the edited version.[187] But Treacy did the opposite of what is conveyed in Ceci and Bruck's edited excerpt; she allowed time for the child to respond to each question, as Poole and Lamb counsel. Moreover, she asked about three objects, two of which would presumably have caused affirmative answers (toys, telephones) if the child thought affirmative answers should be given in order to please the interviewer. Instead, the child said "no," there was no touching with toys or telephones.

There are also two bracketed statements by Ceci and Bruck in this excerpt, both of which insinuate that Treacy implanted ideas into this girl because, in both instances, she "professes no knowledge" about things she later testified to at trial. The first involves abuse with utensils. But a year and a half *before* the session with Treacy, Cassie told Detective Mastrangelo about abuse with utensils.[188] The second involves a "cat game." Again, Ceci and Bruck suggest that because the girl testified at trial about a game in which children licked each other, she must have learned that from Treacy. But Treacy does not mention licking in this excerpt, just the words *cat* and *meow*. Moreover, seventeen months *before* this session, Cassie's mother, when asked about unusual behavior in her daughter that year, replied "she licks me all the time."[189] The implication that Treacy implanted these ideas in the girl does not fit the chronology of the case.

Worse problems plague a second excerpt that Ceci and Bruck offer as evidence of how Treacy "gets the child to say that Kelly's private parts were the same as a little girl's." Curiously, the excerpt does not actually do that (see Figure 5.10). The passage contains ten questions or statements by Treacy, each followed by a response from the child. The passage appears disjointed, the questions are often leading, and the child's responses are vague and practically without substance ("I didn't really do that," "I don't know," "I don't remember about that").

The passage appears disjointed because it was edited that way. The excerpt is largely from pages 6 and 7 of the interview with Treacy, but the final two lines are from page 10. Moreover, critical phrases and lines are omitted without explanation. Consider the first six lines as presented by Ceci and Bruck in Figure 5.10. Here is the same passage directly from the transcript, with the significant material that was omitted or altered highlighted in boldface:

Figure 5.10 Treacy-Child B Excerpt, Reproduced from Ceci and Bruck (1995) with Source Annotations.

Ceci & Bruck Version	ECPO prepared transcript
(1) Treacy: Did Kelly have hair?	
(2) Child B: Nah, 1 know 'cause it's grown ups.... I know about that.	
(3) Treacy: So I guess that means you saw her private pats huh? Did Kelly ask the kids to look at her private parts, or to kiss her private part or....	
(4) Child B: <u>I didn't really do that.... I didn't even do it....</u>	*"I didn't, I didn't really want to do that"*
(5) Treacy: But she made you.	
(6) Child B: She made me. She made me.... But I couldn't do it.... So I didn't even really do it. I didn't do it....	p.6 [12/11/87 interview]
(7) Treacy: Did it smell good?	
(8) Child B: shhh	
(9) Treacy: Her private parts?	
(10) Child B: I don't know.	
(11) Treacy: Did it taste good? Did it taste like chocolate?	
(12) Child B: Ha, ha. No, I didn't even do it.... ————	*"She forced me."* (Missing Text)
	2 lines later
(13) Treacy: You Wee Care kids seem so scared of her.	
(14) Child B: I wasn't. I'm not even....	
(15) Treacy: But while you were there, were you real scared?	
(16) Child B: <u>I don't know.</u>	p.6 [12/11/87 interview] *"Kind of."*
(17) Treacy: What was so frightening about her, B., what was so scary about her?	
	5 pages later
(18) Child B: I don't know. Why don't you ask her?....	
(19) Treacy: Did she drink the pee pee?	
(20) Child B: <u>Please that sounds just crazy.</u> I don't remember about that. Really don't.	p.11 [12/11/87 interview] *"That's how she got crazy."*

JEOPARDY IN THE COURTROOM 118

Italicized text is from the transcript.

[1]   Treacy: Did Kelly have hair?

[2]   Child: Ahh, I know because they're grownups. . . . I know about them.

[3]   Treacy: So I guess that means you saw her private parts huh? Did Kelly ask the kids to look at her private parts, or to kiss her private part or . . .

[4]   Child: I didn't, **I didn't really want to do that—**

[4.1] Treacy: **Do what?**

[4.2] **Child: You know, kiss her private parts. I didn't even do it, I didn't feel like doing it.**

[5]   Treacy: But she made you?

[6]   Child: She made me. She made me but I couldn't do it so I didn't, cause you know I didn't feel like doing it. I didn't even do it.

Note, first, that the child's statement from line 4 actually reads "I didn't, I didn't really want to do that." Ceci and Bruck quote this line as "I didn't really do that. . . . I didn't even do it. . . ." Next, they omit the subsequent two lines in the exchange, labeled 4.1 and 4.2 in the text above. One line involves a simple, open-ended question by Treacy: "Do what?" The child replied: "You know, kiss her private parts. I didn't even do it, I didn't feel like doing it." Ceci and Bruck removed the open-ended question and the child's statement about kissing her private parts.

Later in the same excerpt, the boy's responses reported by Ceci and Bruck vary further from what is contained in the transcript. Ceci and Bruck report that the child answered "I don't know," when asked if he was scared at the time. The transcript indicates the child said "kind of." In other words, the transcript contains a partial affirmation, while Ceci and Bruck's version does not. The transcript also demonstrates that part of the boy's next answer was "She forced me," a phrase that was then repeated by Treacy in the unedited version. But Ceci and Bruck omit this material. Here is the excerpt directly from the transcript, with important material that was omitted or altered highlighted in boldface:

TREACY :   Did it taste good? Did it taste like chocolate?

CHILD B: No I didn't even (inaudible). **She forced me.**[190]

TREACY :   **She forced you.** Let me ask you this, this is one thing I don't understand, why don't you bring Darth Vader over here and help me with this thing. You kids from Wee Care really, really, when I talk to you guys about this. . . .

CHILD B: Yeah

TREACY :   You guys seem to scared of her

CHILD B: (inaudible) I'm not even scared.

TREACY :   But while you were there, were you scared

CHILD B: **Kind of.**[191]

Finally, according to Ceci and Bruck, this excerpt ends with Treacy asking, apparently out of the blue, "Did she [Kelly Michaels] drink the pee pee?" Ceci and Bruck report that the child responded, "Please that sounds just crazy." The authors quote this statement twice in their book, citing it as primary evidence of "a child's horror at the content of the interviewers' questions."[192] But this two-line exchange is actually several pages later than the lines before it. The material in between helps explain the source of Treacy's question. But most remarkably, the *transcript* indicates the child said "That's how she got crazy," *not* "Please that sounds just crazy"—a phrase that sounds suspiciously adultlike.[193] The same line that appears in the transcript— "That's how she got crazy"—also appears verbatim in the report that Treacy wrote shortly after this session in December 1986.[194] (The transcript was prepared more than a year later by a stenographer who never spoke with Treacy.) The childlike explanation that appears in both places does not evince "horror." Moreover, placing this response in context of the entire interview—that is, considering the material Ceci and Bruck omitted between pages 7 and 10—dispels the notion that the interviewer horrified the child. Seven lines *before* the question supposedly causing horror, the child volunteered this: "And then Kelly even tried to make us drink it."[195] The "horrifying" idea, then, came first from the child, not from the interviewer.

Exaggerating the Fantastic

For many, the most persuasive, and certainly the most memorable, argument in the witch-hunt narrative of the Michaels case revolves around the "fantastic" claims made by children in the case. The allegations involving abuse with utensils have been placed in this category. But there were other so-called bizarre claims as well. As Rabinowitz explained it:

> Unnoticed, and on a daily basis, Michaels had also, according to prosecutors, licked peanut butter off the children's genitals, played the piano in the nude, and made them drink her urine and eat a 'cake' of her feces.[196]

Rabinowitz was wrong in several ways. First, prosecutors did not allege that *any* criminal acts happened daily. Second, only a few of "the children" were implicated in the most grotesque charges. Of the 131 counts that went to the jury, there was one lone count about the consumption of feces. To read the witch-hunt narrative, one would think the case was built on these charges. Finally, Rabinowitz was wrong to suggest that Michaels was convicted of the most fantastic claims. The charge just mentioned, possibly the most difficult to believe in the case, was one of the fifteen counts the jury rejected at trial. In short, even though there *were* "fantastic" charges in the case, their role has been inflated and misrepresented. The significance of these charges can be ascertained only by analyzing specific details, something the witch-hunt narrative consistently avoids.

The most widespread claims in the case that have been labeled "fantastic" involve allegations concerning plastic utensils. The word *bizarre* is also used to describe the allegations of sexual abuse with spoons, knives, and forks. The idea that allegations of abuse with utensils emanated from the interviewers has an obvious plausibility, given the ominous claim in Ceci and Bruck's brief that in "17 of the 39 sessions silverware was given to the children with dolls."[197] This is a large enough number to account for all the allegations about sexual abuse with utensils. But some important questions are left unexplored by proponents of the witch-hunt narrative: (1) In how many interviews were utensils introduced by the child? (2) What were the circumstances and content of the first disclosure of each child at trial who alleged abuse with utensils? (3) How many allegations involving utensils came outside the context of the seventeen interviews where they were "introduced by the interviewer"?

The witch-hunt narrative seems to imply that the answer to the first question is zero. At least, it never acknowledges that any child made such statements without prompting. Yet there is compelling evidence from several such children. A careful analysis of when these claims first emerged eliminates "suggestibility" as the original source. The first time utensils were mentioned in the case was May 2, three weeks before Fonolleras entered the investigation. They were mentioned the second day of the investigation, when Sam Raymond, a boy named by Mitchell Pierce, told his father that Kelly Michaels had touched his private parts with a spoon. The boy's father wrote a three-page statement by hand that includes this detail, on the night of May 2, 1985.

Rather than embracing the idea of abuse with a utensil, the authorities responded with skepticism, immediately sensing that these details would probably render the children less credible.[198] The prosecutors would have left those charges out of the case if they could have. The witch-hunt narrative has never explained why, if the interviewers were implanting the whole case, they would choose to include an element likely to make the case less credible. But the fact is that utensils were a consistent feature across children who disclosed earliest and under different circumstances. The idea that all of the statements about abuse with utensils came from leading questions is contradicted elsewhere in the trial transcript. In the initial disclosure to his mother, David Applegate—the child who was never interviewed by DYFS—talked about being penetrated with a "spoon" and with a "stick," which could well be a knife or the handle end of any utensil.

Proponents of the witch-hunt narrative have ignored the most convincing child testimony, but they have simultaneously exaggerated the nature of the claims involving utensils. Those exaggerations transform the allegations from plausible to physically impossible. Rabinowitz has claimed the allegations involved "serrated knives" and "terrible sharp instruments."[199] But she is the one who introduced the language "serrated" knives and "terrible sharp instruments."

Four- to six-year-olds tend not to use words like "serrated." But even if they did, this is not what they said in this case. It was apparent through exhibits used at trial that the utensils at issue were plastic, the kind one finds at a preschool.

In the few places in the investigative interviews where children elaborated on the nature of the utensils, they said things that directly contradicted the descriptors chosen by Rabinowitz. One child, asked to describe what kind of knife, said "like a butter knife."[200] This comes as close as a child possibly could to indicating the knife was *not* serrated or sharp. Another child's mother described her son revealing that "the other end of the knife, not the pointed end, was inserted into his rectum."[201] Most memorably, one child, in an early interview in June, added the phrase "the end you don't eat eggs with," after describing abuse with a fork.[202] In short, what the children actually described were uses of utensils that would not cause serious injuries. Even Dr. Watson S. Price, a physician who testified for the defense, agreed with this assessment. Inserting the handle of a spoon in the anus would "basically cause redness," he testified. Even a dull knife, he continued, would result in "probably nothing, but a little bit of erythema [redness]."[203] The trial record in this case is replete with documented cases of erythema and irritated anuses. This evidence is all missing, however, from the witch-hunt narrative. Moreover, the initial disclosures about "white jean stuff" and "gasoline"— also consistently omitted from the narrative—apparently support the theory that Michaels minimized any acute injuries by using Vaseline.

Another allegation that has become central to the witch-hunt narrative is the claim that Michaels played the piano in the nude. A few children specifically said she had played the song "Jingle Bells." Those claims were nowhere near as pervasive as claims about abuse with utensils. Only a small number of children made such statements. They emerged from multiple sources on June 6 and 7, in claims that were consistent and almost simultaneous. The assertions about eating feces are undoubtedly the most difficult to believe. But the case was *not* characterized by such claims. Two of the children at trial made statements of that kind during the investigation; both emerged late in the investigation, and neither charge resulted in a conviction. One of the charges was dropped; the other resulted in a not-guilty finding by the jury. It is extremely misleading, then, to suggest that such claims were widespread in the case, or that such charges are what resulted in her conviction.

In short, the supposedly fantastic claims in the Kelly Michaels case varied significantly, from being widespread (abuse with utensils) to isolated examples in a few children (allegations involving feces); they also ranged from highly plausible (also the utensil claims), given how they emerged, to much less likely (nude piano playing).[204] Dr. Mark Everson, director of the Program on Childhood Trauma and Maltreatment at the University of North Carolina, reminds us that improbable or fantastic accounts "should not result in an automatic dismissal of the child's report."[205] Everson has proposed twenty-four possible explanations for such statements, urging a balanced approach that includes "multiple dimensions of assessment and investigation" rather than overreliance on the child's statements alone. Critics of the Michaels case have eschewed the idea. Rabinowitz condemned as Orwellian the notion that jurors were told "they didn't need to believe everything the children said."[206] Yet adult witnesses have never been held to the standard that all of their testimony must be rejected if any single statement is not considered credible.

Manufacturing Social Hysteria

An integral part of the witch-hunt narrative is the argument that "social hysteria" inflated and even created an untold number of charges in the Michaels case. This argument postulates social dynamics whereby parents caught up in a frenzy are, at best, less skeptical of children's statements than they would otherwise be, and at worst they actually foment allegations in their own children. On the surface, this claim has an obvious plausibility in the Michaels case because it grew from a 6-count indictment in May to a 235-count indictment in November. Of course, a case involving multiple victims would have to begin somewhere—and no matter how it unfolded, it would apparently be susceptible to a claim that the expansion was enabled or enhanced by social hysteria if the mere fact of expansion is considered enough to prove the claim.

Regardless of the actual evidence in the Michaels case, this claim has been widely accepted. Rabinowitz labeled the case "a condition of national hysteria not unlike the hysteria that seized the Massachusetts Bay Colony" during the Salem witch trials. The state of New Jersey was allegedly in the grips of "a national hysteria" that was "as virulent and contagious as the Asian flu," she continued.[207] Dr. Richard Gardner, who coined the term *sex abuse hysteria* and was hired to worked for the defense in the civil cases against Kelly Michaels, proclaimed that the case had "many of the classic hallmarks" of such "hysteria."[208]

The social hysteria claim plays a critical role in the witch-hunt narrative. First, it provides a kind of catch-all explanation. Any child whose interviews cannot be impugned—or, in the case of David Applegate, who was never interviewed by DYFS—can always be said to have succumbed to vague social forces. The same approach can also be used to explain away the twelve jurors who found Michaels guilty beyond a reasonable doubt. The social hysteria claim is also what makes this case of broader interest. It is a link that arguably ties this case to others across the country. Indeed, critics generally discuss these cases as if they are interchangeable. Debbie Nathan claimed that the Michaels case was "a cookie-cutter copy" of the one she wrote about in Texas.[209] Curiously, she made that pronouncement *before* the brief trip to New Jersey that constituted the research for her first article about the Michaels case in the *Village Voice*.[210] Unfortunately, critics of the case have not supplied a careful, chronological accounting of how the case evolved. Instead, there has been almost indiscriminate use of the word *hysteria*. Law professor Jean Montoya claimed that "the hysteria began" as soon as the letter was sent to parents about unspecified allegations concerning a former employee.[211] But a close examination of the facts reveals that the social hysteria claim is contradicted by the case chronology.

The social hysteria claim is often made such that the initial investigation collapses into the investigation-at-large, making it appear as if Mitchell Pierce's utterance resulted in the decision to interview fifty-one children. "That is how the accusation began," Nathan stated after inaccurately claiming his famous utterance was caused by the nurse rubbing the boy's back. "Detectives and social workers from New Jersey's Division of Youth and Family Services then embarked on a two-month interview process," she continued, without any recognition of the difference between the initial charges and the later investigation. The same mistake was repeated almost verbatim by Justice Clarence Thomas, dissenting from the decision not to hear the case dismissing Michael's civil claims against the state after her conviction was overturned:

> Based solely on [Mitchell Pierce's] statements, a prosecutor and several investigators, respondents here, began an extensive investigation. Respondents interviewed virtually all of the children with whom petitioner could have had any contact.[212]

But this is not how the case evolved. Mitchell's statements resulted in interviewing the two boys he named. One immediately confirmed the claim. Another boy, whose mother was on the Wee Care board of directors, soon emerged to confirm the same. The first phase of the investigation was narrowly focused and quickly brought to an end. The social hysteria arguments simply cannot apply to this stage of the case, and they cannot explain the charges that formed the basis for the original six-count indictment.

The letter to parents of children at Wee Care was sent on May 7. Had the letter named Kelly Michaels, as Nathan erroneously reported in the *Village Voice*,[213] there would have been special reason for concern. But the letter said the investigation was about "a former employee," and it gave no particular reason for parents to assume their children were affected. The first parents' meeting, held on May 15, was more restrained than was often described. There were, of course, some concerned parents, which would happen in any case involving allegations of abuse. There were also many parents who were *not* concerned because the letter specified the investigation concerned "a former employee." Some parents did not even bother to attend the May 15 parents' meeting, and several were on record at the time as being quite restrained about the issue.[214] Moreover, the DYFS investigator did not start interviewing anyone until two weeks after the prosecutor's office had completed the investigation that resulted in the first indictment.

The social dynamics surrounding the case clearly changed during the month of June. Roughly speaking, they went from a targeted investigation based on the content of previously interviewed children to a broad-based investigation, at least by DYFS, seemingly intent on interviewing every child who attended the school. There was also a shift in thinking about the scope and likelihood of the charges against Kelly Michaels. There was clearly a hardening of views about her. Lou Fonolleras displayed this tendency the most. It is fair to say he eventually embodied the kind of "confirmation bias" that taints an investigation. After all, he ultimately "substantiated" abuse claims on virtually every child he interviewed, including ones who denied abuse.[215] But none of the children who were then "substantiated" without regard to the content of their statements was actually in the criminal case. Moreover, there is no reason to conclude that Fonolleras brought this view to the investigation on May 22. Had this been the case, he would have "found" abuse on *that* day and immediately continued interviewing. Instead, he interviewed two children on May 22 and did not return until June 6—only when specifically requested by a parent.

Taking these facts into account, we could say there were three phases to the investigation: the earliest investigative phase, the first part of the DYFS investigation (which soon included the Essex County Prosecutor's Office), and the later part of the DYFS/ECPO investigation. There is not a simple obvious marker for the shift in the DYFS investigation in June. I have selected June 13 for several reasons but acknowledge that it could be drawn somewhat differently.[216] Whatever the boundaries between phases two and three, the social hysteria argument has the greatest plausibility in phase three. Unequivocal denials were prevalent in late June (and early July) but not earlier in the investigation.

The role of the media also changed significantly over this time, and the pattern was completely different from the McMartin case, where intense national publicity preceded the first grand jury by more than a month. In the Michaels case, the initial press coverage was quite restrained, and there was no coverage at all during the first phase of the investigation or through the initial grand jury proceedings. There was a two-hundred-word story in the *Star-Ledger* on June 7 that reported the six-count indictment. They ran a slightly longer story on June 21, reporting that Michaels faced an additional thirty-one charges. This was the first indication in the press that the case extended beyond the original three boys. A longer story, reporting that Michaels was being held at the county jail, appeared in the *News-Record* of Maplewood and South Orange on June 26. There were no statewide stories and no television coverage at the time. Indeed it was more than six weeks before the story was reported elsewhere in New Jersey.

There were few stories before late June and the unsealing of the additional charges in December. Daily stories in the local press did not occur until the case came to trial in 1987. By then, of course, all of the charges had also long since been finalized. These facts illustrate an obvious point that has been overlooked by proponents of the social hysteria claim: the investigation and the surrounding social forces evolved over time. Media coverage went from nonexistent to minimal and, long after the charges were finalized, to intensive. Parental involvement evolved likewise. Many of the charges in the case came long before any arguable signs of so-called hysteria. The evolution of the case must be considered carefully, then, in order to assess when, if ever, broader social forces might have affected it.

But how much of the case was built around children who emerged during the final stages of the investigation? How much was built around children's statements in the earliest stages of the investigation? Those questions have not been addressed by proponents of the witch-hunt narrative, who seem intent on blurring such distinctions. Viewing the investigation in stages, one concludes the likely reason for avoiding such analysis is apparent: the actual patterns in this case contradict what the social hysteria claim would predict. If the case is divided into three phases—May 1 to May 7, May 22 to June 13, June 17 onward—the twenty children at trial were about evenly divided between the first two stages and the third.

Aggregate analysis of the three stages reveals that the interview intensity increased over time while the percentage of children identified as victims dropped significantly in the third phase of the investigation (see Table 5.1). Three of the five children interviewed in phase one (60 percent) ended up at trial. It would likely have been 80 percent if Cody Cook's family had not moved away. Seven of the

Table 5.1 **Kelly Michaels Interview and Charge Information, by Investigative Phase**

	Initial investigation 5/1–5/7	*DYFS/ECPO Phase one 5/22–6/13*	*DYFS/ECPO Phase two 6/17–7/15*
No. children interviewed for the first time	5	13*	33
No. of these children w/ charges resulting	4	9	18
No. of these children at trial (n=19)	3	7	9

* David Applegate emerged in this phase but was not interviewed by DYFS.

thirteen children interviewed during phase two (54 percent) ended up at trial. But only nine of the thirty-three interviews conducted with children interviewed in phase three (27 percent) resulted in charges that went to trial. This pattern runs counter to the social hysteria claim. It is opposite to what happened in the McMartin case. When the social pressures were most apparent, when parents began to organize, when there were stories in the local newspaper about expanding charges, and when interviewer bias apparently became a serious problem and interview frequency intensified, the percentage of children who actually disclosed abuse and were included in the case was less than half the rate of earlier stages.

A handful of children who *did* disclose during the final period later became the basis for some of the most intensive criticism in the witch-hunt narrative. So did other children who were interviewed late in the process—children who were never in the case beyond their initial interview. Given the rising intensity in the prevailing social environment, the charges that emerged during the third phase of the investigation deserve close attention and an extra degree of skepticism. But the fact that ten of the nineteen children at trial were from earlier phases in the investigation is a direct challenge to the social hysteria claim.

The actual verdict in the case also contradicts the claim that the jury succumbed to social hysteria. Had an automatic "believe the children" view captured the jury, they would have found Michaels guilty on all counts. But the verdict clearly reflected child-by-child decisions, not group judgments. The jury found some children's testimony persuasive in relation to all counts charged; this describes the outcome for seven of the twenty children at trial. For two other children, the jury returned guilty verdicts that were, in part, based on "lesser included charges." But for eleven of the twenty children, the jury verdicts were more mixed. In some cases, almost all of the charges were accepted by the jury; in others, either most of the charges were rejected or a guilty verdict was returned on a lesser included charge. This individualized decision making belies assertions of the kind of groupthink that characterizes the hysteria claim.

The Appellate Division Follows Suit

Public opinion about the Kelly Michaels case shifted *before* the case reached the Appellate Division. As Debbie Nathan has since described it, the Rabinowitz article in May 1990 brought national attention to the case. After that, Nathan "was deluged with calls from filmmakers, journalists, and television reporters. Public opinion began shifting in Michaels's favor."[217] By the time the case was actually heard by the Appellate Division in early 1993, Kelly Michaels had become a cause célèbre. There were several stories on national television and in national magazines casting the case as a witch-hunt. There was little or no voice in response, especially since prosecutors are not supposed to argue their cases in the press. The appellate judges in New Jersey, who lived and worked in the greater New York City media market, would already have heard the witch-hunt narrative about the Kelly Michaels case long before it arrived at their court. It appears that the long delay in arrival time was strategic.

If there has ever been an appellate case where it was clear that the decision was made before the oral argument, this was it. Rabinowitz reported, "No one sitting at the February appellate hearing could miss the controlled scorn evidenced by the three judges."[218] "Michaels Case Headed for Remand," the *New Jersey Law Journal* announced with confidence immediately after the oral argument. As they put it:

> Sometimes an appeals court can so telegraph its views on a case that reading its intentions becomes not a question of whether they will, say, overturn a criminal conviction, but rather what new guidelines it will issue in ordering a new trial.[219]

They were correct about the outcome.

Oral arguments in the case were on February 1, 1993. The court issued its 118-page decision in March; it was a resounding victory for the defense. The Appellate Division accepted the arguments about repetitive interviews and child suggestibility; it also held that the expert testimony of Eileen Treacy should not have been allowed. The court ruled that the defendant could not be retried without a "taint hearing"—something not previously recognized in New Jersey law—to assess the reliability of the children's statements. In short, the defense prevailed on every issue except those pertaining to Ralph Underwager; even an Appellate Division that was highly receptive to the defense could not rehabilitate him.

The New Jersey Appellate Division repeated the false claim that "it was patently obvious that the [first] child's comment was misunderstood and that the child was referring to the rubbing of his back and not the anal penetration."[220] The court did not confront the actual content of this child's initial statements or the details of the adult testimony surrounding it. The Appellate Division would have had in its possession the testimony of Laura Hadley, the medical assistant who flatly contradicted this claim. Instead, the judges apparently relied on the pure speculation of Jonas Rappeport, who did not actually review the evidence on this point.[221]

How the case actually evolved was also considered irrelevant by the court, which stated early in the opinion that a "child-specific recitation of the alleged abusive acts would serve no useful purpose at this juncture."[222] This would be true if the only issue before the court was a question of law—the usual function of an appellate court. In fact, the appellate court was substituting its own judgment for that of the trial court on the issue of how the children were interviewed. Indeed, there is significant irony in the fact that the Michaels case is known for the requirement, established by Appellate Division, of a "taint hearing" because there *was* a full airing of the suggestibility issue in a pre-trial hearing in 1987. The proceeding was not labeled a taint hearing, but the pretrial motion by the defense to dismiss the charges contained all of the same arguments.[223] The defense argued that the investigative interviews were unduly suggestive and rendered the children's statements too unreliable to be admitted at trial.

Superior Court Judge William F. Harth, who tried the case, took this issue seriously. He heard days of testimony from two defense psychologists, and he scrutinized the interviews himself, making notes on twenty taped interviews. "Judge Rules Testimony of Children in Day-care Case Wasn't Tainted," the *Star Ledger* reported on May 1, 1987. As explained below, the *Star Ledger's* description is apparently the remaining archival record of this hearing. According to Donna Leusner, who covered the hearing:

> [Judge] Harth read from portions of the preschoolers' grand jury testimony and individually critiqued more than 20 taped interviews conducted by state investigators before the grand jury session. . . . Harth cited numerous examples when questions that could be construed as leading drew negative responses. . . . During some interviews, children corrected or disagreed with investigators.[224]

Such findings of fact are normally accorded substantial deference on appeal because trial judges are closer to the evidence and are better positioned to evaluate the credibility of witnesses. But there was a highly unusual development in this case, one that has escaped notice in the witch-hunt narrative: all of the court records of that important pre-trial hearing disappeared or were mislaid. They were never located during the appeals process. When it became clear on appeal that the official record of this crucial fact-finding hearing was missing, the state moved "for a limited remand before that court to have the record reconstructed."[225] Remarkably, the Appellate Division denied the request. This freed the appellate court to make its own factual findings, unconstrained by what the judge who actually heard the tapes had concluded. Were it not for these highly unusual developments—both the loss of the transcript and the refusal of the Appellate Division to remand the issue to the fact-finding tribunal for the creation of a full record on appeal—this case could not have been overturned on the appellate court's own decision that the interviews were overly suggestive.

The appeal was argued in February 1993; the court issued its decision in March. The court made sweeping factual claims about the interviews after stating that a child-specific analysis "would serve no useful purpose." Sara Sencer-McArdle prepared a long memorandum documenting factual errors in the opinion of the Appellate Division.[226] But history, in this instance, was written by the court. Their factual mistakes are now enshrined in this landmark opinion.[227]

Fearing that this precedent would make it unduly difficult to prosecute child sexual abuse cases, the state appealed to the New Jersey Supreme Court. The court initially declined to hear the case, apparently reasoning that the issues were moot since the state was unlikely to retry Michaels. The court indicated the state could refile its petition for Supreme Court review only if the prosecution declared its intention to retry Michaels. Demonstrating how strong they considered the evidence in the case, the prosecutor's office indicted that it *would* retry Michaels if they won the appeal. The New Jersey Supreme Court agreed to hear the case, and the battleground then shifted to the academic field of psychology.

Academics Enter the Fray

The academic subfield of child psychology was rocked by McMartin. When the case began in 1983, the law was slanted against children as witnesses. Children younger than seven or eight were rarely allowed to testify, juries were often instructed that children were not as trustworthy as adults, and in many states child molestation cases could go forward only if there was some form of corroboration beyond the word of a child. This state of affairs was based more on perception and prejudice than on a proven body of facts, and a few psychologists started doing research that challenged those conceptions. During the mid-1980s, Professor Gail Goodman was considered a leader in the field; her research was featured in a *New York Times* article in November, 1984 captioned "Studies of Child as Witnesses Find Surprising Accuracy."[228] The article summarized studies of children as witnesses from a special issue of the *Journal of Social Issues*. One study found that five- and six-year-olds were as accurate as college students in recounting a staged event in which someone burst into a room and gave a fifteen-second harangue. These studies contributed to legal reforms that allowed younger children to testify, eliminated jury instructions that discounted children as witnesses, and eliminated the requirement that their testimony be corroborated. Those reforms opened the door to the cases that later became the core of the witch-hunt narrative.

In the wake of the McMartin case, it seemed inevitable that the positive view of children as witnesses would be tempered. There was no question that some children had come to believe in things that had not actually happened. There was also no question that adults had misunderstood children in various ways, reading into their responses much more than what the children actually said. How the field of child psychology would respond to those problems was an issue of grave concern, particularly to those who feared an overreaction. Writing in the *Los Angeles Times* on the day after the McMartin verdicts, psychologist Carol Tavris referred to Gail Goodman's research with approval and worried that "legitimate concerns about falsely accusing an innocent adult . . . not cause us to falsely disbelieve an innocent child."[229] This caution did not take hold among child psychologists in the academy. Instead, there was a concerted effort to discredit Goodman's research and promote a new line of studies to emphasize that children were highly suggestible.[230] This included efforts to paint Goodman as an extremist and portray a paradigm shift in the field through a process that, at times, looked more like a political campaign than a scientific endeavor. These developments came to a head in the appellate phase of the Michaels case. Before then, the arguments made on behalf of Michaels and others were largely advanced by the likes of Ralph Underwager, who lacked an academic affiliation and had considerable baggage as an expert witness.[231] All of this changed dramatically in 1993 with publications and related research by a pair of high-stature academic psychologists: Stephen Ceci of Cornell University and Maggie Bruck, then from McGill University, currently at Johns Hopkins University. Ceci and Bruck published two academic articles—one in *Psychological Bulletin*, the other in the *Report of the Society for Research in Child Development*—both of which specifically criticized the Michaels case. They also received significant publicity that year for the "Mousetrap Study," which was linked to the Kelly Michaels case in a front-page story in the *New York Times*. Finally, Ceci and Bruck coauthored a "friend of the court" brief, known to lawyers as an amicus brief, directly in support of Michaels. Though not an academic publication per se, this amicus brief, which came to be known as the "Concerned Scientists" brief, was later published in its entirety in a special issue of *Psychology, Public Policy and Law*, a journal of the American Psychological Association. It has since become a prominent document among academic child psychologists. The brief gave newfound credentials to the witch-hunt narrative about the Kelly Michaels case.

The "Synthesis" in Psychological Bulletin

The first important publication by Ceci and Bruck, "Suggestibility of the Child Witness: A Historical Review and Synthesis," surveyed the literature concerning children as witnesses and concluded that "the field of children's testimony is in turmoil, but a resolution to seemingly intractable debates now seemed attainable."[232] The review began with descriptions of "two recent court cases in which child witnesses provided critical eyewitness testimony"; the first was Kelly Michaels, and the second was Country Walk (the subject of the next chapter). Ceci and Bruck reviewed the literature over seventy years and described examples of five recent studies that supported the idea of children being more suggestible than adults. They also described five studies supporting the view that children are no more suggestible than adults, crediting Goodman with "doing more [than other researchers] to redress the historical imbalance" caused by decades of "research criticizing and belittling the accuracy and suggestibility of child witnesses." Recognizing this accomplishment, Ceci and Bruck nevertheless took a different view of Goodman's work. They also took Gary Melton, a past president of the American Psychological Association's Division on Psychology and Law, to task for criticizing statements, in a dissenting opinion in *Maryland v. Craig*, that children are substantially more suggestible than adults. Acknowledging that there are studies supportive of differing positions on this issue, Ceci and Bruck argued that these schools of thought cannot be resolved by "a point-by-point criticism of the methodological weaknesses of each study.[233] Instead, they proposed examining "the causal mechanisms that may underlie suggestibility effects."

The end of the discussion was also inconclusive, but Ceci and Bruck took the position that "it seems likely" future studies of interviewing techniques will lead to the conclusion that children are more suggestible than previously thought. Somewhat surprisingly, then, the authors go on to say:

> Clearly, more research is needed on this important topic before these conclusions can be accepted, even though many examples consistent with the claim that interview bias has large effects on children's reports can be found in legal case files.[234]

They proceeded to say that "this can be seen explicitly in the Kelly Michaels case," quoting about twenty lines from a single interview in the case. It is the same interview that Rabinowitz excerpted in *Harper's*, where the child was uncooperative and told the interviewer he hated him (and allegedly ended by the interview by saying it was all lies). Ceci and Bruck then claimed that this interview was "characteristic of many of the state's interviews."[235] A systematic analysis of the case demonstrates this child's statements were not characteristic of many interviews; indeed, his interview was unusual in several ways.[236] But the misapplication of laboratory results to specific cases had begun.

The Mousetrap Study in the New York Times

Soon thereafter, Ceci and Bruck were featured on the front page of the *New York Times* in a story headlined "Studies Reveal Suggestibility of Very Young Witnesses."[237] The article described the findings of research by Ceci and Bruck that had not yet been published but would quickly become a staple in the witch-hunt narrative and in defense briefs in child molestation cases. The study is known popularly as "the Mousetrap Study."[238] Children in this study were interviewed about numerous events, after verifying in advance with their parents whether or not these events had ever happened to their child. One of the fictitious events was getting one's hand caught in a mousetrap and having to go to the hospital to have it removed. Faced with children who had never had their hand caught in a mousetrap, the experiment was designed to see whether repetitive questioning over ten weeks would cause children to falsely claim that they had had their hand caught in a mousetrap. When the children were interviewed in this experiment, they were told:

> I am going to read some things that may have happened to you, and I want you to think real hard about each one of them that I am going to read. Try to remember if it really happened.[239]

The children were interviewed seven to ten times over a ten-week period. They were, as it turns out, highly accurate in reporting true, salient events. Approximately one-third of the children, however, falsely assented to questions about an event that had not occurred. Much to the surprise of the authors, the number of false assents did *not* increase over time. The results did not demonstrate the kind of suggestibility they had hypothesized. But there was one particularly dramatic result: a child who originally said he had never been to the hospital spun a detailed story about getting his finger caught in a mousetrap and going to the hospital. The *New York Times* featured a sidebar with excerpts from the weekly progression of that child's answers, titled "How the Questions Become the Answers." It featured the boy's response when asked, in the final interview, "how did it happen?"

> I was looking and then I didn't see what I was doing and it [finger] got in there somehow. . . . The mousetrap was in our house because there's a mouse in our house. . . . The mousetrap is down in the basement, next to the firewood. . . . I was playing a game called "Operation" and then I went downstairs and said to Dad, "I want to eat lunch," and then it got stuck in the mousetrap. . . .[240]

This detailed account seems to provide strong evidence of how children could be led into producing complete narratives of fictitious events through the process of suggestive interviewing. Several months later, the same boy was interviewed on national television by John Stossel, who featured Ceci and Bruck's research in a segment on *20/20* that linked these results specifically to the Kelly Michaels case. Ceci told Stossel:

> What we do [in our experiments] is a pale version of what happens in real cases. It doesn't come close, for example, to what was done in the Kelly Michaels case.[241]

It was a convincing argument. It was also is a serious misrepresentation of what happened in the Michaels case. Children were not told by interviewers that

Kelly Michaels had committed specific acts of sexual abuse, let alone week after week. Moreover, no child in the case was interviewed anywhere close to ten times in the investigation.[242] Surprisingly, the "Discussion" section of the article that reported these results did not focus on the study that, in overall terms, did not confirm their hypothesis. There was a single sentence about the study, followed by a lengthy discussion of something the authors called a "replication study" containing a "modification" in protocol. But the modification made it a significantly different study; the modification was that "each week the interviewer *informed the child that they had actually experienced the fictitious event* and then asked them if they remembered having done so."[243] The results from this study were also published separately.[244]

The "modified" version of the experiment produced much more dramatic results, including "a reliable increase in children's claims of having remembered fictitious events" over a twelve-week period.[245] In the modified experiment, there was also an eleventh interview, conducted by someone different from the earlier interviewer. The authors reported that after ten weeks, "56 percent of children reported at least one false event as true."[246] But the difference between the first study—which did not create the hypothesized results—and the "modified" version, which did, was lost on the media. *New York Times* health columnist Jane Brody made this same mistake, claiming that asking children to "think real hard" about events could cause them to believe fictitious events.[247] The media myth had far outgrown the results of the study. Indeed, in an article that received virtually no attention in the mass media, the child who spun the elaborate tale about getting his finger caught in a mousetrap revealed in a follow-up interview that it was "just a story." Ceci and his coauthors allowed that "the results of this follow-up study show clearly that the source misattributions did not create long-lasting memories."[248] But the study *did* impart a long-lasting sense to the contrary in public discourse about child suggestibility. Long after this child recanted, defense attorneys were still attaching the videotape of his appearance on *20/20* as "evidence" of child suggestibility.

"Translating Research into Policy"

Another important publication that year, also by Ceci and Bruck, came from the Society for Research in Child Development (SRCD). The article, "Child Witnesses: Translating Research into Policy," appeared in the Fall 1993 issue of SRCD's *Social Policy Report*. In this publication, Ceci and Bruck focused largely on "stereotypical knowledge," which they described as "the tendency to extrapolate from stereotypical knowledge to provide erroneous but plausible accounts of non-witnessed events."[249] Could being told that someone is "bad," for example, lead a child to create a whole narrative about sexual abuse? Some children *were* told that Kelly Michaels was "bad" during their interviews in the case. The authors described the "Sam Stone" experiment, not yet published but already in press, which was designed to test the effects of such "stereotype induction." Children were told over a one-month period about Sam Stone, a clumsy clown who often broke things. Sam later visited the nursery school for two minutes, "amiably interacting" but *not* breaking anything or acting clumsy. The next day, children were shown a torn book and a soiled teddy bear and asked about how it happened. In this phase of the experiment, "few children claimed to have seen Sam Stone do these things."[250]

In the second phase of the experiment, children were interviewed five times over ten weeks. They were asked leading questions such as "I wonder whether Sam Stone was wearing long pants or short pants when he ripped the book." At the end of this ten-week period, a different interviewer asked each child what happened when Sam visited their school. As Ceci and Bruck reported:

> When asked, 72% of the 3- and 4-year-olds said Sam Stone had ruined at least one of the items in question (the book or bear). When they were explicitly asked, 45% of the 3- and 4-year-olds replied that they actually had seen him do these things, as opposed to merely being told that he did.[251]

The study was also conducted with an older age group. Only 11 percent of the five- and six-year-olds claimed to have observed Sam damage any items. Ceci and Bruck concluded that "stereotype formation interacts with suggestive questioning to a greater extent for younger than older children." They did not highlight the related result that even among the youngest children almost half of those who *appear* to have adopted a stereotype from external sources readily identified the source when asked. If half of the young children who will adopt a stereotype based on external factors will also make it clear that they learned the information secondhand, then this phenomenon would be apparent in a criminal case through simple cross-examination. But none of the children in the Kelly Michaels trial indicated under cross-examination that what they knew about Michaels came from being told by someone else. There *were* children who said this in the interview process, but they were not included in the case, although some of their interviews have been cited as if they were. Nor were any of the children subjected to five to ten weeks of such questioning before disclosing abuse.

Ceci and Bruck's conclusion about this study is reasonable, but their description of the questions in the study was misleading. The questions were not merely "suggestive"; they actually contained declarative statements. The children were *told repeatedly over time* that Sam Stone had done specific acts. This is important in considering the application of these findings to actual cases. No child in the Michaels case was subjected to such questioning by investigators.

Ceci and Bruck's Brief for the Defense

Why did both of these articles and the *New York Times* story about the Mouse-trap Study refer specifically to the Michaels case? Did Ceci and Bruck have a particular interest in the case? The answer became clearer several months later when the two authored a "friend of the court" brief that supported Kelly Michaels. But even then, the full extent of their involvement with the defense was not disclosed. The brief, which was presented as an independent voice from the scientific community, was filed by Amy Gershenfeld Donella, a former public defender in New Jersey. But it had been requested by Robert Rosenthal, one of Michaels's defense lawyers, who played an active, but undisclosed, role in actually writing the brief. In their 1995 book, Ceci and Bruck state that "transcripts of the children's interviews and of lower court of appeals documents became available to us when we co-authored an amicus brief."[252] But filing an amicus brief does not provide parties with access to a sealed transcript. And even if it did, this brief was written more than two months before the order that permitted the "concerned scientists" to enter the cases as friends of the court.[253]

The email that Bruck sent to solicit signatures for this brief said she "spent a tremendous amount of time" going through the interviews and "in fact every interview is a goldmine of horrifying examples of bad interviewing techniques."[254] However, a draft version of the brief that circulated among defense lawyers before it was filed in the Michaels case contained bracketed comments, in all caps, such as "Robert put in examples, " "Robert is this correct?" and "Robert can you put in a section for [this child]."[255] Robert Rosenthal, the defense lawyer, clearly played a pivotal role in linking Ceci and Bruck's research to the facts of the Michaels case. In their 1995 book, Ceci and Bruck would credit Rosenthal for "verifying information against the trial transcripts."[256] More recently, Ceci's vita was changed to credit Rosenthal *as a co-author* of the Concerned Scientists brief. The designation bears out that Rosenthal played a significant and undisclosed role in crafting the Concerned Scientists brief.

These facts undercut the claim that Ceci and Bruck made to being centrists who were not affiliated with the prosecution or the defense side of the issue. While working with the defense in the Michaels case, Ceci and Bruck sought to paint Gail Goodman as a "pro-prosecution extremist."[257] Goodman was not an extremist, and she was not aligned with the prosecution. But she was opposed to the idea of special taint hearings for children, and she viewed the new wave in child suggestibility research as having a defense slant. She had not testified in several years; before that, she testified three times for the prosecution and three times for the defense.[258] Moreover, she was described as one of the "leading scholars" in the field in a 1991 publication of papers from an APA-sponsored conference on child suggestibility at Cornell University.[259] During this same time period, Ceci, on the other hand, has claimed that he was hired "by both sides" in the Finje case in Florida, when in fact he was hired by the defense.[260] He never disclosed his affiliation with the defense in the Country Walk case (discussed in the next chapter), and, although John Stossel reported that Ceci never testified for the defense, he did so again in the Foeller case in Michigan a month after the program was aired.[261] In a pre-trial deposition, Ceci allowed that his research has a "pro-defense orientation."[262]

The reason these affiliations are important to the Michaels case is that the Ceci and Bruck brief claimed there had been a "paradigm shift" in the field of child psychology. They were essentially claiming there was now a scientific consensus that they were right. But their approach to making the argument looked a lot more like politics than science: they engaged in a signature drive for their amicus brief, and they engaged in negative tactics against the opposition. Forty-three people signed the brief, although many were not actually researchers in the areas covered by it. Indeed, fewer than a third of the signators had published research that was cited in the brief. Moreover, it is not clear who was asked to sign. Ceci boasted that only three people declined to sign the brief, but there are more than three people who had published relevant studies challenging Ceci and Bruck's view whose names do not appear on the brief. The state filed a rare motion opposing the filing of this amicus brief, arguing in part that the excerpts from the child interviews:

> fail to adequately inform the Court of the contexts in which certain questions were asked, and most importantly, fail to inform the Court whether it was the interviewer or the child victim who initiated a discussion of certain allegations.[263]

Courts routinely permit the filing of such amicus briefs, and the New Jersey Supreme Court granted permission for this one to be filed. When prosecutors realized that Goodman, a leading academic in the field, did not sign the brief, they asked the court to reconsider its decision because there was a much larger disagreement in the field than was represented in the brief. The significance of Goodman's work is evident in the fact that her publications accounted for more citations in the reference section of the eventual brief than any other scholar, including Ceci and Bruck. The court, which one would not expect to get involved in an academic dispute, declined the request.

What became known as the Concerned Scientists brief summarized studies that supported Ceci and Bruck's view about the suggestibility of young children, and it weighed in on requiring taint hearings—a mechanism for keeping children's testimony away from the jury in certain cases. The brief described recent experiments, mostly conducted by Ceci and Bruck, about "the conditions under which preschool children are most suggestible."[264] The brief also contained various excerpts from the investigative interviews in the Michaels case and a four-page appendix with information about the interviews and the emergence of allegations made by all twenty children at trial. (The appendix is riddled with errors and misleading statements.[265]) The brief argued that the interviews in the Michaels case were "so faulty that they may have substantially increased the risk that the children's subsequent reports were mere reflections of interviewers' suggestions."[266] It is unclear whether the brief influenced the court, although that has certainly been a central claim in the witch-hunt narrative. But, as law and psychology professor Tom Lyon has pointed out, the New Jersey Supreme Court cited Goodman's work more than it cited Ceci and Bruck's.[267] Its effect on the judiciary remains unclear, but there is no question that the Concerned Scientists brief became highly influential in the field of psychology.

The New Jersey Supreme Court Decides

The New Jersey Supreme Court heard the case on January 31, 1994. Michaels changed lawyers on the eve of the oral argument, discharging Robert Rosenthal and hiring Alan Zegas, who was well known from the Glen Ridge sexual assault case. "The celebrated Margaret Kelly Michaels child sex-abuse case" is how the *New Jersey Law Journal* described it at the time.[268] Four months later, a unanimous court sustained the appellate court's decision.

The immediate significance of the New Jersey Supreme Court opinion was that Michaels could be retried only if the state first conducted a taint hearing to assess whether pre-trial interviews were so suggestive as to render the children's testimony inadmissible.[269] The Essex County prosecutors could still proceed against Kelly Michaels—but they would have to have a hearing to determine child by child whether any had been unduly tainted by the interview process. The prosecutors assessed how many of the children in the case were likely to sustain such a hearing. In their view, a solid case could be built around the original grand jury counts, which came well before any of the contested actions in the child-suggestibility defense, and the counts pertaining to David Applegate, the child who was never interviewed by DYFS. In July 1993, months after the original appellate decision overturning the convictions, Essex County Prosecutor Clifford Minor released a statement, after he consulted the families involved in the matter, explaining that the case would be retried.[270] A year and a half later, after the State Supreme Court had upheld the decision of the Appellate Division, the state decided to drop the charges. Minor said that deciding whether or not to try the case at this point "was the most difficult decision he has faced since taking office." John S. Redden, first deputy assistant prosecutor, elaborated:

While the issue is not one which is free from doubt, and while strong arguments can be made on either side of the issues, the state has decided after careful consideration and reflection that this case, which is nearly 10 years old, should be brought to a conclusion at this time.[271]

Charges against Kelly Michaels were dropped the first week of December 1995. With that, the criminal case was over and New Jersey had become the most prominent state to establish a precedent for so-called taint hearings. Michaels, freed from the possibility of retrial, then filed multiple claims for wrongful prosecution. Some were later dismissed on legal grounds; others were quietly dropped after the state withdrew its demand that Michaels pay the state's attorneys fees for what the state considered a meritless claim. But the victory in the criminal case meant much more than releasing Michaels from jail; it solidified the witch-hunt narrative with the stamp of academic approval.

Conclusion

The Kelly Michaels case represents a turning point in the contemporary history of child sexual abuse in the United States. It was the first well-known case in which a hard-fought conviction was later overturned on appeal. The witch-hunt narrative that has been built around the case claims that the reversal represents a return to reason, a collective coming back to our senses after an era marked by a "believe the children" attitude that accepted sexual abuse allegations without an appropriate degree of skepticism. The result has been portrayed as a triumph of justice, leaving no room for the possibility that *any* of the children in the case had actually been sexually abused.

This chapter has argued that the conventional wisdom is wrong; it is built on misrepresentations about the earliest children in the case and about the investigative interviews that followed. Moreover, it is built on complete denial of the well-documented history of extreme behavioral symptoms and pediatric visits *during* 1984–85. It is also built on gross overgeneralizations from a few children and, worse, on "excerpts" of interviews that have been edited so as to alter their meaning.

Why was this revisionist history possible? Several factors help supply an answer. First, the case was not handled in an ideal fashion. That would have been practically impossible, of course, since multi-victim cases with young children were new and prosecutors were learning how to handle them. Nevertheless, the Essex County Prosecutor's Office did a good job of investigating and presenting the original charges to a grand jury. But when DYFS began its own investigation, there were enormous consequences for the criminal case that were not fully understood at the time. Without a plan for coordinating the investigation, some children were interviewed twice simply because the original DYFS interviews were conducted without anyone from the prosecutor's office being present. This opened the door to erroneous portrayals of these disclosures as coming after "repetitive" interviews. Key children in early June who made statements to Lou Fonolleras and, days later, to an investigator from the prosecutor's office have been inaccurately portrayed as disclosing after multiple interviews.

Second, the case was enormous in scope. Given that there were more than eighty investigative interviews, all it took was a small number of inappropriate interviews to provide enough fodder for a snippet-based argument that such evidence was "typical" or "characteristic" of the entire case. Those possibilities would expand significantly if, as happened on appeal, such arguments relied largely on children who were never in the case. This was made possible, of course, by the worst interviews conducted by Fonolleras, late in the investigation. Had the entire case been based only on the earliest children interviewed, it might well have resulted in a conviction upheld on appeal, on the basis of the cross-corroborating evidence of three or four "untainted" boys. Instead, those children have practically been forgotten; ironically, the legacy of the case is now based largely on the most suspect children, only some of whom were actually in the case.

Those factors alone, however, do not explain the rise of the witch-hunt narrative. After all, even with a flawed case, the prosecution prevailed with the jury. The most important factors in assessing the rise of the witch-hunt narrative were external to the case. Changes in public opinion and changes in the world of academic psychology were both critical. The role of the media in promoting the narrative cannot be overestimated. Neither can the role of the McMartin case, which left the public wondering how such a large case could result in no convictions, and left academic psychologists wondering how their own profession had apparently become complicit in promoting a "believe the children" attitude that was unduly credulous. The significance of the McMartin case is clear in the reactions to the Nathan and Rabinowitz articles about Kelly Michaels. In the environment that prevailed before the McMartin case ended, Nathan's argument did not capture the public imagination, but in the immediate aftermath of the McMartin case the Rabinowitz article did. Both authors, and others, quickly drew direct analogies between the cases. Michaels, we were told, was "another McMartin." The common belief was that there was no evidence in the McMartin case, and so, by analogy, there must not have been any in the Michaels case either. It was a kind of innocence-by-association argument that proved to be extraordinarily persuasive, regardless of the actual facts.

The role of academic psychologists was also crucial. They ultimately provided "scientific proof" that convinced many people of children being so suggestible that virtually every allegation in the Michaels case could be chalked up to "child suggestibility." The defense in the Michaels case had to rely on Ralph Underwager—the discredited psychologist—to make this argument at trial. But Underwager had not actually conducted a single study on child suggestibility. By the time the Michaels case reached the New Jersey Appellate Division, there were television and newspaper reports of a new line of research "proving" that children are highly suggestible.[272] The research even made specific references to the Kelly Michaels case. But those references were based on gross exaggerations of the nature of the interviews in Michaels.

Finally, the witch-hunt narrative was almost literally made for TV. Kelly Michaels won her appeal in the media, and then she won in court. Why the media would so willingly endorse a one-sided view of the case can best be understood in connection with the McMartin case. David Shaw of the *Los Angeles Times* won a Pulitzer Prize for criticizing his own newspaper for credulous acceptance of the initial claims in the McMartin case. The witch-hunt narrative had become an award-winning story. Ceci and Bruck did something similar in the field of psychology: they received awards for arguing that their own field had gotten it wrong about child suggestibility. But like Shaw, they did so by going overboard in the opposite direction. Shaw was alert to coverage that did not challenge the prosecution, but he relied on a perspective that never challenged the defense. Ceci and Bruck's view was that Gail Goodman and others were too quick to accept the testimony of children. Their solution was to brand all of the children in the Michaels case as unreliable, without a careful or fair accounting of the underlying facts.

Everyone agrees that the Kelly Michaels case was a turning point. But the claim that it was a movement toward rationality and common sense is contradicted by the facts of the case. The witch-hunt narrative demonstrates the rise of what I call "disconfirmation bias," an approach to these cases that ignores evidence of guilt and exaggerates anything that might be construed as evidence of innocence. The approach brings biases that are precisely opposite of those brought to the McMartin case by Believe the Children. Instead of a rush to convict despite the lack of evidence, there was now apparently a rush to acquit despite evidence of guilt.

6

Going to Extremes

State v. Fuster

The Kelly Michaels case marked the triumph of the witch-hunt narrative in the media and then among academic psychologists. The concern of psychology professor Gail Goodman and others who declined to sign the famous amicus brief in the Michaels case was that it represented a position that unduly discredited children as witnesses. The argument had almost no traction in the context of the Michaels case, however, because the witch-hunt narrative had prevailed so powerfully in the media that it was inconceivable to anyone familiar with various prominent stories about the case that there actually could be substantial evidence of guilt. The "new wave" of research about child suggestibility, as psychology and law professor Tom Lyon dubbed it a few years later, was focused entirely on the possibility of wrongful allegations; it did not acknowledge, let alone consider, how often children do not disclose real abuse when asked.[1]

Were the arguments made on Michaels's behalf so malleable they could be offered in defense of almost any defendant, no matter how powerful the evidence of guilt? Did the "new wave" of research on child suggestibility mean a broader and unjustified attack on the credibility of children would follow? An initial answer was revealed when the same arguments that had been made on behalf of Kelly Michaels were made on behalf of Frank Fuster.

Fuster was the lead defendant in the Country Walk case, which began in Dade County, Florida, in the summer of 1984. See Figure 6.1 for a timeline. The Country Walk case later appeared on Charlier and Downing's famous list of thirty-six cases because it had several "fantastic" features, particularly allegations that involved feces, masks, and killing a bird to scare the children. Debbie Nathan mentioned the case even earlier, so it is fair to say that it was part of the witch-hunt narrative since shortly after Fuster was convicted in 1985. But Ceci and Bruck presented the Country Walk and Kelly Michaels cases as a contrast in their

Figure 6.1 Comprehensive Case Timelines, Initial Complaint to Jury Verdict.

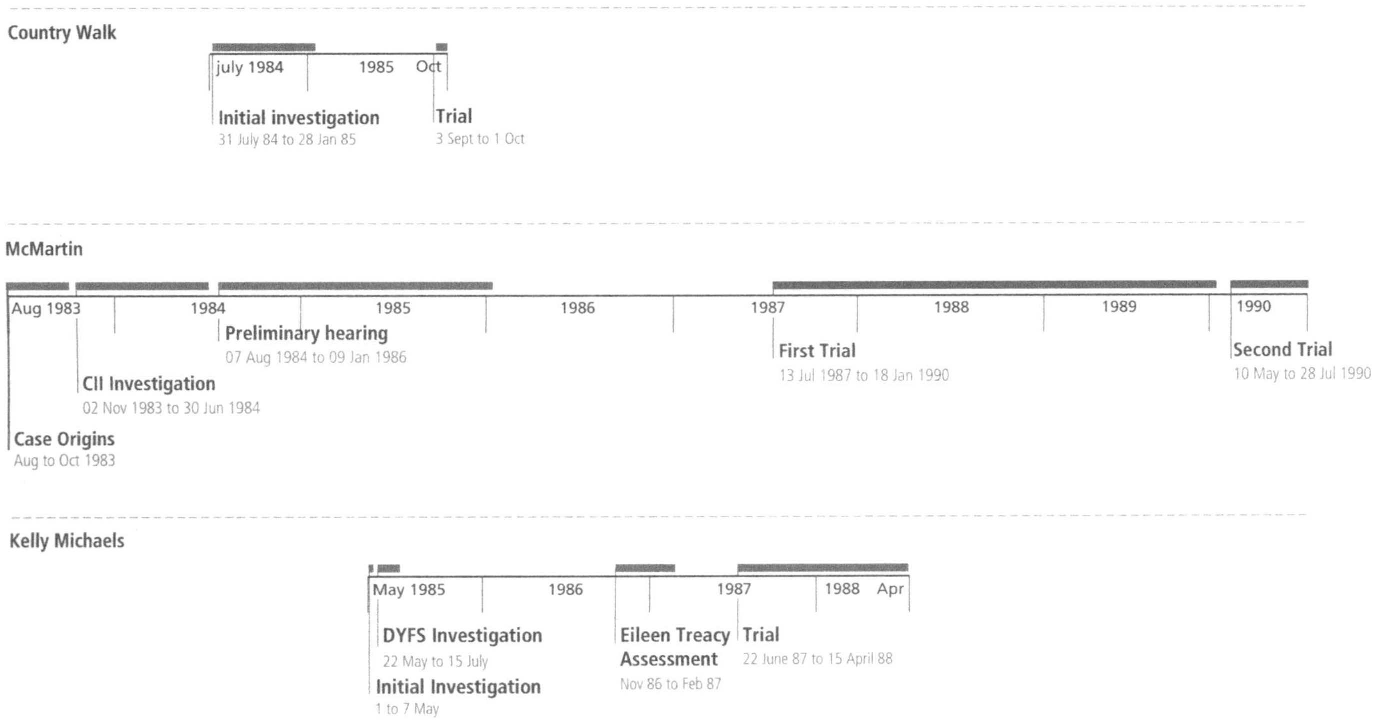

Country Walk

July 1984 | 1985 | Oct

Initial investigation
31 July 84 to 28 Jan 85

Trial
3 Sept to 1 Oct

McMartin

Aug 1983 | 1984 | 1985 | 1986 | 1987 | 1988 | 1989 | 1990

Case Origins
Aug to Oct 1983

CII Investigation
02 Nov 1983 to 30 Jun 1984

Preliminary hearing
07 Aug 1984 to 09 Jan 1986

First Trial
13 Jul 1987 to 18 Jan 1990

Second Trial
10 May to 28 Jul 1990

Kelly Michaels

May 1985 | 1986 | 1987 | 1988 | Apr

Initial Investigation
1 to 7 May

DYFS Investigation
22 May to 15 July

Assessment
Nov 86 to Feb 87

Eileen Treacy Trial
22 June 87 to 15 April 88

famous review of the literature in 1993. Under this view, the Country Walk case demonstrated clear limits to the suggestibility arguments. Even if the interviews with the children could be criticized in various ways, it was clear that those arguments should not be taken too far. At least this is what Ceci and Bruck said in 1993.

Their position changed between the publication of that article and the publication of *Jeopardy in the Courtroom* two years later. In the book, the Country Walk case is presented as another Kelly Michaels case. Indeed, Maggie Bruck filed an affidavit on behalf of Fuster in 1999, arguing that the results of her laboratory research with Ceci supported the conclusion that the children's statements in the Country Walk case were unreliable. Nathan and others took an even stronger view, painting the Country Walk case as an outrageous miscarriage of justice.

This chapter argues that the Country Walk case demonstrates quite the opposite. There was overwhelming evidence of guilt against Frank Fuster. The case originated in a spontaneous disclosure, and it was built on detailed statements made by children who were *not* subjected to repetitive interviews. Fuster's seven-year-old son tested positive for gonorrhea of the throat, and Fuster had a prior record that included a recent conviction for lewd and lascivious sexual assault on a nine-year-old girl. This evidence and much more is detailed in the first part of this chapter. It takes a significant distortion of the evidence to suggest this case was anything but a solid conviction.

One of Ceci and Bruck's primary concerns about the kinds of cases discussed in this book is "confirmation bias," the tendency of investigators and interviewers to seek and recognize only things that confirm their existing inclination toward finding abuse. How the Country Walk case has been portrayed in the witch-hunt narrative demonstrates the opposite problem: *disconfirmation bias*. Those who claim this case was a false conviction have looked only for evidence that might support that claim, and they have distorted or overlooked the vast evidence to the contrary. This chapter demonstrates the problem; the final chapter in this book considers the larger implications of this kind of bias on the problem of child sexual abuse.

Part One: The Original Case (1984–85)

Origins of the Country Walk Babysitting Service

The Country Walk housing development was built in Dade County, Florida, during the late 1970s by the Arvida Corporation in association with the Disney Corporation. The development had upscale suburban homes with large yards and picket fences. The logo for the development was a Tom Sawyerish boy, flopped back in a straw hat with a fishing pole. The development was designed to evoke a kind of country ideal.

Frank Fuster bought a house in the development with his second wife, Martha. They had been married since 1976 and had a son, Noel, who was born in October 1977. Frank and Martha were divorced in 1982, after he was convicted of a sex crime against a child, but the three of them continued to live in the same house. In the summer of 1983, while Martha was in New York City visiting family, Frank met Ileana Flores. Frank and Ileana were married several weeks later at the Country Center, the recreational center at County Walk. Frank was thirty-four, Ileana was sixteen. Martha moved out of the house and Frank retained custody of Noel, then six years old.

Frank Fuster had a small home-remodeling business in the early 1980s called Kendall Decorators. He closed this business and started another one, called Mobile Showroom, in 1983. He operated the business out of a warehouse space where he also had an office. In 1984, however, he gave up the warehouse office and converted a playroom in their house into an office. The business barely brought in any income, according to documents that became part of the later legal proceedings; it was unclear how the Fusters could afford to live in Country Walk in 1983–84. In fact, Frank Fuster said in a civil deposition that he had serious financial problems and was "always trying to borrow money."[2] This undoubtedly helps explain why Ileana Fuster started a babysitting service in December 1983. The Fusters took out advertisements in the *Country Times*, a newsletter for the development. And even though commercial businesses were not officially allowed in the development, the director of the Country Walk Center, Joanne Menoher, gave the Fusters' name out to interested parents. Frank had business cards printed up that said "Country Walk Babysitting Service: *We don't say we're the best, but people do talk.*"

The children who attended the babysitting service between December 1983 and August 1984 ranged significantly in age and duration of attendance. Some attended only in the winter or spring. Others were still attending at the Fusters right up to August 8, the last day that any children were there for babysitting. The frequency of attendance at the Fusters varied significantly, with a handful of children attending daily (that is, five days a week) for at least ten weeks. Others went only occasionally. A striking number of children, it was established after the Fusters were arrested, had attended once or twice and never returned (see Figure 6.2). The ages ranged from infants to five years old. Many were preverbal. There were also a few older children at the Fuster house on occasion. The Fusters' son, Noel, was generally home. A neighborhood friend of his, Ned Unger, a nine-year-old, spent time at the Fuster house in the spring of 1984.

Figure 6.2 Overall Attendance Patterns at Country Walk Babysitting Service.

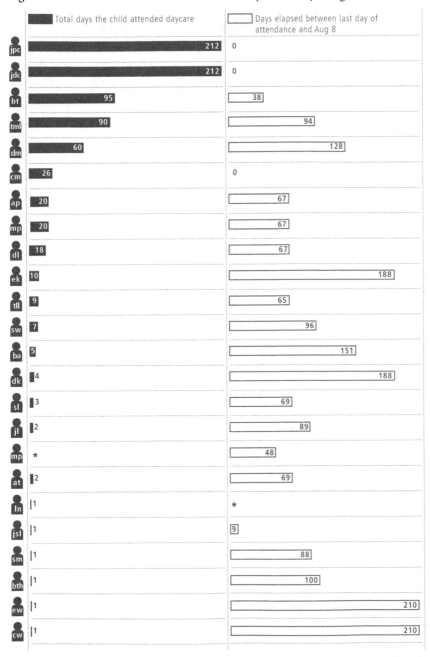

★ *Missing data.*
Compiled by author from original documents.

Four or five months after the babysitting service began, young Donald Menninger made a spontaneous statement that shook his mother. The boy had been attending the Fusters regularly for two months. After spending the day at their house, he casually asked his mother to "kiss my body." His mother, whose family used the term *body* to refer to genitals, asked her son why he would ask such a thing. "Ileana kisses my body," he replied. "Ileana kisses all the babies' bodies." Menninger, who later said she tried hard to maintain her composure, inquired whether Ileana did this to Tom Leventhal, the son of a good friend of hers. Donald said she did. Menninger later testified that Donald awkwardly denied his disclosure hours later. Nevertheless, she pulled her son from the babysitting service immediately and told her friend Betsy Leventhal about the matter, swearing her to secrecy.[3] The information bothered Leventhal so much that she later called the child protective service agency to make an anonymous complaint. An inspector made a cursory visit while Frank Fuster was not home, and the unlicensed babysitting service remained in business.[4] Meanwhile, the operators of the Country Walk development suddenly became quite uncomfortable with the babysitting service. Two letters were sent to the Fusters in July from the managers of the development, informing them that the business was not permitted and must be closed. But it remained open.

At the end of July, a mother whose child had just spent his first day at the Fusters became extremely concerned that something bad had happened to her son there. On July 31, after Emma St. Lorenzo picked up her eighteen-month-old son, John, from the Fusters' she noted to a friend that her son "looked funny."[5] The presence of a rash around John's anus, which she later noticed, raised more concern. At home, St. Lorenzo observed her son hitting himself on the head repeatedly with a wooden block. She had never seen him behave like this. She examined him more closely and concluded that his eyes looked "very glazed."[6] After taking the wooden block away and moving him to another room, she observed the boy banging his head into a sliding glass door. At this point she "became convinced . . . he had been drugged."[7] She contacted her husband and their son's pediatrician, who told her that too much time had passed to make a blood test reliable. Though this may have been true, it seems more likely that the pediatrician's goal was to calm down a seemingly overprotective mother.

St. Lorenzo started asking around about the Fusters. It did not take long before she spoke to Joanne Menoher at the Country Center and learned of a rumor that children had been sexually molested at the Fusters. St. Lorenzo proceeded to call a friend who worked in television news and who had a contact at the state attorney's office.[8] That woman, Jan Hollingsworth, later wrote a book about the case. The police investigation into the Country Walk Babysitting Service began several days later.

The Early Investigation (August 3–8)

On Friday, August 3, 1984, Detective Donna Meznarich was assigned to investigate the possible sexual assault of young children at the Fuster home. Meznarich was an eleven-year veteran of the Miami Dade Police Department; her last seven years had been in the Sexual Battery Unit. But this case would pose investigative challenges she had not previously faced. The children who attended the Fusters' babysitting service were as young as three and a half months. The oldest children using the babysitting service were four or five; most were younger. The police department was not used to interviewing children this young, even in this unit; seven was about the youngest that they tended to see. Older children were much more common, even for child molestation charges. Further complicating the investigation, the children who attended the Fusters' babysitting service ranged widely in attendance patterns. From reports from parents, it was thought that the Fusters had between four and six children in their house on an "average" day; about half would be infants, the other half toddlers. Whether the authorities could even locate all of the children who attended the Fusters was unclear. And whether the children would talk to someone not trained to think about the developmental capabilities of young children was also unknown.

Before leaving the office that day, Detective Meznarich spoke with Allison and Victor Lucas, both of whom were police officers. Their daughter Tammy, who was four years old, had attended the Fusters' nine times in May. The Lucases informed Meznarich that their daughter had an inflamed vaginal itch after going there, but they did not attribute it to the Fusters at the time. While attending the babysitting service, their daughter had also said something about a "big boy" who had a mask and scared her. She even said that she had slept in "big boy's" room. At the time, the Lucases thought those comments referred to Noel. They later learned that Frank Fuster was the "big boy."[9]

The first interview outside the office, later that day, was with Menoher, the recreational coordinator for the Country Center. Detective Meznarich was told about Donald Menninger startling his mother in late April by asking her to kiss his penis one day after attending the Fusters'. Joanne Menoher had heard this story from Betsy Leventhal. Menoher testified that she "told me, as she said, in confidence, that she wanted to get something off her chest."[10] After hearing the story, Menoher made an anonymous report to HRS.[11] Menoher supplied Meznarich with the names of numerous families who had used the babysitting service. She also told the detective that Allison Lucas had said that "the children had secret games that parents don't know about."[12]

In the coming days, the detective visited the homes of several families whose children had attended the Fusters' for a considerable period of time. The Liptons had sent two children to the Fusters; their two-year-old son, Daniel, had attended regularly for months and their four-year-old daughter, Jessie, had attended twice in May. The girl said there had not been any "bad touch" when she was there, and the boy proved nearly impossible to interview. As indicated in the police report:

> Due to his age and the fact that he has a speech impediment, his mother was present. This investigator attempted to ask Daniel Lipton questions; however, he ran around the room ignoring them.[13]

His mother conveyed that the boy was saying "Frank" hurt his "pee-pee" and "toosh," but it is clear the detective could not understand the boy on her own.

She then tried to interview Becky Taylor, a four-year-old girl who attended the Fusters' almost daily for five months. Her name had already come up in several conversations, but she also proved nearly impossible to interview. Meznarich noted: "This investigator attempted to interview Becky Taylor; however, she first hid behind the sofa, then behind her mother."[14] Before the interview was over, Allison Lucas, a friend and neighbor of the Taylors, arrived with her daughter Tammy. Tammy indicated that the Fusters had scared her with a white mask. Becky piped up that it was a green mask. Though Tammy did not disclose anything else, Becky said something about kissing Frank and Ileana Fuster on the lips. What Meznarich had begun to piece together was suspicious but elusive. It was also somewhat bizarre, given the statements about being scared with masks.

Three of the children whom Meznarich had identified and tried to interview were referred to the Rape Treatment Center at Jackson Memorial Hospital. They were seen by Dominique McGinnis, a psychiatric nurse, on August 8. Daniel Lipton, the two-year-old with the speech impediment, was again "interpreted" through his mother. He apparently said that Frank "hit" his "pee pee" and that Ileana had hurt his "toosh."[15] Tammy Lucas, who had earlier disavowed that she experienced anything abusive at the Fusters', also made several incriminating statements. She indicated that "two people at school" had seen her private parts: "Frank and Ileana." According to the nurse's report, the girl also indicated that Frank Fuster had touched her on the "boob" and "climbed" on top of her and kissed her:

> Tammy laid the doll she identified as herself down and placed the large male doll she indicated was Frank on top of her and rubbed the boy doll's penis on the girl doll's vaginal area.[16]

Becky Taylor was also seen that day. Given her age and attendance pattern, she was the child most likely to be able to explain what happened at the Fusters'. But she was extremely avoidant with the detective. The Taylors then brought their daughter to the Sexual Battery Office of the State Attorney's Office, but the girl still had nothing to say. Meznarich described her as "very withdrawn." The interview ended after approximately five minutes. This was not the only failed interview of the day; Meznarich and Assistant State Attorney Christopher Rundle also tried to interview three-year-old Tom Leventhal, the child implicated by Donald Menninger's statements to his mother. The police report indicates simply that the detective "attempted to interview [the boy] but was unable to do so because of his age."[17]

Although there had not yet been any mention of the investigation in the media, word of the investigation was spreading around Country Walk. Fanning the flames of outrage was the discovery that Frank Fuster was on probation for a 1982 conviction for child molestation. Passions were running high among those who had heard about the prior case. A neighbor of the Fusters was arrested outside his house brandishing a gun. Meznarich learned of this unfortunate development while traveling to interview the Cramer family and their two boys. The Cramers did not know the Mennigners or the Leventhals, so they were unaware of the rumors that had been floating around since May. They also did not know about the behind-the-scenes effort by the Arvida Corporation to close the Fusters' illegal babysitting business. They had not even heard about the police investigation in early August. To the contrary, the Cramer children had been at the Fusters' on August 8, the last day the babysitting service was in operation. Sandra Cramer informed the detective that Frank Fuster had told her a day earlier he was discontinuing the babysitting service but that they would continue to babysit her boys anyway.[18]

Meznarich talked with Jason Cramer in his bedroom for fifteen to twenty minutes that night. It was the most substantive statement she had received from any child to date. He was one of the oldest children interviewed and had been there the most recently, literally attending the Fusters' earlier that day. As the detective later reported, Jason disclosed that Ileana had sucked his little brother's penis. He indicated further that she had done the same thing to Donald Menninger and Tom Leventhal. The boy also said that Frank Fuster had taken pictures of children naked.[19] The Cramers were asked to bring their child to the State Attorney's Office the next day for a more formal interview. One might think that the boy's statement would be enough to justify a search warrant. But two days passed before the house was searched. Meanwhile, Meznarich went to the Fuster residence to question the key suspects. The detective did not have a search warrant, so the visit effectively provided the Fusters with an advance warning. Frank denied any wrongdoing and told the detective that "He was never home when the children were there."[20] The detective had already talked to numerous adults and children who said otherwise.

The state attorney for Dade County was Janet Reno, who was appointed U.S. attorney general in 1993. Reno learned in the summer of 1984—primarily from her experience with the inability to prosecute anyone in connection with the Lehrman Day School case[21]—that her office, like most in the country, was ill equipped to handle complaints involving the sexual abuse of young children. Soon thereafter, Reno asked Joseph and Laurie Braga to assist the State Attorney's Office, on an unpaid basis, in interviewing children. The Bragas were adjunct professors at the University of Miami School of Medicine, with training and experience in child development; they had authored a series of books on child development in the 1970s. Jan Hollingsworth later described them as experts in "speaking children." Their philosophy was simple: put the child at ease, assess the developmental level, and engage the child on his or her own level.

The Bragas insisted that all of their interactions with children be videotaped. The primary reason was to reduce the total number of interviews for any given child. They also did not want to leave room for a claim that the children had been coached by the interviewers (an argument that quickly became common in child sexual abuse cases). The idea of videotaping investigative interviews was a first for the office. Hollingsworth later reported that Assistant State Attorney Rundle considered the idea "risky business." He was worried that "any perceived inconsistencies in a child's testimony" could be used against them at trial.[22] This concern seems prescient given the evolution of the witch-hunt narrative, analyzed in the second half of this chapter .

The Initial Braga Interviews (August 9 and 10)

The Bragas interviewed five children on August 9. They had no advance information about the case other than that children had attended the Fusters' for babysitting and may have experienced some form of maltreatment. The children who came to the state attorney's office that day had emerged from Meznarich's investigation. There was a reason for each of these children to be considered worth interviewing formally; what unfolded that first day was enough to sustain the filing of charges against Frank and Ileana Fuster for sexual battery against more than one child. Those charges would take at least two weeks to be considered and crafted. But the first day remains the most important one in the case. It is also the day that would later be overlooked entirely in the witch-hunt narrative about the case.

Four of the five of the children interviewed the first day made statements concerning sexual activities in the Fuster household. The oldest child (Jason Cramer) was by far the most detailed and articulate. The next oldest (Tammy Lucas) also made numerous statements of a sexualized nature. The three youngest children (Joshua Cramer, Tom Leventhal, and Daniel Lipton) were more limited in speaking skills, but at least two of them made statements that appeared to support charges against Frank and/or Ileana Fuster.

Jason Cramer

The first child interviewed by the Bragas was Jason Cramer, an articulate five-year-old. He made detailed and incriminating statements in the first session. Hollingsworth, who later wrote the book *Unspeakable Acts*, described the interview in enough detail to fill thirteen pages.[23] When asked to "show me" what happened at Frank and Ileana's, Jason described something involving his brother: "Iliana's changing his diaper and, uh, playing with his, uh, penis."[24] Unfortunately, this interview was not transcribed into the court record when the tape was played at trial. There were audio difficulties that inhibited the stenographer. Those difficulties have been cited in recent years as a reason the interview cannot be reviewed. But the difficulties were specific to the court reporter, not the videotape. Otherwise it would not have been possible for Hollingsworth to describe this interview in such detail.[25]

Jason Cramer was interviewed again later that day, after the Bragas had interviewed his younger brother, Joshua. The second interview with Jason is arguably the single most important investigative interview in the case. The boy made a remarkably detailed statement about himself and others. This was the primary interview highlighted in the local media when videotapes were made available more than three months later. "The videotapes show low-key conversations between children and Drs. Laurie and Joseph Braga," reported the *Miami Herald*, describing Jason's second session on August 9 as follows:

> The oldest child depicted in the tapes, a pudgy redheaded boy whose name was not released, used anatomically correct dolls in telling the doctors that the Fusters induced the children to play nude games. Those games allegedly led to various sexual assaults on children as young as two years old.
>
> "They were playing ring-around-the-rosy," the child said in the taped interview with the Bragas. "They would dress up naked, all the girls and boys. Frank and Ileana would take their clothes off."
>
> Asked what happened during the game, the child said, "Touch each other." He used the dolls to illustrate the alleged digital penetration of a younger boy's anus. "Frank would stick his finger inside (name deleted) . . . Frank kissed (name deleted) penis."
>
> The boy describes the Fusters engaging in sexual intercourse and other sexual acts with each other in front of the children. He also talks of them sexually assaulting some of the children.[26]

The interview also included disclosures about games involving feces and urine. These statements came after Joseph Braga (JB below; Laurie Braga is LB) asked if Frank Fuster ever just babysat the children or watched movies. This was Jason's reply (JC below), and the questions and answers that followed:

> JC: No he would always play games and stuff. He always played games like pee pee games and ka ka games and butt games. That's what they—
>
> JB: What is the ka ka game?
>
> JC: It's a game where they throw poop at each other. Yes.
>
> JB: You are kidding me?
>
> JC: No
>
> JB: What?
>
> LB: Can you tell us more about that?
>
> JC: They first went to the bathroom and then they started—they took it out of the toilet with some toilet paper and threw it at each other.
>
> JB: Who would do that?
>
> JC: Noel.

The boy's disturbing statements came in response to a simple question of whether Frank Fuster ever babysat the children. And the interviewers did not automatically believe this statement; rather, they sought to assess the statement through the follow-up question, "You are kidding me?" The boy's statements about these grotesque "games" would later be written off as "fantasy" by Dr. Lee Coleman, the defense psychiatrist at trial. But, as documented in the pages to come, these statements were ultimately substantiated in several ways.

The Three Youngest Children

The three youngest children interviewed that day were all too young to testify in court. Joshua Cramer, Jason's one-and-a-half-year-old brother, was interviewed for twenty minutes. He appears to indicate that Ileana took off his clothes and did something with her mouth.[27] The content of his interview is designated as "possible" in Figure 6.5, and he was not interviewed again and played no further role in the case. Tom Leventhal, who had been identified by Donald Menninger months earlier as a victim of Ileana's "body kissing," was three years old, and he provided many one-word responses in his forty-five-minute interview. Tom appears to have conveyed that Frank Fuster touched his penis and had Tom sit on his lap while Frank had no clothes on.[28] Daniel Lipton, the other child interviewed that day, was only two years old and had a speech impediment. Many of Daniel's responses involved taking off clothing. "Take her clothes off," he says at one point after Joseph Braga said: "Show me, Daniel. I want to know. You tell me." There are many references to "pee-pee," enough to infer that there was some kind of pee-pee game. Daniel also clearly said at one point that Becky "took clothes off."[29] But the most seemingly significant statements in this interview were fragmentary. It was clear that this child was never going to play an important role in the case; he was simply too young and too difficult to understand.

Tammy Lucas

The final interview on August 9 was with Tammy Lucas, the daughter of the Miami-Dade police officers. Tammy's fourth birthday was the next day. She had gone to the Fusters' for nine days in May. The interview began with a discussion of Dr. Seuss books and then moved to Peanuts characters and Disney. When the conversation turned to Frank Fuster, Tammy acknowledged knowing him and said "I don't want to go there today." When asked who else went to the same place, Tammy responded with the names Becky and Daniel; but she did not remember Jason or Joshua.

When asked to show "what Iliana would do to Daniel" the girl said "Hit him." Then she added, "Iliana takes her clothes off." It is important to note that there had been no question that contained any kind of reference to nudity or taking off clothing prior to this utterance by the young girl. A few pages later, the girl made a similar statement about Frank Fuster:

> LB: So, show me what they would do to Tammy?
> TL: Something, they did—
> LB: Like that?
> TL: Tickle me.
> LB: Tickle you like that?
> TL: And Frank takes his clothes off.

Soon thereafter, when one of the dolls has been designated as Daniel—one of the children she remembered from the Fusters—Laurie Braga asked simply "Tell me some more, okay?" Tammy's reply: "I will have to take his off, Daniel's clothes off."[30] The girl then got distracted when she has difficulty removing the doll's clothing.

Eventually, once Tammy had acknowledged that the Frank doll should have chest hair (but not a mustache), Laurie Braga asked another open-ended question: "Okay, now show me, would Frank do something to Tammy?" Here is what follows in the transcript:

[1] TL: (Nodding in the affirmative.)
[2] LB: Okay, would you show me?
[3] TL: Oh oh (indicating).

[4]   LB: The bird is biting his hand, huh the bird is mad at his hand?
[5]   TL: (Indicating.)
[6]   LB: Bad hand. What did that hand do? Can you show me?
[7]   TL: Wait a second. (Inaudible.)
[8]   LB: Yes?
[9]   TL: Yuck.
[10] LB: Show me what the hand would do, okay?
[11] TL: Okay.
[12] LB: So you put—would he put his fingers inside?
[13] TL: (Indicating) [Inside of here, Frank did.]

There are three "indicating" notations in this brief and important exchange. A review of the videotape reveals there should be a fourth one, after the "Okay" in line 11. Suffice it to say, the visual content of this videotape is of critical importance. There are pixilated versions of some parts of this interview in circulation because this was one of the portions that the media chose to broadcast when they eventually gained access through a court-mediated agreement. Even without seeing what Tammy was "indicating," it is clear that her memory of the Fuster household was focused on the nudity of children and adults. There is a further deficiency in the official transcription. On line 13 above, where the transcript reads "indicating," the videotape captures the words "Inside of here, Frank did." The girl was interviewed two more times. The second of those interviews was the last investigative interview in the case, conducted on January 28, 1985.[31]

While the initial interviews were being conducted, legal papers were being drawn up to hold Frank Fuster for violating the terms of his probation. He was on probation for a lewd and lascivious assault against a nine-year-old girl in 1981. He had been found guilty by jury in 1982 and was given a suspended sentence. Running a babysitting service out of his home was a serious violation of his probation. So was the fact that he had stopped attending his weekly court-mandated therapy. A prosecutor from the State Attorney's Office telephoned Jeffrey Samek, who was handling Fuster's appeal from the 1982 case, and it was agreed that Fuster would surrender to authorities at 10:00 a.m. on Friday, August 10. With Fuster in custody, Judge Newman had to decide what, if anything, to do with his son, Noel.

Becky Taylor

Shortly after noon on Friday, the Taylors brought their daughter Becky to the State Attorney's Office to be interviewed by the Bragas. Becky was four and a half years old and had gone to the Fusters' five or six days a week from February through June. She even had gone to the beach with the Fusters once. Given her age and her regular attendance, she was one of the most likely children, besides

Jason Cramer, to have relevant information. But she was also the most avoidant child encountered in the investigation. When Meznarich tried to interview her two days earlier, she made no progress. As indicated in the police report: "She hid behind the sofa, then behind her mother." "Refused to sit down." "Ran to the kitchen."[32]

She was interviewed by the Bragas on Friday, August 10, shortly after Frank Fuster surrendered into custody. The interview covers eighty-eight pages of the trial transcript. It is agonizing to read. Becky was avoidant, distracted, and anxious to change the subject. "I hate the question," she says at one point. "Mommy, I am tired of doing this," she adds soon thereafter. Later she says, "I have a hard time talking."[33]

There are isolated moments when a response seems to indicate something untoward. At one point, she talks about Frank and Ileana kissing each other while naked, but when asked on the next page to confirm whether their clothes were on or off, the child says on.[34] She reiterates earlier statements about masks (a white one, and a green one). There are also some frustrating lapses in the stenographic record.[35] Finally, there are statements that clearly suggest the child is holding back; "I don't want you to know" she said at one point, in response to a question about the secret games.[36] And the interview finally ended with the Bragas knowing little more from this child than that she was anxious and not interested in talking about the Fusters.

After this interview concluded, the Bragas interviewed Jason Cramer again with the specific purpose of asking questions that might help support a search warrant. The interview lasted ten minutes. Jason indicated that the children *had* been videotaped by Frank Fuster. Where do they keep the tapes? he was asked. "They hide them in books . . . under the couch," he replied.[37] Also noteworthy in this brief interview is Jason's palpable concern about what would happen to Noel. He seemed particularly worried about Noel getting in trouble for the things that happened at the Fusters'.

Meznarich then joined two state prosecutors and the Bragas to view the videotapes of Jason's interviews on August 9 and 10. The prosecutors concluded that Jason's statements provided probable cause to issue a search warrant for photographs, films, or videotapes. A warrant was prepared to be brought before a judge; it was signed by Judge David M. Gersten at 6:00 p.m. on Friday. The Fusters' house was searched soon thereafter, but the police did not find any evidence of child pornography. This is not surprising since Frank had been given two days of advance notice.

The police took fifty-eight pictures in and around the house, and they seized assorted personal property. Though there was no evidence of child pornography, there were several telling pieces of evidence. First, there were various masks in the house that corroborated the seemingly bizarre statements made about monsters and masks. There was also a crucifix between the mattresses of the Fuster's bed, and some deeply disturbing "family photos." The significance of the crucifix would only be revealed almost a year later, after Ileana pleaded guilty and started talking to prosecutors. The "family photos" contain images that lend support to the idea that Frank might engage in "ca-ca" games. The most unsettling picture recovered was of Noel Fuster perched above a toilet seat, looking scared and confused, in a room with feces smeared on the floor.[38]

The Remaining August Interviews

The first full week of the investigation through the State Attorney's Office was by far the most active interviewing in any week of the entire investigation. There were fourteen videotaped sessions in five days. Eight of the children were being interviewed by the Bragas for the first time. One of those was Noel Fuster, Frank's son. He was seen three times that week by the Bragas, but not as part of the police investigation. Judge Ferguson asked the Bragas to provide an evaluation of where Noel should live. These sessions contained little in the way of incriminating statements beyond a matter-of-fact answer that Frank hit Noel "some days." The boy also said some unlikely things, such as blurting out: "I know how to handle myself. I know how to defend myself." He expressed concern about his father, who he had visited in jail that weekend. He also said things about how he "could save my dad." The Bragas recommended to Judge Ferguson that Noel live with his mother.

The day after the Bragas completed their evaluation, Noel's test results came back. The boy who said his father "never did anything" had gonorrhea of the throat. This was confirmed through a second test. The accuracy, or positive predictive value, of the test that was employed—called RapID/NH—was 99.38 percent.[39]

Seven other children were seen for the first time by the Bragas that week. Only two were later named in individual charges against Frank or Ileana Fuster: Donald Menninger and Jessie Lipton. Three of the interviews that week were one-time-only. Two children who had been interviewed the week before—Jason and Becky—were interviewed again. Jason provided some additional details; Becky remained elusive and uncooperative.

The two children who were later named in individual charges merit further description.

Donald Menninger

Donald Menninger could be considered the index child for the case. His statement to his mother in late April 1984 was the first significant disclosure in the case. That statement caused his mother to remove Donald from the Fusters' care and to warn her friend Betsy Leventhal, whose son Tom was also implicated by Donald as a victim of Ileana Fuster's sexual abuse. The Menningers were on vacation when Meznarich began the formal investigation on August 3. They were contacted—not by authorities, but apparently by a friend or business associate—during their vacation because of media coverage of the case. It quickly became known as the Country Walk case. Donald Menninger's father (who was named Donald Menninger, Jr.) was the director of property management for the Arvida Corporation, owners and developers of Country Walk. If Mr. Menninger had not been in that position, the case might have become public in April, and the St. Lorenzos might never have had a problem. This proposition, and the various facts supporting it, later gave rise to the civil claims for damages against Arvida. In the initial stages of the case, however, the Menningers were cooperative with authorities. They brought their son to be interviewed on August 14, and they brought him back on August 31.

Donald was four years old and on the borderline for being too young to testify. His first interview with the Bragas is difficult to assess on the basis of the transcript alone. There is a moment, for example, when the boy says "She did it to babies." But whether "did it" was meant to carry the kind of meaning that it does for adults is impossible to ascertain from the transcript. The interviewer, who wanted a clearer response, asked an open-ended follow-up: "Will you show me what Ileana would do to the babies." The boy's response in the transcript is reduced to a parenthetic "(*Indicating*)." The transcript leaves the impression of some kind of wrongdoing by Ileana, but the details are unclear. Meznarich later testified that probable cause to charge Ileana Fuster existed on the basis of Donald Menninger's "statement and demonstrations with dolls."[40]

The boy came in again two weeks later. He apparently came at his mother's insistence. This time, he was far more responsive, and at times quite sexually specific. The boy described Frank Fuster taking off his clothing. "All of them," he said at one point; "Even his underwear."[41] After a description of the children and the Fusters without their clothes, the following exchange occurred:

LB: What are they doing, playing a game? What game would they play?

DM: Pee-pee game.

LB: Show me how to play the pee pee game? You can tell me, it's okay. You won't get in trouble.

DM: Do one at a time.

LB: Okay, do one at a time. This is Frank, right?

DM: (Inaudible.)

LB: What did Frank do?

DM: Here, his penis.

LB: Here's his penis, what did you do with his penis?

DM: (Indicating.) To me.

LB: To you, he would rub his penis against your penis?

DM: I would do this. (Indicating.)

LB: You would?

DM: He made me do that.

LB: He made you do that? What else did he make you do?

DM: Nothing.

It would be useful to see the gestures and "indications" in this exchange, but it is clear this boy played a "pee pee game" with Frank Fuster that had sexualized content. This tape was played at Frank Fuster's parole violation hearing, two weeks before his criminal trial began. It was the only child interview tape played in the proceeding. The judge sentenced Fuster to fifteen years.

Jessie Lipton

One of the final interviews of the week was with Jessie Lipton. The girl was four years old at the time. The Bragas had already interviewed her brother, a two-year-old with a speech impediment. Daniel Lipton attended the Fusters regularly for several months; Jessie went only twice in May. This fact is critical to placing her interview in context. Much has been made of the fact that Jessie described the Fusters as "strangers" in this interview.[42] That would potentially be a discrediting statement if made by, say, Jason Cramer (who had attended regularly for months). But Jessie had not seen the Fusters for four months; and she had only been at their house for babysitting *twice*. Under the circumstances, "strangers" is actually quite accurate. The interview did not result in any significant disclosures. Early in the interview, Jessie made an unsettling and unprompted statement about Ileana Fuster: "She gave me a donut once without any poison on it."[43] It is not clear what motivated the statement, and the follow-up questions do not shed additional light. Jessie indicated she liked going to the Fusters' and she flatly denied any abuse: "They did nothing bad to me."[44] One might read this interview as containing a little too much denial by Jessie. "We didn't play any games at all," she said at one point.

Later she allowed that there was a duck, duck, goose game. She did not indicate that there was anything untoward about the game, but she did make an unusual and unclear statement about another game: "sometimes they say that the person is (inaudible). But I am not dead."[45] Presumably, the word that was inaudible to the stenographer was "dead." If so, this comment would corroborate statements about a threatening game that Jason Cramer called "who's gonna lose their head." On the basis of this interview alone, Jessie Lipton would not have been included in any charges. But she came back in January, at the request of her parents, and made a detailed and incriminating statement. It would become the main focus of case critics, so it is important to keep in mind that the January interview occurred five months after most of the charges against the Fusters had been filed. Jessie Lipton was a late addition to the case, and she did not account for many of the charges against the Fusters.

Five children were interviewed the following week. None of these children disclosed abuse, and none was interviewed a second time. They had no further involvement in the case. That week a thirteen-count indictment was prepared against Frank and Ileana Fuster. It contained almost all of the charges that were ultimately brought against them. The investigation was winding down; there were only four interviews the last week in August. One was the first interview with Brian Arrigan, and next was the final interview with Jason Cramer. There was also another interview with Becky Taylor; it was her third interview alone and she remained extremely avoidant, denying that *any* games were played at the Fusters' and refusing to answer many questions. Finally, Donald Menninger came back, at his mother's request, for his second and final interview, already mentioned.

Brian Arrigan was interviewed on Tuesday, August 27. He was a three-year-old boy who had attended the Fusters' from December through April. In this interview, Brian indicated he had been hit at the Fusters', but he made no statements of a sexualized nature. It likely would have ended with that interview, but the parents asked to come back in late October for a second (and final) interview. The boy eventually made several statements that were far more explicit than anything said in his first interview. "They [Frank and Ileana] took off Tom's clothes," the boy said at one point. Though this interview seems to indicate that the boy witnessed naked games, it is also apparent he was too young to testify. This interview contained several statements that were later used to discredit the children. Brian said something about the Fusters' thinking that he was a mouse. He also said something about how, when they gave him a drink, he "would be dead."[46] One could certainly read this exchange as supportive of the idea that children were drugged in some fashion. But this child was seen as too young to testify, and there were no individual charges related to him.

Detective Meznarich continued to investigate the case throughout the month of August. She sought to interview any families with children who attended the Country Walk Babysitting Service. Given that it was August, some families were on vacation. Others had such young children they could not possibly be interviewed; the children were preverbal. A few parents did not want to get involved. That is specifically what Vera Unger told Meznarich; she said she had been caused "great embarrassment" by co-workers at the bank where she worked because they were asking about her connection with Fuster.[47] Though Unger was reluctant to talk, she informed the detective she had taken her youngest child for babysitting at the Fusters' twice. Both times, he had a high fever afterward. It was so bad the second time that she took him straight to the hospital; his fever was 104. Ileana Fuster had not mentioned anything to Unger either time. Her oldest son, Ned, used to play with Noel. But something happened and he stopped going to Noel's house. When interviewed later, Ned provided no information.

By the week of August 20, the State Attorney's Office was prepared to charge Frank and Ileana Fuster with the capital offense of sexual battery on a child. It had been exactly two weeks since the first children were interviewed by the Bragas. Arrest forms were prepared that week, charging each of them with a single count of sexual battery.[48] The charge against Ileana pertained to Donald Menninger, based on his mother's statement and Donald's "demonstration" in the original August 14 interview. The charge against Frank pertained to Noel Fuster and was based on Jason Cramer's statement and the positive STD finding.

"Fusters Charged with Sexual Battery of Children," declared a front-page headline in the *Miami Herald* on Friday, August 24. The story indicated that Jeffrey Samek, Frank Fuster's lawyer, had been informed that the charges involved eight children. The State Attorney's Office filed the first full indictment against Frank and Ileana Fuster on September 5. The document, prepared the third week in August, contained thirteen counts in total: nine were against Frank, three were against Ileana, and one was against both. The indictment named six children. (It seems likely that when Jeffrey Samek said eight children were involved, the count included Joshua Cramer and Daniel Lipton, but both were considered too young to testify.) Ten of the thirteen charges in this indictment stemmed from three children: Donald Menninger (four counts), Jason Cramer (three counts), and Becky Taylor (three counts). Becky's counts were based on statements by Jason. See Figure 6.3 for an elaboration of the general content and sequence of interviews with the four children who were interviewed the most in August. Jason and Donald were ultimately the most significant in the case; Becky and Noel, however, became most significant in the witch-hunt narrative about the case. There were individual counts involving Tom Leventhal, Tammy Lucas, and Noel Fuster. Notably, all of these children were among the first nine interviewed in the case. In short, these charges emerged directly from the earliest stages of the investigation; they did not emerge, as critics would later claim, after extensive, repeated interviews. Unlike cases like McMartin where the interviewing expanded significantly over time, the interviews in the Country Walk case were almost all in August. While two interviews in January became a major focus of the witch-hunt narrative, Figure 6.4 indicates that the interviews in January 1985 were unusual. The most important interviews in developing the evidence against the Fusters were in the first few days of the investigation (see Figure 6.5). None of the disclosures depicted in this figure came after repeated interviews

Figure 6.3 Country Walk, Braga Interview Sequence, Children Interviewed Two or More Times in August.

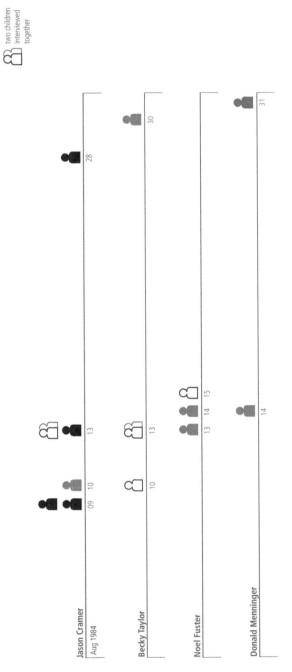

Each icon represents one interview.

Legend

no disclosure

possible sexual abuse

sexual abuse

two children interviewed together

Jason Cramer
Aug 1984   09   10   13

Becky Taylor
10   13

Noel Fuster
13   14   15

Donald Menninger
14

28

30

31

Compiled by author from original documents.

Figure 6.4 Country Walk, Full Braga Interview Sequence.

Each icon represents one interview.

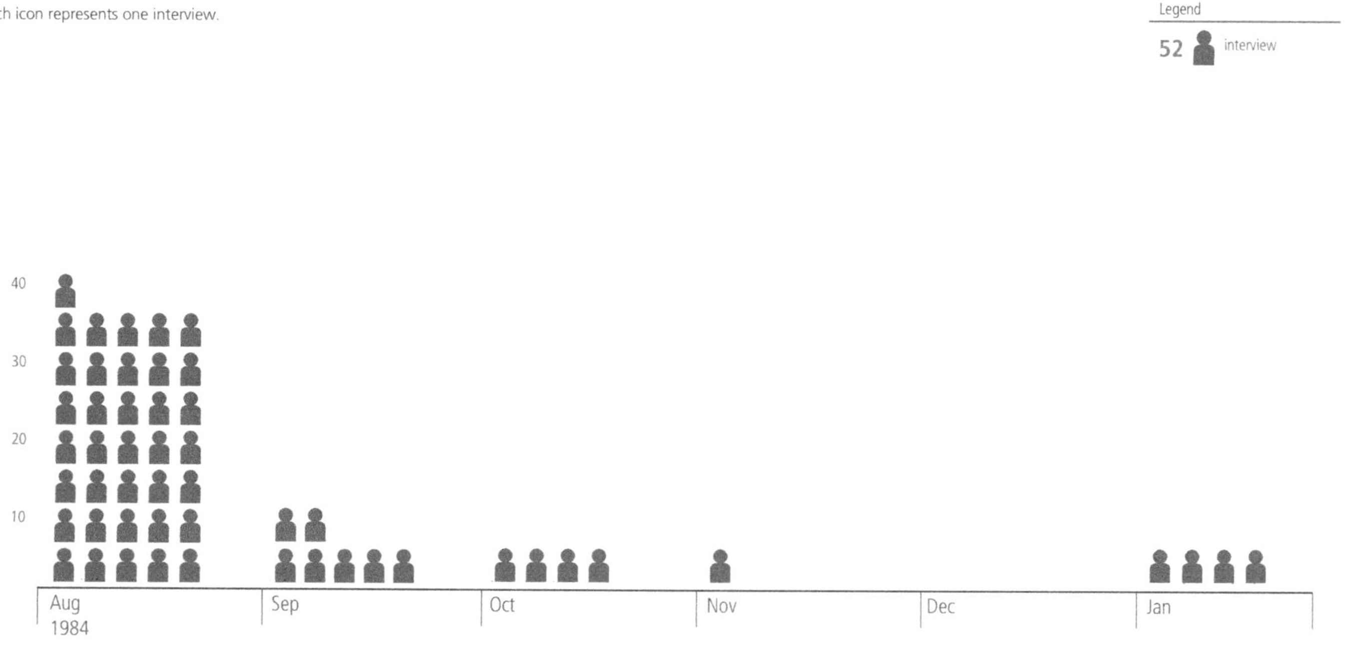

Legend

52 interview

40

30

20

10

Aug
1984

Sep

Oct

Nov

Dec

Jan

Compiled by author from source data.

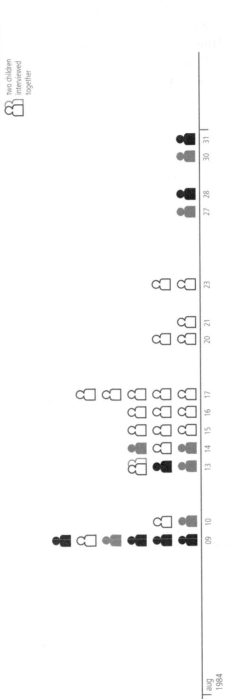

Figure 6.5 Country Walk, Braga Interview Sequence, August Detail.

Each icon represents one interview.

Legend

no disclosure

possible sexual abuse

sexual abuse

two children interviewed together

aug 1984

Compiled by author from original documents.

The Constellation of Other Evidence

While the Bragas were interviewing children in the case, the State Attorney's Office sought additional evidence beyond the children. The primary focus of those investigative efforts was the parents, neighbors, and business associates of the Fusters. Those efforts uncovered a variety of evidence that supported the children's statements.

Medical Conditions: Rashes and Antibiotics

Frank Fuster's son tested positive for gonorrhea of the throat. This was undoubtedly the strongest piece of medical evidence in the case. But it was not the only such evidence. Many of the children had had either vaginal or anal rashes of a nature they had never experienced previously. Tom Leventhal's mother observed what she deemed to be a worrisome rash around the boy's penis; it was unlike anything she had seen in her other boys.[49] Darlene Taylor noted that her daughter Becky was on "ampicillin practically the entire time" she was at the Fusters', and she frequently complained of sore throats and suffered from frequent rashes around her vagina.[50] Carrie Monk developed a rash on her vulva. In the nine days she attended the Fusters', Tammy Lucas had "an inflamed vaginal area."[51] But few of the parents whose children attended the Fusters' actually knew each other, so it was not until investigators documented these disparate incidents that their cumulative weight could be appreciated.

A number of children also had unexplained infections or raging fevers when they left the Fusters' house. Betsy Leventhal testified that, in the five months that her son went there, he had respiratory infections that would clear up with penicillin and subsequently reappear. Vera Unger reported that her son attended the Fusters' for babysitting twice, once in April and once in July 1984. Both times, she said, Charles developed a fever of approximately 104 degrees and stomach and throat infections.[52] Indeed, the children's medical records provide a chilling answer to the question of why none of the other children tested positive for a sexually transmitted disease in August 1984. The answer is that "virtually every child alleged to have been the victim of Frank Fuster putting his penis in their mouth was on antibiotics the entire time."[53] All of these children were tested for strep throat during the year and the tests were all negative, but they were all prescribed antibiotics anyway. Apparently, nobody ever thought to test them for sexually transmitted diseases.

Suspicious Incidents and Unclothed Children

In many child sexual abuse cases, the defense argues that if something untoward had been occurring, surely someone would have noticed something suspicious.

As investigators quickly learned, in the seven months that the Fusters' babysitting service was in operation, there *were* numerous instances that raised suspicions among parents. Indeed, there were a host of families who independently decided to remove their children from the Fusters' care before the case broke.

Nearly all of the parents described waiting a long time at the front door. Some parents reported there were also times when they called the Fuster household during the daytime and got no answer. Ileana told one parent they had disconnected the door bell because they did not want to disturb the children. She told another parent she had unplugged the phone one day for the same reason. Some parents took to calling before they came in order to avoid a long wait at the door. Emma St. Lorenzo called in the middle of the first day that she had taken her son to the Fusters'. There was no answer. She later testified that she was concerned about being an overly protective mother, so she did not rush right over to the house. What happened after she picked up her son, though, caused her to report the Fusters.

Parents did not come in and out of the house freely or unannounced. On the rare occasions when that *did* happen, however, there were various strange circumstances, all involving children in states of undress. For example, Kimberly Porter described twice walking into the home unannounced. Frank Fuster had apparently left the door unlocked, and she let herself in after waiting for five minutes for someone to answer the door. Ileana emerged from the master bedroom and shut the door behind her, locking a whining Tom Leventhal inside.[54] The second time this happened, Ileana did the same thing but failed to properly lock the bedroom door, allowing Tom to open the door and run out totally naked. Porter said that Ileana's hair was "a mess" and she seemed "nervous."[55]

Similarly, Betsy Leventhal—who removed her child in early May—described seeing Becky Taylor naked from the waist down one day when she arrived to pick up her son. This seemed odd enough to Leventhal that she questioned Ileana as to why the girl was not fully clothed. Ileana Fuster explained that Becky's mother had forgotten to pack diapers for her daughter.[56] Only later, after the case broke, did Leventhal find out that Becky did not wear diapers and had not for quite a while.[57] Vivian Pelton also saw a disturbing scene once when she came to pick up her daughter Lacy. Jessie Lipton was standing in a corner of the living room and Frank Fuster was coming out of his bedroom, pulling up his shorts. Pelton thought Jessie was "embarrassed or upset." She was later described as "cowering."[58] She did not make a lot of the incident at the time. But it is worth mentioning since it helps demonstrate how many parents were disturbed at one point or another about something that seemed amiss.

Paula Walker, who took her two-year-old daughter, Sara, to the Fusters' once a week between March and May, had such an incident in early May. Even though she had been told, as other parents were, that Frank Fuster worked outside the home, it was her experience that he "delivered Sara to me at least half the times." She used the word "deliver" because her daughter was routinely so tired that she had to be carried. One time, Walker found Sara in shorts, but without her overalls. She asked Fuster why her daughter was not fully clothed. "Frank told me it was just because it was so hot in the house," she later testified. Walker, who did not consider the temperature in the house to be hot, decided not to bring her daughter back.[59]

Another suspicion that was arrived at independently by several families was that their children had been drugged at the Fusters'. That suspicion was later borne out by Frank Fuster's own lawyer, who argued that Ileana's testimony should not be trusted because *she* had been drugged by Frank.[60] Many parents commented on how tired their children were after leaving the Fusters', and how they sometimes had to carry their children out of the house.[61]

Sexually Precocious Behavior

Donald Menninger's "kiss my body" comment to his mother was only one example of highly sexualized behavior on the part of Country Walk children. A number of parents reported being puzzled as to how their young children learned to French-kiss and why they were acting this way. Betsy Leventhal noticed that Tom began to mimic masturbating "quite a bit" while at the Fusters' for babysitting, though he had not done this before.[62] Roberta Lipton noticed a number of sexualized behaviors in her two-year-old son, Daniel. After he began attending the Fusters', he repeatedly tried to French-kiss his mother, he would "constantly pull on his penis," and once he put her hand on his penis, saying "mommy, rub my pee pee."[63] Kimberly Porter testified that her two-year-old son Malcolm "would do sexual things" to his four-year-old sister.[64] Allison Lucas testified that her daughter asked whether it "was OK to eat shit."[65] Tammy also masturbated in public, French-kissed her parents, and tried on numerous occasions to stick toys into her rectum.[66] Betsy Leventhal testified that her two-year-old, Tom, "would kiss me and then try to stick his tongue in my mouth."[67] Sandra Cramer described her sons, Jason and Joshua, French-kissing, engaging in penile and anal stimulation of each other, and attempting anal stimulation of her. Joshua frequently asked his mother to play with his penis when she changed his diapers.[68] Even the psychiatrist who later testified for the defense allowed that "it would be significant" if numerous children that age started French-kissing.[69] The children who went to the Fusters' exhibited much more overly sexualized behavior than that.

The Final Fifteen Interviews with Children

By the end of August, twenty-four children had been interviewed at the State Attorney's Office. Many were interviewed only once; only two were interviewed more than twice. Two-thirds of all the investigative interviews that would be conducted in the case were complete, and detailed charges had already been drawn up against Frank and Ileana Fuster (see Figure 6.6). There were fifteen more investigative interviews after the last day in August 1984: seven in September, three in October, one in November, and four in January. All charges were finalized thereafter with a second indictment, so those were the last of the investigative interviews.[70] Altogether, then, there were forty-six videotaped sessions of children and the Bragas between August 9 and the end of January 1985. Those sessions involved thirty-one children. Eight of those children ended up with individual, named charges against Frank and/or Ileana Fuster. As Figure 6.6 demonstrates, the earliest children in the investigation were by far the most important children in the case; they accounted for most of the group and individual charges.

Three of the final five investigative interviews in the case later became the focus of substantial criticism. One was with Noel Fuster in late November, and the other two were in late January—one with Jessie Lipton, the other with Tammy Lucas. Two of those interviews are described in detail below. The third contested interview, with Tammy Lucas, is less important to the case. She was a named complainant in the first indictment, on the basis of statements she made then; her third interview did not change things. The charges involving Jessie Lipton, by contrast, were filed on the basis of the January interview. And the November interview with Noel was unlike any other interview in the case.

Confronting Noel

When the charges were filed against Frank and Ileana Fuster in early September, there was a single count naming Noel as a victim of his father. It was based on Jason Cramer's eyewitness account and Noel's positive STD test. There are differing views on how much the prosecution wanted Noel's testimony at trial, though it would be hard to resist calling the oldest possible witness to the allegations. Then again, the boy was clearly conflicted. He had seen his father crying in prison and had told the Bragas something about how he could "save [his] dad."

In late November, Noel's mother, Martha, brought the boy back to the State Attorney's Office for another interview. The session had apparently been requested by Assistant State Attorney Chris Rundle. According to Hollingsworth, Rundle apparently thought he might not be able to proceed with the case "unless he got a statement from Frank Fuster's son as to the source of his gonorrhea." An additional interview could not happen, however, without the support of the boy's mother. Hollingsworth reported that Martha Fuster desperately wanted Noel to be confronted by the psychologists: "Please, I want you to ask him the 'hard' questions," she pleaded with the Bragas before they joined him in the interview room.[71]

Figure 6.6 Country Walk, Full Counts, Frank and Ileana, Individual and Group Charges.

Each icon represents one child. Children are in order of original Braga interview sequence.

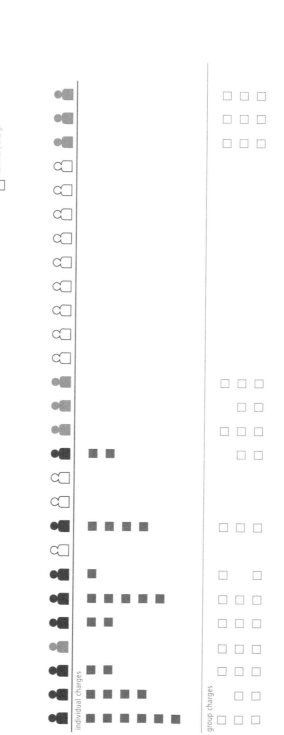

Compiled by author from original documents.

The interview reflected in the court transcript began with Joseph Braga asking Noel about what, if anything, Frank told him *not* to talk about. Noel insisted the only thing he said not to talk about was the fact that Frank was in jail. Since this was widely known, it is unlikely his response reflected the full substance of what Frank Fuster told his son. As the interview progressed, Noel offered some implausible denials; for example, he said he didn't remember *anything* about when he was six, and he denied knowing the word "pee pee."[72] Joseph Braga eventually confronted the boy with the medical evidence:

> The doctors tell me that there's only one way that you can get gonorrhea, and that's if someone puts their penis in your mouth. Do you remember someone ever doing that?[73]

Noel provided a series of evasive answers: "I don't remember, maybe they did, I don't remember . . . ," "Maybe it happened when I was six," "Maybe I was fast asleep. I don't remember. . . ."[74] Perhaps his most revealing statement was: "I do remember. I don't *want* to remember. . . ."[75]

The boy slowly proceeded to acknowledge a number of facts that did not directly involve him. He had already told the Bragas in August that Becky sometimes had no clothes on. This time, when pressed again on the issue, he said she was "running around naked" and "every time she took a shower, she was running around naked." The Bragas expressed obvious surprise at the idea of a four-year-old girl who was left for babysitting taking showers at the Fusters'. "My mom helped her," he added. While continuing to deny any personal involvement in sexualized play, Noel described the actions of other children. He acknowledged that some children went to the bathroom on the floor. In Noel's words, that was a "[g]ame, some people do it as a game or they—some people think it's funny." He also said that "Jason said a lot of things about sexy when Becky was naked." Eventually, at the end of the passage below, Noel made his most incriminating statement yet:

> LB: What do you think is going to happen to you father?
>
> NF: He might stay there forever.
>
> LB: How do you feel about that?
>
> NF: Sad.
>
> LB: I bet you do. Do you think what your father did, that he should be in jail?
>
> NF: Huh? (Inaudible.) Well, what was that? Why did he go to jail?
>
> LB: Well, what we talked about?
>
> JB: What do you think?
>
> LB: Why do you think he went to jail?

NF: Only thing I remember, maybe he did something wrong about the government.

JB: What about with the children?

NF: Children?

JB: Children?

NF: Oh, he (inaudible) that he put his penis in the mouth.

JB: Uh-huh, into the children?

NF: I think he does need to go to jail.

JB: Do you think they can help him there?

NF: (Nodding affirmatively.)

JB: So he will be better and won't do things like this anymore?

NF: I think they would help him.

JB: If you were going to try to help him, what would be some of the things you could say to him?

NF: To tell the truth and don't lie. Like that.

JB: Supposing he could get out of jail, now what were the things he shouldn't do anymore so he wouldn't go back to jail? What are some of the things?

NF: Not to stick his penis in my mouth and not to stick it into little kids, his peeing in their mouth and not to stick any kind of penis (inaudible).[76]

Critics of the case have claimed that the interview up to this point contained nothing of note. The final response just quoted demonstrates this is not true. It is true that the "hard questions" had yet to come. Before taking a break for lunch, Joseph Braga told Noel:

JB: While you are at lunch, I think you ought to think about me asking you questions because I have to tell you this: if the test didn't say you have gonorrhea, then I could believe you. If the other children hadn't told me things that you are a part of, then I would believe you, but all of the children—

NF: I—I (inaudible).

JB: The doctor's tests say that you've got gonorrhea (inaudible).

NF: I think I forgot. Maybe they did.

JB: Maybe you can remember after lunch. Maybe you can remember after lunch. That's what I want you to think about.

After a lunch break, Joseph Braga confronted the boy directly with the implausibility of his denials. Noel then made more detailed statements about his mother kissing Joshua Cramer and his father kissing Becky Taylor on the vagina.[77] He was also more somewhat specific about his father's actions. Noel confirmed that his parents wore masks and scared the children, he said his father "scared me half to death" with a knife, and eventually he said his father put his penis in Noel's mouth "twice."

It still was not clear whether Noel would be a witness at trial. His mother's desire to "ask the hard questions" would not necessarily translate into the willingness to let the boy testify against his father. But Noel had made a vast number of incriminating statements, many of which matched things other children had said.

Jessie Lipton, Again

The most significant interview in January was with Jessie Lipton. She had been interviewed early in the investigation; her interview contained some strange statements that gave pause for concern, but it did not contain disclosures of any sort. Jessie was not named in the original thirteen-count indictment. She had gone to the Fusters' only twice in May, so it was possible that when she was there Frank Fuster was not even home. The state did not ask to interview her a second time. In January, however, her parents contacted the State Attorney's Office to request a second interview. They reported their daughter had "started talking about what happened" at Frank and Ileana's house. There was apparently disagreement among the prosecutors about whether it was advisable to go forward with this interview. The substance of this disagreement was never made public, but it stands to reason that those opposed would be worried that statements in the girl's second interview might somehow be attributed to prosecutors, interviewers, or parents.

The girl comes across in the transcript of this interview as observant and articulate. "In March I'm going to be five and a half," she adds after responding "yes" to the question, "You were just five in September?" She also remembers the State Attorney's Office well enough to know that they were conducting this interview in a different room from the one five months earlier. What Jessie had apparently been saying at home came after Laurie Braga asked what the children did with their clothes off:

> JL: They played cut off your head.
> JB: Cut off your head? Can you show me how they did that?
> JL: Frank would ask them, do you want a cupcake and if they said yes, then he would cut your head off.
> LB: Did he really cut off heads or pretend?
> JL: He was—he put the knife to your neck.
> LB: The knife to the neck (inaudible).
> JL: Yes.

LB: Did he do that to you?

JL: Yes.

LB: What other children did he do that to?

JL: To Daniel, to Joshua.

LB: Uh-huh?

JL: To—to Jason. That's about all I know.[78]

This description was quite similar to one provided by Jason months earlier. Later, Laurie Braga asked Jessie to describe any other games, and Jessie responded, "Duck Duck Goose Goose with their clothes off."[79] She proceeded to indicate that Frank Fuster touched her vagina, although the transcript has some ambiguities that seem to stem from gestures unaccompanied by words.[80] Toward the end of the interview, Laurie Braga raised the question that added something that would later form the basis for a major defense argument: Why didn't she speak earlier?

LB: Okay, do you think—is there anything that you still are a little scared to talk about?

JL: (Shaking head no.)

LB: Uh-uh? Can you tell me what anybody would do to make you scared?

JL: They would put the knife up to your neck.

LB: Up to your neck and what else?

JL: (Inaudible.)

LB: Pull on your pee pee?

JL: That's all.

LB: What did they say would happen if you told?

JL: They would say—they would tell me not to tell but I still tell.

LB: But you didn't tell for a long time, how come, were you scared?

JL: (Shaking head no.)

LB: Do you know why?

JL: Uh-uh, I think I was too young.[81]

Although Jessie described several sexualized or abusive games (Duck Duck Goose Goose; Cut Off Your Head), she also resisted some leading questions at the end of the interview about other games the Bragas had heard about from many children. "What about the pee pee game?" Laurie Braga asks explicitly. "There was no pee pee game," Jessie responded. Similarly, she said that she never saw Frank or Iliana play with ca-ca. Presumably, if the girl was simply trying to please the interviewers, she would have responded affirmatively to those questions. Then Jessie added one more detail:

JL: I will tell you what else happened with my brother. They were dancing
around with my brother, then he was laughing.

LB: Uh-huh?

JL: With his clothes off. He thought that was funny.

LB: He did? Did you think it was funny?

JL: No.

As a result of this interview, Jessie Lipton was added to the second indictment. She later testified at the trial.

"Preparing the Charts"

The Country Walk case was originally investigated and charged by Chris Rundle, under the supervision of Abe Laeser. Janet Reno eventually assigned two more senior prosecutors to the case: John Hogan and Dan Casey. This often happens in high-profile criminal cases; as demonstrated through the McMartin case, however, it is not always a move that improves the chances of prosecutorial success, particularly when sex-abuse prosecutors are replaced with prosecutors who are not experienced with such cases. In the Country Walk case, however, what the new prosecutors brought was a systematic approach that may be what has ensured that the subsequent convictions have not been reversed.

As John Hogan explained in a civil deposition, "When I took over the case I saw as my first priority revamping the charging document."[82] He immediately did something the McMartin prosecutors did not do until long after they filed charges: he actually watched the videotapes of the children's interviews. After reviewing the videotapes, Hogan assigned Rundle and Casey "the task of what we called preparing the charts, and we took each tape and we outlined each and every allegation of sexual misconduct."[83]

There were apparently upward of 450 potential charges. The indictment that the prosecutors produced after their detailed analysis had twenty-eight charges. Eleven of those were against Ileana Fuster alone, fourteen were against Frank Fuster alone, and three were "group charges" that named both defendants and multiple children. "Our goal was to only charge those crimes we thought we had a very good chance of winning," Hogan later testified in a civil deposition.[84] Accordingly, virtually every charge had cross-corroborating evidence from multiple sources. This included statements from other children and statements from adults. This charging strategy also meant the prosecution thoroughly checked its own case for inconsistencies. It was during this process that the State Attorney's Office went to great lengths to establish, as accurately as possible, the precise dates of attendance for every child. The prosecutors were cognizant of the attendance patterns, then, when considering any statement a child made about other children. Only when attendance patterns were kept in mind, for example, did it make sense that certain children did not know other children. The resulting charges were carefully drawn and multiply supported.

Charges were finalized in the Country Walk case with the filing of the second indictment in March 1985. In other day-care sexual abuse cases, particularly McMartin and Michaels, the second indictment vastly expanded the scope of the case. The second indictment in the Country Walk case added *two* children connected to individual counts and thirteen total counts (including group counts, explained below). The individual charges added by the second indictment stemmed almost entirely from children already named in connection with individual charges in the first indictment. There were three additional counts involving Jason Cramer, two additional counts involving Becky Taylor, one additional count involving Tom Leventhal, and one additional count involving Tammy Lucas. There were two more children with individual counts in the second indictment, neither of whom was named in the first indictment. Joshua Cramer was one. Although it was clear he would never testify at trial, an additional charge was added because several children, including Noel Fuster, indicated they witnessed Joshua being sexually abused by Frank Fuster. The other child added to the second indictment was Jessie Lipton. She would later become the most criticized of the children; critics would claim she was typical or representative of the children in the case. Actually, her place in the case was unique.

The prosecutors also filed three group charges, a creative strategy to deal with the fact that many statements involved games or other group activities. Those charges listed as many as fifteen children in one charge—but the children were listed in the alternative, connecting every child with an "and/or." This meant that each of these charges could be proven with evidence about one child alone; but it also allowed for a range of possible testimony. The group charges ultimately added seven children to the case. All of the group charges included children named in the individual counts.

The first group charge was sexual acts between Frank and Ileana in front of children. Thirteen children were listed in the alternate, including all of the children named in individual charges. The second group charge was for aggravated assault stemming from the wearing of masks, displaying weapons, and/or making threats. Fourteen children were listed in the alternate in this count, including all of the named-charge children except Noel Fuster. The third group charge was for lewd and lascivious acts, involving naked dancing and the games with feces and urine.

The case was originally scheduled for trial in January 1985. Several delays were requested by the defense and granted by the judge. Those motions were opposed, with increasing vigor, by the state. The trial ultimately began in September 1985, almost exactly a year after the original thirteen-count indictment. Two pre-trial developments merit discussion.

"Breaking" Jason Cramer

The day-care sexual abuse cases of the 1980s became famous partly because they highlighted questions about how the criminal justice system would accommodate children as witnesses. The issue had scarcely been engaged before the emerging social recognition of child abuse in the 1970s and 1980s. In Florida, there was a legislative effort to allow children to testify via closed-circuit television, an innovation intended to reduce the anxiety of testifying in front of the defendant. There was even hope among some of the parents in the Country Walk case that the videotaped interviews by the Bragas could be introduced into evidence in lieu of actual testimony. The law was unclear, but it seemed likely that the Confrontation Clause in the Constitution would be interpreted to require something more than videotaped statements.

How children would be treated in this process also remained unclear. As the trial date approached, Jeffrey Samek, Frank Fuster's lawyer, obtained an order allowing him to depose children in the case. The judge did not allow Fuster to be in the room for these depositions; instead, he viewed these depositions from an adjacent room where he could watch on closed-circuit television and convey any questions or comments to his attorney. The defense proceeded to take the deposition of Jason Cramer, the most important witness in the case. What unfolded became perhaps the most controversial moment of the case: Samek confronted Jason in an extremely aggressive way. Using a tone that Hollingsworth later described as "sharp, accusatory," Samek said directly to the boy: "I think you're lying." "I don't think Frank ever did anything to you, Frank didn't do anything to you, did he?" However disturbed Jason may have been by the adult's harsh tone, he did not budge. "Yes, he did," Jason replied. As Hollingsworth reports the ensuing exchange:

> "Frank never put his mouth on your penis, *did he?*"
> "Yes, he did," Jason whispered.
> "When did he do it?"
> "Partially." The word barely came out.
> "Huh?"
> "Partially." Jason was on the verge of tears.
> "Jason, *look* at me when you answer—"[85]

An excerpt from a videotape of this interview, later played on television, bears out the Hollingsworth description. Obviously, Samek was confronting the boy in a most unusual way (*Look at me when you answer*); it is unimaginable that a judge would allow an adult witness to be bullied like that. The prosecutors went directly to Judge Newman for a ruling that would prohibit this kind of questioning. Hogan called Samek's tactics "outrageous" and a "travesty." "I have never in my life heard an attorney order a witness that they had to look at him," he told the judge. Samek argued that these tactics were "the only way to have possibility of breaking the spell that has been cast on this child."[86]

Judge Newman declined to stop the deposition entirely, but he agreed to suspend it for a day. The Cramers were unwilling to subject their son to any more of this treatment. They insisted that the matter be appealed. Hollingsworth reported that the Cramers would withdraw from the case if the court did not agree, and it seemed likely that other families might well follow. The viability of the entire case hung in the balance.

The videotape of the confrontation of Jason Cramer was played in an emergency proceeding before the Third District Court of Appeals. Samek claimed that trying to break the child was the only way to get at the truth. Chief Judge Schwartz was unmoved. He called Samek's argument "disingenuous" and said "I am personally going to supply a transcript of this deposition to the Florida bar."[87] The next day, the local section of the *Miami Herald* contained the headline "Judge Seeks Bar Probe of Fuster Lawyer." Samek, who had been appointed by the court to represent Ileana, then tried, without success, to withdraw from the case.

Frank "Freaks Out," Ileana Pleads Guilty

As the September trial date approached, speculation about a possible guilty plea focused on Ileana Fuster. Would she plead guilty and testify against her husband? There was no speculation about whether Frank Fuster would plead guilty; there was nothing the state could offer him. He was a convicted sex offender in a case with STD evidence. The state would seek to imprison him for the rest of his life. His was the kind of case that would go to trial. Matters were much less clear for Ileana, since she had no prior record, she was actually a minor when she was arrested, and it appeared she was also a victim of Frank Fuster. It was likely she would plead guilty.

Yet Ileana Fuster remained an enigma. For months, she protested her innocence and wrote letters to Frank almost daily. But those closest to her in the detention facility later reported that Ileana's marriage to Frank had been precipitated by a rape.[88] Indeed, she began to speak about physical abuse by Frank, but she still denied sexually abusing any children. This left little room for any kind of guilty plea. It also left her lawyer, Michael Von Zamft, wondering whether Ileana was competent to stand trial. There was a competency hearing in early August, where she was found to be competent. It was clear that her own lawyer thought she had no other defense. He then hired two psychologists to start meeting with Ileana in order to get her to face the facts. She had stopped communicating with Frank, and it was apparent that his grip over her was weakening.

Those psychologists would, years later, be accused of "brainwashing" Ileana Fuster. Wild claims—contradicted by all available facts—would be made about how she was treated in prison. And Reno would be blamed for all of it. Those arguments are taken up in Part Two of this chapter, but for now it is important to keep in mind that Ileana Fuster's own lawyer hired the psychologists who would later be described as if they were agents of the prosecution.

Reality started to set in for Frank Fuster. Ileana had stopped communicating with him, and he faced a probation violation hearing stemming from his 1982 conviction for child molestation. Frank then "freaked out." That is how the media described an apparent catatonic trance that Frank Fuster went into, in court in early August. But acting out in court was not going to stop the proceedings. The probation violation hearing was held in mid-August 1985. The three-day proceeding was aimed at deciding whether to revoke the conditions of his probation. During the proceedings, the prosecution played one videotape to the judge, a thirty-four-minute interview with Donald Menninger. Fuster took the stand in his own defense. His testimony was incredible, as he denied that there was a babysitting service in his house. He claimed he was never in the house when children—who were there, of course, for babysitting—were there. All the parents who had seen him when they came or went were, according to Fuster, lying.

The judge sentenced Fuster to fifteen years. A few days later, Ileana pleaded guilty. It was a guilty plea, not a plea agreement, which means she admitted to every fact in the charging documents. She then threw herself on the mercy of the court. Some observers concluded that she was willing to incriminate her husband only once she already knew he was going to prison for many years.

The Trial

Opening arguments in Frank Fuster's trial began on September 3, 1985. Re-markably, the trial lasted less than a month. The case was complicated, but unlike other highly publicized day-care sex abuse cases around the country, it had been charged in a way that was designed to be lean and effective.

The State's Case

The state called thirty-four witnesses in six days. The largest group of witnesses was from among the parents. Fifteen testified about their children's medical and behavior problems that year. A few told stories about occurrences at the Fusters', particularly incidents involving partially clothed or naked children in strange

circumstances. Several parents described incidents that resulted in their pulling
children from the Fusters' care.

The next largest group of witnesses for the prosecution included medical
doctors, and psychologists with doctoral degrees. Two medical doctors provided the details concerning Noel Fuster's STD test, four psychologists testified
as mental health practitioners who had seen one or more of the children, and
both of the Bragas testified about the interview process. The final prosecution
witness was Dr. Roland Summit, a psychiatrist who helped pioneer the study
and treatment of child sexual abuse. Dr. Summit was affiliated with Harbor
UCLA Medical Center in Torrance, California, where he held the unusual title
"community psychiatrist." Two years before the County Walk trial, Summit
published an article that coined the term *child abuse accommodation syndrome*.[89]
That article and his testimony would become focal points for criticisms of the
case years later. Notably, Summit's testimony addressed sexually abused children in general. He explained to the jury the various reasons children might
delay the disclosure of sexual abuse, and why their disclosures might be
equivocal.

The third significant group of witnesses was made up of children who had
attended the Fusters' babysitting service.[90] The potential witness list was conceivably as long as the number of children named in all of the counts, including
the group counts. But some of those children were clearly too young to testify.
The parents of other children were concerned about what it would mean for
their children to testify in open court. Some said they would allow their children
to testify only if the court permitted testimony by closed-circuit television. Several parents helped lobby the Florida legislature for the change that permitted
such testimony in 1985. And two children who could add significantly to the
prosecution's case were in doubt for different reasons. Donald Menninger, the
first child to make a spontaneous disclosure in the case, was unlikely to testify
because his father, an Arvida employee, had divided loyalties in the matter. Noel
Fuster was also unlikely to testify because his mother, Martha, was scared of
Frank Fuster. He had threatened her life over child custody[91] and she could not
risk the consequences of allowing Noel to testify in a case where a conviction
was not assured. Neither of those two boys testified in the case.

Eight children ended up testifying. But three of them were "name witnesses"
only, taking the stand for identification purposes but not providing substantive
testimony. The other five children testified in substance and were subject to
cross-examination: Jessie Lipton, Tammy Lucas, Becky Taylor, Jason Cramer,
and Annie Porter. The children testified about things that happened to them,
and things they witnessed. Annie Porter was named only in group charges; the
other four were named in individual and group charges.[92] They were the core of
the case.

The Defense

Frank Fuster maintained that he was innocent from the time of his arrest. Beyond protesting his innocence, his defense was that the children had been brainwashed. The defense put on a few minor witnesses, but there were basically two important witnesses for the defense: Fuster himself and Dr. Lee Coleman, the psychiatrist from California who described the children as "brainwashed." To lay the foundation for Coleman's testimony, the defense spent more than a week playing almost all of the videotapes of the interviews conducted by the Bragas. Notably, the state did not object to this move. Indeed, according to Jan Hollingsworth, they welcomed it—so long as the defense did not show snippets without any context. The tapes were shown in chronological order. The jury saw thirty-three interviews—virtually every investigative interview with a child connected to any of the charges in the case. By mutual agreement, the defense and prosecution agreed not to show a number of tapes.

The most notable "minor" witness for the defense was Vicki Menninger, mother of the first child to make a disclosure in the case. Attorney Samek asked the court to treat her as a hostile witness. The judge declined the request but indicated he would give the defense considerable latitude in questioning her. Menninger's position had become extremely uncomfortable, since her husband was one of the named defendants in civil suits that had been filed against Arvida and Disney for failing to act on the information that came through his wife. A number of parents were angry that she warned only her friend, Betsy Leventhal, about her son's statement concerning Ileana Fuster "kissing all the babies' bodies." Menninger was in a terrible position. Her husband's job security might be at stake if Arvida lost a huge civil lawsuit because the Menningers—perhaps even thinking they were protecting the company—originally kept this information to themselves (and a close friend). Her statements about the whole matter changed over time. In a deposition in the civil case that occurred after the criminal case was over, her husband denied he or she ever swore anyone to secrecy.[93]

Her description of the original disclosure was unchanged. She allowed, on cross-examination, that there was no doubt her son's statements were sexual, that he had never said anything like this in the past, and that she never sent her son back to the Fusters' house. She claimed, however, his statements were only one factor in the decision. "I really wasn't happy with the babysitting," she testified, claiming that her son spent too much time watching television at the Fusters."[94] On cross-examination, however, Menninger allowed that her son's refusal to go to the Fusters' had escalated in April and become "really bad." And when asked point blank—by the prosecution, not the defense—if she thought her son had been sexually abused at the Fusters, she replied that she did.[95] She may have ultimately been one of the most effective witnesses for the prosecution. Her statements were reluctant; nobody would accuse her of "hysteria" or jumping to conclusions. Indeed, she had financial reasons to side with the defense. But her testimony supported the state's case.

The primary defense expert was Dr. Coleman. The defense had been planning to use Ralph Underwager, who also appeared in the Kelly Michaels case, but he was abruptly dropped by the defense after his deposition was taken.[96] Coleman is a psychiatrist who has made a specialty out of attacking psychiatric diagnoses. For years he appeared as a prosecution witness in cases where the defendant relied on the insanity defense. When changes in California law restricted the use of the insanity defense, Coleman found a new specialty: criticizing the interviews in child sexual abuse cases. Working with the advocacy group VOCAL, he established a new client base. Despite lacking any significant experience with child sexual abuse, Coleman quickly found himself hired by the defense in cases across the country. [97] He qualified as an expert witness in the Country Walk case, even though his credentials for this specific work were limited at best. He agreed, for example, that knowledge of child development would be important in assessing child interviews, yet he could not name any leading figures in the field.[98] The few articles he mentioned about memory issues at trial were all things he had read since his deposition a few months earlier.[99]

Coleman testified that he reviewed sixty hours of videotaped interviews with the Bragas. This would appear to include all of the relevant investigative interviews in the case and some that were not so relevant. There is some uncertainty about whether he reviewed the initial interviews with Jason Cramer on August 9. Coleman testified that he reviewed those interviews and that they contained nothing but "playing."[100] But the key session with Jason Cramer, described at length in Hollingsworth's book, contained the most important disclosures in the case because it was so detailed and it occurred so early.

Coleman testified that all of the investigative interviews were deeply flawed. He argued there was little or no difference between any of the interviews. He reached the conclusion that "in every interview I saw the methods used on the children would render the information unreliable."[101] His basic objection was that the questions were "manipulative" and "leading." He was also dismissive of any interview in which the child referred to an anatomically detailed doll. Dolls are "something you make up stories about," he argued, rejecting the idea that dolls might profitably be used by a child to demonstrate what happened.[102] He also had an extreme view of leading questions. According to Dr. Coleman: "'Show me what Frank and Ileana would do.' That's an example of a leading question."[103] Although that question "leads" the child to speak about Frank and Ileana, it is, of course, otherwise open-ended.

On cross-examination, the limits of Dr. Coleman's analysis were laid bare. Did he have any knowledge whether any of the items he labeled as "fantasy" were reflected in the charging documents? No. Did he ever go through the interviews to determine how often children said no to leading questions? No. Did he go through the tapes and determine how many times a child gave information about sexual acts that was not contained in a leading question? No.[104] It was difficult to conclude that Coleman was anything but an underprepared hired gun. His testimony did not accommodate any of the obvious differences between children or among individual interviews. But then, allowing that any of the interviews were acceptable would lead to the conclusion that the entire case was not a result of "brainwashing" by the Bragas.

The problems with his testimony, as prosecutors pointed out in the state's summation, were much more basic. First, Coleman entirely ignored the most detailed disclosures in the case—those made by Jason Cramer on August 9. Coleman said he skipped that tape because in it the boy was "simply playing."[105] Second, Coleman did not take any other evidence into account. He agreed on cross-examination that there would be cause for concern if a group of three- and four-year-olds started French-kissing their parents and acting in the highly sexualized ways described in the case.[106] But since Coleman never analyzed that kind of evidence in the Country Walk case, he did not know that such evidence pervaded the case. Finally, he wrote off many children because they made statements about feces that *he* considered inherently unbelievable. Again, he was apparently unaware that there was a significant amount of testimony, including a photograph, that substantiated Frank Fuster's strange fascination with the feces. One of the many aspects of this case that has been lost in the witch-hunt narrative is how many claims originally labeled as fantastic—masks, a dead bird, playing with feces—were proven in this case.

The final defense witness was Frank Fuster. His lawyer, Jeffrey Samek, made it clear that the decision whether or not to testify was entirely up to the defendant.[107] It was also apparent from Samek's remarks to the judge that he did not think it was advisable for Fuster to testify. Indeed, there were open arguments between Samek and Fuster during the trial about impromptu press conferences that Fuster held against the advice of counsel. Much of Fuster's testimony was an extended series of negative responses—no, never, absolutely not—to questions from his own lawyer. Samek also tried to defuse a few pieces of physical evidence in the case, including the grotesque picture of Noel in a bathroom covered in feces. This is Fuster's reply to the question, "Why did you take a picture like this?"

> When my wife called me and told me what my son had done, I thought it was funny. I happened to have the camera ready. I took a picture of my son to show it to him when he gets older. I thought it was funny.[108]

On cross-examination, Frank Fuster basically called every other adult in the case a liar. The parents who saw him during the daytime were liars, the parents who saw video equipment in the house were liars, and the business associates of Fuster's who had seen the scary masks that he wore were liars. And the children were all, in Fuster's words, "brainwashed." There were also many exchanges that seemed to involve semantic hair splitting by Fuster. He refused to agree that what Ileana did was a babysitting service, even though the business cards and advertisements for their service used those precise words.[109] The most significant of these verbal contortions involved a visit to his doctor shortly before his arrest. This is when Fuster claimed that he had visited his doctor about diabetes, but the doctor also checked him for venereal disease "since [he] already had the blood." Fuster allowed that he had "a big pain" on his penis at the time as well, but he maintained that this was caused by his zipper and had nothing to do with his visit to the doctor.[110] Neither side ever called Fuster's doctor. Apparently neither side was sure he would be useful as a witness.[111] The defense also chose not to call Noel. They apparently concluded they could not rely on him to present Frank's version of events.

Ileana Fuster, Rebuttal Witness

The prosecution called a few rebuttal witnesses, of which Ileana Fuster was by far the most notable. Even though she had pleaded guilty in August, it was not clear whether she would testify against her husband. This critical point has been lost in a blur of revisionist history addressed later in this chapter. But the simple fact is that Ileana Fuster's plea was "straight up"—she did not agree to testify in exchange for her plea, and the state promised her nothing. It remained unclear through September 1985 whether she would testify. While the trial proceeded in September, Ileana went through several days of deposition. Those depositions apparently convinced prosecutors she would be a good rebuttal witness. But they did not call her as a witness for their case-in-chief. Had Frank not testified, Ileana would not have either. It was Frank Fuster's claims that she rebutted.

When Ileana took the stand, she portrayed her marriage as filled with physical violence, and she testified that the babysitting service was Frank's idea. He was often alone with the children, she testified, recalling Becky Taylor complaining, "She asked me why do I have to leave her with Frank, that she didn't like it, that she was scared of him, things like that."[112] She said that Tammy Lucas had told her much the same thing. Ileana also testified further that Frank would frequently hide in the bedroom when parents came to get their children. This is one of the reasons it took so long to answer the front door.

The moment when Ileana began to implicate Frank in sexual abuse, by saying she had seen Frank in the bedroom with a naked Tom Leventhal, Frank screamed across the courtroom: "You are a liar. You are a liar. God is going to punish you for this."[113] Ileana let out a pained cry in response. The transcript does not contain such information, but this is how a *Miami Herald* reporter described her response: "Ileana Fuster, who was testifying as a prosecution witness, screamed. Her mouth dropped open and she fell back, raising her hands to protect her face."[114] It was one of the defining moments of the trial. Frank displayed his violent temper and Ileana demonstrated an instinctual, cowering response. All three network affiliates in Miami led with the same dramatic footage: Ileana Fuster recoiling under the piercing screams of her fiercely angry husband. The jury was quickly dismissed, the court took a recess, and there was a sidebar about whether to gag the defendant. The judge declined. When proceedings continued, Ileana made it clear that Frank had sucked Tom Leventhal's penis.[115]

The remainder of her direct testimony included many specific, incriminating statements against Frank. She testified that Noel had asked her once "if it was okay for his father to touch his penis."[116] She said that Frank "wanted to see [her] kiss Joshua's penis," so she did it "twice."[117] She described being cut with a knife by Frank and being anally raped with a cross that Frank kept between their bedroom mattresses. (Police found the cross between the mattresses when they searched the house.) And she described finding Frank in the bathroom once, putting his penis in Noel's mouth. Noel subsequently vomited.[118]

Finally, she addressed some of the features of the case that were described as bizarre. She testified about a mask that Frank used to scare the children: "The mask had hair, white hair and front, the front was white and green a little bit and—."[119] (The description bears out the apparent confusion when Tammy Lucas said the mask was white and Becky Taylor said it was green.) She described a bird and a snake, both of which were in the house and both of which died while being handled by Frank.[120]

Ileana Fuster's testimony was damning, to be sure. It was also less than satisfactory. She did not verify all of the things one might think she would have seen. Many of the parents thought she drastically understated her own culpability. In sum, Ileana remained somewhat inscrutable to the end. Asked afterward in a civil deposition whether he thought Ileana was a "willing" participant with her husband, Dan Casey, one of the prosecutors, replied, "I guess it depends on how you define willing."[121]

The Verdict

The jury deliberated for eleven hours over two days. They asked to review tapes or notes six times. Parents of the children in the case were concerned that the jury did not return more quickly. Then again, it seems clear the jury did not rush to judgment. They ultimately found Frank Fuster guilty in some form on all

Figure 6.7 Country Walk, Full Counts, Individual and Group, Frank only, by First Braga Interview, and by Disposition.

Each icon represents one child. Children are in order of original Braga interview sequence.

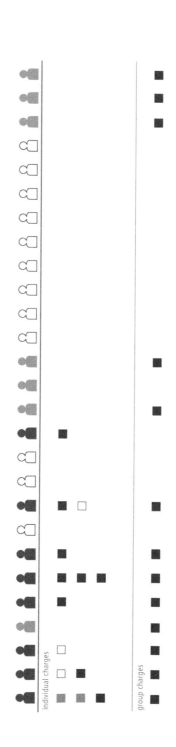

Compiled by author from original documents.

charges. Three charges were dropped before jury deliberations and the jury found Fuster guilty of a lesser included charge in two instances (see Figure 6.7). Fuster was sentenced to 165 years in prison. He appealed his conviction through the Florida courts, ending with the state supreme court declining to review the case. Fuster later pursued it in the federal courts, filing a habeas corpus claim in 1995 that included a supporting affidavit by Maggie Bruck. His federal appeals were unsuccessful. Eventually, the U.S. Supreme Court declined to hear the case, effectively ending the case more than twenty years after the original conviction.[122]

Part Two: Revisionist History (1993–Present)

Just one year after the conviction in Country Walk, there was a story in the *San Francisco Examiner* arguing that "a presumption of guilt" had marked a series of dubious child sexual abuse cases across the country. The emphasis of the series was on "bizarre" features that allegedly tied all of these cases together, and the authors included the Country Walk case. They summarized it as follows: "Allegations included pornography, the drinking of urine, eating of feces and sexual acts during such common preschool games as duck, duck goose and Simon Says."[123] Neither of these lengthy newspaper stories delved into the case in any detail. Two years later, Charlier and Downing included the case in their list of thirty-six.

The first author to cast doubt on the case in the 1990s was Debbie Nathan, who had written an article in the *Village Voice* in 1987 questioning a day-care sex abuse case from El Paso. Nathan used the term "junior McMartins" to describe that case and many others, and the Country Walk case was one of a half-dozen she mentioned by name.[124] Her first writing to mention the Country Walk case in any detail was a chapter on the "Ritual Abuse Scare" in an academic book. She argued that despite widespread claims about ritual abuse, "investigators have uniformly failed to turn up the adult witnesses or physical evidence" one might expect to find in such cases. She allowed in a footnote, however, that in the Country Walk case it "appears that the husband perpetrated sadomasochistic assaults against the wife (who was legally a minor) and possibly against the younger children, including abuse involving urine and excrement."[125]

She abandoned this view in 1993, when Janet Reno was nominated to be attorney general of the United States. That year, Nathan published a detailed critique of the Country Walk case in a journal called *Issues in Child Abuse Accusations*. Although the journal has an impressive sounding title and is sometimes even referred to as "peer-reviewed," it was actually self-published by Ralph Underwager, the psychologist who made his living appearing for the defense in child sexual abuse cases and who Fuster's defense replaced with Lee Coleman after a disastrous deposition in the summer of 1985. In the article that Nathan published in Underwager's journal, she omitted the substance of the footnote quoted above in favor of a blanket critique of the case. Nathan also coauthored a related article about the case with Steven Almond in *New Times*, an alternative weekly newspaper in Miami.[126] A host of writers then relied on Nathan's work to charge Reno with presiding over a gross miscarriage of justice. In 1998 and 2002, the PBS program *Frontline* aired programs assailing the Country Walk case. The case had become a central part of the witch-hunt narrative.

The witch-hunt narrative about the Country Walk case is built on a series of claims, none of which has been closely examined except in the Fuster's federal habeas corpus appeal, where a federal magistrate wrote a 124-page decision in 2002 that rejected all of these arguments.[127] The focus of the revisionist view has been on "child suggestibility." Those arguments are implausible on their face, given that Fuster's son tested positive for gonorrhea of the throat and Ileana Fuster corroborated claims made by the children. In the revisionist view, however, all of this evidence has been dismissed and Frank Fuster has been portrayed as the victim of a "witch-hunt." They make this claim partly because Fuster was an ex-con and partly because of overzealousness by the State Attorney's Office. These arguments, which have been made in condensed form by many writers, require detailed treatment to analyze in full. The six sections that follow each analyze an important element of the witch-hunt narrative about the case.

The "Inaccurate Test" Myth

The single most incriminating piece of evidence against Frank Fuster was that his six-year-old son tested positive for gonorrhea of the throat. Fuster himself did not test positive for gonorrhea at the time of arrest, but it turns out he had recently received a short course of penicillin treatments after seeing his doctor about "a big pain" in his penis.[128] Fuster's account of the treatment would be laughable if the subject matter were not so serious. According to him, the sore on his penis was caused by his zipper, and the doctor prescribed penicillin "just in case." He also claims his visit to the doctor was originally "for diabetic [problems]." Fuster's explanation for how he ended up receiving penicillin is as follows: "My doctor said 'I'm going to check you for syphilis, just in case, since I already have the blood.'"[129]

The positive lab results on Fuster's son were fully documented at trial. The precise test that was used by the laboratory—the RapID/NH System—was evaluated in the *Journal of Clinical Microbiology* in March 1983. In 162 cases of known N. gonorrhoeae, the RapID/NH system correctly identified 100 percent of the cases; the alternative, and more time-consuming, carbohydrate-based method identified 98 percent of the cases.[130] The RapID/NH System was called rapid because the required incubation period was four hours, compared to twenty-four hours for older tests. The positive predictive value of the RapID NH test was found to be 99.38 percent. Accordingly, the positive result on Fuster's son meant there was a 99.38 percent chance that he had gonorrhea. The article concluded: "the accuracy of [the RapID/NH system] is impressive, and the system has been proven to be superior to conventional carbohydrate degradation tests."[131]

Years after the jury verdict, Debbie Nathan claimed that the test used in the Country Walk case "could not distinguish bacteria that cause gonorrhea from other harmless ones that normally live in children's throats."[132] To support this claim she cited an impressive-sounding article from the Centers for Disease Control called "Incorrect Identification of Neisseria Gonorrhoeae from Infants and Children."[133] The article described fourteen cases (out of forty) in which the CDC ascertained that an initial positive test result for gonorrhea was in error. But the article has nothing to do with the Country Walk case. *None of the children with false-positive results were reported as having been tested with the RapID/NH system.* This is not surprising since RapID/NH is used when sexually transmitted diseases *are* suspected, not when a child has conjunctivitis or in a routine exam, as was the case for most of the children described in the article.

To read Nathan and other critics, one would think there was only one STD test used nationwide at the time of the Country Walk case. In fact, there were numerous tests used for different populations according to the circumstances. The CDC article is about a number of tests that may suggest STDs but are generally given for other purposes. Indeed, the authors of the article concluded that "unless there is other evidence of sexual abuse, initiation of formal child abuse investigations should await the confirmed identification of the isolate."[134] Notably, this is precisely what happened in the Country Walk case: the isolates *were* confirmed. Lab technician Freda Burstyn testified that after the Martin Lewis agar results were observed to be positive there was "a biochemical test to confirm it."[135] Moreover, the confirmatory test was processed at a reference laboratory, as recommended by the CDC. In other words, there were two tests on the sample from Noel. The inescapable conclusion is that the positive test result means there was a 99.38 percent chance Noel Fuster had gonorrhea of the throat.[136]

Noel's "Retraction"

Some writers have touted Noel's "retraction" of statements admitting that his father gave him gonorrhea of the throat. Since the underlying claim about the alleged inaccuracy of the test is false, it would appear that any retraction by Noel would fit well into the model of child abuse accommodation syndrome. Instead, his alleged retraction has been offered as evidence of Fuster's innocence. On close examination, however, the retraction itself is not what has been claimed.

The most detailed statement of the claim that Noel Fuster retracted his admissions about abuse by his father was made by Alexander Cockburn in *The Nation*.[137] Quoting selectively from a civil deposition taken years later, Cockburn claims that Noel "unequivocally" retracted any and all claims that he was ever abused by Frank Fuster. The deposition, Cockburn neglected to mentioned, was taken in a civil lawsuit filed *on Noel's behalf* against the Arvida Corporation, the developers and operators of the Country Walk development. The portions that Cockburn cites are entirely from questions asked by the lawyer who was trying to protect Arvida's assets. Apparently abandoning any concern about blatantly leading questions, Cockburn relies on this exchange, reproduced in his article, to support the argument that Noel Fuster had recanted:

Q: It's my understanding and impression from reviewing many documents including lots of reports by psychologists that from the very beginning when you were asked if your father sexually abused you in any way that you were steadfast in saying that he did not; is that correct?

A: Yes, sir.

Q: It's my further understanding that you only said that he did when you felt you essentially had no alternative and if you didn't tell someone what they wanted to hear they would just go on endlessly; is that also true?

A: Yes.

Q: Is it, in fact, true that he did not ever abuse you?

A: Yes, sir.

Cockburn then omits, without the appropriate editorial markings, almost four pages of questions and answers that lead up to this exchange:

Q: Now you initially saw, I think doctor either Miranda or Drs. Braga; is that correct? Do you remember which one was first? I know they were the early ones, Dr. Simon, Marcie Cramer and the two doctors named Braga. Do you have any recollection of that?

A: Are they the ones with the ponytails?

Q: That's right.

A. Yes.

Q: Your memory is pretty good. That's right, they have ponytails. Did they try to change your original statement, that your father had not harmed you?

A: Yes, sir.

Before analyzing the significance of these two snippets, it should be noted that Noel Fuster's "original statement" was *not* that he had never been harmed by his father. To the contrary, the very first day Noel spoke with the Bragas in August 1984, his reply to the question "Does your dad ever hit you?" was "Some days."[138]

Contrary to the self-serving statement that the Arvida lawyer included as a preface to the final question quoted above ("Your memory is pretty good"), the quality of Noel Fuster's memory in this deposition was demonstrably deficient. In the pages Cockburn omitted without editorial indication, Noel said he did not remember *any* of the children who attended the babysitting service over those nine months. The boy who supposedly had a "pretty good" memory could not remember a single person who attended the babysitting service.

Later in the deposition it was revealed that Noel had been hypnotized since the events at issue in the case.[139] This fact alone would disqualify him from testifying in court. Indeed, critics of the Country Walk case claim that Ileana Fuster's confession should be disregarded entirely because the defense psychologists who visited her in prison *essentially* hypnotized her. Though that characterization is contested, there is no question that Noel Fuster *actually* went to a hypnotist.[140] There is a strong argument—generally endorsed by the same people who criticize the Country Walk conviction—that no weight should be given his post-hypnotic statements.

Even accepting the boy's deposition testimony on its face, it is apparent that at age fifteen Noel Fuster was deeply conflicted and extremely confused about what happened eight years earlier. It is also clear that he experienced bizarre treatment at the hands of Frank Fuster. Among the many statements Cockburn does not acknowledge in this deposition are ones confirming several elements of the case Cockburn has ridiculed. For instance, Noel says:

> I was a little traumatized about the gorilla mask he used to put on. He used to put on a gorilla mask and scare the kids and I never really got that out of my head.[141]

Later he recalls that "the kids would scream" when his father scared them with the mask. It should be kept in mind that features like masks are precisely the kinds of "elements" that Charlier and Downing labeled as fantastic and then discounted. Cockburn's summary of this deposition also omits the myriad ways in which Noel expressed uncertainty and ambivalence about what had happened years earlier. At one point Noel refers to "this confusion that I've always had about whether I was sexually abused." He also says "it would be a relief to know" whether he was sexually abused. Later he says that "Everything is so vague" from back then, but he allows, "I sometimes remember things that are extreme."[142] The assertion that Noel has provided an unequivocal retraction simply is not supported by the evidence.[143]

Ileana Fuster's "Coerced Confession"

The revisionist view of the Country Walk case also dismisses Ileana Fuster's guilty plea and subsequent testimony as coerced. These critiques make four related arguments: (1) the state desperately needed Ileana Fuster's testimony, (2) Ileana Fuster was seriously mistreated in prison, (3) she was then brainwashed into pleading guilty, and (4) she has since given a convincing retraction of her guilty plea and related testimony. All four of these claims fail under close scrutiny.

The revisionist view of Ileana's testimony begins with the claim that it was so vital to the state's case that they were willing to obtain it at any cost. According to Nathan, "Reno decided that to get a conviction she would need a confession from Ileana Fuster."[144] The notion that the prosecution had to "break Ileana down" in order to win their case is contradicted directly by the chronology of the case. The case was originally scheduled for trial on January 7, 1985. The defense sought several delays. Every time, the state objected and lost. Reno made what was described as "a rare court appearance" in June to argue strongly against any further delay. She lost the motion, and the trial date was set for September 1985.[145] Ileana Fuster did not decide to plead guilty until the third week in August. Indeed, the psychologists who allegedly brainwashed her into that position had been hired by the defense only two weeks earlier. *But the state was anxious to go ahead with its case months before that.* Their repeated objections to defense motions for continuances clearly contradict the position they would take if Ileana's testimony was considered vital to their case. Nathan's claim is also contradicted by the role that Ileana's testimony actually played in the trial. The state did not include Fuster in the case-in-chief; she was used only on rebuttal. It is not clear that she would have testified at all had Frank Fuster not done likewise; her testimony rebutted his.

Whatever the importance of Ileana Fuster's testimony in proving Frank Fuster's guilt, those who reject the substance of her testimony also argue that she was coerced into making incriminating statements. They maintain that the coercion began with sustained and extreme mistreatment in prison, followed by a series of questionable visits by two psychologists. Her confinement has been described in horrifying terms, including the claim that she was "often kept nude" and was "drugged most of the time."[146] These claims rest entirely on a sworn statement by Stephen Dinerstein, who was hired in 1984 as a private investigator for the defense. Eight years after the conviction, Dinerstein made graphic claims about Ileana's mistreatment in jail that he did not make at the time of the trial.[147] Remarkably, Dinerstein has been accepted as the primary source in the revisionist history, even though there are serious reasons to doubt his credibility.[148]

Dinerstein's claims are contradicted by several credible sources from the time of the alleged mistreatment. First and foremost, the Fusters' own motion about their prison conditions, heard on April 12, 1985, does not support these claims. The claims made by the Fusters under the banner of "cruel and unusual punishment" were actually quite tame. Ileana wanted to be moved out of her "safety cell" into the general population—a request that the judge granted. But her complaints about solitary confinement were ordinary. She complained that she had "only limited access to shower facilities," "only limited access to hot water for coffee," "no access to a day room," and "no access to television."[149] But notably, *there was nothing in her motion in 1985 about drugs, sleep deprivation, or lack of clothing.* Frank Fuster's complaints about his prison conditions were patently absurd and have not been repeated since. He wanted, among other things, two showers a day and cable television. Ileana's letters from prison also contradict the claim made by Frank's lawyer years later.[150]

Evidence from three adults who interacted with Ileana Fuster in 1984–85 contradicts Dinerstein's claims as well. These adults all had more contact with Ileana during this time period than Dinerstein did. First, Shirley Blando, a chaplain in the facility who befriended Ileana, said nothing about her being nude or any of the other wild claims that have been made about her incarceration. To the contrary, Blando recounted frequently sitting outside on a patio with Ileana, including in the months prior to the motion where she complained about lack of access to a "day room."[151] Blando also remarked specifically about how *well* Fuster did while in solitary confinement. A Sergeant Spears, a shift commander at the Detention Center, testified that Fuster "had more recreational time than any other inmate within her cell block, and she spent most of her time with Shirley Blando [assistant chaplain]." She also verified that Fuster made "frequent visits to the sun deck."[152] The Rev. Tommy Watson, who visited Ileana weekly and later assisted in her education, also took strong issue with Dinerstein's years-after-the-fact claims. Watson wrote that during Fuster's period of solitary confinement, "I saw her in the chapel service and in Chaplain Blando's office many times. Ileana asked me to thank the Captain of the detention center for her kind care given while she was in jail."[153]

Ileana pleaded guilty on August 22, 1985. She was not offered anything in exchange for this plea. Judge Newman specifically asked if she understood that she could be sentenced to life in prison. She replied that she did.[154] She later provided detailed testimony against her husband, both in depositions and on the stand for the final day of his criminal trial. When she appeared for sentencing in November, Ileana "repeatedly told [Judge] Newman 'I am sorry . . . I am very sorry.'"[155] In 1993, Debbie Nathan argued that the substance of Ileana's testimony was created by two psychologists hired by Michael Von Zamft, her own lawyer. The psychologists did not testify in the criminal trial, but one of them reportedly told Nathan years later that what he did was "a lot like reverse brainwashing."[156] There is apparently no tape recording of that statement; nor have any written notes ever been referenced by Nathan.

The reason the defense hired these psychologists has been lost in the rush to condemn them. Ileana had been subject to physical threats and psychological control from Frank Fuster. Indeed, Dr. Charles B. Mutter, the psychiatrist who examined Ileana for the court several times between July and November 1985, provided a cogent explanation: "although she played a role in [the abuse], this was not a role of volition, but the role of a terrorized human being."[157]

It also been argued that her guilty plea was "hardly a definitive admission" because of something she said in court the day of her guilty plea.[158] This claim is based on an inaccurate and misleading "quote." Here is a precise quotation from the court proceedings; the words in bold were left out of the "excerpt" that has been reproduced by Nathan, Nathan and Snedeker, and Robert Rosenthal.[159]

> THE DEFENDANT: Judge, I would like you to know that I am pleading guilty, not because I feel guilty, but because I think—I think it's in the best interest. It's the best for my own interest and for the children and for the Court and all the people that are working on the case, but I am not pleading guilty because I feel guilty or because I think I have a criminal mind.
>
> THE COURT: All right.
>
> THE DEFENDANT: **There were circumstances and that—I was raped at sixteen. I was taken away from my home and my school. My attorney said that I am an unlucky person but** I just want you to know that I am pleading guilty not because I feel guilty or that I know I am, that I am guilty. I am inn ocent of all those charges. I wouldn't have done anything to harm those children. I have never done anything in my life. **I have never seen such a case in my life before. I wasn't raised in any environment like it.** I am innocent. I am just doing it— I am pleading guilty you get all of this over **and I think it's best for the parents and everyone.**[160]

What Ileana Fuster said was offered as a reason for a lenient sentence. Not only have Nathan and others omitted the gist of her statement ("there were circumstances," "I was raped"), they have also omitted any reference to what came before and after it. The complete transcript of the proceedings on that day demonstrates that Ileana Fuster first affirmed she was satisfied with her legal representation, she understood the charges, she knew the constitutional rights she was giving up by pleading guilty, *she had not been coerced or promised anything*, she understood exactly what she was doing, she knew she could be sentenced to as much as life in prison, and she was entering the plea because she felt it was in her best interest.[161]

In 1994, years after Ileana had finished her sentence, returned to Honduras, and changed her last name back to Flores, Frank Fuster's lawyers announced she had retracted her trial testimony. The retraction was recorded in Honduras by a defense lawyer named Arthur Cohen, who was working for Frank. It is unclear what Cohen told Ileana Flores that convinced her to attend this meeting. There was no representative for the prosecution present; nor did Flores have her own legal counsel. Nevertheless, Fuster's defense team convinced a federal judge to schedule an evidentiary hearing on the basis of the statement produced by Cohen. On close reading, the statement does not support the claims that have been made about it. First, it is replete with equivocal answers, even though Peter Boyer would later call it an "unequivocal" retraction. Second, Ileana contradicted some of the most vivid claims made about her pre-trial incarceration. For example, she specifically says that she was *not* held naked, contradicting a key assertion made by Nathan, Cockburn, and others who insist that her original confession was coerced. Third, Cohen appears throughout the interview to be looking for evidence to support a preexisting conclusion, and he actively resists answers that incriminate Frank Fuster.[162]

The hearing at which this "new evidence" would have been subject to cross-examination never took place, even though the judge allowed testimony to be taken by satellite from Honduras. As the defense euphemistically put it, Ileana Flores was "unavailable to provide testimony to the court."[163] This is not true. She was available, but she was apparently not planning to say what the defense wanted to hear. She had retracted her so-called retraction. Rev. Watson, who visited Ileana Fuster regularly in prison in Florida, went to see her in Honduras after the stories of her "retraction" surfaced in the Miami media. He returned with a letter signed by Ileana Flores stating she was pressured by Cohen.[164] Watson later testified that Ileana Fuster told him "she was pressured to give statements and that she realized that what she had done was wrong."[165]

Years later, Ileana Flores provided another would-be retraction; this time it was for the television program *Frontline*. As before, the statement was made without any adversarial cross-examination. Ileana had apparently returned to the United States without proper documentation, and as *Frontline* acknowledged, the only way she could ever stay in the country legally would be if somehow her own conviction were overturned.[166] The statement she provided was a last-ditch effort to obtain legal permission to stay in the country. It did not work.

Whitewashing Frank Fuster

Frank Fuster's prior record—which included a recent conviction for child molestation—was undoubtedly one of the most damning pieces of evidence in the court of public opinion. Although for most people it is nearly impossible to imagine an adult having the *inclination* to sexually abuse a child, it is much easier to imagine someone previously convicted of child molestation having such inclinations. This is probably why even critics of the conviction have allowed that some kind of abuse "probably happened" to some of the children at Country Walk.[167] But the jury was never told about the prior conviction, since such information would be considered too prejudicial.

Those endorsing the witch-hunt narrative, however, have gone to considerable lengths to minimize the relevance and the substance of Fuster's prior record. One approach is to claim that his record actually made him a target. "He thought that all was behind him," *Frontline* intoned in their program called *Did Daddy Do It?* "But once word of Frank's record flashed through the neighborhood it was only a matter of time," their narrative continued. "The crusade had the perfect defendant—an ex-con, a convicted child molester."[168] The idea that his status as an ex-con left him targeted for arrest is contradicted by the basic chronology of the case. The two separate incidents that formed the origins of the case—Donald Menninger's spontaneous utterance in April and John St. Lorenzo's appearance of being drugged in late July—both happened *before* anyone was aware of Fuster's criminal record. Emma St. Lorenzo triggered the investigation without the slightest idea about Fuster's record.

Another approach to minimizing Fuster's criminal record has been to minimize or deny the underlying facts of his prior convictions. *Frontline* did that when it reported, without any skepticism, that Fuster's first-degree manslaughter conviction years earlier stemmed from "an accident."[169] His child molestation conviction has also been minimized in the witch-hunt narrative. Author Mark Pendergrast virtually exonerated Fuster of those charges, declaring him to be innocent on the basis of a single interview—with Frank Fuster.[170] Neither of those claims squares with reality. There would be little or no reason to elaborate on these points if the effort to rehabilitate Fuster were not so persistent, and the willingness to accept his dubious denials without any apparent skepticism were not so widespread.

First, the manslaughter charge. Fuster was arrested on January 16, 1969, when a police officer witnessed him shoot a man to death with a rifle after a minor motor-vehicle accident in the Bronx. Fuster was charged with two felonies: manslaughter and reckless endangerment for the "depraved indifference to life" that he demonstrated when pointing his loaded rifle *at the off-duty officer* who arrested him. He eventually pleaded guilty to first-degree manslaughter and served four years of a ten-year sentence. Since then, Fuster has provided differing accounts of the incident—none consistent with official records. In all of his accounts, he bears no responsibility for his actions, even though he pleaded guilty to first-degree manslaughter.[171] When *Frontline* interviewed Fuster in prison in

2001, he described the shooting as "an accident." *Frontline* correspondents Michael Kirk and Peter Boyer accepted and repeated his version without a hint of skepticism, or, apparently, any original research.[172]

The revisionist history of the Country Walk case also includes a whitewashed version of Fuster's prior conviction for child molestation. The case began with the allegations of a nine-year-old girl who told her mother, immediately after the fact, that he had fondled her breasts and genitals through her clothing while he was driving her to her home. Fuster was arrested on September 21, 1981, for lewd and lascivious assault on a minor. At his jury trial in 1982, the girl testified in detail, and she sustained a lengthy cross-examination. Fuster did not take the stand. The jury found the girl credible and convicted Fuster of lewd and lascivious conduct.

The facts of the case have since been distorted beyond recognition by Fuster and his supporters. But a careful examination of his statements to the police officer who arrested him in 1981 reveals the behavior of someone seeking to rationalize sexual contact with a child. Fuster confirmed, but never explained, that he entered the van *through the passenger side*. That is how, according to Fuster, "he may have brushed up against" the nine-year-old girl.[173] Fuster also admitted "that he asked her to sit with him because he was sleepy and wanted someone to talk to and possibly have someone to grab the wheel if he fell asleep." Fuster even acknowledged putting his arms around the girl who *he had made sit on his lap*. Fuster said this was to "keep her from falling off the seat."[174]

As for Fuster's "vehement denial" and the lie detector test he supposedly passed, one can only observe that he did not avail himself of the opportunity to take the stand and try to explain the statements he made to the arresting officer.[175] And there is no evidence in the court file of a lie detector test. But Fuster's MMPI tests (personality tests) *were* revealed through the court proceedings, and they found him to be "compulsive and paranoid" with a "strong need to see himself as extremely virtuous."[176] Remarkably, Fuster has since admitted even more clearly that he committed the basic acts charged in the 1981 case. At one point in his rambling statement at the end of his parole violation hearing in 1985, he demonstrated: "This is how *I* touch her chest area. I don't see any sexual movement here. *I* also touch her in her vagina area. That's it. That was the whole case."[177] One wonders whether Mark Pendergrast and others, who have accepted Fuster's subsequent protestations of innocence, are aware that he admitted in court that in the course of driving a nine-year-old girl home he touched both her "chest area" and her "vagina area."[178]

This is not the full extent of Fuster's criminal record. Police records also indicate that during the investigation of the 1981 child molestation case, Fuster indicated that he had been a suspect in an alleged rape with a girl he had picked up from Central Shopping Center. He confessed to having had intercourse with

her.[179] She was a "very beautiful but demented young woman," according to
Fuster.[180] The case was not prosecuted. During her pre-trial detention, Ileana
Fuster told three separate adults about the violence and abuse she endured at
Frank's hands. There is evidence she was beaten and that she was scared to death
of him, as was his previous wife.[181] Frank was observed striking Ileana in the face
at a Halloween party, and he once pulled a gun on Ileana's stepfather. There was
also evidence that it was his rape of Ileana that led to their marriage. That disclosure predated, by at least two months, the involvement of the psychologists who
the witch-hunt narrative blames for all of the incriminatory statements Ileana
later made in court.[182]

In short, what *Frontline* described as a "fairy tale love story" was much closer
to a horror story from the first day they met. Their marriage was, according to
numerous accounts, precipitated by a rape when Ileana was barely sixteen years
old, and it was punctuated by documented violence and the sexual assault of at
least one minor. None of those things prove that Frank Fuster was guilty of the
Country Walk charges, of course. But the minimization and denial of his criminal record in the witch-hunt narrative is noteworthy. Given Fuster's violent and
dishonest history, one wonders how anyone could cite his denials in the Country
Walk case with utter credulity and without any acknowledgment of the considerable evidence to the contrary.

Manufacturing "Fantastic" Taint

There has been a curious evolution in the argument that "fantastic claims" characterized the Country Walk case. The case was tagged as having several fantastic
elements by Charlier and Downing and others. They included allegations about
feces, masks, and a dead bird. But a close examination of the trial transcript and
related exhibits makes it clear that Fuster actually *had* a perverse interest in excrement, that he owned scary masks and used them to scare children (and
adults), and that he had shown the children a dead bird. Those claims quietly
disappeared from the witch-hunt narrative without any acknowledgment of
their basis in fact.

Proponents of the narrative did not admit that the fantastic elements used to
discredit the case in the 1980s had been proven to be true—and, by implication,
that such things might be true in other cases discredited on the same basis. Instead, the argument shifted and new claims about fantastic elements appeared—
ones that, curiously, were never raised by the defense in the original trial. Ceci
and Bruck claimed in 1993 that "interweaved among the credible allegations" in
the Country Walk case "were ones that seemed fabulous, such as riding on sharks
and eating the head of another person."[183] The authors did not provide specific
citations for either of these claims, let alone excerpts from any relevant

interviews. Indeed, the only source that directly related to the Country Walk case in their 1993 article was Jan Hollingsworth's book, which does not support this claim. Ceci and Bruck made essentially the same claim in their 1995 book, *Jeopardy in the Courtroom*. Immediately after a discussion of satanic and ritualistic abuse—defined in the most extreme terms as cult activities that include witchcraft or animal sacrifice—the authors asserted that the Country Walk case was "characterized by these types of allegations."[184] The authors' only elaboration of this claim, however, makes no reference to witchcraft or animal sacrifice. Rather, the language is almost precisely the same as their 1993 article: "Interleaved among the children's plausible allegations were fabulous ones, such as riding on sharks and eating the head of another person."[185] But the transcripts of the interviews in the Country Walk case do not bear out these claims; there are very few such references to these items and those instances are explainable, not "fabulous."

"Riding on Sharks"

There are approximately eighty hours of interview tapes in the Country Walk case, involving upwards of twenty-seven children. From reading Ceci and Bruck's claim, one would think that these interviews would be filled with references to riding sharks and eating heads. But a full-text search of the interviews that have been transcribed and digitized by Professor James Wood finds only one reference to sharks. It is from Jason Cramer on August 28. The word appears in a statement where the boy was discussing Jacques Cousteau and television programs about whales and sharks. A manual examination of the entire trial transcript, which includes transcriptions of thirty-three videotapes, contains only one other reference to a shark, in an interview with Brian Arrigan, a three-year-old who was not involved in any of the individual named charges. The exchange is nothing more than a simple conversation with a child who is interested in a stuffed- animal shark in the interview room.[186] There is nothing fabulous about these statements; nor are they distributed throughout the children's statements.

"Eating the Head of Another Person"

Ceci and Bruck's other claim about fabulous statements in the Country Walk case involves "eating the head of another person." Again, a full-text search of the interviews compiled by Wood finds no reference to "eating the head" of anything, including a person. There are a few references to either the "cut off your head game" or the "who's gonna lose their head" game. Here is how Jessie Lipton described the game in her January interview:

A: They played cut your head off.

Q: Cut your head off. Can you show me how they did that.

A: They would ask us, "Do you want a cupcake?" and if you said yes, then he would cut your head off.

Q: Did he really cut, cut off heads, or pretend?

A: He would (inaudible) put the knife to your neck.

Laurie Braga then asked further questions to ascertain precisely what the child was saying:

Q: Well, now this a little hard for me to understand. Help me understand, cuz remember I wasn't there so I don't know anything other than what you tell me, okay. You said, they would say, "do you want a cup cake," okay. And if you said yes, then he would hold a knife to your throat? Is that, is that what you said?

A: Yes.

Q: Okay. But if you said yes, and then you wouldn't eat it, that's what I . . .

A: No.

Q: No. Why would he hold a knife to your throat if you said yes you want a cup cake?

A: Cuz is part of the game he was playing.

Q: Is part of the game. Do you think he was trying to scare you?

A: Yes.

Q: Yeah. Did he ever say that he hurt you if you told?

A: Yes.

Q: Can you tell me about that?

A: I said I was going to tell my mom.

Q: Um hum.

A: And, then he said "I'm going to cut your head off."[187]

She never said anything about *eating* the head of another person; rather, she was describing a game that Fuster played apparently to scare the children. Jason Cramer made similar statements in his first interview on August 9.

It remains unclear how Ceci and Bruck came to make the claim about "eating the head of another person." What still requires explanation is why Ceci and Bruck inflated a few small, inaccurate references—one to the cut off your head game, and the other to riding a shark—into the claim that implausible and so-called fabulous claims were interwoven into the statements of "the children" in the Country Walk case.

Suggesting Child Suggestibility

The Country Walk case is one of six "case studies" in Ceci and Bruck's book *Jeopardy in the Courtroom: A Scientific Analysis of Children's Testimony*. Only the Michaels case is cited more often throughout the book. In short, the case became a central part of the argument that children are more suggestible than previously recognized and that adults charged with such crimes are in jeopardy. This is surprising since Ceci and Bruck's review article in *Psychological Bulletin* in 1993 suggested that the Country Walk case was different from the Michaels case. Relying on an excerpt from Hollingsworth's book, they interpreted Jason's consistent replies in response to Jeffrey Samek's "angry and accusatory" questions as evidence that "young children are apparently capable of accurately reporting what they witness at least some of the time." There was a strong hint in the article, however, that Ceci and Bruck were reevaluating their position before the article was published. A footnote indicates that since writing the section about Jason's veracity, "we have learned of arguments" that cast doubt on Ileana Fuster's confession. They put the word *confession* in quotes—and cited Debbie Nathan's article, which had not yet appeared in Ralph Underwager's journal.[188] But by the time *Jeopardy in the Courtroom* was published, Ceci and Bruck were citing the Country Walk case as evidence of many arguments in their book. The case plays such an important role in the book that these arguments merit close attention.

The claim that the children should not be believed was the core of the defense at the original trial. Lee Coleman, the expert for the defense, argued that the children had all been "brainwashed." His testimony was discredited on a number of grounds, among them that it lacked a solid foundation in the scientific literature. Coleman had never done any original research on the issue. More problematic, he appeared unfamiliar with the relevant scientific literature of the day. In Coleman's defense, there was not much literature in 1985 on the suggestibility of children. Maggie Bruck argued years later that Coleman had "provided insightful testimony" that was hampered only by the lack of scientific studies to support it.[189] But the lack of scientific literature was only one of his problems. When the case is analyzed systematically, it is clear that the charges stemmed almost completely from the children who were interviewed at the State Attorney's Office in the first two days of the investigation. More than seventy-five percent of the individual charges in the case were filed in connection with children interviewed the first four days of the investigation. And Coleman had virtually nothing to say about those interviews.

Years later, Maggie Bruck filed a written declaration in support of Frank Fuster's federal appeal. She claimed that Coleman "had the intellectual tools—i.e., intuition—to detect that certain suggestive questioning could shape the child's response" but that no one could provide "scientific data on the actual *impact of* suggestive questioning techniques."[190] The phrase "actual impact" refers to the findings of laboratory experiments, not the particular circumstances of individual children and interviews in the Country Walk case. Indeed, Ceci and Bruck's work has the same flaws that Lee Coleman's did at trial. They never conducted a systematic analysis of the interviews in the Country Walk case, notwithstanding the subtitle of their book (a scientific analysis of children's testimony).[191] Even more surprising, Bruck did not conduct a complete analysis of the interviews and related evidence in preparing her detailed affidavit for Frank Fuster's federal court appeal. Her declaration in federal court listed the items she reviewed, and the list did not include some of the earliest and most important interviews. Bruck did not review the very first interview with Jason Cramer, even though Ceci and Bruck relied heavily on a single sentence from this very interview for their claim that fantastic statements were interleaved among the children's statements. (This is one of the interviews that includes a statement about the "cut off your head" game.) Bruck also neglected to review either of the interviews with Donald Menninger, whose statement in the spring of 1984 caused his mother to remove him from babysitting service and warn her friend. Instead, she took the same approach contained in *Jeopardy in the Courtroom*: citing passages from interviews that she found objectionable without any apparent attention to who was being interviewed, when the interview occurred in the course of the investigation, and what relationship, if any, the interview had on the actual charges in the case. What is lost as a result is any sense of the *actual impact* or representativeness of these disembodied snippets.

Picking and choosing brief snippets of disparate interviews overlooks how and when the claims emerged. The approach also overlooks the corroborating behavioral and medical evidence. It ignores all of the evidence from parents about strange observations at the Fusters, including the numerous independent decisions of various families to take children out of the Fusters' care before August 1984. It also paints a misleading picture of the interview sequence, relying on words like "repetitive," instead of doing actual analysis. A few simple calculations prove the point. The Bragas conducted a total of forty-six interviews with twenty-seven children, or fewer than two per child.[192] Focusing only on the children whose statements formed the basis for individual charges, there were twenty-four total interviews involving eight children. The most important children in the case, in other words, were interviewed an average of three times. A few were interviewed more, and others were interviewed less. These numbers alone belie the claims about highly repetitive interviewing. But the arguments in *Jeopardy in the Courtroom* have been endorsed in so many academic publications that it is worth considering the snippets they cite, and the children they overlook, in more detail.

Irrelevant and Unrepresentative Snippets

One problem with Ceci and Bruck's analysis is that it relies on children who were peripheral to the case to make arguments about children who were central to the case. Four children beyond Noel Fuster account for the seven unidentified snippets from the Country Walk cases that appear in *Jeopardy in the Court-room*.[193] Because the children are never identified in any way, it is not clear to the reader that one child, Jessie Lipton, is the same child quoted four times.[194] It is also not clear that two of the four children had little or nothing to do with the charges in the case. For example, an interview with Ariel Thomas is cited as evidence of the investigators "trying to get the children to disclose by telling them what other children allegedly reported."[195] The authors cite a brief exchange where the interviewer does, in fact, mention things that the girl's sister said. But was this interview actually relevant to the case, and more to the point, was it representative of interviews with "the children"? The answer to both questions is no. No charges were brought in connection with this girl; she was not even named in a group charge. One might assume that if there had been examples of this problem among the children with named charges, Ceci and Bruck would have cited them.

Similarly, Ceci and Bruck use a fairly long excerpt from an interview with Brian Arrigan to demonstrate what they interpret as "the interviewers' pursuit of a single hypothesis that abuse had occurred that involved feeding children poison or drugs and playing games in the nude."[196] In this example, the interviewers ask, "When they gave you the stuff to drink, did you feel dizzy?" Ceci and Bruck note that "drinks were not mentioned previously in the interview." They are correct. And in a perfect interview one would never include a question like that without some prior statement from the child. But they are incorrect that this example is representative of the interviews or that it had any actual impact on the charges in the case. Brian Arrigan, three years old at the time, was clearly too young to be a witness in the case. He was never named in any of the individual charges, and no charges were ever brought in connection with allegedly drugged drinks. Although Frank Fuster was never charged with drugging the children—that is impossible to prove after the fact without forensic evidence—there was considerable evidence to suggest he had done so.

The Most Frequently Criticized Children

One child in the Country Walk case has been the focus of most of the criticisms of the case. This girl, Jessie Lipton, was the only child cited at length in Nathan's long article about the case, she was focus of the snippets in Rosenthal's article, and she is the primary child cited in Ceci and Bruck's book. The reason she is the focus of case critics is that she denied any abuse in her first interview with the Bragas, and then months later indicated she had been sexually abused by the Fusters. Bruck stated in her federal court affidavit that this "pattern has raised the most concerns regarding allegations of abuse." She went on to make the unequivocal claim that "this pattern of disclosure characterizes the child witnesses in *Fuster*."[197] In fact, Jessie Lipton is *the only child whose statements fit this pattern*.

One fact that has been lost in the use of out-of-context snippets is that Jessie Lipton attended the Fusters' only twice. When she was interviewed in August, then, it had been three months since she last attended. This explains a statement that Bruck found odd: that the girl referred to the Fusters as "strangers."[198] Given her brief attendance at Country Walk, what would have been truly odd is if she had claimed to know them well. The interview has also been criticized for references made to statements by other children. "Some of the children said that they were acting like they were monsters and they wore these masks and scared them," Laurie Braga said at one point. "Is that true? Do you know?" the girl replied. Laurie Braga then said: "I'm not sure, but some of the children said so, and I believe the children because I don't think children make up stories like that. Do you?" The stories about the masks were not "made up" and the interviewer began her answer with "I'm not sure"; nevertheless this interview contained too many references to what other children had said. Portions of this interview became the most significant arguments against the interviews in general. But the interview did not result in any disclosures, and the portions that have been cited repeatedly were not representative of the earlier interviews that were the basis for almost all of the charges in the case. Also, the evidence from Noel Fuster and several adults establishes that the masks *were* real; they were not something conjured up by the interviewers.

It is also important to note that the state would have gone ahead without any charges connected to Jessie Lipton had her parents not requested that she be interviewed in January. The reason for the request, according to her parents, was that Jessie had "started talking." There was some debate in the State Attorney's Office about whether to conduct the interview. This indicates that, contrary to various claims, the interviewers did not set out to extract incriminating statements through multiple interviews. They did not initiate this interview and were reluctant to conduct it for reasons that seem prescient given the evolution of the witch-hunt narrative.

What the girl said in January corroborated statements made by Jason Cramer months earlier, particularly with regard to the "cut off your head" game. Those statements came in response to open-ended questions. Critics of the case have argued that the girl's parents pressured her into making these statements. It is impossible to assess the parental pressure claim without at least interviewing the parents. But even allowing for the possibility that one might reach a different conclusion than the jury did, it is clear that Jessie Lipton's circumstances are different from those of all of the other important children in the case. Yet she is frequently cited in various critiques of the case, and the claim is often made that her interview was typical or representative of all of the others.

Becky Taylor is the only other child in the case with named charges who denied any abuse in the first investigative interview.[199] But she had already told Cathleen McGinnis at Jackson Memorial Hospital, when asked if she had ever seen a grown man's penis, that she had seen "her daddy's and Frank's." Her denials in the first interview with Bragas were filled with answers such as "I don't want you to know," "I hate the question," and "I have a hard time telling." Even so, she made references in her first interview to masks and snakes. She also made an ambiguous statement about the "pee pee game."[200]

There is no doubt Becky Taylor was the most avoidant and anxious child in the case. Her mother testified that when Detective Meznarich tried to interview Becky in early August "she started running around the room" as soon as Frank Fuster's name was mentioned. She was "extremely hostile, anxious" and then hit her mother. Dr. Hicks reported that at Jackson Memorial Hospital the girl was "totally uncooperative" and yelled "give me my panties" when the doctor tried to examine her.

Among the many relevant contextual facts that are never mentioned in the witch-hunt narrative about this child are these: no other child in the case had such strong reactions to being interviewed in the case. No other child spent as much time at the Fusters' as she did, either. (She was there weekdays, one weekday evening, and some Saturdays.) She even went on a beach trip with the Fusters. Both Jason Cramer and Tom Leventhal had already said things about her with her clothes off at the Fusters'; and Betsy Leventhal had already told Meznarich about observing Becky once at the Fusters' wearing only a shirt. Ileana "quickly grabbed a towel, wrapped it around her," and told a story, which turned out not to be true, about the girl's mother having forgotten to bring an extra diaper. As the girl's mother later testified, Becky was no longer wearing diapers.[201] There were, in short, myriad reasons to think Becky Taylor might have been abused.

Her August 30 interview was more substantive, but it was also confusing in places and she was still quite avoidant at times. The girl made more statements about the "real snake" and the masks. She also said that Joshua and Tom—the two boys who had mentioned seeing her naked at the Fusters'—had small penises. Critics have emphasized the admittedly leading questions that appear in her interviews, but they have never mentioned the fact that before this girl ever met the Bragas she told a nurse she had seen Frank Fuster's penis and she described the penis of boys who attended the babysitting service. Ileana Fuster later said two words that speak volumes about Becky's behavior: she said that Becky was "Frank's favorite."[202]

Key Children, Overlooked or Downplayed

What is most striking about the critiques by Ceci and Bruck in 1995 is that they overlook the most important statements in the case. Bruck told the federal court that "it is of primary importance to understand the evolution of the child's reports." But her analysis of the case does not follow this advice. The two most important children in the case were Jason Cramer, who made extensive statements on the first day he was interviewed, and Donald Menninger, whose spontaneous utterance in April became the basis for the eventual civil suits against the Arvida Corporation, which employed the boy's father as a property manager at Country Walk. An interview tape of Donald Menninger was the only one played in the parole violation hearing that assured Frank Fuster of a fifteen-year prison term before his criminal trial began. Yet, none of the snippets in *Jeopardy in the Courtroom* are from Donald Menninger or Jason Cramer.

Bruck, who reviewed dozens of interviews and depositions in preparation for her affidavit for the defense, did not review either one of Donald's interviews, both of which were conducted in August 1984.[203] In a systematic analysis of the case—from first disclosure onward in chronological order—Donald is clearly one of the most important children in the case. In the McMartin case, for example, where the mother of the first child in the case became mentally unstable, the index child was the focus of most critiques. In the Country Walk case, however, the index child's mother was the opposite. She was not only lucid but had a clear motive to *deny* that there was abuse. Such a denial would help her husband's defense in the multimillion-dollar civil suits against Arvida and Disney. This is presumably why she was called as a witness for the defense. But Menninger indicated in her testimony that she thought her son *had* been sexually abused by the Fusters. It was perhaps the most powerful evidence for the state. Ignoring this boy's statements, along with his mother's actions in April and her testimony at trial, is an oversight that is difficult to understand.

The most important witness at trial was Jason Cramer. The boy was extremely articulate, and he had made extensive disclosures on August 9, the first day of interviews by the Bragas. The defense clearly saw this boy as the linchpin of the state's case. This is presumably why Samek set out to "break him" in deposition. But the boy withstood a remarkable onslaught by the defense lawyer, who directly accused him of lying. Jason also resisted a clever attempt to trip him up at trial. After Jason testified about the dead bird, Samek asked him, "What about the time they killed the cat?" "They didn't kill the cat," he replied, resisting the temptation to embellish his testimony or to incorporate a false suggestion.[204]

Bruck indicated she reviewed Jason Cramer's most substantive interview on August 9. She claimed she was unable to review his earlier interview that day because of "technical difficulties." But the original tape of the interview was not defective; a technical problem was mentioned in the trial transcript, but it had to do with the ability of the *court reporter* to hear the tape. This issue was discussed on the record, and it is clear that the jury could hear the tape. This is confirmed by the fact that Jan Hollingsworth, who heard the tape in court, quoted from the interview at length in her book. In order to remove all doubt about the integrity of the audio track of this tape, I arranged to have the original played under the supervision of the State Attorney's Office while a stenographer, from the same court reporting firm that transcribed the original trial, transcribed the tape. This transcript bears out the Hollingsworth description. In short, Bruck could have reviewed this tape; instead, she dropped the matter—involving possibly the most important interview in the case—because the tape was not transcribed into the court record. Bruck's lengthy affidavit, with 180 numbered paragraphs, does not contain a single specific criticism of the August 9 interview that she *did* review. She offered one major criticism pertaining to Jason Cramer: she claimed he was induced to talk by "a bag of toys" that the Bragas gave him on August 10.[205]

The interaction that she cites does not support this claim. First, there are no statements to the effect of "we'll give you this if you say something." To the contrary, Jason had already made extensive statements in two sessions on August 9. He came back on Friday the tenth for a brief interview that helped provide the basis for the search warrant of the Fuster house. At the end of the interview, Joseph Braga was talking about some toys. The Bragas had brought a bag of toys to help put the children at ease and to use in rapport building. Jason then said, referring to the bag of toys, "Could I have this?" Joseph Braga responded:

> I need that to show to other kids but what I can give you is let me find it here. You hold the bag. There is a whole bunch of games in there. Here (inaudible).[206]

It is not clear from the transcript what "it"—as in, "let me find it"—means. But from the transcript alone, it is clear that it is *not* the bag of toys. Joseph Braga made this clear when he said "I need that to show to other kids." A review of the videotape indicates the toy was more like the prize in a Cracker Jack box. It was not a "bag of toys." Bruck relied on the "bag of toys" argument to impugn Jason's additional interview on August 13. But the trinket he took with him could not possibly have affected Jason's testimony on the tenth (or the ninth, of course) because it occurred at the very end of the interview. The idea that this trinket alone taints the entire statement of August 13 is both exaggerated and unimportant. In the interviews that Bruck did not review from August 9, the boy gave extensive details that were later corroborated in a variety of ways.

Maligning the Bragas

The Bragas have been the source of relentless criticism in the witch-hunt narrative. The PBS program *Frontline* called them "the Pied Pipers of child abuse in Miami." The attacks on their credibility actually began in 1985 when Stephen Dinerstein, the private investigator employed by Frank Fuster's lawyer, swore that Joseph Braga was a "fraud" and an "impostor."[207] Dinerstein claimed that "the real Joseph Braga" had died years earlier. This provided Dr. Braga with a Mark Twain moment, where he appeared in court and assured the judge that the rumors of his demise were greatly exaggerated. The criticisms of the Bragas intensified when the revisionist view of the case emerged in 1993. There are two related criticisms in the narrative: first, that the Bragas misstated their credentials and were not actually qualified to interview children, and second, that they were inherently biased toward finding sexual abuse.

The criticisms of the Bragas' credentials that have been lodged since 1993 are relentless. Rael Jean Isaac, writing in the *National Review*, called them "self-styled" experts.[208] Robert Rosenthal, writing in *Penthouse* magazine, said "their real expertise" was in "coercing youngsters to talk about sex."[209] Much has also been made of the fact that they were not *licensed* psychologists, although licensing is only necessary to open a private practice (something the Bragas did not do). There were even several ethics complaints filed with the American Psychological Association—almost ten years after the case was over—claiming that the Bragas had misrepresented their credentials. On close examination, none of these claims stood up to scrutiny.

The Bragas both have doctorates relevant to child development. They are among the most highly educated people to interview children in any of the infamous day-care abuse cases of the 1980s. Joseph Braga's doctorate is from the School of Education at Boston University, where his major field was called foundations/educational psychology. His dissertation, an evaluation of an early admissions program in the Lexington, Massachusetts, public schools, is cataloged under the subject heading "Educational Psychology." After completing his doctorate, he was hired as an assistant professor at Boston University, where he taught graduate courses in educational psychology. Laurie Braga's doctorate is from the Graduate School at Northwestern University, where her major field was learning disabilities. Her dissertation involved the development and assessment of a test analysis system for "describing intra-child variables in learning disabled preschool children."[210] Before moving to Miami, the Bragas coauthored four books related to child development: *Child Development and Early Childhood Education* (1973), *Growing with Children: The Early Childhood Years* (1974), *Learning and Growing: A Guide to Child Development* (1975), and *Children and Adults: Activities for Growing Together* (1976). They were also the editors of two series of books for Prentice-Hall, one on human development and the other on the psychology of living.

None of the writers who have challenged the Bragas' credentials has ever engaged the substance of these books. If the Bragas were truly unqualified in the field of child development, these books would presumably be filled with passages demonstrating their incompetence. But not a single passage from any of these books has ever been quoted in support of the claim that the Bragas are unqualified in the areas about which they have written so much.

Instead, there has been a behind-the-scenes effort to damage their reputation through the filing of baseless ethics complaints with the American Psychological Association. Debbie Nathan, the primary writer who has attacked the Country Walk conviction in 1993, initiated this process with a letter to the Ethics Office of the American Psychological Association (APA) exactly one month after Janet Reno was nominated for U.S. attorney general. Nathan stated that her "fact checking" of the Bragas' credentials had revealed that Laurie Braga's Ph.D. was actually in the field of "speech," not learning disabilities. The title page of Laurie Braga's dissertation, which is widely available through interlibrary loan, clearly states that her field of study was, in fact, learning disabilities. An investigator for the APA contacted Northwestern University and received a letter confirming that Laurie Braga's doctorate was in learning disabilities. The APA notified Nathan that it was closing the matter in a letter noting that "this was never a formal ethics case."[211] This is because Nathan did not file a formal complaint. Perhaps she was reticent to take a formal action that would reveal her to be an activist in a story that she claimed to be covering journalistically.[212]

Any presumption of Nathan's impartiality is contradicted by what she then proceeded to do. Working with Frank Fuster's defense lawyer, Robert Rosenthal, Nathan helped orchestrate a behind-the-scenes effort to have a formal ethics complaint filed against Laurie Braga. The effort was timed to coincide with the filing of Frank Fuster's federal habeas corpus appeal. The formal complaint was filed by James Wood, a psychology professor at the University of Texas–El Paso.[213] Wood acknowledged in his complaint that he had never met the Bragas or even tried to contact them, although the APA Ethics Code anticipates such action before filing an ethics complaint.[214] Wood's complaint against Laurie Braga was filed on February 20, 1995 (almost ten years after the Country Walk case had ended). Wood made precisely the same claim Nathan had made earlier: that Laurie Braga had misrepresented her credentials because her doctorate "was in speech" and not in learning disabilities.[215] Wood filed some supplemental materials three months later. Some of those documents were faxed from Rosenthal to Nathan, as indicated by the phone numbers on the faxes.[216]

The supplemental materials filed by Wood included a new and rather stunning claim: that Laurie Braga had been publicly criticized for possible unethical behavior "by the parents of children whom she interviewed in a famous sexual abuse case." To support this charge, Wood attached a 1985 article from the *Miami Herald* that was published three weeks before Frank Fuster's trial began. Curiously, the fifth paragraph in that story directly contradicts Wood's claim:

> People tend to either love them or hate them. Among those in the pro-Braga camp are the child witnesses and parents in the case. Detractors include defense attorneys, a few local psychologists and a former fund-raiser for their nonprofit National Children's Foundation.[217]

Later, under the subheading "Parents' Praise," the article continues: "For their part, the parents of the alleged victims in the Country Walk case are unanimous in their praise of the Bragas." Since Wood submitted nothing else in support of his charge about the parents of the children interviewed by Laurie Braga, it is difficult to imagine on what basis he decided to level this meritless charge.

The APA dismissed his complaint. On August 4, 1995, Professor Wood filed *another* complaint—this time against Joseph Braga. That complaint revived the old charge that Braga had somehow misrepresented the nature of *his* doctorate. This complaint was also ultimately dismissed as baseless. The story of these complaints has never before been made public. The story is noteworthy because it demonstrates the lengths to which some people were willing to go in order to try to discredit the Bragas, regardless of the facts.

The Bragas were also assailed as having a strong predisposition for "finding" sexual abuse in children. "Crucial to the Bragas' technique was their refusal to accept a child's denial of abuse," Rosenthal claimed.[218] It is difficult to square those claims with a systematic view of the Country Walk case. The pattern of interviews and charges in the case demonstrates that almost all of the charges emanated from the children interviewed earliest in the case, when the Bragas knew the least about the allegations. In later interviews, when there is no question the Bragas had concluded that some children *had* been sexually abused at the Fusters, there were few children added to the case. This is hardly what one would expect if there were a powerful "interviewer bias" at work. Indeed, in the Kelly Michaels case, Lou Fonolleras ultimately exhibited a bias toward finding abuse when he "substantiated" findings of abuse on all fifty-one children interviewed, even those who specifically denied any kind of abuse. The Bragas did no such thing in the Country Walk case.

Beyond the Country Walk case, the Bragas further demonstrated a complex view of accusations involving child sexual abuse. They did not always support prosecution; nor did they always find a child's statements about sexual abuse to be trustworthy. Not only did they distinguish carefully among children in the Country Walk case, they also recommended *against* prosecution in other cases during the same time period. Although Peter Boyer claimed on *Frontline* that a pro-prosecution "fever gripped Miami" at the time, the fact is that the Bragas recommended *against* prosecution in a day-care case that arose at virtually the same time as Country Walk. In the Hazel Crawford Day Care, their recommendation against prosecution came over the strong objection of parents.[219] Moreover, the Bragas did not appear exclusively for the prosecution in these cases. Laurie Braga testified for the defense in a child sexual-abuse case in August 1985. An article about her testimony appeared in the *Miami Herald* the same week as the article that James Wood appended to his ethics complaint.[220] These facts contradict the claims of extreme pro-prosecution bias that have been lodged against the Bragas.

Conclusion

Critics of the Country Walk case invoke the concept of "confirmation bias" to explain the allegations in the case. Peter Boyer quoted Professor Ceci saying that confirmation bias is "often exhibited by child advocates whose willingness to believe in child abuse hinders objective analysis."[221] This argument seems to carry a disturbing implication: that what Ceci calls "objective analysis" can only be done by people who are not "hindered" by the "willingness to believe in child abuse." Whether or not this is the intended implication of Ceci's statement, it is clear that those who are *not* willing to believe in child abuse are also hindered in their ability to analyze abuse allegations. They are unlikely to recognize child abuse even in cases where the evidence is overwhelming. When this occurs, "disconfirmation bias" is at work.

The evolution of the Country Walk case—from model prosecution to the revisionist view expressed by Nathan, Ceci and Bruck, and others—demonstrates the problem of disconfirmation bias. Disconfirmation bias involves the systematic discounting of evidence of sexual abuse and the predisposition to find that child interviews are "tainted." If one seeks evidence only for that position, it is likely that any case with as many interviews as Country Walk will contain some snippets that appear to support the preordained conclusion. This is how Lee Coleman approached the case; he admitted having no idea how many statements came as a result of open-ended questions, and he was unaware of the physical evidence that supported the children's statements.[222]

Professor Everson's observation that "fantastic" statements can have a host of origins, with different implications, counsels a close examination of the circumstances and content of children's statements.[223] In the Country Walk case, such an approach would inevitably lead to the conclusion that however unbelievable at first, the children's statements about masks, dead animals, and feces were actually based on reality. In fact, those elements, emphasized as fantastic in early critiques of the case, are not mentioned in the revisionist history of the case. Instead, they have been quietly dropped from the critique without any acknowledgment that they were borne out by extensive evidence.

The first step in the kind of analysis Everson proposed would be a systematic investigation of the children's statements to assess the prevalence and context of fantastic statements. Ceci and Bruck, armed with laboratory studies of child suggestibility and a claim to the scientific method, did not do this. Instead, they made the blanket statement that fabulous statements were "interweaved among the children's statements." But the two examples they cited were dubious at best. No child *ever* said that she or he had "eaten the head of another person." A number of children described a "cut off your head" game, but it did not seem fabulous in light of Frank Fuster's violent and threatening nature. One child uttered a single sentence about riding a shark, but the context of the statement included a discussion of Jacques Cousteau. The possibility that the child was referring to a kiddie ride at the nearby Country Walk Shopping Center provides another reality-based explanation for the statement. But Ceci and Bruck did not consider these explanations; nor did they analyze the interviews systematically in order to assess the frequency of the statements they claimed were widespread. They simply branded the case as being filled with fabulous statements.

The one-sided application of evidentiary standards in the Country Walk case is another indication of disconfirmation bias. People who object strenuously to any kind of post-hypnotic testimony have accepted Noel Fuster's post-hypnotic "retraction" without criticism. People who find bias in almost every question asked by the Bragas have overlooked the clear bias in the interview that Arthur Cohen conducted with Ileana Flores in Honduras. People who claim to embrace science have accepted, without skepticism, an argument about flawed tests that turns out to have nothing to do with the STD test in the Country Walk case. And people who have raised credibility questions about virtually every witness for the prosecution in the Country Walk case have accepted Frank Fuster's protestations of innocence at face value, even though he has a well-documented record of lying about his crimes.

Beyond these biases, there have been dubious tactics employed to discredit the Country Walk case. The Ethics Office of the American Psychological Association received ethics complaints against Laurie and Joseph Braga that were instigated behind the scenes by Debbie Nathan—the primary writer who attacked the Country Walk conviction—and found the complaints to be baseless.[224] There have also been serious misstatements of the facts of the case. Amy Gershenfeld Donnella, Frank Fuster's lawyer in the federal habeas corpus, misstated the origins of the case, telling the court:

It is not clear what triggered the investigation of the Country Walk Babysitting Service. However, at some point in June 1984, a Dade County investigator began interviewing parents who used the service about the possibility that their children had been victims of sexual abuse. Most parents initially turned investigators away. They had no such concerns.[225]

But there is no doubt about what started the investigation: Emma St. Lorenzo's disturbing experience on July 31, 1984, when her son, who had just spent his first day at the Fusters', came home looking "glassy eyed" and with a rash on his anus. There is also no doubt that in the first few days of the investigation, as documented in Detective Meznarich's sixty-page police report, she interviewed numerous parents who had very serious concerns. Several families had independently taken their children out of the Fusters' care, and in one instance it was specifically because of a spontaneous utterance that Ileana Fuster had sexual contact with children. The account provided by Donnella was so disconnected from the record in the case that the judge took the unusual step of highlighting this problem. Magistrate Judge Charlene Sorrentino, who authored a 124-page decision rejecting those claims, noted that Donnella's "purported factual overview is almost entirely devoid of citations to the record, and puts forth numerous sweeping, and sometimes outlandish statements. . . ."[226] The magistrate judge concluded that without any documentation these "hyperbolic statements are unworthy of credence."[227] She noted the same problem in connection with claims about former private investigator Dinerstein, who has been cited for the proposition that Ileana Fuster was drugged and held naked in solitary confinement. After comparing Dinerstein's affidavit from 1985 to the claims made about it by Fuster's lawyer, the magistrate judge conclude that Donnella had "significantly distorted and revised Dinerstein's actual assertions."[228] The PBS program *Frontline* and a host of writers have done the same thing, apparently without checking the original document.

The Country Walk case once stood as an example of how to prosecute cases with young children as witnesses. This conclusion has been challenged by a revisionist view that has been widely accepted in the media and among many academic psychologists. These developments should be seen as a cautionary tale about the dangers of disconfirmation bias. If the overwhelming evidence against Frank Fuster can be spun into a witch-hunt story, then it is unlikely that *any* case based largely on the word of a child will ever be considered sufficient to avoid this kind of treatment. If so, then our society will have come full circle from the early 1980s, when the unwillingness to believe that children were sexually abused in significant numbers resulted in few prosecutions and little recognition of a serious social problem. Those who have promoted the witch-hunt narrative in the Country Walk case offer something quite similar: a world in which a positive STD test, a child's spontaneous utterance, and a web of cross-corroborating evidence are considered insufficient to support a finding of guilt.

Frank Fuster's lawyer argued in 2005, "had this case been tried in 1995 instead of 1985, Fuster would never have been convicted."[229] Unfortunately, given the widespread acceptance of the witch-hunt narrative, that may well be true. The next chapter considers the broader and more current implications of the conclusion.

CONCLUSION II

The significance of the witch-hunt narrative in the academic field of psychology came to a head in the Kelly Michaels case. Not surprisingly, there were divergent views in the field about child suggestibility. Gail Goodman's research in the 1980s had demonstrated that children were, in many ways, as accurate and reliable as adults were as witnesses. But the McMartin case and others challenged this view. Did what happened in the McMartin case have implications for cases all over the country, or was the McMartin case so unique in character and circumstance that its lessons could not be applied to other cases?

Those questions were becoming the focus of academic psychologists in the same year that Charlier and Downing were publishing the claim that at least one hundred cases around the country involving ritual abuse allegations had little or no basis in fact. At the American Psychology-Law Society in Miami in 1988, the "contradictory findings" about child suggestibility were so significant that Stephen Ceci later wrote that he "found the whole ordeal troubling."[1] There was significant disagreement in the field about whether children were highly suggestible and about the applicability, or "ecological validity," of various laboratory experiments demonstrating children's suggestibility. Prompted in part by this experience, the American Psychological Association (APA) sponsored a conference at Cornell University in June 1989 on the suggestibility of children's recollections. Popular interest in this issue was so significant that there was a story in the *Washington Post*, under the headline "Psychologists Divided on Children Testifying," when the volume of papers from that conference was published in 1991. A panel of psychologists at a press conference at APA headquarters conveyed that "the profession is deeply divided" on issues concerning the reliability of young children.[2]

In light of this background, it is surprising, to say the least, that Ceci and Bruck were informing the New Jersey Supreme Court a little more than two years later that there was a consensus in the field around *their* research on child suggestibility. It was either one of the fastest resolutions among deeply divided professionals in academic history or something else was going on. The evidence for a political explanation is elaborated in Chapter Five. In fact, the claim of a "paradigm shift" simply masked the continuing deep divisions in the profession. But the brief (which became known as the "Concerned Scientists" brief) had its desired effect. The court upheld the reversal of Kelly Michaels's conviction and the Michaels case became a turning point in the contested day-care cases from the 1980s.

Ceci and Bruck were successful in convincing many people, both in academia and in the public, that their research demonstrated that the children's statements in the Michaels case were unreliable and that New Jersey should institute a special procedure for "taint hearings" in the future. The argument that their research had direct application to the Michaels case had two simple components: (1) the videotape of the boy spinning a fictitious story, which he apparently believed, about getting his finger caught in a mousetrap; and (2) the statement that what they did in the lab "paled in comparison" to what happened in the Michaels case. The argument succeeded because the videotape was so compelling and the statement about the Michaels case had the appearance of being true, based in part on selected snippets from Lou Fonolleras's interviews. Fonolleras, it should be kept in mind, did not even enter the case until after the six-count indictment in May that was based on an investigation lasting less than one week.

The claims about "paling in comparison" to Michaels were almost impossible to verify. There was no way to check whether the Fonolleras interviews were representative of children in the case. There was no way to check whether those interviews even involved children in the case. There was no way to check whether the claim that disclosures came after "weeks and months" of such interviews was true. And there was no way to check whether there were children in the case who were entirely different in fact and context. At least there was no way to do so without spending years of effort.[3]

The two arguments that were, understandably, so persuasive to academics and others are also deeply flawed. The boy in the Mousetrap Study later told researchers he never got his hand caught in a mousetrap; it was all a story. Moreover, the methods used in the study were misportrayed in the media. Indeed, the article in which they were first published described a much tamer version of the study in the methods section and then discussed the results of a significantly "modified" version in the discussion section. Naturally, this caused some people to think the tamer version of the experiment led to the dramatic results obtained through the modified approach.

The appendix to the "Concerned Scientists" brief did not distinguish between interviews *after* a child had made a disclosure and interviews before that. Once a child has made a disclosure, subsequent interviews cannot be said to have been the cause of the earlier disclosure, but this is the kind of logic one must employ to claim that children in the Michaels case were interviewed for weeks and months. Most of those "interviews" involved testifying at the grand jury, being evaluated by Eileen Treacy, and preparing for trial. From a systematic analysis of the interviews *in the investigative phase* of the Michaels case, elaborated in Chapter Five, the inescapable fact is that *none* of the disclosures came after "weeks or months" of highly suggestive interviews. Many came in the first interview, and most others came in the second. Accordingly, even the modified experiment that produced the dramatic results in the Mousetrap Study did *not* pale in comparison to the Michaels case. The children in Michaels were not told repeatedly that something happened and then asked about it. In actuality, what happened in the Michaels case paled in comparison to the Mousetrap Study.

But it is obvious why the potential signators of the "Concerned Scientists" brief—and the appellate court judges in the case—thought they knew otherwise: they had already been told so by the media. Beginning with the highly publicized Rabinowitz article in 1990 and carrying over to television programs repeating these claims, the witch-hunt narrative about the Michaels case had been adopted and rebroadcast for several years leading up to 1993.

It is clear from their writings that Ceci and Bruck had also adopted this narrative. They described the Rabinowitz article about the case as "seminal," and they relied on Rabinowitz as a source for statements about McMartin. Demonstrating their endorsement of the witch-hunt narrative, Ceci and Bruck argued in their 1993 article for the Society on Research in Child Development (SRCD) that the McMartin case was "not a singular happening." Rather, they said there were *hundreds* of other cases like it. They argued that those cases generally share six elements:

> First, the witnesses were preschoolers at the time of the alleged abuse. Second, the disclosures were not made immediately following the alleged event, but after a long delay. Third, the disclosures were preceded by intensive interviewing of the children by professionals and nonprofessionals. Fourth, the children were the only witnesses to the events, and corroborative physical evidence was lacking. Fifth, none of the defendants ever made a confession. Finally, the major issue before the jury in all of these cases was whether to believe the children.[4]

Applying those elements to the three major cases evaluated in this book yields unexpected conclusions (see Table II-1). First, the paradigmatic case, McMartin, does not itself fit all of the elements. In fact, it fits only three elements without qualification: preschoolers, no confession, and child believability being

Table II-1 **Application of Ceci & Bruck's "Six Elements" to Three Major Cases**

	McMartin	*Michaels*	*Country Walk*
Preschoolers	Yes	Yes	Yes
Disclosures after "long" delay	No for a few; yes for a lot	No	No
Disclosures preceded by intensive interviewing	No for a few; presumably yes for many others	No for several; arguably yes for others	No
Physical evidence lacking	Yes for most; no for a few	Largely yes	No
No confession	Yes	Yes	Yes
Major issue to jury, child believability	Yes	Yes	Yes

a major issue. But those elements do not help distinguish the McMartin case from most of those that goes to trial with young children and sexual abuse allegations. Second, the remaining elements cannot accurately be applied to the McMartin case universally. There are too many differences between children to apply one simple conclusion. For example, "disclosures after 'long' delay" clearly applies to many children in McMartin; it might apply to every child who can be counted as having made a disclosure in February 1984 and later. That is potentially hundreds of children, although there are no available records for most of them and only about a dozen were actually involved in the trial. But even this element is not true of a handful of children in the case, among them Matthew Johnson, some of the September responders, and the Chapman girl in January 1984.

The next element, disclosures preceded by intensive interviewing, is similarly complicated. The description does not fit a small number of children in the McMartin case, which was characterized by children who probably do fit it, although this conclusion is complicated by the lack of information about the nature and frequency of interviewing by "nonprofessionals" (i.e., parents).[5] The same kind of mixed result applies to the element involving physical evidence. There was medical evidence concerning a small number of children in the case that would still be considered meaningful evidence today. This was not true of most children in the case, although many of their parents were told otherwise. Overall, this analysis leads to the self-contradictory conclusion that the

McMartin case itself was not "just like McMartin." Or at least not like the McMartin case that was the basis for the witch-hunt narrative. The case was far more complicated than has been portrayed. If individual differences are not taken into account and, instead, one general designation is required for classifying every element, then the McMartin case "fits" the witch-hunt narrative. But this is not the full story of the case.

The application of these six elements is even more striking for the Kelly Michaels case. The same three elements that clearly fit McMartin also fit Michaels, but those are the elements that do not help distinguish McMartin-like cases from most other sexual abuse trials involving young children. The remaining three elements point out differences between McMartin and Michaels. The Michaels case did not involve disclosures of events that allegedly occurred years earlier, like the McMartin case. The alleged events occurred in the months prior to the investigation, and the only children in the case were those who had encountered Kelly Michaels during the school year. The children whose statements formed the basis for the original indictment were not subject to intensive interviewing in advance of their disclosures. The original charges were based on an investigation that lasted only a few days and began with a spontaneous disclosure. The situation for the rest of the children in the case is less clear. The defense argued that those children disclosed only after intensive interviewing. The facts of the case, as demonstrated in Chapter Five, are more complicated, although the characterization is arguably true for some children. Finally, physical evidence was largely lacking in the case—as it is in most sexual abuse cases—although there was some medical evidence that should not be dismissed out of hand.

Ignoring differences between children makes it easy to characterize Michaels—or almost any case, for that matter—as "just like McMartin." Indeed, the innocence-by-association argument convinced academic psychologists and appellate judges alike. But the story does not do justice to the underlying facts. Accordingly, the Michaels case bears out the concern of those who worried that the "lessons" of the McMartin case would be applied too broadly.

The application of the same elements to the Country Walk case demonstrates how the witch-hunt narrative has gone to extremes to paint cases as "just like McMartin." Although it shares the same three elements that do not help distinguish McMartin from most cases with young children, all three remaining elements point out significant differences. There was a confirmed STD in the Country Walk case, and the disclosures did not generally involve long delays; nor were they preceded by intensive interviewing. The core of the original charges came on the first day of interviewing by the Bragas and involved allegations that had occurred recently. Fuster's defenders have quibbled about whether those descriptions fit the two children who disclosed in January 1985, but the case as a whole does *not* fit any of the three important elements.

A scientific analysis of the child-suggestibility hypothesis would look for evidence that might *disprove* the hypothesis that a case is "just like McMartin." It is a strong indication of disconfirmation bias that not a single proponent of the child-suggestibility view has approached these cases in this fashion. The spontaneous disclosure that began the Michaels case has been distorted such that it completely overlooks the two adults who witnessed the circumstances under which Mitchell Pierce first implicated his naptime teacher, Kelly. Why have those embracing Kelly Michaels favored uninformed speculations over the clear testimony of Laura Hadley, the medical assistant? Similarly, Noel Fuster's positive test for gonorrhea of the throat has been dismissed on the basis of a freelance writer who cited a scientific article that had no application to the actual test used in the Country Walk case. Why haven't any of the academics who embraced Frank Fuster checked the veracity of this claim? Similarly, recognizing the validity of Jason Cramer's testimony alone would result in a rejection of the hypothesis that "child suggestibility" accounts for all of the allegations in the Country Walk case. Although it is predictable that forensic psychologists who generally testify for the defense would avoid this kind of analysis, it is troublesome, to say the least, that academic psychologists have adopted the same position.

The ability of the witch-hunt narrative to paint a persuasive picture that dozens, if not hundreds, of cases are McMartin "clones" is alarming. This narrative has not persuaded any appellate judges in the Country Walk case, but it has persuaded many writers, intellectuals, and academics. This is powerful evidence that concerns about the "lessons" of the McMartin case have been applied too broadly. The literature in psychology is filled with cautions about the need to treat children as individuals and to take individual circumstances into account. Unfortunately, those cautions have not been followed in the extensive writing about the Michaels case or the Country Walk case.

There is a corollary to the importance of treating children as individuals; it is also important to take contextual variables into account. Such variables help account for important differences in how cases are investigated, how they are charged, and what kind of environment surrounds the case. Was there considerable time between the initial complaint and actual charges? If so, there is all the more time for social forces to intensify and affect the case. Was there intense publicity before charges were brought? If so, there is all the more reason that prosecutors might rush to judgment. Did the case spread to other defendants and other locations? If so, those are almost sure signs of some kind of social contagion. These points and several others are elaborated in Table II-2.

This table demonstrates that the Michaels case and the Country Walk case were different from McMartin on virtually every dimension. McMartin is the only one of those cases that (1) had an extended period of time between the first

Table II-2 **Comparison of Key Features of the McMartin, Kelly Michaels, and Country Walk Case**

	McMartin	*Michaels*	*Country Walk*
Length of time from first official complaint to initial criminal charges	28 weeks	3 weeks	2 weeks
Expansion of charges to other defendants?	Yes	No[1]	No[2]
Intense publicity before charges were brought?	Yes	No	No
Number of nearby schools closed, even temporarily, in connection with the case	7	0	0
Parents as investigators?	Yes	No	No
Activist parents without children in the case?	Yes	No	No
Extensive "fantastic" claims?	Yes	No[3]	No[4]
Charges brought without DA reviewing child interviews?	Yes	No	No

[1] Others were considered, but nobody else was charged with sexual abuse.
[2] Frank and Ileana Fuster were both named from the start.
[3] The statements labeled as fantastic were not "extensive."
[4] The statements that were originally labeled as "fantastic" (masks, dead bird, feces play) were all proven at trial. The more recent assertions about "fabulous" statements (riding on a shark, eating the head of another person) were not actually claimed, let alone "extensively."

complaint and the first charges, (2) expanded to multiple defendants not named early in the investigation, (3) had intense publicity before any charges were brought, (4) spread to other preschools, (5) saw parents enlisted by authorities as investigators, (6) had "fantastic" claims that were extensive and never proven, and (7) involved charges brought without an analysis of the children's interviews in the case. Those features are all critical to understanding how the McMartin case evolved and why it resulted in charges that should never have been brought.

Charlier and Downing's series purported to do this kind of analysis, but they lost sight of the fact that almost none of their cases actually fit the "pattern" of charges expanding to other defendants. The case that comes closest is the Georgian Hills case in their backyard, which shares many features with McMartin. Charlier and Downing seem to have viewed the world through the lens of the Ballard case. The same tactic was widely used in many others evaluated in Chapter Three. Other proponents of the witch-hunt narrative have made the same error with the McMartin case. Ceci and Bruck anchored their discussion of Michaels in McMartin. The first nine paragraphs of their SRCD article are about McMartin.[6] This approach makes it easy to claim that even the County Walk case is "just like McMartin." But a host of key features make it clear that McMartin was unique. Beyond the fact that all three cases involved young children, Michaels and County Walk, as demonstrated in these last two chapters, were nothing like McMartin.

If academic psychologists could impugn these cases, they could potentially impugn any child sexual abuse case, regardless of the evidence. The extent to which this has come true is explored in the second half of Chapter Seven.

PART III

RECENT DEVELOPMENTS

The Legacy of the Witch-Hunt Narrative

The triumph of the witch-hunt narrative rested on arguments that have implications well beyond those specific cases. The point of *Jeopardy in Courtroom* was to
convey a view of child suggestibility, not to get to the bottom of the cases studies
used as illustrations. What those cases purported to illustrate were general arguments about child suggestibility and children as witnesses. To others, the witch-
hunt narrative was compelling because it encompassed a political argument
about the overbearing role of government in child protective services, or it expressed a political view about the abuse of power by police and prosecutors. Together, those arguments helped convince people that the witch-hunt narrative
was fitting, even when the facts did not support it. The implications, I argue
below, extend far beyond those cases and that era. This worrisome legacy of the
witch-hunt narrative is elaborated in the second part of this chapter.

But first, there are other recent developments to consider. Even if one agrees
with the argument of the previous chapters—that the witch-hunt narrative
about the 1980s and early 1990s was misplaced *in its time*—several recent developments arguably contradict the claim that those arguments have continuing
impact today. The highly publicized scandals in the Catholic Church and, more
recently, at Penn State seem to demonstrate the ability of our society to recognize and confront sexual abuse without crying witch-hunt. Moreover, there is
evidence in how we treat sex offenders after they are released from prison that
seems to demonstrate an overreaction to sex offenders. Developments since the
enactment of Megan's Law in 1996 and the rise of civil commitment laws appear
to be overly punitive, bearing out a kind of hysteria or overreaction. Finally, a
prominent group of academics and activists argue that witch-hunt-like cases
continue to this day. The significance of these three arguments is analyzed in the
first part of this chapter.

The second part of this chapter elaborates the worrisome legacy of the witch-
hunt narrative: three lingering effects that are underappreciated, understudied,
and potentially quite adverse to the protection of children. This legacy stems
from the same arguments that helped convince people that the day-care abuse

cases were baseless, regardless of the merits. These arguments are alive and well in the contemporary era. They have resulted in a discounting of the reality of continuing day-care sexual abuse. More significantly, they have promoted a general but unwarranted view that children are highly suggestible, that delayed disclosures of sexual abuse are suspect, and that child-abuse professionals constitute a dubious "child abuse industry." In this way, the witch-hunt narrative continues to undermine the credibility of children as witnesses and the institutions that are supposed to respond to the sexual abuse of children.

Recent Developments

Several recent developments contradict the general story of underreaction, minimization, and denial that comprises much of the argument in the last six chapters. A lot has changed since 1995. There have been high-profile cases in involving the Catholic Church and, more recently, Penn State. There have also been crusades of a sort against sex offenders who have completed their prison sentences, suggesting what might be called moral panic. Some also claim that the witch-hunts continued into the contemporary era. This section examines all three of these developments. The Catholic Church cases and the one involving Penn State are both important, but the lessons are much more limited than is widely acknowledged. The crusade against sex offenders is real, and it is worrisome. It focuses too much attention on this population, most of it ultimately counterproductive—but these measures attract strong political support, particularly from conservatives. Finally, the claim that the witch-hunts have continued is not supported by available evidence.

Cases Against the Catholic Church and Penn State

Child sexual abuse is no longer associated with day-care cases. Since those cases faded from public view, there were years when the media coverage of child sexual abuse was minimal. Then a new focus emerged: sexual abuse by Catholic priests. The criminal trial of Michael Jackson generated significant publicity in 2005, but that coverage was fleeting and it did not have nearly the magnitude of the stories in 2002 about sexual abuse by priests.

Those stories were driven largely by civil lawsuits against the church, although there were also criminal cases and grand jury investigations in some jurisdictions. Hundreds of millions of dollars have been paid to victims and more than one thousand priests were removed from their positions as a result of these cases. Documents unsealed in civil cases in Boston in 2002 contained evidence that "Church officials knew about [Father John] Geoghan's pedophilia," which was responsible for more than one hundred victims.[1] There were almost daily stories about these cases in the *Boston Globe* that year. The uproar over these stories created news of its own. Pope John Paul II summoned all of the American cardinals to the Vatican in the spring of 2002 for an emergency meeting on the matter, in no small part because of this publicity. The U.S. Conference of Catholic Bishops met in Dallas in June 2002, under enormous media scrutiny and with the stated intention of approving, for the first time, mandatory rules for how all 194 dioceses in the United States should respond to allegations of sexual abuse. The policy included provisions for mandatory removal of priests who sexually abuse children, reporting to prosecutors, and reaching out to victims. The adoption of this policy must be recognized as a significant event. Through civil litigation, some enterprising lawyers in Boston managed to obtain a surprising measure of accountability from an institution that was historically afforded significant latitude by public officials, including law enforcement. As the *Globe* reported it, "a culture of deference that had taken more than a century to evolve seemed to erode in a matter of weeks."[2]

That does not mean the story was an unmitigated success. The institutional changes adopted in Dallas were not as strong as some thought necessary, and there are forces within the Church hierarchy that remain resistant to these reforms. Indeed, the Vatican expressed the view that the policy adopted in Dallas did not do enough to protect accused priests. By November, the bishops agreed to a narrower definition of sexual abuse, a less burdensome reporting requirement, and a 10-year statute of limitations.[3] It is unclear how well these guidelines have actually been implemented. Moreover, there are several reasons to think these developments say little or nothing about social and legal responses to child sexual abuse in general.

There are three reasons to temper the application of any conclusions about these cases to the broader context of child sexual abuse. First, priests represent a kind of *other*. They wear robes and they take celibacy vows. As disturbing as it is to think that a priest could sexually abuse a child, their *otherness* also makes this thought less threatening and more believable. Add to this the celibacy vows, which many think contribute to priests finding a sexual outlet with children. The issue of celibacy vows has become so mixed up in the discussion of sexual abuse by priests that one might lose sight of the fact that far more child molesters are married men than are unmarried priests. A second distinguishing feature of these cases is that the victims were largely male, both in numbers and in voice. And in many cases it is an adult voice, not a child; the leading voices in 1992 (Frank Fitzpatrick) and 2002 (Greg Ford) were adults. They were far less likely than anyone else to be cast as untrustworthy. Nobody argues that a man would *fantasize* such a thing, or that he might be acting hysterically. Accordingly, most people took the view that these allegations were credible.

Finally, there was a very particular reason these cases exploded in the media in 2002: documents produced through civil litigation proved the extent to which bishops and cardinals transferred priests from one place to another with sufficient knowledge of their abuse histories to know they would be placing children in danger. There was a cover-up. The story of institutional betrayal drove the widespread media coverage in 2002. There had been limited coverage of lawsuits about priests molesting children as early as the Gauthe case in 1984.[4] But the cases from Louisiana were considered "anomalies being blown out of proportion by anti-Catholic elements."[5] They generated only brief coverage. The McMartin case was, at that time, fast defining child sexual abuse in America. There was a much larger cluster of these church-related abuse stories in 1992. The Church viewed this publicity as so unfair that Cardinal Bernard Law famously called down God's power "on the media, particularly the *Globe*."[6] The Cardinal got his wish, for a time. There was a significant lull in stories about this topic for almost ten years, mostly because documents from the civil cases were sealed. When nearly ten thousand pages of documents became public in January 2002, it was clear that the Church had sought to protect its reputation by covering up sexual abuse for decades. That made this a major story. Since the Watergate scandal in the 1970s, it is clear that any cover-up as broad and well-documented as this one will generate significant media attention. The recent events at Penn State bear this out.

What has come to be known as the "Penn State scandal" received massive media coverage in 2011 and 2012. It has largely been a story about justice and accountability. But it was also a story about a cover-up. Jerry Sandusky was convicted in a criminal trial that most observers considered fair and convincing. Efforts by the defense to impugn the testimony of various victims by questioning their motives were unsuccessful. Nobody was distracted by the defense critique of some interviews in the case. Sandusky received a long sentence, and Penn State will apparently pay more than $40 million to settle civil suits by victims. Beyond this, the Freeh Report, commissioned by the university, laid out stark conclusions about the failure of university officials to take appropriate action. The report would have its detractors, but many people welcomed the frank tone and the strong conclusions. The report inspired the NCAA to craft its own wide-ranging penalties, agreed to by the university, including a $60 million fund for child abuse prevention programs. As important and generally uplifting as the developments in this case, it is important to recognize several features that help explain why the case attracted so much attention but was not highly controversial in outcome. These are all factors that limit the applicability of the recent developments to anything beyond the case itself. First, the case did not involve child witnesses. It was adults testifying about what happened to them as children. The case might have been quite different if it had hinged entirely on the testimony of boys age eight to thirteen. Second, the criminal case included an adult witness, the graduate assistant who reported the matter to Coach Paterno. Although there was disagreement about what precise words he used in warning the coach, the point remains that one does not report inconsequential events in this manner. There was also a janitor mentioned in the Freeh Report who declined to report what he saw, for fear of retribution. So the case did not stand entirely on the word of children. Moreover, there was a cover-up. In this way, this story is much like those that drove coverage about the Catholic Church in 2002. It is unclear whether all the attention even led to significantly better procedures or whether it decreased the degree to which this kind of abuse was tolerated in the Church. After ten years, the jury is divided, to say the least. Some think there has been significant slippage in the commitment of the Catholic Church in recent years. And as welcome as many of the developments at Penn State are, the Penn State case was also unusual in many ways.

More broadly, we know that the newfound vigilance against child sexual abuse in the Catholic Church and at Penn State did not permeate the culture. Anyone familiar with the Catholic Church and Penn State stories has to wonder, What institution will next be shown to have covered up the sexual abuse of children? Two recent cases in the Los Angeles School District demonstrate the continued vitality of institutional dynamics that minimize and deny sexual abuse. Both involved sexual abuse by elementary school teachers that went undetected for years. The first case involved Mark Berndt, who had been teaching for thirty-two years and was first apprehended as a result of dozens of photos of blindfolded children that he had commercially developed. Criminal charges are still pending at this writing, but the school district has already agree to pay $27.2 million to settle dozens of civil claims. What is most chilling about Berndt's case is that children reported some his bizarre activities and were reportedly told by a school counselor that "it's not very good to make up stories." Also worrisome is the fact that Berndt was the subject of a criminal investigation in 1993, when a female student reported he tried to fondle her. Prosecutors dropped the matter, stating that "the evidence was insufficient to prove a crime occurred."[7] The second case involved Paul Chapel III, a third grade teacher, who later pleaded guilty to thirteen counts of a lewd act on a child, one for each victim.[8] A civil complaint against the school district claims it had sufficient knowledge to have known that Chapel should not be in a classroom. He lost a civil case in 1987 involving the showing of a sexually explicit video to students. Moreover, he was prosecuted in 1997 for molesting an eight-year-old girl and was placed on administrative duty during those proceedings. But the criminal trial ended in a hung jury, the prosecutor decided not to retry the case, and Chapel was allowed back into the classroom, where, as he later admitted, he went on to molest thirteen students between 2006 and 2010. Both of these cases demonstrate the extent to which child sexual abuse lives on in institutions that one might think had long since confronted and addressed the problem. It has, after all, been a matter of public discussion since 1983, when the McMartin Preschool case began nearby.

Megan's Law and Sex-Offender Politics

A second major development related to child sexual abuse in the contemporary era is the nationwide increase in laws and policies targeting sex offenders. The 1990s were marked by the adoption of sex-offender registration, community no-tification systems, residency restrictions, and the use of civil commitment. Sex-offender registration provisions were incorporated into federal law in 1994 through the Jacob Wetterling Crimes Against Children and Sexually Violent Of-fenders Act. Federal law was amended two years later with the adoption of com-munity notification provisions modeled after Megan's Law from New Jersey. Those provisions were "enhanced" ten years later by the Adam Walsh Protection and Safety Act of 2006, which provides for wider dissemination of information about sex offenders. Although states have differing version of these systems, the use of registries and community notification became nationwide in the 1990s. Residency restrictions and civil commitment are also important developments in the post-Michaels era, but neither has been nationwide. Some residency re-strictions are adopted at the local level; others are statewide, such as the provi-sion in many states that registered sex offenders cannot live within in a specified proximity of schools or parks. Nineteen states have adopted systems for civil commitment.

All of these policies have been criticized extensively in law review articles and other academic literature. Psychiatrist Richard Krueger, in an editorial in the *Los Angeles Times*, called these developments "the new American witch hunt."[9] They are widely seen among scholars from various disciplines as an overreaction that is based on social vilification of sex offenders rather than evidence-based argu-ments about the efficacy of the policies. This is hardly surprising given how so many of these "tribute" laws originated. Megan's Law is probably the best-known example. It was signed into law less than three months after Megan Kanka was murdered by a neighbor who had prior sexual abuse convictions. The defendant had not yet been tried when the law was passed. There are a host of similar laws, such as Jessica's Law in Florida and Ashley's Law in Texas, that were enacted quickly and without serious debate in order to demonstrate some kind of gov-ernment response to a tragedy.

The evaluation research on community notification systems is mixed at best. An early study in the state of Washington concluded that notification did not have an effect on recidivism but offenders subject to community notification were arrested more quickly than those in the comparison group.[10] A more recent study found evidence that might demonstrate a strong effect in recidivism rates, but the study had enough qualifications that more research is necessary.[11] There have also been several studies finding these policies have no effect on recidivism rates.[12] Critics of these policies often display little or no sensitivity to the dynamics of child sexual abuse by placing great significance on the fact that sex offenders tend to have a low recidivism rate. This simple comparison to the recidivism rates for other crimes would make sense if all crimes had an equal chance of detection. But child sexual abuse is secretive by its nature, and disclosure often does not occur during childhood. *There are no serious felonies as underreported as is child sexual abuse.* This fact should affect how one interprets recidivism rates across crimes. Indeed, "correcting" for this dynamic significantly changes any analysis of sex offender registration laws.

Although the benefits of these policies remain unclear, the monetary and administrative costs in keeping a large database accurate and accessible are significant. (There are sixty-three thousand offenders in the database for California.[13]) Some have raised concerns about vigilantism.[14] Even if the concerns have been exaggerated, the benefits of sex-offender registries are mixed, at best. The evidence concerning the efficacy of residency restrictions is even weaker. The benefits seem to be nonexistent, but the (indirect) costs can be significant. These policies find little or no support in the community of professionals who treat sex offenders. A recent collection of scholarship by criminologists concludes that "the misguided and deleterious consequences of residential residency restrictions" call for elimination or dramatic change of these policies.[15] Public support for these policies, however, is strong. This support bears out the idea that the policies are driven by extreme attitudes of sex offenders as "monsters."

This argument fits community-notification laws and a related development in the 1990s: the rise in civil commitment statutes for those labeled as "sexually violent predators." These statutes provide for varied processes, by state, for deciding whether a sex offender is considered sufficiently dangerous to be held after completion of their prison sentence. Typically, the determination must be renewed every two or three years. Civil commitment is extremely expensive, costing three or four times the already high cost of incarceration. Given the costs and the procedural hurdles, only a small percentage of incarcerated sex offenders are ever subject to civil commitment. Sociologist Chrysanthi Leon documents that "just over 2% of the initial referrals were civilly committed" in California, which has the largest program in the country. Between 1998 and 2002, an average of about sixty people per year were admitted to civil commitment in California. A *New York Times* investigation in 2006 concluded that a total of 3,493 men had been confined nationwide under these laws.[16] (Approximately two hundred times that number are subject to sex offender registration.)

The strongest objections to these civil confinement laws are ideological. This makes sense since the number of people actually subject to civil commitment is small. To the disbelief of many civil libertarians, the U.S. Supreme Court upheld these laws in 1996 (by a 5-4 decision) against a constitutional challenge in *Kansas v. Hendricks*. The topic is so ideologically charged that there has been little attention paid to how civil commitment is actually being used.[17] Are offenders being held without strong evidence of dangerousness? Or are offenders with strong evidence of dangerousness failing to be held? Both could be true, of course. Neither is easy to study given the small number of total cases. The number of people subjected to civil commitment nationwide every year is probably smaller than the number of people who sexually abuse children in day-care settings. Either way, it is fair to say both of these groups have, in their own time, received a disproportionate amount of attention in public discourse.

The rise of civil commitment programs and the increased use of community-notification laws are both products of the pernicious politics of sex-offender policies in modern America. The rigid "law and order" positions that largely defined the public discourse over crime policy in the 1970s and 1980s have faded as crime rates have dropped. But the area of sex offenses, particularly against children, is one of the last bastions of these politics. Elected officials want to portray themselves as "tough on sex offenders." Conversely, there are cynical efforts to paint one's opponent as weak on sex offenders. Republicans maneuvered a vote during the recent health care debate that was portrayed as "Viagra for child molesters."[18] Beyond posturing, there is the problem that ratcheting up laws to demonstrate "toughness" can be counterproductive. The most recent efforts to "improve" community notification provisions under the Adam Walsh Act include notifying employers and the public where sex offenders work. These provisions seem likely to make it harder for those released from prison to find and maintain jobs, which is counter-productive to the goal of a safe transition back to society. But political forces make it unlikely that any elected official will voice those concerns for fear of being portrayed as "weak" on sex offenders. In short, the critique of overly punitive policies concerning sex offenders is well taken. The laws are dubious in many respects and often the product of shameless politicking.

While many people express dislike, even hatred, of sex offenders when asked about the subject in the abstract, it is important to remember that such attitudes can coexist with the embrace of perpetrators in specific cases. Leon reveals how the "moral panic" over sex offenders that is reflected in media stories between the 1930s and the mid-1950s did *not* translate into increased arrests and convictions in criminal court, which seems to be assumed in so many academic writings.[19] The "desire to protect reputable citizens" in specific cases, Leon explains, often trumps the general desire to treat child molesters severely. In the contemporary era, though, punishment is seen as the overriding quality of the criminal justice system. It defines much of the scholarship about the era.

Actual punishments in the post-McMartin era have not been as strict as is often claimed. Though commenters continue to emphasize the "punitive" treatment of sex offenders, these perceptions seem to be driven by highly publicized cases rather than aggregate data. Harsh sentences are publicized; lenient ones prevail. This is what I discovered after testing Richard Gardner's claim that our country has become so hysterical over the sexual abuse of children that child molesters receive longer sentences on average than murders. Admittedly, this claim, if true, would constitute strong evidence of an unreasonably punitive approach toward sex offenders. But Dr. Gardner was off by a factor of hundreds.[20] Professor Theodore Cross and colleagues, in their meta-analysis of child abuse prosecutions, found that the incarceration rate for child abuse cases was "lower than all three comparison categories and significantly lower than violent crimes and rape and sexual assault."[21]

There is little reason to think that the overreaction to sex offenders' being released from prison translates into greater willingness to report or act on suspicions of sexual abuse. An eight-month investigation by two reporters at the *Arkansas Democrat-Gazette* examined allegations of sexual misconduct against school teachers. They concluded, "When teachers are accused of sexual misconduct, some school officials and school boards quietly sidestep legal and ethical issues to protect their schools from scandal."[22] The study was published in 1996, four years after Gardner flatly asserted it is "no longer the case" that those revealing sexual abuse will be met with a disbelieving community. Gardner claimed the opposite was true, that police and child protective services were more likely to "accept as valid even frivolous and absurd accusations."[23] But Hargrove and Roth found that "sexual allegations by students have been greeted with shrugs, although a teacher's files indicated previous sex-related complaints."

There is no reason to think this phenomenon was peculiar to Arkansas. Indeed, in a more recent case from California, an appellate court declined to hold the Anaheim School District liable in a case where there was, as the court agreed, "evidence of obliviousness—perhaps the better word would be cluelessness—on the part of several of the district's teachers" who might have surmised sexual abuse had they "put two and two together."[24] The case has been described as encouraging a see-no-evil ethic.[25] That ethic stands alongside the punitive attitudes toward convicted sex offenders.

Overreaction at the back end of the criminal justice system—when sex offenders complete their prison term—is politically easy. We have been doing it with sex offenders since the 1990s through sex offender registries and related policies such as residency restrictions. These policies accomplish little in the way of public safety. But there is an enormous difference between being tough on incarcerated sex offenders upon release and confronting sexual abuse at the moment a child discloses it. Confronting the problem as a whole would require acknowledging the fact that most child molesters remain unapprehended and that most child sexual abuse is not reported. But proponents of the witch-hunt narrative would apparently rather challenge the evidence than agree that Roland Summit was correct when he wrote that child sexual abuse has two important preconditions: secrecy and helplessness.

The paradox of the contemporary sex offender in America is that we treat the group with leniency in many ways—failing to report suspicions, rallying around "upstanding" defendants, and meting out lenient punishments on many occasions—but we overreact about their release from prison. This gives an appearance of severity. Politicians have managed to exploit this in various ways. The appearance is also useful as a social salve since we are so willing to ignore child sexual abuse in the specific. The witch-hunt narrative glosses over the issue, just as scholars who characterize the modern era as a "punishment boom" miss the myriad ways in which the criminal justice system continues to be surprisingly lenient in child sexual abuse cases.

Persistent "Witch Hunt" Claims

The witch-hunt narrative described in this book revolved around cases from the McMartin era. But there have also been persistent witch-hunt claims in the years since then. Those claims have not received the publicity of the cases from the McMartin era; nor have they been grouped together by a common feature such as the day-care setting. Nevertheless, the cases have been offered as evidence of continued *overreaction* to child sexual abuse. Indeed, some of the same activists from the Day of Contrition—an event held in Massachusetts in 1997 that sought to link many of the cases discussed in this book directly to the Salem witch trials of the 1690s—formed a non-profit organization with the Orwellian name the National Center for Reason and Justice (NCRJ). The NCRJ provides legal assistance and other support to defendants in child sexual abuse cases that they claim were injustices. Their current president is Michael Snedeker, the defense lawyer who coauthored *Satan's Silence* with Debbie Nathan. Nathan and two other writers are on the board of directors. So is Professor Elizabeth Loftus, the highly acclaimed memory researcher. One of the first cases that the NCRJ sponsored (which apparently means providing support with legal fees) was that of Frank Fuster, the subject of Chapter Six. The NCRJ sponsors a number of lesser-known cases discussed in Chapter Three, including Robert Halsey, Lynn Malcom, Francis and Daniel Keller, and Nancy Smith and Joseph Allen. The NCRJ also sponsors a host of defendants from more recent cases. There is no question that defendants in child sexual abuse cases continue to *claim* they are victims of a witch-hunt.

What kind of evidence is there to support the witch-hunt claims that have emerged since the Michaels case? Eight examples are discussed here. This assortment of cases comes from a variety of sources, including writers Debbie Nathan, Mark Pendergrast, Thomas Sowell, activist Carol Hopkins, and the NCRJ. Some of Robert Rosenthal's recent appellate cases are examined as well, since he has claimed that his own practice is made up of defendants who experienced grave injustices in child sexual abuse cases. (Rosenthal represented Kelly Michaels and Frank Fuster at the appellate level.) These sources should yield the bess possible evidence of modern witch-hunts. But in all eight of these examples, it appears that the witch-hunt claim is overblown and distorts or entirely overlooks significant evidence of guilt. Accordingly, these cases are most notable for what they demonstrate about the continuing political interest in rallying around defendants, regardless of the facts, in child sexual abuse cases.

Neil Shumate

Neil Shumate was a popular kindergarten teacher in Pleasanton, California, which makes the origins of his case all the more surprising. A first-grader at Fairlands Elementary School, named Kimberly, told a yard-duty teacher, in a conversation about which teachers they did and did not like, that she did not like Shumate because he "puts his hands down my pants."[26] There was no doubt in the teacher's mind as to what the girl said or meant. Indeed, the teacher knew she was duty-bound to report suspected abuse to the principal. The principal spoke to Kimberly and her older sister, Cathleen. Cathleen apparently reported that Shumate had touched her bottom on many occasions. On the basis of those statements, the principal made reports to the police and child protective services. Through the investigation that followed, it emerged that this was not the first time such complaints had come to the principal. But it *was* the first time she called law enforcement.

The police investigation began with the original two sisters and expanded to other kindergarten, first-, and second-grade students. In additional to the original girls, four other children reported sexual touching by Shumate inside their outer clothing. A complaint was filed soon thereafter charging him with seven counts of child molestation during 1991–92 and 1992–93. A few weeks later, charges were added in connection with a boy who was in Shumate's class in 1988–89. Further investigation identified three additional male victims, all of whom who been molested at Shumate's home while living there as foster children. Two of those boys were added to the criminal charges.

The portrait that emerged of Neil Shumate was of a teacher everyone agreed was "affectionate." Children often sat on his lap, and he regularly hugged and patted children. He was known for administering spankings on children's birthdays, one spank for every year. He was also known for giving "slobbery kisses." A room mother raised concerns with Shumate and others that he was "too affectionate."[27] But he also had a following of admiring parents and teachers. Even so, a mother who weighed in *against* Shumate's being imprisoned told authorities she was uncomfortable when helping in his class because of how he physically handled children. She hoped that he "got help."[28]

Shumate would argue on appeal that "touching [was] an inextricable part of teaching kindergarten" and that five-year-olds "need help with zippers and belts and shirttails on a daily basis."[29] But those kinds of innocuous actions were not the nature of the claims against Shumate; he was charged with rubbing penises and buttocks, over the clothing or over the underwear, and sticking his fingers inside children's pants and underwear.

The children testified at trial and were subject to cross-examination. The defense presented Lee Coleman, who testified for Frank Fuster, to criticize the investigation and opine that the children were not reliable. A brief exchange in cross-examination revealed the extreme implications of Coleman's position. When asked if he had ever conducted an interview of a child for the purposes of determining whether or not the child had been molested, Coleman said "absolutely not" because doing so "would be a contradiction of everything" he believes.[30] He holds it is impossible to "get at the truth of whether a child was molested by a psychiatric examination." In short, he does not believe in interviewing children. It is no wonder he always has something to say for the defense in cases where, inevitably, children have been interviewed.

The biggest surprise at trial was Daniel Bromberg, who had been an aide in Shumate's class in 1981 and testified about a conversation that opened with Shumate saying "You like boys, don't you?" and included Shumate describing how he tries "to be as affectionate with the girls as with the boys" in case the parents of any boys complain.[31] Bromberg's testimony was particularly compelling because he had pleaded guilty to child molestation elsewhere two years later. Shumate's defenders have claimed that this case amounts to making it a crime to be an affectionate teacher. But an examination of the charges and testimony demonstrates that this case is about much more specific touching than is normal, and that Shumate's history was filled with red flags, minimization, and denial. The case began with a spontaneous disclosure, and a quick investigation turned up multiple other charges.

Shumate was convicted by a jury of all the charges. Immediately after his conviction, he tried the innocence-by-association approach, filing these items with the court: Nathan's *Redbook* article about the Kelly Michaels case, several of Rabinowitz's *Wall Street Journal* articles about the Amirault case, and some printed copy from Jonathan Harris's internet Witch-Hunt Information Center. The site contained a list, prepared by Nathan, of cases with allegedly "compelling evidence" of false convictions. Shumate's name was on the list, although he was not included on the dedication page of her book with Snedeker. Shumate also received a surprising level of support from the community. Before sentencing, the court received more than four hundred letters from parents and teachers "stating emphatically that [Shumate] is incapable of such crimes."[32] (An almost equal number of people signed a petition urging a strict sentence.) Shumate's conviction was upheld on appeal.

Christopher Ferrara

Christopher Ferrara was introduced sympathetically by Carol Hopkins at the "Day of Contrition" in Salem, Massachusetts. Ferrara had recently been released from the New York prison system, where he served four years for attempted first-degree sexual abuse. He had been a special deputy in the "Officer Bill" program of the Wyoming County Sheriff's Department, visiting schools and, according to one news story, warning children about "the dangers of talking to strangers."[33] Ferrara was indicted on seven felony counts of first-degree sexual abuse involving boys between nine and fourteen. Ferrara brought boys to his apartment and sometimes "bathed them" and gave them presents. His defenders classify these acts as befriending underprivileged boys. But nobody has explained why a twenty-five-year-old police officer would be "bathing" a fourteen-year-old boy—underprivileged or not—in his apartment. Ferrara served his full sentence because he was unwilling to admit to the parole board that he committed any crime. He was introduced at the event in Salem as a witch-hunt victim who "had not yet had his conviction overturned."[34]

This is not surprising, since his conviction was the result of a guilty plea.[35] What is surprising is the unquestioning acceptance of Ferrara by those at the Day of Contrition. Child molesters often emphasize how they never intended any *harm*. They view their sexual activities as love or education. This may well be true for Christopher Ferrara, and that would undoubtedly be useful information for the purposes of sex-offender treatment. But treatment is meaningless for those who deny their crimes. And the misguided thinking that may help explain how or why Ferrara talked himself into giving young adolescents baths in his apartment is irrelevant to the question of innocence or guilt. Those promoting the witch-hunt narrative at the event in Salem, however, were apparently too intent on their political cause to exercise skepticism or seek to verify claims.

Robert Lawton

Another one of the lesser-known people introduced as a witch-hunt victim at the so-called Day of Contrition is Robert Lawton. Carol Hopkins did not explain why

Lawton deserved to be honored, but Mark Pendergrast had earlier associated Lawton's case, in his book *Victims of Memory*, with the idea that "little children can be led into stating and believing the most outrageous falsehoods."[36] Pendergrast did not provide any details beyond the fact that Lawton had been convicted of sodomizing his three sons.

Lawton's case did not involve young children or repetitive, coercive interviews. The oldest boy was nine years old when he testified, and the case had strong physical evidence. There were deeply disturbing anal findings in all three sons.[37] Dr. Paul Young, a former Burlington area pediatrician who had trained medical students and residents in the areas of physical and sexual abuse of children, testified that the oldest boy, Greg, did not have normal anal findings. There was unusual venous engorgement, physical findings that that were "abnormal and consistent with a history of rectal penetration."[38] His observations on David were similar, but the engorgement was elevated, suggesting that the injury had occurred numerous times. Dr. Young described this "as a strikingly abnormal finding," most likely to have been caused by penetration.[39]

Pendergrast implies that Ceci and Bruck's arguments were responsible for overturning Lawton's conviction in Vermont. Actually, the court did not rule on those issues; instead, it overturned Lawton's conviction because the prosecutor went overboard while cross-examining Lawton. But the decision highlights the range of evidence against him: direct testimony, hearsay, and medical evidence. There was also evidence about an event years earlier in California, when the defendant's brother-in-law walked into a room in his sister's house and allegedly observed Lawton sitting in the middle of a circle of children with an exposed erection.[40] The prosecutor made *three* references to that matter during the trial. The Vermont Supreme Court thought the three references were inflammatory. The court agreed that the incident was "probative," so mentioning it once might have been acceptable. There was also an extended analysis of the motion for acquittal on the charge involving Lawton's youngest son. The court concluded that the child's statements were trustworthy and that there was sufficient evidence to support a conviction, but for the overzealous conduct of the prosecutor.[41]

Was Lawton the victim of a witch-hunt, or did a group of academics and activists embrace a man whose three sons all had strong physical evidence of anal rape, whose brother-in-law reported suspected child sexual abuse years earlier in California, and whose wife took out a restraining order against him in order to protect the children? There is no evidence in the appellate record of anything other than overzealousness on the part of a prosecutor who was apparently outraged at Lawton's misleading testimony on the witness stand.[42] But Lawton was not retried, and the charges were ultimately dismissed, providing an argument for those who would label the case a witch-hunt.

Charles Bighead

Charles Bighead was convicted in 1994 of sexually abusing his daughter, Rita Bighead Eison. She testified that the abuse began when she was seven years old, and that by age eleven she was forced to have sexual intercourse with her father regularly. He would often pay her small sums of money afterward. Bighead was a tribal police officer and was described as "a strict disciplinarian" who punished his children physically and apparently once injured Rita's eye in the process.[43] When Rita was seventeen years old, she insisted that her father stop his sexual assaults. Later that year, she confided in a tribal police officer about the abuse. This set the wheels in motion for Bighead's prosecution. The officer was the first adult Rita had ever told about the abuse.

A federal jury eventually heard from Rita, two of her childhood friends, and Tasha Boychuk, the director of forensic services at the Child Advocacy Center in Phoenix. The childhood friends both testified to statements that Rita made *at the time* about sexual abuse by her father. Boychuk, who testified as a rebuttal witness, spoke only about the general characteristics of sexually abused children, not about Rita in particular. Boychuk told the jury that, on the basis of her experience interviewing more than a thousand children, it is not unusual to delay disclosure of sexual abuse. She was rebutting the defense argument that Rita's credibility was dubious because she delayed reporting the abuse. Bighead denied any wrongdoing. He was convicted, and his conviction was subsequently upheld 2-1 on appeal.

The dissenting opinion in the Ninth Circuit Court of Appeals was written by Judge John T. Noonan, who was apparently incensed that Boychuk was allowed to testify. Noonan invoked the Salem witch trials and expressed his broad dissatisfaction with various "cultural changes" that have nothing to do with the evidence against Bighead.[44] He also railed against those who would claim or believe in satanic ritual abuse but then allowed that such claims were not actually part of this case. He further relied on Richard Gardner's *Sex Abuse Hysteria* to criticize "the kind of persons engaged in the kind of work that Tasha Boychuk is engaged in."[45] In other words, Judge Noonan took the position that Boychuk, whose psychology doctorate involved a field-based validation study of children's statements about sexual abuse, had "remarkable bias" *because she had professional training and experience with child sexual abuse.* The power of crying witch-hunt did not go unnoticed. Thomas Sowell quickly followed suit, editorializing in *Forbes* about the "legal lynching" of Charles Bighead. Sowell bemoaned how "in some cases, even a daughter's own denial that anything happened is not enough to override the suspicion and presumptions of social workers."[46] But this description has nothing to do with the case against Bighead. His daughter was clear and consistent from the moment she disclosed as a seventeen-year-old. What she delayed reporting to any adult she had told to two separate friends during childhood, and both of them verified that fact. Bighead's case had nothing to do with lynching or witch-hunts, but it nevertheless demonstrates how effective those images can be in mobilizing people with a larger agenda against social workers and "survivors" of sexual abuse.[47]

Elsie Oscarson

Elsie Oscarson was convicted of sexually abusing her two sons in Vermont in 2003. Her case is one of the recent "sponsored cases" of the NCRJ, which places her squarely in the contemporary witch-hunt narrative. Her case was located by Pendergrast, who also lives in Vermont. His limited account of the case—based largely on attending a sentencing hearing and talking to the defendant—provides no evidence on which to conclude that her conviction was an injustice. To the contrary, he allows that it was "a messy case" and that "it may be a good thing that [Oscarson's] children were taken from her in Tennessee," years before the case in Vermont.[48] It is not clear why Pendergrast says this since he also apparently thinks that Oscarson was falsely accused in the case. His overall theory is that she has been falsely convicted twice—and that proving the first conviction was wrong might have affected the second case, even though there were far apart in miles, years, and facts.

Is there anything beyond conjecture to support this theory? Pendergrast says there is a memorandum describing the first case as involving "horrendous abuse." He transforms this phrase into the supposition that this earlier case was a "classic satanic ritual abuse" case, but he does not provide a single quote to back up this charge, and the mystery memo is never actually cited. But this conjecture alone is apparently enough for adherents to the witch-hunt narrative. Oscarson passed muster with the "criteria" that the NCRJ claims to employ before deciding whether to sponsor a case. Daniel Patrick Moynihan worried years ago about "defining deviancy down."[49] In the contemporary era, it seems that "witch hunts" are being defined down. Little more than a protestation of innocence by the defendant and some assorted innuendo is necessary for many activists, writers, and academics to cry "witch hunt."

Robert Rosenthal's cases

Robert Rosenthal, who most famously represented Kelly Michaels and worked with Ceci and Bruck on the "Concerned Scientists" amicus brief, has claimed that cases he and others were recently litigating across the country are "testament" to continuation of "witch hunts" involving child sexual abuse. In a letter to the *Wall Street Journal* in 2003, Rosenthal claimed that those like Frank Fuster—who is, in his view, wrongfully imprisoned—"continue to be joined by others like them all too often."[50] He did not mention any of these recent cases by name. But looking at his appellate practice, one finds little evidence to support his claim.

One of Rosenthal's clients was Jose Serrano, convicted by a New York jury of eighteen child sexual-abuse counts in connection with male foster children placed in his home. Serrano had requested that only male foster children be placed in his house. In 1997, a fourteen-year-old identified as Cody O. reported that Serrano had forced him to engage in oral sex. According to Magistrate Judge Victor Bianchini's Report years later, "the authorities told Cody O. he was a liar, and ruining a 'good man's life,' and he recanted his allegations." Another fourteen-year-old, Daniel, reported much the same thing two years later, followed by a third report, by a twelve-year-old named Glen. A police investigation was commenced after a *fourth* report, in 2000, by a twelve-year-old named Edward. The police interviewed other children who had resided in Serrano's home, and two other boys reported sexual abuse. They then interviewed Serrano, and he confessed to the abuse of four boys who had been identified by the police, and one who had not. That boy, who was twelve years old at the time, later confirmed he had been sexually abused by Serrano. Beyond the lack of any reason to think it was a wrongful conviction—one of Serrano's main appellate arguments was to object to his own confession—what is striking about this case is how many children were sexually abused and did not disclose anything at the time.[51] And that some did and were ignored.

Rosenthal also represented Frederick Weber, who had been indicted on thirty-seven counts involving sexual contact with thirteen young girls at his home in Nassau, New York, between 1996 and 2000. Some counts were dismissed for overlapping with each other, others were severed (meaning they would have to be tried separately), and Weber was tried on thirteen counts related to three girls. He was convicted of all counts on one girl, and acquitted on the charges connected to her sister and her friend. Rosenthal argued that the time frame specified in the counts was insufficiently specified and that the trial court should have had a "taint" hearing. The appellate court ruled that the claim of the victims having been subjected to undue suggestion was "speculative" and upheld the conviction, noting that the children and the police investigators had all been subject to cross-examination.[52] Another of Rosenthal's appellate clients was Tyler Lupoli, who was convicted of sexual abuse charges in connection with four girls outside Portland, Oregon. After an appellate court reversed the decision, Lupoli offered to plead guilty to three counts of attempted first-degree sex abuse and two counts of harassment for intimate touching in order to avoid going through another trial. There isn't the slightest hint that the gist of the charges against Lupoli was wrongful. He admitted he touched three young girls inappropriately.[53] These are not witch-hunts, and Rosenthal's arguments are not about factual innocence.

The only possible exception is *State v. Carol M.D.*, the strange case from Wenatchee, Washington.[54] It is strange because one of the children in the case, Susan "Sam" Doggett, ended up in the custody of Carol Hopkins, who had formed an organization devoted to alleged injustices to defendants in child sexual abuse cases. Hopkins, who lived more than a thousand miles from Wenatchee, offered to take custody of the girl, and later she told CBS News she wanted the girl to become "the poster child for the cause."[55] "Sam" apparently recanted claims against her parents while living with Hopkins. Rosenthal's successful appeal, filed before the recantation, included arguments that appear to undercut the claim that there was no abuse in the family. His first argument on appeal was against the use of testimony from a counselor to Doggett's youngest daughter concerning incriminating statements the girl apparently made about her parents.[56] Although excluding such evidence might be appropriate in all fairness to a criminal defendant, it is not the kind of defense that suggests Rosenthal's client was being subjected to a witch-hunt. Charges were eventually dropped and the Doggetts filed suit in federal court claiming their constitutional rights had been violated by the investigation. U.S. District Judge Alan MacDonald ruled the lawsuit "frivolous" and ordered their lawyer to pay the City of Wenatchee's legal fees.[57]

The Wenatchee cases at large are similarly complicated. Much like what came to be known as the Jordan, Minnesota cases, the Wenatchee cases are actually a series of loosely connected cases that should not all be grouped under one heading. It would take years of research to examine the cases thoroughly, but there is readily available evidence to suggest that labeling the entire matter a witch-hunt is inappropriate. A local television station broadcast a prison interview with an adult woman who had pleaded guilty and, even after all the criticism of the case, maintained she and other adults *had* engaged in sexual contact with numerous children.[58] Moreover, a jury in a highly publicized civil trial related to the Wenatchee cases ruled that various public officials did *not* violate the civil rights of eight plaintiffs. The judge had instructed the jurors that if were "facts that would cause a reasonably cautious office to believe that the person had committed the crime for which they were arrested," they should rule for the defendants—the public officials.[59] But it is also clear that there were false convictions in Wenatchee, spurred by an overzealous sheriff, Robert Perez, who would later be discredited for his behavior, including the fact that two key witnesses in several cases were foster children in his home. Perez was also accused of trying to coerce children's testimony and destroying evidence.[60] The false conviction problem has been expounded on in the media and in a book by a defense lawyer, Kathyrn Lyon, called *Witch Hunt*.[61] What has been lost in those accounts is any sense that some of the cases were well founded, some were rightly not overturned, and some were never even challenged. The witch-hunt narrative about these cases paints with such a broad brush that it cloaks the guilty with the veneer of innocence. David Horsey of the *Seattle Post-Intelligencer* drew a cartoon about Wenatchee that featured judges, police, and social workers in bed together. It was titled "The Real Incest," as if the far more widespread type of incest, including Wenatchee defendants who never challenged their convictions, was not real. In this regard, the current discourse has the same imbalance that the witch-hunt narrative brought to cases like those in Jordan, Minnesota, where the tragedies connected to actual abuse were quickly lost to history.

The period of infamous day-care sexual abuse cases ended almost twenty years ago. Yet there are still respected academics, judges, and other professionals carrying the mantle of the witch-hunt narrative. The power of claiming innocence-by-association while employing the rhetoric and imagery of the Salem witch trials is undeniable. Those claims have not met with much success in court, but they have nevertheless helped to mobilize a divergent coalition of interest groups, from father's rights advocates and the False Memory Syndrome Foundation to defense lawyers and assorted academics. These diverse groups share a strong interest in continuing to promote the witch-hunt narrative.

There is also a significant and unexpected convergence of the left and the right around these issues that helps explain why there have been so few skeptical voices about the witch-hunt narrative. Those on the right rally against witch-hunts on the part of child protective services agencies because they do not think that government involvement in the family is legitimate, even to protect children. Those on the left find the witch-hunt narrative compelling because they are already well versed in the abuse of power by police and prosecutors. Accordingly, there is no skepticism of the witch-hunt claim. Both of these political viewpoints are prone to believe the cry of witch-hunt, even if the evidence is as strong as in the cases against Robert Lawton, Christopher Ferrara, Jose Serrano, and others.

The Legacy of the Witch-hunt Narrative
Discounting the Reality of Day-care Sexual Abuse

The infamous day-care sexual abuse cases occurred in the 1980s and early 1990s. There has not been a highly publicized day-care sexual abuse trial in twenty years. The witch-hunt narrative employs this fact as proof that the original cases must have been baseless, creatures of a particular time and place. As one commenter put it, the "sudden absence of new cases" is evidence that "the tumult has subsided."[62] But, just as there were day-care sexual abuse cases *before* the McMartin case (see Chapter Four), there have been day-care sexual abuse cases ever since. It is impossible to ascertain how the overall number of such cases has changed over time. What is clear is that the cases ending up in court are different in two ways. First, prosecutors do not bring massive indictments involving large numbers of children; instead, they are more likely to pare cases down to the strongest counts. Second, if the case goes to trial, it is likely to receive only local publicity; none of the sexual abuse cases in day-care centers since the end of the Michaels case has received significant national coverage. In this way, the perception that these cases have disappeared is actually evidence of a change in our primary window into understanding the issue: media coverage. (Hence the attention earlier in this chapter on the Catholic Church cases and Megan's Law, major topics of media interest in the post-McMartin era.)

A few examples illustrate the reality of day-care sexual abuse in the post-McMartin era. The Oak Tree Day Care Center case in Yucaipa, Arizona, began in 1997 when Nathan Martindale, who was working in his parents' day-care center, was arrested after the parents of three children reported possible abuse. Martindale eventually admitted to some of the allegations, including performing oral copulation on the children (a feature deemed fantastic by Charlier and Downing). In a reflection of how prosecutors tend to handle these cases now, the charges were reduced to apply to one child who was considered the strongest witness. The local newspaper—there was no significant media coverage—reported "investigators were having trouble obtaining clear-cut testimony from other young victims."[63] A decade earlier, many prosecutors would have put those children on the stand. The case would likely have been the kind of perplexing mixture that characterized many in the 1980s, and it might well have been labeled a "hoax." Instead, it is a little-known case that ended in a noncontroversial guilty plea.

A similar result occurred in the Children City Learning Center case in Reno, Nevada, where Gary Hanneman, thirty-three, was arrested and charged in February 2001 with, among other things, ten counts of sexual assault on a child and one count of using a child to produce pornography. Hanneman had been working since 1999 at the center, across the street from the University of Nevada, Reno, campus. Hanneman was well liked, he had no criminal record, and many adults who worked there apparently never saw anything abnormal. He allegedly molested dozens of children over three years without any complaints until the very end of that time. And when the children were finally interviewed, some said "fantastic" things about games with feces. If this had happened in the late 1980s, it would probably be on Charlier and Downing's list of dubious ritual abuse cases from around the country. But the Hanneman case happened ten years later, at a time when video equipment had gone from expensive and novel to affordable and extremely portable. And Hanneman had videotaped some of his crimes. This is probably why he also quickly confessed to molesting twenty-eight children at the day-care center. When explaining why a plea agreement would spare the families involved, the prosecutor made note of Hanneman's form of pedophilia, which "involves a fetish with human excrement." Presumably the videotapes document this supposedly fantastic element. In short, everything about this case that could have been cast as dubious was actually true. Hanneman entered a guilty plea in November 2001. None of the sensational evidence was aired in court, and there was almost no publicity beyond Nevada.

Other recent cases also emphasize the number of victims that can be involved in day-care abuse cases and the number of years such abuse can go still unapprehended in the post-McMartin era. Larry Akins was apprehended in August 2007 for abusing children ranging in age from three to eight over a period of years at the Gingerbread Day Care in Van Buren, Arkansas. He had been operating the center with his wife since 2000. Akins pleaded guilty to charges involving eight children; his lawyer read a statement saying he "took full responsibility."[64] A similar case, but with a much longer history of untold abuse, unfolded in Ste. Genevieve, Missouri, where William E. Huck, Sr., was apprehended in March 2007 for sexually abusing a four-year-old boy at an in-home day care run by his wife. Huck confessed to the crime and provided "a detailed account of how he engaged in sexual contact with the boy twelve different times."[65] He had apparently been doing the same thing for almost thirty years without detection. Officials estimated that approximately forty children had been molested. Neither case received significant media coverage.

A final case is noteworthy because it emanates from Wenatchee, Washington, the location of probably the worst excesses in a sexual abuse investigation in the mid-1990s and possibly since. The day-care case had nothing to do with those earlier ones. The defendant, Agustin O. Barragan, pleaded guilty in 2010 to two counts of third-degree assault of a child in an Alford plea that acknowledged that the state had sufficient evidence to convict him. The abuse occurred at the Barragan's in-home day care in Wenatchee. According to a local newspaper account, Child Protective Services records entered in this case indicate there had been complaints against Barragan in 1994, 1995, and 2003.[66] *None of those investigations resulted in any charges or loss of license.* Given his eventual admission in the 2010 case, one wonders whether the earlier investigations were dropped in error, the kind of thing that never gets mentioned in the witch-hunt narrative, where "unsubstantiated" is frequently conflated with "untrue."[67]

These anecdotes illustrate the continued existence of sexual abuse in day-care centers. They also demonstrate something about the power of the secrecy and related forces against children disclosing such abuse even in the post-McMartin era. They all involved multiple victims, and yet none were quickly exposed. The fact that prosecutors are savvier and the media is less obsessed with these cases is beneficial. What is unclear is whether those improvements occurred alongside a decrease in the likelihood of investigating and prosecuting sexual abuse in day-care settings. The question is impossible to answer with existing data sources. There is no national archive of data on state prosecutions of this crime, and the state-level data from Child Protective Services agencies are scattered and tend to lump day-care abuse into the broader category of "institutional abuse." Nevertheless, there are a variety of reasons to postulate that the official number of cases involving day-care centers has gone down more than the actual incidence of such abuse.

First, original data obtained from DYFS in New Jersey suggest a worrisome trend. There were twenty-five cases of substantiated sexual abuse in day-care centers in New Jersey in 1986. One of those involved Wee Care in Maplewood, New Jersey (the Kelly Michaels case), and that year was the high water mark. There were ten substantiated cases in 1992 and nine in 1993, the year the Michaels case was overturned on appeal. The following year, there was only one substantiated case statewide. *There were none in the three years after that.* From those data, it would appear that either sexual abuse in day-care centers stopped occurring in New Jersey after 1993 or it stopped being investigated and recognized. There is no reason to think it is the former and there are very specific reasons to think that DYFS might try to avoid such cases in the years after Michaels. These data from a single state over ten years need to be supplemented by studies of multiple states in more recent years.

Second, empirical studies of case flows in criminal courts bear out the hypothesis that cases with younger children are more likely to be dismissed by prosecutors. Stroud and her co-authors in New Mexico conducted one of the only studies to compare cases referred to prosecutors against those that were not.[68] They found that 32 percent of the dropped cases involved children age four and under, while only 9 percent of the criminal cases involved children that age. In another study, prosecutors accepted 35 percent of the sexual abuse referrals in cases involving children four to six and 69 percent for ages seven to twelve.[69] Ellen Gray's study of eight jurisdictions across the country described cases involving victims five years old or younger as "notoriously difficult to prosecute effectively."[70] Not all studies find such a clear result. William Tucker obtained strikingly different results in comparing information from child advocacy centers in Minnesota and Wisconsin in order to analyze the possible effect of age and other variables on the likelihood of a case moving forward in the criminal justice system.[71] But the consensus of existing literature is that cases involving young children are much less likely to move forward in the criminal justice system.

Finally, there is survey evidence that prosecutors have internalized these values. In one survey, 62 percent of prosecutors said "too young" was sometimes or very often a reason for rejecting a child sexual abuse case.[72] Tucker's survey of prosecutors in eleven states found that, with controlled vignettes, younger age was clearly associated with decrease in likelihood to prosecute.[73] Since vignettes hold facts constant and vary only designated variables, these findings reflect a general attitude about the age of child witnesses.

The concern that screening mechanisms might screen out good cases is rarely discussed in the existing literature in law and psychology, where the implication of the witch-hunt narrative is that day-care sexual abuse charges are "bizarre" and to be discredited. In 2004, Ceci and Bruck wrote that a "disproportionate number of studies of preschool children at the end of the 20th century" was "directly motivated by forensic concerns of the day."[74] Those concerns were exclusively about defendants, and this book argues they were misplaced. Moreover, an imbalance still exists in the psychology literature. As Professors Tom Lyon and Kathy Pezdek have pointed out, there is much more attention paid to what is wrong with interviews than there is to how to make them better.[75] In the meantime, there are several reasons to be concerned about whether sexual abuse cases involving young children, in and out of day care, are less likely to be acted on now than they were in the 1980s.

Undermining the Credibility of Children

The witch-hunt narrative came out of cases from the 1980s and prevailed in the court of public opinion, in many criminal courts, and in the field of psychology in the 1990s. But what started as a contest over highly publicized day-care cases in the 1980s has turned out to have ramifications far beyond those cases. One lasting effect is in the field of psychology, where the idea that children are "highly suggestible" has taken hold largely because of the persuasive, but inaccurate, portrayal of the Michaels case. A group of activists and academics have mobilized around this narrative to promote various agendas and support cases that seek to discredit children.

The first sign of this political mobilization came when the television program *Nightline* set out in 1996, a year after the Michaels case was over, to examine whether children's testimony was being unduly discredited. They wondered whether one effect of the witch-hunt narrative was that it was harder to bring and win cases that were based on the word of a child. This concern had been expressed during the years when Ceci and Bruck's position started dominating the field. The decision by Gail Goodman and others not to sign the "Concerned Scientists" brief in the Michaels case was based on similar concerns. A single-minded and exaggerated view of child suggestibility was bound to have negative consequences on children as witnesses.

The ABC network quickly discovered there were writers and academics so devoted to the witch-hunt narrative that they mobilized to object to a program about whether children's testimony was being unduly discounted *before* the program was aired. There was an organized campaign to discredit Civia Tamarkin, a journalist who contributed to the program and had once been an advisory board member of Believe the Children. Tamarkin had also said, in a speech about

ritual abuse cases that was later published in article form, that she was "unequivocally . . . convinced that these crimes do occur."[76] Peter Freyd, a mathematics
professor at the University of Pennsylvania who helped form the False Memory
Syndrome Foundation (FMSF), sent an email labeled "Nightline Alert" through
the FMSF-News distribution list. The message claimed that Tamarkin was the
producer of the upcoming program and the message contained "background
information assembled by Debbie Nathan," along with copies of two separate
letters from Nathan to *Nightline*. In those letters, Nathan painted Tamarkin as
espousing "discredited and downright bizarre child abuse theories."[77] This effort
did not succeed in keeping the program off the air, but it demonstrated surprisingly strong resistance to asking questions about whether the witch-hunt narrative has had negative effects.

When the program aired, Ted Koppel began with an unusual preface that
gently scolded those who so strongly protested against a program they had not
yet seen. Correcting the misimpression that Tamarkin produced or reported
the story—she had acted only as a consultant—Koppel expressed the view that
the story is "important" and "had been compiled as fairly and cleanly as possible."[78] The program opened with television footage from a highly publicized
case from Broward County, Florida, where two girls had been raped and murdered by a man whose long record of sex crimes against children had been met
by lenient, even lackadaisical, responses by the state. On New Year's Eve 1995,
an eleven-year-old girl was assaulted by a man who took off his clothes, carried
her into his bedroom, and tried to rape her. They struggled and she managed to
kick him hard enough that he stopped. As she left the room, the man said to
her: "Tell somebody about this. It was a bad thing that I did; I shouldn't have
done it."[79] The girl told her father, who filed a police report within two hours,
identifying Howard Steven Ault as the assailant. A detective took a taped statement from the girl and her father, and then the case languished for more than
ten months.

It was later revealed that Ault was on probation at the time for sexual assault
on a six-year-old girl in 1994.[80] He had also been convicted of attempted sexual
battery of a twelve-year-old girl in Lauderdale Lakes in 1988. But Ault was not
arrested on the New Year's Eve charges. No action was taken until ten months
later, when he was in custody at the Oakland Park Police station in connection
with the kidnapping, rape, and murder of two homeless sisters, age eleven and
seven. Only then did Broward County detectives—embarrassed by their failure
to take the other eleven-year-old girl seriously—rush to try to cover themselves
for all those months of inaction. "A Child's Word" used the case to point out the
potential costs of discounting or failing to act on the word of a child. They also
quoted prosecutors who argued that it had become more difficult to bring sexual
abuse cases because people were unduly dismissive of children as witnesses.

"Distorted Journalism," Nat Hentoff titled his *Village Voice* column the following week—the first of two columns he devoted entirely to an attack on "A Child's Word." "Why was not a single abandoned case mentioned?" Hentoff protested, labeling the program "propaganda" for asserting that lives had been lost because of the discrediting of child witnesses.[81] Hentoff was apparently unaware that the videotape at the beginning of the program was from the Ault case—a highly publicized case that illustrates in gruesome detail how discounting the word of a child ultimately cost the lives of two children.[82] But their story, which generated considerable publicity when the girls were found murdered, was quickly lost in the popular discourse about child sexual abuse. There has not been a serious engagement of the questions raised in "A Child's Word," in print or broadcast, since. There have been flashes of media attention to more recent Ault-like stories, such as the Avila case in California in which Samantha Runnion's life would have been spared had the word of two eleven-year-old girls been taken more seriously a year earlier.[83] But these grim cases have not generated much commentary or attention to the general question of child credibility and whether the word of a child is too quickly doubted or dismissed.

The same people who objected to "A Child's Word" gathered the following year in Salem, Massachusetts, for an event they called the Day of Contrition. Held on the three hundredth anniversary of a day of remorse for the Salem witch trials, they could not have been more direct in trying to associate their own causes with the righteousness of being against the witch trials. The event was ostensibly organized by Carol Hopkins, an activist from San Diego who had formed something she called the "Justice Committee."[84] Her organization generated the most exaggerated estimate of wrongful convictions in the 1980s, claiming there were "thousands" of such cases. Hopkins described the purpose of the Day of Contrition as addressing "the reasons and remedies for the nationwide epidemic of spurious accusations and prosecutions."[85] The event featured writers, academics, and former defendants connected to all of the major cases in this book: McMartin, Michaels, and Country Walk. Ralph Underwager led a prayer at the event and Richard Gardner, a frequent defense expert in these cases, gave a fiery speech that argued "a whole industry has been spawned" as a result of the Child Abuse Prevention and Treatment Act (CAPTA) and that "hysteria is being fueled by the money." The audience applauded when he said "children are liars!"[86]

Gardner is perhaps best known for coining the phrase "parental alienation syndrome," which attributes a child's statements about sexual abuse, most often in the context of a divorce case, to the "alienation" of the hostile parent, almost always the mother. PAS, as it has come to be known, does not have a scientific basis in the literature, but it had an enthusiastic following in Salem.[87] Supporters of "false memory syndrome," which suffers from the same problem, were also active participants in the conference.[88] These groups sought to gain credibility and acceptance by associating themselves with the imagery of Salem. That much was public. What was not publicized is that Herman Ohme—an activist with the False Memory Syndrome Foundation, and one of the behind-the-scenes organizers of the event—with assistance from Carol Hopkins and Richard Gardner had been working closely with a staff member of Illinois Senator Dan Coats, a conservative Republican, to water down the Child Abuse Treatment and Prevention Act.[89] They did not succeed in eliminating the statutory mandate to report suspected child abuse, but the larger agenda of these activists endured.

Eileen McNamara wrote a column for the *Boston Globe* about the Day of Contrition titled "Hardly a Case of Persecution." Arguing that there is no evidence we are preoccupied with protecting children, she criticized those at the event for seeing "rampant hysteria" where it does not exist.[90] She did not use the strident language of the witch-hunt narrative, but she did experience the same kind of wrath that came down on Koppel when ABC asked whether a child's word has become unduly discredited because of the efforts of people to associate more and more cases with the imagery of Salem.[91] It was becoming apparent that there was intense opposition to anyone who questioned the exaggerated claims advanced by these groups.

The Marzolf Case: Expansive Efforts to Label Children as "Tainted"

One of the worries of those who opposed the idea of "taint hearings" in the Michaels case was that a process arguably justified by the most extreme cases would be imposed on cases where it did not belong. Taint hearings are a special procedure that allows defendants to argue a child has been so "tainted" by the interview process that the child is not reliable enough to testify at trial; these hearings came about in New Jersey as a result of the Michaels case. The Marzolf case, the first taint hearing held in New Jersey after Michaels, provided the first test of those concerns. The case arose under circumstances that would seem to eliminate the need for a taint hearing, to wit, it began when James Marzolf, twenty-nine, had his hands down the pants of his young nephew when the boy's stepfather, Mark Glazer, walked into the room. Marzolf thought he was alone with the seven-year-old Tyler, on the third floor of an empty house. Glazer testified that after registering what he was seeing, he backed up and announced his presence from the hallway, whereupon Marzolf came out of the room looking startled and saying something about "wrestling" with Tyler.[92] Glazer told his wife about the incident an hour later; they called DYFS the next day and asked advice about what to do. DYFS referred them to the police, who arranged to interview the boy and both parents a few days later.

Tyler was shy and reticent to talk. Most of his answers in the twenty-seven-page interview transcript are single words or phrases. Even so, occasional answers included details that speak volumes. "What did he do with his hand when he touched you?" the boy was asked after he had said he was touched and pointed to his "pee-pee." Tyler did not respond by saying tickle, or pinch, or something vague; he answered, "He went up and down."[93] Near the end of the interview, Tyler indicated that Uncle Jimmy bought "special" underwear for him, he got the underwear "from a closet," the underwear were "too small" for Tyler, and Uncle Jimmy made him wear them when he was "at his house." When police executed a search, the colorful, "too small" bikini underwear was located in the closet where Tyler said it would be. The boy gave a second statement on September 14 that had much more detail and included additional allegations against Marzolf. Criminal charges were ultimately based on these two statements and the stepfather's statement about observing the original event.

It seems strange that this case would even be subject to a taint hearing given a level of corroboration that would have allowed it to go to trial even back when the word of a child alone could not sustain charges. Yet the defendant was able to convince a judge to have a taint hearing, referred to as a Michaels hearing by the court.[94] What could possibly be said in a case where the child made a statement promptly and there was an adult witness? As it turns out, Maggie Bruck appeared for the defendant and offered the opinion that "there is a high degree of possibility" that the evidence from the boy is "unreliable."[95] He was so unreliable, she argued, that the judge should prohibit him from testifying at trial.

Bruck had criticisms of every step of the investigation. She viewed the five days between the initial report and the first police interview as "problematic." Ideally, she said, the interview should have been done "immediately."[96] She criticized the first interview as having too many directed questions. She allowed, in cross-examination, that the interviewer was sensitive in this interview, he did not pressure Tyler, and she would not likely have been able to conduct a better interview. Still, she considered it "biased." As for the much more detailed statements in the boy's second interview, Bruck opined that "one should really be concerned about the accuracy" of the second interview—*because* it was the second interview.[97]

The most striking part of Bruck's position is the contention that disclosing sexual abuse is a simple process normally done in one fell swoop. Referring to cases she "had been involved with" in which she thought there *was* sexual abuse—but without providing any actual case names—Bruck described the process of disclosure as follows: "it is sort of like the story just comes out and it is there."[98] Under that view, any child who does not disclose everything in the first interview is apparently suspect. Bruck's involvement in cases, it should be noted, was not as a clinician. She is not in the practice of evaluating children for suspected abuse or treating children who have been sexually abused.

Bruck also made several critical judgments about the boy's mother and step-father. She discredited the account of the stepfather, who said he witnessed Mar-zolf with his hands down the boy's pants, on the grounds that he had allegedly changed his story. "I think their reporting two years later just sounded very dif-ferent to what it was in the police reports five days later," she asserted. "And I think that the way they present the situation now it looks more—it looks cleaner," she continued, "than what was in their original statements."[99] But a direct comparison of the police report on August 25, 1995, and the stepfather's testimony on May 5, 1997, reveals that the two are extremely consistent.[100] Bruck focused her critique on the mother, who had the most interactions with her son about these events between his first and second interviews with the police. Bruck's position was predicated on the argument that the boy was "primed" by his first interview because, as she put it, Tyler was "asked to in fact engage in, you know, circling things and showing things on the doll."[101] There wasn't actually a doll. Sargent Hassim had a diagram, and he asked the boy to circle anywhere he had been touched. The boy circled the place he called his "wiener." Bruck cited recent work by Jane Rawls for the proposition, "when chil-dren are interviewed with line drawings, that line drawings can increase sugges-tiveness."[102] But the Rawls study actually differentiated between open-ended questions and directed questions and found the former to be much more accu-rate. Those *were* the kinds of questions Tyler was asked when he was given the line drawing.[103] After this "priming," Bruck's argument continued, a certain amount of suggestive questioning from the mother could account for Tyler's statements in the second interview. How did Bruck justify the conclusion that the mother was likely to have questioned her son in a way that tainted his testi-mony forever? The passage in which she justified her conclusion reads exactly as follows:

> I just—I mean, I can't be sure exactly what she said, but I think my—my feeling was that there were just enough hints in this record that she had certain fears and certain premises she was asking Tyler about.[104]

Elsewhere, Bruck is adamant that she represents the voice of science, and that clinicians, who do not conduct controlled laboratory experiments, do not. Yet in rendering her professional opinion that a mother's questions had likely tainted her son forever, Bruck relied on a *feeling*. That feeling did not strike Judge Cole-man as plausible, particularly in light of the mother's actual testimony.[105] He ruled that the state had presented "clear and convincing evidence that the state-ment is reliable," which meant the case could proceed to trial. He based the deci-sion in part on two common-sense ideas that were voiced by the psychologist who testified for the state. First, children are not disposed to believe bad things about someone they love; and by all accounts, Tyler loved "Uncle Jim." Second, people "aren't always willing to come forward with all of the information [about sexual abuse] on the first instance."[106] Disclosures often occur over time; this fact alone should not be taken as suspect. The outcome in this case was sensible enough, but one wonders whether it also means any defendant in New Jersey with the resources and the inclination can subject any child, and the adults with whom have the child has had contact, to a taint hearing. It would appear so.

The taint hearing took a toll on the boy's family. It constituted only a handful of court days but ended up being spread out over almost two years. By the time it was over, the parents did not want to go through an actual trial, having already endured a trial-like hearing that treated them as if they were the defendants.[107] The Glazers moved away and declined to cooperate any further with the prosecution.[108] Accordingly, charges against Marzolf were dropped in December 1997. The taint hearing was a success, at least in terms of the outcome. But the prosecution had won the battle and lost the case. One of the worries among those who argued against taint hearings at the time of the Michaels case was that they would impose needless and discouraging costs on children and their families. The Marzolf case bears out the concern.

The eventual consequences in the Marzolf case were worse. Marzolf moved to Pennsylvania and opened a karate school. In 2002, he was arrested and charged with possession of child pornography and nine counts of sexual abuse of children.[109] He eventually pleaded guilty to single felony counts of child pornography and child molestation.[110] This case demonstrates the real cost of failing to hold someone like Marzolf accountable for the events in New Jersey; the price was paid by children in Pennsylvania.

It is surprisingly difficult to ascertain how often taint hearings have been held in New Jersey and to what end. Cases that are dropped as a result of taint hearings would be most difficult to find, since they do not reach trial and would never produce any appellate documents. There would be an appellate opinion only in cases where children's testimony was admitted after a taint hearing and the defendant was subsequently convicted and then appealed. One case that fits this description involved former school psychologist James Krivacska, who published an article in Underwager's journal in 1991 about the "dangers" of informing children about sexual abuse.[111] Although he did not mention this in his article, Krivacska had been arrested for child sexual abuse in 1986 and was acquitted in a trial that pitted his word against a single child's. His conviction in 1998, stemming from allegations at another school, was based on the testimony of two children, who were subjected to a taint hearing that concluded with the decision that both boys could testify at trial. Krivacska was then convicted by a jury and sentenced to twenty-six years in prison. One might think Ceci and Bruck would be satisfied with this outcome, since there *was* a taint hearing. But

Ceci, Bruck, and eight other psychologists filed a brief at the U.S. Supreme Court in April 2002 in an effort to overturn Krivacska's conviction.[112] They described their research as "uncontroverted within the scientific community" and branded Kathryn Hall, who testified for the state, as a "self-styled 'expert'" who "propounded junk science."[113] Hall, who has a doctorate in psychology, acknowledged Ceci and Bruck's work, but she did not agree on how it applied to this case. The U.S. Supreme Court declined to hear the case, ending Krivacska's appeals. After a hearing in 2008, the Special Classification Review Board in New Jersey found that Krivacska, who they declined to release on parole, had acknowledged he "created victims and admits to some guilt."[114] Krivacska is still listed as one of the "sponsored cases" by the NCRJ, the organization headed by Michael Snedeker.

Although the controversy over whether to have special procedures for vetting children's testimony remains alive, the danger for children lies as much in the taint *rhetoric* as it does in court holdings about taint hearings.[115] By framing the issue about children's testimony in terms of *taint*, the concepts of gradations and degrees are glossed over with a rhetorical sleight of hand. Children are either tainted, or they are not. And given that defense experts seem to have enough targets in virtually any interview to support a conclusion that a child is tainted, the taint rhetoric often predestines the result. Children do not live in laboratory experiments; they populate the real world, where interviews and other human interactions are always subject to criticism. The important question is whether legitimate concerns about suggestibility are so strong that children should be prohibited from testifying. Though it would seem wise to reserve this argument for the most extreme cases, it has increasingly been applied to everyday child sexual abuse cases, including those with strong corroborative evidence. In no other area of law do we require a test like this before allowing a member of a class to testify. The taint arguments are distinctively anti-child.

The Rouse Case: Contesting Child Abuse Accommodation Syndrome

Another post-Michaels development is the widening attack on child abuse accommodation syndrome (CAAS), a theory put forth by Roland Summit in 1983 about how children disclose abuse and why it often remains secret. The theory was developed through clinical observation and was presented along with some empirical support from published studies.[116] Summit never claimed the theory was diagnostic. Though it is best known for what it predicts about disclosure, the foundation of the theory is that there are preconditions to the occurrence of sexual abuse. In other words, there are reasons inherent to the commission of the act itself that suggest disclosure would be difficult and slow. This was a large point of Summit's conceptualization. Two of the five components in CAAS are preconditions: secrecy and helplessness. They help explain how sexual abuse occurs in the first place and why eventual disclosure does not come quickly and easily. The final three components of the syndrome are (3) entrapment and accommodation, (4) delayed disclosure, and (5) retraction.

Child abuse accommodation syndrome is dismissed wholesale in the witch-hunt narrative. The concept and its author are both seen as contributing causes to the worst injustices of those years. According to the narrative, Summit's conceptualization, which considers retraction as a normal part of the disclosure process, results in a kind of catch-22, where if a child says he was abused, then he should be seen as abused, but if a child denies he was abused, then he is probably in denial and was actually abused. But Summit never made this claim, which conflates denials with retraction. Nevertheless, Lawrence Wright blamed Summit for precisely this kind of catch-22 logic in a blistering editorial in the *New Yorker*. (Wright had to issue a rare retraction later.[117]) The apparent desire to discredit child abuse accommodation syndrome at all costs lives on.

Ceci and Bruck have joined this campaign. In an article called "Unveiling Four Common Misconceptions," they argue that "recent developments in forensic psychology" challenge four misconceptions about children's disclosures. The first is, in their words, that "sexually abused children do not disclose their abuse."[118] After labeling child abuse accommodation syndrome as "the most popular embodiment of this idea," Ceci and Bruck argue that the theory is not well supported by empirical studies. They criticize various studies because participants who reported delayed disclosure were never asked whether they had specifically been asked about abuse earlier. In other words, even though many respondents did not disclose their abuse, this does not mean they would deny it if asked directly. Possibly so. But it hardly provides sufficient evidence to claim it is a *misconception* to say that "sexually abused children do not disclose their abuse." The authors' own meta-study concluded that "only 33% of adults remembered disclosing the abuse in a timely fashion."[119] In other words, more than two-thirds of sexually abused children delay the disclosure of sexual abuse. What Ceci and Bruck label as "Misconception #1" is actually true. A significant majority of sexual abuse victims do not disclose their abuse, and for most others there is a delay between the abuse and telling someone about it.[120]

Nothing in Summit's elaboration of child abuse accommodation syndrome says that denials should be taken as evidence of abuse, although he and his theory are both frequently accused of proposing this kind of circular logic. But Summit's view is more problematic on the matter of recantations. Recantations involve children who have already disclosed something to someone. If considered a normal part of the disclosure process, then almost any child who recants could be seen as doing something that sexually abused children are likely to do. As a result, recantations might not be taken seriously enough. That is, they could automatically be *disbelieved* because there is an expectation that children who have disclosed abuse will also recant at some point in the process. Summit never said it this strongly, and his discussion was specifically about sexual abuse within a family context and in situations where two other conditions were met. But those subtleties are consistently glossed over in the witch-hunt narrative

Ceci and Bruck argue that the studies with the highest reported recantation rates among abused children are methodologically the weakest. One of those studies involves children from the McMartin case, and another involves children who were apparently all from the practice of Barbara Snow, a therapist in Utah. Their critique, along with London and Shuman, of these studies is well taken.[121] But those are not the only studies on the matter. Ceci and Bruck conclude that studies with stronger methodologies report recantation in less than 10 percent of cases, while there are widespread claims that it happens at least 25 percent of the time.

If recantation is not a normal part of disclosure, does that make it more likely to be accurate? Is it more likely a child who recants an allegation was not actually abused? It would seem so. But it appears some have taken the position that recantations almost always mean the initial disclosure was false, evincing a willingness to disregard corroborative evidence of abuse as well as evidence concerning pressures brought upon the child who recanted. This may seem like a particularly surprising position for Ceci and Bruck, who seem attuned to every possible way in which children's statements about abuse might have been tainted. But in cases where recantations seem to have been produced by family pressure and other forms of coercion, Bruck, acting as an expert witness, has been willing to overlook corroborative evidence of abuse rather than recognize the existence of coercion on behalf of those who become defendants.

These issues are highlighted in the Rouse case, as it is known in legal filings, an interfamilial sexual abuse case involving four defendants (Desmond and Jessie Rouse, and Garfield Feather and Russell Hubbeling) from the Yankton Sioux Reservation in South Dakota. The four were convicted in 1994 of sexually abusing Rebecca, Tiffany, Lacey, and Joanie Rouse, who were all between four and seven at the time.[122] The complainants were all grandchildren of Rosemary Rouse, whose house they were living in along with two of the defendants. The other two defendants—Feather and Hubbeling, their uncles—came to the house to drink beer, and occasionally they stayed over.

The case began when Rebecca Rouse, five, was removed from her grandmother's home in November 1993, after a teacher at her school filed a report of suspected neglect.[123] The girl made statements to her foster mother two months later about sexual abuse by her uncles. The foster mother called child protective services, and arrangements were made for Rebecca to be interviewed the next day by therapist Ellen Kelson. On the basis of Rebecca's statements on January 10, 1993, the other children in the house were quickly removed. Some adamantly denied that there had been any sexual abuse; they were returned. Others made incriminating statements that constituted the basis for the criminal case. The children were all examined by pediatricians, and the results were so striking that they bear recounting in some detail. Moreover, they include statements by the girls themselves that are closest to the events in time and possibly most damning in terms of content.[124]

Dr. Kaplan found signs of recent trauma including a bruise or contusion on the left labia, inside the majora, of 4½-year-old, Joanie Rouse. Pointing to her labia, the girl told Dr. Kaplan "Uncle Jessie hurt me."[125] Dr. Kaplan found a large bruise on the right labia of 6-year-old, Lacey Rouse.[126] It was an acute injury sustained within the last week. Dr. Kaplan noted a readily open hymen and a midline scar on the anus at the 6:00 o'clock position on Rebecca Rouse, the 5-year-old who made the first accusations in the case. Pointing to her vagina, the girl told Dr. Kaplan that she had a bruise "where my uncle put his private spot."[127] Dr. Kaplan also found contusions on the right inner labia majora and considerable tenderness in 7-year-old Tiffany Rouse. The contusions were evidence of recent trauma. Dr. Randall Alexander, board certified in pediatrics, reviewed the files and confirmed how strongly they indicated sexual abuse. Responding to the defense claims that these injuries might have happened accidentally, Dr. Alexander testified that "it's a pretty rare event" to see a girl with a labial injury from an accidental source.[128] There were three girls with such injuries in this case. None presented any kind of history that included some kind of freak accident.

The prosecution's case was based on the testimony of these children—three of whom were allowed to testify by closed-circuit television after the court found they were afraid of the defendants—and on related medical testimony. The defense focused on events that happened after the initial disclosures. They engaged Ralph Underwager to offer his opinion that:

> children in this case have been subjected to massive and coercive social influence by adults . . . such as to make it highly likely that any statements are so contaminated by adult behaviors as to be unreliable.[129]

It was a clever way of acting as if claims about reliability were not really claims about credibility. Expert witnesses are not supposed to offer judgments on whether to believe a particular witness. This was the criticism of Eileen Treacy's testimony in the Michaels case—that her testimony "essentially" did so. In the Rouse case, the judge limited the scope of Underwager's testimony to avoid statements that would specifically impugn the child witnesses. The limits on his testimony became a major issue on appeal.

A divided three-judge panel in the Eighth Circuit Court of Appeals overturned the verdicts in November 1996. Judge Myron Bright's majority opinion adopted the witch-hunt narrative in literal terms. "With respect to conditions that can influence children's memories," the judge notes, "we are mindful of a historical event of some three hundred years ago," the Salem witch trials. After stating that nineteen adults were put to death as alleged witches, the judge noted: "This case, of course, is not a Salem Witch Trial, but that history must remind us that memory, particularly children's memory, may be falsely induced."[130] Returning to the matter at hand, the judge ruled it was prejudicial error to prohibit Underwager from relating his general testimony about suggestibility to the specific facts of this case. The witch-hunt digression is notable primarily because it flies in the face of the evidence in the case, including spontaneous statements to pediatricians and overwhelming medical evidence of sexual abuse. Chief Judge James B. Loken's dissent points out, bluntly and with detailed documentation, that "the majority takes liberties with the record in attempting to cast doubt on the jury."[131]

The decision would be cited in the APA Monitor as evidence of Ceci and Bruck's effect on the field.[132] But the decision was short-lived. Less than three months later, the decision was vacated by the grant of a motion for rehearing[133]. On rehearing, the three-judge panel issued a new opinion *affirming* the original convictions. Judge Loken was now writing for the majority and Judge Bright was the dissenter. As Loken put it, "It is clear from the record that [Underwager] was intent upon expressing his ultimate opinion that the victims' accusations of sexual abuse were not credible."[134] Loken considered this to be the domain of the jury. While allowing that Underwager might have been given wider latitude to testify about suggestibility issues, the judge concluded it would not have altered the result of a trial with such strong medical evidence and contemporaneous statements.

Two years later, the defendants made a motion for a new trial, arguing that there was new evidence in the form of recantations from all the original child witnesses. The recantations were captured on a videotaped interview conducted by none other than Ralph Underwager, on January 30, 1999. The court held an evidentiary hearing on the matter, and Maggie Bruck appeared for the defense. She summarized the literature on recantations and criticized, for sound and well-taken reasons, two of the studies often relied on by clinicians. Bruck's position, based on a meta-study she coauthored, was that recantation rates are quite low and could *not* be said to be "a natural part of the process," as Summit postulated in child abuse accommodation syndrome.

Bruck went one bold step further. She "did the math" and—relying on the assumption that the five recantations were independent events—testified there was a "one in nine hundred" chance of this many witnesses recanting.[135] The prosecutor called it "mysterious math." Chief Judge Lawrence L. Peirsol, who was generally complimentary to Bruck, told her he was "troubled" with these calculations. "These are not independent events," he said; they are "in a family situation." Bruck eventually backed down and called the math "a logical exercise."[136] She settled for the idea that the odds of at least one child recanting in this case are, given the literature, as big as one in four, or more likely about one in ten.

But even if there is only a 10 percent chance that a sexually abused child will recant a true accusation, isn't there every reason to conclude *under the facts of this case* that the recantations were likely to be in this group? As Judge Piersol noted:

> The children did not recant until they were sent home and were being cared for by the mothers and grandmothers who did not believe the abuse occurred and who made it known to the children that they missed their sons and brothers.[137]

Moreover, there was a telling incident on December 6, 1999, after the motion for a new trial was filed, between Joanie Rouse and a school counselor who knew nothing about the case.[138] The counselor testified that Joanie told her she was afraid for the upcoming Christmas break because her uncles were coming home. When the counselor asked why this was worrisome, Joanie reportedly said because they touched her private parts and would be mad at her for her telling.[139] These "recantations" are also suspect thanks to the earlier involvement of Underwager, who "interviewed" two of these girls in 1996. The tape is under seal, but according to Judge Peirsol, Underwager told the children "he was there to help the children get the defendants out of prison and he talked at length of the prison sentences imposed."[140] Having a stated purpose and actively enlisting the assistance of the children in meeting the purpose is presumably just as inappropriate when it is done by the defense as when it is done by the prosecution. But even though the Rouse defendants have been embraced as the "Yankton Four," nobody writing about this case has criticized Underwager's heavy-handed efforts. Instead, Maggie Bruck and Hollida Wakefield, Underwager's wife, have continued to champion the case, with the support of Michael Snedeker's organization.[141]

This case evokes the grand conflict between different ways of knowing in psychology. If Bruck's way is the only true claim to knowledge, then until there are laboratory experiments about family dynamics and sexual abuse—something that will never occur, given ethical and practical limitations—we will not be able to recognize that pressures exist within a family to recant abuse allegations. Requiring a deliberate blindness to such things because they have not been measured in a controlled experiment seems eerily like adopting the mindset that existed before we "recognized" the sexual abuse of children. The consequences would certainly be quite similar.

More generally, popular writing and academic studies that played a foundational role in the witch-hunt narrative have since been used to discredit children as a class. In *Kennedy v. Louisiana*, the U.S. Supreme Court cited "serious systematic concerns" in child rape cases, particularly the "problem of unreliable, induced, and even imagined child testimony."[142] The court cited Ceci and Freidman's *Cornell Law Review* article stating that "there is strong evidence that children, especially young children, are suggestible to a significant degree."[143] Law professor Samuel Gross and his coauthors wrote about this issue in 2005, appropriately holding the claim of exoneration to cases involving "an official act declaring a defendant not guilty of a crime for which he or she had previously been convicted." Employing this definition, the authors allowed that almost none of the famous child abuse cases from the 1980s and early 1990s qualify as "exonerations." Neverthelesss, relying on Nathan and Snedeker's book, they opined that "there is *no doubt* that most were falsely convicted" (emphasis added).[144] The shortcomings of that assertion have been elaborated elsewhere in this book. But the witch-hunt narrative nevertheless provides the basis for the majority's opinion in *Kennedy* concerning a "special risk of wrongful execution." Yet, there have not been *any* studies that actually document a significant difference between the accuracy of criminal court outcomes in cases involving children and those involving adults. Instead, this widespread belief, cited by the Supreme Court as if it were fact, apparently stems from the saliency of the witch-hunt narrative in "explaining" the day-care sexual abuse cases from the 1980s and early 1990s. What the opinion expresses is a kind of return to the disfavored jury instruction that used to tell jurors to discount children as a class. In its place, the U.S. Supreme Court relied on the stereotype of children as significantly less reliable. There are plenty of arguments for opposing the death penalty in general. But the claim there is a "serious systemic concern" for child rape convictions that does not exist for murder is without a solid factual basis.

Moreover, this argument takes a one-dimensional view of "reliability," focusing on false positives without apparent regard for the problem of false denials. A "gold standard" study on the failure to disclose known abuse involved a population of young children with sexually transmitted diseases that were considered diagnostic of sexual abuse. Only 43 percent disclosed abuse in the first interview.[145] This finding contradicts the claim that children generally disclose in one fell swoop. It also suggests a reason to worry that concerns about "repetitive" interviews may have gone too far, especially in those instances impugning a second interview with a child who did not disclose in the first interview. That is what a majority of the children with sexually transmitted diseases did. The "systemic" error that has been left unrecognized, then, is how the "pro-defense orientation" in the field of psychology results in the failure to inquire about false denials of abuse, about false determination that a case is unsubstantiated, or about acquitting defendants by unduly discounting the word of a child.

The Backlash Against Institutions and Professionals

Beyond the arguments about child suggestibility, the witch-hunt narrative also contained an antigovernment message that attracted a variety of interests, right and left wing. One strand of this argument, expressed by the Eberles as early as 1987, claimed that the child-abuse "industry" was a scheme, created by Congress, that enriched state agencies and related nonprofit institutions, who had a financial interest in "finding" abuse. Accordingly, the Child Abuse Prevention and Treatment Act (CAPTA) became the scapegoat for various complaints about false accusations. Critics routinely refer to the law as the Mondale Act, named for the liberal Minnesota Democrat who introduced the legislation (which was signed into law by President Nixon). Blaming CATPA is far-fetched, to say the least, but this argument nevertheless galvanized conservative interests. It has since engaged father's rights groups that challenge the legitimacy of government regulation of the family. Liberals have also been attracted to aspects of this antigovernment critique, particularly when it focuses on police and prosecutorial abuses. Although this kind of rhetoric was a staple of the witch-hunt narrative, the critique was always much broader than the day-care sexual abuse cases. The agenda, which has not gained sufficient political support to prevail, involves the elimination of mandatory child-abuse reporting and a massive defunding of federal support for child protective services and foster care. One of the three major organizers of the Salem Day of Contrition in 1997 worked closely with conservative Republican Senator Coats from Indiana in an unsuccessful attempt to achieve those goals.

Those institutional goals remain out of reach, but there has also been a powerful attack on child abuse professionals in court. The witch-hunt narrative focused on child interviewers and social workers, who did not necessarily have advanced degrees or specialized training. But those arguments have expanded in recent years to cover child-abuse pediatricians and forensic child interviewers with advanced degrees. One of the first high-profile cases to illustrate this assault on child abuse professionals was the so-called British Nanny case, involving Louise Woodward. Woodward was convicted of murder, but Judge Hiller B. Zobel sentenced her only to time served, apparently moved by the defense claims that rejected the collected wisdom and understanding of child-abuse pediatricians.[146] More recently, some of the same academic psychologists who focused on child suggestibility in the 1990s have also challenged the expertise of child-abuse doctors.[147] A horrific child-murder case from Harrington, Maine, demonstrates the lengths to which advocates of the child-suggestibility framework have gone to reject clinical judgments, even involving battered child syndrome.

Robert Ardolino was charged with beating his nine-year-old son, Matthew, to death in late June 1993. Ardolino was divorced and living with his sons Matthew

and David; the latter was about to turn twelve. Matthew Ardolino died of peritonitis, an inflammation of the lining of the bowel. Peritonitis is caused when di-
gestive juices and bacteria from the intestine leak into the abdominal cavity; the
result is a massive inflammatory reaction. The cause of his condition was blunt
force trauma to the stomach. The blow had to be so hard that it squeezed the je-
junum (lower intestine) between the back of the abdominal wall and the spine
with enough force to puncture it. A child's heart would then start to race, he
might vomit—as Matthew did several times that day—and he would be in severe
pain. The treatment, as Dr. Lawrence Ricci testified, is "very simple and straightforward and almost uniformly successful."[148] But left untreated for twenty-four
hours, it is inevitably fatal. This is what happened to Matthew. As Dr. Ricci later
testified, Matthew would have looked "seriously ill" during much of those
twenty-four hours.[149] He vomited bile that evening, yet his father did not seek
any medical attention. Matthew died before daybreak.

     When David was interviewed, he told the police the same thing his father
said: Matthew had fallen out of the tree house. David denied that his father had
harmed Matthew in any way. Given the surrounding circumstances, David's
statements were not credible. First, there were witnesses who heard Robert
Ardolino berating Matthew from a distance when they went out clamming that
Saturday morning. This indicates there was more to the story than David was
saying. Second, Matthew's body was covered in bruises of different ages—bruises
in places where children are rarely injured once, let alone multiple times. This
made the blanket denial of any physical abuse highly suspect. Third, the internal
injury to Matthew's bowel was not consistent with falling out of a tree.[150] It also
turns out the clothes he wore that day were not consistent with this story.[151]

     Dr. Ricci, a pediatric child-abuse specialist, eventually reviewed the medical
records and concurred that this was a classic case of battered-child syndrome.
One reason for the conclusion was that there were "multiple injuries that are
unexplained by the history, on multiple planes of the body in assaultive, rather
than accident location, of multiple ages." Specifically, there were truncal injuries
"in a particular location consistent with punches along the flank, lower lateral
back, and abdomen region" and "multiple punctuate bruises on the chest and
abdomen such as from poking." Matthew also had bruises about the arms "in
possible self-defense location." Another reason factoring into Dr. Ricci's equa-
tion was a "history of delay in seeking treatment" and then providing a history
that is inconsistent with the extent and severity of the injuries.[152]

     But the medical evidence alone would not support charges against Ardolino.
Accordingly, the police requested another interview with David in January 1994.
They interviewed him for more than three hours, making it clear they did not
consider his answers about Matthew falling out of the tree to be credible. David
stuck by the story and insisted that his father never did anything abusive to

Matthew or to him. It should be kept in mind that Ardolino was still free at this point, although David had been removed from his custody. Six months later, the state police were contacted by David's foster mother and told that David wanted to tell the real story.

David then gave a detailed statement on July 14, 1994, about what happened on the fateful Saturday. He reported that in the morning, Robert Ardolino was unhappy with how Matthew had made a milkshake, so he kicked him in the stomach. When they went clamming after breakfast, his father was upset at Matthew and threw him against a boat, injuring the boy's back. Matthew threw up that afternoon while hanging up laundry. He kept reverting to the fetal position—a natural response to the pain of peritonitis—and his father got angry about that as well. Robert Ardolino then went out to sell some clams, and while he was gone there was a phone call in which someone asked for Matthew and hung up when David asked who was calling. David said his father was enraged when he was told about this because he thought Matthew had called child protective services. He ordered David to get his baseball bat from the shed. When asked to describe what his father did with the bat, this is what David said:

> DAVID: It was like a poking motion at his stomach.
> QUESTION: Did he hit him?
> DAVID: Yes.
> QUESTION: Can you give us an estimate of how many times?
> DAVID: No. It was a lot.[153]

David testified that "it went on for a while." Then his brother "threw up green throw-up and dad got mad at him for throwing up."[154] Within about six hours, Matthew was dead.

The criminal trial included David's testimony, but the emphasis was on the medical evidence. There were lengthy arguments about whether photos of the bruises would be so inflammatory they would prejudice the jury. Some photos were kept out on that basis. But the jury received detailed descriptions of the range and types of bruises on Matthew's body. And they heard from several medical experts. Ardolino was convicted of "depraved indifference" murder.

As with the Marzolf case in New Jersey, where there was an adult eyewitness, there would seem to be no place for child-suggestibility claims in the Ardolino case, with its extensive medical evidence of physical abuse. If anything, the case seems to speak volumes about the power of fear, secrecy, and denial. Those influences were strong enough that David was steadfast in his denials, even in the face of authority figures who cajoled him and expressed outright disbelief during the interview of January 7, 1994.

Robert Rosenthal represented Ardolino in federal court, where he challenged his state conviction. Rosenthal engaged Maggie Bruck as an expert, and she provided the opinion that the first interview with David, immediately after his brother died, was the most reliable one.[155] He should never have been interviewed again, she concluded—certainly not, according to Bruck, after having "contact only with adults who believed that his statements that Mr. Ardolino had not beaten Matthew were false."[156] Bruck saved her outrage for the police interviewers who pushed David in January. This was apparently the only possible abuse she detected in the case. One might be particularly skeptical of Bruck's position since it was raised on behalf of Robert Ardolino, the one person who stood to lose the most if David's story aligned with the physical evidence. In this sense, the case also threatened to provide a powerful example of how a child might *falsely deny* there was any abuse even in the face of extremely aggressive questioning.

The remarkable blind spot in Bruck's position is how it failed to apply her vast knowledge and concern about *coercion* to the most likely and powerful source in the case: the man who used a baseball bat to make his points. In Bruck's view, the interview of July 14, 1994, was completely tainted because in the preceding months David had had contact only with adults who believed Ardolino was guilty. Bruck never explains why this is so objectionable, while an interview conducted immediately after years under the control of the defendant doesn't rate any similar concern—even when the allegation, backed up with medical evidence, is that the defendant slowly beat his brother to death. Apparently, even a witness to such horror is suspect in Bruck's view if he does not disclose the abuse immediately, on the first interview, and all in one piece.

There is, of course, a hidden value choice in the position—one that deems the coercive effects of the police interview as a far greater concern than the coercive effects of living with Robert Ardolino for years. In that respect, Bruck's position is *de facto* pro-defense. This is the only explanation that makes this position consistent with the Rouse case, where Bruck readily accepted recantations that occurred *only after the children moved back into a residence where the adults did not believe their original claims*—the mirror image of the reason she used to reject David Ardolino's testimony. So Bruck does not see the Rouse adults as tainting the recantations in that case, yet she sees David's foster mother as tainting his testimony, which was, in effect, a recantation of his earlier denials. These positions are logically incompatible, except to the extent they both favor defendants. This "pro-defense orientation" is precisely how Ceci described the design of his research studies when testifying in the Foeller case in Michigan.[157] Why so many psychologists have aligned themselves with the defense, to the point of demonstrating and even admitting bias in that direction, is a puzzle for another time. What matters for this book is that these politics exist and work to diminish the credibility, and ultimately the safety, of children.

The more radical aspect of Bruck's position is the assault on battered child syndrome. Rosenthal argued in post-conviction proceedings that Ardolino's original lawyer should have challenged the admissibility of the syndrome itself. Bruck's affidavit actually criticized the medical examiner for not adequately considering "fights with neighbors," "bicycle accidents," and the "active life of a 9-year-old boy" before reaching the conclusion that Matthew had been beaten to death.[158] Bruck, a developmental psychologist without medical training, suggested the medical examiner jumped to the conclusion that it was battered child syndrome. But Dr. Ricci, the pediatric child-abuse expert who later reviewed all of the medical evidence, testified that he knew about all of the information Bruck mentioned, that he took it all into account in reviewing the case, and that it did not change his conclusion of a clear-cut case of battered child syndrome.[159]

Bruck's dispute is not so much about pediatrics as it is about forms of knowledge in psychology. Even though battered child syndrome is much more concrete than syndromes based on psychological factors alone, it involves a clinical judgment about patterns of injuries. Bruck is among a group of academic psychologists who minimize the value of clinical judgments. Indeed, she and a few others have gone to great lengths to attack such clinical judgments. Bruck filed an affidavit in support of a motion to disqualify Constance Dalenberg in a case in California, even though Dalenberg has a doctorate in clinical psychology and heads a research institute that specializes in child abuse research. Dalenberg also teaches courses in the treatment of child abuse victims and perpetrators, she spends one day a week in a child abuse clinic, and she teaches graduate-level statistics. But in a case where she declined to view a child's statements as the product of suggestion, Bruck and five others, among them the writer Carol Tavris, opined that Dalenberg's views were "unfounded, unscientific, unreliable, and unprofessional."[160]

Bruck's position in these cases is not based on science alone. The position that challenges the ability of child-abuse specialists to diagnose battered-child syndrome is part of a broader attack on child-abuse professionals. Arguments against them are a foundational element of the witch-hunt narrative. When the Eberles first wrote *The Politics of Child Abuse* in 1986, they claimed that the underlying problem was CAPTA, the Child Abuse Prevention and Training Act. Eleven years later, Richard Gardner, a frequent defense expert in these cases, gave a fiery speech at the Salem Day of Contrition, where he argued "a whole industry has been spawned" and that "hysteria is being fueled primarily by funding from the federal government under the Child Abuse Prevention and Treatment Act."[161] This position is now a mainstay of father's rights groups and right-wing activists who lobby against child protective service agencies as a violation of family privacy. Painting in broad pejorative strokes, the witch-hunt narrative refers to those who investigate, treat, or prosecute child abuse as "the child-abuse industry." Curiously, the professionals who consistently appear on the other side are rarely, if ever, called an industry, and their financial rewards are never scrutinized. In the witch-hunt narrative there is a "child abuse industry" but not a "child-abuse *defense* industry."

Conclusion

The witch-hunt narrative continues to have a significant impact on social and legal responses to child sexual abuse in America. Activists with varied agendas continue to use the imagery of Salem to promote their causes. The media generally view these claims with utter credulity. This has resulted in a surprising amount of positive press for child molesters, from Frank Fuster to Charles Bighead. The judiciary has not fallen for these stories as readily as the media, but judges like John T. Noonan in the Bighead case and Myron Bright in the Rouse case demonstrate that the judiciary is not immune to this rhetoric.

There have also been developments to the contrary. The cases against the Catholic Church demonstrate a willingness to confront sexual abuse in places where it would have been unimaginable in the not-too-distant past. Those developments are admirable, but their application is limited. They do not necessarily suggest anything about allegations made by children; moreover, the impetus for recognizing and addressing those cases was a proven cover-up. There is also evidence of overreaction to child sexual abuse since the end of the McMartin case. The widespread implementation of Megan's Law demonstrates how our society has overreacted to sex offenders after their release from prison. But the "lesson" from that phenomenon has been applied too broadly, leading some to characterize our social response to sex offenders in general by the way we treat the very small percentage of offenders who get imprisoned. Leon suggests that the movie *The Woodsman* is indicative of a dominant discourse that now sees sex offenders as monsters. But there was a more popular movie during the same era, *Capturing the Friedmans*, which retold a child molestation case from the 1980s through the lens of the witch-hunt narrative, notwithstanding all the facts to the contrary. Just as supporters of Megan's Law take too much comfort in symbolic acts that do little to address sex offenders at large, those who focus on Megan's Law to characterize social response to child molesters as "highly punitive" similarly miss the point. The witch-hunt narrative directs our attention away from the reality of child sexual abuse, which remains widespread, underreported, and generally punished quite leniently. But that is an uncomfortable reality. It is easier just to favor—or disdain—policies like Megan's law.

In the field of psychology, Ceci and Bruck continue to be viewed by many as the leading experts on "child suggestibility." Their work is now a primary source on child suggestibility in psychology textbooks. But there have also been some prominent critics of the general direction of the field, among them Professor Tom Lyon, who has pointed out the biases of the "new wave" in child-suggestibility research.[162] These disagreements among academics are not generally reflected in media stories about the subject, but they are more apparent in scholarly journals. Less apparent, except to the closest observers, are three developments discussed in this chapter. First, there has been an expansive effort to employ child-suggestibility concepts to keep children from testifying in court in a broad range of cases. Those who originally argued that suggestibility claims belonged only in cases with extremely coercive interviewing were now applying the same arguments to cases with strong corroborative evidence of abuse and far less in the way of coercive or repetitive interviews than anything that was claimed in the Michaels case.

Second, there has also been a surprising attack on the conventional wisdom—conventional, at least, to those in the clinical world—that sexual abuse disclosures are often delayed and then disclosed in bits and pieces. Those attacks threaten to undermine the vast majority of victims of sexual abuse, who delay disclosure and are therefore considered suspect. Ceci and Bruck's own meta-study found that two-thirds of sexual abuse victims delay reporting the fact, but Bruck and others have demonstrated a willingness to impugn children who do not report fully and immediately.

Finally, there has been a surprising effort to undermine the professionals who conduct the front-line work in this area, such as pediatricians who operate child-abuse clinics and psychologists who direct forensic interviewing programs at child advocacy centers. The disdain that Judge Noonan registered for Tanya Boychuk in the Bighead case reflects this disturbing trend. So does Maggie Bruck's willingness to second-guess the medical examiner who concluded that Matthew Ardolino had been beaten to death. These developments are a function of a witch-hunt narrative that sees these professionals as an "industry" and that threatens to undermine the front-line workers and institutions responding to the sexual abuse of children in the United States.

ACKNOWLEDGMENTS

The effort that I expended on this book pales in comparison to the debts that I incurred along the way. So many people helped on this project in so many ways that a brief acknowledgment cannot possibly convey the full extent of their contribution or my gratitude. First and foremost are the extraordinary undergraduate students at Brown University. This book could not have been researched so extensively without the incredible work of students from almost a generation of the university. More than eighty of them worked on this project in one way or another. Some worked on a single case for as long as two years. Others took on the challenge of obtaining information from court clerks while in hometowns across the country. They came back to campus with docket sheets, transcripts, and stories about the surprising challenges of this kind of original trial court research. Or they came back with nothing but determination to crack the puzzle next time they were home.

With enduring gratitude to all of the Brown undergraduates who helped give "extreme research" its name, in simple alphabetical order: Brian Agboh, Tamiz Ahmed, Dena Aufseer, Evelyn Avila, Zoe Billinkoff, Sarah Blum-Smith, Nicole Boucher, Caroline Burnett, Sarah Coburn, Dara Cohen, Dave Cooker, Stephanie Czech, Julia Dahlin, Brandi Davis, Brittany Davis, Joe Davis, Marta DiSilva, Javier Dominguez, Jessica Dubin, Brett Eggleston, Cara Farber, Shae Fitzpatrick, Amanda Freedman, Emily Geldwert, Erica Goldschmidt, Debra Greenspan, Hillary Gross, Chris Hartman, Elia Herman, Kate Herts, Beth Hollander, Morriah Horani, Jennifer Hutchinson, Ivalya Ivanova, Nicole Janisiewicz, Carey Jaros, Darren Jorgenson, Katherine Kosub, Lauren Kupersmith, Damian Lara, Liz Leidel, Vanessa Lipschitz, Jesse Maniff, Andrea Matthews, Chelsea McCarron, David Mervis, Jocabel Michel, Alec O'Neill, Sarah Olverson, Ben Petrosky, Katya Potkin, Felisa Preskill, Adam Reich, Zachary Reiss-Davis, Margaret Rose, Elizabeth Root, Sarah Rubin, Jacquelyn Rudis, Dan Sack, Rebecca Santoro, Catherine Schaper, Aaron Scherzer, Katie Schlicter, Danny

Schneider, Mark Scott, Amy Senia, Felica Sexsmith, Jesse Shapiro, Reece Smith, Savannah Smith, Claudia Solari, Veena Srinivasa, Katherine Stewart, Nicole Stock, Jen Swearingen, Ilana Streit, Eric Tucker, Will Tucker, Emily Walsh, and Stacy Yen.

Ten Brown undergraduates did senior theses that contributed in various ways to this book. Thank you to each of you for your hard work and your insights: Karen Tumlin, Sasha Grief, Rebecca Santoro, Miranda Galindo, Margaret Merrifield, Sarah Squire, Margaret Rose, Dara Cohen, Julie Gottlieb, and Will Tucker.

There are several other Brown students who inspired me and supported me along this journey. Special thanks to Allison Smith-Estelle, Jennifer Sigall, Meg McGrath, Jake Gersen, Karen Tumlin, Beatriz Lorenzo, and Rebecca Bradburd.

One Brown undergraduate has become a long-time collaborator. Arthi Krishnaswami, who is credited on the cover for the illustrations: thank you for helping me think and see more clearly. You are an ideal colleague and it made a world of difference to this book.

The Taubman Center for Public Policy and American Institutions and the Political Science Department at Brown have long supported my work and the spirit of interdisciplinary studies. I am particularly indebted to Jim Morone for his interest and encouragement of this book, whether or not he necessarily agreed with all of the arguments. Mark Blyth, Roger Cobb, Beverly Haviland, Sharon Krause, and Rose McDermott have also gone out of their way to be encouraging along the way. I am always thankful for the efforts of Patti Gardner at the Department of Political Science and Isabel Costa and Jack Combs at the Taubman Center for assisting in so many of the details of this project.

Significant costs were incurred in this project, particularly to acquire documents, some of which had to be transcribed by court reporters. I am grateful to a host of sources for providing financial assistance for this work: the Taubamn Center at Brown University, the John and Happy White Internship program, the Undergraduate Teaching and Research Assistants (UTRA) program, the Dean of the Faculty, the Office of the Provost, the Department of Political Science, the Goldschmidt Book Fund, and a stipend from the Carnegie Foundation. The most significant single source of financial support for this research was Earl and June Cheit, my parents, without whom this book would not have been possible. Thanks, Mom and Dad, for believing in this project.

The Brown Library has helped me in countless ways over the years, handling requests for obscure small-town newspapers on microfiche, for assistance with state court libraries, and other unusual requests with aplomb. Thank you to Beth Beretta, Beth Coogan, Michael Jackson, and Anne Nolan.

Thank you to everyone who talked with me off the record. Those conversations were most useful in helping to locate documents. There were also two formal interviews that are cited directly in the text. One was with Joseph Braga, who helped clear up a mystery about a videotape aired on a San Francisco television station and provided information about various (unfounded) ethics complaints. The other was with Maggie Bruck, who generously agreed to answer a variety of questions about issues in this book. Thank you to both of you for agreeing to be interviewed. (These interviews were conducted with an approved protocol from the IRB at Brown University.)

I had the good fortune to present pieces of this research at various venues, including Harvard Medical School, the University of Oregon, Duke University, the University of Auckland, the Roger Williams University School of Law, the New England School of Law, University of Nevada Las Vegas William S. Boyd School of Law, the University of New Hampshire, and various meetings of the Law and Society Association. I also presented versions of this work at several venues at Brown University, including the Warren Alpert Medical School and the Lipsitt-Duchin Lectures. Thank you to the audiences at those venues. Thanks also to the students in my Children and Public Policy class and in a graduate seminar on the Politics of Child Abuse with Kate Murphy, Miranda Turner, Darren Jorgensen, and Eric Tucker.

Thanks to Dave McBride at Oxford University Press for accepting this book and for working tirelessly through its endless challenges and complexities. Thanks also to Liz Hasse and Mark Fowler for their sage counsel. I am also extremely grateful to Thomas Finnegan for his expert copy editing.

I owe an enormous debt to those who read the entire manuscript, sometimes more than once, with great care. Heartfelt thanks to Elizabeth Mertz, Jennifer Freyd, Jim Morone, Wendy Murphy, Ken Pope, Jennifer Hoult, Andrea Matthews, Nancy Feinstein, Hayley Goldbach, Jeffrey Masson, Morriah Horani, Will Tucker, Eric Tucker, Peter Loss, Dave Cheit, and Kathleen Odean. I greatly appreciate all of your efforts, even if I did not always take your suggestions. Any remaining errors, of course, are mine. Thank you also to the reviewers at Oxford University Press who made useful suggestions for improving the book.

This book is also a product of Rhode Island, a wonderful and quirky state that serendipitously provided me with some remarkable resources. The earliest ideas in this book were formed at the Trauma Breakfasts led by Paul Block. Two of the most important contributors to this book were professionals in Rhode Island. First, I am forever grateful to Dr. Carole Jenny, a nationally recognized expert in pediatric child abuse, who graced our presence in Providence for almost the entire duration of this book. Carole answered questions, reviewed testimony, and answered more questions with patience and good humor. She also advised an undergraduate thesis that examined medical testimony in several cases in this book, and then read and reread key sections of this manuscript. Dr. Tom Roesler, who I met through Carole, has also provided valuable insight and assistance to this project. Thanks very much to both of you.

Peter Loss, director of the Sex Offender Treatment Program at the Rhode Island Department of Corrections, also saw this book through from start to finish. He answered endless questions and provided me with an extraordinary opportunity for a kind of continuing weekly education about sex offenders for the last fourteen years. Thanks, Pete, for your friendship and your careful read of countless drafts. The book is much better with the benefit of your lens. Thanks also to Professor Carl Bogus of the Roger Williams University School of Law for supporting this project and organizing a fabulous conference on children as witnesses. You are another Rhode Island treasure.

Finally, I express my lasting gratitude to Kathleen Odean, who continued to believe in this project long after it had consumed an unreasonable number of years. Thanks for your support, dear, and for providing such as an astute reading of the almost-final version. I promise not to do another project like this one. Dave Cheit also helped at every stage of this project. Dave, thank you for your level-headed advice and your willingness to engage this project more times than I should have asked. You are a great lawyer and a wonderful brother. Finally, I am extremely grateful to W.F.G. for your boundless support and assistance. You strengthened this book in so many important ways. I hope that it lives up to your high standards and ideals.

BIBLIOGRAPHIC NOTES

Most of the research for this book was case-based, and most of the sources cited in the book are primary documents from criminal cases. The challenges of this research are described in detail in an article that is mentioned in the Preface. The notes below elaborate on the primary source materials for the three chapter-length case studies.

State v. Buckey (Chapter Two)

The transcript of the preliminary hearing and the transcript of both criminal trials in *State v. Buckey* are housed at the Los Angeles County Hall of Records under docket number A750900. There is no official index to the thirty-two boxes that I identified and inventoried. The Preliminary Hearing covered 489 (thin) volumes of testimony. Some of those volumes are either misplaced or missing entirely; specifically, vols. 74–146, 181–253, and 323–445 are not located in the boxes that are filed together with this case. The trial covered 456 volumes. Volumes 90–146, much of the testimony between July and September 1987, are either misplaced or missing entirely. Fortunately, I was able to locate some of these volumes elsewhere. The retrial of Ray Buckey covered forty-nine volumes; and all are included in the boxes at the Hall of Records. There was a Protective Order in the case to protect the children's names and to protect the CII videotapes, but the trial transcript uses children's initials throughout and can be reproduced without breaching confidentiality of identities. No videotapes are included in the materials at the Hall of Records. The Superior Court may still be in possession of videotapes of the trial testimony, but I was not able to obtain a definitive answer to that question.

The most significant sources for the analysis in Chapter Two were documents generated *before* any charges were filed in the case. Through independent research I located multiple sources of documents from the investigation. I amassed seventeen boxes of materials, including several devoted to media coverage. The most significant documents I obtained were the Manhattan Beach Police Department Call Log in response to the letter sent to the community, the Information Form and Medical Report for children referred to CII and various internal CII memos, the District Attorney's Investigator Notebooks, and the grand jury transcripts. I also obtained copies of the Manns-Stevens tapes, along with competing transcriptions of the tapes. I also located medical records for numerous children, including photographic slides for one of the girls involved in both trials. Finally, I obtained copies of videotaped interviews with fifteen assorted children at CII. I believe I am the first researcher to locate and view any of these tapes. I did not get to select the specific interviews, but they included a range of dates, among them five from November and early December 1983. (These tapes are low-quality and would need to be enhanced in order to be analyzed in greater detail. They also need to be pixilated to mask the children's faces.) Further, I obtained transcriptions of fifty-three CII interviews from Professor. Maggie Bruck, who sent them in response to requests to view the archives described in Nathan and Snedeker's *Satan's Silence*.

State v. Michaels (Chapter Five)

The trial transcript in the Michaels case is sealed by order of the trial judge. The *Village Voice* challenged the seal in a case that was decided by the New Jersey Supreme Court two years after Debbie Nathan wrote about the case in the *Village Voice*. See *In re VV Publishing Corp.*, 120 N.J. 508; 577 A.2d 412; 1990 N.J. LEXIS 82 (1990). The court agreed that the petitioners were entitled to a redacted version of the transcript, so long as they paid for the cost of redacting. Relying on the reasoning in that case, I obtained access to the trial transcript and many related documents by negotiating an agreement with the state to provide unfettered access to the prosecutor's files in exchange for assurances that the children's identities would never be revealed. (This assurance was guaranteed by a research protocol approved by the Institutional Review Board at Brown University.) The trial transcript was complete, but there was no record of the pre-trial taint hearing discussed in the text. The prosecutor's files contained all of the motions and correspondence concerning the amicus brief, including the letter to peer-reviewed journals that was dismissive of Professor Gail Goodman's work. It also contained extensive documentation used to cross-examine Ralph Underwager. Tape recordings of interviews with children were also contained in these files. The audio quality is very poor, and I relied largely on transcriptions. Transcriptions of some DFYS interviews are contained in a three-volume appendix to the defendant's appeal; many have handwritten corrections and other notations presumably written by the defense. Transcriptions of Eileen Treacy's evaluative interviews, prepared at the Essex County District Attorney's Office, were also in these files. I was unable to locate the early videotape in the case that is discussed in the text. I did obtain various useful documents from the discovery phase of *Michaels v. New Jersey,* an unsuccessful attempt by Michaels to obtain damages from various parties.

State v. Fuster (Chapter Six)

The trial transcript in the Fuster case is available for public inspection through the Dade County Archive. Files from Fuster's earlier criminal case can be viewed at the Dade County Superior Court. I obtained a copy of the complete transcript and, through independent research, located a host of ancillary court documents, including affidavits and depositions from the criminal case. I also obtained records from Frank Fuster's parole violation hearing in August 1985 and from his aggravated manslaughter case in New York. Finally, I viewed (but was unable to obtain copies of) the videotapes of all of the interviews in the case. As described in the text, I had one of the original videotapes (still in state storage) transcribed by a court reporter to verify its contents. There is a Protective Order in the case aimed at protecting the children's names and the videotapes of their interviews (although several families identified themselves to the media and, surprisingly, a federal magistrate used virtually all of the names in a decision upholding the verdict). I also obtained depositions and related documents from several civil cases, including *[Mayor] v. Fuster-Escalano* (Case No. 84–42560, Dade County) and *N.G v. Arvida Corp.* (Case No. 91–35636, Dade County).

NOTES

Preface

1. Freeh Sporkin & Sullivan, Report of the Special Investigative Counsel Regarding Actions of The Pennsylvania State University Related to the Child Sexual Abuse Committed by Gerald A. Sandusky (July 12, 2012). Commonly known as the Freeh Report. Available at http://progress.psu.edu/the-freeh-report
2. Suzanne Sgroi, "A National Needs Assessment for Protecting Child Victims of Sexual Assault," Introduction to Anne Wolbert Burgess, et. al., *Sexual Assault of Children and Adolescents* (Lexington Books, 1978).
3. *State v. Dunn*, 726 A.2d 1142 (R.I. 1999).
4. Many of the cases listed on the dedication page were not contained in the index of the book. Many of those that were listed in the index were mentioned in the text in a single sentence. Only a few cases were discussed in any detail with footnotes from original sources.
5. Ross E. Cheit, "The Legend of Robert Halsey," *Journal of Child Sexual Abuse* (2001), 9(3/4): 37–52.
6. Stephen J. Gould [Letter to the editor], *New Yorker* (December 26, 1994).
7. Mike Stanton, "Bearing Witness," *Providence Journal* (May 4–6, 1995).
8. Ross E. Cheit, "The Elusive Record: On the Difficulties in Researching High-Profile Child Sexual Abuse Cases from the 1980s," *Justice System Journal* (2007), 28(1): 79–97.
9. William Blackstone, *Commentaries*, Volume 4, On Public Wrongs, 358. ("Better that ten guilty persons escape than that one innocent suffer"). Quoted in Alexander Volokh, "*n* Guilty Men," *University of Pennsylvania Law Review* (1997) 146, 173.
10. Professor Fred Schauer's brilliant article explains the logic of this and other outcomes that turn on the standard of proof. "Slightly Guilty," *University of Chicago Legal Forum*, 1993, 83–100.

Chapter One

1. An example of the KABC coverage in February 1984 can be viewed at http://youtu.be/e4d2cIoZwBs.
2. Michelle Green, "The McMartins: The 'Model Family' Down the Block That Ran California's Nightmare Nursery," *People* (May 21, 1984).
3. Stan Katz, "Stop the Witch Hunts for Child Molesters,"*New York Times* (June 20, 1984).
4. David Shaw, "Where Was Media Skepticism?"*Los Angeles Times* (January 19, 1990).
5. A. S. Ross, "Satanism or Mass Hysteria?"*San Francisco Examiner* (September 28, 1986) A8.
6. The rest of the thirteen cases on the map of "sensational cases across the county" involved child sexual-abuse charges, but not in a day-care setting.
7. Her most significant article that year was about the Kelly Michaels case, the subject of Chapter Five.

8. Mary A. Fischer, "Flip-Flop," *Los Angeles Magazine* (December 1988), 33(12): 85–94.

9. Mary Pride, *The Child Abuse Industry* (Crossway Books, 1986), 31.

10. Pride is editor of *Practical Homeschooling Magazine* and the website *Homeschool World* http://www.home-school.com.

11. The witch-hunt narrative has generally overlooked questions about the Eberles' background; or it has been claimed that the Eberles' previous publications were the kind of "soft porn" often associated with the advertising section in free weekly newspapers. That may be true of the *L.A. Star*, a more recent publication of the Eberles, but it is decidedly not true of their earlier publication, called *Finger*. In her book about the Michaels trial, Lisa Manshel described how prosecutor Glenn Goldberg confronted Dr. Jonas Rappeport with this evidence after Rappeport recommended *The Politics of Child Abuse* (Lyle Stuart, 1986), another book by the Eberles (Manshel, 284–285). This is Manshel's description of the publication, as illustrated at trial: "On the inside pages were photographs of children being raped, a child standing over an adult and urinating into the adult's mouth, written pieces detailing sexual experiences with young children . . ." (285). I have confirmed this information independently, obtaining an inventory of slides from *Finger* magazine that begin with a two-page spread called "Baby Fucking." See also Maria Laurina, "Paul and Shirley Eberle: A Strange Pair of Experts," *Ms.* (December 1988). Confronted with this issue on *Larry King Live* in 1988, Paul Eberle did not distance himself from the content of his former publication; rather he scolded lawyer Gregory Mooney for bringing it up, as if this was an unfair attack on their character. But the issue—whether the Eberles had a demonstrated acceptance of the idea of sexual contact between adults and children—goes directly to their credibility as reporters of these cases. The Eberles were never convicted of any crime in connection with publication of *Finger* magazine, although it should be noted that there was not a specific prohibition against child pornography in the United States until passage of the Protection of Children Against Sexual Exploitation Act of 1977 (Public Law 95–225, codified in Title 18, Chapter 110, Section 2251 of the U.S. Code). Before then, prosecution was possible only through general obscenity laws, which were notoriously vague and difficult to enforce. After passage of the 1977 law, "commercially produced magazines such as Lollitots, Baby Love and Nudist Moppets—in which children as young as 3 years old were shown performing sex acts with adults—have virtually vanished from adult bookstore shelves." Carol McGraw, "Child Smut Business Going Underground," *Los Angeles Times* (September 16, 1985), 3.

12. There is a second relevant book, published in 2001 by the University Press of America, called *The Anatomy of the McMartin Child Molestation Case*. But the book focuses on jury issues, not on issues of fact. The authors are quite clear about their allegiance; the book is dedicated to Virginia McMartin. The coauthors, including high-profile jury consultant Jo-Ellan Dimitrius, worked for the defense in the McMartin case.

13. David Shaw, "Where Was Media Skepticism?" *Los Angeles Times* (January 19, 1990).

14. Debbie Nathan and Michael Snedeker, *Satan's Silence: Ritual Abuse and the Making of a Modern American Witch Hunt* (Basic Books, 1995).

15. Steven Mintz, *Huck's Raft: A History of American Childhood* (Harvard University Press, 2004), ch. 5, "Parental Panics and the Reshaping of Childhood." He relies entirely on Nathan and Snedeker's chapter and the Eberles' book for his account of McMartin.

16. Rabinowitz was not the first to write about Kelly Michaels through the witch-hunt frame. Nathan did so in August 1988, long before Rabinowitz. But the Rabinowitz article was longer, it had more materials from the case, and it was better-timed.

17. Amy Driscoll, "State Won't Retry Officer in Abuse Case," *Miami Herald* (November 21, 1998).

18. The first program, "The Child Terror" (1998), focused on three cases from Dade County: Frank Fuster, Grant Snowden, and Bobby Finje. The second program, "Did Daddy Do It?" (2002), was devoted entirely to the Fuster case. That case is the subject of Chapter Six in this book.

19. Lawrence Wright, "Remembering Satan, Part II," *New Yorker* (May 24, 1993).

20. Ceci and Bruck, "Suggestibility of the Child Witness: A Historical Review and Syntheses," *Psychological Bulletin* (1993), 113(3): 403–439.

21. The movie opens with the statement "This story happened in America in our time." The producer and director presented the work as fully documented at a press conference promoting the movie. A statement at the end of movie read "Court transcripts and actual videotapes were among the sources used in telling the story."

22. A review of the movie in their newsletter, which had a circulation of approximately five hundred, attracted the attention of the Manns' "litigation counsel," as they identified themselves in a letter threatening the organization and its directors with litigation for libel and other claims. The organization issued a correction of several statements. A second letter rejected these corrections as insufficient and again threatened litigation if more changes were not forthcoming. I could find no record of any additional charges or any actual litigation over this matter. Correspondence from Lavely & Singer to Executive Director, Children's Civil Rights Fund, April 21, 1995. A follow-up letter on May 2, also from Lavely & Singer to multiple parties (seven board directors and fifteen advisory board members of Believe the Children). More significantly, this was an obscure fight. By 1995, there was no serious credence given to those who might defend even some aspect of the prosecution in the McMartin case.

23. Ellen Willis, "The Media and McMartin," *Village Voice* (May 30, 1995) 40(22): 8.

24. Jim Okerblom and Mark Sauer, "Was Akiki Inquiry Rush to Judgment?" *Union-Tribune* (November 2, 1993).

25. Martin Gardner, "The Tragedies of False Memories," *Skeptical Inquirer* (Fall 1994).

26. Thomas Sowell, "Legal Lynchings," *Forbes* (January 26, 1998).

27. Trevor Armbrister, "Justice Gone Crazy," *Reader's Digest* (January 1994).

28. Andrew Schneider and Mike Barber, "The Power to Harm," five-part series in the *Seattle Post-Intelligencer* (February 23–27, 1998). Defense lawyer Kathyrn Lyon also wrote a book about these cases, called *Witchhunt: A True Story of Social Hysteria and Abused Justice* (Avon, 1998).

29. Home page, Witch-Hunt Information Center. Old MIT URL, circa 1993–2000.

30. I have a copy of the list, but the various sites that used to reprint it are all apparently gone right now. Nathan's list is a major source for the list compiled at this site: http://www.solresearch.org/~SOLR/rprt/bkgrd/FalsAcCases.htm#Sct_1_explain. The list is divided into two pieces, both are linked, but both of the links are dead (as of August 24, 2012).

31. Frederick Crews, Response to Letters to Editor, *New York Review of Books* (January 12, 1995), 42–48.

32. All messages came addressed "Sender: Is there a child sex abuse witchhunt?" <WITCHHNT@MITVMA.MIT.EDU>.

33. Local coverage painted a more favorable view of the prosecution. See e.g., UNC-TV, *North Carolina Now* (November 23, 1997, critiquing the PBS program "Innocence Lost").

34. Post to witch-hunt list: "Re: day care cases" from Ralph Underwager (April 23, 1995). The message is signed by his wife, Hollida Wakefield.

35. Stephen Maher, "The Bizarre World of 'WITCHHUNT,'" *Wenatchee World* (October 17, 1999).

36. www.religioustolerance.org/ra_case.htm (accessed March 25, 2012).

37. Philip Jenkins, *Moral Panic: Changing Conceptions of the Child Molester in Modern America* (Yale University Press, 1998), 278, 21.

Chapter Two

1. The first book about the case, *Abuse of Innocence: The McMartin Preschool Trial* (Prometheus Books, 1993), was written by Paul and Shirley Eberle, who reportedly attended much more of the trial than any of the reporters. The book is impressive for its lengthy quotations directly from their courtroom observation. But the book has no footnotes, and it contains some clearly dubious claims. For example, the Eberles suggested that the cause of Judy Johnson's death was more nefarious than alcohol poisoning and that network executives manipulated the airing of a movie to affect the McMartin verdict. See also text accompanying footnotes 180–181. A second book about the case, *Anatomy of the McMartin Child Molestation Case*, was published more than ten years after the case ended. There are four coauthors, including Jo-Ellan Dimitrius, the jury consultant for the defense in the McMartin case. The book is dedicated to Virginia McMartin. The text includes only one

reference to the underlying transcript. Instead, the authors offer the defense view of the case as fact without any critical inquiry into areas in which there was conflicting evidence. There is a third book that is at least half about the McMartin case, but it has been relegated to obscurity because it takes a credulous view of the McMartin case as a large-scale ritual abuse case. By way of comparison, the book analyzes children from the Papoose Palace Academy case in Nevada, a case discussed in Chapter Four of this book. Waterman, Kelly, Oliveri, and McCord, *Behind the Playground Walls: Sexual Abuse in Preschools* (Guilford Press, 1993). The movie about the case is *Indictment*, a 1995 HBO movie by Abby and Myra Mann. (The Manns announced they were writing a book in 1986, when they also announced plans for the movie. They announced a book deal with Random House in 1993, but the book was never published.)

2. Pseudonyms have been given for first and last names of almost all of the children mentioned in this book. In this chapter, the only exception is Judy Johnson's son—only his first name is a pseudonym. (So, too, with Frank Fuster's son Noel in Chapter Six.) The same pseudonyms used by Nathan and Snedeker for the McMartin case have been employed for children in this chapter; the remaining pseudonyms, for the children not mentioned in *Satan's Silence*, are new. Throughout the book, the pseudonyms that I have assigned preserve the initial letters in the real first and last name.

3. The case is often described as having forty-four children at its height. Bob Williams, a *Los Angeles Times* reporter, prepared a list of forty-four that includes three children who testified before the grand jury but were not later listed as one of the forty-one complainants.

4. See footnote 207 and accompanying text in this chapter.

5. Paul Bynum, a police officer turned private investigator, committed suicide the night after Judge Pounders ruled his testimony could be presented to the jury the next day. Michael D. Harris, "McMartin Witness Commits Suicide," UPI (December 11, 1987, PM cycle.) Robert Hamill Winkler, charged with two other defendants of molesting seven children at the Coco Palms Hotel, died of a drug overdose the day he was to stand trial. David Hall, "Molestation Suspect Dead of Apparent Drug Overdose; Had Been Linked to McMartin Preschool Case," *Daily Breeze* (November 13, 1985), A3. Neither suicide was ever shown to be linked to the McMartin case, although the implication has repeatedly been made about Bynum.

6. Norma Meyer, "McMartin Case Renews Interest in 1976 Slaying," *Daily Breeze* (March 31, 1984), A1 (discussing the unsolved rape and murder of Karen Sue Klaas; the crime occurred after she dropped a child off at the McMartin preschool).

7. That result was upheld on appeal. *McMartin v. County of Los Angeles*, Court of Appeal of California, Second Appellate District, Division One, July 6, 1988. 202 Cal. App. 3d 848; review denied, Supreme Court of California, 1988 Cal. LEXIS 1280 (October 12, 1988).

8. *Spitler v. Children's Institute International*, 11 Cal. App. 3d 432, (Court of Appeal of California, Second Appellate District, Division One) (December 1, 1992).

9. *McMartin v. Currie*, Superior Court for Los Angeles Court, Case No. C751559. (Complaint concerning accusations made by Robert Currie on the following programs, which occurred immediately after the verdicts were announced in the McMartin case: *Geraldo, Sally Jesse Raphael, The Jane Wallace Show*, and *L.A. in the Morning*).

10. Carol McGraw, "McMartin Figures Win $1 in Civil Trial," *Los Angeles Times* (May 8, 1991), B1.

11. Robert Safian, "McMartin Madness: Ten Days in the Life of the Longest, Most Gruesomely Difficult Criminal Trial Ever." *American Lawyer* (October, 1989) 9:46.

12. Cynthia Gorney, "The Terrible Puzzle of McMartin Preschool," *Washington Post* (May 17–18, 1988).

13. Cynthia Gorney, "We All Wanted the Truth, But Must Settle for Justice," *Los Angeles Times* (January 19, 1990), 7.

14. Douglas Besharov, "The McMartin Case: Protecting the Innocent," *National Review* (February 19, 1990), 44.

15. Debbie Nathan. "What McMartin Started: The Ritual Abuse Hoax," *Village Voice* (June 20, 1990).

16. Carol Tavris, "A Day-Care Witch Hunt Tests Justice in Massachusetts," *Los Angeles Times* (April 11, 1997), B9.

17. Carol Tavris, "Beware the Incest-Survivor Machine," *New York Times Book Review* (January 3, 1993), 1, 9.

18. Carol Tavris, "A Day-Care Witch Hunt Tests Justice in Massachusetts."

19. Stephen Ceci and Maggie Bruck, *Jeopardy in the Courtroom: A Scientific Analysis of Children's Testimony* (American Psychological Association, 1995), 8–9.

20. Willis, "The Media and McMartin," *Village Voice*, 8.

21. Rabinowitz, *Wall Street Journal* (May 15, 1995).

22. Nathan and Snedeker, *Satan's Silence*, 69.

23. Memorandum by Dr. Richard Segal, Kaiser Permanente, MR# 664-20-82; August 12, 1983.

24. Summarized in *State v. Buckey* at tr. 61584 ("band of redness, erythema encircling his rectum") and tr. 61587 ("appeared to be some friction like trauma").

25. Quoted in *State v. Buckey* at tr. 61587, lines 21–24.

26. Nathan and Snedeker, *Satan's Silence*, 70.

27. Nathan and Snedeker, *Satan's Silence*, 70. Nathan and Snedeker refer to the clinic as the "Marion Davies Clinic," omitting one word from its actual title, the word that describes the clinic's specialization: the Marion Davies Children's Clinic.

28. *State v. Buckey*, Grand Jury tr. 9, lines 1–8 (bruising); trial tr. 61602 (discoloration).

29. MBPD D.R. No. 83-04288, 16, line 23.

30. *State v. Buckey*, tr. 62,146.

31. A study by McCann et. al. (1988) is widely known for providing the first reliable comparisons of abused and non-abused children. McCann et al., "Perianal Findings in Children Selected for Nonabuse: A Descriptive Study," *Child Abuse & Neglect* (1988) 13(2): 179–193. The study provides evidence that some "signs" thought to be associated only with sexual abuse also appear in non-abused children. For example, almost 30 percent of the non-abused sample exhibited intermittent dilation and relaxation of the anal sphincter, something that Hobbs and Wynne (among others) considered a sign of sexual abuse. Similarly, 30 percent of the non-abused sample had increased pigmentation, another sign often connected to sexual abuse. But the witch-hunt narrative has dismissed medical evidence that is not challenged by McCann's findings. As the authors make clear, they did not find any abrasions, hematomas, or fissures in the non-abused sample. This strengthens the significance of such findings, although it is never acknowledged in the witch-hunt narrative. Butler and his coauthors also claim that McCann's findings were "not admitted at the trial." Actually, Judge Pounders declined to let the defense subpoena Dr. McCann. That decision was eminently reasonable since Dr. McCann had no specific knowledge about the McMartin case. But the content of his studies of "normals" *was* included in the cross-examination of Dr. Heger in the second McMartin trial. The questions did not catch her off-guard. She was most familiar with the work—having served as one of the peer reviewers for the journal that published it.

32. Nathan and Snedeker, *Satan's Silence*, 227.

33. Mann-Stevens Tapes, Defense No. 25, August 4, 1986, 36.

34. Willis, "The Media and McMartin," *Village Voice*, 8.

35. D.A. Investigator Notebooks, 8–30 [1985] notation.

36. Shawn Hubler, "Driven to Her Death," *Los Angeles Herald-Examiner* (March 8, 1987), A1.

37. *People v. Buckey*, Preliminary Hearing, tr. 3139.

38. Mann-Stevens Tapes, Defense No. 6 (April 30, 1986), 64.

39. Mann-Stevens Tapes, Defense No. 17 (July 28, 1986), 20.

40. Nancy Hill-Holtzman, "'Poison' of the McMartin Case," *Los Angeles Herald-Examiner* (October 14, 1988), 1; Times Wire Services, "McMartin Judge Says Case 'Has Poisoned Everyone'," *Los Angeles Times* (October 14, 1988).

41. Letter to Parents from MBPD, September 7, 1983.

42. The MBPD Police Report on Matthew Johnson indicates that on August 24 and 25, 1983, "Det. Dye in R/O's absence" contacted several families. Although all of these adults were reportedly sworn to secrecy, someone informed Virginia McMartin, who called the station to inquire about the matter on August 28. Det. Hoag's entry of August 30, 1983, states: "R/O thinks that [named parent] told Peggy." Ray Buckey was on vacation in South Dakota at the time; he was arrested (and released) on September 7.

43. For example: "This letter, combined with a local television report about possible links between the preschool and a pornography ring in nearby Los Angeles, touched off a panic." Steven Mintz, *Huck's Raft: A History of American Childhood* (Harvard University Press, 2004), 335. But the first media stories were five months after the letter was sent. If the combination of the two touched off the panic, then there were five months of "pre-panic" developments to examine.

44. [Anonymous], "McMartin: Anatomy of a Witch-Hunt," *Playboy* (June 1990), 45, 49.

45. Mary A. Fischer, "A Case of Dominoes?"*Los Angeles Magazine* (October 1989), 131. James Rainey, "L.A. Magazine Meets, Beats Economic Challenges," *Los Angeles Times* (June 25, 2011).

46. See e.g., Wakefield and Underwager, "Assessing the Credibility of Children's Testimony in Ritual Sexual Abuse Allegations" ("The McMartin case was made at CII"). http://www.tc.umn.edu/~under006/Library/Assessing_Crediblity.html

47. "Students of Virginia McMartin Pre-School," DR#83-04288, 288 PC Investigation; Manhattan Beach Police Department.

48. Nathan and Snedeker, *Satan's Silence*, 72.

49. MBPD, D.R. No. 83-04929, 3.

50. The Mergilis had not informed anyone at the preschool of their decision to withdraw. Quite to their surprise, then, Peggy Buckey called Mrs. Mergili on Tuesday, September 13, to find out if the reason Tanya had not been in attendance "had to do with that letter." Without going into any details, Mrs. Mergili told her it did. What happened next became a major issue in the case, with the defense trying to keep these facts from the jury: according to Mrs. Mergili, Peggy Buckey said she "would hate to have Tanya put through" what would happen if this became a legal case. Mrs. Mergili testified that she considered the remark to be a threat. The defense argued vigorously, but unsuccessfully, that any description of the conversation should be kept out of the case.

51. The latter version contains comments and descriptions by someone on the defense team. Unfortunately, neither document meets professional standards of transcription; each version has missing dialogue and appears more like contemporaneous notes than an actual transcription. These are apparently the only available records of this vital September interview. The videotape was never introduced as evidence because Tanya eventually dropped out of the case.

52. Court reporters do not tend to record such information, beyond a parenthetic with the words *indicating* or *child indicating*.

53. Transcript of the Audio Portion of a Videotaped Interview of Tanya Mergili by [Dr.] Mary Wilson, UCLA Hospital, September 20, 1983, 15.

54. Transcript of the Audio Portion of a Videotaped Interview of Tanya Mergili by [Dr.] Mary Wilson, September 20, 1983, 15.

55. Transcript of the Audio Portion of a Videotaped Interview of Tanya Mergili by [Dr.] Mary Wilson, Septembers 20, 1983, 17.

56. Medical Report—Suspected Child Abuse. UCLA Hospital, September 20, 1983. Hospital ID No. 136-07-50, 2.

57. Mergili family Information from Parents or Caretakers, Children's Institute International, 4. Handwritten, undated. Likely completed the same day as Tanya's CII interview (December 8, 1983).

58. Nathan and Snedeker, *Satan's Silence*, 85.

59. *California v. Buckey*, Grand Jury, tr. 339.

60. Diary of Gloria Barton, 3. The diaries of several mothers were obtained through discovery and over strenuous objection of mothers who never considered their own diaries possibly subject to "discovery" in a criminal case.

61. "Information Form," [J and D] Gregg. Contained in "Parent Lists and Responses to Letter," Manhattan Beach Police Department, 1983.

62. MBPD report 83-06235 (1-24-84) Det. Hoag unnumbered.

63. Police Report D.R. 83-05464, Manhattan Beach Police Department (9-23-1983), 3.

64. Police Report D.R. 83-05464, 3.

65. Police Report D.R. 83-05464, 4.

66. Police Report D.R. 83-05464, 5.
67. C.I.I. November. Four-page document with paragraph-length summaries of twelve November CII interviews. The author has clearly viewed the videotapes, and the summaries contain a significant amount of editorializing. This would seem to be a document created by the defense, as that is the substantive orientation of the editorial remarks.
68. "Mary Gordon Interview 11/16/83," 2–3. Note: this twelve-page typed transcript is a truncated transcription of the full interview, which I have seen on videotape. This transcript is not in the same format as other CII transcripts, and it is not clear who prepared it.
69. "Mary Gordon Interview 11/16/83," 3.
70. "Mary Gordon Interview 11/16/83," 5.
71. "Mary Gordon Interview 11/16/83," 7.
72. "Mary Gordon Interview 11/16/83," 7.
73. Information Form, [G.] Ingram. Contained in "Parent Lists and Responses to Letter," Manhattan Beach Police Department, 1983.
74. Police affidavit, unnumbered. S/Judge Schulte 5/5/84.
75. *State v. Buckey*, Grand Jury, tr. 129–140. There is also evidence that Dr. Mary Wilson examined Amy Goldman on September 20 and was told by Amy that she kissed Ray's penis. However strong the evidence in September, it was mitigated by a series of reports from this family as early as mid-January 1984 when one of their children identified "Fireman Pete" from Nautilus Club and two others. By February 4, one of the parents was reporting something about lions and about being "married" at church.
76. Police Report D.R. 83-04932, Manhattan Beach Police Department, 3.
77. Letter from Jean Matusinka, Deputy in Charge, Los Angeles District Attorney's Office to Kee MacFarlane, Child Sexual Abuse Diagnostic Center, Children's Institute (October 17, 1983).
78. Mann-Stevens Tapes, Defense No. 16 (July 28, 1986), 7.
79. "McMartin: Trial and Errors," a 1990 program on public television in Los Angeles, included an interview with a mother who had moved to Hawaii before the McMartin case broke in the news. According to the program, her son corroborated some of the allegations in the case. There was also a family that was in the Far East and one that moved to Oregon before the case broke. There would be numerous other leads to follow if one is looking for evidence that might contradict the claim that the case was created at CII. In one early list of 153 McMartin parents, four families were listed with "no address available," one was listed in Paradise Valley, and another in Bend, Oregon. This kind of inquiry went beyond the scope of my research paradigm and expertise.
80. "Believe the TV Movie," *Village Voice* (May 23, 1995) 40(21), 46. The title is a snide rejoinder to the organization called Believe the Children.
81. Nathan and Snedeker, 80.
82. Nathan and Snedeker, 79–80.
83. After saying that she still likes Ray, Tanya volunteers "He did some bad things, so I don't like it" (34, lines 16–17). MacFarlane's first mention of "bad secrets" comes *after* that (34, lines 27–28).
84. Nathan and Snedeker, 80.
85. Nathan and Snedeker also say that "The girl was mute. She only nodded" (80). There is no explanation why nodding, a universally recognized sign of affirmation, should not be considered affirmation in this instance, other than an unexplained observation about her open mouth.
86. P. 76, lines 5–7.
87. P. 76, lines 16–19.
88. Trisha Walters interview transcript, 82, 85.
89. Police Report D.R. 83-06218, Manhattan Beach Police Department (12–29–83), 1.
90. *State v. Buckey*, Grand Jury, tr. 61 (lines 12–16).
91. Dr. Paul on Trisha Walters. *State v. Buckey*, Retrial, tr. 6679.
92. CII interview (November 7, 1983), 29, 31.
93. CII interview (November 1, 1983), 71.
94. CII interview (November 29, 1983) [Defense description], 3, 4.
95. CII interview (November 30, 1983), 11.

96. CII interview (December 1, 1983).
97. CII interview (December 7, 1983), 61 (won't help) and 62 (scaredy cat).
98. Tanya Mergili was identified in September and videotaped being interviewed by a pediatrician at UCLA Medical Center.
99. "First Implication of Female Teacher Perpetrators." Prepared by Kee MacFarlane (April 5, 1984). Handwritten.
100. Videotape of CII interview (December 5, 1983) (swimming, at 39 min.; saw a movie, at 40 min.; Did Miss Peggy? at 45 min.).
101. Transcription of the Audio Portion of a Videotaped Interview of Tanya Mergili by Kee MacFarlane, Children's Institute International (December 7, 1983), tr. 50–51.
102. "First Implication of Female Teacher Perpetrators." Prepared by Kee MacFarlane (April 5, 1984). Handwritten.
103. Videotape of Charles Sanders interview at CII (January 7, 1984; Peggy naked horsey rider at 33 min).
104. The grand jury notebooks are included with other pre-trial materials at the Los Angeles County Archives. The Mike Wallace reference is apparent in a full transcript of the interview that Wallace did with Lael Rubin. The reference to this incident was not included in the program, which was extremely defense-oriented. Although not disclosed in the program, the interview was staged at the house of Myra and Abby Mann. Glenn Stevens confirmed this information at the 401 hearing. Trial transcript: vol. 25, tr. 3884 (January 28, 1987).
105. Transcript of interview with Terrence and Ellen Chapman, by Bill Brunetti and Detective Augusta Bell, 12.
106. Ellen Chapman later testified that Peggy Buckey told her "she would always continually watch Ray when the children were sitting on his lap or hanging on his neck, um, that if he ever had a hard-on, that she would have noticed it." *State v. Buckey*, vol. 168, tr. 24545–6 (December 16, 1987).
107. Testimony of Ellen Chapman, Grand Jury proceedings, tr. 528 (lines 10–14).
108. Testimony of Ellen Chapman. Grand Jury proceedings, tr. 528 (lines 18–20).
109. Transcript of interview with Terrence and Ellen Chapman, by Bill Brunetti and Detective Augusta Bell, 17.
110. Transcript of interview with Terrence and Ellen Chapman, by Bill Brunetti and Detective Augusta Bell, 21–22; see also Testimony of Ellen Champan at Grand Jury proceedings, tr. 529–530. Chapman wasn't the only witness to these statements; they were made in the presence of her friend, Mary Walker. Interview tr. 19–20.
111. Testimony of Dr. Heger at Grand Jury proceedings, tr. 533–534.
112. *State v. Buckey*, Grand Jury, tr. 524–535.
113. Transcript of interview with Terrence and Ellen Chapman., by Bill Brunetti and Detective Augusta Bell, 42–3.
114. The soundtrack of a videotape of a CII interview with Charlie Marks on February 4, 1984.
115. CII interview with Miranda Chase (April 3, 1984). Quotes in text from notes of videotape.
116. The medical evidence in the McCuan case, which is analyzed in Chapter Three, is much stronger than has been portrayed in the witch-hunt narrative.
117. Bruce Woodling and Astrid Heger, "The Use of the Colposcope in the Diagnosis of Sexual Abuse in the Pediatric Age Group," *Child Abuse & Neglect* (1986), 10(1), 111–114.
118. John McCann, Robert Wells, Mary Simon, and Joan Voris, "Genital Findings in Prepubertal Girls Selected for Nonabuse: A Descriptive Study," *Pediatrics* (1990) 86: 428–439; John McCann, Joan Voris, Mary Simon, and Robert Wells, "Perianal Findings in Prepubertal Children Selected for Nonabuse: A Descriptive Study," *Child Abuse & Neglect* (1989) 13(2): 179–193.
119. Ross E. Cheit, "The Elusive Record: On the Difficulties in Researching High-Profile Child Sexual Abuse Cases from the 1980s," *Justice System Journal* (2007), 28(1) 79–97.
120. Sources official and otherwise: grand jury transcripts, trial transcripts, investigator's notebooks, MBPD reports, CII documents, and internal documents from both the prosecution and the defense, including the Mann-Stevens tapes and transcriptions made by the defense.

121. Nathan and Snedeker cite the 80 percent figure in their book; their footnote is to Mary Fischer's article in *Los Angeles Magazine*. The article does not provide a source or footnote. Nathan and Snedeker, *Satan's Silence*, 293 (fn. 42).

122. Statement of Kee MacFarlane, Child Abuse and Day Care, Joint Hearing before Subcommittee on Oversight of Committee on Ways and Means and Select Committee on Child, Youth, and Families. Ninety-Eighth Congress, Second Session (September 17, 1984), 43.

123. Bruce Woodling and Astrid Heger, "The Use of the Colposcope in the Diagnosis of Sexual Abuse in the Pediatric Age Group," *Child Abuse & Neglect* (1986), 10(1), 111–114.

124. McCauley, J., R. L. Gorman, and G. Guzinski. "Toluidine Blue in the Detection of Perineal Lacerations in Pediatric and Adolescent Sexual Abuse Victims," *Pediatrics* (December 1986), 78(6), 1030–1043.

125. McCauley, Gorman, and Guzinski, 1042. (The control group consisted of "girls 0 to 10 years of age, who presented to the pediatric emergency room or the well-child clinic with a non-acute complaint and no history or suspicion of child abuse"; 1040.)

126. Astrid Heger, Lynne Ticson, Oralia Velasquez, and Raphael Bernier, "Children Referred for Possible Sexual Abuse: Medical Findings in 2384 Children," *Child Abuse & Neglect* (2002), 26(6–7), 645–659.

127. Hendrika Cantwell, "Vaginal Inspection As it Relates to Child Sexual Abuse in Girls Under Thirteen," *Child Abuse & Neglect* (1983), 7, 171–176.

128. John McCann, Robert Wells, and Joan Voris. "Genital Findings in Prepubertal Girls Selected for Nonabuse: A Descriptive Study," *Pediatrics* (1990), 86, 428–439. See also Heger et al., "Appearance of the Genitals in Girls Selected for Nonabuse: Review of Hymenal Morphology and Nonspecific Finings," *Journal of Pediatric and Adolescent Gynecology* (February 2002) 15(1), 27–35.

129. Shireen Atabaki and Jan Paradise, "The Medical Evaluation of the Sexually Abuse Child: Lessons from a Decade of Research," *Pediatrics* (1999).

130. Nathan and Snedeker, *Satan's Silence*, 70.

131. W. D. Erickson, N. H. Walbek, and R. K. Seely, "Behavior Patterns of Child Molesters," *Archive of Sexual Behavior* (February 1988) 17(1), 77–86.

132. One study concluded that 45.5 percent of male sex-abuse victims do not sustain such injuries. Another study found that "two-thirds of children under 6 years of age [in Rimza and Neggerman's report] had normal physical exams" despite having been sexually abused. Rimza and Neggerman also found that genital trauma was "more common in assaults by strangers, occurring in 25% of the cases with stranger assailants and in only 12% of the cases involving known assailants." Cited in W. D. Erickson, N. H. Walbek, and R. K. Seely, "Behavior Patterns of Child Molesters," 79–80. In other words, the kind of abuse that Judy Johnson suspected would likely *not* leave the child seriously wounded. The claim that such abuse "often maims or kills" is utterly fantastic. An epidemiologic study of child sexual abuse in Minneapolis found two deaths in a period with approximately twenty-four hundred reported cases of child sexual abuse. Both were due to strangulation during attempted rape. Arthur C. Jaffe, Lucille Dynneson, and Robert ten Bensel, "Sexual Abuse of Children: An Epidemiological Study," *American Journal of Diseases of Child,* (June 1975), 690.

133. Dr. Paul was asked whether "in cases of acute sodomy which might result in fissures" the gait of the child might be affected. His answer was: "No. Funny enough, it isn't." Vol. 406 at 55574 (August 7, 1989).

134. Mary Gordon, one of the September responders discussed earlier in this chapter, also had significant medical findings. Dr. Heger reported "a large scar measuring between a 1½ and 2cm at 6 o'clock extending through the posterior forchette and crossing the hymen and extending into the vagina." This kind of scar has never been reported in any study of "normal" (non-abused) children.

135. The CII process was not a directed investigation; rather, they responded to referrals. Presumably, the Gregg family did not obtain a referral to CII until after sometime in late November, or possibly even December.

136. *State v. Buckey*, Grand Jury, 74, lines 23–28; 75, lines 1–2.

137. *State v. Buckey*, tr. 61629 (as described in summation).

138. *State v. Buckey*, tr. 61632 (as described in summation).

139. *State v. Buckey*, tr. 61632 (as described in summation).

140. Dr. Paul amended his view in the second trial. He testified that the white marks on pictures of Sally were not scars but tiny drops of mucous reflecting light. He also blamed any "irregularity" of the posterior fourchette on Dr. Heger pulling on the area. This was pure speculation on the part of Dr. Paul, who provided no basis for reaching this new conclusion about slides he previously testified were "perfectly normal."

141. *State v. Buckey*, Second trial, tr. 3432, lines 6–14.

142. *State v. Buckey*, Second trial, tr. 3634.

143. *State v. Buckey*, Second trial, tr. 3635.

144. *State v. Buckey*, Second trial, tr. 3636.

145. *State v. Buckey*, Second trial, tr. 3432, lines 15–21.

146. *State v. Buckey*, Second trial, tr. 3633, lines 7–25.

147. *State v. Buckey*, Grand Jury, tr. 61, lines 12–16.

148. *State v. Buckey*, Grand Jury, tr. 61, lines 19–28; 62, lines 7–9.

149. *State v. Buckey*, Grand Jury, tr. 62, lines 1–5.

150. *State v. Buckey*, Second trial, tr. 3420, lines 1–3.

151. *State v. Buckey*, Second trial, tr. 3420, lines 10–11.

152. *State v. Buckey*, Second trial, tr. 3421, lines 16–19.

153. *State v. Buckey*, Second trial, tr. 3421

154. *State v. Buckey*, tr. 61555, lines 23–28; 61556, lines 1–2.

155. *State v. Buckey*, Second trial, tr. 6418.

156. *State v. Buckey*, Second trial, tr. 6649.

157. The medical report on Allison contains two relevant findings: (1) a 1.0–2.0 cm scar crossing the posterior forchette totally and entering and crossing the hymen into the vagina (98, line 27 to 99, line 3); and (2) a small anal scar (0.5 cm) at 12 o'clock.

158. Heger testimony described at tr. 61489-90.

159. Cited in Lois Timnick, "Doctor Testifies for Defense in McMartin Trial," *Los Angeles Times* (August 9, 1989).

160. Astrid Heger, S. Jean Emans and David Muram, *Evaluation of the Sexually Abused Child* (Oxford University Press, 2000), 7.

161. *Satan's Silence*, 187. As chief medical examiner in Sao Paulo, Brazil, Dr. Teixeira wrote an article that Nathan and Snedeker described as "instructing colleagues how to do virginity checks on girls and women" with a colposcope. The authors claimed that Teixeira had done hundreds of these dubious examinations. "If an accused wife denied indiscretions before marriage," Nathan and Snedeker explained, "[Dr. Teixeira] attempted to distinguish the fresh irritations inflicted by her husband's penis from other infinitesimal wounding that might have been wrought by a former boyfriend." But the article that Dr. Teixeira wrote is called "Hymenal Colposcopic Examination in Sexual Offenses" and is based on the examination of 500 patients during a six-month period, all of them "actual or supposed victims of sexual offenses." There is a single mention of the civil law that allows a husband to request annulment up to ten days after the wedding "under the special circumstance of his wife not being virgin without his previous knowledge." Notably, Teixeira describes this as "a very uncommon situation" and makes no statement to indicate he has ever had a single case like that. He certainly does not describe one. Wilmes Teixeira, "Hymenal Colposcopic Examination in Sexual Offenses," *American Journal of Forensic Medicine and Pathology* (September 1981), 213.

162. Woodling and Heger, "The Use of the Colpscope in the Diagnosis of Sexual Abuse in Pediatric Age Girls," *Child Abuse & Neglect* (1986), 10(1), 112.

163. This case, like McMartin, is far more complicated than has been portrayed in the witch-hunt narrative. See Ross E. Cheit and Andrea Matthews, "Revisiting the Jordan, Minnesota Cases," *Roger Williams University Law Review* (forthcoming, 2014).

164. *State v. Buckey*, Second trial, tr. 6334 ("a liar will avoid your eye contact at some time or another").

165. Astrid Heger, S. Jean Emans, and David Muram, *Evaluation of the Sexually Abused Child: A Medical Textbook and Photographic Atlas*, 2nd ed. (Oxford University Press, 2000); see also John Wilkens and Jim Okerblom, "Wrong Photos Utilized in Child-Abuse Trial," *San Diego Union-Tribune* (January 21, 1992), B1 (describing how Heger's evaluation identified the error in the Poway case).

166. *State v. Buckey*, Second trial, tr. 3620.
167. A brief synopsis of five other children in the preliminary hearing or trial whose medical evidence merits further consideration:

Cindy Ennis. Among the remaining children, the medical evidence was strongest in the case of Cindy Ennis. Cindy was nine years old when she was interviewed at CII on March 14, 1984. Four doctors eventually testified she had an extremely enlarged hymenal opening (2.0 cm). Although studies on the range of "normal" hymenal openings in girls with no suspected history of sexual abuse later challenged the earlier notions of what constituted possible signs of abuse, even those studies agreed that a 2 cm. opening is not normal. (At the time of the trial, many pediatricians considered a hymenal opening of more than 0.5 cm. to be enlarged. McCann's subsequent studies indicate that openings up to 1 cm. could well be normal. But the evidence on Cindy E. was twice that number.) There was also extensive scarring evidence noted through colpscopic pictures. Of the eight colposcopic findings, six would still be considered highly significant under current standards. All of those involved scarring. Defense lawyer Danny Davis, who rarely gave any points to the prosecution, described the medical evidence on Cindy Ennis as "serious and convincing." In his closing argument, he offered only the technical defense that 62 percent of the time Cindy attended the preschool was outside the scope of the statute of limitations. In other words, Ray Buckey could not be convicted for those acts if the jury concluded they occurred during those times. *State v. Buckey*, tr. 62094.

Bill Sandel. Probably the most notable remaining child, from the point of view of medical evidence, was Bill Sandel. He was the second child to testify at the preliminary hearing, so his testimony received extensive media coverage. The medical evidence, which was presented separately, received much less attention. According to Bill's mother, who was then a nurse, the boy complained of rectal bleeding while he attended the McMartin Preschool. She testified this was a recurring problem and she observed "excoriated areas around the anus." She entertained the possibility of pinworms, never even considering sexual abuse as a possible cause. Three doctors testified Bill had significant anal scarring in a most suspicious location (between 6 and 7 o'clock). Dr. Heger originally examined the boy, and Dr. Gordon testified that he agreed with her findings. The boy was also seen separately by Dr. Berkowitz, who took her own photographs with a colposcope and verified the scarring.

Dr. Paul concurred that there were anal injuries but he argued they likely occurred more recently than when Bill attended the preschool. At one point he argued that the injuries were acute; nobody else took the claim seriously. Indeed, Dr. Paul's assertion does not explain the source of the problems Bill experienced in his anal area while attending the McMartin Preschool. Nor does it indicate how Bill sustained the injuries Dr. Paul acknowledges, especially given that Bill's only explanation to the pediatrician involved Ray Buckey.

Kristy Walters. There was strong disagreement over the medical evidence concerning Kristy Walters, Trisha's older sister. Trisha is the one child at trial who emerged from the initial CII interviews in November. She was attending the school at the time, which indicates how strongly her family supported the McMartins before Trisha made her statements on November 22, 1983. Dr. Heger examined Kristy when she was seven and a half years old. The girl had last been in attendance at the McMartin Preschool two and a half years earlier. Dr. Heger testified at the grand jury that Kristy had a very relaxed hymenal opening, which she said was one and a half times the normal size. She testified further that there was general rounding of the hymen and skin tags (McMartin Grand Jury, tr. 64, lines 18–28). These findings would not be considered important today; they can all be found in "normals."

There were other findings, however, that would be considered significant indicators of abuse by today's standards. Most significantly, Dr. Heger observed a long scar at 6 o'clock that was greater than 2 cm. It extended through the antichamber, across the hymen, and into the vagina (McMartin Grand Jury: 65, lines 1–4). Six o'clock is the most common place for injury to occur in a penetrative assault; a large scar in that location is practically diagnostic of sexual abuse. Dr. Heger also testified that Kristy had other scars perpendicular to the opening of the vagina. She described them as typical of "a blunt object pushing against delicate tissue" (McMartin Grand Jury: 65, lines 22–28).

Dr. Heger further testified that there was a depression near the anal verge. Dr. Gordon, who examined the photographs, testified he also saw scars that were consistent with sexual abuse (McMartin First Trial: summarized at 61521, lines 9–12). Dr. Paul testified he could not see any of the supposed scars (tr. 56385–56387); nor could he draw any conclusions from the depression on the anal verge. It is impossible to assess whether this was an abnormal finding that was due to trauma or merely a congenital defect, without having an independent medical expert examine the photographs. The jury never heard about the "well-healed anal scars"—scars consistent with the penetration of a blunt object—because Kristy never disclosed anal abuse in her testimony; the defense won its fight to keep this evidence from the jury. There is no medical doubt that Kristy Walters sustained serious anal injuries. But because she never disclosed them, the jury never heard the medical evidence.

Ariel Marks. Ariel accounted for twenty-one of the fifty-two counts against Ray Buckey at trial. The ten other children accounted for between one and six counts each against him. She was the child with the longest period of attendance at McMartin, which helps account for the large number of criminal counts. Curiously, Ariel has not played prominently in the witch-hunt narrative; nor was she one of the three girls who convinced enough jurors to result in a mistrial on those charges. The documents I was able to review provide sufficient details to understand what Dr. Heger originally reported. They do not provide details about Dr. Paul's responses.

Dr. Heger testified before the grand jury that Ariel had recurrent vaginitis and bladder infections while enrolled at the McMartin Pre-School. This is relevant but not particularly strong evidence since sexual abuse is one of many possible explanations. The significance of Dr. Heger's testimony about "rounded tissue remnants around the hymen" and about a "very relaxed hymenal opening" has been contradicted by research conducted since 1984. Similarly, the findings concerning "neovascularization" would not have been considered notable under current knowledge. Had these questionable findings been the only signs of abuse, then Ariel's medical evaluation would have been seriously impugned under today's state of knowledge. But the evaluation also found signs of trauma that remain solid signs of abuse today. Dr. Heger testified further that there was scar tissue at various locations surrounding the opening of the vagina; there was a "remarkable scar which streams from 3:30 across the hymenal orifice into vagina." The significance of this kind of evidence of physical trauma has not been diminished by subsequent research. That is, vaginal scars have not been found in non-abused populations in controlled studies unless the child had a well-defined episode of previous vaginal trauma. Ariel Marks did not have a previous record of vaginal injury.

Daniel Acorn. Daniel was first interviewed at CII on March 1, 1984. He was nine years old and had not been at the McMartin preschool for almost three years. His medical evaluation by Drs. Woodling and Heger was conducted on May 26. Testimony much later in the case suggests that Dr. Woodling's employment for the prosecution was discontinued after this date, although it is not at all clear why. Dr. Woodling's report describes the medical examination as follows: "A general physical examination is performed by Astrid Heger, M.D. Careful inspection of the perianal area reveals a small, old well-healed fissure at 12 o'clock. Multiple photographs are taken using a colposcope. No other genital injury or scarring is present. Internal examination is not performed at the request of both the patient and his mother." The colposcopic findings described "a six o'clock scar with loss of tissue integrity," "loss of rugal patterns with hypertrophy, palor and underlying erythema" at 4 o'clock, and "scarring with rugal interruption" at 12 o'clock. There is still a debate in the field about the significance of "rugal patterns"; therefore much of what he described might be irrelevant to proving sexual abuse. Scarring, however, is always suspicious, especially at the 6 or 12 o'clock position. Dr. Paul admitted there could be "a scar or scars" on one slide, but he said it had "little significance either way." Dr. Heger ultimately presented these findings merely as "consistent with" sexual abuse, which is not any kind of diagnostic claim. It is difficult to ascertain more without being able to submit the slides at issue to an outside expert, but it is safe to say the significance of the findings on this child was probably overblown.

168. Sara Barton, one of the very first positive responders in September 1983, demonstrated several notable medical signs of sexual abuse. Dr. Heger noted one finding—"rounding" of the

tissue—that has since been considered an unreliable indicator of sexual abuse. She also noted scarring, which is still considered strong evidence of sexual abuse. Mary Gordon, another September responder, was examined by Drs. Heger and Woodling on January 7, 1984. Dr. Heger reported scarring in the area outside the hymen at 4 o'clock, 5 o'clock, 7 o'clock, and 8 o'clock. She also observed a large scar measuring 1.5-2 cm at 6 o'clock, extending through the posterior fourchette and into the vagina. These findings, if confirmed today, would be considered strong evidence of sexual abuse.

169. The mother who testified at Congress as "Mrs. Deborah Smith" had taken her child to the pediatrician, who observed "considerable redness and swelling in her genital area." At the next visit, a routine visit for her younger brother, the pediatrician noted vaginal discharge. The girl's stepfather, a general practitioner, diagnosed vaginitis.

170. Grand Jury, tr. 46–47. Also at 50, lines 12–16: "And so with Kathy, she definitely had the scarring, she definitely had a large scar at the point of 6 o'clock that crossed all the way across and went right into the vagina. You could see the scar very, very noticeably."

171. This was described by Debra Mergili in the Preliminary Hearing, vol. 139, October 1, 1984.

172. Jeffrey Victor, "Satanic Cult Rumors as Contemporary Legend," *Western Folklore, Contemporary Legends in Emergence* (January 1990), 49(1): 51–81, 69.

173. Investigator Worksheets, V. Harper (replaced January 19, 1984, by A. W. Brunnetti).

174. Investigator Worksheets, A. W. Brunnetti (February 16, 1984).

175. The most vocal of the parents involved in the dubious tunnel dig after the first trial was Jackie McGaulie, whose daughter was never part of the criminal case. One of the most vocal of the parents during the trial was Tim Wheeler, who appeared on the *60 Minutes* program about the case; he too did not have children in the case. Neither did Bob Currie, who became famous both for the reward he posted without success for evidence of commercial pornography at the McMartin Preschool and for being featured as a rabid parent in the movie *Indictment*.

176. Richard Beck, "Willis and Happiness," *n + 1* (November 18, 2011). The statement of purpose is from the organization's Fall 1993 newsletter. I reviewed twenty-three newsletters from 1986 to 1997 and did not find any references that bear out the claim they were "right wing." In the only year an actual budget was published in the newsletter, the organization had an annual income of $15,917 and it expended of $19,816. (Believe the Children newsletter, Winter 1996, 7.) Although various cultural theorists have claimed, retroactively, that this organization was an important influence on American society, the claim is difficult to square with their small membership and the content of their newsletter, which largely reproduced articles published elsewhere and did not take credit for any actual legislation or other outcomes. Moreover, Nancy Whittier's detailed account of the social movements around child sexual abuse in the United States provides no support for the claim that these organizations were right-wing. Rather, they represented feminists and victims, whose politics were, if anything, left-leaning. Nancy Whittier, *The Politics of Child Sexual Abuse* (Oxford University Press, 2009).

177. A handmade typed spreadsheet of all the children at trial, apparently prepared by the LADA, lists the therapist for each child. Nine went to C. Kent; two others went to J. Kent. The three remaining children were seen by Jane McCord, Noel Plourde, and Michelle Dugan. See Eberle and Eberle, *Abuse of Innocence*, 18, 20, 49, 59, 72, 75, 139.

178. Mann-Stevens Tapes, No. 17, 8 (July 28) and No. 18 (July 30), 3. Stevens uses the plural more than once in this conversation, making it clear he was implicating both therapists, even though Kent saw far more children. Kent and Dugan contributed to a chapter in Waterman et. al.'s *Behind the Playground Walls*, wherein they provide a clinical view of children in the McMartin case. Two clinical examples involved children who reportedly were forced to kill animals (248–249). Though duly noting that nobody in the case was convicted in criminal court, the chapter in Waterman does not entertain the possibility that stated reports about killing animals might have been factually incorrect.

179. In 2008, the Santa Cruz Ritual Abuse Task Force posted a credulous summary of the claim that there had been tunnels under the McMartin Preschool. It was contained on a Word Press blog about the McMartin Preschool trial that no longer exists. The Task Force is credited with writing the introduction to a section called "Archaeological Investigations of the

McMartin Preschool Site" on a Ritual Abuse website. http://ritualabuse.us/ritualabuse/articles/mcmartin-preschool-case-what-really-happened-and-the-coverup/.

For a sense of the conspiracy theories that can be associated with such task forces, see Aaron Curtis, "Some on Ritual Abuse Task Force Say Satanists Are Poisoning Them," *Los Angeles Times* (December 1, 1992).

180. Eberle and Eberle, *Abuse of Innocence*, 19–20.

181. He was a previously convicted arsonist who was apprehended after setting another fire, on May 17, at the home of a former companion who provided the police with evidence linking him to the McMartin fire. See David Hall, "McMartin Fire Suspect 'Full of Violence,'" *Daily Breeze* (May 26, 1984), A3.

182. Documents from the arson investigation reveal that Mann claimed the U.S. attorney was "biased" against them and the investigation when they concluded there was no connection to the McMartin case. Report of Investigation, Dept. of Treasury, Bureau of Alcohol, Tobacco and Firearms, Investigation No. 93110-95-0011-D (December 12, 1995), 5.

183. Lisa Belkin, *Show Me a Hero: A Tale of Murder, Suicide, Race, and Redemption* (Little Brown, 1999), 69.

184. See e.g., KABC arraignment story from March 1984 that ends with anchorwoman saying "this is your story [Wayne], it's all your story" and endorsing the need for contributions to CII. Available at: http://youtu.be/MD5aT6kZ5MQ.

185. The relationship between Kee MacFarlane and Wayne Satz became a major part of the witch-hunt narrative largely because it was eventually revealed that the two were linked romantically. Although much has been made about the relationship, by all indications their romantic involvement began long after the initial stories on KABC and after the first few months of CII interviews. One full day of cross-examination of MacFarlane was devoted to her relationship with Satz (*State v. Buckey*, reporter's daily transcript, Tuesday August 9, 1988). Judge Pounders ruled that their romantic relationship was off-limits because it did not bear sufficient relevancy to issues about the CII interviews. As to MacFarlane's role in the original stories, she denied leaking information to Satz, but she acknowledged that she spoke with him several times during the development of the story, that she knew the story was coming out in advance of February 2, and that she participated in a live TV interview with Satz after one of the stories in March (tr. 38534). In short, she worked closely with him. None of which excuses the obvious impropriety of discussing a confidential investigation with Satz, but the reasons for doing so were apparently not related to the relationship that later formed between the two.

186. Notation, Investigator's Notebooks, February 2, 1984.

187. Philip Jenkins, *Moral Panic*, 276, fn. 5.

188. Since Judy Johnson was not the only one with a fanciful version of the case by then, this issue is far less important than has been represented in the witch-hunt narrative. Johnson's behavior in February 1984 does not prove anything about what three separate doctors saw in August 1983. Instead, it helps prove that social forces surrounding the case were taking hold shortly after the media coverage began.

189. The cut-off date for the second round of charges was early May 1984. There had been 178 children evaluated at that point. This was about half the number of children who would ultimately be evaluated. The children who were interviewed later played no role in the legal proceedings, and none of the multiple sources of documents located for this research included any information about them, beyond transcripts of some CII interviews.

190. Ilyce Meckler's rarely cited investigative report for PBS ("McMartin Trial and Errors") in January 1990 demonstrated that the DA's office viewed very few of the children's interviews before taking the case to the grand jury. Instead, they relied on the videotape log notations.

191. Mann-Stevens Tapes, Defense No. 22 (August 16, 1986), 22 ("it was just awesome").

192. Carol McGraw, "McMartin Pupil, 10, Tells of Bizarre Rite; Forced to Drink Blood, Witness Claims," *Los Angeles Times* (February 21, 1985), 6.

193. Mann-Stevens Tapes, Defense No.4 (March 22, 1986), 17.

194. John A. Jackson, "Trial by Ordeal: The McMartin Court Has Its Way with One Small Girl," *Daily Breeze* (May 16, 1985), 1, 18 +.

195. William Plummer and Joshua Hammer, "The Young Witnesses in the McMartin Sex Abuse Case Undergo a Legal Battering in Court," *People* (July 8, 1985), 26.

196. Mann-Stevens Tapes, Defense No. 29 (June 11, 1986), 25.

197. Mann-Stevens Tapes, Defense No. 4 (March 22, 1986), 10.

198. Lois Timnick, "McMartin Defense Investigator Coerced Witness, Judge Finds," *Los Angeles Times* (September 13, 1989), Metro, Part 2, 3.

199. See testimony of Wesley Sorenson, September 22 and 25, 1989. Volumes 431 and 432 of the trial transcript, *State v. Buckey*. The incident, which Virginia McMartin reported in her dairy, involved the Sorenson's daughter touching Ray's genitals in the spring of 1983. Virginia described the incident as inadvertent, and in a conversation with Mrs. Sorenson Virginia learned that the girl had apparently tried to touch her father's genitals in the shower on one or two occasions. Those incidents, which the father considered both private and irrelevant to the charges in the McMartin case, were eventually the focus of many questions in court. Welsey Sorenson testified that the defense investigator who approached him about these issues made him "uneasy" and gave him the "feeling" that the defense was warning him that if he testified it would be very embarrassing for him (tr. 59953). The detailed and repeated questioning about his occasional showers with his small daughter bears this out.

200. Marcia Chambers, "Questions Arise About Investigation of Coast Molestation Case," *New York Times* (October 22, 1985).

201. Transcripts of the Mann-Stevens tapes, covering conversations over several months in the late spring and summer of 1986, indicate Stevens told the Manns on several early occasions that he thought there was sufficient evidence of guilt against Ray Buckey. Mann eventually says that the success of the movie depends on all the defendants being acquitted. Stevens famously drank a toast with the Manns to the acquittal of both defendants, even though Stevens later allowed under oath that he still believed Ray Buckey was guilty at the time. Stevens eventually adopted the witch-hunt narrative wholesale, arguing that Ray Buckey was also factually innocent.

202. Michael Reese, "A Child-Abuse Case Implodes," *Newsweek* (January 27, 1986), 26. This view had been building in the press coverage for more than six months. See John Crewdson, "California Abuse Case May Be Unraveling," *Chicago Tribune* (May 17, 1985).

203. The Manns announced their intention to make a movie and write a book in a press release on November 3, 1986. "Abby Mann Plans Book, Feature Film on 'McMartin Preschool Case,'" Solters, Roskin, Freidman, Inc. (November 3, 1986). The agreement they signed with Stevens, which became an exhibit in the hearing on the motion to dismiss, was dated April 1, 1986. The conversations took place largely in June and July of 1986.

204. The Manns said they "agonized" about the decision, particularly since they promised Stevens the tapes would be confidential, but decided they could not withhold evidence—evidence that they created. Richard Layco, "Hollywood Tapes and Testimony," *Time* (December 15, 1986).

205. Mann-Stevens Tapes, No. 29, 37.

206. *State v. Buckey*, Pre-trial hearing, tr. 3876 (January 28, 1987).

207. Memorandum to: Gilbert Garcetti. From: Glenn E. Stevens. Subject: Analysis, Recommendation and Revised Summaries *People v. Raymond Buckey et al.*, January 10, 1986. 3. He recommended "a simple case against Raymond Buckey with six victims all supported by medical evidence" and concluded that the evidence "should lead any jury or court to conclude that he is guilty as charged" (8).

208. Mann-Stevens Tapes, No. 20, 29.

209. Fischer, "A Case of Dominoes," [Figure] "Where Was Ray?" 130.

210. James Rainey, "L. A. Magazine Finds Its Way Back," *Los Angeles Times* (June 25, 2011), D1 (naming the McMartin "debunking" article as one of the most important articles in the magazine in its fifty years).

211. A mother whose two children attended McMartin between 1975 and 1980 said "Ray came to the school right as they were leaving" (Response of. L. B.). Another mother specifically placed Ray at the school in the fall of 1980 (Response of D. E.). A mother whose daughter attended only in 1980–81 told the police a specific story about how Ray was "real mean" to the kids (Response of J. P.). A man whose son attended from 1978 to 1981 also verified that

his son had contact with Ray Buckey (Response of D. S.). Tara Duncan, who had come to McMartin for observation from El Camino College, testified Ray was there in the fall of 1980. Trial testimony, vol. 259 (July 27, 1988).

212. *State v. Buckey*, tr. 36701–36702.

213. Nathan and Snedeker, *Satan's Silence*, 71.

214. The footnote to Nathan's claim references an entire article and not a particular passage. The article is an "exclusive" interview with the Buckeys by a writer clearly sympathetic to the defense. Nathan and Snedeker, *Satan's Silence*, 268, fn. 16.

215. Scott Moniak told the MBPD he "used to hang around with Ray," and that Ray "drank in the daytimes" and was "out of control" and "into magic mushrooms." MBPD interview, November 22, 1983.

216. Virginia McMartin testified she put things about the preschool in her diary "if they were important." *State v. Buckey*, tr. 60271. On April 8, 1981 she wrote: "Ray had troubles. Several calls from Peg. Steve came from work and helped P. A. with him. Poor dear." When asked to explain the notation years later, Virginia McMartin testified she "hasn't the slightest idea" what the entry meant, remarking that "all young people have troubles." Tr. 60, 374–60375.

217. Major Jon L. Lightner, JA, "The McMartin Pre-School Case," JAG School (March 1993), 13.

218. Statement of Cindy and Jacob Dale, November 9, 1983, MBPD.

219. "It came across to me in that moment of time as if the exposure was intentional," she testified. She thought about calling the police but did not do because she "care[d] about the family." *State v. Buckey*, tr. 58474 (September 12, 1989).

220. *State v. Buckey*, tr. 58444, lines 18–19 are the quote. Her testimony begins 58440 and includes Buckey's response: "I never wear underwear."

221. *State v. Buckey*, tr. 40338; *State v. Buckey*, Second trial, tr. 3348.

222. Sorenson took great issue with Virginia McMartin's account. See tr. 60084–60085.

223. Sorenson testified that this was the only time he saw Ray "exposed" in this fashion, that he said something to Ray, and that Ray responded he didn't have any clean underwear that day. Sorenson testified he "thought it might just have been a simple mistake." Tr. 60018–60019, 60021. In other words, he gave Ray the benefit of the doubt—at the time. Sorenson later came to a different position and testified for the prosecution.

224. *State v. Buckey*, Trial tr. 24545–46.

225. *State v. Buckey*, Second trial, tr. 5008, 5010.

226. Specific details about the divided votes were not announced. The jury foreman reported that the jury was divided eight to four but did not indicate which direction or specify whether the vote was consistent for each of the twelve charges.

227. The jurors spoke at a press conference shortly after announcing their verdicts. Seth Mydans, "For Jurors, Facts Could Not Be Sifted from Fantasies," *New York Times* (January 19, 1990), A18. This simple, verifiable fact is important in assessing one of the strangest claims in the witch-hunt narrative to be made about this press conference: that jurors' statements should be discounted because they might have been "self-serving" responses to the public criticism they felt after the verdicts had been announced. Ceci and Bruck made this argument, attributing it to an unnamed "close observer" of the trial. Stephen J. Ceci and Maggie Bruck, "Child Witnesses: Translating Research into Policy," *Social Policy Reports* (Society for Research in Child Development, Fall 1993), 25, fn. 1. This unnamed source did not reconcile this speculation against the fact that the press conference occurred *before* there were any headlines about the case or even any television programs with outspoken parents as guests. There was actually very little public outcry over the verdict as a whole; but more importantly, the various developments after the verdicts were announced, however they are characterized, are irrelevant to explaining any behavior at the press conference because it came immediately after Judge Pounders dismissed the jury.

228. "McMartin Jury: Prosecution Never Proved Case," *United Press International* (January 19, 1990), Domestic News Section.

229. Transcript, *MacNeil Lehrer News/Hour* (January 18, 1990), 8.

230. "The McMartin Jury's Trial," *Washington Post* (January 20, 1990), A18.

231. Paul Pringlee and Dolores Wood, "Jurors' Quest for Agreement Ends in Futility," *Daily Breeze* (July 28, 1990), 1.

232. Her license was reinstated by Administrative Law Judge Ronald M. Gruen. *In re Peggy Ann B.*, California Commission on Teacher Credentials (No. L-42932), November 24, 1988.

233. Peggy Buckey was charged with conspiracy as well as child molestation. As reflected in the jury's verdict in the first trial, the evidence for the conspiracy charge was stronger than the evidence of child molestation.

Chapter Three

1. Debbie Nathan, "The Making of a Modern Witch Trial," *Village Voice* (September 29, 1987), 20.

2. Mark Sauer, "Decade of Accusations: The McMartin Preschool Child Abuse Case Launched 100 Others," *San Diego Union-Tribune* (August 29, 1993), Part 1, D1.

3. Mary De Young, *The Day Care Ritual Abuse Moral Panic*, 3.

4. Ceci and Bruck, "Child Witnesses" (emphasis added), 3.

5. Carol Hopkins Press Release. Repeated credulously in Humes, *Mean Justice*, 572, fn. 76.

6. Paul Craig Roberts, "False Memories, False Prosecutions," *Washington Times* (January 20, 1998), A12. Roberts asserts that the "Justice Committee has files on some 2,000 innocents whose lives were ruined and families destroyed by the accusation." According to Philip Kaushall, a forensic psychologist in San Diego who took possession of those files after the "Justice Committee" was disbanded, the files represent a survey of prisoners whose claims of innocence have not been independently examined (Kaushall, private communication).

7. There were fifty-one names in the hardcover edition, fifty-four names in the paperback edition. This page was removed from later editions.

8. The *San Francisco Examiner* published a similar article in 1986, but the focus was not national. A. S. Ross, "Ritualistic Child Abuse? A Presumption of Guilt," *San Francisco Examiner* (September 29, 1986). Almost all of the cases contained in the article were included in Charlier and Downing's list of thirty-six. Curiously, Charlier and Downing chose to exclude the case in which five members of a Wicca coven "were convicted or pleaded guilty to several hundred counts of sexual abuse involving teen-age boys going back to 1979."

9. See e.g., Jason Fine, "Seeking Evil: The Hell of Prosecuting Satanic Ritual Abuse," *California Lawyer* (July 1994), 90; Interview, Michael Phillips, *Whole Earth Review* (December 22, 1998), 104. Alexander Cockburn also relied extensively on the series with utter credulity in "Abused Imaginings," *New Statesman & Society* (January 1990).

10. Ellen Willis, "As Child-molestation Cases Fall Apart, Who's Watching Now?" (Minneapolis) *Star Tribune* (June 5, 1995), 5A.

11. See footnote 20, John Earl, "The Dark Truth About the 'Dark Tunnels of McMartin,'"*Issues in Child Abuse Accusations*, Vol. 7 (1995).

12. Denis Brion, "The Hidden Persistence of Witchcraft," *Law and Critique* (1993); Mary de Young, "Another Look at Moral Panics: The Case of Satanic Day Care Centers," *Deviant Behavior* (1998).

13. Jeffrey Victor, *Satanic Panic: The Creation of a Contemporary Legend* (Open Court, 1993): Appendix V, 355–361.

14. Barbara Fister, "The Devil in the Details: Media Representations of 'Ritual Abuse' and Evaluation of Sources," *Studies in Media & Information Literacy Education* (May 2003), 1–14.

15. Three of the "cases" are presented without a single proper name or related feature that would facilitate any kind of fact checking. The defendant is not named in the Bouse, Arizona, case; nor are the names given of anyone else involved. None of the accused are named in the Atherton, California, case either, or the woman who allegedly accused them. Similarly, there are no identifying features in the Richmond, Virginia, case.

16. Two prominent examples are explained in detail in later chapters: the Kelly Michaels case (Maplewood, New Jersey) in Chapter Five and the Country Walk case (Miami) in Chapter Six.

17. Charlier and Downing, "Patterns Emerge Across Nation," *Commercial Appeal* (January 1988), A3.
18. Charlier and Downing, "Patterns," A3.
19. Some newspaper articles at the time said the house had been abandoned by LeRoy Freeman. Other reports said a neighbor, who apparently did not know Freeman, resembled him. Chris Evan and Ted Wendling, "Bedeviled Searchers Call It Off," *Plain Dealer*, June 22, 1985, A1, 14. A 1986 article, however, said Freeman had lived in the house before this person moved in; and it apparently was abandoned by Freeman and later purchased from the bank. See "Fruitless Dig for Victims of Cult Leaves Family Angry," *Plain Dealer* (July 22, 1986), B2.
20. Jim Sielicki, "General News," UPI (Toledo, Ohio, June 21, 1985, PM cycle).
21. Deputies watched and tape-recorded an outdoor ritual service near the areas searched on April 30, 1985. It was attended by about one hundred people. "The two-hour ceremony featured chanting, but no sacrifices," deputy sheriff Trilby Cashin was quoted as saying. Chris Evan and Ted Wendling, "Hunt Near Toledo Fails to Find Human Sacrifices," *Plain Dealer* (June 21, 1985), 1, 16A.
22. Arthur Lyons, *Satan Wants You: The Cult of Devil Worship in America* (Mysterious Press, 1988). These items were also mentioned in newspaper articles at the time. See e.g., Chris Evan and Ted Wendling, "Bedeviled Searchers Call It Off," *Plain Dealer* (June 22, 1985), A1.
23. "Grandfather, LeRoy Freeman, Is Sentenced for Kidnapping," *Plain Dealer* (January 31, 1987), B4.
24. Charlier and Downing, "Similar Tales" *Commercial Appeal* (January 1988), A8.
25. Denis Brion, "The Hidden Persistence of Witchcraft,"*Law and Critique* (1993).
26. Seven cases account for two-thirds of the entries in this table: McMartin, Kern County, Memphis, Niles, Chicago, and two cases never actually discussed in the article; Torrance and Rolling Hills (discussed in Chapter Four of this book), which were near the McMartin Preschool.
27. Interview, Michael Phillips, *Whole Earth Review* (December 22, 1998), 104.
28. See e.g., J. Frazier Smith, "Child Admits Testimony Lie at Abuse Trial," *Cincinnati Enquirer* (August 10, 1985), C1; J. Frazier Smith, "Mother Didn't Think Child Was Abused," *Cincinnati Enquirer* (August 15, 1985), D3; J. Frazier Smith, "Lawyer Saw Mom's Journal as Key," *Cincinnati Enquirer* (July 24, 1985), C1.
29. Faizah Alim, "'Snuff' Case Thrown Out," *Sacramento Bee* (October 26, 1985), A1.
30. The licensing proceedings were against Barbara Orr, owner and operator of the Jubilation Day Care Center in Ft. Bragg. I obtained 537 pages of documents on the case from the California Department of Social Services (DSS). Those records indicate that Administrative Law Judge Michael C. Cohn initially issued findings of fact that Orr's niece had "engaged in sexual acts with K.B. a six year old boy being cared for at the facility." (Para V, p. 2.) Decision, *In the Matter of the Accusation Against Barbara Orr DBA Jubilation Day Care Center*, No. LC 1269-0584, California Department of Social Services, July 30, 1984. Those findings were not contested, the niece was placed in some kind of therapy, and an order was issued prohibiting the niece from having any contact with children at the day care. Orr's license was placed on two-year probation. During this time, the allegations surrounding the case grew and Barbara Orr and her sister were named as potential suspects. Tom Hine, "Ex-Coast Day Care Center Hit by Abuse Charges," (Mendocino) *Grapevine* (July 11, 1985), 3. The DSS files document that therapist Pamela Hudson was a key actor in the case. The earliest investigative document in the file is a letter from Hudson recommending an investigation into possible abuse by the young niece. Letter to Child Protective Services (March 23, 1984, Bates No. 000033). There also typed summaries labeled "Taped Statements by Pamela Hudson" covering three days in January 1985 (Bates No. 000041-42). As her role in the case continued, the claims she reported became stranger. A Mendocino County Sheriff's Report in April 1985 includes details, provided to the Sheriff's Office by Hudson, about a child allegedly hung by a cross and adults allegedly killing animals to scare children (Bates No. 000470). Hudson published a credulous "Survey of Ritual Abuse Cases" in 1988 that counted the Fort Bragg "case" as a ritual abuse case with ten or eleven child victims. But Barbara Orr was never charged with any acts of physical or sexual abuse, only with violating the conditions of her probation.

A hearing that would have presented the evidence for revocation was canceled when Orr voluntarily agreed to a permanent license revocation. Decision and Order, *In the Matter of the Accusation Against Barbara Orr*, California Department of Social Services, No. LC1269-0584 (December 16, 1985). Her sister was never formally charged with any kind of wrongdoing.

31. Correspondence from Cheryl Hays (Criminal Investigator, Shelby County DA) and W. L. Callicott (Shelby County Sheriff's Office) to Ken Lanning FBI. February 5, 1985; Part I, 4.

32. *State v. Ballard*, Criminal Court of Tennessee, Thirtieth Judicial District (Case No. 84-04893). Tr. F11: 1357–1374, 1413, 1421, 1436, and 1485.

33. Ballard testified she said "Satan in the name of Jesus and by His shed blood I rebuke you, you have no place in my life." She denied accounts that she told Satan to get out of her body. *State v. Ballard*, tr. F11:1473.

34. *State v. Ballard*, tr. A6I: 23. (Chris Brown).

35. Correspondence from Cheryl Hays: Part II, 2.

36. Gail Goodman, et. al., "Children's Religious Knowledge: Implications for Understanding Satanic Ritual Abuse," *Child Abuse & Neglect*, (1997); 21(11):1111–30.

37. One of the members of a task force that investigated this case testified she and other task force members were instructed by an assistant district attorney to prepare narratives to tape-recorded interviews with the child victims and then reuse the tapes of the interviews of these children so that the tapes would not be available for discovery by the defense. *State v. Ballard*, 714 S.W.2d 284 (Tenn.Cr.App.1986). The decision to overturn the verdict and remand the case for a possible retrial was upheld by the Tennessee Supreme Court. *State v. Ballard*, 855 S.W.2d 557 (1993). The case was not retried, charges were dropped and Ballard eventually had her conviction expunged.

38. Interview with Wayne Hargrove: June 16, 1984, by Jackie Allen Hammer.

39. *State v. Ballard*, tr. C5: 772–775.

40. *State v. Ballard*, tr. C5: 833, 837; C6: 930.

41. *State v. Ballard*, tr. C5: 802–803 ("rectum showed a large scar between eleven and twelve and some dilation").

42. *State v. Ballard*, tr. C6: 784–787, 874, 948.

43. *State v. Ballard*, tr. A10: 45. (Wayne Hargrove).

44. *State v. Ballard*, 855 S.W.2d 557 (Tennessee Supreme Court, 1993).

45. David Peterson, "Child Abuse Cases Remain Tricky Terrain," *Star-Tribune* (October 16, 1994), 14A; "Ten Reasons Why It Happened" [Sidebar], *Star-Tribune* (October 16, 1994), 14A.

46. Minnesota Attorney General, "Report on Scott County Investigations" (February 12, 1985). Popularly known as the Humphrey Report.

47. Philip Jenkins and Daniel Maier-Katkin, "From Salem to Jordan," *Augustus*, (1986), 9(6): 22.

48. Commission Established by Executive Order No. 85–10 Concerning Kathleen Morris, Scott County Attorney, "Report to Governor Rudy Perpich" (October, 1985). Popularly known as the Olson Commission after the chair, Judge Lynn Olson.

49. *Myers v. Morris*, 810 F.2d 1437 (8th cir. 1987).

50. Humphrey Report, 9.

51. Ross E. Cheit and Andrea Matthews, "Revisiting the Jordan Minnesota Cases," *Roger Williams University Law Review* (forthcoming, 2014).

52. Josephine Marcotty, "Bentzes Join Donahue to Talk About Abuse," *Minneapolis Star & Tribune* (January 16, 1985), 1.

53. Charlier and Downing, "Patterns Emerge," A3.

54. Debra Cassens Moss, "Are the Children Lying?" *ABA Journal*, (May 1, 1987), vol. 73.

55. Marianne Taylor, "State Calls Sex Abuse Charges Unfounded," *Chicago Tribune* (October 4, 1984).

56. Lynn Emmerman and Marianne Taylor, "'Expert' in Day-care Probe Can't Back up His Resume," *Chicago Tribune* (April 19, 1985); Lynn Emmerman and Marianne Taylor, "Day-care Probe Rife with Errors," *Chicago Tribune* (April 21, 1985).

57. There was no transcript made for appeal because the case ended in an acquittal. Under Illinois procedures, the original stenographic record stays with the court reporter, even when

the person retires. We were able to locate only one of the two court reporters from this case and accordingly could have only portions of the proceedings converted to hard copy.

58. Report of Proceedings, *State v. Parks*, Cook County Circuit Court, Second Division, Case No. 84C5544, September 23, 1985. Tr. 20–21.

59. As reported in Robert Enstad, "Doctors Saw 'Possible Abuse' of Pupil," *Chicago Tribune* (September 24, 1985).

60. Medical Report on Sophie Voigt. Jeffrey Grabenstein, M.D. (May 8, 1984).

61. Medical Report on Sophie Voigt, 2.

62. Supplemental Report, Polygraph Tech. Walsh, Chicago Police Department, RD#F 133–047 (April 15, 1984).

63. Quoted in Gary Wisby, "Janitor Not Guilty in Rape of Girl, 7; Parents Bitter," *Chicago Sun-Times* (October 3, 1984), 16.

64. Robert Enstad, "Janitor Cleared of 1 Sex Charge; 'I Have No Choice,' Judge Says." *Chicago Tribune* (October 3, 1985).

65. Lisa Leff, "Howard County Sex Abuse Trial Starts Today," *Washington Post* (March 16, 1987), 1. Charges in the original case were dropped "after the teenager was placed in a psychiatric hospital and ordered to stay away from the school." The county settled financially with families for failing to handle the complaint adequately.

66. Theresa E. Grace (children taken upstairs to Craig's office "three or four times a week") tr. 3–162; Theresa Louise Weyer ("we would send [disciplinary cases] up to Mrs. Craig's office" about five times a week) tr. 3–177–78; Shannon Kelly ("if the kids did something wrong we were to send them up to her office") tr. 3–189.

67. Karen Almonte, tr. 4–114. Cynthia Miller testified that the "usually gentle" Craig was "cold and angry" with children who were disruptive, and that she "did not understand" why Craig insisted on taking children upstairs. Tr. 4–141, 143.

68. Lisa Leff, "Child, Experts Cited in Craig Conviction," *Washington Post* (April 3, 1987), C1.

69. *Maryland v. Craig*, Dr. Shubin, tr. 2–170, 2–173.

70. There was considerable testimony about Craig obsessing over a "dowel stick" that was missing from a toy. The stick would be consistent with the injuries described by Dr. Shubin, who testified there was "remarkable consistency in patterns to these four injuries and each of them the genital tissue had an object rammed into it with enough force to cause an injury that we can see healed scars from." *State v. Craig*, Trial transcript, vol. VI (March 23, 1987), tr. 21.

71. *Maryland v. Craig*, Exhibit 5–15.

72. *Maryland v. Craig*, tr. VI-56 to 58.

73. *Maryland v. Craig*, 497 U.S. 836 (1990).

74. China Myers, "Jamal Craig Innocent in Child Abuse Case," *Baltimore Afro-American* (August 1, 1987): 1,2. The headline of this article conflates having charges dismissed with a finding of innocence.

75. Complaint, Washington Department of Social and Health Services, 1978. The doctor is described on the complaint as "Dr. Burham," without any designation of his first name. In none of the voluminous materials I located about this case was this doctor's name listed in full.

76. Cora Priest deposition, *T.R. v. Cora Priest's Day Care*, 1994.

77. Call for Service Report, Sequim Police Department, 1985.

78. Psychological/Psychiatric Evaluation of Ralph Priest, Washington State Department of Social and Health Services, 1985.

79. *Issues in Child Abuse Accusations*, 4(1), 32–44. 1992. Underwager and Wakefield use a pseudonym for Ralph Priest, but the facts match this case, and Hollida Wakefield confirmed by email correspondence that the case was Cora's Day Care and they were employed by the insurance company.

80. Charlier and Downing, "Legal Soundings Hit Same Depths from Case to Case," *Commercial Appeal* (January 1988), A15.

81. "Abuse Charges Against Day-Care Center Dropped," *Seattle-Post Intelligencer* (April 22, 1987).

82. Deborah Bybee and Carol T. Mowbray, "An Analysis of Allegations of Sexual Abuse in a Multi-Victim Day-Care Center Case," *Child Abuse & Neglect* (1993), 17: 774.

83. Unpublished opinion, *State v. Barkman*, Michigan Court of Appeals (September 13, 1988). The trial judge had applied a standard interpretation of the "rape shield" law to prevent inquiry into a complainant's sexual history. The defense wanted to inquire about an allegation the boy allegedly made about abuse by Rebecca Barkman.

84. "Probation Term Ends Smallworld Molestation Case," *UPI* (June 11, 1990, BC cycle). In announcing this deal, chief county prosecutor Dennis Wiley acknowledged that some parents were "not happy with the outcome." At the same time, he emphasized "the inherent problems in trying to resurrect a case that is now six years old."

85. There were also children who were never involved in the civil or criminal processes who apparently made disclosures concerning sexual abuse. The MDMH Report indicates that 62 children made explicit disclosures, meaning there were 24 such children who were not involved in civil or criminal proceedings. Their absence in any proceedings is impossible to interpret without further information. The MDMH report is based on "case records" documenting 1,393 official contacts with 106 children and their families. Bybee and Mowbray, "Analysis," 772.

86. MDMH report, viii.

87. A nine-page "Summary of DSS Records on Small World Victims," presumably prepared as part of the civil litigation, describes each child in brief. One child (H.C.) said, among other innocuous things, that "during lunch they took chickens to the farm" (2). This child did not say anything that indicated she had been sexually abused. Another child (M.P.) said "Richard hurt chickens and would cut their wings off." This boy also said that Richard went "potty" on his face behind the baseball diamond and there was "white stuff" on his face. There may have been more fantastic claims about chickens, but they did not characterize the case enough for there to be any reflection in a summary of each child.

88. Bybee and Mowbray, "Analysis," 774.

89. Subject Report, State of Michigan Department of State Police, Complaint No. 53-3736-84 (December 6, 1984), 4.

90. Mediation Summary, *Risenhoover v. Small World Pre-School*, Berrien County Circuit Court, Case No. 84-3573-NO-2 (September 2, 1986), 21.

91. Mediation Summary, *Risenhoover v. Small World Pre-School*, 21–23.

92. *Newsweek* (July 8, 1985). See also January 1986 *Redbook*; and David Hechler, *The Battle and the Backlash: The Child Sexual Abuse War* (Macmillan, 1989). None of these secondary sources are the primary source for any claims in this section. I obtained 490 pages of documents from the FBI investigation through the Freedom of Information Act, along with original documents saved by several sources at the time, including documents connected to the civil litigation.

93. Charlier and Downing, "Patterns Emerge," A3.

94. Emergency Care and Treatment (Medical Report) by Dr. David Suttle, July 27, 1984.

95. That is what the administration appears to have done in 1983 when an army employee, convicted in a court martial of killing a child, was given a dishonorable discharge but did not serve any time in jail. See Memorandum from Col. Richard E. Eckert, M.D., Chairman, Child Protection Case Management team to the Superintendent, West Point Military Academic, Subject: Appeal for Command Support on Child Abuse (8/1/83).

96. Memorandum from FBI NY to Director of FBI, November 23, 1984, 2.

97. Quoted in *Redbook*, 142.

98. The perpetrator was apparently Jeanette Martin's fourteen-year-old son. Newspaper stories indicate the boy was adjudicated in confidential proceedings in Family Court. He testified in the criminal trial that he raped the three-year-old at his mother's direction.

99. Dr. Jeffrey Gilbert's testimony about these findings is on transcript pages 11773–11789.

100. "Victims' Testimony Key to Child-Abuse Cases," *New York Times* (February 15, 1987).

101. Andrew Blum, Regional News, *UPI* (March 12, 1987).

102. *People v. Watt*, 84 N.Y.2d 948; 644 N.E.2d 1373 (Court of Appeals of the State of New York, 1994).

103. Members.shaw.ca/imaginarycrimes/jameswatt.htm. Quotation from "Victims' Testimony Key to Child Abuse Cases," *New York Times* (February 15, 1987).

104. *New York Times* (July 21, 1985) and *New York Times* (October 31, 1985). The fact that six children contracted venereal diseases was also mentioned in an Associated Press story that appeared in newspapers across the country in the end of March 1986. See e.g., "Testimony of Children Key in Trial," *Charlotte Observer* (March 31, 1986), 6A.

105. Quote from "Imaginary Crimes" website, which mentions that Watt tested negative for venereal disease but omits the fact that the test was ordered so long after the events that Watt's own lawyer argued, before the court order, that the "test was not relevant." UPI, August 2, 1985 (AM cycle).

106. Judith Levine, "Abuse of Justice," *Women's Review of Books* (June 1996), 8.

107. The twelve cases are (alphabetically) Figured/Hill, Friedman, Halsey, Malcom, Parkers, Perkins, Runyan, Schildmeyer, Smith, Souzas. Toward, and Watt.

108. One simply does not appear on the page claimed (Wilcox); the other (the Kellers) appears in a single phrase (where they are called the Kellners) not containing any facts about the case.

109. Nathan and Snedeker, *Satan's Silence*, 246.

110. The list includes Nancy Smith but not her co-defendant, Joseph Allen, who was implicated in the same case. Similarly, it includes Jenny Wilcox, but not her co-defendant Robert Aldridge. Since these cases are never discussed in the book, it is impossible to ascertain whether those distinctions were intentional or accidental. The convictions for both Smith and Allen have withstood post-conviction judicial challenges; as this book was being completed both were initiating petitions to the state clemency board. The convictions of Aldridge and Wilcox were set aside by a presiding judge in a proceeding where that remedy had not even been requested. The state chose not to appeal this unusual ruling. Although Aldridge and Wilcox claimed vindication from the outcome, this claim is contradicted by the outcome of their civil claim for damages. That case, which involved witnesses who were not present when the criminal charges were dismissed, resulted in a judicial decision specifically citing evidence of guilt. Before concluding that "the evidence fails to support their claims" for wrongful imprisonment, Judge Gregory J. Frost made a point of stating, quite bluntly, "the court is convinced that the plaintiffs engaged in criminal conduct, at least in relation with V. P. and C. B., for which the plaintiffs were initially charged." Accordingly, he concluded that "the evidence fails to support their claims" for wrongful imprisonment and he assessed costs against the petitioners, Aldridge and Wilcox. Judgment Entry, *Aldridge v. Ohio*, Case No. 98-0774, Court of Common Pleas, Montgomery County, Ohio.

111. Two of the four were major day-care cases: Amirault and Edenton. Both require extensive research. I have done much of that research for Amirault and some of the necessary research for Edenton. I plan to write about one or both in the future. The other two cases (Perkins and Souzas) were not day-care cases and they did not involve ritual abuse. I plan to write about one or both of those in the future as well.

112. My view is tentative because I have been unable to arrange for transcription of the four-day hearing that resulted in the decision described in footnote 110. The decision relies on the assessment of two witnesses whose testimony is critical to analyzing the case. The court reporter no longer has the stenographic tapes. The hearing was more than ten years ago, and state law requires stenographers to keep such records for only ten years. Nor have I been able to obtain the trial transcript from the case discussed in footnote 115.

113. The Wright articles were published in the *New Yorker* on May 17 and 24, 1993. Wright expanded those articles into a book called *Remembering Satan* (Knopf, 1994). This view of the case has been called into serious question in Karen A. Olio and William F. Cornell, "The Façade of Scientific Documentation: A Case Study of Richard Ofshe's Analysis of the Paul Ingram Case," *Psychology, Public Policy, and Law* (1998), 4: 1182.

114. Gardner relied entirely on newspaper accounts to support his conclusion that the jury was "gullible." But his summary of those accounts omitted these two sentences from one story: "A Rutherford County doctor who examined the boy said it was the worst case of sexual abuse he had seen in 25 years. Another Rutherford County doctor who examined the girls said they also showed signs of sexual abuse." *Times-News* on February 3, 1994. Testimony cited in the state's appellate brief indicates that one boy's "anus muscles were so stretched that he had severe problems with bowel control."

115. This case is particularly unusual because the court's copy of the transcript either is missing or is the one the defense lawyer has in his possession; moreover, the original court reporter (who is duty-bound to save the underlying materials) says she threw them away. The reluctance of the defense lawyer to provide me with access to the transcript, while working on an appeal, is understandable; his duties are to his client. But this speaks volumes about what assurances Snedeker had that his clients would be protected by Nathan's writing.

116. The local broadcast can be viewed here: http://youtu.be/Y2cSpKPY1XM.

117. Detective Perez was criticized for being a foster parent to the initial children who made charges in the case, which could give rise to a conflict of interest. Perez was also criticized for pressuring and coercing other children. Mike Barber and Andrew Schneider, "Detective a Man Who Charmed, Harmed; Trouble Follows on and off Job," *Seattle Post-Intelligencer* (February 23, 1998), A7; "With Every Step, Rights Were Trampled," *Seattle Post-Intelligencer* (February 25, 1998). In the Everett case, the first in the cluster of Wenatchee cases, the Court of Appeals of Washington eventually ordered the Chelan County Superior Court to conduct a hearing to determine whether the state's investigative techniques improperly influenced the statements and testimony of M.E. and her sister D.E. After six days of testimony, the court "found it likely that M.E.'s and the other children's statements were obtained by the State's use of improper interrogation techniques." The Court of Appeals concurred with this decision, citing evidence that Detective Perez had "refused to believe the children when they denied abuse," and Idella Everett's testimony that she was "bullied by Detective Perez" and that Perez "implied that he would harm" her child. The Court of Appeals concluded that "the evidence of Detective Perez's tactics is sufficient on its face to support a finding of impropriety." *In the Matter of the Application from Relief from Personal Restraint of Harold E.*, Court of Appeals of Washington, Division Three, Panel Seven (September 15, 1998). 1998 Wash. App. LEXIS 1351.

118. [Sidebar] "Kern's Long List," in "Stolen Innocence, Part II," *Bakersfield Californian* (January 28, 1985).

119. Edward Humes, *Mean Justice: A Town's Terror, a Prosecutor's Power, a Betrayal of Innocence* (Simon & Schuster, 1999).

120. Maggie Jones, "Who Was Abused?" *New York Times Magazine* (September 19, 2004).

121. Humes, *Mean Justice*, 265. Nathan and Snedeker's chapter on the Bakersfield cases is called "Beginnings: Mary Ann Barbour."

122. Dr. Squyres testified that when she informed Deborah McCuan that her daughter had been sexually abused, McCuan responded "I don't believe that" and said she felt the injuries could have been caused by falling on a fence. *State v. Kniffen*, tr. 2666.

123. In the Matter of Darla and Bobbie McCuan. Report of Social Service Worker, 10.

124. The April 4, 1979, Medical Report by Dr. Fred Miller, Valley Medical Clinic, People's Exhibit No. 47, is discussed by Dr. Carol Squyres at tr. 2654–2663. The 1979 report indicated: "large ecchymosis with no hematoma. Edema of the labial area. No cuts or abrasions seen." Tr. 2657–2658. In lay terms, Bobbie was black and blue in the labia area of the vagina. The lack of cuts or abrasions is why Dr. Squyres concluded those injuries were "not consistent" with falling on a fence. Tr. 2662. The four hundred pages of testimony by Dr. Squyres is not cited or acknowledged by Humes or Nathan and Snedeker, who wrote about the case in some detail. (Nathan and Snedeker obliquely mention "early findings in the case" without any citation or details. *Satan's Silence*, 188.)

125. Dr. Squyres testified that when she informed Deborah McCuan that "a fall" could not have caused the injuries she observed in 1980, McCuan "was not happy with what I said and had nothing more to say and hung up." Tr. 2666. Nevertheless, in a version of the Kniffen-McCuan case that she prepared for a class at McGill University, Bruck characterized Deborah McCuan as "concerned enough to follow-up by getting counseling for her daughter." She provided no documentation for this characterization. Bruck, "Kern County Assignment," Psychology 204-438A (The Child Witness) McGill University (1997).

126. Crime or Incident Report, Kern County Sheriff's Office, KC 81–41195 (October 20, 1980), 3.

127. Ruling on Evidentiary Hearing in Habeas Corpus Matter, *In re the Matter of Scott and Brenda Kniffen*, Kern County Superior Court, No. HC 5528 A (August 12, 1996).

128. Decision and Findings of Fact, Ruling on Evidentiary Hearing in Habeas Corpus Matter, *In re the Matter of Scott and Brenda Kniffen*, Kern County Superior Court, No. HC-5528-A (August 12, 1996) 4.

129. Humes, *Mean Justice*, 271.

130. *State v. Kniffen*, Dr. Woodling testimony (September 15, 1983), tr. 623–625.

131. Joyce Adams, et. al.: "Guidelines for Medical Care of Children Who May Have Been Sexually Abused." *Journal of Pediatric & Adolescent Gynecology* (2002) 20:163–172 See also text and accompanying footnote 135.

132. There are no references in the medical literature to Dr. Paul's "lateral traction test," described at tr. 10410–10411. Nor do any accepted medical protocols call for inserting fingers to test anal tone, described at tr. 10326. The results of such a "test" would be too subjective. Dr. Paul's testimony contains many other dubious statements. He employed several terms that do not appear anywhere in the medical literature, including "frenulum" and "vaginal bulge."

133. Judge Stuebbe also noted "there is disagreement over whether Woodling observed dilatation of over 12 mm" (9). One would need to obtain the slides to allow an independent medical assessment of this disagreement. Those slides were created by a colposcope—the device that Nathan condemns.

134. Humes claims that Barbour had engaged in "two years of amateur gynecological examinations," noting the defense asserted on appeal that Barbour may have caused the injuries. Humes, *Mean Justice*, 266–267. There is no evidence in the trial transcripts to support these assertions, also made by Nathan and Snedeker, which likely explains why the only citation is to a defense brief. Humes, 555, 48. Briefs are not findings of fact; to the contrary, they tend to involve *assertions* about the facts, sometimes linked by citations to actual evidence in the case. The assertions about Barbour do not include this kind of support.

135. Adams et. al., "Guidelines," 166.

136. Squyres, tr. 2643. She also observed Gardnerella and interpreted it as evidence of sexual activity. Though that is possible, Gardnerella can also be caused by poor hygiene or be an unexplained finding in a non-abused child.

137. The slides were entered as exhibits at trial, but they are not part of the permanent record. I was unable to obtain them and therefore could not arrange for an independent medical assessment of this testimony. Such an assessment could have shed light on the testimony about anal fissures. It is not clear from the testimony whether Dr. Squyres saw fissures, which would be an indication of abuse, or normal folds.

138. Squyres, tr. 2860.

139. Nathan and Snedeker, *Satan's Silence*, 189.

140. Judge Stuebbe said: "It is clear that the families of the petitioners have used their own techniques to 'adjust' the stories told by the Kniffen boys over the years." He went on to find: "The Kniffen boys themselves have changed their stories so many times, both before and after adulthood, both orally and in writing, that present testimony is found to be an indecipherable mix of memory, wish, remorse and guilty." Ruling on Evidentiary Hearing, 3.

141. Ruling on Evidentiary Hearing, 6.

142. *People v. Stoll*, 49 Cal. 3d 1136 (1989, reversing the convictions against defendants Grafton and Palomo, upheld by the Court of Appeal).

143. "The Myth of the Sex Offender Profile," Center for Sex Offender Management, http://www.csom.org/train/etiology/3/3_1.htm#backtrack2.

144. *People v. Stoll*, 49 Cal. 3d 1136 (1989) at 1163. (Lucas, C.J. dissent).

145. *Self v. State*, Petition for Writ of Habeas Corpus, Case No. HC-10529A, Kern County Superior Court, Metropolitan Division. March 10, 2008.

146. Gretchen Wenner and James Burger, "County Settles Overturned Molestation Suit for $5.5 Million," *Bakersfield Californian* (September 15, 2009). "It doesn't come out of anyone's budget," the county's chief deputy counsel is quoted as saying. The settlement was paid entirely by insurance money. The article also indicates that Stoll's lawyers acknowledged that Stoll's son has never recanted his claim.

147. Justice Committee Press Release posted by Carol Hopkins, circulated to "Fellow Witchhunters" on the Witchhunt List on September 12, 1995. Subject: Help on Kern County Cases.

148. De Young cites an internet-based account called "Frame Up Through Fantasy" as her source for concluding that Grant Self's conviction should have been overturned. She labels this source "an exposé," without providing any independent analysis. This is another example of the witch-hunt narrative growing and expanding through easily available, but unreliable, "information" on the web. De Young, *The Day Care Ritual Abuse Moral Panic,* 232, fn. 2.

149. Maggie Jones, "Who Was Abused?" *New York Times Magazine* (September 19, 2004).

150. *State v. Self,* Supplemental Clerk's Transcript on Appeal, DCA No. F037537, California Court of Appeal, Fifth Appellate District. July 18, 2000.

151. *People v. Manners,* 180 Cal. App. 3d 826, 225 Cal. Rptr. 798 (1986).

152. *People v. Manners* (1986).

153. In an account of the case circulated on the WITCHHUNT-List, Nicholas Peters states that Self "continued to rent the pool house" after he moved to live with his girlfriend and her children, in order "to comply in form with the terms of his parole." Peters asserts that Stoll was not aware of his parole status, or presumably of the fact that Self was not actually living in the pool house. Nicholas Peters, "Frame Up Through Fantasy." Revised version posted to Witchunt-L on April 15, 1997.

154. OCRT cite http://www.religioustolerance.org/ra_baker.htm.

155. There were apparently photographs in more than just the 1979 case. An evaluation report prepared in 2000 states: "He denied ever taking picture of children, other than those in 1979. He said since they had pictures showing him engaging in sexual activities, he can't deny he did it, although he said he doesn't recall doing it." WIC 6600 Evaluation Report on Grant Self, June 5, 2000, 53. The report constitutes 32–68 of the Supplemental Clerk's Transcript on Appeal, *People v. Self,* Fifth Appellate District of California (DCA No. F037537).

156. WIC 6600 Evaluation Report on Grant Self, June 5, 2000, 54.

157. Lois Henry, "Kern County Settles Last of Molestations Conviction Suits," *Bakersfield Californian* (March 26, 2013).

158. Judgment, *State v. Self,* Case No. 125187FE (Oregon Circuit Court, Jackson County) (July 17, 2013), 1–3.

159. For details about his case see, Kathy Freeman, "Photos of Sex Acts Freeze the 'Moment' for Child Molester," *Bakersfield Californian* (January 30, 1985). See also testimony of Dr. Robert Halon, who was called by the defense in a 1999 hearing but testified that Bishop told him "there wasn't anything wrong with" adults having sex with children. Reporter's Transcript, *State v. Bishop,* California Fifth Appellate District (March 2, 1999), tr. 104.

160. Humes, *Mean Justice,* 286. See also *People v. Pitts,* 223 Cal. App. 3d. 606 (1990). By 1994, all six of the children connected to this case had reportedly recanted. *Pitts v. County of Kern,* 17 Cal. 4th 340; 949 Cal. Rptr. 2d 823; 1998 Cal. LEXIS 21 (1998), 345–346. The Pitts and the McCuans are the only ones named in a March 2013 story in the *Bakersfield Californian* who did not succeed in collecting *any* money from the county through civil suits. I have not examined the case against George and Anthony Cox but Humes, who criticized many of the child sexual abuse prosecutions in Kern Conty from that time, described the evidence against them as "compelling." Humes, *Mean Justice,* 486. The Coxes succeeded in having their convictions overturned, however, and were part of a multi-million dollars settlement with the county. Lois Henry, " Kern County Settles Last of Molestations Conviction Suits," *Bakersfield Californian* (March 25, 2013).

161. Jay Matthews, "In California, a Question of Abuse," *Washington Post* (May 31, 1989), D1.

162. *Commonwealth v. Baran,* 74 Mass. App. Ct. 256, 265, fn. 11 (2009).

163. One-page document, stamped "Patient Allergic to Penicllin," without date or heading, containing Baran's name, birthdate, and notations for visits as an adolescent.

164. In the competency hearing on January 18, Angela B. gave incorrect answers to many questions about the difference between truth and a lie. Her direct testimony on January 25 was even less responsive. In a five-page exchange in the transcript, she refuses to "promise to tell what really happened" or answer questions, saying only that "she doesn't like it." *Commmonwealth v. Baran,* 85–827, tr. 175–80.

165. Competency Hearing, *Commonwealth v. Baran* (January 18, 1985), tr. 25.

166. Mehegan, "Firm Convictions," *Boston Globe* (October 1, 2000).

167. *Commonwealth v. Baran*, 2006 Mass. Super. LEXIS 393 (June 16, 2006, granting a new trial) affirmed by *Commonwealth v. Baran* 2009 Mass. App. LEXIS 652 (May 15, 2009). Charges were subsequently dismissed. See also, Ross E. Cheit, "The Blight of the Baran Case," *Berkshire-Eagle* (July 16, 2004).

168. JoAnne Marez, "BI Mother Testifies 4-year-old Was Abused," *The Sun* (October 1, 1986), 6.

169. *State v. Runyan*, Kitsap County Superior Court, Washington (No. 85-1-00463-7).

170. Mark Pendergrast, *Victims of Memory: Sex Abuse Accusations and Shattered Lives* (Upper Access Book, 1996), 387.

171. JoAnne Marez, "Day Care Operator Convicted of Rape, Sexual Abuse." *The Sun* (January 18, 1986), 1. See specifically *State v. Runyan*, tr. 1668–9, 1681–2, 1709.

172. "Woman Gets 13-year Term for Sex Abuse," *Spokesman Review* (March 13, 1986), A13.

173. JoAnne Marez, "Day Care Operator's Attorney Suddenly Withdraws," *The Sun* (March 5, 1986), 1.

174. Unpublished Opinion, *State v. Runyan*, Washington Court of Appeals (Division Two) (No. 9719-2-II) (July 8, 1998), 8.

175. Unpublished Opinion, *State v. Runyan*, 5.

176. The decision requiring the Superior Court hearing is *In the Matter of Personal Restrain of Debbie Runyan*, 121 Wash. 2d. 432, 853 P.2d 424 (Washington Supreme Court, 1993).

177. Quotes in both sentences from JoAnne Marez, "Girls Says She Saw Children Tied Up," *The Sun* (January 16, 1986), 2.

178. Findings of Fact and Conclusions of Law, Judge Rosanne Buckner (signed October 13, 1995), *State v. Runyan* (No. 85-1-00463-7), 3. See also Order Denying Defendant's Motion to Vacate the Conviction on Count Three (October 18, 1995).

179. Transcription, "Frame by Frame: 'Capturing the Friedmans' Workshop," October 18, 2003 (New York City), 11, 20. Jarecki has always said he stumbled into the sexual abuse story after approaching David Friedman—Arnold's son and Jesse's brother—to make a film about birthday clowns. If Jarecki's story is true, it would be interesting to know how Nathan became "an intermediary," why it was even necessary, what she did in that role, and why it was never fully disclosed.

180. Jarecki told an audience in New York: "I generally don't mention his name just because, I don't know. I just don't. He's not in the film because he didn't want to be in the film." Transcription, "Frame by Frame," 32. Note: when the movie was later released on DVD there was an "extra feature" that included Goldstein.

181. Friedman post-conviction motion, 25.

182. Sharon Waxman, "Victims Say Film on Molesters Distorts Facts," *New York Times* (February 24, 2004; "Asked repeatedly by The Times whether he knew of a lie-detector test that Jesse Friedman took and failed while he protested his innocence in the 1980's, Mr. Jarecki said he did not. But in an interview on a Web site, Mr. Jarecki spoke in detail about the lie-detector test, saying he considered it inconclusive.").

183. "What Was Left Out? A Critique of 'Capturing the Friedmans'" http://youtu.be/qj YWOZgMbHQ.

184. Nathan, "Ritual Child Cases Need Investigation." Witchhunt post (May 28, 1994).

185. Jesse Friedman later claimed he gave this interview because he thought it would help improve his treatment in prison. I have never heard of anyone, before or after this assertion, claim that admitting one is a child molester would somehow be useful in prison.

186. The Conviction Integrity Review covered this issue in detail, including a full-page reproduction of a hand-written statement by Jesse Friedman on February 6, 1989 admitting that "against the advice of my attorney, Peter Panaro, Esq." that "I will voluntarily appear on the Gerlado Rivera show." "Conviction Integrity Review," 44–46.

187. As described in Paul Vitello, "Interesting, But Not Quite Accurate," *Newsday* (July 23, 2003), A8.

188. Jesse Friedman protested on his own website, created after the film, that the computers in the classroom "were not loaded with pornographic video games. They were on five inch floppy disks in a file box." http://www.freejesse.net/component/content/article/2-regular-page/23-faqs (In answer to "What about the pornographic computer games?").

189. Corey Kilgannon, "Hypnosis Rigged Sex Case Against Him, Man Says," *New York Times*, October 20, 2007.

190. Affidavit of Joyce W. Parks, Ph.D., *People v. Friedman*, April 14, 2004.

191. Transcript of Motion, *Friedman v. Rehal* (October 3, 2007), tr. 12.

192. Waxman, "Victims Say Film on Molesters Distorts Facts."

193. Affidavit of Andrew Jarecki, *People v. Friedman*, paragraph 4.

194. *Friedman v. Rehal*, 618 F.3d 142 (2d Cir. 2010) (stating there was a "reasonable likelihood" that Friedman was wrongfully convicted).

195. Nassau County District Attorney, "Conviction Integrity Review: *People v. Jesse Friedman*," June 2013. The full report and a 917-page appendix are available at www.nassauda.org.

196. Conviction Integrity Review, 37–39 (discussing the evaluation by Dr. David Pogge, a psychiatrist and a specialist in the psychopathology of teenage sex offender diagnosis); 116–118 (discussing the statements of Howard Friedman). It should be noted that whether or not one finds Howard Friedman's hearsay statement persuasive, it would not be admissible in a criminal case.

197. Conviction Integrity Review, 83–86. The Review Team indicated that the filmmakers "were not forthcoming with evidence under their control" and that although Jarecki promised to provide access to information he claimed "would greatly impact the re-investigation," that he never shared key interviews, including those with Jesse Friedman and Ross Goldstein. (153).

198. One of the reasons the review team found the recantation unreliable is that it was contradicted by notes from a conversation between Goldstein and Marc Smerling, a producer of *Capturing the Friedmans*, who was trying to convince Goldstein to appear in the movie. Smerling told Goldstein "we have found quite a bit of exonerating stuff" and Goldstein characterized such evidence as "completely untrue" and said that he could not help Jesse. Goldstein was "unable to explain" these statements when he later recanted. Conviction Integrity Review, 137. (Notably, the filmmakers did not provide the notes of that conversation to the review team.) The report also details how Goldstein's recent recantation is contradicted by statements from Witness 29, a close friend of his from sixth grade through high school. See 140–143.

199. "Statement of the Friedman Advisory Panel," iii. This statement is included as a preface to the report.

200. "Subject of Oscar-nominated 'Capturing the Friedmans' vows fight for exoneration will go on," Associated Press (June 25, 2013).

201. Presentence and Intake Report, Washington Department of Correction. January 5, 1988, 2. Exhibits 23 and 25 in Clark County Prosecuting Attorney's Office Opposition to the Petition for Clemency by Marilynn Rose Malcom (August 15, 1997).

202. Interview and Contact Summary, Office of the Clark County Sheriff, MC #593, 3. Exhibit D in Petition for Clemency by Marilynn Malcom (August 15, 1997).

203. Interview and Contact Summary, Office of the Clark County Sheriff, MC #593, 3. Exhibit D in Petition for Clemency by Marilynn Malcom (August 15, 1997).

204. Testimony of Dr. Brigitte Mengelberg, Exhibit H in Petition for Clemency by Marilynn Malcom (August 15, 1997).

205. Utility Report, Clark County Sheriff's Office, MC #593 (April 20, 1987), 2. Contained within Exhibit D in Petition for Clemency by Marilynn Malcom (August 15, 1997).

206. Brief of Appellant, *Malcom v. State*, No. 11735-5-II (Washington Court of Appeals; September 19, 1988), 3.

207. Psychological/Psychosexual Evaluation of Marilynn Malcom (December 7, 1987), 8. Exhibit 25 in Clark County Prosecuting Attorney's Office Opposition to the Petition for Clemency by Marilynn Rose Malcom (August 15, 1997). There was additional evidence of Malcom's dishonesty in court records. Her bail was revoked after she violated the stipulation that she live at the residence of Cheryl Ducett, a professional counselor. Ducett called the court after Malcom went missing for a week. She then told prosecutors: "Now I believe she (Lynn, the defendant) has a sociopathic personality disorder." She stated further that "based upon the things she has learned about Lynn Malcom since she took responsibility for her, that she no longer wants to take responsibility for her care." Motion and Affidavit for Bench Warrant, *State v. Malcom* (August 18, 1987), 2.

208. Marilynn Malcom, "Clemency Denied," *The Columbian* (September 26, 1997), B8. ("The report by Dr. Steve Jensen was not accepted by Judge Dean Morgan.")

209. Paragraph 4, page 2, specifically states, "This finding is based upon the combined factors of two psychological reports corroborated by the facts presented at trial." Findings of Fact and Conclusions of Law, *State v. Malcom* (No. 87-1-00339-6).

210. Unpublished opinion, *State v. Malcom*, Washington Court of Appeals (February 13, 1991).

211. Clark County Prosecuting Attorney's Office Opposition to the Petition for Clemency by Marilyn Rose Malcom, August 15, 1997, 19.

212. Affidavit of Scott Campbell Re: Attempt to Interview Jane Malcom. *State v. Malcom.* August 8, 1997. 2. Exhibit 28 in Clark County Prosecuting Attorney's Office Opposition to the Petition for Clemency by Marilynn Rose Malcom (August 15, 1997).

213. Minutes of Meeting of September 5, 1997. Clemency and Pardon Board, Office of the Governor, State of Washington, 11.

214. Affidavit of Kevin Malcom, Exhibit 9 in Clark County Prosecuting Attorney's Office Opposition to the Petition for Clemency by Marilynn Rose Malcom (August 15, 1997), 2 (lines 16–20).

215. Affidavit of Rebecca Neville, Exhibit 8 in Clark County Prosecuting Attorney's Office Opposition to the Petition for Clemency by Marilynn Rose Malcom (August 15, 1997), 1, 3.

216. Minutes of Meeting of September 5, 1997. Clemency and Pardon Board, Office of the Governor, State of Washington, 16.

217. Jill Taylor, "Shocking Actions Raised Suspicions About Glendale, Parents Testify," *Palm Beach Post* (June 13, 1989), 1B. See also Complaint Affidavit, Stuart Police Department (February 29, 1988), attachment, 1.

218. Complaint Affidavit, Stuart Police Department (February 29, 1988), attachment, 2.

219. Complaint Affidavit, Stuart Police Department (February 29, 1988), 3.

220. Jill Taylor, "Downfall of an 'English Gentleman,'" *Palm Beach Post* (January 15, 1989), 1A.

221. Jill Taylor, "Prospective Toward Juror to Be Witness, Clerk Says Child-Sex Suspect Bought Polaroid Camera," *Palm Beach Post* (June 1, 1989), 1B.

222. Taylor, "Prospective Toward Juror," 1B.

223. Jill Taylor, "Police Search for Videos in Child-Sex Case," *Palm Beach Post* (January 5, 1989), 1B.

224. Taylor, "Police Search for Videos," 1B.

225. Jill Taylor, "Glendale Case Settled Before Trial," *Palm Beach Post* (June 5, 1996), 1B.

226. In "Another Look at Moral Panics," De Young states that she included only cases where "there are sufficient archival data in the form of court transcripts, legal briefs, investigative reports, interview transcript, and local and national news articles to assess the case" (259). The bibliography for this article does not cite any court transcripts, legal briefs, investigative reports, or interview transcripts from the Toward case. Since the newspaper coverage alone is insufficient for concluding that this was a false conviction, it is unclear on what basis De Young assessed the case and reached this conclusion.

227. "Glendale Montessori School Case Resurfaces," False Memory Syndrome Foundation Newsletter (Spring 2008) 17(2), 3–8. These snippets constitute the vast majority of an article that has fourteen footnotes, but there is not a single footnote for the interview. This interview is not part of the public record. Without additional information it is impossible to check its accuracy or context.

228. Transcript of Proceedings for Change of Plea and Sentencing, *State v. Toward*, Martin County Circuit Court, Florida (Case Nos. 88-927-CF, 88-926-CF, 88-285-CF, June 14, 1989).

229. Meredith Maran, *My Lie: A True Story of False Memory* (Jossey-Bass, 2010), 214–216. There is no indication in the book that Maran posed any questions about the safety deposit box, the cowboy hats, the character evidence, or the reports to the child abuse registry before the case broke. Demonstrating her nonjournalistic approach, Maran later told an interviewer how much she admired Toward's "courage" and hoped her "meetings with Mrs. Toward over the past year" had lent her "a bit of strength." Interview by Margaret Renki (www.chapter16.org).

230. Exhibits D and E, *In re: The Commitment of James Toward*, Martin County Circuit Court (Petition No. 99-0517-CAR) July 19, 1999.

231. http://ra-info.org/faqs/ra-convictions/.

232. Hubert, C. (1989). "Day-care Abuse Stuns Iowa Town."*Daily Herald*, December 4.

233. *State v. Schildmeyer*, tr. 327–337.

234. Unpublished opinion, *State v. Schildmeyer* (Court of Appeals of Iowa). December 27, 1990, 2.

235. Unpublished opinion, *State v. Schildmeyer*, 5–7.

236. Correspondence from Virginia Barchman, Assistant Attorney General, Iowa Dept. of Justice, to James Nussle, Delaware County Attorney, August 13, 1990, 1.

237. Unpublished opinion, *State v. Schildmeyer*, 8.

238. Allison Hall, "DCI Joins Child-abuse Investigation," *Des Moines Register* (October 12, 1989), 1M.

239. Correspondence from Virginia Barchman, 2.

240. Correspondence from Virginia Barchman, 4.

241. Front page, Witch-Hunt Information Center. Hosted while Jonathan Harris was affiliated with MIT at web.mit.edu/afs/athena.mit.edu/user/h/a/harris/…/witchhunt.html.

242. *State v. Figured*, 116 N.C. App. 1; 446 S.E.2d 838 (Court of Appeals of North Carolina, 1994). This opinion was upheld by the North Carolina Supreme Court. 339 N.C. 617, 454 S.E.2d 261 (1995). The court recently upheld, without a published opinion, the dismissal of Figured's effort to appeal his conviction post-conviction. 718 S.E.2d 404 (November 9, 2011).

243. *State v. Figured*, Trial tr. 511–520.

244. *State v. Figured*, Trial tr. 524.

245. *State v. Figured*, Trial tr. 585–608.

246. Gary Cartwright, "The Innocent and the Damned,"*Texas Monthly* (April 1994), 22(2): 100.

247. *Keller v. State*, No. 3-92-603-CR and No. 3-92-604-CR, Court of Appeals, Third District of Texas (October 26, 1994), slip opinion, 2.

248. *State v. Keller*, November 17, 1992, Trial tr. 167.

249. *State v. Keller*, November 17, 1992, Trial tr. 184, lines 16–17.

250. The substance of this paragraph comes from that story. See Denise Gamino and Pamela Ward, "Speaking the Unspeakable: Nightmares of Fran's Day Care Stalk Families," *Austin American-Statesman*, December 13, 1992, 1.

251. The case was included on a "Conviction List" of "Ritual Abuse cases" compiled by Believe the Children. The single citation provided to support the claim is the lengthy newspaper article after the criminal case was over. The list is still on the Web at http://ra-info.org/faqs/ra-convictions/.

252. Denise Gamino, "5-year-old Testifies in Day-care Abuse Case," *Austin American-Statesman* (November 19, 1992), 1.

253. Pamela Ward, "Charges Dropped in Child Abuse Case," Austin American Statesmen, B1 (quoting Assistant D.A. Byran Case that "it was not a prosecutable case").

254. *Keller v. State*, Court of Appeals, Third District of Texas, 2.

255. *Nash v. Keller*, Fourth Amended Original Complaint (September 29, 1995), 53rd Judicial District, Travis County Texas, No. 93-10045, 2.

256. "Difficult Child Abuse Line," editorial, *Austin American-Statesman* (January 12, 1988), A6.

257. Cartwright, "The Innocent and the Damned," *Texas Monthly* (April 1994).

258. Cartwright, "The Innocent and the Damned."

259. Jordan Smith, "Believing the Children,"*Austin Chronicle* (March 27, 2009).

260. Jonathan Harris, "Ritual Abuse Is Alive and Well in Western Massachusetts," posting to Witch-hunt list on June 10, 1994.

261. More information about this and many other details of the case are elaborated in Cheit, "Legend of Robert Halsey."

262. *Commonwealth v. Halsey*, Trial tr. 4:626.

263. The National Center for Reason and Justice, http://ncrj.org/robert-halsey/.

264. *State v. Smith*, 1996 Ohio App. LEXIS 241 (Court of Appeals of Ohio, January 24, 1996); *State v. Allen*, 1996 Ohio App. LEXIS 385 (Court of Appeals of Ohio, February 7, 1996). The testimony about the 1985 child rape was allowed because there were striking similarities to the allegations in the Head Start case. Allen had "parties" for the girl, and he tied her up before sexually assaulting her.

265. They were entered as State Exhibits 3 and 9, respectively, at trial.

266. The proceeding was based on the defense claim that the judgment of conviction had never been made final because it did not contain an explicit statement of the "manner of conviction"—that the defendants had been found guilty by jury. Judge Carr, in a dissent that agreed with the outcome of the appellate court, reasoned that this claim "elevates form over substance to a new level" and that since it was apparent to the defendants "and to anybody who glanced at the record" that the conviction was by jury, the resentencing hearing itself was improper. The majority of the court simply found that the resentencing judge had no authority to vacate the sentences. *State v. Allen*, 2010 Ohio 2990 (Court of Appeals of Ohio, Ninth Judicial District, June 30, 2010).

267. *State v. Allen*, 128 Ohio St. 3d 442; 2011 Ohio 1838 (2011).

268. Smith served approximately fifteen years in prison. Visiting Judge Virgil Sinclair resentenced her to twelve years, meaning that Smith would not return to prison. Smith agreed, as part of this deal, not to sue for wrongful imprisonment. Brad Dicken, "Deal Means Nancy Smith Will Remain Free," *Chronicle-Telegram* (June 4, 2013).

269. Kaylee Remington, "Parole Board Votes Against Pardon for Nancy Smith," *Morning Journal* (August 9, 2013). That recommendation was passed on to Governor John Kasich who had not made a final decision when this book was being copy edited.

270. Brad Dicken, "Joseph Allen Cuts Deal for Reduced Prison Sentence," *Chronicle-Telegram* (October 2, 2013); Kaylee Remington, "Head Start case: Joseph Allen Sent Back to Prison," *Morning Journal* (October 1, 2013). The recommendation against Allen's clemency petition was passed on to Governor John Kasich who had not made a final decision when this book was being copy edited.

Chapter Four

1. See, e.g., Pamela Freyd, "Problem Is with Priorities, Not Denial," Letter to the editor, *Toronto Star* (September 28, 1996), C3.

2. De Young, "Another Look at Moral Panics," 260.

3. Debbie Nathan, "Sex, the Devil, and Day Care," *Village Voice* (September 29, 1987), 23.

4. Richard Beck, "Willis and Happiness," *n + 1* (November 18, 2011).

5. Debbie Nathan, "What McMartin Started," *Village Voice* (June 12, 1990).

6. The Kniffen and McCuan cases in Kern County definitely predated McMartin. The charges were brought in 1982. But Charlier and Downing tagged the Kern County cases with a June 1984 date, corresponding to the charges in a much later case, and placed McMartin first.

7. Mitchell Landsberg, "Daycare Teacher Charged with Sex Abuse," *Philadelphia Inquirer* (May 11, 1983), A2.

8. "Convicted Child Abuser Waives Hearing on Similar Felony Charges," UPI (September 25, 1981, BC cycle).

9. "Ex-School Operator Gets Term in Facility for Sex Offenders," *Philadelphia Inquirer* (April 27, 1984).

10. "Charges Filed in Niles Twp. Day-Care Case," *Detroit Free Press* (October 2m 1984), 8C. Guilty plea indicated in Berrien County Justice System Public Access Defendant History Report, Person ID: 40001533. Accessed June 15, 2000.

11. Findings of Fact, Conclusions of Law and Judgment, *Iowa v. Warnock*, Iowa District Court for Polk County Criminal (November 5, 1982). Warnock was charged again in 1991 with sexually abusing young children in her care. State investigators found "as many as 10 cases of possible abuse" but most of the children were too young to testify. There were evidence problems in the case, including a defective search warrant, and charges were dropped in exchange for her "agreement to follow a judge's order and stop caring for children without their parents present." Lane Beauchamp, "Child Abuse Charges Dismissed Against Day-care Operator," *Kansas City Star* (February 4, 1992), A10. Associated Press, "Parents Ask for Help of Officials to Reopen Miller County case," *Kansas City Star* (February 5, 1992), C6.

12. Gregory Byrnes, "N.J. Man Charged in Child Abuse," *Philadelphia Inquirer* (October 17, 1981), B3. See also "Sex Crime Children Abuse Sentence," *Philadelphia Inquirer* (April 27, 1984), B2.

13. UPI, Domestic News; San Diego, California (November 4, 1982, BC cycle). Hetherington's parole eleven years later received more widespread publicity. See e.g., Judi Villa, "Arizona Rejects Child Molester; California Con's Request Refused," *Arizona Republic* (February 10, 1994), B1.

14. Regional News: New Mexico, UPI (June 23, 1982, BC cycle); Regional News: New Mexico, UPI (February 18, 1983, AM cycle).

15. Lorraine Bennett, "Child Abuse Probe Reveals Litany of Injury, Deprivation,"*Los Angeles Times* (December 8, 1981), 3, 18–19.

16. Nathan and Snedeker, 279, fn. 70. (Criticizing Waterman et. al. because their study "lumps children and parents in its Manhattan Beach sample to those from a verified sexual-abuse case from another state.")

17. "Sex and Satan." [Interview with Debbie Nathan.] *The Guide* (May 1996).

18. Finkelhor and Williams, *Nursery Crimes: Sexual Abuse in Day Care* (Sage, 1988).

19. Finkelhor and Williams, *Nursery Crimes*, 17–20.

20. Finkelhor and Williams, *Nursery Crimes*, 61–63.

21. In *Jeopardy in the Courtroom*, Ceci and Bruck are dismissive of the study of 270 cases because, in their words, it includes "many" cases where there was no "hard evidence" (27). The authors then point to the McMartin and Michaels cases as their proof.

22. All quotes from *Seering v. Department of Social Services*, 194 Cal. App. 3d 298; 239 Cal. Rptr. 422 (Court of Appeal of California, First Appellate District, 1987).

23. *State v. Walter*, Change of Plea (San Diego Municipal Court, Department No. 18, Case No. F91843).

24. Frederick Crews letter, *New York Review of Books* (January 12, 1995).

25. *Fischer v. Walter*, Verified Petition of Guardian Ad Litem for Compromise of Disputed Claim of Minor (Case No. 585495), 4–5.

26. "Day Care Operators Face Abuse Charges," *Miami Herald* (April 6, 1985), 2D. See also *State v. Mitchell*, Judgment of Guilt Placing Defendant in Community Control, filed March 26, 1986. (Case No. CRC85-03645CFANO-D).

27. Proposed Decision, *In the Matter of Bo Peep Day Care Nursery*, Maryland Department of Health and Mental Hygiene (Docket No. 88-M-028) (August 23, 1988), 3.

28. Proposed Decision, *In the Matter of Bo Peep Day Care Nursery*, 7.

29. Proposed Decision, *In the Matter of Bo Peep Day Care Nursery*, 38.

30. *Maryland Department of Human Resources v. Bo Peep Day Nursery*, 565 A.2d 1015, 1021 (1989).

31. UPI, Regional News (June 9, 1988).

32. The decision was not about the underlying merits; indeed, the court of appeals assessed costs against the state for devoting so much time to the substantiality of the evidence "despite the fact that neither the circuit court nor Bo Peep has questioned the revocation order on that ground" (1032).

33. Lisa Perlman, "Boy Tells Court How He Molested Preschoolers, Then Threatened Them," *Associated Press* (March 29, 1990, a.m. cycle).

34. National Center for the Analysis of Violent Crime, *Investigator's Guide to Allegations of "Ritual" Child Abuse* (FBI Academy, Quantico, Va., January 1992).

35. Daniel Goleman, "Proof Lacking for Ritual Abuse by Satanists," *New York Times* (October 31, 1994). The headline is explained by the fact that the report found no evidence of such abuse being perpetrated by organized groups.

36. Goleman, "Proof Lacking."

37. Goleman, "Proof Lacking."

38. Utah Attorney General's Office, *Ritual Crime in the State of Utah: Investigation, Analysis & A Look Forward*, (Prepared for the Utah State Legislature, 1995), 3.

39. Utah Attorney General's Office, *Ritual Crime*."

40. FBI, *Investigator's Guide*, 18.

41. A. S. Ross, "Satanism or Mass Hysteria?" *San Francisco Examiner* (September 28, 1986).

42. Post to Witchhunt list, HFJustice (July 30, 1999). Fishman, whose email address matches the witchhunt post, is listed as a "national forensic consultant in the areas of child custody, abuse and neglect" in Missouri on a website called Child Abuse Defense Kit. http://cadkit. tripod.com

43. The "Similar Tales" sidebar in their series includes tattooed man or woman; activities in basement; assaults during naptime or trips to bathroom; children choked, pinched, or physically abused; foreign objects inserted in rectum or vagina; Barbie dolls; nude games.

44. "Man Convicted of Torturing 14-year-old Boy," *Associated Press* (August 19, 1998, AM cycle). An appellate court upheld the conviction, finding specifically that there was sufficient evidence to constitute "cruel abuse or torture" as required by statute. *Ohio v. Dillard*, 1999 Ohio App. LEXIS 2546 (July 23, 1999).

45. "Parents Charged with Torturing Their Children," *Associated Press* (November 25, 1991).

46. *Commonwealth v. Gaddis*, 432 Pa. Super. 523; 639 A.2d 462 (Superior Court of Pennsylvania, March 22, 1994).

47. Sue Carlton, "Sextons Face Another Charge," *St. Petersburg Times* (June 23, 1994).

48. Unpublished opinion, *People v. Wilkins* (Division One, Fourth Appellate District Court of Appeal) No. D007162 (Super Ct. No. CR85004) Lori Elizabeth Bartz was co-defendant.

49. Bill Callahan, "El Cajon Woman Sentenced to 48 Years; Used Satanism in Sex Abuse of Children," *San Diego Union-Tribune* (March 26, 1988), B1.

50. Unpublished opinion, *People v. Wilkins*, 14.

51. Trial Brief, *State v. Ball*, Case No. 14750-C (Sonoma County Superior Court), 1.

52. Trial Brief, *State v. Ball*, 5 (describes a five-year-old boy who "was unable to testify beyond direct so the People requested that he be dismissed and his testimony was then stricken from the record.")

53. Nurse Practitioner Gail Jackson testified to evidence of chronic anal penetration, penetration of hymen consistent with sexual abuse, anal scarring, and other marks consistent with repeated penetration by a foreign object. Preliminary hearing transcript summarized in Trial Brief, 5.

54. Change of Plea, *State v. Ball and Thrailkill* (Reporter's Transcript of Proceedings of Monday June 6, 1988), Court No. 14750-C (Sonoma County Superior Court).

55. Clark Mason, "Thrailkill a Sexual Predator," *Press Democrat* (September 9, 1998).

56. One verified case of cult activity involving the sexual abuse of children emerged in October 1983, when police raided the headquarters of the Neo-American Church in Harrisburg, Pennsylvania. Material seized in the raid demonstrated that the cult, run by George Feigley, believed that "you were closest to God at the point of sexual climax." A four-year-old boy and three girls (ages four, five, and sixteen) were placed in foster care after "hundreds of pictures were found showing the sexual abuse of children." William Heineke, "Authorities Say Cult May Have Used Children in Sex Rituals," *Associated Press* (November 23, 1983). Feigley was convicted of raping three girls and served twenty-five years in prison. He was released without restrictions in 2008 because his crimes predated sex-offender registration requirements. Robin Acton, "'70s Child Rapist Freed Without Restrictions," *Pittsburgh Tribune Review* (August 16, 2008). Another verified case of sexual abuse in an organized context involved the "Zion Society" in Utah, a self-proclaimed "secret society" governed by Arvin Shreeve, who convinced his followers that children in the group should be involved in the sexual practices that he preached. Twelve adults in this polygamous cult were charged with felonies involving child sexual abuse. Shreeve pleaded guilty to sodomy and child sex abuse charges in 1991. "Alleged Cult Leader Pleads Guilty to 4 Sex-Abuse Counts," *Salt Lake Tribune* (November 7, 1991), B3. At least ten other cult members later pleaded guilty. More recently, an investigation of a break-in at an animal shelter in Murray, Kentucky—where two puppies were mutilated and their body parts taken—led police to a group known as the "Vampire Clan," which committed a series of crimes with satanic overtones. Sondra Gibson, thirty-five, pleaded guilty to enticing a fourteen-year-old boy into having sex during a blood-sucking initiation rite known as "crossing over." Rod Ferrell pleaded guilty to two counts of murder. Mike Schneider, "Vampire Cult Leader Pleads Guilty," Associated Press (February 5, 1998). See also for example, Judgment on Jury Verdict of Guilty, *State v. Rogers*, Cause No. 18,738 (91st District, Eastland County, Texas), December 14, 1992 (Indecency with a Child

Younger than 17 Years, Committed During the Court of a Ritual); Lisa Roose Church, "Man Gets 24 Years for Satanic-ritual Rape of 10-year-old Girl," *Tennessean* (September 30, 2000).

57. See Lawrence A. Stanley, "The Child Pornography Myth," *Playboy* (September 1988). Cited with approval in Jenkins, *Moral Panic*, 272; Levine, *Harmful to Minors*, 37–38; Kincaid, *Erotic Innocence*, 326; Best, *Threatened Children*, 224.

58. Debbie Nathan, "Justice in Wenatchee," *New York Times* (December 19, 1995), A25.

59. This case is discussed in Chapter Three, 126.

60. This case is discussed in Chapter Three, 123–26.

61. *People v. Meacham* (California Court of Appeals; Second Appellate Division, Division Three) 152 Cal. App. 3d. 142, 199 Cal. Rptr. 586 (1984).

62. "Teacher Sentenced for Abuse," *Washington Post* (February 16, 1984), C2; Rosa Michnya, "Ex-Daycare Teacher Held on New Charges," *Washington Post* (May 10, 1983), C5.

63. Curtis Morgan, "Afraid for the Children Parents May Have Trouble Responding to Abuse," *Miami Herald* (March 11, 199), 11.

64. Steve Rothaus, "Legal Mix-Up Aided Child-Porn Suspect; Preschool Owner Paid $200 and Left Hawaii," *Miami Herald* (February 5, 1990), 1B. See also Order of Probation, *State v. Shaver*, Circuit Court, 17th Judicial Circuit, Broward County, Florida (Case No. 90-2105) August 21, 1991.

65. Order of Probation, *State v. Shaver*, Circuit Court of the 17th Circuit in and for Broward County, Florida. Case No. 90-2105. Filed August 21, 1991. (Guilty plea to one count of sexual performance by a child.)

66. Renee Graham, "Parents Used Day Care Knowing It Was Illegal,"*Boston Globe* (December 23, 199).

67. Patricia Nealon, "Arlington Man Is Sentenced for Sexual Assault of Two Girls," *Boston Globe* (September 16, 1992), 20.

68. "Coast Inquiry Is Pressed into Child Sexual Abuse," *New York Times* (April 1, 1984).

69. Carol McGraw, "Child Smut Business Going Underground; Grows Uglier as Customers Trade Children, Not Just Pictures, Police Say," *Los Angeles Times* (September 16, 1985), Part I, 3.

70. Stanley's article won an award from the Free Press Association in 1989. Debbie Nathan presented him with the award. See David Hechler, "Awkward Award," *Columbia Journalism Review* (September/October 1990).

71. Stanley is described as "publisher of *Uncommon Desires*" in a story describing a warrant for his arrest in Canada for allegedly sexually abusing a girl under the age of fourteen. Gene Mustain, "Man-Boy Love Lawyer Wanted in Girl Abuse," *Daily News* (September 21, 1995), 34. For additional information see the WCBS news report, digitized at http://youtu.be/kcVTCfkCAXk. Stanley was later convicted in absentia in a Dutch court for sexual abuse of three girls, ages seven to ten. In 2002, he was arrested on child pornography charges in Brazil. Robert Stacy McCain, "Porn Lawyer Charged in Brazil Girls Case," *Washington Times* (July 24, 2002). The popular Brazilian magazine *Epoca* reported, after a four-month investigation, how Stanley "produces, publishes and markets" photos of nude girls age six to thirteen, "controlling an international network of child pornography." http://blog.newtonpaiva.br/pos/wp-content/uploads/2013/02/E3-SI-20.pdf.

72. For a recent example of this tactic, see http://blogs.brown.edu/recoveredmemory/2013/02/09/ncrj-reveals-itself/.

73. See e.g., Transcript, (n.d.) [Likely summer 1995] Francis interview with Stephen Ceci about the Christchurch case in New Zealand (for "Assignment" David McLoughlin, a television program), 11 ("this case has the same constellation of ingredients that ninety-plus percent of mass allegation crèches cases have ... there is this air of accusation").

74. "Children Were Swapped for Sexual Abuse, State Alleges," *Los Angeles Times* (August 4, 1984).

75. Richard Wexler, *Wounded Innocents*, 147.

76. Child number four's mother indicated the daughter of a neighbor had recently "become hysterical about going to the Peninsula Montessori School." This child was not on the list supplied by Krikorian. See Decision, *In the Matter of the Application Against Claudia Krikorian*, Department of Social Services, State of California, September 30, 1985, para. 23 (informing

the man that he was a suspect "was an irresponsible act on the part of the respondent" and "may have resulted in the destruction of incriminating evidence"), para. 25 (refusing to provide names and class schedule was "irresponsible" and constituted a failure to cooperate with the sheriff).

77. Declaration of Susan McGirt, *State v. Krikorian* (November 14, 1984), 3.
78. Decision, *In the Matter of the Application Against Claudia Krikorian*, 4.
79. Decision, *In the Matter of the Application Against Claudia Krikorian*, 7.
80. Declaration of Susan McGirt, *State v. Krikorian* (November 14, 1984), 9.
81. Medical Report—Suspected Child Abuse, Re: Montessori, Harbor UCLA Medical Center (June 22, 1984), 1, 2.
82. Decision, *In the Matter of the Application Against Claudia Krikorian*, 4.
83. "Molestation Suits Settled," *Los Angeles Times* (October 20, 1987).
84. Tim Waters, "Judge Drops Molestations Charges," *Los Angeles Times* (December 7, 1985), A1, 8.
85. One child in the preliminary hearing in the McMartin case testified about witnessing satanic rituals at the church including black robes and drinking blood.
86. Faye Fiore, "Men Confess Molestations—Too Late to Prosecute," *Daily Breeze* (October 18, 1985).
87. Lois Timnick, "Police Appeal for Help in Pre-School Case," *Los Angeles Times* (November 1, 1984), D3.
88. Decision, *In the Matter of the Accusation Against Claudia Krikorian*, No. LD-1539-0215. Department of Social Services, State of California (December 12, 1985).
89. Announcement of Intended Decision, *Krikorian v. Department of Social Services*, No. SW-C-82343, Los Angeles Superior Court (June 30, 1986).
90. Bob Williams, "Abuse Cases Ebb," *Los Angeles Times* (May 12, 1988), V20.
91. Bob Williams, "McMartin Fallout Eases,"*Los Angeles Times* (May 1, 1988), R4.
92. Greenup's first trial ended in a mistrial with nine jurors voting for conviction and three for acquittal. Jurors were at odds over Greenup's "intent in placing [girls] on his lap and caressing them." "Mistrial Declared in Molestation Case," *Los Angeles Times* (May 15, 1986). Jurors in the second trial heard expert testimony about how Greenup had altered a key piece of evidence in the case, a large green chair. Paul Feldman, "Jury Convicts Ex-Teacher in Molestations," *Los Angeles Times* (April 3, 1987). The "political witch-hunt" claim stemmed from the media appearances that District Attorney Robert Philibosian made when the case was originally filed. At sentencing, Greenup's lawyer argued for lenience in part because his client had "shown remorse." Terry Pristin, "Teacher Gets 36 Years for Molesting Girls," *Los Angeles Times* (May 5, 1987).
93. Rabinowitz, "From the Mouths of Babes to a Jail Cell: Child Abuse and the Abuse of Justice," *Harper's* (May 1990), 56.
94. Rabinowitz, "From the Mouths of Babes," 56.
95. "Name Confusion Causes Woes for Clifton Daycare Center," *The Record* (August 25, 1985), C3.
96. The Country Walk case is the subject of Chapter Six. The Snowden case involved two separate criminal trials and cannot easily be summarized. From research to date, I think there are many reasons to doubt the witch-hunt narrative about this case, but those arguments require detailed elaboration and documentation. This case will be the subject of a future publication.
97. Jane Daugherty, "Boy, 2, Believed Attacked at Temple,"*Miami Herald* (August 7, 1984), 1B.
98. Miami Beach Police Department Report Supplement, Complaint No. 84-25307, May 6, 1984 (indicating that one suspect was deceptive in his polygraph exam); Polygraph Report, Miami Beach Police Department Report Supplement, Complaint No. 84-25307, May 25, 1984 (indicating that the second suspect scored "conclusive of deception" on his polygraph exam); Miami Beach Police Department Report Supplement, Complaint No. 84-25307, May 16, 1984 (describing victim identifying the primary suspect).
99. Nery Ynclan, "Care Center Shut in Spanking Probe,"*Miami Herald* (August 24, 1984), 1D.
100. Nery Ynclan, "Judge Says Child Care Center Can Reopen Despite New Claim of Child Sexual Abuse," *Miami Herald* (September 15, 1984), 2B.
101. Jane Daughterty, "HRS Seeks Psychiatric Tests for 2 Daycare Operators," *Miami Herald* (October 25, 1984), 2B.

102. Jane Daugherty and Christopher Wellisz, "Daycare Operator Is Charged with Molesting Girl, 4," *Miami Herald* (July 17, 1985) 1B.

103. Jay Ducassi, "State Is Dropping Child Abuse Case," *Miami Herald* (August 20, 1985) 1B.

104. "Former Day Care Operator Cleared in Civil Suit over Alleged Abuse," *Miami Herald* (April 1, 1989) 2B.

105. Dorothy Rabinowitz, "Kelly Michaels Orwellian Ordeal," *Wall Street Journal* (April 15, 1993) A15.

106. Martie Barnes, "Mass. Continues to Get Reports of Day Care Abuse," *Boston Globe* (January 20, 1985).

107. Recommended Decision, *Office for Children v. Wingard*, Division of Administrative Law Appeals (Docket N. OFC-8640), Commonwealth of Massachusetts, July 31, 1985, 13.

108. John J. O'Connor, "'Amelia' on ABC, A Movie About Incest," *New York Times* (January 9, 1984).

109. Ralph Blumenthal, "Freud: Secret Documents Reveal Years of Strife," *New York Times* (January 29, 1984), C1.

110. Jenkins, *Pedophile Priests*, 91.

111. Masson, *Assault on Truth*, 35.

112. John Caffey, "Multiple Fractures in the Long Bones of Infants Suffering from Chronic Subdural Hematoma," *American Journal of Roentgenology* (August 1946) 56: 163–173.

113. "Subtle inferences to that effect could be drawn by experienced clinicians." John Rust, "No Easy Answers: Why the Word of Children Aren't Convicting their Abusers," *Los Angeles Daily Journal* (April 28, 1986).

114. C. Henry Kempe et. al., "Battered-Child Syndrome," *Journal of the American Medical Association* (July 1962) 181(1):17–24.

115. Lynn Sacco, "Sanitized for Your Protection: Medical Discourse and the Denial of Incest in the United States, 1890–1940," *Journal of Women's History* (Autumn, 2002), 14(3).

116. Judith Herman, *Father-Daughter Incest* (Harvard University Press, 1982).

117. Dianna Russell's book *Secret Trauma: Incest in the Lives of Girls and Women* concluded that the true incidence rate of incestuous abuse was about one in six women. If that is true, then the one-in-a-million claim would be off by a factor of 166,000. Nathan has criticized Russell's survey for having "extravagantly broad definitions" because it includes "even distant relatives" and did not exclude "botched attempts." Nathan, "The Ritual Sexual Abuse Hoax"; Nathan, "Cry Incest." It is not clear how many cases Nathan thinks would be eliminated by excluding "distant relatives" or why she would think those should not count as incest. But her quibbles about definitions distract from the magnitude of the original error. Even if we assume her objections would eliminate *half* of the reported cases, then the old estimate of incest prevalence would still be off by a factor of 88,000.

118. Linda Gordon, *Heroes of Their Own Lives: The Politics and History of Family Violence, Boston 1880–1960* (Viking Press, 1988).

119. Estelle Freedman, "'Uncontrolled Desires': The Response to the Sexual Psychopath, 1920–1960," *Journal of American History* (June 1987), 102.

120. Roland C. Summit, "The Child Abuse Accommodation Syndrome," *Child Abuse & Neglect* (1983), 7: 177–193.

121. Coleman's remarks are summarized in detail on pp. 150–169 of Paul and Shirley Eberle's book *The Politics of Child Abuse* (1986).

122. Charles Krauthammer, "Defining Deviancy Up," *New Republic* (November 22, 1993): 20–25.

123. Patrick Boyle, *Scout's Honor* (Prima Publishing, 1994).

124. Barry Siegel, *A Death in White Bear Lake* (Bantam, 1990).

125. Richard Firstman and Jamie Talan, *The Death of Innocents* (Random House, 1997).

126. Marjie Lundstrom and Rochelle Sharpe, "Getting Away with Murder: Easy to Kill a Child—and Bury the Secret," Gannett News Service (December 12, 1990). This story won the 1991 Pulitzer Prize for National Reporting.

127. Jenkins, *Moral Panic*, 10.

128. Carla Van Dam, *How Child Sexual Molesters Groom Adults to Gain Access to Children* (doctoral dissertation, Union Theological Institute, 1996). See also "Techniques of Deception," chap. 3 in Anna Salter, *Predators: Pedophiles, Rapists, and Other Sex Offenders* (Basic Books, 2003).

129. William Nack and Don Yaeger, "Who's Coaching Your Kid?" *Sports Illustrated* (September 13, 1999).

130. Richard Hoffman, *Half the House* (Mariner Books, 1996). See also "Ex-coach, 68, Gets Jail Time for Molesting Four Boys," *Philadelphia Inquirer* (August 23, 1996).

131. Nathan, "Making of a Modern Witch Trial," 20.

132. Prosecutor cited in Charlier and Downing. Van Dam, *How Child Sexual Molesters Groom Adults.*

133. *State v. Kelly*, Superior Court Division, Pitt County, North Carolina (July 21, 1991). File Nos. 91-CRS-4250-4363, Vol. LXVII, tr. 15185.

134. One study documented the average wait between cessation of abuse and disclosure to be fourteen years. Roesler and Wind, "Telling the Secret: Adult Women Describe Their Disclosure of Incest," *Journal of Interpersonal Violence* (1994) 9, 327.

135. Stephen Fried, "Boy Crazy," *Philadelphia* (October 1987).

136. Fried, "Boy Crazy."

137. Charles Walston and Ralph Ellis, "Broken Trust," *Atlanta Journal-Constitution* (August 20, 1995): H5. Remarkably, West's name has appeared on at least one "false conviction" list— without any explanation. C. Ronald Huff, Martin Killias, *Wrongful Conviction: International Perspectives on Miscarriages of Justice* (Temple University Press, 2008), 25, fn. 5.

138. Calvin Trillin, "Outdoor Life," *New Yorker* (August 11, 1986).

139. Trillin, "Outdoor Life," 66.

140. Susan Duerksen, "Health Professionals Reluctant to Report Abuse, Study Finds," *San Diego-Union Tribune* (January 19, 1990), A-16.

141. Joe Dirck, "Another Abuse Tale: Author Loses Gamble on Boys Scouts and Pedophilia," *Plain Dealer* (July 17, 1994), 10J.

142. Christopher Wellisz and Gelareh Asayesh, "Cops Assail School in Abuse Probe," *Miami Herald* (April 23, 1988), 1A.

143. Carolyn Pesce, "Town Grapples with Dirty Little Secret; Male Teacher Abused Boys, Parents' Trust," *USA Today* (November 19, 1990) 3A.

144. "Sex Case Teacher Gets 20 Years' Jail," *Herald Sun* (November 16, 1990).

145. "Montana Teacher Molested Generations of Students," *Associated Press* (November 25, 1990, BC cycle.)

146. Mary Hargrove and Susan Roth, "Preying on Pupils," *Arkansas Democrat-Gazette* (September 8, 1996).

147. [The Gardner contribution] Amicus Curiae Brief for the New Jersey Council of Child and Adolescent Psychiatry [in *State v. J.Q.*], n.d. [circa summer 1992], 12. Dr. Gardner sent me this document; the words "The Gardner contribution" are handwritten on the first page.

148. Allison Klein, "Family's Ordeal Nearly Over," *Miami Herald* (November 17, 1997), 1B.

149. Bittenbender is the central character in Patrick Boyle's 1994 book *Scout's Honor*, which provided the first public account of the Boy Scouts' "confidential files." Files on 231 leaders banned from scouting for sexual misconduct were obtained in connection with a civil suit involving a Reston, Virginia, youth who was molested by Bittenbender in the early 1970s. *Infant C. v. Boy Scouts of America*, 239 Va. 572, 391 S.E. 2d 322 (1990). Bittenbender was convicted of charges involving sexual conduct with three members of that scout troop. The book details later abuse by Bittenbender in Wilmington, Delaware, and in Rhode Island. Boyle, who interviewed Bittenbender many times in prison, writes that "Carl is candid about many acts of abuse, most of which are not on the public record" (329). Boyle, *Scout's Honor*, 81–95, 113–123.

150. Charlier, "Prosecutors Honing Edge in Duel of Reforms, Right," *Commercial Appeal* (January 1988), A12.

151. Nathan, "Making of a Modern Witch Trial."

152. *Dove v. Texas*, 768 S.W. 2d 465 (March 31, 1989). The trial judge ruled that charges involving other children had to be tried separately, but evidence concerning some of those children was admitted in the case. There was never a trial involving any of the charges concerning other children. Those charges were eventually dropped.

153. Susan Krohn, "Parents: Presidio Day Care Probe Inadequate," UPI (April 19, 1988); see also, "Third Presidio Tot Has Venereal Disease," UPI (August 14, 1987).

154. Cheryl McCall, "The Cruelest Crime," *Life* (December 1984): 35.

155. Affidavit in Support of Probable Cause, Palm Beach County, November 23, 1988 (88-15245CF).

156. Affidavit in Support of Probable Cause, Palm Beach County, December 12, 1988 (88-217661); Affidavit in Support of Probable Cause, Palm Beach County, December 12, 1988 (88-217663). (Affidavit 88-217662 was not in the materials that I obtained on this case.)

157. The Investigative Decision Summary states that "medical evidence corroborates molestation" and "credible statements" were given to a pediatrician, two psychologists, law enforcement, "and this investigator." Abuse Report (Report No. 88-086445), Florida Protective Services System, 6.

158. Presentment, *In re Grand Jury Proceedings* (Circuit Court, Fifteenth Judicial Circuit; Palm Beach County) March 17, 1989.

159. Glenn Collins, "The Child's Word Isn't Enough," *New York Times* (July 11, 1983), B4.

160. California Jury Instructions—Criminal 10.37 (as it existed in 1984). This specific section has a different meaning now, although the section is still about sex offenses.

161. The California Supreme Court ruled that this instruction was inappropriate, in *People v. Rincon-Pineda*, 14 Cal. 3d 864 (1975).

162. *People v. Algarin*, 166 A.D.2d 287; 560 N.Y.S.2d 771 (Supreme Court of New York, Appellate Division; 1990).

163. *Maryland v. Craig*, 497 U.S. 836 (1990). The Confrontation Clause also became a significant argument in the Amirault cases. In 1995, Judge Robert A. Barton granted a motion for a new trial based on the argument that the seating arrangements in the original trial violated the Confrontation Clause. *Commonwealth v. Amirault*, 4 Mass. Legal. L. Rep. 245; 1995 Mass. Super LEXIS 434 (August 25, 1995). The Massachuetts Supreme Judicial Court vacated that order. *Commonwealth v. Amirault*, 424 Mass. 618, 677 N.E.2d 652 (1997).

164. *Maryland v. Craig*, 497 U.S. 836, 110 S. Ct. 3157 (1990).

165. Harry Stein, "Presumed Guilty; the Charge of Sexual Abuse of Children Is the Dirtiest, Deadliest Trick in Divorce Court,"*Playboy* (June 1992), 74.

166. William Tucker, *"The Effect of Victim Age and Gender on Prosecutor's Willingness to Prosecute Cases of Child Sexual Abuse."* Unpublished undergraduate thesis, Brown University, 2004.

167. Matthew Brelis, "Lynn Officer Charged with Abusing Girl," *Boston Globe* (March 17, 1989) 1.

168. *State v. Curlew*, 459 A.2d 160; 1983 Me. LEXIS 644 (1983).

169. Michael deCourcy Hinds, "Delaware Case Shows Difficulty in Proving Child Sex-abuse," *Chicago Tribune* (November 22, 1992), 11.

170. Mary Hargrove, "The Courtroom Ordeal," *Miami Herald* (November 7, 1993), 28A (Part of *Stolen Innocence* series).

171. Paul Wilkes, "Unholy Acts," *New Yorker* (June 7, 1993), 77.

172. The conviction was upheld on appeal. *Commonwealth v. Provost*, 418 Mss. 416, 636 N.E.2d 1312 (1994).

173. "Details Given in Prosecutor Sex Abuse Case," *Detroit Free Press* (January 13, 1983), 3A.

174. John F. Harris, "Va. Girl Who Leaped in Train's Path Wrote of Sex Abuse Fear,"*Washington Post* (July 31, 1986), C1.

175. Suzanne M. Sgroi, "A National Needs Assessment for Protecting Child Victims of Sexual Assault," Introduction to Anne Wolbert Burgess, et. al., *Sexual Assault of Children and Adolescents* (Lexington Books, 1978).

176. Martin John Costello, *Hating the Sin, Loving the Sinner: The Minneapolis Children's Theatre Company Adolescent Sexual Abuse Prosecutions* (University of Minnesota, 1987).

177. "Children's Theatre Founder Accused of Molesting 3 Boys," *New York Times* (April 19, 1984).

178. *Hating the Sin*, 90.

179. *Hating the Sin*, 103.

180. *Hating the Sin*, 146.

181. Brawley and Smist, "Convicted Child Molester Reaping Strong Support from Norman Church," *The Oklahoman* (June 30, 1985).

182. Grant, "Support for Child Molester Angers Family," *Citrus Times* (July 3, 1994), 1.
183. Personal correspondence from Richard A. Gardner, M.D., to Professor Ross Cheit (August 21, 1995).
184. Ross E. Cheit and Erica Goldschmidt, "Child Molesters in the Criminal Justice System: A Comprehensive Case-Flow Analysis of the Rhode Island Docket (1985–1993)," *New England Journal on Criminal and Confinement* (1997), 23(2): 267–301.
185. "Probation for Child Molester," *Philadelphia Inquirer* (October 30, 1983), A4.
186. "Gold Gets Probation in Fondling of Child," *New York Times* (October 21, 1983).
187. Kathleen O'Steen, "Sex Offender Gets Probation as Mom of Victim Protests," *Los Angeles Daily News* (June 15, 1984).
188. John Corry, "4-part Series on Child Sexual Abuse," *New York Times* (September 17, 1984), C18.
189. Barbara E. Smith and Sharon Goretsky Elstein, ABA Center on Children and the Law, *The Prosecution of Child Sexual and Physical Abuse Cases: Final Report* (American Bar Association 1993). This report was submitted to the National Center on Child Abuse and Neglect.
190. Smith and Goretsky Elstein, *The Prosecution of Child Sexual and Physical Abuse Cases*, 118.
191. Those were equally divided between sentences in excess of twenty years (4 percent) and life sentences (4 percent). Smith and Goretsky Elstein, *The Prosecution of Child Sexual and Physical Abuse Cases*, 118.
192. "Child Abuse: The Crimes of the 80s," *Boston Globe* (November 8–11, 1987).
193. Neil Roland, "Daycare Workers Detailed Concerns," *Fort Lauderdale Sun-Sentinel* (May 15, 1990).
194. David Rhode, "Probation for Teacher Guilty of Abuse at Stuyvesant," *New York Times* (August 18, 1999).
195. "Molester Sentenced to Psychiatric Treatment," UPI (April 3, 1984).

Conclusion I

1. See footnote 210 and accompanying text in Chapter Five.

Chapter Five

1. Open letter to parents from Kelly Michaels dated May 17, 1985. I obtained a copy of this letter in the course of my research but never found any information about who actually received the letter.
2. Stephanie Lorman, Reinterview (October 7, 1987) by Investigator Noreen Catarino, Office of Public Defender.
3. Testimony of Madeline Sullivan, August 11, 1987, tr. 118.
4. The first and last names of all of the children involved in this case have been changed to pseudonyms that maintain the original initials of their actual first and last names.
5. *State v. Michaels*, June 25, 1987, tr. 198, line 25. (The trial transcript, which is approximately fifty thousand pages long, was prepared daily. Every day begins with page 1, and sometimes the afternoon session begins with page 1. The date is included with every transcript cite. There is a fully stamped transcript on appeal, but I could gain access only to the dailies.)
6. *State v. Michaels*, June 25, 1987, tr. 199, lines 1–4.
7. *State v. Michaels*, June 25, 1987, tr. 36.
8. She was married during the many years that this case lasted; her name became Sara Sencer-McArdle. She is referred to as Sencer-McArdle throughout.
9. Lisa Manshel, *Naptime: The True Story of Sexual Abuse at a Suburban Day Care Center* (William Morrow 1989). Some critics of the case are also extremely critical of the book. I found it accurate on every fact that I was able to check, but I relied on original documents for almost every claim in this chapter. Ceci and Bruck also cited *Naptime* as a source in *Jeopardy in the Courtroom*.
10. McGrath notes from Mitchell Pierce interview.
11. *State v. Michaels*, June 29, 1987, tr. 86.
12. Statement to Detective R. Mastrangelo, May 3, 1985, 1.

13. Andrew Cook, handwritten statement, May 2, 1985, 1.
14. Cook, handwritten statement, 2.
15. Cook, handwritten statement, 2.
16. Cook statement to Det. Richard Mastrangelo, May 3, 1985.
17. Patricia Crowley, *Not My Child* (Doubleday, 1989), 49. This book has been criticized for lack of objectivity. I have not relied on it for any significant factual statements in this chapter, but this is the longest available account concerning the Rooneys. I located only a few documents about this child.
18. Crowley, *Not My Child*, 49–50.
19. *State v. Michaels*, Grand Jury, July 10, 1985, tr. 16.
20. Letter to Wee Care Parents, May 8, 1985.
21. Manshel, *Naptime*, 24.
22. Minutes, Wee Care All-Parent Meeting, May 15, 1985, 1.
23. Minutes, Wee Care All-Parent Meeting, May 15, 1985, 1.
24. Mitchell Pierce's mother testified: "I was instructed by a social worker from United Hospital that I was not to try to elicit any kind of information from Mitchell. I was just to, if he talked, listen to him and not pry at all, and just be a supportive listener." *State v. Michaels*, June 24, 1987, tr. 143.
25. Crowley, *Not My Child*, 44.
26. Manshel, *Naptime*, 36.
27. *State v. Michaels*, Grand Jury, November 4, 1985, tr. 27.
28. *State v. Michaels*, Grand Jury, November 4, 1985, tr. 27.
29. Manshel, *Naptime*, 37.
30. Oralee Wachter and Jane Aaron, *No More Secrets for Me* (Little Brown, 1983). Annotation: four short stories about situations that children may find themselves in regarding abuse and how these children find a way out of harm's way.
31. *State v. Michaels*, Grand Jury, November 4, 1985, tr. 27.
32. Testimony of Lou Fonolleras in *State v. Michaels* (November 16, 1987; afternoon), tr. 35.
33. Julia Tilden police statement, June 12, 1985.
34. Eileen Treacy, Report on Nora van Haley, November 16, 1986.
35. *State v. Michaels*, Grand Jury, July 10, 1985, tr. 63.
36. Crowley, *Not My Child*, 51.
37. Donna Leusner, "Nursery Ex-teacher Indicted in Sex Abuse of 3 Children," *Star Ledger* (June 7, 1985).
38. Memorandum from Karen Burton to Jonas Rappeport (September 11, 1986), 1.
39. Donna Leusner, "Ex-nursery School Teacher Faces 31 Sex Abuse Charges," *Star Ledger* (June 21, 1985).
40. There are three children in the overall case with the initials B.M. Two are boys. The one referred to here was not included in any charges.
41. Brian's father did not object to this interview. Indeed, he testified about two mysterious oval-shaped bruises that he saw on his son's back in the spring. They were consistent with an injury by a wooden spoon. *State v. Michaels* (August 25, 1987), tr. 110–114.
42. Fonolleras Summary DYFS Report. It should be noted that no charges were ever brought in connection with this child.
43. Fonolleras notes on Elliot Shandley interview (June 19, 1985). This is one of a handful of children who were not part of the fifty-one children included in Ceci and Bruck's numbering of children in the case. None of these children were involved in any charges and none had multiple interviews. Most likely, these children were interviewed once by DYFS and never by law enforcement.
44. Fonolleras report on Clare Williams (June 20, 1985). It should be noted that no charges were ever brought in connection with this child either.
45. This child's name appears in DYFS notes but not on the list of fifty-one.
46. Clare Williams (June 20), Andrea Towne (June 20), Michelle Marshall (June 24), Shayla Palimieri (June 24), Ruby Watson (June 26), and Margaret Selby (June 27).
47. Original sources conflict on whether the number of interviews was eighty-two, eighty-three, or eighty-nine. I have located original documents to support all of those aggregate totals. The

difference between eighty-two and eighty-three depends on how one counts an interview in which two children were interviewed together. The difference between eighty-three and eighty-nine involves children who were most marginal to the case.

48. Manshel, *Naptime*, 111.

49. *State v. Michaels* (August 18, 1985), a.m. session, tr. 82.

50. *State v. Michaels* (August 18, 1985), a.m. session, tr. 85.

51. *State v. Michaels* (August 18, 1985), a.m. session, tr. 100.

52. *State v. Michaels* (August 18, 1985), a.m. session, tr. 85.

53. Concerned Scientists brief, published in *Psychology, Public Policy, and Law* (1995) 1(2): 272-322, 285.

54. She told Rebecca Flora's mother, who called her in May when Rebecca said she had seen David naked at school, not to jump to conclusions. Judy Applegate assumed there was an innocuous explanation and did not follow up with her son or attend the first parent's meeting a week later.

55. Debbie Nathan addressed this child in an article written in 1998, long after the case was over and it was clear David Applegate would not testify again. Nathan claimed to have discovered evidence that Michaels's "inexperienced and overworked public defenders" never considered, to wit: . . . on the tape of an interview of another Wee Care student, Lindsay, I heard her father say that she and [David] played together. The point: [David] could have picked up the details of the alleged abuse from his playmate." This assertion is contradicted by various testimonies at trial. First, the extent to which David had contact with children outside of school was not something that escaped the notice of Kelly Michael's defense team. The boy's mother was specifically questioned about the subject at trial. Judy Applegate would no doubt be surprised by Nathan's unsubstantiated claim that her son "regularly played" with any other child from Wee Care. Her testimony at trial was that "once, maybe twice he played with Debra Schultz, and I think there was once a day when Diane Plunkett had him over after school a little bit." Second, David contracted chickenpox and was out of school in early June, when word of the case might conceivably have become a topic of discussion among children. It is curious that proponents of the child-suggestibility defense, normally acutely attuned to whether events are literally possible, apparently missed the fact that there were few or no opportunities for the conversations that Nathan hypothesizes. There is no evidence that the details of the allegations against Michaels were a topic of conversation between children before David Applegate got chickenpox. One child told interviewers she learned from her friend that Kelly "had been bad." Several others allowed that they learned this from their parents—but *all of those were in late June.* David Applegate had been out of school for weeks by then and had been isolated from all possible playmates.

56. *Matter of Nicole V.*, 71 N.Y.2d 112 (1987). The decision of the Court of Appeals, New York's highest court, supported the approach Treacy used. The case stemmed from a Family Court proceeding held in early 1985.

57. *State v. Michaels* (June 25, 1987), tr. 15, 31–33, 64–65.

58. Summit, "The Child Sexual Abuse Accommodation Syndrome."

59. The defense relied on David M. Brodzinsky, a Rutgers psychology professor who argued that a behavioral checklist used in the case was subject to measurement error. On the basis of a small survey that he conducted at the Rutgers University Day Care Center, Brodzinsky argued that mechanical use of this checklist would cause 28 percent of so-called normal preschoolers to be suspected of having been sexually abused or at least of having experienced some similar trauma. He did not comment on how much more prevalent the symptoms were in the Kelly Michaels children than in his "normal" survey. Nor was this informal survey—conducted for the defense, although this was not disclosed to those surveyed—apparently subjected to peer-review or apparently published in any academic journal.

60. She could not rule out other possible causes of the child's behavior.

61. Eileen Treacy, [Report] "Interview #2 2–17–87," David Applegate, 1, 2.

62. Institutional Abuse Report, n.d. Exhibit S-233 in *State v. Michaels*.

63. The agency could have taken some kind of licensing action. But Kelly Michaels left before the allegations surfaced, and the school ended up closing.

64. This is my own position concerning the ethical duty of prosecutors. Many, possibly most, legal ethicists maintain an even stricter position: that charges should be brought only if the prosecutor personally believes the defendant is guilty. In a fascinating essay, law professor Alafair Burke reviews those arguments and argues instead for prosecutorial agnosticism. Alafair S. Burke, "Prosecutorial Agnosticism," *Ohio State Journal of Criminal Law* (2010), 8: 79–100. All commenters agree that prosecutors are obligated to "do justice," not simply win cases. And whatever the ethical standard, criminal cases require a higher level of proof than civil or administrative cases.

65. *In the Interest of K.A.W.*, 104 N.J. 112, 515 A.2d 1217 (Supreme Court of New Jersey, 1986).

66. Manshel, *Naptime*, 98.

67. Manshel explained that the appellate section instructed prosecutors to charge by the instrument. "Instead of charging one count of vaginal penetration and one count of anal penetration for each girl, Sara was to charge up to three separate counts for vaginal penetration (fork, knife, and spoon) and up to three separate counts for anal penetration (fork, knife, and spoon)." *Naptime*, 98.

68. Fifty-four of the counts that went to the jury were for aggravated sexual assault. Keep in mind that, given the multiple ways of charging the details of sexual abuse, a single incident could account for up to six counts. Again, spread across nineteen children, these fifty-four counts translate into a handful of incidents.

69. Typologies of sex offenders distinguish between kinds of abusers. "Opportunistic" abusers are "impulsive, unplanned, and driven by opportunity as a means of seeking immediate gratification." CSOM Etiology. http://www.csom.org/train/etiology/4/4_1.htm.

70. Manshel, *Naptime*, 133.

71. The second interview was requested by John's mother, not by authorities. She said John wanted to come back and talk to "the man with the dolls." But he did not disclose anything in his second interview.

72. Crowley, *Not My Child*, 204.

73. *State v. Michaels*, Grand Jury (November 6, 1985), tr. 26–29.

74. *State v. Michaels* (June 29, 1987), tr. 47.

75. *State v. Michaels*, Grand Jury (July 10, 1985), tr. 73.

76. *State v. Michaels*, Grand Jury (July 10, 1985), tr. 101.

77. Julie Gottlieb, *From the Courtroom to the Newsroom: An Analysis of the Print Media Coverage of State of New Jersey v. Margaret Kelly Michaels*. Unpublished undergraduate thesis, Brown University 2000, 53.

78. She testified: "The first day [that she came back to work in early May] I remember it very clearly because Brenda was there with me and I said to her, I said this is strange, these kids are all asleep and in the winter they didn't sleep."

79. This document can be found on p. 347 of the three-volume exhibit attached to the defense brief on appeal.

80. Jacob Peyton interview, June 20, 1985, 26.

81. *State v. Michaels*, Concerned Scientists brief, 31.

82. *State v. Michaels*, Concerned Scientists brief, 31. Citing Ceci and Bruck (1993), "Child Witnesses: Translating Research into Policy," *SRCD Social Policy Reports*, (Fall 1993) VII(3): 1–12.

83. *State v. Michaels* (October 21, 1987), tr. 17.

84. *State v. Michaels* (November 3, 1987), tr. 58.

85. Typed synopsis of interview on July 2, 1985. Institutional Abuse Report. Exhibit S-233 in *State v. Michaels*.

86. John Allister interview (July 15, 1985), tr. 7.

87. *State v. Michaels* (November 16, 1987), tr. 70–71.

88. *State v. Michaels* (September 9, 1987), tr. 32.

89. Frank Lindblad et. al., "Preschoolers' Sexual Behavior at Daycare Centers: An Epidemiological Study," *Child Abuse & Neglect* (1995) 19(5):569–577. Cite at 575.

90. *State v. Michaels* (October 13, 1987), tr. 39.

91. *State v. Michaels* (June 24, 1987), tr. 142–43.

92. *State v. Michaels* (August 18, 1987), tr. 75.

93. *State v. Michaels* (July 28, 1987), tr. 144, 157.

94. *State v. Michaels* (November 19, 1987), tr. 18–21.
95. *State v. Michaels* (February 23, 1988), tr. 13.
96. *State v. Michaels* (February 23, 1988), tr. 35–53.
97. *State v. Michaels* (November 19, 1987), tr. 23–24.
98. *State v. Michaels*, Grand Jury (July 10, 1985), tr. 98.
99. *State v. Michaels*, Grand Jury (July 10, 1985), tr. 70.
100. Rabinowitz described Michaels as "pretty in a traditional, American girl sort of way." *Harper's*, 54. The *60 Minutes* program about the Michaels case was called "The Girl Next Door." The view that Michaels could not possibly have abused children because of her appearance conveyed the same stereotype that Nathan betrayed when, in her first contribution to the witch-hunt narrative, she referred to "sleazy trench coats"—as if child molesters were actually identifiable by their outerwear.
101. Murray Bartky, Ph.D., Psychological Evaluation (n.d.), 3. Exhibit D5 in *State v. Michaels*. This three-page document was also included in an appendix to the first defense brief on appeal and is numbered A-79 to A-81.
102. *State v. Michaels*, December 1, 1987, tr. 11, lines 9–13.
103. Although the witch-hunt narrative dismisses the testimony of Charlene Munn out of hand, no evidence has ever been offered to support the insinuation that her ten-year sentence for aggravated manslaughter was a "deal." Sentencing agreements that are contingent on cooperation generally hold sentencing in abeyance until after the person testifies. Munn testified after she had been sentenced and she received a substantial sentence.
104. In one of many claims of memory lapse while testifying under oath, Michaels, a nonsmoker, would assert she "could not remember" whether she had bought sixteen separate packages of cigarettes for Munn that she had charged to her prison account.
105. M.A.R.C.I.S. Incident Report Supplement, December 19, 1985, submitted by Det. Sgt. John J. Noonan.
106. *State v. Michaels* (November 30, 1987), tr. 85.
107. *State v. Michaels*, Transcript of Proceedings (February 15, 1991), tr. 111. Note: Dr. Brodsky examined Michaels for three and a half hours on August 7, 1990. He made no audio or video record of the interview.
108. *State v. Michaels* (March 7, 1988), tr. 64.
109. It is thirty-seven words long, not altogether coherent, but possibly copyright-protected by Kelly Michaels. Accordingly, I will simply describe it as strange. The final phrases are about "the smell of your flesh" and "your body will leave me." The poem is included in Manshel, *Naptime*, 319.
110. *State v. Michaels*, March 2, 1988, tr. 49–50.
111. Manshel, *Naptime*, 259.
112. The only other child to have only a single count presented to the jury was Martin Zeitz, who did not actually testify. Jacob Peyton and Martin were first interviewed quite late in the investigative sequence.
113. "Lawyer Quitting Sex Abuse Case," *Star Ledger* (June 3, 1986).
114. *State v. Michaels* (June 22, 1988), tr. 187.
115. *State v. Michaels* (June 22, 1988), tr. 234, 237.
116. *Phil Donahue Show* on the Jordan, Minnesota cases, January 15, 1985.
117. "Interview: Hollida Wakefield and Ralph Underwager," *Paidika* (1993), (3)2: 3–4. This now-defunct magazine had a line drawing of a naked prepubescent boy on the cover. Underwager would later argue that this was a "primary prevention effort" somehow aimed at preventing pedophilia. The claim is difficult to square with the purpose of the magazine; moreover, his wife distanced herself from the remarks and Underwager was forced to resign from the advisory board of the False Memory Syndrome Foundation when this interview became known in the United States.
118. See generally Diane Curcio, "Lawman Hammers at Nursery Sex Case," *Star Ledger* (February 7, 1988), 62. Among the materials still in storage in this case is testimony from other cases around the country and investigative documents concerning his marriage (to a former marriage counseling client) and business (which include a farm implement business just a year before he became an "expert" in the Jordan case). There was also documentation of the

close relationship between Underwager and the activist group VOCAL (Victims of Child Abuse Laws), which had office space in Underwager's house.

119. Underwager said "a scientist who bases an opinion upon unchecked subjective experience has regressed to the level of the witch doctor." The prosecutor pointed out how some of Underwager's claims in the case were entirely subjective.

120. Angela Stewart, "Judge Prohibits Psychiatric 'Profile' in Sex Abuse Trial of Day-care Teacher," *Star Ledger* (May 15, 1987), 35.

121. Manshel, *Naptime*, 283.

122. Jonas Rappeport, "Psychiatric Evaluation of Margaret Kelly Michaels," *State v. Michaels* (February 2, 1987), 15, Exhibit D-3.

123. *State v. Michaels* (June 25, 1987), tr. 198–199.

124. Quoted in Manshel, *Naptime*, 287.

125. All of these details were contained in Alfonso A. Narvaez, "Former Day-Care Teacher Denies Sexually Abusing Schoolchildren," *New York Times* (February 28, 1988), 37.

126. *State v. Michaels* (March 7, 1988, afternoon session), tr. 22.

127. *State v. Michaels* (March 7, 1988, afternoon session), tr. 43, 49, 73.

128. Mary de Young, *The Day Care Ritual Abuse Moral Panic.*

129. The inconclusive result is acknowledged in *Michaels v. New Jersey*, 50 F. Supp 2d 353, 354 (May 29, 1999).

130. Associated Press, "Jury Method Fought," *News Tribune* (March 31, 1988), A7.

131. Those counts were charged as third-degree "child endangerment," since they did not actually involve sexual contact.

132. Debbie Nathan, "Victimizer or Victim?" *Village Voice* (August 2, 1988).

133. Debbie Nathan, "Day-Care Witch Trials," *Village Voice* (April 26, 1988), 17.

134. Nathan, "Victimizer," 38.

135. Nathan, "Victimizer", 34.

136. Nathan did not reveal that those were some of the same interviews already criticized; nor did she mention that none of those interviews resulted in charges at the trial.

137. This is what he said, in a portion of the transcript that was underlined in the annotated version of the interviews filed by the defense on appeal: "So I just want you to know that I lived through it when I was a kid and I remember how hard it was to talk about it and how scary it was to talk about it." But the story that Fonolleras actually proceeded to tell did not involve his disclosing sexual abuse. Actually, he said that "somebody hurt me [sic] brother real bad" and he adds that "they threatened me." Natalie Jenkins interview (6/24/85), 11. Fonolleras told at least one other child something about his own abuse history. Defense counsel insinuated at one point, on the basis of Fonolleras having "told [Natalie Jenkins] and at least one other" child, that he had a preconceived determination in sexual abuse cases. *State v. Michaels* (October 28, 1987), tr. 66. Fonolleras denied the charge, and the prosecution argued that anything about interviews with those children should be kept out of the case because they were not children named in the actual indictment. The judge let the evidence in, so the jury was fully aware of this issue.

138. Rabinowitz, "From the Mouths of Babes to a Jail Cell," *Harper's*, May 1990.

139. Nathan has written that this group first met in January 1990, four months before the Rabinowitz article was published. But since Rabinowitz apparently had difficulty placing the article, an early draft could well have been central to the mobilization of other people in New York City. The collapse of the McMartin case might also explain why this group coalesced in January 1990.

140. For example, Deirdre Donahue said that "Rabinowitz persuasively argues that a new McCarthyism has taken hold of our national psyche," in the "Magazines" column in *USA Today* (May 11, 1990), 4D.

141. Rabinowitz, "From the Mouths of Babes," 56.

142. See the text and accompanying footnotes in this chapter describing testimony of Mrs. Pierce (fn. 7) and Laura Hadley (fn. 5, 6).

143. Rabinowitz, "From the Mouths of Babes," 56.

144. Rich Lowry, "Creating Victims," *National Review* (December 5, 1994).

145. "The Case of Kelly Michaels, Accused of Sex Abuse," *48 Hours* (June 19, 1991), CBS News Transcripts, 1.

146. "The Case of Kelly Michaels," 3.

147. Debbie Nathan, "Sweet Justice: My Fight to Free Kelly Michaels," *Redbook* (June 1995), 85 (original emphasis).

148. Rabinowitz, "From the Mouths of Babes," 60.

149. Nat Hentoff, "Once More the Witch Hunt," *Washington Post* (May 23, 1992), A31.

150. Sources vary slightly on the total number. I have been able to account for eighty-three interviews using multiple sources. Many children were later interviewed by Eileen Treacy and by the prosecutor's office, but the investigative phase accounts for the initial disclosures and charges.

151. He did not disclose anything in his first interview on June 10; he was interviewed again on June 17, after his mother called to report that John had asked to come back and talk to the man with the dolls; but John did not disclose anything in his second interview. His mother provided an extensive statement on July 3 about statements John had been making at home. There was a final interview with John on July 15; he did not disclose anything and he was not part of the trial.

152. Interview with Rebecca Flora (July 3, 1985), 6.

153. Interview with Rebecca Flora (July 3, 1985), 11. Note: the name of the child she mentions has been blacked out and "1C" has been put in its place. But 1C is a boy, so it is unclear whether the defense misidentified this child or whether the gender confusion was Rebecca's.

154. *State v. Michaels*, Grand Jury (November 4, 1985), tr. 27.

155. Nathan, "Victimizer."

156. Rabinowitz, "From the Mouths of Babes," 58.

157. The Rabinowitz version makes it appear that the child provided a meaningless answer in the following exchange:

> FONOLLERAS: What color did Kelly have down there? Brown like her head? Did she have hair under her arm?
> LUKE: My daddy do.

The transcript of this interview, however, which is appended to the defense briefs on appeal, describes the exchange differently. It reveals that the child's answer came to an earlier question, changing the meaning significantly:

> [67Q] LOU: That is hair because she is a grown up, right and what color did Kelly have down there?
> [67A] CHILD: Brown.
> [68Q] LOU: Brown? Like her hair on her head. Did she have hair under her arms?
> [68A] CHILD: Ooh, my daddy got those.

158. Interview with P. J. Isaacs, 15; stamped as 58. June 27, 1985.

159. Vincent Caroll, "The Tragedy of a Modern-Day Witch Hunt," *Rocky Mountain News* (June 19, 2003), 40A. This editorial includes a lengthy interview with Rabinowitz.

160. Nat Hentoff, "Anna Quindlen Doesn't Get It," *Village Voice* (June 23, 1992).

161. Manshel, 1990, 99. Manshel's account includes descriptions of the child's demeanor that I could not verify—that "he answered softly in an uncontorted voice." But the grand jury transcript, which I obtained, verifies Manshel's description. *State v Michaels*, Essex County Grand Jury (July 11, 1985), tr. 92, lines 1–2.

162. Caroll, "Tragedy of a Modern-Day Witch Hunt," 40A.

163. This story was reported by Lisa Manshel in "Reporters for the Defense," *Washington Journalism Review* (July/August 1991), 20.

164. Manshel, *Washington Journalism Review*, 20.

165. Transcript of *Booknotes*, CNN (May 4, 2003), 5.

166. Transcript of *Booknotes*, CNN (May 4, 2003), 6.

167. Manshel, *Naptime*, 238.

168. Manshel, *Naptime*, 238.

169. Associated Press, "Jury Method Fought," A7.
170. *State v. Michaels*, Brief on Behalf of Amicus Developmental, Social and Psychological Researchers, Social Scientists and Scholars, 48. [Hereinafter "Concerned Scientists brief"]
171. *State v. Michaels*, Concerned Scientists brief, 1, fn 2.
172. Nathan, "Victimizer," 38.
173. Posting by Jonathan Harris, Friday, February 25, 1994, on the electronic "witchhunt" list that he created while at MIT. Subject: "Another fruitcake (a dangerous one at that)."
174. Transcript of *Booknotes*, CNN (May 4, 2003), 4.
175. Eileen C. Treacy, "Foster Parenting the Sexually Abused Child: The Evaluation of Two Specialized Parent Education Programs," doctoral dissertation, Fordham University (filed February 8, 1995).
176. Nathan also complained: "While Treacy says she received 'ongoing training' from two Columbia professors in the field of child sex abuse, this instruction did not involve her enrolling in a single accredited Columbia course." Note the clever construction: Nathan does not deny that Treacy received ongoing training from two Columbia professors; her quibble is that the training "did not involve her enrolling in a single credited course"—something Treacy never claimed.
177. Rabinowitz, "From the Mouths of Babes," 61.
178. "Abuse Petition Is Dismissed for Insufficient Corroboration; Matter of Maria B. (Juan T.), Supreme Court, Judge Lefkowitz," *New York Law Journal* (September 1, 1989), 21.
179. Rich Lowry, "Creating Victims," *National Review* (December 5, 1994), 66.
180. *Matter of Evelyn C.*, reported in *New York Law Journal* (January 11, 1994), 21.
181. *People v. Taylor*, 75 N.Y.2d 277, 552 N.E.2d 131 (1990).
182. Ceci and Bruck, *Jeopardy in the Courtroom*, 296.
183. These page-long excerpts involve children labeled "A" and "B." The children are not otherwise identified by Ceci and Bruck even with initials or interview date; but through painstaking checking of interview transcripts, the passages were identified as coming from Cassie Bond-Foley and Ralph Gans, respectively.
184. The Essex County Prosecutor's Office arranged to have these tapes transcribed and provided to the defense. These transcriptions were not entered into evidence.
185. Ceci and Bruck, *Jeopardy in the Courtroom*, xiv–xv.
186. Cassie Bond-Foley, November 23, 1986 Transcript of interview by Eileen Treacy prepared by the Essex County Prosecutor's Office, 20.
187. Debra A. Poole and Michael E. Lamb, *Investigative Interviews of Children: A Guide for Helping Professionals* (American Psychological Association, 1998), 170.
188. Cassie Bond-Foley, Statement, June 13, 1985. This statement was entered at trial as Exhibit D-36 and is contained in the defense brief that Ceci and Bruck cite in their *Psychological Bulletin* article. See Supplementary Appendix Volume I, 10.
189. *State v. Michaels*, Grand Jury (July 19, 1985), tr. 50.
190. Ralph Gans Statement #2, December 11, 1987. Transcript of interview with Eileen Treacy prepared by the Essex County Prosecutor's Office. Hand-numbered p. 7, line 10. (The typed page numbers are one page off after the first p. 4.)
191. Ralph Gans Statement #2, hand-numbered p. 7.
192. Ceci and Bruck, *Jeopardy in the Courtroom*, 73 and 118. This quote is also highlighted in the Concerned Scientists brief and has become a staple of the witch-hunt narrative about the case. See, e.g., Robyn N. Dawes, *Everyday Irrationality* (2001), 165.
193. I asked Professor Bruck, in a personal interview on October 12, 2009, if she could explain the difference between the transcript and the account in their book. She had no explanation and expressed the view that the differences were not significant. She did not respond to repeated requests for a more detailed explanation of why their account varies from the transcript that was prepared by the state.
194. Treacy, Report on Ralph Gans, 1.
195. The boy said "And then Kelly tried even to make us drink it" on p. 10 (as indicated by hand numbering), line 23. The response that contains the word *crazy* is on p. 11, line 5.
196. Rabinowitz, "From the Mouths of Babes," 52.
197. *State v. Michaels*, Concerned Scientists brief, 32.

198. See Manshel, *Naptime*, 17.
199. Dorothy Rabinowitz, "Kelly Michaels's Orwellian Ordeal," *Wall Street Journal* (April 15, 1993).
200. Shayla Palmieri interview, June 24, 1985, 17.
201. *State v. Michaels* (June 29, 1987, A.M. session), tr. 114.
202. Sadie Gaffney interview, June 11, 1985, 1. This interview is hardly a secret. It appears on p. 43 in the defendant's three-volume appendix on appeal, but it is not otherwise mentioned in the witch-hunt narrative.
203. *State v. Michaels* (September 23, 1987, P.M. session), tr. 19, 21.
204. The FBI tested the piano bench for traces of feces, which had been alleged by at least one child. The results came back negative.
205. Mark Everson, "Understanding Bizarre, Improbable, and Fantastic Elements in Children's Accounts of Abuse," *Child Maltreatment* (May 1997), 2(2): 134.
206. Rabinowitz, "Kelly Michael's Orwellian Ordeal."
207. Rabinowitz, "From the Mouths of Babes," 56.
208. Richard Gardner, "Apparatchiks Turn 'Child Abuse' into 'Witch Hunt,'" *New Jersey Law Journal* (March 1, 1993), 17. It turns out Gardner exaggerated when he said, "After examining the alleged victims, the accusing parents, and Ms. Michaels, I was convinced that she did not engage in the variety of abominable acts attributed to her." Aware that few children and no parents were examined in the civil cases, I wrote Dr. Gardner and inquired about how many children and parents he interviewed. His response indicates he "only evaluated two children" and that he did not evaluate any parents. Correspondence from Richard Gardner to Ross Cheit, September 6, 2001.
209. Nathan, "Day-Care Witch Trials," *Village Voice* (April 26, 1988), 17.
210. Nathan made the "cookie-cutter copy" claim on April 26, 1988, two months before the "12 days" of research she apparently did in the Michaels case. Nathan, "Sweet Justice: My Fight to Free Kelly Michaels," *Redbook* (June 1995), 86 ("the 12 days I needed to do the reporting").
211. Jean Montoya, "Something Not So Funny Happened on the Way to Conviction: The Pretrial Interrogation of Child Witnesses," *Arizona Law Review* (Winter 1993) 35, 927, 928. Even if her description were accurate, it would not account for the four disclosures before that.
212. *Michaels v. McGrath*, 531 U.S. 1118 (2001, Justice Thomas dissent from denial of certiorari).
213. Nathan, "Victimizer," 34 ("sent a letter to parents, telling them Michaels was being investigated for sexual abuse").
214. For example, David Applegate's mother did not attend the first parent's meeting because she had no reason, on the basis of the letter to parents, to think her son was somehow involved. Indeed, this is the response Mrs. Applegate provided when Rebecca Flora's mother called to inform her that Rebecca had seen David's penis: "I actually said to her, you know kids go to the bathroom. . . . I'm not going to get upset over it and she shouldn't either." *State v. Michaels*, August 18, 1987 (A.M. Session), tr. 80, 82.
215. DYFS Institutional Abuse Report, 40. ("Evaluation: The investigation has substantiated the following: (1) Sexual Abuse on the part of Margaret Kelly Michaels against 51 children, (2) Physical Abuse against those same 51 children by the same perpetrator, (3) Emotional Abuse against those same 51 children by the perpetrator, and Institutional Neglect on the part of the Wee Care Administration . . ."). (N.D., but likely November 1985 as the final page (42) mentions the November 8 Grand Jury and indicates "we are awaiting [additional] indictment.") Exhibit S-233 in *State v. Michaels*.
216. There is a three-day break in the interviewing after June 13. Moreover, there were two significant parents meetings after June 13 that increased the social awareness and pressures around the case.
217. Nathan, "Sweet Justice," 122.
218. Rabinowitz, "Kelly Michael's Orwellian Ordeal."
219. Richard Pilskin and Jeffrey Kanige, "Michaels Case Headed for Remand," *New Jersey Law Journal* (February 8, 1993), 6.
220. *State v. Michaels*, Superior Court of New Jersey, Appellate Division, 264 N.J. Super. 579, 625 A.2.d. 489 (1993).

221. Rappeport allowed on cross-examination that he had not reviewed any of the testimony or other documentation related to this incident, although it was potentially available to him.

222. *State v. Michaels*, Superior Court of New Jersey, Appellate Division, 264 N.J. Super. 579, 625 A.2.d. 489 (1993).

223. Donna Leusner, "Judge to Decide if Interviews by Probers in Day-care Sex Case Were 'Tainted,'" *Star Ledger* (April 30, 1987), 36.

224. Donna Leusner, "Judge Rules," *Star Ledger* (May 1, 1987), 24.

225. Supplemental Brief on Petition for Certification to Review a Final Judgment of the Superior Court, Appellate Division, *State v. Michaels* (Docket No. 36, 633) (October 12, 1993), 2.

226. Memorandum from Sara Sencer-McArdle to John S. Redden (Deputy First Assistant Prosecutor) re: Inaccuracies in the Appellate Division Opinion in *State v. Michaels*, March 30, 1993.

227. When Michaels's civil claim was dismissed in 1999, Judge Barry began her opinion with the statement "The facts of this case are, by now, well known." Citing the two New Jersey appellate court decisions in the case, she went on to say, "This court will not attempt to recap every nuance of the case's history, and that history is well documented in the various opinions which have preceded this opinion." *Michaels v. State of New Jersey*, 50 F. Supp. 2d 353, 356 (1999).

228. Daniel Goleman, "Studies of Children as Witnesses Find Surprising Accuracy," *New York Times* (November 6, 1984).

229. Carol Tavris, "Do Children Lie? Not About This," *Los Angeles Times* (January 19, 1990), 7.

230. The initial effort took the form of the APA sponsored conference on child suggestibility at Cornell in 1989. The unusual nature of the conference is captured in a subsequent article in the *APA Monitor*. Tori DeAngelis, "Controversy Marks Child Witness Meeting," *APA Monitor* (August 1989), 1: 8–9. Before the conference proceedings were published, *Time* magazine reported that "a psychologist involved in the project says the book shows 'there are definite limits to knowledge about whether children are telling the truth.'" Jerome Cramer, "Why Children Lie in Court," *Time* (March 4, 1991).

231. Years later, in the U.S. Court of Appeals for the Armed Services, Judge H. F. Gierke concluded there was a "reasonable basis" for a defense lawyer's decision not to use Ralph Underwager as a witness because "the credibility of the defense might be undermined if the defense was perceived as using a 'quack' as a witness." *U.S. v. Grigoruk*, 52 M.J. 312 (C.A.A.F. 2000)

232. Ceci and Bruck, "Suggestibility of the Child Witness: A Historical Review and Syntheses," *Psychological Bulletin* (1993), 113(3): 403–439.

233. Ceci and Bruck, "Suggestibility of the Child Witness," 411.

234. Ceci and Bruck, "Suggestibility of the Child Witness," 422.

235. Ceci and Bruck, "Suggestibility of the Child Witness," 423.

236. Lou Fonolleras described it as the "most disturbing [interview] of his professional life." Manshel, *Naptime*, 86. The length, content, and tone are different from all of the earlier interviews in the case.

237. Goleman, "Studies Reveal Suggestibility of Very Young Witnesses," *New York Times* (June 11, 1993). It is not clear how the *New York Times* became aware of this article so far in advance of publication.

238. Stephen Ceci, Mary Crotteau-Huffman, Elliott Smith, and Elizabeth Loftus. "Repeatedly Thinking About Non-events." *Consciousness & Cognition* (1994), 3, 388–407.

239. Ceci, Crotteau-Huffman, Smith, and Loftus, 394.

240. "How the Questions Become the Answers," Chart, *New York Times* (June 11, 1993), A23. Description of study: "In weekly sessions, the researchers reviewed the list with the child, asking for each event: 'Has this ever happened to you?'" Reported result: "56 percent of children reported at least one false event as true." This is 20 percentage points higher than the results reported for the first study, where children were simply told to "think real hard" about whether the fictitious event had occurred.

241. "From the Mouths of Babes," ABC News *20/20* (October 22, 1993), 3.

242. Defending themselves against criticisms by law professor John E. B. Myers about the applicability of these studies, Ceci, Bruck, and Rosenthal referred to an estimate that "the typical child witness was interviewed between 4 and 11 times prior to offering in-court testimony."

Ceci, Bruck, and Rosenthal, "Children's Allegations of Sexual Abuse: Forsensic and Scientific Issues: A Reply to Commentators," *Psychology, Public Policy, and Law* (June 1995), at 500. But the claim glosses over the question of when they first disclosed abuse. It has nothing to do with the emergence of a claim. If the first disclosure is in the first few interviews, as it often was in the Michaels case, then later interviews cannot be considered the cause of the disclosures.

243. Ceci, Crotteau-Huffman, Smith, and Loftus, 397.
244. Stephen Ceci, Elizabeth Loftus, Michelle Leichtman, and Maggie Bruck. "The Role of Source Misattribution in the Creation of False Beliefs Among Preschoolers." *International Journal of Clinical and Experimental Hypnosis* (1994), 62, 304–320.
245. Ceci, Loftus, Leichtman, and Bruck, 304–320.
246. Ceci and Bruck, "Child Witnesses."
247. Jane Brody, "Memories of Things That Never Were," *New York Times* (April 25, 2000), F8.
248. Mary L. Huffman, Angela M. Crossman, and Stephen J. Ceci, "'Are False Memories Permanent?': An Investigation of the Long-Term Effects of Source Misattributions," *Consciousness and Cognition* (1997) 6, 482–490, 488.
249. Ceci and Bruck, "Child Witnesses" Translating Research into Policy," *SRCD Social Policy Reports* (1993) 7(3).
250. Ceci and Bruck, "Suggestibility of the Child Witness: A Historical Review and Syntheses," *Psychological Bulletin* (1993) 113(3): 423.
251. Ceci and Bruck, "Child Witnesses."
252. Ceci and Bruck, *Jeopardy in the Courtroom*, xiv.
253. It appears that Ceci and Bruck had some connection with the defense years earlier than was disclosed. The excerpt from the Michaels case that they included in their *Psychological Bulletin* article ends with what appears to a citation in parentheses, reading "(6/27/85 Appellate Court Brief)." That was not the date of the brief, however; it was the date of the interview. The brief does not appear in the references section of the article, but the order allowing the defense to attach copies of interview transcripts to their appellate brief was issued on December 15, 1992, seven months *after* Ceci and Bruck submitted the final version of this article.
254. Maggie Bruck, "Here it is," email to assorted academic psychologists, October 21, 1993, posted to the APLS B-Board.
255. For example, the draft of this brief appeared on the website of Barbara Johnson, a "father's rights" advocate in Massachusetts. http://falseallegations.com/amicus.htm, confirmed January 5, 2012. This draft has also been filed in court. See e.g., Appendix, Appellee's Merit Brief, *State v. Silverman*, Supreme Court of Ohio (Case No. 2008-0582).
256. Ceci and Bruck, *Jeopardy in the Courtroom*, preface.
257. Correspondence from Maggie Bruck to Professor Susan Somerville, editor, *Child Development*, January 27, 1993. It should be noted that Goodman was unaware of this letter before I asked her about it.
258. Interview with Gail Goodman (October 9, 2004).
259. *The Suggestibility of Children's Recollections*, ed. John Doris (American Psychological Association, 1991), Foreword.
260. Ceci quote from PBS, "The Child Terror."
261. Deposition of Stephen Ceci, November 22, 1993. *State v. Foeller*, File No. 93-64975-FC (Fourth Judicial Circuit Court for Jackson County, Michigan).
262. Deposition of Stephen Ceci, *State v. Foeller*, 133.
263. *State v. Michaels*, Motion for Reconsideration and to File Such Motion Nunc Pro Tunc, Supreme Court of New Jersey, Docket No. 36,633. January 27, 1994.
264. *State v. Michaels*, Concerned Scientists brief, 1.
265. The appendix is labeled "Attempts to Reconstruct Interviews and Emergence of Disclosure." The appendix obscures the issues involving the emergence of disclosures by listing children in a numerical order that is not related to how the case evolved. Conventionally, the first child to make a statement—the index child—would be numbered one. For the purposes of this appendix, the first child to make a disclosure in the Michaels case is numbered sixteen because the numbering turns out to be alphabetical, rather than numerical, although

this is never explained in the appendix. The appendix also misstated important facts surrounding several children. For example, the appendix states that child 4C's initial disclosure was "a few days" after being interviewed by Lou Fonolleras. In fact, she made an initial disclosure after her mother received the letter from Wee Care about "serious allegations concerning a former employee." The statement was well documented because it was made in front of her mother and a neighbor, Dale Skolnick, who both testified about it at trial. The girl said she had "played doctor" with Kelly Michaels; she also said there was a "secret room" at Wee Care. By the time she was interviewed in early June, she had also told her mother about children being hit with spoons and forks. None of those details had been made public by then. Lucy Deacon also "had a documented history of vaginal soreness" during the year. Her mother was concerned enough to have raised it with her pediatrician three or four times that school year.

There are two material misstatements in the brief description of Mitchell Pierce's (16C) outcry at the pediatrician. The appendix claims his statement occurred before the pediatrician's assistant inserted the thermometer. In fact, her testimony is that it was after the thermometer had been inserted for thirty seconds. This is relevant to the meaning of Mitchell's statement that Kelly did the same thing to him at school. The appendix also states, erroneously, that "no further notice was taken at that visit," when in fact there was conversation between Laura Hadley and Mrs. Pierce. There are similar errors in the description of child 11C. The appendix states "first disclosure after Lou interview," when in fact the interview came to pass because of a statement she made spontaneously to her mother.

The appendix repeatedly claims that transcripts and records of interviews do not exist when, in fact, those records do exist. The appendix even claims there are "no documents" pertaining to Treacy's interviews with five children (2C, 6C, 8C, 14C, 15C) whose interviews with Treacy are excerpted and cited in a defense brief on appeal!

All of the errors that I have identified in the appendix are in the same direction: they all promote the witch-hunt narrative.

266. *State v. Michaels*, Concerned Scientists brief, 1.
267. Tom Lyon, "The New Wave in Children's Suggestibility Research: A Critique," *Cornell Law Review* (May 1999), 1086 ("By repeatedly quoting Goodman . . . the court clearly hoped to render its conclusions uncontroversial").
268. Tim O'Brien, "Defense Team Dumped in Wee Care Case; Counsel Switch on Eve of Argument Fuels Feud over Fees and Egos," *New Jersey Law Journal* (January 31, 1994), 3.
269. *State v. Michaels*, 136 N.J. 299, 642 A.2d 1372 (1994).
270. Diane C. Walsh, "Essex to Retry Michaels on Abuse Charges," *Star-Ledger* (July 16, 1993).
271. Diane C. Walsh, "Judge's Dismissal of Charges Ends 10-year Ordeal for Accused," *Star-Ledger* (December 3, 1994).
272. Tom Lyon identified and critiqued this line of research in "The New Wave in Children's Suggestibility Research."

Chapter Six

1. Lyon, "The New Wave of Suggestibility Research," 1004–1087.
2. *[Lucas] v. Fuster*, Case No. 84032827 (11th Judicial Circuit for Dade County, Florida). Deposition of Frank Fuster (October 31, 1985), tr. 279. Frank Fuster's last name is sometimes referred to Fuster Escalona (or Fuster-Escalona) in court documents. In case captions in this book, I will generally use Fuster.
3. State v. Fuster, Trial tr. 4144–4179.
4. Margaret Butler did the inspection. She had worked at the department for seven years; this was her first sexual abuse complaint. She did not interview any children, and the children who were there that day were not identified in her report. The visit was so cursory that she did not even realize the license tacked on the wall was for Frank Fuster's decorating business, not for the day care. Butler apparently later told Meznarich, "Due to the fact that the house was neat and clean, and everything seemed to be in order, the complaint had been unfounded." *State v. Fuster*, Meznarich deposition (Part I, January 25, 1985), tr. 148.
5. *State v. Fuster*, St. Lorenzo deposition (July 11, 1985), tr. 13.

6. St. Lorenzo deposition, tr. 13–16.
7. St. Lorenzo deposition, tr. 17.
8. St. Lorenzo deposition (July 11, 1985), tr. 19–22.
9. *State v. Fuster*, Deposition of Donna Meznarich (Part I, January 22, 1985), tr. 90.
10. Menoher deposition, *State v. Fuster* (July 18, 1985), 39.
11. Incident Report, Subject: Frank Fuster, Case No. 287537-E, Metro-Dade Police Dept., September 7, 1984, 4 (hereinafter Fuster Police Report).
12. Menoher's cooperation also waned over time. As it became clear that her behavior helped implicate the Arvida Corporation—because she had recommended the (illegal) babysitting service to Country Walk residents—Joanne Menoher denied referring parents to the babysitting service. When asked about Menoher in a civil deposition after the criminal case was over, prosecutor John Hogan said he could not answer the questions because there was an ongoing investigation of Menoher "in connection with a potential claim of perjury." Deposition of John Hogan, *Marks v. Fuster*, June 24, 1986, tr. 50–51. (No perjury charges were ever brought.)
13. Fuster Police Report, 20.
14. Fuster Police Report, 21.
15. Fuster Police Report, 20.
16. Miami Dade Police Department, Incident Report, October 1, 1984, No. 312747-E, 5.
17. Miami Dade Police Department, Incident Report, 5.
18. Meznarich deposition (Part I, January 22, 1985), tr. 165.
19. Fuster Police Report, 29–30; Meznarich deposition (Part I), tr. 168–170.
20. Meznarich deposition (Part I), tr. 174.
21. This case is discussed in Chapter Four, 174.
22. Hollingsworth, *Unspeakable Acts*, 52.
23. Hollingsworth, *Unspeakable Acts*, 54–66.
24. This is cited in Hollingsworth, *Unspeakable Acts*, 56. I arranged to have this videotape transcribed by a court reporter under the supervision of the court. This precise line appears at the top of page 28. Transcription of a Videotape Interview [with JPC], *State v. Fuster*, Case No. 84-19728 (Transcribed by Elaine Crandall, November 17, 2006).
25. Moreover, Dr. Roland Summit reviewed a copy of the same tape and testified about specific details in his testimony. Trial tr. 4746, lines 8–11.
26. Jane Daugherty, "Day Care Videotapes Released; Kids Describe Sex at Country Walk," *Miami Herald* (December 21, 1984), 1A.
27. The trial transcript contains an "inaudible" marking where the actual videotape seems to say "takes off clothes"; Trial tr. 2265 (line 7). That response fits what the interviewer then said: Takes off clothes?
28. Trial tr. 2249–2250, 2255–2260.
29. Trial tr. 2312.
30. Trial tr. 2944.
31. The other interview with Tammy was on September 10. She was extremely avoidant in that session, telling the interview directly "I don't want to talk about that." Later, when asked if she was scared to talk, the girl nodded affirmatively. But the conversation meanders many times, and when this interview was shown in court, the judge instructed that the tape be fast-forwarded four times.
32. Fuster Police report, 25. When her parents brought her in the next day to be interviewed by Assistant State Attorney Chris Rundle, Becky was "very withdrawn." They gave up trying to interview her in less than five minutes. The following week, on August 14, when Becky was seen at Jackson Memorial Hospital, she was so uncooperative that she refused to be examined.
33. Trial tr. 2447, 2449, 2475.
34. Trial tr. 2437, 2438.
35. "There's no pee-pee game," the girl says at one point. "I call it (inaudible) game," the transcript continues. Trial tr. 2440. It is impossible to know what to do with this answer without decoding the inaudible portion.
36. Trial tr. 2439.

37. Trial tr. 2369.
38. As Jan Hollingsworth described some other photos: "Posteriors, in fact, comprised a large portion of the Fusters' collection, many of them tightly framed by telephoto lens." One picture was a rear view of a woman at the Fusters' kitchen sink, alongside Fuster's son; "He had been posed lifting the back of the skirt to reveal her panties, which were heavily soiled with what appeared to be either menstruum or feces." Hollinsworth, *Unspeakable Acts*, 443.
39. Mary Jo Robinson and Thomas R. Oberhofer, "Identification of Pathogenic Neisseria Species with the RapID NH System." *Journal of Clinical Microbiology* (1983), 3, 400–404.
40. Meznarich deposition (Part II, January 23, 1985), 95.
41. Trial tr. 3468.
42. *Fuster v. Singletary*, Case no. 97-1369-Civ-LENARD. Affidavit of Maggie Bruck (February 2, 1999), para. 96.
43. Trial tr. 2902.
44. Trial tr. 2905.
45. Trial tr. 2910.
46. Trial tr. 3223.
47. Fuster Police report, 26.
48. The charge against Frank Fuster was supported by Jason's statement. MDPD Case No. 312759-E. The charge against Ileana was supported by Donald's mother's statement and by Donald's demonstration in 8/14 tape. Case No. 312752-E.
49. Trial tr. 989–90.
50. Trial tr. 1806.
51. Meznarich deposition (Part I, January 22, 1985), tr. 90.
52. Trial tr. 1374; Lee deposition, tr. 12–14.
53. Trial tr. 5061–62.
54. Trial tr. 1034.
55. Trial tr. 1035.
56. Trial tr. 994.
57. Trial tr. 1815.
58. Trial tr. 1656.
59. Trial tr. 1522–1524.
60. "She was dizzy. She had been drugged," Fuster's lawyer allowed, while arguing against her recollection of seeing Frank sexually abuse various children. Trial tr. 4993.
61. For example, Becky Taylor's mother described picking her up after her first day at the Fster and Becky was napping, which was unusual, because Becky hadn't napped since she was two and half. Darlene Taylor asked Ileana about the fact that Becky was napping. "She [Ileana] said Frank had played with her [Becky]". She tried to wake Becky up to leave, but couldn't wake her so Darlene carried her out. Deposition of Darlene Taylor, *State v. Fuster*, (February 7, 1985), 34–35.
62. Trial tr. 992–993.
63. Trial tr. 1102–1103.
64. Trial tr. 1403. She described two differing, equally disturbing, actions: "He would try to spread her legs apart and put his mouth on her vagina" and "He would try to pull her head towards his penis."
65. Hollingsworth, *Unspeakable Acts*, 444.
66. Trial tr. 1565–1566.
67. Trial tr. 991.
68. Trial tr. 2017.
69. Coleman deposition, tr. 78.
70. There were several other sessions videotaped in later months, well after the charges had been finalized; one was with Elmo Slade on March 12, 1985. His name does not appear anywhere else in the case; nor are the contents of this interview described in the trial record. The second was with Jason Cramer on April 9, 1985, after he had had a problem at school involving inappropriate sexualized play. His parents wanted "Joe" to talk with Jason about the incident and about sex education in general. This Cramer tape was later misrepresented on

television by Lee Coleman, the defense psychiatrist in the case. Coleman claimed the tape was "typical" of the investigative interviews in the case, and he shocked the daytime television audience of "People Are Talking" with the excerpt where Joseph Braga is explaining the concept of sexual response to the child. The content of this excerpt does not appear in the trial transcript because it was not one of the investigative interviews. Joseph Braga confirmed from contemporaneous notes that this brief meeting occurred on April 9, 1985, was at the request of Jason's parents, and had nothing to do with the investigation of the case (Braga interview, July 4, 2012.)

71. Hollingsworth, *Unspeakable Acts*, 491.

72. There had been an incident in the spring of 1984 where Noel called Becky "sexy." He also told Sally Leventhal in the spring of 1984 that she had "a nice pussy."

73. Trial tr. 3769.

74. Trial tr. 3770.

75. Trial tr. 3772, lines 19–24 (emphasis added).

76. Trial tr. 3805, line 4 to 3807, line 2.

77. Trial tr. 3851–2.

78. Trial tr. 4642, line 17 to 4643, line 11. The third, fourth, and fifth lines in this excerpt have been edited slightly to reflect what is apparent on the videotape of this interview. In the third line, the child said "cut your head off" not "cut off your head" as indicated in the transcription. In the fourth line, the interviewer said "Did he really cut off heads or pretend?" The transcription omits the word "really." In the fifth line, the child starts an answer "He was" and then seems to start the word "pointing" before saying "he put the knife to your neck." The court reporter, who transcribed while the tape was playing in court, (inaccurately) wrote "He was—he put some ice on a knife to your neck." That is what appears in the trial transcript. The corrcted version in the text connected to this footnote reflects the words heard on the videotape. This excerpt is described in a newspaper article and it was broadcast on the local news. Nery Ynclan, "Fusters Face New Charges," *Miami Herald* (March 29, 1985). The new broadcast proves that the transcribed version is inaccurate; the child did *not* make a confusing reference to ice. See, http://youtube/nAwE3jjmRS8.

79. Trial tr. 4648.

80. See especially Trial tr. 4650.

81. Trial tr. 4655, lines 3–25.

82. Hogan civil deposition, 29.

83. *Marks v. Fuster*, Case No. 84-42560 (11th Judicial Circuit for Dade County, Florida). Deposition of John Hogan (June 24, 1986), 30 (Hogan civil deposition).

84. Hogan civil deposition, 31.

85. Hollingsworth, *Unspeakable Acts*, 349–350.

86. All the quotes about this incident are from Hollingsworth, *Unspeakable Acts*, 350.

87. Hollingsworth, *Unspeakable Acts*, 365.

88. See text accompanying footnote 182.

89. Summit, "The Child Sexual Abuse Accommodation Syndrome."

90. The other three witnesses for the state were a social worker and two police officers.

91. *State v. Fuster*, Martha Gonzales Fuster deposition (August 8, 1985), tr. 57.

92. The other children who were named in individual charges were Noel Fuster, Joshua Cramer, and Tom Leventhal. The charges related to Leventhal were dropped at the conclusion of the state's case because Jason Cramer, who had described Tom's abuse in earlier interviews, did not mention those statements in his testimony at trial. Donald Menninger was the other child who most clearly substantiated the charges involving Leventhal, but his parents were no longer willing to assist the prosecution. Jason Cramer provided extensive evidence, however, concerning the abuse of his younger brother, Joshua. And the charges involving Noel were substantiated through the testimony of several children and through the positive STD test.

93. Donald Menninger, Jr. (the father) denied he told his wife not to say anything about it, and says "she did not" give anyone such instructions either. *[Lucas] v. Fuster* deposition, February 12, 1985, tr. 118. But his wife testified six months earlier, "I felt really bad that it would end up being very slanderous statement about someone, so, I said [to Betsy Leventhal], 'I just

don't want it spread around.'" *State v. Fuster*, deposition. July 23, 1985, tr. 20. Betsy Leventhal's testimony at the time matches this description.

> Q: Did they ask you not to pass this information along?
> A: Yes, they did.
> Q: Did you promise that you wouldn't?
> A: Yes, I did.
> Q: But you did?
> A: Yes, I did.

State v. Fuster, Betsy Leventhal deposition. July 10, 1985. tr. 29.

94. Trial tr. 4157.
95. Trial tr. 4165 ("really bad"); tr. 4174 ("yes, I do").
96. Hollingsworth provides a long excerpt from the deposition, in which Underwager allowed that he did not know the average number of words a three-year-old child might be expected to understand, he did not know any studies on the matter, and he could not say anything "right now" about the cognitive development that takes place between and three and four years of age. Hollingsworth, *Unspeakable Acts*, 393–395.
97. Coleman testified he could remember "two or three patients" in the course of his twenty-year professional career who were victims of child sexual abuse. None of those cases involved children under the age of eight. He could not remember if he had treated any victims of child sexual abuse in the last five years (tr. 4207, lines 3–16). Coleman also testified that he had developed "a special interest" in how children were interviewed in sexual abuse cases "about 9 or 10 months ago" (tr. 4208).
98. *State v. Fuster*, Coleman deposition (August 12, 1985), tr. 38.
99. Trial tr. 4381.
100. *State v. Fuster*, September 24, 1985, tr. 75.
101. Trial tr. 4256.
102. Trial tr. 4243, line 15.
103. Trial tr. 4284.
104. Trial tr. 4410.
105. Trail tr. 4270.
106. Trial tr. 4424.
107. Trial tr. 4667 ("I advised him yesterday that the only witness he could compel me to call is him and that's what I did").
108. Trial tr. 4465, lines 16–18.
109. See e.g., 4577 ("That was not a business." "You keep calling it a babysitting service. You want to make it sound like a daycare center, which it wasn't.").
110. Trial tr. 4596–4599. ("since I have the blood already," tr. 4596, line 5; "suffered a big pain" on my penis, tr. 4597, lines 21–23; "I did not go there for that reason" tr. 4598, line 4).
111. The doctor was apparently a family friend of Fuster's and accordingly the state was worried he might slant his testimony accordingly. There are indications that Fuster's STD test came back "borderline," and the defense was apparently worried this information would be incriminating.
112. Trial tr. 4812, lines 7–9 (Becky), and line 13 (Tammy).
113. Trial tr. 4817.
114. Messerschmidt, A., and M. Ducassi. "Wife: Fuster Beat Me Soon After We Met," *Miami Herald* (September 13, 1985), 1B.
115. Trial tr. 4820, line 12.
116. Trial tr. 4822, lines 15–17.
117. Trial tr. 4835, lines 1–4.
118. Trial tr. 4852, lines 12–20.
119. Trial tr. 4853, lines 19–20.
120. Trial tr. 4864 (snake).
121. *[Mayor] v. Fuster*, Case No. 84-42560, 11th Judicial Circuit, Dade County, Florida, Deposition of Dan Casey (June 24, 1986), tr. 95.

122. *Fuster-Escalona v. McDonough*, No. 06-6916, U.S. Supreme Court. Cert. denied, 549 U.S. 1213, 127 S. Ct. 1251 (February 20, 2007).
123. Charlier and Downing, "Patterns Emerge," 43.
124. Nathan, "The Making of a Modern Witch Trial," 20.
125. Debbie Nathan, "Satanism and Child Molestation: Construction the Ritual Abuse Scare," in James Richardson, Joel Best, and David G. Bromley, eds. *The Satanism Scare* (New York: Aldine de Gruyer, 1991), 88–89, fn. 1.
126. Debbie Nathan and Steve Almond, "Reno Reconsidered," *Miami New Times* (March 3–9, 1993).
127. *Fuster-Escalona v. Singletary*, Report of Magistrate Judge Charlene H. Sorrentino (March 8, 2002, hereinafter Magistrate Report).
128. Trial tr. 4597.
129. Trial tr. 4595.
130. Robinson and Oberhofer, "Identification of Pathogenic Neisseria Species," Table 1.
131. Robinson and Oberhofer, "Identification of Pathogenic Neisseria Species," 404.
132. Nathan and Almond, "Reno Reconsidered"; Nathan and Snedeker, *Satan's Silence*, 195.
133. Whittington, W. L. H., Rice, R. J., Biddle, J. M., and Knapp, J. S., "Incorrect Identification of Neisseria Gonorrhoeae from Infants and Children," *Pediatric Injections Disease Journal*, 7(1): 3–10.
134. Whittington et al., "Incorrect Identification," 8.
135. *State v. Fuster*, Deposition of Freda Burstyn (July 24, 185), tr. 11.
136. The "unreliable test myth" has mysteriously been given a boost by Wil Whittington, the lead author of the CDC article (who has since left the CDC). But Whittington's declaration is misleading, at best. It relies on, and does not take issue with, the same 1983 article that concluded the RapID/NH test was 99.38 percent accurate.
137. Cockburn, "Reno's Victim," *Nation* (September 20, 1993), 272.
138. The first session with Noel was largely rapport building. There were pages and pages of discussion of *Star Wars* and *Cat in the Hat*. Noel then drew a spaceship. Later he drew a Super-Noel. Super-Noel, as Hollingsworth described it, "could do things that little Noel could not. Like protect himself." The drawing activities continued for a long time without any pointed interviewing. One of the few revealing passages in this interview occurred, ironically, immediately after Noel said, "Nothing concerns me." Then the following exchange ensues:

> LB: Do you know what has been happening?
> NF: Happening?
> LB: Yes, since, you know, where your dad is.
> NF: In jail.
> LB: Do you know why?
> NF: (Inaudible.)
> LB: Do you know why?
> NF: Somebody put a lie on him.
> LB: (Inaudible.)
> JB: Who told you that, that somebody put a lie on your dad?
> NF: My mom. The whole car's apart.
> JB: Now, the hard part is putting the car back together (inaudible).
> NF: It's easy. See this?
> JB: Yes.
> NF: That little hole?
> JB: Yes?
> NF: This has to go over those two holes, okay, and go inside. You're right it's hard.
> JB: Has your mom ever (inaudible).
> NF: No.
> JB: Has your dad ever hit you?
> NF: Some days.

139. *N. G. v. Arvida Corp.*, Case No. 91-35656 (11th Circuit for Dade County, Florida), Deposition of N.F.G. (October 29, 1992), tr. 48.
140. Deposition of N.F.G., tr. 48–49.
141. Deposition of N.F.G, tr. 59.
142. Deposition of N.F.G., tr. 47, 60, 73, 125.
143. Some political activists who have embraced Noel Fuster's "retraction" decided to include him as a speaker at the so-called Day of Contrition, an event designed to link cases like Country Walk to the Salem witch trials. Given the opportunity to provide a clear retraction to an audience that wanted to hear one, Noel Fuster did not deliver. Here is a complete, verbatim transcription of Noel Fuster's rambling, equivocating statement:

> Hello. My name is Noel Fuster. I don't have the knowledge or the know-how to opt really for any good solutions or anything like that, but I can offer one thing, and that's experience. My experience has shown me that a lot of times doctors do have the way of knowing what's wrong. One example, me, they found a virus or some type of sickness, and it could have been any number of things. I could have had a cold, a sore throat, or anything, but within really human error, or I don't know exactly what happened, I was suddenly diagnosed with gonorrhea. I got a multitude of shots. I could go all into that explanation, but it's just I feel if you have a solution, scientists, let's have an answer, but people will end up finding a way to kind of mess that up somehow, you know, and the way, I guess, our emotions carry us or what-not, I think it's really important to try to get the message out to people, and we can find a way, but even if we had the way of finding out, would we still get the answer out there and would the right things be done? People most of the time do the right things that need to be done, but I'm glad there's so much care and so much, you know, want to do something, and something needs to be done, something needs to be done. Noel Fuster, Salem Day of Contrition (January 13, 1997, Forum B), [transcription], tr. 77.

144. Debbie Nathan, "Janet Reno has a Child Care Skeleton," *Capital Times* (February 17, 1993), 9A.
145. Jane Daugherty, "Baby Sitters' Sexual Abuse Trial Is Delayed," *Miami Herald* (June 3, 1985), 3B.
146. Rael Jean Isaac, "Abusive Justice: Janet Reno's Dirty Secret," *National Review* (June 30, 1997), 31–35, 32; Debbie Nathan, "Revisiting Country Walk," *Issues in Child Abuse Accusations* (Winter 1993) 5(1): 1–11, 5 (kept nude); Robert Rosenthal, "Janet Reno's Child Abuse" (May 1996), 27–37 35 (drugged).
147. *State v. Fuster*, Dinerstein statement, 4–5.
148. First, Dinerstein lost his private investigator's license years before making his claims about Ileana Fuster. See Complaint (Information Report), Bureau of Regulation and Enforcement. Report of Investigator Tom Murray (stamped March 17, 1989, indicating that "Mr. Dinerstein has been uncooperative in the past with both the Miami Regional Office and the West Palm Beach Office"). See also Final Order, *Department of State v. Stephen M. Dinerstein, Linda Dinerstein, Classic Detective Agency* (Case No. C89-264). It is unclear from these public records why his license was revoked. Dinerstein's credibility was also damaged early in the Country Walk case when his "sworn statement" that Dr. Joseph Braga was an impostor proved to be completely false.
149. Motion to Prohibit Cruel and Unusual Pre-trial Detention, *State v. Fuster*, (April 10, 1985).
150. On March 17, 1985, for example, she wrote: Well baby, I'm fine. I got up at 11:30 this morning, late lunch, then you wouldn't believe it but we had to wash our clothes in the shower ... the laundry was broken." The reflects the strongest objections she lodged at the time about conditions at the prison.
151. *State v. Fuster*, Shirley Blando deposition, (August 1, 1985), tr. 21, 38, 55.
152. Blando deposition, tr. 6, 11.
153. Rev. Tommy Watson, Correspondence to State Attorney's Office, Miami Dade County (August 28, 1985), 3.
154. *State v. Fuster*, Proceedings of August 22, 1985, tr. 7.

155. Messerschmidt and Ducassi, "Wife," 1B.
156. Nathan and Snedeker, *Satan's Silence*, 174. The quote is attributed to "telephone interview with author, August 1991." Ibid., 291, 68.
157. C. B. Mutter, Correspondence to the State Attorney's Office, Miami Dade County, about Ileana Fuster (November 7, 1985), 3.
158. Nathan and Snedeker, *Satan's Silence*, 175.
159. Nathan, "Revisiting Country Walk," 6; Nathan and Snedeker, *Satan's Silence*, 175, Rosenthal, "Janet Reno's Child Abuse," 36.
160. *State v. Fuster*, Proceedings, August 22, 1985, tr. 10.
161. *State v. Fuster*, Proceedings of August 22, 1985, tr. 5–8.
162. One of Ileana Flores's answers, for example, twice included the phrase "those things proba- bly happened"—but Cohen's follow-up question changed the subject away from "those things." There are also numerous instances in which in which Cohen interrupted an answer that did not appear to support Frank Fuster's cause. For example, at one point, Ileana Fuster said: "No, they just told me if I recognize him. And because I 'was so afraid of him I would break down. You know, even today I . . . .'" This "statement"—it cannot be called a deposition because there was no cross-examination—was reproduced in *Issues in Child Abuse Accusa- tions*, vol. 6, no. 4 (1994), 192–206. The interruption is on 204, "those things probably hap- pened" is on 195.
163. *State v. Fuster*, Prehearing Proffer, 5.
164. Rev. Tommy Watson's characterization was "they badgered her and badgered her." Manny Garcia, "Molester's Ex-wife Tells New Story," *Miami Herald* (March 21, 1995), 2B. Flores's letter says "I told the lawyers to stop bothering me." It also says she was "in a state of total confusion" when Arthur Cohen arrived "unannounced into my life." The letter ends with this paragraph: "I am sorry for the embarrassment that I may have cause to anyone that try to help me in time past. I do not wish to give any other deposition that could be different than the one given 10 years ago. Again, Frank Fuster did horrible things to me and I know he did the same to the children, he deserves to be where he is now. I don't want to be a victim any- more and I wish his attorneys to leave me alone please." Letter of March 18, 1995 "To whom it may concern," signed by Ileana Flores.
165. *State v. Fuster*, Watson deposition (May 9, 1995), tr. 32–33. This deposition is described in foonote 19 of the Report of the Magistrate Judge, *Fuster v. Singletary* (2002), 93.
166. "Did Daddy Do It?" transcript, 30.
167. Debbie Nathan, "Satanism and Child Molestation: Construction the Ritual Abuse Scare," in James Richardson, Joel Best, and David G. Bromley, eds. *The Satanism Scare* (New York: Aldine de Gruyer, 1991); Consultants on Religious Tolerance, "'Country Walk' case in Maimi [sic], FL." Written November 2000. Available at: http://www.religioustolerance. org/ra_fuste.htm# ("In our opinion, fondling did occur at Country Walk.") But they assert it was because of a cultural misunderstanding involving Ileana. The author is apparently un- aware that the cultural practice that would supposedly excuse sexual fondling would *not* be acceptable with girls. See, Elena Padilla, *Up from Puerto Rico* (Columbia Univerity Press, 1958), 186.
168. "Did Daddy Do It?" 10.
169. "Did Daddy Do It?" 10.
170. Pendergrast, *Victims of Memory*, 372.
171. In all of Fuster's accounts, he bears no responsibility for his actions, even though he pleaded guilty to First Degree Manslaughter. In 1982, Fuster told Dr. Seth Krieger that:

> The other man pulled a gun, threatened him, and then started to leave the scene. Mr. Escalona [Fuster] grabbed a rifle he had within reach, and pointed it at the other man, trying to "make an arrest." The other man yanked on the barrel of the gun, it went off, and he died of the resulting wound.

Note how Fuster could not bring himself to say that he shot his own rifle. Yet witnesses, in- cluding the off-duty police officer, all agree that Fuster shot an unarmed man in cold blood. Dr. Krieger concluded that Mr. Fuster "developed a lifestyle and world view characterized by compulsive and paranoid features." Those features were borne out in the Country Walk case, where Fuster argued that all of the parents had conspired against him, even including those who did not bring civil suits or have children in the criminal case.

When Fuster testified in the Country Walk case, his misstatements about the manslaughter case became more fantastic. Fuster claimed under oath "when I was twenty years old, couple of months before becoming a New York City police officer, I'm accused of being a murderer." But Fuster was not in training to become a New York police officer. Instead, he was working at the time as a salesman for the Minx Fur Company. Fuster also blamed his conviction on the District Attorney. "The office of the district attorney induced perjury," Fuster asserted, professing that he was "free of guilt." Fuster made the absurd claim that the off-duty policeman in the case "set him up." He also claimed that the man he killed was "armed" and shot first, neither of which were borne out by the evidence at the scene. Fuster's refusal to accept any blame for this death is consistent with the conclusion of his parole assessment upon release from New York:

> Fuster is a tall, well-built man who is almost a compulsive talker. He goes into great details about everything that he discusses and much of the information that he provides differs from that available in the Probation Report. It does not appear that he accepts full responsibility for killing the victim of the instant crime, indicating that the individual threatened him with a weapon and the rifle that the subject had discharged it when it was grabbed by the victim. It does not appear that he has a great deal of remorse over the fact that he killed a man." [New York] Institutional Record–Parole. (HS. No. 1056-627) D: 6/10/70; T: 7/15/70, 5.

When Frank Fuster was standing before the judge in his probation violation hearing in August 1985, he referred to Mr. Isenbek's death by rifle shots as "a crime that did not take place." When *Frontline* interviewed Frank Fuster in prison in 2001, he described the shooting as "an accident."

172. Michael Kirk also erroneously claimed that the conviction was for "involuntary manslaughter." Michael Kirk and Peter J. Boyer, "Did Daddy Do It," *Frontline* (April 2002).
173. Deposition of Detective Bradley Marshall, *State v. Fuster*, No. 81-21904 (December 17, 1981), 35.
174. Deposition of Detective Marshall, 35.
175. He later blamed his lawyer for "not letting him take the stand." But Fuster could have done so if he desired, as he acknowledged in a statement at his probation violation hearing. Fuster's exact words were that his lawyer told him "If you want to testify you got to sign documents for me, release, blah, blah." The release was to indicate that his lawyer advised against such an action. Fuster chose not to sign the release. He apparently decided he would rather claim later he had wanted to testify than actually testify at the time.
176. Hollingsworth, *Unspeakable Acts*, 208.
177. *State v. Fuster*, Parole Violation Hearing, August 13, 1984, tr., 140, 19–21.
178. Pendergrast asserts in his book, *Victims of Memory*, that Fuster was wrongfully convicted of the charge—apparently on the basis of a telephone interview he had with Fuster. 372.
179. Deposition of Detective Bradley Marshall, December 17, 1981, 38–39.
180. The young woman's mother reported the alleged rape, but the prosecution did not go forward. The police suspected that a similar kind of incident might have precipitated the gunshot wound Frank Fuster received in a confrontation at his workplace.
181. Deposition of Martha Gonzales Fuster, *State v. Fuster*, (August 8, 1985), tr. 58–60 ("he told me that he would kill me," "if I ever took Noel away," "he would kill me if I took Noel," "afraid of him.")
182. Shirley Blando, the assistant chaplain who spent the most time with Ileana, verifies that in June—two months before her lawyer called in the psychologists—"she said that he had forced sex on her." Deposition of Shirley Blando, August 1, 1985, tr. 76. "The first time she talked about it with me and Reverend Watson, it was an unbelievable struggle," Blando continued (tr. 78). Jo Anne Berg, a psychiatric nurse, visited Ileana four times during this period.

She indicated in a pre-trial deposition that "Ileana shared with her mother—for the first time—her initial contact with Frank, when she was raped." The transcript continues:

> Question: Was that her word, "raped"?
> Answer: Yes. (Deposition of Jo Ann Berg, August 1, 1985, 25.)

183. Ceci and Bruck, "Suggestibility of the Child Witness," 113, 3.
184. Ceci and Bruck, *Jeopardy in the Courtroom*, 27.
185. Ceci and Bruck, *Jeopardy in the Courtroom*, 15. (They used the word *interweaved* in 1993 and *interleaved* in 1995.)
186. The only shark reference in the interviews later transcribed by Professor Wood comes from an interview with a child who was not involved in the trial and who was clearly referring to a stuffed animal in the interview room (Interview [Wood's transcription] 082784C1, 27-8). The exchange begins when the boy says to the interviewer "you know what?" The following ensues:

> Q: What?
> A: I'm scared of that shark.
> Q: Are you really?
> A: Yeah.
> Q: Yeah? You wanna go and look at it closely 'cuz its not scary? Not really. Its kinda friendlly. Come here, let me show you from this angle. Give me your hand.
> A: No.
> Q: Okay. Well, look, let me show you. See? Its not really a shark. See its kinda friendly. Its got a nice eye, see, and its got a fin here.
> A: Yeah., but it looks like a . . .
> Q: Its just kinda nice. Here. You can touch it, it won't hurt. Yeah.
> A: Ooo, like a real fish!
> Q: Is it like a real fish?
> A: Yes, but its not.

What is obvious from this exchange is that the child is referring to a stuffed animal in the interview room, not to a real shark. Moreover, he clearly knows the difference between the two (it's *like* a real fish, "but its not").

187. Interview 01785C1 [Wood's transcription], 5-7. This videotape was transcribed into the trial record on pages 4642-4643. The transcription at trial contains several errors which are detailed in fn. 78 of this chapter.
188. Ceci and Bruck, "Suggestibility of the Child Witness," 423, fn. 5. The article refers to the Fusters as the "Fursters" throughout.
189. Bruck affidavit, para. 150, p. 52.
190. Bruck affidavit, para. 9, p. 4.
191. They refer to their case studies as "brief summaries" and "sketches." Ceci and Bruck, *Jeopardy in the Courtroom*, 7, 18. They allow that their analysis is "not based on a quantitative analysis of all of the interviews" (82).
192. There were a handful of additional interviews after the second indictment was filed; the defense agreed they were irrelevant to the child suggestibility defense.
193. The excerpts were identified through the painstaking process of looking through the trial transcripts of the interviews for passages that match the excerpts in the book.
194. (1) excerpt on 112, identified as J.L., can be found at testimony of J.L., tr. 2905; (2) excerpt on 122-123, identified as "child," can be found at testimony of J.L., tr. 4653-4654; (3) excerpt on 136 identified as "child," can be found at testimony of J.L., tr. 2942; and (4) excerpt on 147, identified as "child," can be found at testimony of J.L., tr. 4663-4664.
195. Ceci and Bruck, *Jeopardy in the Courtroom*, 148.
196. Ceci and Bruck, *Jeopardy in the Courtroom*, 98.
197. Bruck affidavit, para. 18.
198. Bruck affidavit, para. 96.

199. Noel denied sexual abuse in his initial interview, but he acknowledged serious physical abuse in the same interview.

200. "There's no pee pee game," she told the interviewer. "I call it (inaudible) game." This seems to be an acknowledgment of some sort, but obviously it is impossible to know without ascertaining what the court reporter found inaudible.

201. Trial tr. 1815.

202. Deposition of Dan Casey, tr. 59–60.

203. Neither of the Menninger interviews is mentioned in para. 5 of Bruck's 1999 affidavit in Fuster's federal habeas petition, which details, in Bruck's words, the materials "sent for my review" by counsel, Robert Rosenthal.

204. Trial tr. 1981–1982.

205. Bruck affidavit, 83: "At the end of JC's interview on August 10, 1984, the Bragas gave JC a bag of toys and told him there were a whole bunch of games in the bag. (9/12/85, 198–199). JC returned to the Bragas three days later, having done a lot more talking in the meantime. (9/13/85, 182)."

206. Trial tr. 2375, lines 11–15.

207. *State v. Fuster*, Affidavit of Stephen M. Dinerstein, filed February 6, 1985 ("confirming" that "the real" Joseph Braga is dead).

208. Rael Jean Isaac, "Abusive Justice," *National Review* (June 30, 1997).

209. Robert Rosenthal, "Janet Reno's Child Abuse," *Penthouse* (May 1996).

210. Laurie Davis Braga, "Development and Evaluation of a Test Analysis System for Describing Intra-Child Variables in Learning Disabled Preschool Children," unpublished dissertation, Northwestern University, August 1972.

211. Correspondence from Patricia Green, investigator, Office of Ethics, American Psychological Association to Laurie Davis Braga, Ph.D., October 13, 1993.

212. Nathan informed the APA that she had "no personal interest in filing a complaint" and she specifically declined to do so, while noting that she assumed the APA "would have its own interest" in taking any appropriate disciplinary action. Correspondence from Debbie Nathan to Stanley E. Jones, director, Office of Ethics, American Psychological Association. The letter is dated "March 29, 1992" by Nathan, but the year is in error. The letter states it is in response to correspondence from Jones on March 23, 1993, and the Nathan response was stamped as received by APA on April 1, 1993.

213. Nathan, who lived in El Paso at the time, has since acknowledged that she regularly met with James Wood during this time.

214. Section 8.04 of the code [in 1992] provided: "When a psychologist believes that there may have been an ethical violation by another psychologist, they attempt to resolve the issue by bringing it to the attention of that individual. . . ."

215. Ethics Complaint Form [against Laurie Braga], American Psychological Association. Signed by James Wood on February 15, 1995.

216. The telephone number matched the 1995 El Paso telephone book listing for Deborah Nathan. The address in the phone book matches the return address Nathan listed in the letter she sent to the APA in 1993.

217. Jane Daugherty, "County Walk Case Spotlights Psychologist Couple," *Miami Herald* (August 12, 1985), B1.

218. Rosenthal, "Janet Reno's Child Abuse," *Penthouse*, 30.

219. Jay Ducassi, "State Is Dropping Child Abuse Case," *Miami Herald* (August 20, 1985), B1.
220. Patrick May, "Specialist Switches in Rape Case," *Miami Herald* (August 15, 1985), 2BR.

221. Boyer, Children of Waco, *New Yorker* (May 15, 1995), 44.

222. Coleman testimony, Trial tr. 4410.

223. Mark D. Everson, "Understanding Bizarre, Improbable, and Fantastic Elements in Children's Accounts of Abuse," *Child Maltreatment* (May 1997): 134–150.

224. See text accompanying footnotes 212–217.

225. *Fuster Escalona v. Singletary*, Petitioner's Reply Brief and Amended Petition for Habeas Corpus, 3.

226. Report of Magistrate Judge, *Fuster v. Singletary*, Case No. 97-1369-Civ-LENARD (March 8, 2002), slip opinion, 93.

227. Report of Magistrate Judge, 93.
228. Report of Magistrate Judge, 70.
229. Initial Brief for Petitioner Appellant, 4.

Conclusion II

1. Stephen J. Ceci, "Some Overarching Issues in the Children's Suggestibility Debate," ch. 1 in John Doris, ed., *The Suggestibility of Children's Recollections: Implications for Eyewitness Testimony* (American Psychological Association 1991), 1. See also, Tori DeAngelsi, "Controversy Marks Child Witness Meeting,"*APA Monitor* (August 1989): 1, 8–9.
2. Liz Hunt, "Psychologists Divided on Children's Testimony," *Washington Post* (July 26, 1991), A3.
3. I obtained unfettered access to the transcript and related materials after signing an agreement, verified by the Institutional Review Board at my university, that I would never disclose the names of the children in the case. The agreement honored the spirit of the protective order and of the decision in *In the Matter of Application of VV Publishing Co.*, 120 N.J. 508; 577 A.2d 412 (1990).
4. Ceci and Bruck, "Child Witnesses," 2.
5. The term is Ceci and Bruck's. It is not clear whether they consider any inquiry by a parent to qualify as an "interview," but there is no doubt that parents exercised considerable influence in how the McMartin case evolved.
6. There are no citations or footnotes in those paragraphs save a final footnote attributed to a "close observer of the trial." I asked Professor Bruck to clarify the nature of this source. She replied that she could not remember., and promised to follow up on this question and several others; she did not respond to repeated efforts for a substantive response after the interview in October 2009.

Chapter Seven

1. Investigative Staff of the Boston Globe, *Betrayal: The Crisis in the Catholic Church* (Back Bay Books, 2002), 23; Walter V. Robinson, "$20m Accord Seen in Geoghan Cases," *Boston Globe* (March 5, 2002), A1.
2. Investigative Staff of the Boston Globe, *Betrayal: The Crisis in the Catholic Church* (Back Bay Books, 2002), 120.
3. Frank Bruni and Laurie Goodstein, "Rome Withholding Endorsement of U.S. Abuse Plan," *New York Times* (October 18, 2002); Joan Rivera, Bishops to Revisit Policy on Sex Abuse," *Baltimore Sun* (November 11, 2002).
4. See generally Jason Berry, *Lead Us Not Into Temptation: Catholic Priests and the Sexual Abuse of Children* (Doubleday, 1992).
5. Investigative Staff of the Boston Globe, *Betrayal*, 6.
6. Investigative Staff of the Boston Globe, *Betrayal*, 7.
7. Howard Bloom, Richard Winton, and Alan Zarembo, "Accused Teacher Drew Sheriff's Scrutiny in '94," *Los Angeles Times* (February 2, 10212), AA1.
8. Jason Kandel, "Telfair Elementary Teacher Sentenced in Sex Abuse Case," NBCLA.com (Thursday, September 20, 2012).
9. Richard Krueger, "The New American Witch Hunt,"*Los Angeles Times* (March 11, 2007), M1.
10. Donna Schram and Cheryl Milloy, "Sexually Violent Predators and Civil Commitment," Washington State Institute for Public Policy (February 1998).
11. Robert Barnoski, "Sex Offender Sentencing in Washington State: Measuring Recidivism," Washington State Institute for Public Policy (August 2005).
12. "Sex Offender Sentencing in Washington State."
13. http://www.meganslaw.ca.gov/ (visited September 30, 2011).
14. A 1996 study into the success of Washington's notification laws revealed that 3.5 percent of sex offenders, subject to notification laws, had been harassed by the public (Scott Matson and Roxanne Lieb, "Community Notification in Washington State: 1996 Survey of Law

Enforcement," Washington State Institute for Public Policy, November 1996). But there have been a few terrible cases of vigilantism, including a double murder.

15. Richard Tewksbury, "Policy Implications of Sex Offender Residence Restrictions," *Criminology & Public Policy* (May 2011) 10(2).

16. Monica Davey and Abby Goodnough, "Doubts Rise as States Hold Sex Offenders After Prison," *New York Times* (March 4, 2007), 1.

17. A very recent exception is Rachel Aviv's article in the *New Yorker*, which highlights someone whose main offenses involved child pornography and has been subject to civil confinement in Minnesota. Rachel Aviv, "The Science of Sex Abuse," *The New Yorker* (January 14, 2013). But Aviv plays down the defendant's guilty plea for enticing a child, focusing instead on the child pornography charges. Court records indicate that the defendant —whose identity Aviv chose to shield—"talked specifically with 'Sarah,' the fourteen-year-old, about engaging in sexual acts together" before driving to an agreed meeting place. He had "lingerie and sex toys" with him when he was arrested approaching two undercover officers. Findings of Fact, Conclusions of Law, and Order for Judgment, *U.S. v. Volungus*, Civil Action No. 07-12060-GAO (U.S. District Court, District of Massachusetts) March 8, 2012, 4. In his ruling, Judge George A. O'Toole noted that it was "uncontested" that Volungus had attempted "to meet what he thought was a fourteen-year-old girl for the purposes of having sex with her." 12.

18. Senator Tom Coburn introduced an amendment: "To reduce the cost of providing federally funded prescription drugs by eliminating fraudulent payments and prohibiting coverage of Viagra for child molesters and rapists and for drugs intended to induce abortion." This was intended to force supporters of the Obama Administration, whose plan would treat all Americans the same, to have to cast a vote that would be portrayed as "Viagra for child molesters." Supporters of the president's bill were later subjected to that charge, which was rated as false by Politifact.com (October 26, 2010). For another example of these misleading tactics, see Politifact column, "Cicilline 'argued against Megan's Law and voted against mandatory registration of sex offenders'" *Providence Journal* (October 27, 2010) (Ruled "mostly false").

19. Chrysanthi S. Leon, *Sex Fiends, Perverts, and Pedophiles: Understanding Sex Crime Policy in America* (NYU Press, 2011).

20. Ross E. Cheit and Erica Goldschmidt, "Child Molesters in the Criminal Justice System: A Comprehensive Case-Flow Analysis of the Rhode Island Docket (1985–1993)," *New England Journal on Criminal and Confinement* (1997) 23(2), 267–301.

21. Theodore Cross et. al., "Prosecution of Child Abuse: A Meta-Analysis of Rates and Criminal Justice Decisions," *Trauma, Violence & Abuse* (October 2003), 323, 333.

22. Mary Hargrove and Susan Roth, "Preying on Pupils,"*Arkansas Democrat-Gazette* (September 8, 1996).

23. Amicus Curiae Brief for the New Jersey Council of Child and Adolescent Psychiatry in *State v. J.Q.*, 130 N.J. 554; 617 A.2d 1196 (New Jersey Supreme Court, 1993).

24. *Steven F. v. Anaheim Union High School District*, 112 Cal. App. 4th 904; 6 Cal. Rptr. 3d 105 (2003).

25. "More Guidance for Teachers," Editorial, *Los Angeles Times* (November 11, 2003), B12.

26. *People v. Shumate*, Reporter's Transcript on Appeal, Vol. II, tr. 564 (line 28)–565 (line 1); testimony of Jill Paddack, first-grade teacher on yard duty on February 2, 1994.

27. *People v. Shumate*, Probation Officer's Report and Recommendation, Alameda County Superior Court (August 17, 1995), 11.

28. Handwritten letter to Lesley Pankopf (Deputy Probation Officer) dated March 28, 1995. Name redacted. Attached to *People v. Shumate* Probation Officer's Report and Recommendation.

29. *People v. Shumate*, Appellant's Opening Brief, Court of Appeals of the State of California, First Appellate District, Division Two (November 4, 1996); Michael Snedeker co-counsel for the defendant.

30. *People v. Shumate*, Reporter's Transcript on Appeal, Vol. IX, tr. 2298.

31. *People v. Shumate*, Reporter's Transcript on Appeal, Vol. VI, tr. 1390 (lines 24–26). He also testified that Shumate told him "he got involved with one of his foster kids, and his wife found out. And they sent the foster kid away" (tr. 1391).

32. Elaine Herscher, "Molest Sentence May Be Delayed," *San Francisco Chronicle* (August 17, 1995), A21.

33. Matt Gryta, "Man Pleads Guilty to Molestation; Ex-Officer Gets Jail for Abusing Boys," *Buffalo News* (January 9, 1993): 4.

34. Carol Hopkins, Salem Day of Contrition (January 14, 1997) [transcription], tr. 52.

35. There is no appellate decision in this case because Ferrara pleaded guilty.

36. Mark Pendergrast, *Victims of Memory*, 496.

37. Dr. Young testified "that B.L.'s physical condition was consistent with a history of rectal penetration, and that the best explanation for the physical condition of all three boys was that they had been victims of sexual abuse." *State v. Lawton*, 164 Vt. 179; 667 A.2d 50; 1995 LEXIS 88 (1995), 182, 54.

38. *State v. Lawton*, Trial tr. 139.

39. *State v. Lawton*, Trial tr. 142.

40. This evidence came in through the testimony of Mark Williams, the mother's counselor. Williams testified that when the mother told him this story (and one other) he became convinced she had an obligation to report the matter to child protective services (*State v. Lawton*, Trial transcript, tr. 222–223). This is how the case in Vermont began. Since the defendant's theory of the case blamed the therapist in part, there is considerable irony in the fact that the defendant objected to this testimony. As the state pointed out in its brief, the defense opened the door to this testimony through the theory of the case it advanced at trial. Brief of Appellee, *State v. Lawton*, Vermont Supreme Court, Docket No. 93-098, 18–37.

41. *State v. Lawton*, 164 Vt. 179; 667 A.2d 50 (1995; "B.L.'s statement was not the product of repeated interviewing, nor was any evidence of coercion or manipulation present. Given the circumstances, the statement was trustworthy").

42. Asked when he first became aware of the abuse allegations, Lawton gave a misleading answer about "three mild accusations" contained in divorce papers. There were actually four allegations and, as the prosecutor apparently emphasized too much, they were not "mild"; they involved anal sex, and Lawton knew that.

43. *U.S. v. Bighead*, 128 F.3d 1329, 1332 (9th cir. 1997).

44. *U.S. v. Bighead*, 1338.

45. *U.S. v. Bighead*, 1336.

46. Thomas Sowell, "Legal Lynchings," *Forbes* (January 26, 1998).

47. Noonan noted that "being a victim has become a popular calling" and "those who have complained of such abuse are identified by their therapists as 'victims,' or, more dramatically, as 'survivors.'" *U.S. v. Bighead*, 1338.

48. Pendergrast, "The Case of Elsie Oscarson," http://ncrj.org/Oscarson/Oscarson.html.

49. Daniel Patrick Moynihan, "Defining Deviancy Down," *American Scholar* (Winter 1993).

50. Letter to the editor from Robert Rosenthal, *Wall Street Journal* (November 7, 2003), A11.

51. Report and recommendation, *Serrano v. Kirkpatrick*, Federal District Court for the Southern District of New York (06-CV-990), 2.

52. *State v. Weber*, 807 N.Y.S.2d 222, 25 A.D.3d 919 (2006).

53. Emily E. Smith, "Hillsboro Man, Convicted of Sex Abuse in 2006, Shortens Sentence with Plea Deal," *Oregonian* (September 2, 2010).

54. *State v. Carol M.D.*, 983 P.2d 1165 (Court of Appeals of Washington, Division Three, Panel Five, September 14, 1999). Robert Rosenthal was of counsel.

55. CBS *48 Hours* transcript (April 3, 1997), 18. Hopkins also told CBS News that she coached the girl for speeches before Congress and for a press conference by the Justice Committee, the organization Hopkins founded (19, 20). It is not clear why this unusual foster placement was approved, but the placement is particularly ironic in light of Hopkins's editorial favoring "the all too obvious recommendation that foster children should not be placed with a person who has a conflict of interest and is in a dual role." Carol Hopkins, "Wenatchee Case Demands Reform of Child-Protection System," *Seattle Post-Intelligencer* (March 4, 1998), A13. CBS News reported that Sam Doggett eventually ran away from Hopkins's home "with an unknown man in an unknown car" (21).

56. *State v. Carol M. D.*, 89 Wn. App. 77; 948 P.2d 837; 1997 Wash. App. LEXIS 2012 (December 9, 1997), 841–842. The court also concluded that the defendants should have been authorized funds to hire an expert on false memory. In discussing that claim, however, the court noted "there is evidence that M.D. [the youngest child] stated from the beginning that her parents had abused her" (844). The court also quoted from the Kelly Michaels case in New Jersey with approval and ordered a so-called taint hearing (845). The Supreme Court of Washington granted review and remanded the case in light of the *In Re the Dependency of A.E.P.*, 135 Wash.2d 208, 956 P.2d 297 (1998), a case in which the court *declined* to adopt taint hearings. *State v. Doggett*, 136 Wn. 2d 1019; 967 P.2d 548; 1998 Wash. LEXIS 782 (1998). The court of appeals subsequently withdrew the portion of its earlier opinion concerning taint hearings, and adhered to the decision to reverse the convictions on other grounds and remand the case for retrial. *State v. Carol M.D.*, 97 Wn.App. 355; 983 P.2d 1165; 1999 Wash. App. LEXIS 1840 (1999).

57. AP, "Judge Denies Family's Claim in Child Sex-Abuse Investigation," *The Columbian* (November 21, 2004): C4.

58. The interview in which this woman makes the admission from prison is contained in a local TV news story that can be viewed at http://youtu.be/Y2cSpKPY1XM.

59. Andrew Schneider, "Jury Rejects Wenatchee Suit; Verdict Jolts the Accused in Child Sex Cases; City and Police Are Absolved," *Seattle Post-Intelligencer* (June 30, 1998), A1.

60. Barber and Schneider, "Detective a Man Who Charmed," A7; "With Every Step, Rights Were Trampled."

61. Kathyrn Lyon, *Witch Hunt: A True Story of Social Hysteria and Abused Justice* (Avon, 1998).

62. Philip Terzian, "The Witchcraft Trials of the '80s," *Providence Journal* (May 31, 1995), A11.

63. Joe Strupp, "Molester Sentenced to 6 Years in Prison," *Press-Enterprise* (Riverside, California, November 21, 1998), B2.

64. Dave Hughes, "Man, 61, Admits Molesting Kids," *Arkansas Democrat-Gazette* (May 19, 2007).

65. Todd C. Frankel, "Town in 'Shocked Silence,' Ste. Genevieve Struggle with Report from Authorities That Trusted Man Molested 40 Children over 30 Years," *St. Louis Post-Dispatch* (April 6, 2007), A1.

66. Michele Mihalovich, "Man Accused of Molestations at Day Care Pleads Guilty to Lesser Charges," *Wenatchee World* (September 18, 2010). The lesser charge was third-degree assault of a child. The information about previous complaints was contained in an affidavit filed by a Child Protective Services investigator.

67. There are some states with a three-tier system that allows a middle category between substantiated and unsubstantiated, where there is evidence of abuse but not enough to "substantiate" the case—these are designated "indicated." Without the distinction, the "unsubstantiated" category lumps together everything from cases determined to be untrue to those where there was definite evidence, but not enough to "substantiate." A study of "unsubstantiated" cases reveals that many unsubstantiated reports involve either some form of maltreatment or preventive service needs appropriate to CPS intervention, and that using substantiation as a means of gauging the validity of a CPS referral is therefore intrinsically fallacious. Brett Drake, "Unraveling 'Unsubstantiated'," *Child Maltreatment* (August 1996) (1), 3, 261–271.

68. Delores D. Stroud, Sonja L. Martens, and Julia Barker, "Criminal Investigation of Child Sexual Abuse: A Comparison of Cases Referred to the Prosecutor to Those Not Referred," *Child Abuse & Neglect*, (2000), 24(5): 689–700.

69. Theodore P. Cross, Debra Whitcomb, and Edward DeVos, "Criminal Justice Outcomes of Prosecutions of Child Sexual Abuse: A Case-flow Analysis," *Child Abuse & Neglect* (1995), 19(12), 1431.

70. Ellen Gray, *Unequal Justice: The Prosecution of Child Sexual Abuse* (Free Press, 1993).

71. In Minnesota, there were no statistical indications that the age of the victim affected the likelihood of prosecution. In Wisconsin, cases involving very young children were approximately four times less likely to be referred for prosecution than cases in the middle age group (six to twelve). Tucker, "The Effect of Victim Age and Gender," 109.

72. Barbara Smith and Sharon Goretsky-Elstein, "The Prosecution of Child Sexual and Physical Abuse Cases: Final Report" (American Bar Association, 1993).

73. Tucker, "The Effect of Victim Age and Gender."

74. Bruck and Ceci, "Unveiling Four Common Misconceptions," *Current Directions in Psychological Science* (2004), 13(6), 229, 231.

75. Lyon and Pezdek, "From Post-Mortem to Preventive Medicine: Next Steps for Research on Child Witnesses," *Journal of Social Issues* (2006), 62(4), 833.

76. She proceeded to discuss the McMartin case and the Jordan, Minnesota, cases in some detail, blaming investigators for the lack of criminal convictions. Civia Tamarkin, "Investigative Issues in Ritual Abuse Cases, Part I," *Treating Abuse Today*, 4(4): 15. The two-part article was an edited and abridged version of an address to the Fifth Regional Conference on Abuse and Multiple Personality, June 1993, Alexandria, Virginia.

77. Correspondence from Debbie Nathan to Richard Harris, *Nightline*. October 2, 1996. Reproduced in FMSF-News email from Peter Freyd (October 12, 1996).

78. "A Child's Word," *Nightline*, ABC News (November 14, 1996). Transcript #4039-1, Koppel quote.

79. Complaint Affidavit, Broward County Police Department, Offense Report LL95-12-2769 November 5, 1996, 2.

80. Offense Incident Report, Sunrise Police Department, Report No. 94-17243 (includes physical evidence conveyed by Sandra Gibson, Nurse Practitioner).

81. Nat Hentoff, "Distorted Journalism," *Village Voice* (December 17, 1996), 22.

82. There were more than fifty stories in the Lexis/Nexis newspaper database about the case on December 1, 1996—two weeks before Hentoff's column was published—including one in his local newspaper. See Mireya Navarro, "Roses and Outrage at Funeral for 2 Young Girls," *New York Times* (November 13, 1996), A14.

83. Larry Welborn et. al., "Verdict in the Samanatha Runnion Killing: Guilty," *Orange County Register* (April 29, 2005), 1. See also Arlene Getz, Jennifer Barrett, and Geoffrey Gagnon, "The Top Stories of 2002," *Newsweek* (December 26, 2002).

84. Hopkins had served on a special grand jury in San Diego that criticized prosecutors, pediatricians, and child protective service workers for how they handled child sexual abuse cases. Although seldom noted when this report is mentioned, a grand jury the following year issued a report that criticized this report as exaggerated and inaccurate.

85. "Protesting Modern Witch Hunts," Press Release, January 14, 1997. Justice Committee, Carol Lamb Hopkins, executive director.

86. Richard Gardner, Salem Day of Contrition, Afternoon session (January 14, 1997) [transcription], 332, 361.

87. Jennifer Hoult, "The Evidentiary Admissibility of Parental Alienation Syndrome," *Children's Legal Rights Journal* (Spring 2006) 26(1).

88. "False memory syndrome" dismisses reports of sexual abuse by adults, generally blaming them on the therapist of the person making the accusation. Strangely, this syndrome is often claimed to exist solely on the basis of the denial of the person accused.

89. Ohme described himself as "the silent man behind the scenes who was going to change the CAPTA law." He said Dorothy Rabinowitz was going to write an article about him, but "I told her that I could not do it because it would blow our cover." Email correspondence from Herman W. Ohme to Earl Rogers, Subject: "Confidential, Please" (November 19, 1999). On a now-defunct website from an organization that called itself the Ohio Association of Responsible Mental Health Practices, Ohme described his involvement with this issue: "When the Republican Party took control of the U.S. House of Representatives in 1994, after 40 years as the Minority political party, I saw the opportunity to change the CAPTA laws (Mondale Act of 1974) which had been the root cause of the child sex abuse hysteria and false accusations. I had been an active member of the RNC (Republican National Committee) for years and had some voice with the new party in control. I enlisted the help of nationally known CAPTA experts, Richard Gardner, M.D., Carol Hopkins, San Diego Grand Jury Foreman, to testify before the U.S. House and Senate Committee's to overhaul the Mondale Act of 1974. Our team was successful in correcting some of the worst features of the old CAPTA law but were blocked from deleting the 'mandatory reporting' feature." WWW. LTECH.NET/OHIOARMHP (accessed April 5, 2002).

90. Eileen McNamara, "Hardly a Case of Persecution," *Boston Globe* (January 15, 1997), B1.

91. See e.g., "Complaint to Boston Globe for McCarthyite Smear," http://mysite.verizon.net/vzex11z4/globsmer.html; Alexander Cockburn, "Our Little Secret," *Counter-Punch* (May 1-15, 1997).

92. Voluntary Statement of Mark Glazer, Somerset County Prosecutor's Office, August 25, 1995. 7.

93. Voluntary Statement of Tyler Glazer, Somerset County Prosecutor's Office, August 25, 1995, 8(19).

94. Under the Michaels decision, the defendant must make a showing of "some evidence" that the victim's statements were the product of "suggestive or coercive interview techniques." Then the burden shifts to the state to prove the reliability of the statements by "clear and convincing evidence."

95. *New Jersey v. Marzolf*, Michaels Hearing, Somerset County Superior Court, Indictment No. 96-01-0055 (August 12, 1997), tr. 12, 18, 109.

96. *New Jersey v. Marzolf*, Michaels Hearing (August 12, 1997), tr. 14, 93.

97. *New Jersey v. Marzolf*, Michaels Hearing (August 12, 1997), tr. 37–38.

98. *New Jersey v. Marzolf*, Michaels Hearing (August 12, 1997), tr. 88.

99. *New Jersey v. Marzolf*, Michaels Hearing (August 12, 1997), tr .54.

100. Here is a side-by-side comparison.

Statement to police, August 25, 1995 (p.4)	Testimony in court, May 5, 1997 (p.6)
I went in the house to get my shoes on, and come to realize that Travis and Jimmy, my wife's brother, were still in the house, but nowhere to be found. It was very quiet and I had made my progress to go up to the second story of the house into the living room, where Travis and Jimmy were last seen. Were not there. Got to the third landing, and to my left is Jimmy's room and I had noticed that it was very quiet as I got to the bedroom, I noticed Jimmy hovered over Travis from behind Travis with his hands in his pants.	I basically went into the house and to go get shoes on to go look at a shed that was in the backyard with his father. Knowing Travis and James were in the house still, as I approached, I proceeded into the house, I did acknowledge that it was very quiet. And when I went up to the third landing of the house, I had viewed that Travis was standing in front of James. As I saw that James was hovered over with his hands in his pants.

101. *New Jersey v. Marzolf*, Michaels Hearing (August 12, 1997), tr. 35.

102. *New Jersey v. Marzolf*, Michaels Hearing, (August 12, 1997), tr. 95,4–6.

103. Jane Mary Rawls, "How Questions and Body-parts Diagrams Could Affect the Content of Young Children's Disclosures," *Lawtalk New Zealand* (April 1996), 28–29. She concludes: "open-ended questions only is by far the safest option when interviewing children as it results in greater accuracy of reports." (It is not clear whether this study was ever published in a peer-reviewed journal.) Quote from interview with Tyler: "Now I want you to take my pen and circle anywhere on these, this diagram that anybody touched you."

104. *New Jersey v. Marzolf*, Michaels Hearing, (August 12, 1997), tr. 36, lines 20–24.

105. The judge took note of the fact that Professor Bruck had not actually heard the mother's testimony, although it was apparently available to her on tape.

106. *New Jersey v. Marzolf*, Decision on Michaels Hearing, (August 14, 1997), tr. 9.

107. The father was asked why he waited an hour to call his wife. The defense tried to get into the boy's school records and counseling records—all under the rubric of examining the "totality of the circumstances." Professor Bruck made derogatory comments about the parents when I interviewed her on October 12, 2009. "They were calling the police all the time," she asserted. No evidence of that was presented in court.

108. Affidavit of Probable Cause, Lower Pottsgrove Police Department, October 29, 2002, (Comp/Inc. #D-685/10290257), 1.
109. Police Criminal Complaint, Montgomery County, Pennsylvania, Incident No. 02-17153 January 17, 2003.
110. Criminal Docket, Court of Common Pleas of Montgomery County, Docket No. CP-46-CR-0000587-2003.
111. James J. Krivacska, "Sexual Abuse Prevention Programs: Can They Cause False Allegations?" *Issues in Child Abuse Allegations*, (1991), 3. He published another article in this journal written while an inmate at the Adult Diagnostic and Treatment Center at Avenel, New Jersey. James Krivacska, "Societal Myths About Sex Offending," *Issues in Child Abuse Accusations* (2001), vol. 11. The article warned, among other things, that "after-the-fact association of 'trauma' of sexual abuse with the pleasant genital stimulation [a child] may have experienced (in, for example, a case on fondling) may ultimately interfere with their later experience of sexual pleasure as an adult."
112. The other eight signatories were Charles Brainerd, Kathleen Clarke-Stewart, Melvin Guyer, Timothy Moore, Peter Ornstein, Debra Poole, Amye Warren, and James Wood.
113. Motion of the Scientists Concerned for Reliability of Children's Reports, Accusations and Testimony for Leave to File Amicus Curiae, *State v. Krivacska*, U.S. Supreme Court, Docket No. 01-1326, April 2, 2002, paras. 5, 7.
114. Unpublished Decision, *Krivacska v. Special Classification Review Board*, Superior Court of New Jersey Appellate Division, Docket No. A-1217-08T3, August 24, 2011.
115. Many states have declined to institute taint hearings. The largest state that has followed New Jersey's lead is Pennsylvania. *Pennsylvania v. Delbridge*, 855 A.2d 27 (Penn. 2003).
116. Summit, "The Child Abuse Accommodation Syndrome," 171–193.
117. Lawrence Wright, "Child-Care Demons," *New Yorker* (October 3, 1994). In a letter to the editor published on November 28, 1994, Wright acknowledged his claims were "wrong in every particular." He admitted that Summit "did not in fact testify at the Michaels case" and that Summit's original article "does not claim that denial is evidence of abuse." Lawrence Wright, "Mistaken Identity," Letter to Editor, *New Yorker* (November 28, 1994), 15–16.
118. Maggie Bruck and Stephen Ceci, "Forensic Developmental Psychology: Unveiling Four Common Misconceptions," *Current Directions in Psychological Science* (2004) 13(3): 229.
119. Bruck and Ceci, *Current Directions in Psychological Science* (2004), 13(3): 230.
120. Thomas A. Roesler and Tiffany Wind, "Telling the Secret: Adult Women Describe Their Disclosure of Incest," *Journal of Interpersonal Violence*, (1994), 9: 327–338.
121. Kamala London et. al., "Disclosure of Child Sexual Abuse: What Does the Research Tell Us About the Ways That Children Tell?" *Psychology, Public Policy, and Law* (2005) 11(1): 211–213. The extended criticism of the Sorenson and Snow study appears to be well-taken, although original research into the Hadfield and Bullock cases would be necessary to justify a firm conclusion. Snow was censured for unprofessional conduct in 2008 and her license was suspended subject to a term of four years probation. Stipulation and Order, *In the Matter of the License of Barbara W. Snow*, Case No. DOPL 2007-7 (Division of Occupational and Professional Licensing, Utah Department of Commerce) February 15, 2008. Snow's defense against these charges makes it clear that additional research would be required to justify a firm conclusion about what this license proceeding proves about Snow's judgment and practice. Response to Notice of Agency Action and Answer to Petition, *In the Matter of the License of Dr. Babara Snow* (February 12, 2007).
122. There were five defendants at trial. Duane Rouse was acquitted. The case name is the last name of two of the defendants. The first names of all the children in this case have been changed.
123. She had previously been removed from her mother's home. The record in this case does not indicate the reasons for removal.
124. *U.S. v. Rouse*, 329 F. Supp. 2d 1077 (South Dakota, 2004). Judge Piersol concluded that "the trial testimony of Dr. Kagan and Dr. Farrell established that the children had been sexually abused. The children described the abuse to Dr. Kaplan shortly after they were removed from their home." The judge quoted six paragraphs from the state's brief summarizing the

testimony from both doctors as to what they found and were told while examining the children.

125. *U.S. v. Rouse*, Jury Trial, U.S. District Court for South Dakota, (CR 94-40015, July 27, 1994), tr. 205.

126. When first interviewed about this case by the FBI, Desmond Rouse reportedly told Special Agent Pritchard that he "probably" touched Lacey's "groin area." He also reportedly said that if he abused the children he "must have been pretty drunk." He later denied making the first statement; he said the second statement was taken out of context. *U.S. v. Rouse*, Jury Trial (August 8–9, 1994), tr. 1597.

127. *U.S. v. Rouse*, Jury Trial (July 27, 1994), tr. 219.

128. *U.S. v. Rouse*, Jury Trial (August 10, 1994), tr. 1908.

129. *U.S. v. Rouse*, Jury Trial (August 9, 1994), tr. 1768–69.

130. *U.S. v. Rouse* (8th. cir. November 12, 1996), slip opinion, text accompanying fn. 2. This opinion was reported at 100 F.3d 560. It was depublished less than three months later when the court granted a motion to rehear the case, so that only the orders and subsequent history now appear in the Federal Reporter. The "depublished" opinion still resides on the web at this address: https://law.resource.org/pub/us/case/reporter/F3/100/100.F3d.560.95-1559.95-1558.95-1556.95-1554.htm.

131. *U.S. v. Rouse*, (8th cir. November 12, 1996; Loken, dissent). The majority does not attempt to respond to the factual details provided in this dissent. Instead, they allow, glibly, that "We do not quarrel with the sufficiency of the evidence" (fn. 20 in the [depublished] slip opinion).

132. Judicial Notebook, *APA Monitor* (June 1997). The article emphasized how the court "relied heavily" on Ceci and Bruck's 1993 article in *Psychological Bulletin*; it did not mention that the decision as vacated in early February 1997. The same claim was repeated in 1998, again without any mention that the decision was quickly vacated and then overturned. Metta Winter, "Children as Witnesses," *Human Ecology Forum* (Winter 1998) 26(1): 8–12.

133. The 2-1 decision issued November 16, 1996 was vacated on February 6, 1997 by an unusual grant of rehearing. 107 F.3d 557; 1997 U.S. App. LEXIS 2190. The case was set for oral argument on April 14. On March 3, the court issued a second order, stating "upon further consideration, the petition for rehearing is granted" but the order to schedule oral arguments was rendered moot and the hearing was cancelled. The same three-judge panel that overturned the convictions in November decided, again in a 2-1 split, to uphold the convictions. Judge McMillian switched positions by concurring with the majority decision written by Judge Loken. *U.S. v. Rouse*, 111 F. 3d 561; 1997 U.S. App. LEXIS 6659 (8th cir. 1997).

134. *U.S. v. Rouse*, 111 F. 3d 561, 571.

135. *U.S. v. Rouse*, Hearing on Motion for a New Trial, U.S. District for South Dakota, CR. 94-40015 (September 5, 2001), tr. 27.

136. *U.S. v. Rouse*, Hearing on Motion for a New Trial, tr. 96.

137. *U.S. v. Rouse*, 329 F. Supp. 2d 1077 (South Dakota, 2004), 1088.

138. *U.S. v. Rouse*, 329 F. Supp. 2d 1077, 1080.

139. *U.S. v. Rouse*, 329 F. Supp. 2d 1077, 1081. When the counselor met with J.R. to inform her that her uncles would *not* be coming home, J.R. told the counselor "that both her mother and R.R. had told J.R. to lie to the social worker in the summer of 1999." This direct evidence of pressure to recant has gone unacknowledged in the witch-hunt narrative.

140. *U.S. v. Rouse*, 329 F. Supp. 2d 1077, 1081. The court also noted that "R.R. did not recant her testimony during her interview with Underwager." Indeed, "R.R. responded affirmatively when Dr. Underwager asked if Jesse did things to her that were not right."

141. Stephanie Woodward, "Yankton Sioux Seek Justice for 17-year Old Case at the White House Tribal Nations Conference," *Indian Country Today* (December 6, 2011). See also, http://ncrj.org/the-ncrj-is-sponosring-the-yankton-four/.

142. *Kennedy v. Louisiana*, 554 U.S. 407 (2008), 411 ("systemic concerns in prosecuting child rape").

143. Stephen J. Ceci and Richard D. Friedman, "The Suggestibility of Children: Scientific Research and Legal Implications," *Cornell Law Review* (2000), 86: 33–108.

144. Samuel R. Gross et. al., "Exonerations in the United States 1989 Through 2003." *Journal of Criminal Law & Criminology* 95, no. 2 (2005): 523–553, 524. Gross now edits a project called The National Registry of Exonerations, which employs a much looser definition of exoneration, one that arguably negates the meaning of the word itself. Cases dismissed without any official finding of innocence are included, *even when the dismissal was not based on evidence of innocence.* https://www.law.umich.edu/special/exoneration/Pages/glossary.aspx.

    Using that definition, the Registry (as of September 28, 2013) included Kelly Michaels as "exonerated" despite: (1) the evidence of guilt elaborated in Chapter Five, (2) the lack of *any* recantations, (3) the fact that Michaels lost her civil suit, and (4) the lack of any official finding of innocence. Under the same dubious approach, the Registry also lists Sandra Craig (discussed in Chapter Three) as exonerated, despite the medical evidence and the lack of any official finding of innocence, and it lists Deborah and Alvin McCuan (also discussed in Chapter Three), despite the fact the neither of their daughters has ever recanted and the McCuan's lost their civil suit. It appears that the desire to fit cases into the witch-hunt narrative continues to be much stronger than the facts that support such claims, even twenty years after the narrative first took hold.

145. Louanne Lawson and Mark Chaffin, "False Negatives in Sexual Abuse Interviews," *Journal of Interpersonal Violence* (1992) 7, 532–542. Bruck and her co-authors minimized the significance of this result, arguing that because very few children contract STDs "this sample again is not representative of the CSA population." The authors offered no reason why children contracting STDs would be different from all other sexually abused children in some meaningful way that affects the pattern or likelihood of disclosure. The children in this study stand out for the strength of our certainty that most of the significant number of nondisclosures in the first interview were false denials, a problem never acknowledged in the witch-hunt narrative.

146. Carey Goldberg, "Pediatric Experts Express Doubt on Au Pair's Defense," *New York Times* (November 12, 1997). Forty-seven pediatric experts signed the letter to the editor, published in *Pediatrics* (February 1, 1998) 101(2): 321–323.

147. Battered-child syndrome is probably the oldest and most widely recognized syndrome involving child abuse. It was first described by this name in 1962 in a landmark article. C. Henry Kempe et. al., " Battered-Child Syndrome," *Journal of the American Medical Association* (July 1962) 181(1):17–24.

148. *State v. Ardolino,* Docket No. CR-95-478, Penobscot [Maine] County Superior Court, (March 8, 1996), vol. IV, tr. 132.

149. *State v. Ardolino,* vol. IV, tr. 131.

150. Dr. Kristin Sweeney, deputy chief medical examiner for the state, went to the house and examined the root structure below the tree house to see if the roots protruded enough to cause a localized deceleration impact injury. She concluded they could not. The roots are "fairly broad and flat" and "they're not protruding." Tr. 55–56; Vol. VII, March 13, 1996.

151. William Harwood, forensic chemist at the Maine State Police Crime Lab, examined eight containers and one envelope of leaves, twigs, bark, and fiber taken from the area under the tree. None of those items were found to be consistent with anything on the clothing Matthew was wearing that day. Where there should be extensive physical evidence, if Mathew had fallen, not a single fiber was found that linked the clothes he was wearing to the scene Tr. 119–124; Vol. VII, March 13, 1996.

152. All quotes in this paragraph from letter from Dr. Ricci to William R. Stokes re *State v. Ardolino* (January 19, 1995), 2–4.

153. *State v. Ardolino,* Excerpt: Testimony of David Ardolino (March 7, 1996), tr. 53.

154. *State v. Ardolino,* Excerpt: Testimony of David Ardolino, tr. 54.

155. *Ardolino v. Maine,* Affidavit of Maggie Bruck (on Motion for Post-Conviction Review), Penobscot County Superior Court, Docket No. CR-98-430, 32 ("we can have more confidence in a child's spontaneous statements made prior to any attempt by an adult to elicit what they suspect may be the truth—such as David's initial statement in this case").

156. *Ardolino v. Maine,* Affidavit of Maggie Bruck, 32.

157. Deposition of Stephen Ceci, November 22, 1993. *State v. Foeller*, File No. 93-64975-FC (Fourth Judicial Circuit Court for Jackson County, Michigan), 133.

158. *Ardolino v. Maine*, Affidavit of Maggie Bruck, 15.

159. Ricci testified that he knew Matthew was "an active nine-year-old child" when he examined the records (tr. 149). He also spoke directly to the injuries that could have been accidental. Ricci identified such injuries (bruises and abrasions round the ankle, knees, elbows, and forehead; tr. 134).

160. Declaration of Maggie Bruck, *In the Matter of Riley B.*, Case No. CK40772/CK40775 (Los Angeles County Superior Court, July 25, 2001).

161. Richard Gardner, Salem Day of Contrition, Afternoon session (January 14, 1997) [transcription], tr. 340. The witch-hunt narrative is filled with claims that CAPTA created financial incentives for "finding" abuse. In fact, the funding for CAPTA has always been miniscule compared to the massive changes it supposedly caused. Moreover, the largest portion of CAPTA money went to demonstration projects, which usually meant programs to prevent child abuse. Little CAPTA money has ever gone to state programs or services. There was a deliberate decision when the bill was crafted to provide only token funding of state programs. By statute, there was a mandate to spend 5 percent of the CAPTA budget on existing programs. The allocation of that money has *never* been based on the number of abuse cases, although that claim is often made by proponents of the witch-hunt narrative. To the contrary, there was a provision "to establish criteria designed to achieve equitable distribution of assistance under this section among the States." HHS determined that "equitable funding" would be provided through a per child funding formula. The funding formula, in other words, is a function of "the number of children under 18 residing in the state."

162. Thomas Lyon, "The New Wave of Suggestibility Research: A Critique," *Cornell Law Review* (1999) 84, 1004–1087.

INDEX

ABC Scholar Day Care Center, 164

ABC television
  on Believe the Children, 387–88
  on child's word, 390
  McMartin Preschool case, 6, 19, 72–73

Abuse of Innocence (Eberle and Eberle), 7, 418n1

Accommodations for children as witnesses, 187–88

Acorn, David, 428n167

Activist therapists, 69–72

Adam Walsh Protection and Safety Act of 2006, 370, 372

Aldridge and Wilcox case, 117

Alexander, Randall, 397

Allen, Joseph, 149–50, 374, 438n110. *See also* Head Start Program case

Allister, John
  dropped from case, 226, 247
  extreme behavioral evidence, 230

Almond, Steve, 328

American Academy of Pediatrics, 148–49

American Bar Association
  Center on Children and the Law, 194

American Lawyer, 21

American Psychological Association (APA), 349–50
  APA Monitor, 398
  Cornell conference, 355
  Division on Psychology and Law, 273
  Ethics Office, 352
  Nathan, Debbie and, 475n212

American Psychology Law Society, 355

Amirault case, 438n111
  championing of, 8
  "hysteria," Boston allegedly in grip of, 176–77
  information on, 11–12
  Satan's Silence, dedication page, 115
  "sex abuse hysteria" and minimal punishment, 194
  Wall Street Journal article, 376

"Anal wink," 62

Anatomy of the McMartin Child Molestation Case, 418–19n1

APA. *See* American Psychological Association (APA)

Applegate, David
  contested actions and, 279
  extreme behavioral evidence, 229
  Fonolleras, Lou, interview with, 220–21
  interview of, 245
  medical evidence, 231
  testimony of, 238, 456n55
  Treacy, Eileen on, 223
  verdict and, 240
  witch-hunt narrative and
    medical evidence, 262
    sex-abuse hysteria, use of term, 264

Applegate, Judy, 221, 231, 462n214

Ardolino, David, 402–4

Ardolino, Matthew, 401–5, 407

Ardolino, Robert case, 401–5

Arkansas Democrat-Gazette
  school teachers, sexual misconduct of, 373
  on sexual misconduct allegations, 184

Arlington, Massachusetts, child pornography case, 165

Armbrister, Trevor, 11

Arrigan, Brian, 339, 343

Arvida Corporation, 285, 291, 330, 346

Ashley's Law, 370

The Assault on Truth: Freud's Suppression of the Seduction Theory (Masson), 177

Associated Press
  Michaels, Kelly case, 239, 253

Atherton, California case, 92

Atkins, Larry, 385

Atlanta Constitution
  West, Walter P., 182

Ault, Howard Steven, 388

Austin American Statesmen
　Fran's Day Care case, 146
Austin Chronicle
　Fran's Day Care case, 146
Austin, Texas. *See* Fran's Day Care case
Aviv, Rachel, 477n17

Bach, Richard, 185
Bailey, Penny, CII evaluation, 46
Bakersfield, California case, 100
Bakersfield Witch Hunt, 119. *See also Mean Justice*
　(Hume)
Baldwin, Ella, CII evaluation, 45
Ballard, Frances, 96–100. *See also* Georgian Hills
　Early Childhood Center case
Ball, Daryl, Jr., 162–63
Baran, Bernard, 11, 126–28, 155. *See also* Early
　Childhood Development Center
Barber, Mike, 439n114, 440n134
Barbour, Gene and Linda, 119
Barbour, Mary Ann, 119–22, 440n134. *See also*
　Mean Justice (Hume)
Barkman, Rebecca, 108–9
Barkman, Richard. *See* Small World Preschool case
Barragan, Agustin O., 385
Barry, Helena, 169
Barry, Judge, 463n227
Bartky, Murray, 233
Barton, Gloria, 32–33
Barton, Sara
　CII interview with, 47–50
　early investigation, 32–33, 428–49n168
Bartz, Lori, 162
The Battle and the Backlash (Hechler), 111
Baughan, William, 126–27
Beck, Richard, 71, 152, 429n176
*Behind the Playground Walls: Sexual Abuse
　in Preschools,* 419n1
Believe the Children
　ABC network and, 387–88
　McMartin Preschool case, 4, 10–11, 71, 85–86
　ritual abuse case, 163
　Rogers Park case, 71
Belkin, Lisa, 72
Benedek, Elissa, 238–39
Bennett, Cameron, 99
Bentz, Robert and Lois, 100–103, 236. *See also*
　Jordan, Minnesota cases
Berent, A. Andrew, 175
Bergman, Stephen, 175
Berkowitz, Carol, 169
Berndt, Mark, 369–70
Berry, Jason, 183
Besharov, Douglas, 22
Bianchini, Victor, 381
Bighead, Charles case, 379–80, 406
Bikel, Ofra, 8–10, 12
Bishard, Beryl, 153

Bishop, Richard Charles, 126, 164
Bittenbender, Carlton, 185, 452n149
Blando, Shirley, 473–74n182
Boatwright, Stephen, 153
Bobb, Judge Aviva, 19, 79
Bond-Foley, Cassie
　medical evidence, 232
　subsequent investigation, 215
　verdict and, 242
Bo Peep Day Nursery, 158–59
Boston, Amirault case, 176–77
Boston Globe
　Amirault case, 176, 194
　Day of Contrition, 390
　Lanesborough Elementary School case, 147
　Law, Cardinal Bernard and, 368
Boulder, Colorado. *See* Marks, Douglas
Boychuk, Tasha, 379–80, 407
Boyer, Peter, 9, 174, 183, 337, 351
Boy Scout Troop 26, 182–83, 452n149
Brackenridge Hospital, 144
Braga, Joseph and Laurie
　early investigation, 292
　ethics complaints against, 352
　interviews by
　　criticisms of, 344
　　final interviews, 308–15
　　initial interviews (August 8 and 10, 1984),
　　　292–98
　　later August 1984 interviews, 298–305
　　sequences of, 303–5
　　later interviews (August 1984), 298–305
　　maligning of, 348–51
Braintree, Massachusetts. *See* Caring for Kids, Inc.
Brainwashed, use of term, 41
Breto, Albert, 193
Bright, Judge Myron, 397–98, 406
British Nanny Case, 401
Brodsky, Stanley, 234
Bromberg, Daniel, 376
Broward County, Florida
　rape and murder, 388–89
Brown, Allison, 66–68
Brown, Jenny, 46
Brown University, Institutional Review Board, 413
Bruck, Maggie. *See also* Ceci and Bruck
　implication regarding Lawton, Robert case;
　Ceci and Bruck on child abuse
　acccommodation syndrome; Ceci and Bruck
　on Country Walk case; Ceci and Bruck on
　Kelly Michaels case; Ceci and Bruck on "Six
　Elements to Three Major Cases; *Jeopardy in
　the Courtroom: A Scientific Analysis of
　Children's Testimony* (Ceci and Bruck)
　Ardolino, Robert case, 404–5
　Coleman, Lee, 341–42
　on forensic concerns, 387
　Fuster, Frank, affidavit on behalf of, 285, 327

on Goodman, Gail, 22–23
Marzolf case and, 391–92
on McMartin case, 87
on personality of sex offenders, 181
on Rainbow Christian Daycare case, 136–37
on recantation rates, 396
Rouse case, 398–99
Bruneau, David, 108
Buckey, Peggy. *See also* McMartin Preschool case
acquittal of, 83
CII interviews with victims and, 48–51, 56
indictment of, 19, 76
libel suit against, 21
Manhattan Beach Police Department (MBPD) letter, response to, 82
Mergili, Mrs., call to, 422n50
paranoia of, 27
statements of, 20
Buckey, Peggy Ann. *See also* McMartin Preschool case
indictment of, 19, 76
libel suit against, 21
results of case, 84
Buckey, Raymond. *See also* McMartin Preschool case
acquittal of, 83
arrest of, 27
character and behavior, evidence regarding, 81–82
evidence against, 23, 42
indictment of, 19, 76
initial claims against, 4
interviews with victims and, 35, 44–45, 55–59
retrial of, 413
strength of evidence, 20
trial of, 5, 80–84
Burstyn, Freda, 329
Burton, Karen, 215
Butler, Margaret, 466n12
Bynum, Paul, 27, 420n5

CAAS. *See* Child abuse accommodation syndrome (CAAS)
California
Arkansas Democrat-Gazette, 373
civil commitment, 371
California Penal Code, 28
California Supreme Court, 187
Canada, Ontario Consultants for Religious Tolerance, 13
Cantwell, Hendrika, 61–62
CAPTA. *See* Child Abuse Prevention and Treatment Act (CAPTA)
Capturing the Friedmans (Jarecki), 11, 130–33, 443n198
Caring for Kids, Inc., 176
Carl Sandburg Junior High School, 192
Carroll case, 254

Cartright, Gary, 145–46
Cases, listings of. *See* 36 cases, list of by Charlier and Downing
Casey, Dan, 315, 327
Catholic Church cases
denial, 177–78
exposé of, 183
scandals, 365–68, 384, 406
U.S. Conference of Catholic Bishops, 367
CBS
48 Homes, 478n55
Michaels, Kelly case, 252
News, 382
CDC. *See* Centers for Disease Control (CDC)
Ceci and Bruck implication regarding Lawton, Robert case, 378
Ceci and Bruck on child abuse acccommodation syndrome, 395–400
"Unveiling Four Misconceptions," 395
Ceci and Bruck on Country Walk case
as contrast to Michaels, Kelly case, 283, 285
"fantastic" elements, 338–40
"objective analysis," 351
suggestibility claims, 252, 341–46
"Suggestibility of the Child Witness: A Historical Review and Synthesis, 272–73
Ceci and Bruck on Kelly Michaels case
on affiliations, 278
brief for the defense by, 277–79
"Child Witnesses: Translating Research into Policy," 275–76
dismissal of children's testimonies, 221–22
"Mousetrap Study," 273–75, 356
policy implications, 275–76
"Suggestibility of the Child Witness: A Historical Review and Synthesis," 272–73
Treacy, Eileen, inaccurate claims about, 253, 255, 257–69
"fantastic" elements, claiming, 262
Treacy-Child A excerpt, 256
Treacy-Child B excerpt, 258
Ceci and Bruck on "Six Elements to Three Major Cases, 337–59, 358
Ceci, Stephen. *See also* Ceci and Bruck implication regarding Lawton, Robert case; Ceci and Bruck on child abuse acccommodation syndrome; Ceci and Bruck on Country Walk case; Ceci and Bruck on Kelly Michaels case; Ceci and Bruck on "Six Elements to Three Major Cases; *Jeopardy in the Courtroom: A Scientific Analysis of Children's Testimony* (Ceci and Bruck)
on "air of accusation," 167
on child suggestibility claims, 355–56
on forensic concerns, 387
on Goodman, Gail, 22–23
on recantation rates, 396

Center on Children and the Law, American Bar Association, 194

Centers for Disease Control (CDC), 329

Channel 10, McMartin Preschool case, 72

Chapel, Paul III, 369–70

Chapman, Breanna, 55–56

Chapman, Ellen, 55–56, 82

Charlier, Tom and Downing, Shirley, 11
 Country Walk case, 283, 327
  "fantastic elements," 338
  "Justice Abused: A 1980s Witch-Hunt," 88, 92
 on ritual abuse allegations, 355, 384
 36 cases, list of, 87–115. See also 36 cases, list of by Charlier and Downing

Chase, Miranda, 57–59

Chicago. See also Rogers Park Jewish Community Center case
 Department of Children and Family Services, 103–4

Child abuse accommodation syndrome (CAAS), 157, 178–79
 contesting, 394–400

The Child Abuse Industry (Pride), 7

Child Abuse Prevention and Treatment Act (CAPTA), 389, 401, 405, 480n89, 485n161

Child Abuse Registry Hotline, 137

Child Advocacy Center, 379

Child pornography, 94, 130, 132
 as "myth," 163–67

Child Protective Services, 385–86

Children City Learning Center, 384–85

Children's Institute International (CII)
 contested medical evidence and, 59–60
  overdiagnosis issue, 61–62
 evaluations, 33, 40–59. See also *specific victim*
  November 1983, 44–46
  December 1983, 46–51
  January 1984, 51, 55–56
  February 1984 onward, 57–59
 forces beyond, 68–77
 interviews by
  early investigation, 34–37, 42
  generally, 17, 19
  sequence of interviews, 52–54
 McMartin Preschool case. See *Lines throughout this topic*
 neglecting to supervise process, 74–75
 preliminary hearing, interview sequence, 53–54
 retrial, interview sequence, 53–54
 trial, interview sequence, 53–54

Children's Path Preschool, 170–71

Child suggestibility claims, 16, 355, 360, 365–66, 406–7
 Country walk case, 283, 341–52
  Braga, maligning of, 348–51
  children most criticized, 343–45
  overlooked or downplayed children, 346–47

"A Child's Word," 388–89

"Child Witnesses: Translating Research into Policy" (Ceci and Bruck), 275–76

CII. See Children's Institute International (CII)

Cincinnati, Isaac Wise Temple summer camp case, 95

Civil commitment, 371

Clarksville case. See Craig's Country Pre-School case

Clemency and Pardons Board, 136–37

Clinton, New Jersey. See Wee Care Child Care Center

Coats, Dan, 390

Coburn, Tom, 477n18

Cockburn, Alexander, 330–31

Coffee, John, 178

Cohen, Arthur, 335, 352

Cohen, Lucy, 148

Coleman, Judge, 392

Coleman, Lee, 351
 Bruck, Maggie on, 341–42
 Country Walk case and, 179
 on other child abuse cases, 469n97
 on "People are Talking," 469n70
 Shumate, Neil case, 376
 testimony of, 321–23
 Underwager, Ralph, replacement of, 328

Colposcope, 56–57, 66, 122, 427n167

Commercial Appeal
 "Justice Abused: A 1980s Witch-Hunt" (Charlier and Downing), 88, 92
 36 cases, list of, 87–115
 on witch-hunt narrative, 11

Community notification systems, 371–72

Concerned Scientists brief, 277–79, 356–57, 380, 387

"Confirmation bias," 285

Contested medical evidence, McMartin case. See McMartin Preschool case

Contra Costa County, CA. See Seering Family Day Care

Cook, Cody
 dropped from case, 226
 initial phase of investigation, 208–9
 subsequent investigation, 216

Cook, Debbie, 208

Cora's Day Care case, 107–8

Cordova, Sally, 83

Cornell Law Review, 400

Cornell, William, 117

"Corroboration" requirements, 187

Costello, Marvin, 192

Country Walk case, 15, 283–354, 414. See also Fuster, Frank; Fuster, Ileana (Flores)
 attendance patterns, 287
 Ceci and Bruck and, 272–73, 278
  "Six Elements" to Three Major Cases, 359
 charges, 315–16
  full counts, *310*

"coerced confession" of Ileana Fuster, 332–35
defense, 179, 321–25
evidence, 306–15
  medical conditions, 306
  sexually precocious behavior, 308
  suspicious incidents, 306–8
  unclothed children, 306–8
"fantastic" elements, 283, 331, 338–40, 351–53
full counts, 326
"hysteria," Dade County, Florida allegedly in
  grip of, 174–75
"inaccurate test" myth, 328–29, 470n130
interviews
  Braga interviews, initial (August 8 and 10,
    1984), 292–98
  final interviews, 308–15
  later August 1984 interviews, 298–305
key features of, 360–61, 361
medical conditions, 306
original case (1984-85), 285–327
  aggressive questioning of child witness,
    317–18
  Braga interviews, initial (August 8 and 10,
    1984), 292–98
  charges, 315–16
  early investigation (August 3-8, 1984), 285,
    289–92
  evidence, 306–15
  guilty plea, 298, 318–19
  later August 1984 interviews, 298–305
  origins of Country Walk babysitting service,
    285–305
  trial, 319–25
  verdict, 325, 327
origins of Country Walk Babysitting Service,
  285–305
  Arvida Corporation, 285, 291, 330, 346,
    466n12
  Disney Corporation, 285, 346
revisionist history (1993-present), 327–51
  "coerced confession" of Ileana Fuster, 332–35
  Fuster, Noel, retraction by, 329–31, 471n143
  "inaccurate test" myth, 328–29, 470n130
  prior record of Fuster, minimizing, 335–38
sexually precocious behavior, 308
state's case, 319–20
STD findings, 302, 320, 352
suggestibility claims, 341–52
  Bragas, maligning of, 348–51
  children most criticized, 343–45
  overlooked or downplayed children, 346–47
"Suggestibility of the Child Witness: A
  Historical Review and Synthesis" (Ceci
  and Bruck), 272–73, 406–7
suspicious incidents, 306–8
timelines, 284
trial, 319–25
  defense, 321–24

full counts, 326
overlooked or downplayed children, 346–47
state's case, 319–20
verdict, 325, 327
unclothed children, 306–8
verdict, 325, 327
victims and family. See Arrigan, Brian; Cramer,
  Jason; Cramer, Joshua; Leventhal, Betsy;
  Leventhal, Charlie; Leventhal, Tom;
  Lipton, Daniel; Lipton, Jessie; Lipton,
  Roberta; Lucas, Allison; Lucas, Tammy;
  Lucas, Victor; Menninger, Donald;
  Menninger, Donald, Jr.; Menninger, Vicki;
  Monk, Carrie; Pelton, Vivian; Porter,
  Annie; Porter, Kimberly; Porter, Malcolm;
  St. Lorenzo, Emma; St. Lorenzo, John;
  Taylor, Becky; Thomas, Ariel; Walker,
  Paula; Walker, Sara
Craft, Daryl, 184
Craig, Sandra, 105–7. See also Craig's Country
  Pre-School case
Craig's Country Pre-School case, 105–7, 189,
  436n70
Cramer, Jason
  Braga, Joseph and Laurie, interviews, 292–95,
    297, 301, 309, 311–12, 339
  counts involving, 316
  criticisms of interview(s), 345
  cross-examination of, 320
  early investigation, 291
  ignoring of, 323
  overlooked or downplayed testimony, 346–47
  sexually precocious behavior, 308
  tapes made by, ignoring of
    aggressive questioning of, 317–18
  validity of testimony, 360
Cramer, Joshua
  Braga, Joseph and Laurie, interviews, 294
  sexually precocious behavior, 308
Cramer, Sandra, 308
Cranshaw, Jane, 104
Credibility of children, undermining, 387–406
  child abuse accommodation syndrome,
    contesting, 394–400
  institutions, backlash against, 401–6
  professions, backlash against, 401–6
  "tainted," labeling children as, 390–94
Crews, Frederick, 12, 157
Crime Library website, 17
Croskey, Judge H. Walter, 171–72
Cross, Theodore, 373
Crowley, Patricia, 453n17
Currie, Robert, 21, 69–70, 73

Dade County, Florida. See also Country Walk
  case; Finje, Bobby case
  "hysteria," allegedly in grip of, 174–75
Daily Breeze, McMartin Preschool case, 79

Dalenberg, Constance, 405
Davis, Danny, 20, 78
Daybridge Day Care Center, 177
Daybridge Learning Center, 97
Day care abuse, 1980s, 152–59. *See also specific cases*
    during McMartin, 155–59
    pre-McMartin, 152–55
The Day Care Ritual Abuse Moral Panic (Young), 87
"Day care sexual abuse cases of the 1980s," use of term, 87
Day care workers as "symbols," 152
Day of Contrition (linking cases to Salem witch trials of 1690s), 374, 377, 389–90, 401, 485n161
Dayton, Ohio. *See* Aldridge and Wilcox case
Deacon, Lucy
    extreme behavioral evidence, 231
    subsequent investigation, 215, 216
A Death in White Bear Lake (Seigel), 179
Denial and silence on child sex abuse cases, 15, 151–95
    "air of denial," 177–85
    day care abuse, 1980s, 152–59
        during McMartin, 155–59
        pre-McMartin, 152–55
    denial, use of term, 151
    "fantastic" elements, 154, 159–67
        child pornography "myth," 163–67
    "hysteria," use of term in witch-hunt narrative, 167–85
        Amirault case, Boston during, 176–77
        Country Walk case, Dade County, Florida during, 174–75
        Kelly Martin Day care case, New Jersey during, 173–74
        McMartin era, 167–73
        places allegedly in grip of, 167–77
        Southern California, 167–73
    leniency for child molesters, 191–95
    prosecuting child abuse, difficulties, 185–91
Department of Social Services (DSS)
    California, 154, 172–73, 434n30
    Massachusetts, 126–28, 165
    Michigan, 110, 437n87
Des Moines Register, 141
Dillard, Michael Paul, 161
Dimitrius, Jo-Ellan, 419–20n41
Dinerstein, Stephen, 332–33, 348, 353, 471n148
Discounting reality of day-care sexual abuse, 383–87
Disney Corporation, 285, 346
Doe, Gregory, 132
Doggett, Susan "Sam," 382
Domestic Violence Prosecution Unit (Westchester County), 187
Donahue, John, 192

Donnella, Amy Gershenfeld, 277, 352–53
Dove, Gayle, 185
Downing, Shirley, 11
    Charlier, Tom and Downing, Shirley. *See* Charlier, Tom and Downing, Shirley
    "Justice Abused: A 1980s Witch-Hunt," 88, 92
    36 cases, list of, 87–115. *See also* "Justice Abused: A 1980s Witch-Hunt" (Charlier and Downing); 36 cases, list of by Charlier and Downing
Drew, Dana, 226
Drummond, Donald T., 186
DSS. *See* Department of Social Services (DSS)
Dugan, Michele, 71
Duke Child Protection team, 143
Duke Medical Center, 143
Dye, Detective, 34, 37, 421n42
Dyer, Ed, 182–83
DYFS. *See* New Jersey Department of Health and Family Services (DYFS)

Early Childhood Development Center, 126–28, 155
Eberle, Paul and Shirley, 7, 71–72, 405, 418n11
Edenton, North Carolina. *See* Little Rascals day care center case
Edgewood, Iowa. *See* Sunshine Preschool and Day Care Center case
Eison, Rita Bighead, 379–80
Ennis, Cindy, 427n167
Ennis, Donna, 82
Esquilin, Susan, 217
Essex County Prosecutor's Office, 280
    cross examinations, 236
    decision on who would be included in case, 224
    evidence allegedly kept from jury, 252
    Sexual Abuse unit, 206–7
Everson, Mark, 263, 351–52
Evidence. *See specific case*

Fairmont Baptist Church, 157
Falls-Lakeview School, 192
False Memory Syndrome Foundation (FMSF), 12, 139, 383, 388, 390
Famous Trials website, 17
"Fantastic" elements
    Country Walk case, 283, 331, 338–40, 351–53
    McMartin era, 154, 159–67
        child pornography "myth," 163–67
    Michaels, Kelly case, 261–64
FBI
    Georgian Hills Early Childhood Center case, 97
    Investigator's Guide to Allegations of "Ritual" Child Abuse, 160–61
    McMartin Preschool case, 70, 72
    West Point Child Development Center, 112
Feather, Garfield, 396
Feifel, John E.., 180

Feigley, George, 448–49n46
Fells Acres Day School case, 176
Felsten, Anne, 229–30
Ferguson, Judge, 298
Ferrera, Christopher case, 377, 383
54 names listed in *Satan's Silence: Ritual Abuse and the Making of an American Witch-Hunt* (Nathan and Snedeker)
    dedication page, 115–50. *See also specific names and cases*
        details on names listed, *116*
        wrongful convictions, cases with, 117–18
Figured, Patrick, 11, 142–44. *See also* Miss Polly's Day Care Center
Finje, Bobby case, 174–75
Finkelhor, David, 155–57, 163
Fiore, Faye. *See* St. Cross Church
Fischer, Mary, 6, 7, 28, 81
Fitzpatrick, Frank, 367
Fitzpatrick, Janet, 141
Flora, Rebecca
    extreme behavioral evidence, 230–31
    Fonolleras, Lou, interview with, 221
    interview of, 247, 249
    medical evidence, 231–32
    verdict and, 242
Flores, Ileana. *See* Fuster, Ileana (Flores)
Florida. *See also* Country Walk case; Dade County, Florida; Finje, Bobby case; Glendale Montessori School
    Jimmy Ryce Act, 140
FMSF. *See* False Memory Syndrome Foundation (FMSF)
Foeller case, 278, 404
Fonolleras, Lou
    bias, 350
    initial phase of investigation, 206–7
    interviews by, 217, 219–21, 226, 281
        criticisms in witch-hunt narrative, 249–51, 266
        sequence of, *218*
    Nathan, Debbie, criticisms by, 243
    own abuse, telling children about, 243, 459n137
    subsequent investigation, 213–16
    substantiation of sex abuse by, 224
    testimony, 228
Ford, Daniel, 127
Ford, Greg, 367
Fort Bragg case. *See* Jubilation Day Care Center case
Fort Lauderdale, Florida. *See* Rainbow Christian Day Care case
48 Hours (tv show), 244, 478n55
Foster case, 10
Foster, Peg, 212–13, 228–29, 247
Fox, David, 186
Fran's Day Care case, 144–47
Freeh Report, 368–69

Freeman, Clara, 93
Freeman, James, 114
Freeman, LeRoy, 93, 434n19
Freud, Sigmund
    seduction theory, suppression of, 3, 177
    writings against, 12
Freyd, Peter, 12, 388
Friedman, Arnold and Jesse case, 11, 130–33
    Capturing the Friedmans (Jarecki), 11, 130–33, 443n198
    Innocence Project, 133
    website, 442n188
    "Witch Hunt Information Center" and, 130
Fried, Stephen, 182
Frontline (PBS program), 8–11, 174
    Country Walk case, 336, 338, 348, 351, 353
Fuster, Frank
    affidavit on behalf of by Bruck, Maggie, 285, 327
    as defense witness, 323
    First Degree Manslaughter plea, 472–73n171
    information on, 11
    Kendall Decorators, 286
    manslaughter charges, prior, 336–37
    marriages, 286. *See also* Fuster, Ileana (Flores)
    Mobile Showroom, 286
    prior record of, minimizing, 335–38
    rape, as prior suspect in, 337–38
    Satan's Silence, dedication page, 115
    sentencing of, 319
Fuster, Ileana (Flores). *See also* Country Walk case; Fuster, Frank
    guilty plea, 298, 318–19
        as "coerced confession," 332–35, 341
    marriage of, 286
    as rebuttal witness, 324–25
    statements from children regarding, 288
    testimony of, 472n162
Fuster, Martha, 309
Fuster, Noel
    abuse by father
        Braga interview, 298, 302
        Fuster, Ileana testimony, 325
        retraction by, 329–31, 471n143
    birth of, 286
    interview, 309, 311–13, 470–71n138
    quotes used in trial, 343
    STD findings, 302, 309, 320
Futrelle, David, 161

Gabaeff, Steven, 136
Gaddis Rickie Jay, 161–62
Gannet News Service, 179–80
Gans, Ralph
    extreme behavioral evidence, 230
    interviews of, 249–50
    subsequent investigation, 213–14, 216
Garcetti, Gil, 80
Gardner, Martin, 11, 117

Gardner, Richard
   Day of Contrition, 405, 485n161
   on jury, 438n113
   Michaels, Kelly case, exaggerations pertaining to,
      462n208
   parental alienation syndrome, 389–90
   on police and child protective services, 184
   on punitive treatment of sex offenders, 373
   sex-abuse hysteria, coining of term, 193–94,
      264
   Sex Abuse Hysteria: Salem Witch Trials Revisited,
      179, 379
   Watson, Norman case and, 180
Gauthe case, 368
Geoghan, Father John, 366–67
Georgian Hills Early Childhood Center case,
      96–100, 362
   numbers of perpetrators, 89
   in 36 cases, list of by Charlier and Downing, 94
Gersten, Judge David M., 297
Gingerbread Day Care, 385
Giuliani, Rudolph, 112
Glazer, Mark, 390, 393
Glendale Montessori School, 137–40
Gloucester County
   Maryland day care centers, 153
   New Jersey nursery schools, 153–54
Goldberg, Bernard, 244–45
Goldberg, Glenn, 239, 417n11
Gold, Eugene, 193
Goldman, Amy, 423n75
Goldstein, Ross, 131, 443n198
Goodman, Gail, 22
   child suggestibility claims and, 355
   Country Walk case, 283
   Michaels, Kelly case, 271–72, 277, 282, 387,
      413
Gordon, Linda, 25, 178
Gordon, Mary
   CII evaluation, 44
   contested medical evidence and, 64,
      428–29n167
   early investigation, 34–37
Gorney, Cynthia, 21
Grafton, Margaret, 123
Great Neck, New York. *See* Friedman, Arnold and
      Jesse case
Green, Judge Robert, 193
Greenup, Campbell, 172, 450n92
Green, Wade, 71
Gregg, Barry
   CII interview with, 47, 50
   contested medical evidence and, 63–64, 67
Gregg, Darlene, 81
Gregg, Sally, 33
Gross. Samuel, 400
Guild, Greg, 229, 232

Hadley, Laura, 36, 206, 238, 269
Haley, Nora van, 214–15
Halsey, Robert case, 12, 147–49, 157, 374. *See also*
      Lanesborough Elementary School
      case
Hamrick, Robert, 34
Hankin, Richard, 130
Hanneman, Gary, 384–85
Harbor-UCLA Hospital, 169
Hargrove, Wayne, 98–99
Haroutunian, Anna, 231–32
Harper's
   McMartin Preschool case, 8
   Michaels, Kelly case, 22, 243, 273
Harrington, Maine. *See* Ardolino, Robert case
Harrisburg, Pennsylvania. *See* New American
      Church
Harris, Jonathan, 11–12, 142–43, 147, 254, 376
Hartford County, MD. *See* Bo Peep Day
      Nursery
Harth, Judge William, 234, 237, 239, 270
Hart, Kim, 185
Hart, Lisa, 170
Harwood, William, 484n151
Hassim, Sargent, 392
Hating the Sin, Loving the Sinner, 192
Hayes, Tracy, 219
Hazel Crawford Day Care, 351
Head Start Program case, 149–50
Hearsay evidence, 191
Hechler, David
   The Battle and the Backlash, 111
Heger, Astrid
   CII interviews, 45
   colposcopic exam by, 56–57
   contested medical evidence and, 59–68,
      427–28nn167 and 168
   on evolution of medical knowledge, 197
Hentoff, Nat, 245, 251–52, 389
Herman-Giddens, Marcia, 143
Herman, Judith, 178
Hermosa Beach, California. *See* Children's Path
      Preschool; St. Cross Church
Hetherington, Thomas Max, 154
Higgins, Charlie, 99
High Society magazine, 150
Hight, Judge Bob T., 170, 187
Hill, Sonja, 11, 142–44. *See also* Miss Polly's Day
      Care Center
Hoag, Detective, 38, 40
Hoffman, Richard, 180
Hogan, John, 315
Hollingsworth, Jan, 288, 292, 309, 347, 467n38
   Unspeakable Acts, 293, 341
Hollywood, Florida. *See* Nativity School
Holtzman, Elizabeth, 187
Home day care case, 128–29

Home day care center, White Plains, New York, 113–15
Homophobia, 127
Honolulu, Hawaii. *See* Kailua Beach Preschool
Hopkins, Carol, 12, 375, 377–78, 382, 389–90, 478n55
Horsey, David, 383
Hoyt, Wanda, 179–80
Hubbeling, Russell, 396
Huck's Raft: A History of American Childhood (Mintz), 8
Huck, William F., Sr., 385
Hume, Edward, 121–22, 126, 440n134
    Mean Justice, 118–19, 440n134, 441n160
Humphrey, Hubert III
    Report on Scott County Investigations, 101–3
Hypnosis, 132
"Hysteria," use of term in witch-hunt narrative, 15, 156, 167–85
    "air of denial" and, 179
    Amirault case, Boston during, 176–77
    Country Walk case, Dade County, Florida during, 174–75
    Kelly Martin Day care case, New Jersey during, 173–74
    McMartin era, 167–73
    Michaels, Kelly case, 264–68
    places allegedly in grip of, 167–77
    sex-abuse hysteria, coining of term, 193–94
    Southern California, 167–73

Implanted, use of term, 7, 41
Incest. *See also* Fuster. Noel
    Secret Trauma: Incest in the Lives of Girls and Women (Russell), 451n117
    Something About Amelia (tv movie), 3, 177
Indictment (film), 9–11, 23
    described, 419n1
    fire in school, depiction of, 72
    Johnson, Judy, portrayal of, 25
    Stevens, Glenn, interviews with, 20
    on trial and retrial, 81
Ingram case, 117
Ingram, Kathy Kae
    CII evaluation, 44
    contested medical evidence and, 68
    early investigation, 37–40
Ingram, Paul, 9
Institutions, backlash against, 401–6
Inverness, Florida. *See* Matthews, Mitchell case
Investigator's Guide to Allegations of "Ritual" Child Abuse (FBI), 160–61
Iowa Department of Human Services, 141–42
Iowa Department of Justice, 141
Iowa v. Warnock. *See* Warnock, George and Betty
Isaac, Rael Jean, 348

Isaacs, P. J.
    extreme behavioral evidence, 231
    Fonolleras, Lou, interview with, 220
    interviews of, 250
    testimony of, 238
Isaac Wise Temple summer camp case, 95
Isabel's Day Care, 164
Issues in Child Abuse Accusations (Nathan), 327

Jackson, John, 78
Jackson, Mary Ann, 19, 76. *See also* McMartin Preschool case
Jackson Memorial Hospital, 345
Jackson, Michael, 366
Jacob Wetterling Crimes Against Children and Sexually Violent Offenders Act, 370
Jarecki, Andrew, 442n180
    Capturing the Friedmans, 11, 130–33, 443n198
Jenkins, Natalie, 243, 459n137
Jenkins, Philip
    Catholic Church and, 177–78
    on child pornography, 163
    on homicide, 180
    on media reports, 73, 101
    Moral Panic: Changing Conceptions of the Child Molester in Modern America, 13
Jeopardy in the Courtroom: A Scientific Analysis of Children's Testimony (Ceci and Bruck)
    children's testimony, article on, 23
    child suggestibility claims and, 9–10, 365
    Country Walk case, 15, 285, 341–43, 346
Jessica's Law, 370
Jimmy Ryce Act, 140
John Paul II, 367
Johnson, Judy
    beginning of case, 24–27
    behavior of, 430n188
    contested medical evidence and, 63
    death of, 20, 24, 26
Johnson, Kirk, 135
Johnson, Matthew, 24–27, 358
    contested medical evidence, 59, 63
    examinations by physicians, 25
    MBPD report on, 421n42
Johnston, Pennsylvania, ritual abuse, 161–62
Jones, Dennis, 242
Jones, Kimmy, 242
Jones, Maggie, 124
Jones, Samuel L., 193–94
Jordan, Minnesota cases, 100–103, 163
    highlighting of in 36 cases, list of by Charlier and Downing, 94–95
    leniency for child molesters, 191–92
    numbers of perpetrators, 89
    Olson Commission, 101–2
    prior apprehending of defendants, 194

Jordan, Minnesota cases (*continued*)
  Report on Scott County Investigations
    (Humphrey), 101–3
  Satan's Silence, dedication page, 115
Journal of Clinical Microbiology
  Country Walk case, 328
Journal of Social Issues
  Michaels, Kelly case, 271
Jubilation Day Care Center case, 96, 434–35n19
"Junior McMartins," use of phrase, 87, 152–54,
    180–81, 327
"Justice Abused: A 1980s Witch-Hunt" (Charlier
    and Downing), 88, 92
Justice Committee, 12, 389

KABC television. *See* ABC television
Kailua Beach Preschool, 164–65
Kaiser Permanente, 24
Kanka, Megan, 370
Kaplan, Dr., 396
Kauffmann, Kristi, 191
Kauffmann, Paul, 191
Keenan, Detective, 104
Keller Army Hospital, 112
Keller, Daniel and Francis, 144–47, 374. *See also*
    Fran's Day Care case
Kelly Michaels Defense Committee, 243
Kelly, Robert. *See also* Little Rascals day care
    center case
  conviction of, 8–9
  information on, 11
  sex-abuse hysteria, coining of term and, 193
Kelson, Ellen, 396
Kempe, Henry, 178
Kendall Decorators, 286
Kennedy v. Louisiana, 400
Kent, Cheryl, 71
Kentucky, "Vampire Clan," 448–49n46
Kern County, California cases, 11, 100, 164, 197.
    See also Kniffen case; McCuan case; Self,
    Grant; Stoll, John
  numbers of perpetrators, 89
  *Report on the Kern County Child Abuse
    Investigations*, 118
  wrongful convictions, 118
Kern, David A., 157
Key, Bradley James, 161
Kidnapping case
  Huntington Beach, California, 93
"Kinder Orgy" (film), 166
Kirk, Michael, 337
Kniffen, Brian and Brandon, 120–21
Kniffen case, 59, 118–23, 126
Koppel, Ted, 388, 390
Krause, Sharon, 134, 136
Krauthammer, Charles, 179
Krebs, Sandy, 57–59
Krieger, Seth, 472–73n171

Krikorian, Claudia, 168–72
Krivacska, James, 393–94
Kropinack, Leslie, 173
Krueger, Richard, 370
Kuemin, Raymond, 153

Lake Worth, Florida. *See* Sugar Plum School
    House case
LA Magazine
  McMartin Preschool case, 81
Lamb, Michael, 257
Landell, Sonny, 45
Landez, Martha
  initial phase of investigation, 210
  interview of, 247
  subsequent investigation, 215–16
  verdict and, 240
Lanesborough Elementary School case, 147–49
Lang, Justin, 230
Lanning, Kenneth, 97, 160
Larry King Live (tv show), 417n11
L.A. Star, 417n11
"Lateral traction test," 440n132
Law, Cardinal Bernard, 368
Lawson, Henry, 172
Lawton, Betsy, 47, 50
Lawton, Otis, 47, 50
Lawton, Robert case, 377–78, 383
Learning Game preschool, 170–71
Lee, Skipper, 162
Legacy of the witch-hunt narrative, 363–407
  credibility of children, undermining, 387–406
  overview, 383–406
  reality of day-care sexual abuse, discounting,
    383–87
Lehrman Day School, 174, 292
Leniency for child molesters, 191–95
Leon, Chrysanthi, 371–73
Leventhal, Betsy, 288, 306–8, 321
Leventhal, Charlie, 306
Leventhal, Tom
  Braga, Joseph and Laurie, interviews by, 293–95,
    299, 302
  counts involving, 316
  criticisms of interview(s), 345
  early investigation, 291
  medical conditions, 306
  sexually precocious behavior, 308
  statement of other child, 288
  unclothed, incident, 307, 324–25
Licht, Allan, 166
Linder, Douglas, 17
Ling, Lorraine, 104
Lipton, Daniel
  Braga, Joseph and Laurie, interviews, 293, 294,
    300–302
  early investigation, 289–90
  sexually precocious behavior, 308

Lipton, Jessie
  Braga, Joseph and Laurie, interviews, 298–99,
    313–15
  criticisms of interview(s), 343–45
  cross-examination of, 320
  early investigation, 290
  quotes used in trial, 343
  suspicious incident, 307
Lipton, Roberta, 308
Lists of case names
  54 names in Nathan/Snedeker book, 87–88. See
    also 54 names listed in Satan's Silence:
    Ritual Abuse and the Making of an American
    Witch-Hunt (Nathan and Snedeker)
    dedication page, 115–50
  36 cases, Commercial Appeal, 87–115. See also 36
    cases, list of by Charlier and Downing
  chronology of cases, 153
  settings of cases, 155
Little Angels Preschool, 172
"Little But Lewd" (film), 166
Little Rascals day care center case, 8–10
Llewellyn, Richard, 184
Loftus, Elizabeth, 374
Logan, Mary, 169
Loken, Chief Judge James B., 398
Lopez, Judge Richard, 171
Lorain, Ohio. See Head Start Program case
Lorman, Stephanie, 204
Los Angeles County. See also McMartin
    Preschool case
  Sheriff's Ritual Abuse Task Force, 4, 85, 197
Los Angeles District Attorney's Office
  McMartin Preschool case, 68, 74–75
  political factors and, 76–77
Los Angeles Herald Examiner
  on Johnson, Judy, 26
Los Angeles Magazine
  McMartin Preschool case, 6
Los Angeles School District, 369–70
Los Angeles Times
  on child pornography, 166
  McMartin Preschool case, 6, 21–22, 74, 172
  Michaels, Kelly case, 271–72, 282
  sex-offender politics and, 370
Lowry, Rich, 254
Lucas, Allison, 289–90, 308
Lucas, Judge Malcolm M., 123
Lucas, Tammy
  Braga, Joseph and Laurie, interviews, 292,
    295–96, 302, 466n31
  counts involving, 316
  cross-examination of, 320
  early investigation, 289–90
  Fuster, Ileana testimony, 324–25
  medical conditions, 306
  sexually precocious behavior, 308
Lucas, Victor, 289

Lupoli, Tyler case, 381–82
Lynwood, California. See Little Angels
    Preschool
Lyon, Kathryn, 382
Lyon, Tom, 279, 283, 387

MacDonald, Alan, 382
MacFarlane, Kee, 7
  CII interviews, 42–51, 57, 75
    overdiagnosis issue and, 61
  early investigation, 34–36
  interview transcripts and, 41
  in preliminary hearing, 78
  Satz, Wayne, relationship, 430n185
  Stevens, Glenn and, 40
Maine Supreme Court, 190
Making Monsters (Ofshe and Watters), 9
"The Making of a Modern Witch Hunt"
    (Nathan), 6
Malcom, Julia, 134, 136
Malcom, Kevin, 134–35
Malcom, Lynn case, 374
Malcom, Marilynn, 133–37, 443n207. See also
    Rainbow Christian Daycare case
Malden, Massachusetts. See Amirault case
Mandatory Reporting Act, 192
Manhattan Beach, California. See Learning Game
    preschool
Manhattan Beach Police Department (MBPD).
    See also McMartin Preschool case
  Buckey, Peggy, response to letter, 82
  contested medical evidence and, 59
  early investigation, 27–28
    responses to letter, 30, 32–34, 37–40, 414
    sequence of events, 29
  "hysteria," alleged and, 167–68
  Johnson, Matthew, report on, 421n42
  notification of injuries by Simpson-Savary, Jean
    H., 25
  photos from, 69–70
Manhattan Ranch Preschool, 170, 187
Mann, Abby, 9–11, 23. See also Indictment (film)
  fire in home of, 72
  on Johnson, Judy, 25, 26
  Stevens, Glenn and, 19–20, 40, 80
  testimony of children and, 78–79
Manners, Glenda, 123–25
Manning, Lona, 115
Mann, Myra, 20, 80
Manshel, Lisa
  on charges, substantiation of, 234
  on Fonolleras, Lou, 207, 220
  on The Politics of Child Abuse (Eberle and
    Eberle), 417n11
  Rabinowitz, Dorothy, criticisms by, 251–52
  on Sencer-McArdle, Sara, 225
Maplewood, New Jersey. See Michaels, Kelly case;
    Wee Care Child Care Center

Maran, Meredith, 444n229
Marcotty, Josephine, 102
Marion Davies Children's Clinic, 25
Marks, Douglas, 184
Martindale, Nathan, 384
Martin, Harold, 114
Martin, Jeanette, 113–15, 437n98. *See also*
    Unlicensed day care centers
Maryland, University of, 61
Maryland v. Craig, 106, 273
Marzolf case, 390–93, 403
Massachusetts
    Day of Contrition (linking cases to Salem witch
        trials of 1690s), 374, 377, 389–90
Masson, Jeffrey
    *The Assault on Truth: Freud's Suppression of the
        Seduction Theory*, 177
    on Freud suppression of seduction theory, 3
Mastrangelo, Richard
    initial phase of investigation, 206, 209
    interview with child, 257
    state's case and, 228–29
Matthews, Mitchell case, 192–93
Matusinka, Jean, 40, 73
McCann, John
    contested medical evidence, 66–67
    studies, 60, 62, 67, 143, 421n31
McCormick, Robert, 164
McCuan, Bobbie and Darla, 119–22
McCuan case, 119–23, 126
McCuan, Deborah and Alvin, 59, 118–23
McGaulie, Jackie, 429n175
McGeary, Scott, 25
McGinnis, Catherine, 345
McGirt, Susan, 169
McGrath, George, 207, 209, 228, 247, 249
McGraw, Carol, 166
McKeg, Thomas, 154
McMartin era, 151–95. *See also* McMartin
    Preschool case
    day care abuse, 1980s, 152–59
        during McMartin, 155–59
    "fantastic" elements, 154, 159–67
        child pornography "myth," 163–67
    "hysteria," Southern California allegedly in grip
        of, 167–73
"McMartin Madness: Ten Days in the Life of the
    Longest, Most Gruesomely Difficult
    Criminal Trial Ever" (Safian), 21
McMartin Preschool case, 17–86, 413–14. *See also*
    Buckey, Peggy; Buckey, Peggy Ann; Buckey,
    Raymond; McMartin era; McMartin,
    Virginia
    beginning of case, 17, 19
    Believe the Children, 4, 10–11, 71, 85–86
    Ceci and Bruck on "Six Elements to Three Major
        Cases, 358–59

Children's Institute International (CII). *See*
    Children's Institute International (CII)
children's statements, generally, 189
    contested medical evidence, 59–68
        overdiagnosis issue, 60–62
        relevant evidence, 62–68
    early investigation, 27–40
        September responders, 39
        sequence of events, 29
    evaluations at CII, 40–59. *See also* Children's
        Institute International (CII) *for detailed
        treatment*
evidence
    contested medical evidence, 59–68
    failure to review, 75–76
evolution of witch-hunt narrative and, 21–23
excesses of the case, 197
fire at school, 71–72
forces beyond CII, 68–77
grand jury, 17, 19
graphic stories, television reporting, 3
initial acceptance of charges, 5–6
jurors, 432n227
key features of, 360–61, *361*
made-for-tv-movie on, 9–11
media coverage, 72–74. *See also specific
    newspaper and television station*
number of complainants, 19, 41
numbers of perpetrators, 89
overview, 4–5, 14
parent-investigators, 69–72
photo lineups, 75
preliminary hearing, 77–79
    interview sequence, 53–54
    testimony of children, 78–79
prosecutorial failures, 74–77
    CII process, neglecting to supervise, 74–75
    evidence not reviewed, 75–76
    political factors and, 76–77
relevant medical evidence, 62–68
retrial, 80–84
"ritual abuse" claims, 4, 85
Sheriff's Task Force
    "ritual abuse" claims, 4, 85, 197
testimony of children, 22–23
therapists, activist, 69–72
in 36 cases, list of by Charlier and Downing, 94
timeline, *18*, 196–97
transcripts, 198
trial, 80–84
verdicts, 7, 20, 83–84
victims and family. *See* Acorn, David; Bailey,
    Penny; Baldwin, Ella; Barton, Gloria;
    Barton, Sara; Brown, Jenny; Chapman,
    Breanna; Chapman, Ellen; Chase,
    Miranda; Ennis, Cindy; Ennis, Donna;
    Gordon, Mary; Gregg, Barry; Gregg,

Darlene; Gregg, Sally; Ingram, Kathy Kae;
Johnson, Judy; Johnson, Matthew;
Landell, Sonny; Lawton, Betsy; Lawton,
Otis; McGaulie, Jackie; Mergili, Tanya;
Sandel, Bill; Van Holden, Bobby; Van
Holden family; Van Holden, Valerie;
Vickers, Bobby; Walters, Kristy; Walters,
Trisha
as "witch hunt," 5–6
McMartin Task Force, 19
McMartin, Virginia, 4. *See also* McMartin
Preschool case
Anatomy of the McMartin Child Molestation Case,
dedication, 419–20n1
on Buckey, Ray, behavior of, 82
CII interviews with victims and, 51, 58
indictment of, 19, 76
learning of investigation, 27
libel suit against, 21
Sorenson, Wesley, testimony of, 431n199
McNamara, Eileen, 390
MDMH Report, Small World Preschool case,
109–10, 437n85
Meacham, Edwin James, 164
Mean Justice (Hume), 118–19, 440n134,
441n160
Meckler, Ilyce, 430n190
"Media Flip-Flop: Why Four Years Later the Press
Is Taking a Strikingly Different Approach to
the Martin Preschool Scandal," 6
Medical evidence, contested in McMartin case. *See*
McMartin Preschool case
Megan's Law, 365, 370–74, 384, 406
Meltzer, Harvey, 236
Memphis, Tennessee. *See Commercial Appeal;*
Georgian Hills Early Childhood Center case
Mendes, Brenda
extreme behavioral evidence, 231
Fonolleras, Lou, interview with, 220
medical evidence, 232
Mengelberg, Brigitte I., 134
Menninger, Donald
Braga, Joseph and Laurie, interviews, 298–99,
301–2
early investigation, 289, 336
overlooked or downplayed testimony, 346
statement to mother, 288, 291, 308
substantation of charges, 468–69n92
Menninger, Donald, Jr., 468–69n93
Menninger, Vicki, 321
Menoher, Joanne, 288, 289, 466n12
Mergili, Tanya
CII interview with, 42, 47–51
contested medical evidence and, 67–68
early investigation, 30–32
parent-investigator and, 70
withdrawal of parents from case, 422n50

Meznarich, Donna
August 1984 interviews and, 299, 301–2
early investigation, 289–91
interviews, 345
Miami Herald, 190
Country Walk case, 293, 302, 325, 350–51
Michaels, Kelly case, 8, 203–82, 414–15
academics. witch-hunt narrative and, 271–79
brief for the defense, Ceci and Bruck, 277–79
Concerned Scientists brief, 277–79, 356–57,
380, 387
effect of, 281–82
"Mousetrap Study," 272–75, 356
research, translating into policy, 275–76
"Suggestibility of the Child Witness: A
Historical Review and Synthesis" (Ceci
and Bruck), 272–73
appeals (Appellate Division), 268–71
decision, 279–80
April 1985 (key events), 204–6
belief system, 233
Ceci and Bruck on "Six Elements to Three Major
Cases, 359
charges, actual, 224–25
children at trial by status of charges, 235
children dropped from case, 226, 227
children interviewed, 217, 219–21
initial phase of investigation, *211*
sequence of, *218*
child suggestibility claims, 16, 355
civil claim, 463n227
criticisms of interview(s), 10, 198
defense, 236–39
depositions by charge, by child, *241*
deterioration of investigation, 217, 219–22
dropping of charges, 280
evidence allegedly kept from jury, 252–53
extreme behavior evidence of children, 228–31
"fantastic" elements, 261–64
Fonolleras, Lou, interviews by. *See* Fonolleras,
Lou, interviews by
"hysteria"
Boston allegedly in grip of, 176–77
New Jersey allegedly in grip of, 173–74
influence of, 200
information on, 11
initial phase of investigation, 206–12
children interviewed, *211*
intensity of investigation, increase of, 217, 219–22
interview and charge information by
investigative phase, *267*
interviews, inaccurate claims about (post-
conviction), 245–52
"repetitive interviewing" claim, 247
sequence of interviews, *246, 248*
job change by Michaels, 204
Kelly Michaels Defense Committee, 243

Michaels, Kelly case (*continued*)
  key features of, 360–61, *361*
  media on, 22
  medical evidence, 231–32
  motive of, 232–34
  "Mousetrap Study," 272–75, 356
  Munn, Charlene, letter to, 239
  number of charges convicted of at trial, 242
  psychological evaluation of, 233–34
  Satan's Silence, dedication page, 115
  sentence, trial, 239–42
  social hysteria, manufacturing, 264–68
  state's case, 226, 228–35
    children at trial by status of charges, *235*
    extreme behavior evidence, 228–31
    medical evidence, 231–32
    motive, 232–34
  subsequent investigation, 212–16
  timeline, *205*
  Treacy, Eileen on case. *See* Treacy, Eileen
  trial
    children at trial by status of charges, *235*
    defense, 236–39
    depositions by charge, by child, *241*
    number of charges convicted of, 242
    state's case, 226, 228–35
    verdict and sentence, 239–42, 268
  as turning point, 15
  verdict, trial, 239–42, 268
  victims and family. *See* Allister, John; Applegate,
      David; Applegate, Judy; Bond-Foley,
      Cassie; Cook, Cody; Cook, Debbie;
      Deacon, Lucy; Drew, Dana; Flora,
      Rebecca; Gans, Ralph; Guild, Greg; Haley,
      Nora van; Hayes, Tracy; Isaacs, P. J.;
      Jenkins, Natalie; Jones, Dennis; Jones,
      Kimmy; Landez, Martha; Lang, Justin;
      Mendes, Brenda; Murphy, Brian;
      Nathanson, Eddie; Palmieri, Shayla;
      Peyton, Jacob; Pierce, Dorinda; Pierce,
      Mitchell; Raymond, Jackie; Raymond,
      Sam; Rooney, Max; Sanders, Elliot;
      Schultz, Debra; Shaw, Jessie; Tilden, Julia;
      Watson, Ruby; Williams, Clare; Wolfe,
      Clare; Zeitz, Martin
  witch-hunt narrative following conviction
      (rewriting story of case), 242–68. *See also*
      Ceci and Bruck on Kelly Michaels case;
      Nathan, Debbie; Rabinowitz, Dorothy
    academics and, 271–79
    evidence allegedly kept from jury, 252–53
    "fantastic" elements, 261–64
    interview and charge information by
        investigative phase, *267*
    interviews, inaccurate claims about, 245–52
    social hysteria, manufacturing, 264–68
    Treacy, Eileen, inaccurate claims about,
        253–61

Michigan Supreme Court, 191
Minimization of child sex abuse cases, 151–95
  day care abuse, 1980s, 152–59
    during McMartin, 155–59
    pre-McMartin, 152–55
  "fantastic" elements, 154, 159–67
    child pornography "myth," 163–67
  Fuster, Frank, prior record of, 335–38
  "hysteria," use of term in witch-hunt narrative,
      167–85
    Amirault case, Boston during, 176–77
    Country Walk case, Dade County, Florida
        during, 174–75
    Kelly Martin Day care case, New Jersey
        during, 173–74
    McMartin era, 167–73
    places allegedly in grip of, 167–77
    Southern California, 167–73
  leniency for child molesters, 191–95
  prosecuting child abuse, difficulties, 185–91
Minneapolis Children's Theatre case, 192,
      199
Minor, Clifford, 279
Mintz, Steven, 8
Miss Polly's Day Care Center, 142–44
Mitchell, Richard J., 158
Mitzenmacher, Myron, 56
Mobile Showroom, 286
Mondale Act. *See* Child Abuse Prevention and
      Treatment Act (CAPTA)
Monk, Carrie, 306
Montessori School No. 2, 168–71
Mooney, Gregory, 417n11
*Moral Panic: Changing Conceptions of the Child
      Molester in Modern America* (Jenkins), 13
"Moral panic," use of term in witch-hunt narrative,
      156
Morgan, Judge J. Dean, 135
Mormon Church, 182–83
Morris, Kathleen, 101–2, 163
"Mousetrap Study," 272–75, 356
Mouw, Dr., 146–47
Moynihan, Daniel Patrick, 380
Munn, Charlene, 233–34, 239
Muram, David, 99
Murphy, Brian, 219
Mutter, Charles R., 334
Myrhow, Paul, 184

Nanny's Day Care, 153
Nassau County District Attorney's Office, 133
Nathan, Debbie. *See also Satan's Silence: Ritual
      Abuse and the Making of an American Witch-
      Hunt* (Nathan and Snedeker)
    on Buckey, Raymond, character of, 81
    "child pornography myth," 164
    contested medical evidence and, 63, 66
    Country Walk case, 283

American Psychological Association (APA),
  correspondence, 475n212
  Bragas, maligning of, 349, 352
  Fuster, Ileana (Flores), "coerced confession"
    of, 332–35
  "inaccurate test" myth, 329
  "junior McMartins," use of term, 327
  suggestibility claims, 341
day care workers as "symbols," 152
on Early Childhood Development Center, 155
Issues in Child Abuse Accusations, 327
on Johnson, Matthew, examinations of, 25
"Junior McMartins," use of phrase, 87, 152–53,
  180–81
"The Making of a Modern Witch Hunt"
  (Nathan), 6
Michaels, Kelly case, 8
  appeals and, 268
  on Applegate, David, testimony of, 456n55
  criticisms of, 243, 397
  effect of articles, 281
  Fonolleras, Lou, criticisms of, 243
  interviews, inaccurate claims about, 245, 250
  Redbook article, 376
  social hysteria, manufacturing, 264–65
  Treacy, Eileen, criticisms of, 243, 254,
    461n176
  witch-hunt narrative following conviction,
    generally, 242–43
National Center for Reason and Justice (NCRJ),
  374–75
Nightline (tv program), letter to, 388
omissions of facts, 33
on Papoose Place Academy, 155
on personality of child molesters, 193
on prosecution, 185
on West Point Child Development Center, 111
"What McMartin Started: The Ritual Abuse
  Hoax," 22
Nathan, Eleanor, 154
Nathanson, Eddie
  initial phase of investigation, 207
  interviews of, 249
  medical evidence, 231
  subsequent investigation, 213–14, 216
  verdict and, 240
The Nation
  Country Walk case, 330
National Center for Reason and Justice (NCRJ),
  114–15, 149, 374–75
National Center on Child Abuse and Neglect
  (NCCAN), 160–61
National Children's Foundation, 350
National Review
  Country Walk case, 348
  McMartin Preschool case, 22
  Michaels, Kelly case, 244, 254
National witch-hunt, evidence of, 87–150

lists of case names
  54 names in Nathan/Snedeker book, 87–88,
    115–50. *See also* 54 names listed in
    *Satan's Silence: Ritual Abuse and the
    Making of an American Witch-Hunt*
    (Nathan and Snedeker)
  36 cases, *Commercial Appeal*, 87–115, 153. *See
    also* 36 cases, list of by Charlier and
    Downing
Nativity School, 183
NCAA, 368
NCCAN. *See* National Center on Child Abuse and
  Neglect (NCCAN)
NCRJ. *See* National Center for Reason and Justice
  (NCRJ)
Neovascularization, 68
New American Church, 448–49n46
New Hampshire, University of
  Family Research Laboratory, 155
New Jersey. *See also* Michaels, Kelly case; Wee
  Care Child Care Center
  "hysteria," allegedly in grip of, 173–74
  Special Classification Review Board, 394
New Jersey Department of Health and Family
  Services (DYFS), 206, 207, 390
  findings of, 224
New Jersey Division of Youth and Family Services,
  265
New Jersey Law Journal
  Michaels, Kelly case, 269, 279, 462n208
New Jersey Supreme Court
  Michaels, Kelly case. *See* Michaels, Kelly case
Newman, Judge, 317–18, 333
New Mexico day care center, 154
News-Record
  Michaels, Kelly case, 26
Newsweek
  McMartin Preschool case, 79
  West Point Child Development Center, 111
New Times
  Country Walk case, 328
New York City Advisory Task Force on Rape, 255
New Yorker
  on child abuse accommodation syndrome, 395
  Ingram case, 117
  on Provost, Father Ronald, 190
  witch-hunt narrative and, 9
New York Law Journal
  Michaels, Kelly case, 254
New York Review of Books, 12, 157
New York Times
  on civil commitment, 371
  on corroboration requirements, 187
  Friedman, Arnold and Jesse case, 132
  Michaels, Kelly case, 271–72
    "Mousetrap Study," 273–75, 356
  Minneapolis Children's Theatre case, 192
  Self, Grant, 124

New York Times Book Review
  McMartin Preschool case, 22
  unlicensed day care center, White Plains, New
    York, 115
New York Times Magazine
  Stoll, John case, 119
"Nightline Alert," 388
Nightline (tv program), 387–88
Niles, Michigan. *See also* Small World Preschool
    case
  day care center, 153
Nixon, Richard M., 401
Noble, Mickey, 185
No More Secrets for Me, 213
Noonan, Judge John T., 11, 379, 406, 407
Norman, Oklahoma. *See* Trinity Baptist Church
North Carolina. *See* Parker case
North Carolina, University of
  Program on Childhood Trauma and
    Maltreatment, 263–64
Northern California, ritual abuse case, 162–63
North Miami Police Department, 175
Not My Child (Crowley), 453n17
Numbers of child sex abuse cases, 15. *See also* 54
    names listed in *Satan's Silence: Ritual Abuse
    and the Making of an American Witch-Hunt*
    (Nathan and Snedeker); 36 cases, list of by
    Charlier and Downing
Nussle, Jim, 141

Oak Tree Day Care Center, 384
O'Boyle, James Joseph, 182
Ofshe, Richard, 9
Ohio Parole Board, 150
Ohio Supreme Court, 150
Ohme, Herman W., 390, 479n89
Okerblom, Jim, 11
Olio, Karen, 117
Olson Commission, 101–2
Olympia, Washington. *See* Ingram case
Olympic Memorial Hospital, 107
Ontario Consultants for Religious Tolerance, 13
Orr, Barbara, 434–35n19
Oscarson, Elsie, 380
Overdiagnosis issue, 60–62
Owen, Nina, 38
Owen, Roseanne, 38

Paidika: The Journal of Paedophilia, 236–37
Palmieri, Shayla, 219
Palomo, Timothy, 123
"Panic," use of term in witch-hunt narrative, 15,
    156
Papoose Place Academy, 153, 155, 199, 419n1
Parental alienation syndrome, 389–90
Parent-investigators, McMartin Preschool case,
    69–72
Parker case, 117

Parks, Deloartic, 103–5. *See also* Rogers Park
    Jewish Community Center case
Paterno, Joe, 369
"Patricia Crowley" book, 210
Paul, David, 24, 427–28n167
  contested medical evidence and, 63–64, 66–67
  "lateral traction test," 440n132
Pearl Lee Mitchell licensed day care center, 158
Peirsol, Chief Judge Lawrence L., 398–99
Pelton, Vivian, 307
Pendergrast, Mark, 375
  "child pornography myth," 164
  Fuster, Frank, exoneration of, 336
  Lawton, Robert case, 378
  Oscarson, Elsie case, 380
  Victims of Memory, 129
Peninsula Montessori School No. 1, 171–72,
    449–50n76
Penn, Sean, 11, 119
Penn State scandal, 365–66, 368–69
"People are Talking" (tv program), 468n70
People Magazine
  McMartin Preschool case, 6, 78
People v. Taylor, 255
Perez, Detective, 439n114
Perez, Robert, 382
Perpich, Rudy, 101
Perry, David H., 153–54
Perry, Douglas, 144–46
Personalities of sex offenders, 181, 185
Peters, Nicholas, 441n153
Peterson, Anita, 136–37
Peyton, Jacob, 229–30, 234
Pezdek, Kathy, 387
Phelps, Rod, 119–21
Philibosian, Robert, 19, 76–77
Phillips, Michael, 94
Pierce, Dorinda, 206–8
Pierce, Mitchell, 206–7
  extreme behavioral evidence, 228–29
  first implication of teacher, 360
  Fonolleras, Lou, interview with, 220
  medical evidence, 231
  medical examination of, 238, 244
  subsequent investigation, 213
  witch-hunt narrative and
    "fantastic" elements, claims of, 262
    medical examination of, 244
  sex-abuse hysteria, use of term, 265
Pike County, Ohio, ritual abuse, 161
Pirro, Jeanine, 187
Pittsfield, Massachusetts. *See* Early Childhood
    Development Center
Plass, Richard, 195
Playboy magazine, 82–83
  "child pornography myth," 163, 166
Political factors, McMartin Preschool case,
    76–77

The Politics of Child Abuse (Eberle and Eberle), 7, 405, 417n11
Polk County, Iowa, unlicensed day care centers, 153
Poole, Deborah, 257
Poole, Warren, 189–90
Porter, Annie, 320
Porter, Judge Charles Jr., 192
Porter, Kimberly, 307, 308
Porter, Malcolm, 308
Post-Intelligencer
  Cora's Day Care case, 108
Pounders, Judge, 27, 83, 419n5, 430n185
Presidio Child Development case, 186
Price, Winston S., 232, 263
Pride, Mary, 7
Priest, Cora, 107–8. *See also* Cora's Day Care case
Priest, Ralph, 107–8. *See also* Cora's Day Care case
Prince George's County, Virginia. *See* ABC Scholar Day Care Center
Professions, backlash against, 401–6
Prosecuting child abuse, difficulties, 185–91
  accommodations for children as witnesses, 187–88
  "corroboration" requirements, 187
Prosecutorial failures
  McMartin Preschool case, 74–77
    CII process, neglecting to supervise, 74–75
    evidence not reviewed, 75–76
    political factors and, 76–77
Protection of Children Against Sexual Exploitation Act of 1977, 417n11
Provost, Father Ronald, 190
Psychological Bulletin
  Country walk case, 341
  Michaels, Kelly case, 272–73
Punitive treatment of sex offenders, recent developments, 373

Rabinowitz, Dorothy, 22–23, 173
  on Amirault case, 176
    Wall Street Journal article, 376
  Michaels, Kelly case, 8
    appeals and, 268–69
    effect of articles, 281, 357
    evidence allegedly kept from jury, 252–53
    "fantastic" elements, claiming, 261–64
    Harper's article and, 273
    interviews, inaccurate claims about, 245, 250–52
    social hysteria, manufacturing, 264
    Treacy, Eileen, inaccurate claims about, 254
    witch-hunt narrative following conviction, generally, 243–44
  Ohme, Herman W. and, 479n89
Radcliff, Kentucky. *See* Nanny's Day Care
Raidor, Betty, 195. *See also* McMartin Preschool case

on Buckey, Ray, behavior of, 81
  indictment of, 19, 76
Rainbow Christian Daycare case, 134–37, 164–65, 194–95
Rameriz-Brouwer, Ada, 140
Ramona, California day care center, 154
Randle, Madeline, 70
Rape and murder cases, Florida, 388
RapID/NH System, 328–29
Rappeport, Jonas, 237–38, 269, 417n11
Rawls, Jane, 392
Raymond, Jackie, 207
Raymond, Sam
  initial phase of investigation, 207, 209–10
  medical evidence, 231
  subsequent investigation, 213–14
  witch-hunt narrative, "fantastic" elements, 262
Reader's Digest, 11
Reality of day-care sexual abuse, discounting, 383–87
Recent developments, 363–407. *See also specific cases*
  Ashley's Law, 370
  Catholic Church scandals, 365–68, 384, 406
  community notification systems, 371–72
  Jessica's Law, 370
  Megan's Law, 365, 370–74, 384, 406
  Penn State scandal, 365–66, 368–69
  punitive treatment of sex offenders, 373
  sex-offender politics, 370–74
  "witch hunt" claims, persistence of, 374–83
Redbook
  McMartin Preschool case, 22
  Michaels, Kelly case, 376
  West Point Child Development Center, 111
Redden, John S., 279–80
Redmond Oregon. *See* Mormon Church
Reiner, Ira, 19, 77
Reiter, David, 184
"Reliability," 400
Rempell, Jeryl, 230–21
Reno, Janet
  contested sex abuse cases, 9
  Country Walk case, 292, 315, 318, 327, 332, 349
  Hazel Crawford Day Care Center, 175
Reno, Nevada. *See* Children City Learning Center; Papoose Place Academy
Report on Scott County Investigations (Humphrey), 101–3
Report on the Kern County Child Abuse Investigations, 118
Ricci, Lawrence, 402, 405
Richmond, Virginia case, 89, 93–94
Ritual abuse
  allegations, Charlier and Downing and, 355, 384
  claims, 156
  "fantastic" elements, 154, 159–67
Ritual Abuse Task Force, LA County, 4, 85, 197

Roberts, Paul Craig, 87
Robie, Judge Ronald, 95
Robinson, Bruce, 13
Rogers Park Jewish Community Center case, 103–5
  Believe the Children, 71
Rok, Richard, 162
Rolling Hills, California. *See* Montessori School No. 2
Rooney, Max, 209–10, 215
Rosenthal, Robert
  Country Walk case, 350, 380–81
  Lupoli, Tyler case, 381–82
  Michaels, Kelly case, 277, 279, 375
  Serrano, Jose case, 381
  Weber, Frederick case, 381
  Wenatchee, Washington cases, 382–83
Ross, A. S., 6, 10, 161
Rouse case, 394–400
Rouse, Desmond and Jessie case, 396, 404, 406
Rouse, Joanie, 399
Rouse, Lacey, 396
Rouse, Rebecca, 396–97
Rouse, Tiffany, 396
Rubin, Lael, 424n104
Ruby, Michael, 170, 187
Rud, James, 100, 194. *See also* Jordan, Minnesota cases
Rundle, Christopher, 175, 291–92, 315, 466n32
Runion, Samantha, 389
Runyan, Debbie, 128–29
Russell, Dianna, 451n117

Sacco, Lynn, 178
Sacramento, California case, 95
Safian, Robert, 21
Salem Day of Contrition. *See* Day of Contrition (linking cases to Salem witch trials of 1690s)
Salon, 161
Samek, Jeffrey, 302, 317–18, 321, 341
Sandel, Bill, 427n167
Sanders, Elliot, 219
San Diego, California. *See also* Fairmont Baptist Church
  ritual abuse case, 162
San Diego Union-Tribune
  on satanic rituals, 162
  on witch-hunt narrative, 11
Sandusky, Jerry, 368
San Francisco, California. *See* Presidio Child Development case
San Francisco Examiner
  Country Walk case, 327
  McMartin Preschool case, 6, 10
San Mateo, California day care center, 154
Santa Cruz Ritual Abuse Task Force, 429–30n179

"Satanic ritual abuse cases of the 1980s," use of term, 87
Satanism allegations. *See also* Ritual abuse
  Cora's Day Care case, 108
  36 cases, list of by Charlier and Downing, 94
  West Point Child Development Center, 113
Satan's Silence: Ritual Abuse and the Making of an American Witch-Hunt (Nathan and Snedeker), 8, 9, 374
  dedication page, 115–50
  54 names listed in, 87–88, 115–50
  on MacMartin preschool case, 23, 42–43, 87–88
  dedication page, 114
Satz, Wayne
  MacFarlane, Kee, relationship, 430n185
  McMartin Preschool case, 3, 6, 72–73
  in preliminary hearing, 79
Sauer, Mark, 11
Schachter, Daniel, 12, 13
Schauer, Fred, 417n11
Scheck, Barry, 133
Schildmeyer, Kim, 140
Schildmeyer, Michael Joseph, 116, 140–42. *See also* Sunshine Preschool and Day Care Center case
Schneider, Andrew, 439n114
School teachers, sexual misconduct of, 369–70, 373
Schultz, Debra
  extreme behavioral evidence, 229
  medical evidence, 232
  testimony of, 243
Schuster, Marilyn, 239
Scientific American, 11
Scott County, Minnesota. *See* Jordan, Minnesota cases
Scout's Honor, 183
Seattle Post-Intelligence, 11, 383
Secret Trauma: Incest in the Lives of Girls and Women (Russell), 451n117
Seering Family Day Care, 157
Seering, Flora and William, 157
Segal, Richard, 24
Seigel, Barry
  A Death in White Bear Lake, 179
Selected day care sexual abuse cases (1980s and 1991), 5
Self, Grant, 119, 123–26, 164
Sencer-McArdle, Sara, 207, 225, 270
Sequium, Washington case. *See* Cora's Day Care case
Serrano, Jose case, 381, 383
Sex Abuse Hysteria: Salem Witch Trials Revisited (Gardner), 179, 379
Sex offender databases, 370–71
Sex-offender politics, 370–74

Sexton, Eddie Lee, 162
Sexually precocious behavior, 308
Shaver, John W. "Jack," 164–65, 194, 199
Shaw, David, 22, 74, 282
  on McMartin Preschool case, 6–8
  Where was Media Skepticism?, 7–8
Shaw, Jessie, 215
Shell, Paul, 97
Shell, Robert, 165
Sheriff's Task Force
  McMartin Preschool case, "ritual abuse" claims,
    4, 85, 197
Shubin, Charles, 106, 158, 436n70
Shumate, Neil case, 375–77
Silence on child sex abuse cases, 15, 151–95
  day care abuse, 1980s, 152–59
    during McMartin, 155–59
    pre-McMartin, 152–55
  "fantastic" elements, 154, 159–67
    child pornography "myth," 163–67
  "hysteria," use of term in witch-hunt narrative,
    167–85
    Amirault case, Boston during, 176–77
    Country Walk case, Dade County, Florida
      during, 174–75
    Kelly Martin Day care case, New Jersey
      during, 173–74
    McMartin era, 167–73
    places allegedly in grip of, 167–77
    Southern California, 167–73
  leniency for child molesters, 191–95
  prosecuting child abuse, difficulties, 185–91
Simons, Judge William, 127
Simpson-Savary, Jean H., 25
60 Minutes
  McMartin Preschool case, 6
Skeptical Inquirer, 11, 117
Slade, Elmo, 467–68n70
Slater, David, 195
Slone, David, 192
Small World Preschool case, 108–11
  DSS interviews, 110
  MDMH Report, 109–10
  Satan's Silence, dedication page, 115
Smerling, Marc, 443n198
Smith, Nancy, 149–50, 374, 438n110. *See also*
  Head Start Program case
Smithville, North Carolina. *See* Miss Polly's Day
  Care Center
Snedeker, Michael. *See also Satan's Silence: Ritual
  Abuse and the Making of an American Witch-
  Hunt* (Nathan and Snedeker)
  on Buckey, Raymond, character of, 81
  contested medical evidence and, 63
  on Johnson, Matthew, examinations of, 25
  Malcolm, Marilynn, clemency petition,
    135–36

National Center for Reason and Justice (NCRJ),
  374
  omissions of facts, 33
  Rouse case, 399
Snow, Barbara, 395, 396
Snowden, Grant, 8, 175
Social hysteria. *See* "Hysteria," use of term in
  witch-hunt narrative
Society for Research in Child Development
  (SRCD), 275, 357, 362
Something About Amelia (tv movie), 3, 177
Sonoma County, California, ritual abuse cases,
  163
Sorenson, Wesley, 431n199
Sorrentino, Judge Charlene, 353
South Bay, California
  preschool cases, 168–72
South Dakota
  Yankton Sioux Reservation, 396
Southern California
  "hysteria," allegedly in grip of, 167–73
Southern California, child pornography cases,
  165–66
South Orange, New Jersey. *See* Wee Care Child
  Care Center
Sowell, Thomas, 11, 375, 379
Spears, Sergeant, 333
Special Classification Review Board (New Jersey),
  394
Spector, Arlene, 208, 213
Spencer, Township case, 92–93
Spitler, Babette. *See also* McMartin Preschool case
  indictment of, 19, 76
  results of case, 84
  at trial, 82
Spitler, Donald, 82
Sports Illustrated, 180
Squyres, Carol, 120, 122, 439nn122 and 124
SRCD. *See* Society for Research in Child
  Development (SRCD)
Stanley, Lawrence, 163, 166, 449n71
Star Ledger
  Michaels, Kelly case, 217, 270
Star Tribune
  Jordan, Minnesota cases, 100, 102–3
State Department of Health and Rehabilitative
  Service (DHRS), 175, 186
State v. Buckey. See Buckey, Raymond; McMartin
  Preschool case
State v. Carol M.D., 382
State v. Figured, 143
State v. Fuster. See Country Walk case; Fuster,
  Frank
State v. Michaels. See Michaels, Kelly case
St. Claire, Sherry L., 143
St. Cross Church, 170
STD findings, 128, 302, 311, 320, 328, 352

Stein, Judge Jack G., 105
Stereotypes of sex offenders, 180–81
Stevens, Glenn
  CII evaluations and, 40, 44
  conversations with Mann, Abby and Mann,
    Myra, 80
  Mann, Abby, interviews with, 19–20, 26
  media coverage and, 73
  preliminary hearing, 78–79
  on therapists, 71
St. George's Episcopal Church. *See* Wee Care Child
  Care Center
Stimson, Betty, 97–98
Stimson, Jeff, 97
St. Lorenzo, Emma, 288, 307, 353
St. Lorenzo, John, 288, 307, 336
Stoll, John, 119, 123–26
Stone, Oliver, 10, 23
Stossel, John, 274
St. Petersburg, Florida. *See* Pearl Lee Mitchell
  licensed day care center
Stuart, Florida. *See* Glendale Montessori
  School
Stuebbe, Judge, 120, 440nn133 and 140
Sudden Infant Death Syndrome, 179–80
Sugar Plum School House case, 186–87
Suggestibility claims. *See* Child suggestibility
  claims
"Suggestibility of the Child Witness: A Historical
  Review and Synthesis" (Ceci and Bruck),
  272–73
Summit, Roland, 178–79, 320, 394–95, 397
Sunshine Preschool and Day Care Center case,
  140–42
Sweeney, Kristin, 484n150

Taibbi, Mike, 244, 252
"Tainted," labeling children as, 390–94
Tamarkin, Civia, 387–88
Tardieu, Paul, 178
Tavris, Carol, 21–22, 271–72, 405
Taylor, Becky
  Braga, Joseph and Laurie, interviews, 296–98,
    302, 311–12
  counts involving, 316
  criticisms of interview(s), 345
  cross-examination of, 320
  early investigation, 291
  first day at Country Walk, 467n60
  Fuster, Ileana testimony, 324–25
  medical conditions, 306
  Rundle, Christopher, interviews, 466n32
Taylor, Darlene, 306, 467n60
Teixeria, Wilmes, 66, 426n161
Telb, James, 92–93
Temple Emmanuel, Miami, 174
"The Terrible Puzzle of McMartin Preschool," 21

Texas Monthly
  Fran's Day Care case, 144, 146
Texas Supreme Court, 146
36 cases, list of by Charlier and Downing, 87–115.
  See also specific cases
  child pornography as "myth," 163
  chronology of cases, 153
  by date and case features, *90–91*
  on defense lawyers, 189
  details on 11 cases highlighted by, 95, 96
  "elements" of cases, 93–94
  "fantastic" elements, 154, 159–67, 338–40
    child pornography "myth," 163–67
  on hearsay evidence, 191
  "hysteria" and, 173, 176–77
  plot of, *90*
  pornography, allegations of, 94
  on prosecution, quotes in series, 185
  satanic exaggeration, 94
  settings of cases, 155–56
Thomas, Ariel, 343
Thomas, Justice Clarence, 265
Tilden, Julia, 214
Torrance preschool, 172
Toward, James, 137–40. *See also* Glendale
  Montessori School
Toward, Rosario, 139
Treacy, Eileen
  Ceci and Bruck, inaccurate claims about, 253,
    255, 257–61
    "fantastic" elements, claiming, 262
    Treacy-Child A excerpt, 256
    Treacy-Child B excerpt, 258
  evaluation of children, 222–23, 357
  Nathan, Debbie
    criticisms by, 243, 253–61, 461n176
    inaccurate claims about, 245, 250
  Rabinowitz, Dorothy, inaccurate claims about,
    254
  state's case and, 228
  subsequent investigation, 215
Trials. *See specific case*
Trillin, Calvin, 182
Trinity Baptist Church, 192
A True Story of False Memory (Maran), 444n229
Tucker, William, 386
Turtle Top Day Nursery, 175

UCLA Medical Center, 30–32
Uncommon Desires (Stanley), 166, 449n71
Underwager, Ralph
  on Charlier and Downing list of thirty-six cases,
    88
  Country Walk case, 322, 327–28, 341
  Day of Contrition, 389–90
  discrediting of, 203
  Kelly Michaels case and, 173

Michaels, Kelly case
  appeals and, 269
  arguments advanced, 272
  cross-examination of, 413
  expert witness, 236–37
  Rouse case, 397–99
  VOCAL, launching of, 101–2
Unger, Ned, 286
Unger, Vera, 301–2
Unlicensed day care centers
  Polk County, Iowa, 153
  White Plains, New York, 113–15
"Unreliable test" myth, 328–29, 470n130
Unspeakable Acts (Hollingsworth), 293, 341
U.S. Conference of Catholic Bishops, 367

"Vampire Clan," 448–49n46
Van Buren, Arkansas. *See* Gingerbread Day
  Care
Vancouver, Washington. *See* Rainbow Christian
  Daycare case
Van Dam, Carla, 181
Van Holden, Bobby, 38, 40
Van Holden family, 38, 40
Van Holden, Valerie, 38, 40
Vermont Supreme Court, 378
Vickers, Bobby, 47–50
Victims of Memory (Pendergrast), 129
Victor, Jeffrey, 70
Village Voice
  Country Walk case, 327
  "Distorted Journalism" article, 389
  on *Indictment* (film), 23
  on on "Justice Abused: A 1980s Witch-Hunt," 88
  McMartin Preschool case, 6, 7, 22
  Michaels, Kelly case, 243, 251–52, 265
VOCAL (Victims of Children Abuse Laws), 85,
  101–2, 179, 185
Voigt, Brenda, 103
Voigt, Sophie, 103, 104–5
Von Zamft, Michael, 318, 333–34

Wakefield, Hollida, 399
Waldman, Alan J., 140
Walker, Paula, 307–8
Walker, Sara, 307–8
Wallace, Mike, 424n104
Wall Street Journal, 8
  Amirault case, 376
  Country Walk case, 380–81
  Michaels, Kelly case, 244
  sex-abuse hysteria, coining of term,
    193
Walsh, Adam, 370, 372
Walters, Kristy, 427n167
Walters, Trisha, 44–45, 65
Walter, Vasco W., Jr., 157
Warnock, George and Betty, 153, 446n11

Washington Post
  on children testifying, 355
  Craig's Country Pre-School case, 105–6
  on Kauffmann, Kristi, 191
  McMartin Preschool case, 21, 84
  Michaels, Kelly case, 245
  on numbers of cases, 87
Watkins, Alex and Wade, 147–49
Watson, Norman, 180
Watson, Reverend Tommy, 333, 335, 472n164
Watson, Ruby, 219
Watters, Ethan, 9
Watt, James, 113–15, 149. *See also* Unlicensed day
  care centers
Weber, Frederick case, 381
Websites
  Crime Library, 17
  Famous Trials, 17
  Friedman, Arnold and Jesse case, 442n188
  Ontario Consultants for Religious Tolerance, 13
  Witch Hunt Information Center, 11–12
Wee Care Child Care Center, 173–74, 386
Weisberg, Brett, 82
Wenatchee, Washington cases, 382–83
  Satan's Silence, dedication page, 117–18
Western State Hospital, 107
West Point Child Development Center,
  111–13
  Satan's Silence, dedication page, 115
West, Walter P., 182
Wexler, Richard, 168
"What McMartin Started: The Ritual Abuse
  Hoax" (Nathan), 22
Where was Media Skepticism? (Shaw), 7–8
White, Edward Charles, 183
White Plains, New York. *See* Home day care
  center, White Plains, New York
Whittier, Nancy, 429n176
Wilcox, Karen, 33
Wilkes, David, 190
Wilkins, Robert, 162
Williams, Bob, 172
Williams, Brenda, 138
Williams, Clare, 219
Williams, Linda Meyer, 155–57
Williams, Mark, 478n40
Willis, Ellen, 11, 23, 25, 88
Wilson, Catherine Stubblefield, 166
Wilson, Mary, 30–32, 423n75
Wingard, Deborah, 176
Witch Hunt (documentary), 11, 119
Witch Hunt Information Center
  Baran case and, 155
  Shumate, Neil case, 376
  Treacy, Eileen, inaccurate claims about, 254
  webmaster, 142, 147
  website, 11–12
Witch-Hunt List, 131, 441n153

Witch Hunt (Lyon), 382
Witch-hunt narrative, generally. *See also* Legacy of
    the witch-hunt narrative; National witch-
    hunt, evidence of
  evolution of, 21–23
  rise of, 5–6
Witnesses, accommodations for children as,
    187–88
Wolfe, Clare
  Fonolleras, Lou, interview with, 219
Wood, James, 339–40, 349–51, 474n186
Woodling, Bruce
  contested medical evidence and, 59–62, 64–65,
    429n168

Kniffen and McCuan cases, 121–22
Woods, James, 81
Woodward, Louise, 401
Wright, Lawrence, 117, 397

Yankton Sioux Reservation (South Dakota),
  396
Young, Mary de, 87, 139, 152, 441n148
Young, Paul, 378
Yucaipa, Arizona. *See* Oak Tree Day Care Center

Zegas, Alan, 279
Zeitz, Martin, 228
Zobel, Judge Hiller B., 401